GEORGETOWN UNIVERSITY PRESS
Romance Languages and Linguistics Series

A COURSE IN ROMANCE LINGUISTICS. VOL. 1: A SYNCHRONIC VIEW
Frederick B. Agard

A COURSE IN ROMANCE LINGUISTICS. VOL. 2: A DIACHRONIC VIEW
Frederick B. Agard

PASSIVE SENTENCES IN ENGLISH AND PORTUGUESE
Milton M. Azevedo

A CONTRASTIVE PHONOLOGY OF PORTUGUESE AND ENGLISH
Milton M. Azevedo

FROM LATIN TO ROMANCE IN SOUND CHARTS
Peter Boyd-Bowman

THE SOUND SYSTEM OF FRENCH
Jean Casagrande

A DICTIONARY OF INFORMAL BRAZILIAN PORTUGUESE
Bobby J. Chamberlain and Ronald M. Harmon

SPANISH IN THE AMERICAS
Eleanor Greet Cotton and John M. Sharp

SPANISH PHONOLOGY AND MORPHOLOGY: A GENERATIVE VIEW
William W. Cressey

INTRODUCCION A LA HISTORIA DE LA LENGUA ESPAÑOLA
Melvyn C. Resnick

SYNTAX AND SEMANTICS OF SPANISH PRESENTATIONAL
SENTENCE-TYPES
Margarita Suñer

SPANISH/ENGLISH CONTRASTS: A COURSE IN SPANISH LINGUISTICS
M. Stanley Whitley

See p. 399 for additional titles of interest.

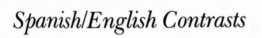

Spanish/English Contrasts

Spanish/English Contrasts

A Course in Spanish Linguistics

M. Stanley Whitley

Georgetown University Press, Washington, D.C.

Library of Congress Cataloging-in-Publication Data

Whitley, Melvin Stanley, 1948-
  Spanish/English contrasts.

  Bibliography: p.
  Includes index.
  1. Spanish language—Grammar, Comparative—English.
2. English language—Grammar, Comparative—Spanish.
I. Title.
PC4099.W45   1986   468.2'421   86-22917
ISBN 0-87840-095-8

10 9 8 7 6 5 4 3

To Mary Jo, Steven, and Philip
for the warmth of their love.

Contents

Foreword

This book seeks to provide in a single basic text a comprehensive survey and synthesis of scholarly work on the Spanish language. Since many users will be teachers of Spanish to English speakers, it focuses on pedagogical implications and the particular problems native speakers of English encounter in learning Spanish. But it also introduces those interested in research to many of the important sources of data and to many of the current issues in Spanish linguistics. It presents consensus where this exists; it integrates disparate works whose substance (if not approach or theory) is compatible; and, where debates have occurred, it reviews issues and viewpoints so that readers may form their own views and develop their own applications. In addition, its exercises promote analysis both of language data and of student errors, stimulate discussion of issues and questions, and suggest further directions for exploration.

As in any other linguistic description of a particular language, some acquaintance with general linguistics is basic to the study of Spanish linguistics. Specifically, *Spanish/English Contrasts* builds on the sort of coverage encountered in the typical one-semester introductory course in general and/or English linguistics, e.g. one based on a text such as Fromkin and Rodman 1983. To duplicate such backgrounding in fundamental linguistic principles in a book devoted to Spanish linguistics would have necessitated many tangents and would have crowded out a number of interesting topics in the particular description of Spanish.

Nevertheless, this book does not presuppose advanced preparation, and it reviews and explains basic linguistic terms and formalisms as they occur. Wherever possible, technical points and theoretical refinements are held to a minimum so as to make the material accessible to different kinds and levels of audiences. In addition, the Introduction presents a descriptive framework for linguistic comparisons, and Chapters 1, 5, and 14 discuss in a general way the notions to be developed in the chapters that follow them. For those classes with some prior experience in linguistics, these reviews should suffice for proceeding to a description of Spanish in contrast with English. For those classes with no prior study of linguistics, however, the instructor might wish to comment more amply and in greater depth on the terms and concepts that are introduced.

As explained in the Introduction, the various systems of any language are interconnected, and while it is expositorily useful to study, say, word order and sentence types in one chapter, this topic bears on subjects from other chapters such as intonation, verb endings, pronoun usage, and the speaker's communicative strategy. The Index summarizes such ramifications, but for greater convenience to the reader a direct cross-indexing is provided within the exposition itself. A reference such as (v. 12.1.2)—'see (*vide, véase*) 12.1.2'—indicates that the point under discussion has been reentered from, or will be treated more fully in, section 12.1.2 of Chapter 12. Readers may read on without disruption from the parenthesized reference, or follow up on it without having to flip back to the Index first for one particular point. It is hoped that this feature will combine the merits of a reference work with the smoother development of a text.

As in all surveys, the tremendous debt owed to the research of others is obvious. The references given at the end of this book cannot substitute for a complete bibliography of research in Spanish linguistics, but the list collects those contributions I have found especially useful for mention here. The special debt to the giants of the field—Bello, Ramsey, Stockwell et al., Bull, Gili Gaya, Navarro, etc.—is evident from the frequency of their citation. Thanks are also due to the many colleagues and informants whose feedback helped to eliminate several oversimplifications in the discussion of Spanish data, and to Richard J. O'Brien, S. J. and the Georgetown University Press for their extensive assistance in transforming a manuscript into a book. Lastly, I acknowledge the contributions of my students, whose problems and probing questions have stimulated my own work as a Spanish teacher and linguist. Often it is those 'simple' questions—'Why did you use *que* there?'—that make teacher-linguists realize how much of this fascinating *idioma celestial* is yet to be explored.

M. Stanley Whitley
The University of North Carolina at Charlotte

Chapter 0
General introduction:
Language and linguistics

0.1 Language and linguistics. Language can be thought of as a communication system that conveys meaning via some medium such as sound, as depicted in Figure 0.1. It consists of at least six interdependent components: PHONOLOGY, the speech sounds and rules governing them; MORPHOLOGY, the inflection and derivation of words; SYNTAX, the principles of word order and of phrase and sentence construction; LEXICON, the vocabulary system; SEMANTICS, word and sentence meaning; and PRAGMATICS, the sociocultural conventions for using the output of the other components.

Figure 0.1 A simple model of language.

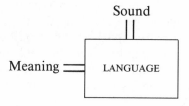

The past century has witnessed a variety of proposals as to precisely how these components function and interact with one another, and several distinct schools have emerged. The model shown in Figure 0.2 synthesizes many of these proposals, chiefly on the basis of one of the most influential theories, that of generative transformational grammar.

Although Figure 0.2 is more detailed than Figure 0.1, it still oversimplifies by omitting many internal mechanisms, glossing over issues that have been controversial, and depicting in two dimensions a part of human behavior that is quite multidimensional; but it should suffice for our purposes in this book.

Figure 0.2 A model of the component systems of language. Arrows indicate mutual input between the components.

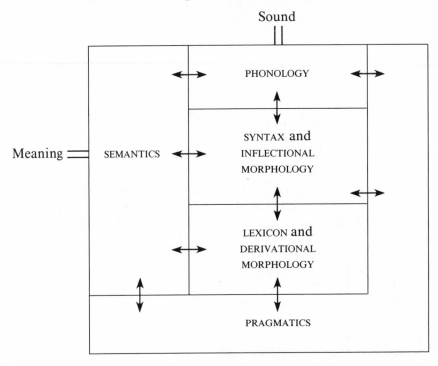

THEORETICAL LINGUISTICS focuses on the nature of these components against a general background of language and cognition. DESCRIPTIVE LINGUISTICS studies how one or more of the components is manifested in particular languages and dialects by describing the patterns revealed through analysis of data from native speakers. APPLIED LINGUISTICS takes the insights of theoretical and descriptive linguistics and applies them to such areas as translation, speech pathology, literary analysis, sociopolitical issues, and language instruction. This last area will be of special interest in this book.

0.2 Comparing and contrasting languages. One useful tool of linguistics applied to language instruction is CONTRASTIVE ANALYSIS, which compares and contrasts two language systems. For there to be any meaningful comparison at all, it is assumed that languages share much the same basic architectural plan: similar components, types of rules, units, constraints on these units, functions of the system, and cognitive bases. What differs is not the overall plan, but the details of layout and furnishings. Contrastive analysis takes a description of language A and one of language B, compares them, notes similarities and differences, and proceeds to predict the problems of A-speakers when they study B and vice-versa. Contrastive analysis is thus two-way, at least ideally; in practice, though, most such work in the United States understandably posits English as the SOURCE LANGUAGE (i.e. the students' native or primary language, sometimes abbreviated 'L1'), and some other language as the TARGET LANGUAGE (the foreign or secondarily acquired language, 'L2'). This book follows this orientation since we are interested in information that might improve Spanish instruction in an English-speaking country. For our purposes, then, English is the source language and Spanish the target language. But occasionally, it is helpful to reverse these roles; teachers who wonder why their students persist in confusing *ser* and *estar* may obtain a fresh perspective on the problem by imagining how they would go about explaining to Spanish-speaking students of English the similarly perplexing distinction of *make* vs. *do*.

0.2.1 Correspondences between languages. Contrastive analysis discerns at least three categories of correspondences between two languages as it predicts problems in language acquisition and proposes strategies for overcoming them.

(1) Language A has a feature (unit, distinction, pattern) *x* matched rather closely by an *x* in language B. Such a convergence can come about in several ways. First, *x* may be a UNIVERSAL OF LANGUAGE: all languages have verbs, pronouns for 'I' and 'you', a syntactic unit definable as 'sentence', procedures for negating and conjoining, and certain constraints on grammatical operations. Linguists take special interest in such universals because of what they indicate about human language in general, apart from the 'particular grammar' of each language. Second, *x* may be shared because A and B are linguistic relatives that inherited *x* from their common ancestor. This is why Spanish, English, and other descendants of Proto-Indo-European (circa 4000-3000 B.C.), have irregular paradigms for *be*, relative pronouns, similar number and tense systems, a pervasive masculine/feminine gender distinction in their lexicons, and much else. Third, *x* may be shared because of later linguistic and cultural cross-fertilization; English and Spanish have directly exchanged some words, and share article systems, perfect tenses, and a linguistic ritual involving *thanks/gracias* because of their West European upbringing. And fourth, the sharing of *x* may be a coincidence: English and Spanish both have a *ch* sound (/č/) for no particular reason at all.

(2) Language A has a feature *x* that resembles an *x* in B to some extent, but differs in several details of form, function, distribution, or conditions on usage. Examples here are legion for Spanish and English: their use of

stress, their assignment of the roles of subject and object to nouns, their formation and use of passives, their pronunciation of the vowel /u/ in *tú* and *two*, etc.

(3) Language A has a feature *x* which B lacks or which can be rendered only in terms of B's *y*, which operates according to different principles. Spanish has a personal *a* that English lacks, but English has two-word verbs (*stand up*) and Spanish does not. Spanish distinguishes the sounds *r/rr*, *ser/estar*, preterite/imperfect; English distinguishes the sounds *b/v*, *make/do*, and *his/her/their*.

0.2.2 Pedagogical implications of the correspondences. When A-speakers study B, contrastive analysis predicts that features of Category 1 can be carried over with little modification, i.e. with little comment from text or teacher. These are sometimes described as having POSITIVE TRANSFER value. Features found to belong to Categories 2 and 3, however, have NEGATIVE TRANSFER value, and require more pedagogical attention and practice; they may cause interference in the acquisition of B, so that entrenched habits, rules, and patterns must be blocked and new ones must be practiced extensively. In a broad sense, none of this is really new; traditional pedagogy has implicitly recognized the difference by giving more attention to the pronunciation of *r/rr* and the meaning of *tú/usted* (Category 3) than to the pronunciation of /č/ and the meaning of *yo* (Category 1). Where contrastive analysis potentially has more to offer is in areas such as the following.

(1) Distinguishing degrees of difficulty. If, within Category 3 above, A has an *x/y* distinction that B merges into its *z*, then generally it will be easier for A-speakers to learn to use B's *z* for both 'x' and 'y' than for speakers of B to master an *x/y* contrast they have never used. More concretely, English distinguishes comparative/superlative and Spanish does not (*más* for both 'more' and 'most'; v.13.4.1); Spanish distinguishes pre- and postposed adjectives and English does not (*altos precios, precios altos, high prices;* v.11.3.2). Learning both *más* and adjective position takes effort; but one predicts that English speakers will need more help with the latter than with the former.

(2) Identifying specific problems. Every grammatical description is rather skeletal, and foreign language students must flesh out such descriptions through induction, deduction, communicative experience, and source language transfer. Given the limited contact time available to students in class situations, contrastive analysis suggests that the points of grammar to be addressed should be primarily the more salient ones of Categories 2 and 3. That is, the entire language need not (and cannot) be covered, but one should address just those specific points identified as posing special problems, given the students' source language.

For example, French-speaking students of Spanish can pass lightly over *saber/conocer* since their *savoir/connaître* matches this distinction well enough (Terrell and Salgués 1979:8); but Spanish *he hablado/hablé* is merged by their *j'ai parlé,* and the contrast between present perfect and preterite must receive considerable attention in the course syllabus for French speakers. For English-speaking students, however, the relative status of these two cases is exactly reversed. The contrast between *he hablado* and *hablé* is clear to users of *I've spoken* and *I spoke,* but not the contrast between two kinds of knowing. Consequently, Spanish teachers in France and their colleagues in the United States will not present exactly the same 'grammar' of Spanish; nor should they, since their students come from different backgrounds.

In this regard, mention should be made of the special case in which source equals target, i.e. materials about *castellano* for native Spanish speakers. Such materials are designed for an audience that has spoken the language since childhood but needs guidance on certain standard usages: the preposition used with a verb, the plural of *frenesí* and *memorándum,* the forms of the uncommon verb *placer,* subtleties of punctuation, the syllabification of *construir,* where to write *b* and *v* and accent marks, certain literary tense usages, etc. Such texts tend to be silent on matters that natives get right intuitively but nonnatives are baffled by. Consequently, applied linguistics in the United States often relies on studies about Spanish by English-speaking teachers and linguists, who have posed and explored questions that may not occur to native grammarians. To return to an earlier example, *ser/estar* is taken for granted by native Spanish speakers, and the Real Academia (i.e. the Real Academia Española, or RAE) has relatively little to say about it; but English-speaking linguists, for whom *ser/estar* usage is not obvious but must be discovered and carefully described by analyzing data from Spanish speakers, have turned up a great deal of information about the two verbs. In contrast, a Costa Rican student of English linguistics who investigates *make/do* might visualize the problem better, and shed more light on it, than English-speaking grammarians. It undoubtedly helps to have an intuitive 'feel' for the language one is exploring, but sometimes the perspectives of outsiders are illuminating.

(3) Determining how a unit works within its own system. Linguists since Saussure (1915/1959) have stressed that the 'value' or function of any unit of language must be defined in terms of the role it plays within its own system; units from different languages may not be equated just because they appear alike. In short, an apparent correspondence of Category 1 may turn out to be of Category 2 or even 3. For instance, both English and Spanish have progressive verb forms; they are formed similarly, and a situation described by *está lloviendo* can usually be described by *it's rain-*

ing also. Most texts therefore equate them and assume that students who learn the morphology of *está lloviendo* will grasp its use implicitly. But contrastive analysis reveals that these progressives fit into their respective systems differently (v. 7.2.2): *¿llueve?* and *¿está lloviendo?* can be synonymous, whereas *does it rain?* and *is it raining?* never are. Hence, it is quite possible for the beginner to get along without the Spanish progressive; but when it is eventually taken up, it should be presented within the context of the Spanish tense system, not within the differently operating system of English.

(4) Assigning priorities on the basis of functional load. Some distinctions have a larger communicative role or FUNCTIONAL LOAD than others; they are more fundamental, more frequent, even indispensable. Although two languages may share a distinction (Category 1), they may assign it different functional loads. For example, mood contrasts are possible in both languages (v. 7.3), but the functional load of the English subjunctive is quite low and almost negligible, whereas the Spanish subjunctive contrasts sharply and abundantly with the indicative, and cannot be bypassed in many contexts. Though all texts devote some attention to mood contrasts, one could argue that this topic deserves an earlier position in the syllabus than is usual.

(5) Dealing with variation. Some grammarians have attempted to sort out variants on the basis of some prescribed distinction: use *x* here, *y* there, but never *z* because it is improper. Linguists prefer to accept variations where they exist and to interpret them as options the language sets up for expression or as socially linked variables of a dynamic system. For instance, many texts include an elaborate account of where to use each relative pronoun in Spanish, and despite its intricacy, students should try to master this account if it reflects native usage. But often it does not; as one native-speaking teacher once said of such a lesson, '¡no decimos esto!' In many instances, two, three, or four of the supposedly distinct forms can be used interchangeably (v. 13.3), while in other instances a trend is emerging that is not reflected by the traditional rules. Contrastive analysis would identify the problems of English speakers (whose relative forms vary too, but differently) if they transferred their native system to the target one, and within Spanish it would distinguish those cases in which the grammar is relatively fixed from those in which it sets up options.

0.3 The limits of linguistics in language pedagogy. Like any other pedagogical tools, contrastive analysis and other applications of linguistics have their limits. Linguistics provides information on language, but (as explained in Chapter 16) there is far more to what happens in the foreign language classroom than the imparting and receiving of new words, new endings, new sounds, and new structures. The ways in which the individual learner is internalizing and using the material can also be an important variable, and this fact is not always taken into account when linguists make generalizations about interference between linguistic systems. Among the special problems noted by van Els et al. (1984) are the following. First, not all errors which one might anticipate on the basis of contrastive analysis will actually occur, and different learners will evince different degrees of interference. For example, some English speakers try to use a -'s possessive on Spanish nouns, but most seem to accept the *de* possessive with little difficulty. Second, many errors have an intralingual source (within L2) rather than an interlingual one (transfer from L1). Thus, when English speakers confuse *sentir* with *sentar* or overgeneralize their *sient-* (*sientía sientaba* for *sentía sentaba*), the problem is not due to English (except insofar as English *feel* and *sit* are less similar and lack *ie* stem changes). Third, instead of projecting L1 patterns onto L2, students may just avoid those L2 patterns that give them trouble. For example, to the frustration of the teacher who sets up a drill to practice Spanish object pronouns, English speakers often repeat the full nouns: '¿Terminaste el examen de estadística?' 'Sí, terminé el examen de estadística.' Finally, language learners from all language backgrounds exhibit certain similarities in the course of developing their L2 skills. One such similarity is a tendency, at certain levels, to omit 'grammatical words' (functors) such as articles, prepositions, and auxiliaries, even when their L1 has some equivalent of these. Consequently, the L1 interference described by contrastive analysis undoubtedly exists in L2 study, but it is not the only source of difficulty; teachers must also consider the roles played by general cognitive processes, social interaction, and even personal idiosyncrasies in learning a language.

Moreover, although some of the facts revealed by linguistics can be directly translated into improved presentations, activities, syllabi, and remediations, others will be more useful to teachers as background information for the decisions they must make; such is the case, for example, with much of the dialect variation surveyed in Chapter 3. Finally, linguists have generally had more to say about models of language and of language acquisition than about teaching styles, drilling techniques, philosophies of education, and methods for stimulating student interest and progress. They are among the first to admit that knowledge of *ser* vs. *estar*, for instance, does not by itself ensure the ability to teach and practice this distinction successfully in the classroom. The methodology of foreign language pedagogy is complemented by linguistics, but is generally recognized as a distinct discipline with its own contributions to teacher preparation and training.

But what value linguistics does have in pedagogy is predicated on the assumption that correct information about source and target languages is a necessary, if not sufficient, condition for successful teaching; teachers are not mere parrots mindlessly modeling to younger parrots, but knowledgeable professionals who efficiently and effectively *teach*. Whatever information is offered to them, they are able to evaluate it in light of their goals and their own students' problems, and to apply it in the manner they deem best.

Part One: Phonology

Chapter 1
Introduction to phonology

1.0 Phonology vs. orthography. Human messages are sent by sound, gesture, written marks, eye contact, body movement, and electronic impulses; but for most of us the main channels are speech sounds and writing. When reflecting on language, some people may confuse the two by taking speech as an imperfect rendition of the 'real' language, the written one. Yet phonology and orthography are rather distinct systems, and if either depends on the other, the latter should be assumed to be based on the former. Facts such as the following support this assumption.

(1) Humans normally learn their language orally (and aurally) years before learning its orthography. In fact, billions of perfectly knowledgeable language users communicate throughout their lives with no assistance from written marks.

(2) Many areas of language are communicated in speech but ignored in writing. One example is intonation, the pitch inflection of the voice; English stress (as with the difference between the noun *object* and the verb *object*) is another.

(3) Certain principles are difficult to state in terms of orthography alone. For example, the Spanish conjunction *y* 'and' is often said to change to *e* before the vowel *i*. What is actually meant is the sound [i], not the letter *i*, since the change also occurs before *hi*: *hijos e hijas*. But it would still be wrong to state the change as occurring before the spellings *i* and *hi*, for it does not occur in *agua y hielo* (where *hi* represents a sound that is not [i] at all).

Consequently, linguists regard the phonology of a language as the primary or more basic output component, and attempt to study it apart from orthography.

1.1 Review of phonetics. The study of speech sounds, or PHONES, is called PHONETICS; and any indication of all discernible details of a given pronunciation is called a PHONETIC REPRESENTATION (or phonetic transcription). Bypassing the letters of orthography, linguists adopt specially defined phonetic symbols in order to represent the speech sounds they describe, and enclose them in square brackets ([]) for a phonetic representation. Although there are noteworthy variations in symbol preference, the most widespread transcriptional system is that of the International Phonetic Alphabet (IPA), a version of which is adopted in this book. Whenever possible, symbols chosen for the IPA were drawn from the Roman alphabet if these were fairly consistently used in the alphabets of Europe; thus, for the sound spelled *b* in Eng. *bat* (Fr. *bas*, Ger. *böse*, Span. *bajo*, etc.), there was early consensus on the symbol [b]. But for many of the phones to be taken up in this book's discussion of English and Spanish, the IPA arrived at symbols that are unusual, given English or Spanish orthography. For reference a complete list of symbols is given in Appendix 2.

It is not enough merely to symbolize phones; their articulation must also be described. [b], for example, is a consonant made by stopping the airstream with the lips while the vocal cords are vibrating, a description that is conveniently summarized by the label 'voiced bilabial stop'. The next sections will review the descriptive terms found in most introductory courses in linguistics.

1.1.1 Classes of sounds. The three major classes of phones are vowels (V), glides (G), and consonants (C). VOWELS include sounds such as the [i] of Eng. *see* (*sea*) and Span. *si*; they typically function as the peaks of syllables (v. 2.3). GLIDES include sounds such as the [j] beginning Eng. *you* (and occurring after the *f* of *few*), and the [w] of Eng. *woo*; they are also called semivowels (or in Spanish, *semivocales* when they precede vowels and *semiconsonantes* when they follow vowels). Such sounds are brief transitional glidings toward a vowel; unlike true vowels, they are never syllabic, and one key difference between [i] and [j] is the syllabicity of the former. CONSONANTS are characterized by greater and more deliberate constriction in the vocal tract than glides, and they occur around vowels in the formation of syllables.

Consonants, in turn, can be broken down into three main subclasses. In NASALS (or nasal stops), the airstream is blocked somewhere in the oral cavity and the air is deflected through the nasal cavity. Nasals can be symbolized as a group by N. Examples include the [m] and [n] of Eng. *man* and Span. *mano*. In LIQUIDS (symbolized L), there is some kind of [l] or [r] articulation with a characteristic resonance that is both vowel- and consonant-like; but 'liquid' is articulatorily vague, given the variety of *r*-sounds found in language. In OBSTRUENTS (O), the airstream is obstructed (but not deflected through the nose), either completely as with the [t] of

Eng. *stew* and Span. *tú*, or just to the extent that friction-like noise results, as with the [s] of Eng. *see* and Span. *si*.

1.1.2 Voicing. There are two muscle folds within the larynx, the vocal cords, that may come together and vibrate as air passes between them. This vibration is called VOICE. Sounds having this feature are called VOICED; sounds in which the vocal cords are spread apart (as in normal breathing) are called VOICELESS. V, G, N, and L are normally voiced in all languages, and these sound classes are acoustically perceived as resonance resulting from the passage of a voiced airstream through the nasal or oral cavities. Because of this resonance, they are sometimes called SONORANTS. Obstruents may be either voiced or voiceless, and many languages have pairs of obstruents contrasting in voicing: the [f] and [s] of Eng. *fat* and *race* are voiceless as opposed to the [v] and [z] of *vat* and *raise*, which are voiced.

The rate and energy of vocal cord vibration can be modulated and finely controlled. When the vocal cords are made to vibrate faster, the pitch rises (as in the question *Do you see?*); when made to vibrate more energetically, their voicing is louder and may be perceived as stress, as in the difference in syllable loudness between Eng. *object* (verb) and *object* (noun). Stress can be shown either by an accent on the vowel (*objéct, óbject*) or by a raised vertical stroke before its syllable (*obʹject, ʹobject*); lack of stress can be indicated by a breve or left unmarked (*ŏbjéct = objéct*).

1.1.3 Place and manner of articulation. Consonants and glides are described in terms of two other parameters: where they are made (place or point of articulation) and how they are made (manner of articulation). The place of articulation is taken to be the point in the vocal tract where a constriction occurs. For sounds such as the [p] of *pat* and the [f] of *fat*, this is LABIAL (made with the lips), specifically BILABIAL ('both lips') for [p] and LABIODENTAL ('lip plus teeth') for [f]. For sounds such as the [t] of *tin*, the [θ] represented by the *th* of *thin*, and the [š] (also symbolized [ʃ]) spelled by the *sh* of *shin*, the articulation is CORONAL, meaning that the forward part of the tongue approaches or contacts some point in the area between the teeth and hard palate. Within this area, finer points of articulation are customarily distinguished: DENTAL when there is contact with the upper teeth (as in [θ]), ALVEOLAR when there is contact with the gum ridge (alveolae) behind the teeth (as in Eng. [t]), and ALVEOPALATAL when there is contact with both the gum ridge and the forward part of the palate (as in [š]). Coronal sounds further require at times the specification of which part of the tongue (tip or blade) is used, and whether the tongue surface is relatively flat or curled back.

Five other major points of articulation are palatal, velar, labiovelar, uvular, and glottal. In PALATAL articulations, the middle (not the tip) of the tongue rises to or towards the palate; English has only one palatal, [j], but as a glide this sound never quite reaches the palate. In VELAR articulations, the back of the tongue rises to or toward the soft palate (velum); this is where Eng. [k] (spelled *c* in *cut*, *k* in *book*, *q* in *quit*) is pronounced. In LABIOVELAR articulations there is simultaneous labial and velar constriction; Eng. [w] is labiovelar, but like [j] it is only a glide that approaches a point of articulation. UVULAR articulations are made on the uvula, the pendulous extension of the velum; English makes no consistent use of the uvula in speech, although some varieties of Spanish do (v. 3.1.8). Finally, in GLOTTAL articulations there is no oral constriction at all; instead, the vocal cords modify the sound without voicing it. Eng. [h] as in *hat* is often termed a glottal fricative since it is just the 'aspiration' or rushing of air through the open larynx and vocal tract.

Manners of articulation are named for the degree of constriction or obstruction. In STOPS (or plosives, or occlusives) such as [t], there is a complete blockage of the airstream; in FRICATIVES (or spirants) such as [f] and [s], the airstream continues through with relatively noisy turbulence due to a constriction that narrows the passage without blocking it. These two types of obstruents are analyzed as differing in their 'continuance'. Many subtypes are distinguished: the stop can be imploded or exploded, released or unreleased, pronounced with or without an [h]-like puff of aspiration, and so on. Likewise, the fricatives may be SIBILANT ('hissy'), as with [s] and [š], or nonsibilant, as with [f] and [θ]. Finally, it is possible to articulate a stop released as a fricative, a manner of articulation called AFFRICATE. The consonant spelled *ch* in Eng. *chat* and Span. *chato* is an affricate, and is symbolized [č]; alternatively, it can be shown as a kind of stop-fricative compound, [tš] (or [tʃ]).

There are various manners of sonorant articulation. NASALS, as described earlier, involve the deflection of the airstream through the nasal cavity; this results from a slight dropping of the velum, which otherwise (i.e. in nonnasal or ORAL sounds) is raised to shut off the nasal chambers. With LATERALS such as [l], the tongue firmly contacts a point of articulation, but unlike stops, laterals allow the airstream to continue over the side(s) of the tongue. With *r*-sounds, several manners of articulation are involved, and these will be dealt with in detail in a fuller comparison of English and Spanish (v. 2.1.3).

1.1.4 Vowels. Vowels are described in terms of their tongue position. For the vowel called 'schwa', [ə], occurring in the last syllable of Eng. *idea* and *circus*, the tongue is roughly in its rest position: it is MID (neither raised nor lowered) and CENTRAL (neither advanced nor retracted). The terms FRONT, BACK, HIGH, and LOW, respectively, indicate a vowel articulation in which the tongue moves forward, pulls back, is raised, or is lowered from this mid central position. Alternatively, since raising and lowering the tongue may be accompanied by the raising and lowering of the jaw, high and low vowels are sometimes called 'close' and 'open' vowels. In addition, the lips may be pursed out (ROUNDED) or spread (UNROUNDED)for any tongue position. Four vowels shared by English and Spanish (aside from details to be explained later) can be described as follows:

[i] (Eng. *see, tea*, Span. *si, ti*): high front unrounded
[e] (Eng. *they, day*, Span. *de*): mid front unrounded
[o] (Eng. *toe, tow, though*, Span. *todo*): mid back rounded
[u] (Eng. *Sue, zoo, do*, Span. *su*): high back rounded

In the tongue's low position, English distinguishes a front [æ] (*sack*) from a back [ɑ] (*sock, car*); Span. [a] (*saca*) is roughly central or front-central.

In the articulation of DIPHTHONGS, the tongue begins in one vowel position and then glides away toward another. For instance, the vowel of Eng. *night* or in the first syllable of Span. *naipe* begins with a fairly low front tongue position and then moves into a higher position approaching the palatal glide [j]. Some phoneticians symbolize such a diphthong with two vowel symbols representing the beginning and ending of the movement: [ai], [aɪ], [ae]. Others use a vowel symbol for the beginning tongue position followed by a glide symbol for the direction of movement: [aj]. The latter practice will be followed in this book.

English furthermore distinguishes TENSE and LAX articulations. The vowels [ɪ] of *bit*, [ɛ] of *bet*, [ɔ] of *caught*, and [ʊ] of *look* are, respectively, like the [i] of *beat*, the [e] of *bait*, and the [o] of *coat*, and the [u] of *Luke*, except that [ɪ ɛ ɔ ʊ] are laxer or pronounced with a more relaxed articulation than the tense [i e o u]. Although not all phoneticians agree that tenseness is the key distinction in these vowels, many believe that it is specifically the tongue root that contracts or relaxes to bring about the contrast. Tense and lax are also applied at times to consonantal articulation, in which case they may be termed FORTIS and LENIS: in general, voiceless stops tend to be more fortis (tenser) than voiced ones.

The traditional terminology for phonetic description leaves consonants and glides labeled with one set of terms (e.g. 'voiceless velar stop' for [k]), and vowels with an entirely different set ('rounded tense high back vowel' for [u]). This makes it difficult to describe the effects of one group on the other. For example, [k] commonly changes its place of articulation, becoming almost palatal before [i] (as in Eng. *key*, Span. *quiso*), but staying fully back before [u] (as in Eng. *cool*, Span. *culto*). Apparently, the [k] ASSIMILATES somewhat to the tongue position of the vowel, adapting to it or becoming more like it, and this fact is lost as long as C and V are handled with different parameters. As a remedy, some Spanish phoneticians carry over consonantal terms to vowels; front vowels are *vocales palatales* and back vowels are *vocales velares*. Recent American phoneticians use 'back' for both back vowels and velars, and 'nonback' for front vowels and palatals, in order to explain the same relationship.

1.2 Phonemes, allophones, and rules. Although the linguist refers to phones in describing pronunciation, the basic units of phonology are more abstract entities called PHONEMES. Phonemes are shown by symbols in diagonals: /i/, /č/, /t/, etc.; so are the PHONEMIC REPRESENTATIONS of words (/tič/ for *teach*). Every language has a finite set of phonemes, about 17 to 50 or so, even though the actual number of recorded phones may number in the hundreds. On the surface of a language (i.e. the sounds emitted by the speakers), a trained phonetician can perceive many different phones, but its native speakers will interpret those phones as variants of the underlying phonemes of their language, ignoring differences that do not 'count' in listening for the differences between words. For example, English speakers round their lips in saying the /r/ of *rack*, devoice (make voiceless) the /r/ of *track*, and neither round nor devoice the /r/ of *car*. In a phonetic representation, the three sounds could be recorded, respectively, as [rʷ], [r̥], and [r]. But English speakers react to them as variants (ALLOPHONES) of the same phoneme, /r/; without training, they do not hear the differences and are unaware of making them. The /r/ can become rounded [rʷ] or voiceless [r̥] without any confusion with other English phonemes that signal different words. Yet, if the articulation of the /r/ were to intrude into the articulatory space of /l/, English speakers would readily perceive the change: /r/ and /l/ are used to contrast MINIMAL PAIRS in English, i.e. words whose distinguishability depends on the phonetic difference, such as *rack* and *lack*, *berry* and *belly*, *write* and *light*. Thus, [rʷ] and [r̥] are not separate phonemes but allophones of one (no English minimal pair ever hinges on that difference), whereas /r/ and /l/ are distinct phonemes. Japanese speakers, in contrast, perceive [r] and [l] as the same phoneme, hearing no more difference between them than English speakers do between [r] and [r̥]. While phonological structure is not entirely different from one language to the next, what is phonemically contrastive in one language may be allophonic in another.

As another example, consider the English minimal pairs *den/then, day/they, ride/writhe*. These show the distinction between the two phonemes /d/ and /ð/ in English, and it can be predicted that English speakers will be alert to the difference between *She's riding* and *She's writhing*. Spanish speakers, however, will not readily sense the difference since their language organizes [d] and [ð] as allophones of the same phoneme. There are no minimal pairs such as /rajd/ (*ride*) vs. /rajð/ (*writhe*) in Spanish, and in fact, the same word can be pronounced with either phone, depending on its environment: *dónde* is [dónde] in *¿Dónde está?* but [ðónde] in *¿De dónde es?*, and native speakers are unaware of the change in pronunciation unless they have received phonetic training. On the other hand, Spanish makes a phonemic distinction between the velar stop /k/ and the corresponding velar fricative /x/ (spelled *jota*), as in the minimal pair *carro/jarro*. English does not make this distinction, and although English speakers occasionally use a *jota* sound in a relaxed pronunciation of the medial /k/ of *recognize*, they interpret it as representing English /k/, not some other phoneme.

In order to explain the difference between the underlying phonemic representation of a word and its phonetic representation, many linguists posit PHONOLOGICAL RULES. For example, one can state as a general process for Spanish that /d/ changes to [ð] in certain environments (v. 3.1.6), as in /dónde/ → [ðónde] in *de dónde*, /déxes/ → [ðéxes] in *¡no lo dejes!*, and /adjós/ → [aðjós] in *adiós*. The various allophones of Eng. /r/ are similarly explained as arising from the application of phonological rules. English lacks a /d/ → [ð] rule, these being distinct phonemes in its system; and Spanish lacks an /r/-rounding rule. Consequently, a student who transfers his English rules to Spanish may have an 'accent' or nonnative pronunciation, or may even obliterate the distinctions among Spanish phonemes, making word recognition difficult. Moreover, by failing to acquire the phonological rules that are peculiarly Spanish, the learner may again have an accent or may misunderstand Spanish phonemes when they appear in their altered phonetic guises: '[ðéxe]? What's a *they-kay*?' Such interference between source and target language phonologies will be the focus of attention in the following three chapters.

Chapter 2
Phonemes

2.0 Comparing phonemic systems. This chapter first compares the consonant and vowel systems of Spanish with those of English. Next, it discusses the different ways in which the two languages join phonemes to form syllables and words. Finally, since pedagogy usually takes up Spanish phonemes in terms of their orthography, spelling conventions are described and distinguished from phonological processes. The classical methods of contrastive analysis (v. 0.2.1) have been particularly successful in this arena of phonology, because a comparison of phonemic systems readily reveals cases of shared elements (e.g. Span. /m/ = Eng. /m/), of similar elements with different form or function (e.g. /t/ and /j/ in the two languages), and of wholly different elements or patterns (e.g. the Spanish *eñe* and *erre* sounds, which English lacks).

2.1 Consonants. English and Spanish share many of the same consonants and spell them similarly. The major problems center on shared phonemes with different articulations, Spanish phonemes that are absent from the English system, and dialect variation at two major points in the Spanish system.

2.1.1 General comparison of consonant systems. Figures 2.1 and 2.2 present the consonant systems of Spanish and English. The two systems are constructed similarly: both make voiceless/voiced distinctions in their stops (/p t k/ vs. /b d g/), both distinguish two glides (/j w/) and three nasals, and there is much direct overlapping in that /f m l s č n g . . . / occur in both. In learning the consonant phonemes of Spanish, therefore, the English speaker need not start from scratch, and this fact is regularly exploited by pedagogical instructions such as 'Span. *f* is pronounced like the *f* of Eng. *find*'.

Figure 2.1 Spanish consonant and glide phonemes. (Symbols in parentheses represent phonemes that do not occur in all dialects.)

		bil.	labd.	dent.	alv.	alvp.	pal.	vel.	labv.
Stop	vl.	p		t		č		k	
	vd.	b		d				g	
Fricative (vl.)			f	(θ)	s			x	
Nasal (vd.)		m			n		ɲ		
Lateral (vd.)					l		(ʎ)		
Tap/flap (vd.)					r				
Trill (vd.)					r̄				
Glide (vd.)							j		w

16

Figure 2.2 English consonant and glide phonemes.

		bil.	labd.	dent.	alv.	alvp.	pal.	vel.	labv.	glot.
Stop	vl.	p			t	č		k		
	vd.	b			d	ǰ		g		
Fricative	vl.		f	θ	s	š				h
	vd.		v	ð	z	ž				
Nasal (vd.)		m			n			ŋ		
Lateral (vd.)					l					
Approximant or glide (vd.)					r		j		w	

Abbreviations of places of articulation (v. 1.1.3):

bil.: bilabial   alv.: alveolar   vel.: velar
labd.: labiodental   alvp.: alveopalatal   labv.: labiovelar
dent.: dental   pal.: palatal   glot.: glottal

Abbreviations of voicing state (v. 1.1.2):
vl.: voiceless   vd.: voiced

2.1.2 Consonants with different articulations: /t d/. One must be careful in equating phonemes because of their symbols alone. Both languages have two phonemes conventionally symbolized /t/ and /d/, but this does not mean that they are identical. One difference is articulatory: these stops are dental in Spanish but alveolar in English. That is, the Spanish speaker pronounces them with the apex (tip of the tongue) against the edges of the inner surfaces of the upper front teeth, an articulation symbolized [t̪ d̪] in a detailed (or NARROW) phonetic transcription. The English speaker, on the other hand, articulates them with the apex or blade on the alveolar ridge just above and behind the upper teeth, as shown in Figure 2.3. Another difference is distributional: Spanish /t d/ readily occur before the glide /j/ as in *tierno* and *diente* /tjérno djénte/, but English /t d/ do not;[1] this is treated as a matter of PHONOTACTICS (v. 2.3). Still other differences are introduced by the application of phonological rules, whereby Spanish /d/ more often appears as a fricative than as a stop (v. 3.1.6), and English /t/ in various positions is aspirated, flapped, or preglottalized (v. 3.2.1-3.2.3).

Transferring an alveolar /t d/ to one's Spanish causes a slight accent but no serious misunderstandings. Whatever their phonetic realizations, the phonemes /t d/ are present in both languages and have similar functional roles: they contrast in minimal pairs (*tía/día*, *tie/die*) and occupy roughly the same positions in their respective systems. More problematic are those phonemes which are present in one system but not in the other, and these receive more pedagogical attention.

Figure 2.3 Dental and alveolar /t d/.

Dental [t̪ d̪] as in *té, de*   Alveolar [t d] as in *stay, day*

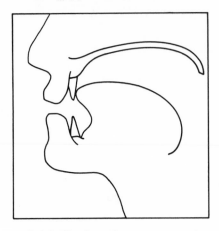 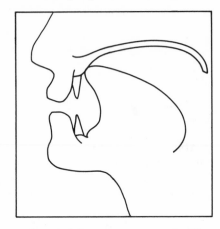

2.1.3 Unshared consonants. A comparison of the two systems in Figures 2.1-2.2 reveals that the consonants /v ð z ž š ǰ h ŋ/ are present in English but not in Spanish. As will be shown in Chapter 3, many of these consonants do occur phonetically in Spanish as allophones of other phonemes: [ŋ] occurs for the /n/ of *cinco* and [ð] for the /d/ of *cada*. But they do not contrast with other phonemes as in English nor do they form minimal pairs like English /n/ vs. /ŋ/ in *run/rung*, or /d/ vs. /ð/ in *dough/though*. Thus one might forget about these un-Spanish English phonemes in pedagogy and dispense with seemingly lame statements such as 'the English *sh* sound does not occur in Spanish.' Yet they do cause some interference in at least two ways. First, orthography may cue the use of an English phoneme that the student has never heard in the teacher's model; for instance, Spanish has no /v/, but the spelling of *conversar* and *invitar* seems to demand one instead of Spanish /b/. Second, several Spanish phones may be equated with English phonemes because of a real or perceived acoustic resemblance. Thus, many students hear the fricative allophone [β] (v. 3.1.6) of /b/ in *saber* or *nueve* not as a new sound to be acquired, but as some kind of English /v/, and they so pronounce it.

2.1.3.1 The *eñe* /ɲ/. The Spanish phonemes or phonemic distinctions lacking English counterparts are /ɲ/, /x/, /r/ vs. /r̄/, and in some dialects the *elle* (v. 2.1.4.1). /ɲ/ is the palatal nasal spelled ñ. Contrary to the descriptions of many texts, it is not the English *ni* or *ny* of *onion, canyon*, but a single nasal sound formed by pressing the middle of the tongue firmly against the palate, with the apex tucked down behind the lower teeth. English *ni* or *ny* represents a sequence of two sounds, the /n/ of *can* followed by the /j/ of *you*: the apex contacts the alveolar ridge and then pulls away as the middle of the tongue briefly rises toward the palate and glides back down, never touching it. There is some acoustic similarity between /ɲ/ and /nj/, but they are distinct, as illustrated in Figure 2.4, and Spanish contrasts them in minimal pairs; *uñón* vs. *unión, huraño* vs. *uranio.*[2]

Figure 2.4 Palatal nasal vs. alveolar nasal + palatal glide.

/ɲ/ in Span. *cañón, huraño*   /nj/ of Span. *uranio,* Eng. *canyon*

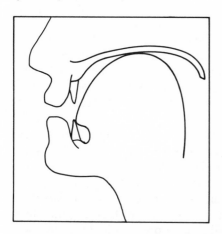
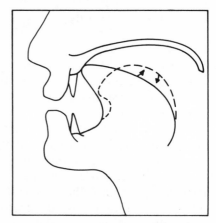

2.1.3.2 The *jota* /x/. The symbol *x* in phonology represents a voiceless velar fricative, not the /ks/ of Eng. *box* of Span. *éxito,* and it transcribes the *jota* (and *g* before *e* or *i*) of most Spanish speakers. /x/ is the fricative counterpart of the stop /k/; with /k/ the back of the tongue (dorsum) presses firmly against the velum so as to stop the airstream there, but for /x/ it comes just close enough to the velum (or for some speakers, the uvula) to constrict the airstream and cause turbulence. The two contrast in numerous minimal pairs: *carro* vs. *jarro, coco* vs. *cojo, quema* vs. *gema, cura* vs. *jura,* etc. English speakers may miss the contrast and perceive /x/ as some kind of /k/, just as they usually hear and reproduce the same sound in the German name *Bach* as Eng. /k/. If the friction of the /x/ is weaker, they may interpret it as a raspy /h/. In fact, in southern Andalusia, the Caribbean dialects, and much of Central America, Colombia, Venezuela, Spanish /x/ does weaken to the glottal fricative or aspiration [h].[3] This variant will obviously be easier than [x] for English speakers, but it is not the typical *jota* of most Spanish speakers.

2.1.3.3 The flap and trill. English has only one *r* phoneme, and although it is symbolized /r/, it is not a Spanish /r/. In American English, /r/ is phonetically a RETROFLEX APPROXIMANT. It is retroflex in that the apex curls up and back (or, for some speakers, the tongue bunches up), and approximant in that the tongue vaguely 'approaches' the roof of the mouth without making contact; it is really more like a glide (/j w/) than a true consonant. In a narrow transcription, this articulation is shown by the symbol [ɹ]. Moreover, it is reinforced by lip rounding before a vowel, as in *rack* or *around*; since lip rounding is indicated by a raised *w*, this phone can be shown as [ɹʷ]. The two are allophones of one English phoneme, /r/.

Spanish distinguishes two *r* phonemes, neither of them rounded, retroflex, or approximant. With /r/ as in *caro*, the apex flaps once against the alveolar ridge: this is a FLAP (or tap, or *vibrante simple*), symbolized in a narrow transcription by [ɾ]. With /r̄/ as in *carro*, the apex flutters rapidly against the alveolar ridge; this is the TRILL (or *vibrante múltiple*). For lovers of detail, Navarro (1967:122) has calculated that the trill normally has two vibrations after /n/ (*honra* /ónr̄a/), three initially or before a stressed vowel (*roca* /r̄óka/, *corremos* /kor̄émos/), and four after a stressed vowel (*carro* /kár̄o/, *corre* /kór̄e/). Nevertheless, what matters is not the exact number of vibrations in the trill, but only that it have perceptibly more than the one of /r/.

No other Spanish phonemes cause so many American students to balk right away. The flap [ɾ] should not be articulatorily difficult for them since they have almost exactly the same sound for their intervocalic *t, tt, d, dd* in *Betty, water, latter=ladder, seating=seeding* (v. 3.2.3). The problem with [ɾ] is phonemic and orthographic: students can and do use it, but they resolutely regard it as a /t/ or /d/ according to the laws of English phonology and spelling, not as an /r/. But the trill is the more formidable of the two, and many students have a ready rejoinder when they are introduced to it: 'I can't do that!' It may be useless to instruct them to imitate motors, since (1) those who cannot trill even for motors will give only an earnest '[ɹɹɹ]' instead of '[r̄r̄r̄]' and (2) those who *can* imitate motors with a trill do not view onomatopoeic sound effects as likely phonemes combinable with other phonemes to form words, any more than they would accept hiccups and cockadoodledoos in human speech. To perceive their difficulty, the reader might try trilling the lips as for 'brrrr!' or clicking the tongue as for *tch-tch*, and try using these consonants in fluently articulated 'words'; both are so used in some languages, but they seem bizarre as phonemes to Spanish and English speakers alike.

The pronunciation of /r̄/ requires the following articulatory steps:

(a) The apex must rise to the alveolar ridge, as for Spanish and English [ɾ]. Seen from above, the tongue would look concave (Navarro 1967:122), with the tip up and the rest down. The whole tongue is, and remains, relaxed, for it is not its musculature that initiates the trilling.

(b) A voiced airstream must rush through at high velocity, i.e. under increased pressure from the lungs. The apex, instead of tapping once on the alveolar ridge, as in a normal airstream, will vibrate against it. Without the additional air pressure, there will be no trill but only a flap or series of flaps, [ɾəɾəɾə ...].

Most defects in students' articulations of /r̄/ come from a lack of one or both of the above components. The apex may be wrongly placed, the body of the tongue may be too high, airflow may be too weak, or the tongue may be tensed up in anticipation of the legendary *bête noire* of Spanish. Students can usually master /r̄/ if they know precisely what to do (with more precision than most texts offer), truly wish to do it, practice doing it, and do it with guidance from a teacher who can diagnose the problem and who insists on mastery.

Of the two vibrants, only /r̄/ occurs word-initially (*roca, riesgo*) and after /n s l/ (*honra, Israel, alrededor*), despite the orthographic *ere*. After other consonants (*cobro, creo, otro*), only /r/ appears. Word-finally or before a consonant (*armar, servir, ardar*)—i.e. syllable-finally—the flap is usual, but for emphasis it can be strengthened to [r̄]; the contrast being neutralized[4] here, the substitution of a trill for the flap does not disrupt intelligibility. Intervocalically, though, the two contrast in abundant minimal pairs: *caro/carro, pero/perro, coro/corro, vara/barra, quería/querría, enterado/enterrado, mira/mirra*, etc.

2.1.4 Dialect variations. In English, vowels show considerable dialect variation while consonants are fairly stable and uniform; in Spanish, it is the consonants that vary more. Those variations that involve phonological rules will be taken up in the next chapter, but there are two points at which the phonemes themselves vary: (1) presence vs. absence of a /ʎ j/ distinction (*calló/cayó, valla/vaya, halla/haya, arrollo/arroyo, llena/hiena*), and presence vs. absence of a /θ s/ distinction (*caza/casa, vez/ves, cierra/sierra, bazo/baso*). According to most texts, both distinctions are maintained in Spain and both are lost (merged) in the New World, but the actual situation is not so straightforward.[5]

2.1.4.1 *Lleísmo* vs. *yeísmo.* The symbol ʎ represents a palatal lateral for what is spelled as the *elle*, and this sound is often equated with the *li* (/lj/) of English *million*. As with the similar matching of /ɲ/ with /nj/, this is incorrect. /lj/ in *million* is a sequence of two sounds, an alveolar lateral followed by a palatal glide; /ʎ/ is one sound, articulated (like /ɲ/) with the apex down and the middle of the tongue pressed against the palate. There are some minimal pairs for /lj/ vs. /ʎ/ in Spanish, *polio/pollo, aliar/hallar*, that demonstrate the difference.

Dialects that distinguish /ʎ/ in *calló* from /j/ in *cayó* are called *lleísta*, and include northern Spain, marginal pockets of Andalusia, northern Argentina, northern Chile, and most of the Andean highlands from Bolivia to Bogotá. All other dialects are *yeísta*, merging /ʎ/ with /j/ so that *calló* is pronounced like *cayó*. Even in northern Spain, *yeísmo* is pushing back *lleísmo* in urban centers and radiating outward into the countryside. *Lleísmo* is definitely a recessive feature in modern Spanish, and for the vast majority of speakers the /ʎ/ has become /j/.

2.1.4.2 /s θ/: *Distinción, seseo, ceceo, ceseo.* One of the best known features of 'Peninsular' Spanish is the use of the voiceless dental fricative /θ/ for the sound spelled by *z* or (before *e* or *i*) *c*: *cierra* and *vez* /θjér̄a béθ/ vs. *sierra* and *ves* /sjér̄a bés/. /θ/ is not distinguished from /s/ in any part of

Spanish America, and there *cierra* and *sierra*, *vez* and *ves*, and so on are homonyms: /sjéřa bés/. This merger of /θ/ with /s/ is called *seseo*; maintenance of a distinction is called simply *distinción* (not *ceceo*, which refers to a different situation discussed below).[6]

Crosscutting this dialect difference in *distinción*/merger of *cierra* and *sierra* is a second one involving the articulation of /s/. Spanish speakers make a variety of fricatives in the dental-to-alveolar area. The three main types are described below, and are pictured in Figure 2.5.[7]

(a) LAMINOALVEOLAR. This is the /s/ that English speakers typically use. The blade (lamina) of the tongue is in light contact with the alveolar ridge and forms a back-to-front groove against it. Air is forced through this little

Figure 2.5 Three fricatives used in *cierra* and/or *sierra*.

(a) Laminoalveolar [s]

(b) Apicoalveolar [ś]

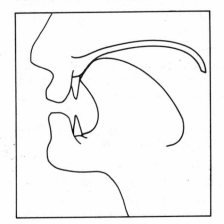
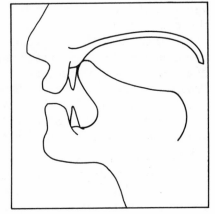

(c) Apicodental [θ]

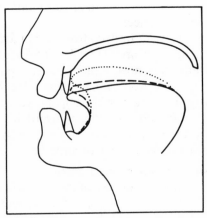

groove, resulting in hissiness (sibilance) that is markedly high-pitched and noisy. In Spanish, laminoalveolar /s/ is found in most of Spanish America, central Andalusia, and among some Castilians.

(b) APICOALVEOLAR. In this articulation, the apex alone rises to the alveolar ridge and forms a groove there; the blade and middle of the tongue are not used, but are dropped, yielding a concave tongue shape. Its sibilance is lower-pitched, reminding English speakers faintly of their /š/ in *shut* (which, however, is made quite differently). Apical /s/ may be symbolized [ś] phonetically, and it goes by several names: *ese apical, ese espesa, ese cóncava, ese castellana*. It is the /s/ used by most northern and central Spaniards, but it is found in scattered parts of Spanish America, including western Colombia, the Ecuadorian and Peruvian uplands, and western Puerto Rico. Despite the latter distributions, most nonusers associate it with Castile, whence *ese castellana*.

(c) APICODENTAL. In this articulation, represented by /θ/, the apex advances to the upper teeth and the blade is not used. Unlike both of the preceding sounds, it is not a sibilant, there being no hiss-making groove down the middle of the tongue. The apex may (1) protrude through the teeth (INTERDENTAL), (2) just touch the teeth edges without protruding, or (3) lightly touch the backs of the upper teeth. Type (2) is the usual one in English *thing, Cathy*, and Type (1) in Castilian *cinco, caza, cierra*; but in both the other types can also be heard.

As opposed to *distinción, seseo* means the use of some kind of sibilant /s/ for both *cierra* and *sierra*, usually the laminoalveolar one; and *ceceo* ('lisping') means the use of some kind of dental /θ/ for both. Dialect surveys earlier this century showed Andalusia to be three west-to-east bands in this regard. The northern one, northern Huelva province arching over to Almería, practices *distinción* of /θ/ vs. some kind of /s/ (*cierra* /θjér̄a/, *sierra* /sjér̄a/); the central one, around Córdoba and Sevilla, has *seseo* (*cierra=sierra* /sjér̄a/); and the southernmost one (Cádiz, Málaga, Granada) uses *ceceo* (*cierra=sierra* /θjér̄a/). Yet Dalbor (1980a:14) finds the current situation more variable, even 'chaotically' so; a single speaker alternates among *distinción, seseo, ceceo*, and aspiration (v. 3.1.5), so that *luz* is [luθ luś lus luh]. Dalbor believes that *distinción* is gradually permeating Andalusia from the north, but is not yet consistently used; a variable rule (v. 3.0), dependent on style, class, and situation, may be the only way to describe the current situation. As a convenient shorthand, though, Obaid (1973:63) has proposed the term *ceseo*.

2.2 Vowels and diphthongs. The vowel phonemes of the two languages are compared in Figure 2.6.[8] The English system is visibly the more complex one, making more vocalic distinctions than the Spanish system. In fact, English has two more vowels not shown in Figure 2.6. The first is schwa, [ə], which is a short, very lax, mid central vowel occurring in the unstressed syllables of *about, believe, item, gallop, suppose*, etc. It resem-

Figure 2.6 Spanish and English vowel phonemes.

Spanish vowels				English vowels (stressed)		
Front	Back			Front		Back
i	u	High	tense	i		u
			lax	ɪ		ʊ
e	o	Mid	tense	e		o
			lax	ɛ	ʌ	ɔ
a		Low		æ		ɑ

bles the /ʌ/ of *must*, which occurs in stressed syllables and is somewhat more open, longer, and more backed than the muffled schwa. Some phonologists have treated [ə] and [ʌ] as allophones of one phoneme; alternatively, schwa is more often treated today as an allophone of almost all English vowel phonemes, since they reduce to [ə] when unstressed (v. 3.2.7): *phon*[á]*logy* but *phon*[ə]*lógical*. The other additional vowel is /ər/, as in *her, fir = fur, word, murder, were*. Phonetically, /ər/ is really a single sound, a schwa with the curled-back apex of /r/, and this can be shown by the special symbol [ɚ] (or [ɝ]) in narrow transcription.

2.2.1 General comparison of systems. A glance at the two vowel systems suggests that it might be easier for English speakers to learn Spanish vowels than vice-versa. On a gross phonemic level, this is generally true. For the Spanish student of English, the contrasts between *beat* and *bit* (/i ɪ/), *pool* and *pull* /u ʊ/), *boat* and *bought* /o ɔ/), and *cat* and *cot* and *cut* /æ ɑ ʌ/) are notoriously troublesome, primarily because of a tense/lax distinction not used in Spanish. The English speaker, however, easily perceives the Spanish contrasts in *piso/peso/paso/pozo/puso*, and if he uses his English /i e a o u/ in Spanish, he will be understood (provided that he avoids reducing them to [ə] when they are unstressed).

But a direct transference causes at least a perceptible accent since the Spanish vowels are not exactly the same articulatorily. Spanish /a/ is equated with the English /ɑ/ in *father, cot* in most texts, but it is pronounced more in the front of the mouth than most English speakers' /ɑ/; it will seem between their /æ/ and /ɑ/—i.e. *saca* will sound like a cross between *sack* and *sock*.[9] /i e o u/ are pure vowels (MONOPHTHONGS) in Spanish, pronounced with a steady tongue position; but they are usually DIPH-THONGS in English, with the tongue (and lip) position changing during their articulation (v. 3.2.6). For English /i e o/, the tongue starts near Spanish /i e o/ and glides upward toward the palatal [j] position for /i e/, and back toward [w] for /o/: phonetically, they are [ij ej ow]. English /u/ is glided or diphthongized like /o/ but its beginning is not as well rounded or fully backed as Spanish /u/; it is centralized, as indicated by the symbol [ʉ] in the narrow phonetic transcription [ʉw].

If transferred to Spanish, English diphthongal /i u o/ sound strange but are recognizable. This is because Spanish has no diphthongs [ij uw ow] (except in *bou*) which might contrast in minimal pairs with /i u o/. But Spanish does distinguish /e/ from /ej/, and the English speaker who diphthongizes in *reno, pena, le, ves* will actually say *reino, peina, ley, veis*.

2.2.2 Diphthongs. In addition to its diphthongized /e i o u/ = [ej ij ow uw], English has the three diphthongs /aj/ (*buy = by, lie = lye, hi = high, eye = I*), /ɔj/ (*boy, noise*), and /aw/ (*now, loud, bow down*). In all three, the speaker begins with a vowel sound and then glides off toward a higher tongue position, whence the transcription of vowel plus glide, VG. But it is also possible to make a diphthong the other way around, starting with a glide and sliding down into a more open vowel; this is essentially what English speakers do in the /ju/ of *music* /mjúzɪk/, *cute, beauty*.[10] The first kind of diphthong, VG, is RISING (or upgliding), and the second, GV, is FALLING (or downgliding).

Although Spanish has only five simple vowel phonemes, it abounds in diphthongs of both kinds:

VG[11]		GV	
/aj/	hay, naipe, traigo	/ja/	piano, Asia, copia, diablo, lidiar
/ej/	reina, rey, ley, seis	/je/	pie, siete, fiel, pierdo, serie
/oj/	soy, oigo	/jo/	odio, idioma, acción, Dios, comió
/aw/	auto, auge, cauteloso	/ju/	diurno, ciudad, triunfo
/ew/	Europa, deuda	/wa/	cuajar, mutua, graduado, actual
/ow/	bou	/we/	puedo, juez, sueño, averigüe
		/wi/	muy, fui, cuidado, ruina
		/wo/	cuota, arduo, continuo, averiguo

Even with shared diphthongs—/aj/, /aw/, [ej]—there is a slight difference in that the upgliding is much faster and more definite in Spanish than in English. In English *eye*, the tongue dwells on the [a] and glides up a short way toward an indistinct position; in Spanish *hay*, this movement is quicker and it reaches a fairly high position. For the phonologist, however, the main problem is that the glides of Spanish diphthongs are not always phonemic glides, as shown in the next section.

2.2.3 Hiatus, syneresis, and the analysis of glides. Adjacent vowels may count as two separate syllables or they may blend into a diphthong as one of them loses its syllabicity and becomes a glide. The former condition, VV, is traditionally called HIATUS, and the latter, VV → GV or VG, is called SYNERESIS.[12] The rule laid down in many texts is as follows:

(a) A E O are STRONG vowels, and I U are WEAK;

(b) two adjacent strongs form separate syllables, i.e. stand in hiatus: *ca-e, pro-a*;

(c) strong + weak or weak + strong form one syllable, the weak becoming a glide (i.e., there is syneresis of the two vowels): *cai-go, grue-so*;

(d) . . . unless the weak one carries an accent: *ca-í, grú-a.*

This analysis is phonologically unclear because it is letter-based. The Strong-Weak rule 'changes' the vowel *i* to a glide ([j]) in *caigo*, making *ai* a diphthong instead of two syllabic vowels standing in hiatus. Yet *ai* in *caigo* spells exactly the same sound as *ay* in *hay*, namely /aj/, and neither can ever be pronounced [a-i]. *Caigo* does not 'start' as /ká-i-go/ and 'become' [káj-go]; it is /kájgo/ phonemically and undergoes no *ai* → [aj] rule at all in phonology. Likewise, the [we] of *grueso* does not come from a rule that changes two individual vowels, /u/ and /e/, to a diphthong; *grueso* is always pronounced [grwéso] and it is phonemically /grwéso/ too. AI = /aj/ and UE = /we/ are simply letter pronouncing instructions, like X = /ks/ and QU = /k/.

Nevertheless, there are cases in which the [j w] of Spanish diphthongs should be analyzed as allophones of the vowel phonemes /i u/, with a phonological rule that—like the Strong-Weak rule—changes unstressed high vowels to glides when next to another vowel. In one widespread analysis,[13] glides are regarded as phonemically /j w/ if and only if they are always pronounced as glides or consonants, never as real vowels; but they are treated as allophones of /i u/ if they do appear as full, syllabic vowels in some morphological or stylistic variants of the word. The following examples may clarify the application of this criterion.

(1) Always [j w], hence phonemically /j w/:

caigo, naipe, hay: always [aj], therefore /kájgo nájpe áj/.

peinar, causar, cuajar, copia: always [ej aw wa ja], therefore /pejnár kawsár kwaxár kópja/.

estudiar, averiguar: throughout the paradigms of these verbs, stem-final *i* and *u* spell glides and are never pronounced [i u], therefore /estudj- aberigw-/.

(2) Alternating with high vowels, hence phonemically /i u/:

aislar, aullar, prohibir: [aj aw oj] in these forms and others with unstressed stems, but [aí aú oí] in *aíslo, aúllo, prohíbo* (and others with stressed stems); therefore /aislár aujár proibír/.

enviar, continuar: [ja wa] in these forms (and others with unstressed stems), but [ío úo] in *envío, continúo,* and others with stressed stems; therefore their stems end in vowels, /embi- kontinu-/.

espiritual, melodioso: [wa jo] here, but corresponding to the glides [w j] are the vowels [u i] in *espíritu, melodía*; therefore /espiritu+al melodi+oso/.

The Gliding Rule needed for /i u/ → [j w] in (2) will be discussed in more detail in the next chapter (v. 3.1.10).

Even granting that the Strong-Weak rule is a partly true orthographic reflection of a phonological Gliding rule, there are three sets of data it cannot handle. First, contrary to its predictions, adjacent strongs also undergo syneresis; the expected hiatus is maintained in slow speech, but in faster (and normal) styles there is gliding here too: *oasis* → [wásis], *teatro* → [tjátro], *qué hay* → [kjáj], *qué hubo* → [kjúβo] (v. 3.1.10). Second, adjacent identical vowels are merged almost universally, whether strong or weak: *alcohol* /alkól/. According to Quilis and Fernández (1975:149), pairs such as *corte/cohorte*, *pasé/paseé*, *azar/azahar*, *de su uso/desuso* are distinguished only in 'un lenguaje muy cuidado o enfático,'[14] and otherwise are homonyms. Third, several normative phoneticians have recommended hiatus in a handful of words for which the Strong-Weak rule predicts syneresis: Navarro (1967:155, 158-59, 167) specifies *cru-el*, *fi-ar*, *su-ave*, *di-ario*, *vi-aje*, *bri-oso*, *tri-ángulo*, *avi-ón*, *ru-ido*, *jesu-ita*, *hu-ir* (and other *-uir* verbs), and *hi-ato* itself. Quilis and Fernández (1975:71) add a few others (*bi-óxido, cu-ota, di-edro* . . .) and the Real Academia (1979:48-57) quite outdoes itself in hiatophilia. If these hiatuses are actually practiced, and with consistency, then they throw a small monkey wrench into the Gliding Rule analysis as well as the Strong-Weak analysis, both of which predict diphthongs in all of these. But in fact, native speakers do not follow all these recommendations,[15] and the norm givers disagree anyhow; Quilis and Fernández prescribe *ruido* and *ruina* with [wi], but Navarro says [u-i].

2.2.4 Linking (liaison). Even with hiatus of adjacent vowels, the English speaker must learn to link them smoothly. Especially in slower styles (oral reading, emphatic or cautious speech, dictation, etc.), English speakers often separate the following with a catch in the voice, i.e. a glottal stop [ʔ]:

(1) the final vowel of one word and the initial one of the next: *two ʔeggs*
(2) the final consonant of one word and the initial vowel of the next: *ten ʔeggs, these ʔeggs, an ʔaim* (≠ *a name*).

Outside these slower styles, glottal stop insertion is rarer and *an aim* then converges with *a name*. But as teachers are well aware, the speech style of foreign language students is typically slow, especially at first; consequently, glottal stop insertion may appear more often in their Spanish than in their English. By contrast, Spanish requires full linking (LIAISON, *enlace*) among all consonants and vowels in a phrase. Thus, *tu éxito, ten éxito, un ama* will differ from *two eggs, ten eggs*, and *an aim* in their lack of glottal stop insertion.

2.3 The combining of phonemes into syllables and words. Traditional authorities such as the RAE (1979:44-63) have devoted much attention to syllabification, i.e. the rules for breaking words into their syllables and fixing syllable boundaries. The syllable boundaries are variously symbolized with hyphens, periods, or (especially in recent linguistic work) dollar signs. One well-known Spanish rule, for instance, concerns the treatment of medial consonants: VCV (as in *pasa*) is syllabified as V.CV, VCCV (*pasta*) as VC.CV (unless the second C is /l/ or /r/ as in *abre*, in which case V.CCV), and VCCCV (*instinto*) as VCC.CV (but again as VC.CCV if the last C is a liquid, as in *empleo*). As a result, the prefix *trans-* forms one syllable in *transnacional* /trans.na.θjo.nál/ but is broken up in *transeúnte* /tran.se.ún.te/.

For many decades, linguists gave only passing mention to the syllable, but many current phonologists (e.g. Harris 1983) have shown renewed interest in it. The syllable is now seen not only as a unit demarcated by boundaries, but as a phonological constituent characterized by internal structure. The central, most resonant part of the syllable is the PEAK (or NUCLEUS); what follows this peak (if anything) and completes the syllable is the CODA, and the peak and coda together comprise the RIME (this being that portion which words share when they are said to 'rhyme'). That part of the syllable that precedes the rime (if anything) is the ONSET, and it may contain several phonemes forming a CLUSTER. The only required constituent is the peak, which is always a vowel in Spanish; the onset and coda are optional, and they are always a consonant, glide, or cluster thereof. This constituent analysis of the syllable can be represented in a tree-like branching diagram (like the diagrams for syntactic structure, v. 5.2), such as that in Figure 2.7 for the syllables of *transeúnte*. (The sigma, σ, stands for 'syllable'.)

Figure 2.7 Syllable structure of *transeúnte*.

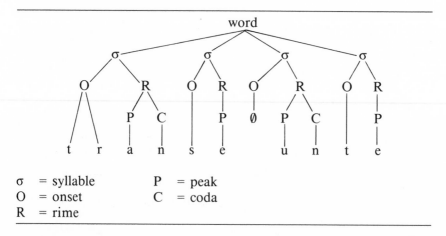

σ = syllable   P = peak
O = onset   C = coda
R = rime

English syllables are similarly constructed, and in fact, the onset + rime configuration seems universal; different languages will differ primarily in the phonemes they allocate to each part. But syllable boundaries are not as clear in English as in Spanish. A dictionary may syllabify *very* and *any* as /vér.i/ and /én.i/, but intervocalic consonants in English often seem to belong to both syllables, functioning both as the coda of one and as the onset of the next. Indeed, a spectrographic analysis shows the retroflexion of the /r/ and the nasality of the /n/ 'smearing' into both syllables. The term AMBISYLLABIC ('both syllables') has been applied to such fence straddlers.

The study of syllable structure is related to PHONOTACTICS, the description of how phonemes combine to form words. Syllable structure and phonotactics are not quite identical in their specifications; for one thing, Spanish liaison is so strong that words in a phrase are 'resyllabified' (Harris 1983:43) as if the word boundaries of phonotactics did not exist: *las hijas irán en el auto* thus becomes /la.sí.xa.si.rá.ne.ne.láw.to/. Consequently, it is difficult to study the phonemic structure of words apart from the phonemic combinations of syllables, and phonotactic generalizations (e.g. about how words begin and end) must take into account syllabic principles (e.g. onset and coda patterns).

In one way, namely, the distribution of glides, Spanish phonotactics is less constrained than English phonotactics. Spanish has more GV combinations than English, and these occur more freely after consonants. The /pw/ of *puerta*, the /trw/ of *trueco*, the /trj/ of *triunfo*, the /plj/ of *pliego*, and the /mw/ of *muero* are phonemic clusters that are rare or impossible in English, and they can give students trouble not because their phonemes are odd but because pronouncing them together in an onset is un-English. The /mw/ of *muero* thus becomes [mu-] or [muw-] in adaptation to English phonotactics. (Cf., however, the students' ease in pronouncing the English-like /kw/ of *cuero*.)

On the other hand, there are at least three ways in which Spanish is more phonotactically constrained than English. First, the only consonants that commonly end a word (and therefore final syllables) are /d s n r l (θ)/. Others are rare in final position, as with the /x/ of *reloj* or the /b g k t f č p/ of the borrowings *club, zigzag, coñac, complot, rosbif, sandwich, jeep* (*yip*). In fact, many of these words are commonly pronounced without their final C, and words spelled with final *m* (*álbum, referéndum*) are pronounced with /n/. Spelling sometimes recognizes such adaptations: *compló, carné, coñá*. Medially, too, syllable codas such as /b g k p t f č p/ are unusual in Spanish, existing primarily in learnèd words borrowed from Greek and Latin. When these consonants meet with others medially, they form clusters called *grupos cultos* that sit astride the syllable boundary: /b.s/ (*absoluto*), /k.s/ (*éxito*), /k.t/ (*pacto*), /p.s/ (*cápsula*), /t.l/ (*atlas*), /t.n/ (*étnico*). Outside of a fairly *culta* pronunciation, the initial C of the cluster tends to be pronounced as a weak fricative or glide, or to be dropped entirely, and this results in a simplified and more normal syllable structure: *extraño* /eks.trá.ɲo/ → /es.trá.ɲo/. Again, spelling may recognize the simplification: *se(p)tiembre, su(b)scripción, su(b)stituir*, and formerly, *estraño*.

Second, clusters of two or more C at the end of the word are frequent in English up to a maximum of four (*sixths* /síksθs/); but these are absolutely forbidden in Spanish phonotactics, and quite rare as syllable codas as well. Loanwords conform to this constraint in pronunciation (and eventually in orthography too) by losing all but one consonant or by adding a protective vowel:

record → /r̄ékor/   tank → /tánke/
zinc → /θin, sin/   trust → /trúste/
bíceps → /bíθes, bíses/ film → /fílme/

Third, initial clusters of /sC/ are commonplace in English but again forbidden in Spanish. Since Roman times, the Iberian solution has been the addition (EPENTHESIS) of an initial /e/. The Real Academia adopts the e- in the orthography of its dictionary once the word is felt to be naturalized.

station = estación   Slav = eslavo   scanner = escáner
slogan = eslogan   spy = espía   stress = estrés
sphere = esfera   ski = esquí   spasm = espasmo
special = especial   snob = esnob   status = /estátus/

But Spanish and English phonotactics are not completely different. For example, in neither language are double (GEMINATE) consonants commonly used. What is spelled as a double consonant is either phonemically one:

funny /fʌ́ni/   committing /kəmítɪŋ/   carro[16] /kár̄o/
borrow /báro/   assured /əšúrd/   cuello /kwéjo, kwéʎo/
or corresponds to two separately pronounced phonemes in different syllables:

suggest /səg.jést/   acción /ak.sjón, ak.θjón/

The only instances of true, phonemically geminate consonants are found where a stem or prefix ending in a consonant joins with a stem beginning with the same one. For example, English has /kk/ in bookcase and /ss/ in misstate; and though they may simplify in faster pronunciation, in slower speech Spanish has /nn/ in innumerable and /bb/ in obvio and subversivo.

2.4 Phonemic vs. orthographic representation. Although they are distinct components, orthography is at least partially based on phonology in alphabetic systems. Thus, the spelling of English fat is close to its phonemic representation /fæt/, and the spelling of Spanish puso is identical to the IPA symbols used for its phonemic representation, /puso/. Of course, there is a greater 'phonemic fit' or phonological fidelity in Spanish orthography, and perhaps this is why the language is chosen by some students as a relatively 'easy' foreign language—a mistaken impression, as they soon discover. Like English, Spanish orthography has silent letters (h), two-letter combinations for one sound (the digraphs ch, qu), useless letters (x = cs), two or more symbols for one phoneme (b and v = /b/), and two or more phonemes handled by the same letter (/x/ and /g/ = g). Even where the language is internally consistent, as with ñ for /ɲ/, its conventions may not match those of English. For illustration, Figure 2.8 contrasts orthographic and phonemic representations for selected Spanish and English words.

In both languages, there are orthographic rules whereby one spelling changes to another. In English, for example, a final *y* becomes *i(e)* before a suffix (*ie* before a consonant, *i* before a vowel), but stays *y* before *i*: *carry*,

Figure 2.8 Orthographic vs. phonemic representations of selected words.

(a) Spanish:

araña /aráɲa/	horario /orárjo/
aunque /áwnke/	huérfano /wérfano/
bautizar /bawtisár/, /bawtiθár/	idioma /idjóma/
cañería /kaɲería/	joyero /xojéro/
cenizas /senísas/, /θeníθas/	juguete /xugéte/
chorro /čór̄o/	lleven /jében/, /ʎében/
desagüe /deságwe/	Marruecos /mar̄wékos/
Enrique /enr̄íke/	quién /kjén/
fuego /fwégo/	quincuagésimo /kinkwaxésimo/
giroscopio /xiroskópjo/	rayaba /r̄ajába/
guardia /gwárdja/	suave /swábe/
hollín /ojín/, /oʎín/	viraje /biráxe/
hielo /jélo/	yunque /júnke/

(b) English

above /əbʌv/	live /lív/ (verb), /lájv/ (adj.)
abroad /əbrɔ́d/, əbrád/	Mexico /méksɪko/
allergy /ǽlərǰi/	musician /mjuzíšən/
bathe /béð/	natural /nǽčərəl/
cartoon /kɑrtún/	phase, faze /féz/
channel /čǽnəl/	roughly /rʌ́fli/
clock /klák/	seasonal /sízənəl/
crumbs /krʌ́mz/	shroud /šráwd/
equality /ikwáləti/	stranger /strénǰər/
fusion /fjúžən/	Thomas /táməs/
gesture /ǰésčər/	though /ðó/
growled /gráwld/	thought /θɔ́t/, /θát/
hanger /hǽŋər/	treasures /tréžərz/
height /hájt/	use /júz/ (verb), /jús/ (noun)
huge /hjúǰ/	usually /júžuəli/
idea /ajdíə/	would, wood /wúd/
judging /ǰʌ́ǰɪŋ/	whose /húz/
kitchen /kíčən/	youth /júθ/

carrie-s, carri-ed, carri-er, carry-ing; bury, buri-ed, buri-al, bury-ing. The main Spanish rules are as follows:

(1) *i* (if spelling /j/) → *y* after a vowel or word-initially:
com-ió but *ca-yó*
durm-iendo, but *yendo, ca-yendo*
cerrar (*ie*) → *cierro*, but *errar* (*ie*) → *yerro*

(2) *r* for /r̄/ word-initially → *rr* intervocalically:
romano, but *prerromano*   *regla*, but *arreglar*
revolución, but   *Puerto Rico*, but
  antirrevolucionario   *puertorriqueño*

(3) *g* for /x/ → *j* before *a, o, u*:
corregir, corrijo, corrija

(4) /k/ is *qu* before *e, i*, but *c* elsewhere:
chico, chiquito   *rico, riqueza*
marcar, marqué   *delinco, delinquir*

(5) /θ/ (=/s/ in *seseo*) is *c* before *e, i*, but *z* elsewhere:
lápiz, lápices   *empezar, empecé*

(6) /g/ is *gu* before *e, i*, but *g* elsewhere:
lago, laguito   *pago, pague*

(7) /gw/ is *gü* before *e, i*, but *gu* elsewhere:
averiguo, averigüé   *lengua, lengüita*

These rules are not phonological rules and do not change pronunciation in any way. If anything, they are an awkward way of maintaining a record of pronunciation in a system in which one letter has more than one value. That is, since *ga ge gi go gu* are /ga xe xi go gu/, then the syllables /ga ge gi go gu/ will be spelled *ga gue gui go gu*; and since this preempts *gu* for /g/ before *e, i, gü* will be needed for /gw/ before those vowels. It should also be noted that these changes are not verb irregularities since—in terms of the Spanish system—they are regular in the first place, and they occur with other parts of speech as well. The student of Spanish who finds orthographic changes strange might recall his own language, in which *carry* is a regular verb, and the *y* → *i(e)* change is a regular spelling adaptation; it is still /kǽri/, regardless of what suffix is added. Moreover, the same change occurs in adjectives (*sloppy, sloppier, sloppily*) and nouns (*party, parties*). Rules that change pronunciation are wholly different, as will be shown in Chapter 3.

Even after a student has satisfactorily mastered the phonemes and orthography of a second language, regressions may be frequent in cognates. Cognates may be 'free' as lexical items with carried-over meanings (v. 15.2), but they are very deceptive phonologically. For some students, it may be easier to reproduce an alien pronunciation for an alien word, e.g. *hoyuelo* or *reja*, than to revise their pronunciation for an old friend such as *general* or *probable*. The following are noteworthy examples whose similarity of spelling is belied by difference in phonemic representation. (For others, see Stockwell and Bowen 1965.)

radio = *radio* but /r̄ádjo/ ≠ /rédio/
usual = *usual* but /uswál/ ≠ /júžuəl/
acción = *action* but /aksjón/ ≠ /ǽkšən/
conversación = *conversation* but /kombersasjón/ ≠ /kànvərséšən/
automático = *automatic* but /awtomátiko/ ≠ /ɔ̀təmǽtɪk/
hospital = *hospital* but /ospitál/ ≠ /háspɪtəl/
Europa = *Europe* but /ewrópa/ ≠ /júrəp, jə́rəp/
causa = *cause* but /káwsa/ ≠ /kɔ́z/
ángel = *angel* but /ánxel/ ≠ /énjəl/
acusación = *accusation* but /akusasjón/ ≠ /æ̀kjuzéšən/

Notes for Chapter 2

1. Many southern U.S. and most British speakers do use /tj- dj-/ in *tune, duty*, but only before /u/.

2. The contrast between /ɲ/ and /nj/ holds in most varieties of Spanish, but there are a few dialects in which /nj/ is merged with /ɲ/ (Boyd-Bowman 1960:83): *nieto, tinieblas, junio, opinión* → [ɲéto tiɲéβlas xúɲo opiɲón].

3. Many of these aspirated *jota* dialects retain Old Spanish /h/ (now silent in most dialects) in *harto, heno, hembra, hilo, hediondo, huir*, and a few other words. Thus, a word such as *halar* 'pull' is pronounced [halár] there, and often spelled *jalar* since /x/ has merged with the [h]. But the old /h/ has also been kept in some /x/ dialects too: [xalár] (Boyd-Bowman 1960:65-68).

4. NEUTRALIZATION means the merger or canceling-out of a contrast maintained elsewhere. An English example is that the vowels of *beat* vs. *bit* are meticulously distinguished in most environments, but not before /r/ (*beer*) or /ŋ/ (*Bing*); here, speakers use the /i/ of *beat* or the /ɪ/ of *bit* or some vowel in between them. Neutralization will be encountered in other parts of language structure also.

5. For more information on the geographical distribution of the dialect variants discussed here, see Resnick 1975, Canfield 1981, Zamora-Vicente 1967, Navarro 1967 and 1975, and the *Atlas lingüístico de la Península Ibérica*.

6. By saying that /θ/ is 'merged' with /s/ in *seseo*, we are not claiming that *seseantes* historically had a /θ/ that they changed to /s/. Actually, the Old Spanish distinction was four-way: two sibilant affricates, /ts/ in *caça* (>*caza*) vs. /dz/ in *hazer* (>*hacer*) and two sibilant fricatives, /s/ in *passa* (>*pasa*) vs. /z/ in *casa*; there was no /θ/ at all. But at the time that Spaniards began to colonize the New World, /dz/ and /z/ had merged with /ts/ and /s/, respectively, and the remaining /ts/ and /s/ were on the way to further merger. The merger of /ts/ with /s/, i.e. *caza* with *casa*, won out in

Andalusia and America, but in northern Spain the dental onset of /ts/ dentalized its /s/ before dropping, yielding /θ/ in *caza* and *hacer*. For further information, see Harris 1969:189-206 and A. Alonso 1967:84-122.

7. There are many subtypes, especially in southern Spain, and Navarro (1975:21-80) confirms them with detailed palatography (a technique that records precisely where the speaker's tongue makes contact). The reader with advanced knowledge of phonetics can appreciate the variety by bearing in mind that the tongue can be grooved or ungrooved; that the tip, blade, or both can be used; that the tongue shape can be convex, concave, or rather flat; and that contact can be anywhere from the teeth to the postalveolar area just behind the gums. All of the following are therefore possible, and apparently all can be found in Andalusia. (Phonetic symbols are omitted; the needs of Spanish phoneticians in discriminating fricatives long ago surpassed the capacity of the IPA.)

1. Grooved (sibilant)
   1.1 Alveolar
      1.1.1 Apical (concave tongue)
      1.1.2 Laminal
         1.1.2.1 Tip down, resting close to lower teeth; tongue is convex, with predorsal contact
         1.1.2.2 Tip up, resting close to upper teeth roots; flattish tongue, coronal contact
   1.2 Dental: groove formed by blade, but the tip is close to the teeth, giving simultaneous [s] and [θ] turbulence
2. Ungrooved (slit)
   2.1 Apical: tip touches teeth, tongue is flat
      2.1.1 Tip protrudes between teeth
      2.1.2 Tip touches edges of front teeth
   2.2 Laminal: predorsal contact with inner teeth surfaces; convex tongue

8. With dialect variation (see Kurath and McDavid 1961, Wells 1982), it is hard to portray ONE vowel system for English. I have selected the system that dominates in much of the U.S. But many speakers no longer have a contrast between /ɔ/ and /ɑ/ and their *caught, hawk, chalk, naughty, dawn* merge with *cot, hock, chock, knotty, Don.* Figure 2.6 also does not show the effects on English vowels of the 'r-dropping' of some dialects, whereby *farther, tuber, court* merge with *father, tuba, caught.*

9. But in northern England, eastern New England, and the Great Lakes area many speakers use a fronted /ɑ/ that is much closer to Spanish /a/.

10. Further diphthongization of /u/ yields an English TRIPHTHONG of GVG: /ju/ = [jʉw]. Spanish has triphthongs mainly in certain *vosotros* verb forms: *averiguáis* /-wajs/, *averigüeis* /-wejs/, *estudiéis* /-jejs/.

11. Old Spanish also had /uj/ and /iw/, and some dialects retain them in *muy* and *ciudad*, respectively; but most dialects (including the standard) replaced them with /wi/ and /ju/.

12. Spanish phonologists usually distinguish *sinéresis* from *sinalefa* for word-internal position (*teatro*) vs. across word boundaries (*te atreves*), re-

spectively. Since the same process is involved and a general term would be useful, 'syneresis' will be adopted for both.

13. See Harris (1969:20-36, 122-24), who explains this analysis and summarizes alternatives.

14. Yet Navarro (1967:153-54) insists on hiatus for identical vowels when one of them begins a suffix, as in *lo-or, cre-encia, moh-oso*. Dalbor, on the other hand (1980b:183), believes stress to be the key: unstressed double vowels (*creería*) are 'usually' one vowel in pronunciation, but if one is stressed (*creéncia, creér, crée*), they are pronounced as one long vowel in careful speech, one short one in faster speech.

15. None of the native speakers I consulted pronounced all (or even most) of these words with hiatus, even in a careful oral-reading style. Educated speakers adopted the hiatus mainly in a slower pronunciation of *-uir* verbs and with some learnèd prefixes (*bi-óxido*), but otherwise with little consistency.

16. But see Harris (1983:67-78) for a revisionist defense of [r̄] as phonemically /rr/.

Exercises for Chapter 2

1. Some books claim that Spanish and English have five vowels (a e i o u). What kind of confusion does this indicate?

2. Which Spanish phonemes have no equivalents in English? List them, and indicate the strategies you might use in teaching their (usual) articulation. (Note: phonetic information is a means to the end of establishing correct articulatory habits; students are studying Spanish, not general phonetics, so as a teacher you must use terms that are precise and useful, but understandable to students.)

3. Give at least one minimal pair in Spanish for each of the following phonemic distinctions. Example: /p b/ *pez, vez.*

(1) /t č/	(4) /p f/	(7) /j w/	(10) /a o/,	unstressed
(2) /r r̄/	(5) /n ɲ/	(8) /o u/	(11) /j ʎ/	in dialects that
(3) /k x/	(6) /k g/	(9) /e i/	(12) /s θ/	have these

4. What differences exist in the Spanish and English articulations of /t/, /d/, /r/? Where should these differences be presented in an introductory course, and how much emphasis should be given to each of them? Why?

5. According to the analysis presented in this chapter, what criterion is used to determine whether Spanish [j w] are phonemically /j w/ or /i u/? Applying this criterion, how would you analyze the indicated glides of the following words?

(1) de[w]da	(6) polic[j]al	(11) resfr[j]ar	(16) amá[j]s
(2) antig[w]o	(7) jag[w]ar	(12) arg[w]ir	(17) ma[j]zal
(3) act[w]ar	(8) ba[w]llero	(13) ad[j]ós	(18) farmac[j]a
(4) pa[j]sano	(9) re[j]naba	(14) grad[w]ado	(19) anunc[j]ado
(5) camb[j]ar	(10) s[w]egro	(15) conf[j]ado	(20) re[w]nir

6. The following words are in Spanish phonemic representation for a

dialect that lacks /θ/ and /ʎ/. Pronounce them, and identify them by re-writing them in their normal orthography.

(1) /kostíja/ (7) /kombídan/ (13) /kořjénte/ (19) /jwébe/
(2) /xwísjo/ (8) /biráxe/ (14) /umijár/ (20) /aberigwé/
(3) /řixjéron/ (9) /wélga/ (15) /xenxíbre/ (21) /jéřo/
(4) /jábe/ (10) /čéke/ (16) /bergwénsa/ (22) /kawdíjo/
(5) /čantáxe/ (11) /paɲwélo/ (17) /asjénda/ (23) /bírxenes/
(6) /exérse/ (12) /bóses/ (18) /wéko/ (24) /ɲoɲés/

7. Vice-versa, convert the following to phonemic representation.

(1) enviudar (7) chapucear (13) quizás (19) jueguen
(2) alcohólico (8) redacción (14) invierno (20) huevos
(3) oveja (9) rapiña (15) quiñón (21) cuello
(4) sugiero (10) horquilla (16) anhelado (22) guitarra
(5) guerrero (11) éxito (17) jerarquía (23) convicción
(6) anzuelo (12) valle (18) yegua (24) auge

8. Aside from gross phonemic accuracy, how will English speakers tend to pronounce the following differently from Spanish speakers?

(1) Él está en ese hospital. (3) Me he enterado de ello.
(2) ¿Qué es un artista? (4) Los han oído.

9. Although we are focusing on the problems English speakers have with Spanish, sometimes the reverse approach can provide insight into the Spanish system. Explain why Spanish-speaking students of English might have trouble with the following contrasts.

(1) bowel, vowel (4) set, sat, sot (7) yet, jet
(2) peat, pit (5) cheat, sheet (8) esteem, steam
(3) fool, full (6) boat, bought, butt (9) band, ban

10. Take each of the consonant phonemes of Spanish and list the ways that it is rendered in the orthography. Do the same for English conso-nants, and then indicate what the major patterns of interference might be. For example,

Span. /k/: C, QU
Eng. /k/: C, CK, K, Q. Interference: K will not be used in most Span. words, and QU will render /k/, never /kw/.

11. What is meant by the 'phonemic fit' of a spelling system? To what extent is the fit obvious to nonnative speakers?

12. Find derivatives of the following nouns and adjectives which show the same spelling changes as in verbs. For example: vago, vaGUedad, as in pagar, paGUe.

(1) raza (4) bazo (7) trigo
(2) agua (5) poco (8) rico
(3) antiguo (6) pez (9) perspicaz

13. Predict how unwary students might mispronounce the following Spanish cognates. A precise way of showing sources of error will be to con-trast the Spanish phonemic representations with those of the English cognates.

(1) oxígeno	(6) residuo	(11) millón	(16) abusar
(2) exterior	(7) musical	(12) hotel	(17) biología
(3) anual	(8) presente	(13) digestión	(18) quieto
(4) higiene	(9) tranquilizar	(14) series	(19) visitar
(5) usado	(10) humano	(15) equilibrio	(20) autor

14. A U.S. ship with a Spanish name, the *Pueblo*, was pronounced by newscasters in this country 'the [puwéblow].' Also, a tire named *Tiempo* was advertised as '[tijémpow].' Why did Spanish /pwéblo/, /tjémpo/ come out in this way?

15. At least for the phonemicization of Spanish words in slow speech, it might be necessary to distinguish single and double phonemes, as in the following:

(1) /unómbre/ *un hombre*, /unnómbre/ *un nombre*

(2) /elóro/ *el oro*, /ellóro/ *el loro*

(3) /lasálas/ *las alas*, /lassálas/ *las salas*

(4) /labenída/ *la venida*, /laabenída/ *la avenida*

(5) /desúso/ *desuso*, /desuúso/ *de su uso*

But as pointed out earlier, double vowels are merged in faster styles, and Quilis and Fernández (1975:149) note the same for double consonants. Have a native speaker pronounce these examples (and any others you might wish to add) and determine whether the speaker uses geminates. Instead of using directly contrastive pairs—which might induce an atypically careful pronunciation—embed the cues in sentences and mix them up.

16. We noted that Spanish allows glides to occur in clusters (/trw plj mw/ etc.) that are absent in English. List as many Spanish clusters of consonant + /l r j w/ as you can think of (there are about four dozen of them), and circle those that English speakers would probably have trouble with.

17. Each of the following shows dialect variation in Spanish. Which variant would you select for your classroom, and why?

(1) articulation of /s/   (3) articulation of /x/

(2) distinction of /θ/ and /s/   (4) distinction of /ʎ/ and /j/

18. Some texts use phonetic symbols to bring the student's attention to precise sound values in descriptions of pronunciation, especially when spelling is unhelpful. In your opinion, to what extent (if any) should text and teacher make use of special symbols (IPA or improvised) alongside orthography?

19. Many texts discuss Spanish syllabification, usually in terms of orthography. Students learn, for instance, that *estudiante* is *es.tu.dian.te*, *agua* is *a.gua*, and so on. If the only purpose of a lesson on syllabification were how to split words at the end of a line, it would have little utility. Does a description of syllabification serve some other purpose? Which one, and why?

Chapter 3
Phonological rules

3.0 Types of rules: Categorical and variable, general and dialectal. The pronunciation of phonemes changes in a fairly regular fashion that depends on the phonetic environment. For example, in both English and Spanish a vowel (V) becomes somewhat nasalized (Ṽ) when a nasal consonant (N) follows, as in *moon* and *mundo*. Thus, /mundo/ → [mũndo]. Linguists formalize such a rule by using an arrow for 'becomes', a slash for 'when in the environment of . . . ', and a blank that specifies the environment. Thus, 'a vowel becomes nasalized when preceding a nasal' is written as follows:[1]

V → Ṽ / ____ N

This format can also be used for the insertion or deletion of sounds. As noted in the preceding chapter (v. 2.3), Spanish inserts /e/ in front of initial *s*C (cluster of *s* plus consonant): *ski* → *esquí*. This EPENTHESIS rule can be stated as follows: 'where there was nothing preceding *s*C, insert /e/':

∅ → e / ____ sC

Yet this is too general as it stands, for it will insert /e/ before every *s*C cluster, giving not only *ski* → *esquí*, but also *chispa* → *chiespa* and *asco* → *aesco*. The rule must be confined or constrained so as to apply just when the *s*C is word-initial, i.e. when it follows a word boundary. The symbol for word boundary is #. Hence,

∅ → e / # ____ sC

To express another rule taken up in Chapter 2, namely, the simplification of a final CC in Spanish (*récord* →/r̄ékor/), we state that a C deletes or drops (becomes zero) when it follows another C and is word-final (i.e. precedes #):

C → ∅ / C ____ #

The # is not the only boundary that plays a part in phonology. A plus, +, represents a morpheme boundary, the grammatical stitch or 'juncture' between stems and affixes within a word. A double vertical line, ‖, stands for a phrase boundary, the slight pause between 'breath-groups'. Some phonologists may also state rules in terms of syllable boundaries (represented by . or $) where these are identifiable.[2]

Some phonological rules are general throughout all (or almost all) varieties of a language, while others are limited to a few dialects. Crosscutting this classification is another one, categorical rule vs. variable rule. A CATEGORICAL rule applies across the board, so that when it can apply it regularly does apply; Vowel Nasalization and *E*-epenthesis are categorical in this sense. A VARIABLE rule applies some of the time, and its frequency drops off or picks up according to factors such as social class, sex, style, and age. A well-known example from English is 'G-dropping,' whereby words such as *nothing, playing, singing* become *nothin', playin', singin'*; more precisely, final /ŋ/ becomes [n] when following an unstressed vowel (V̆):

ŋ → n / V̆ _____ #

Thus, *nothing* /nʌ́θɪŋ/ → [nʌ́θɪn].

Many English speakers regard G-dropping as substandard or indicative of slovenly or careless articulation, and they deny ever doing it themselves. In fact, variable rules that have become salient to native speakers are often dismissed in this way, acquiring a strong attitudinal component and status as social markers. Yet careful studies of actual speech have confirmed that virtually all native English speakers alternate between [ŋ] and [n], with upper classes using more [ŋ] than lower classes and with all speakers using relatively more [ŋ] in their formal speech. That is, this rule has a variable output depending on class and style. Variable rules are of intense interest to linguists and sociologists, but because of the attitudinal element, some of the literature on dialect variation is not completely objective. Scholars will often deny with great vigor that their group (class, country, stratum, *patria chica*, etc.) ever uses a certain *vulgarismo* when in fact, at least informally, they do.

3.1 Spanish rules. Sections 3.1.1 through 3.1.8 describe rules that apply to consonants and glides. Sections 3.1.9 and 3.1.10 focus on vowel variations. To the extent that published studies permit, the application of each rule will be identified as general or dialectal, and as categorical or variable.[3]

3.1.1 Glide Strengthening.

$$w \rightarrow \text{w̶} \atop j \rightarrow \text{j̶} \Bigg\} \; / \; \begin{cases} V \; \underline{\quad} \; V \\ V \; \underline{\quad} \; +G \\ \# \; \underline{\quad} \; V \\ C+ \; \underline{\quad} \; V \end{cases}$$

(general but not universal, some variability in output)

English /w j/ are weak 'semivowels' or glides, as are Spanish /w j/ when they are word-final (*rey, hoy*) or next to a consonant (*naipe* /nájpe/, *pie* /pjé/, *causa* /káwsa/, *aduana* /adwána/). But in the following positions, Spanish glides are pronounced with greater articulatory tension and friction in most regions.[4]

  Intervocalic: Chi*hua*hua, a*hue*car, ho*y*o, va*y*a, a*y*udar, re*y*es (and ca*ll*e, cue*ll*o in yeísta zones)
  Stem-final before another glide: ho*y*uelo /oj+wélo/
  Initial: *hue*so, *hue*vo, *hua*rache, *y*erno, *y*ate, *hi*erro, *y*ugo (*ll*amar, *ll*evar)

Furthermore, /j/ is strengthened postconsonantally if it begins a stem, as in ab*y*ecto, des*h*ielo, and in*y*ección.[5]

/w/ is labiovelar; when strengthened to [w̯] (/wéso/ → [w̯éso], /awekár/ → [aw̯ekár] etc.), it takes on labial or velar friction, typically the latter. In trying to render the velar friction, some dialect writers respell *huevo*, *hueso* as *güevo*, *güeso*; indeed, since /g/ becomes a fricative (v. 3.1.6), there is little or no difference between the /gw/ of *agua* and the /w/ of *Chihuahua*. In the case of palatal /j/, strengthening consists in the tongue rising a bit higher to the palate, which yields a voiced palatal fricative symbolized [ɟ]. Thus, *yerno leyes* /jérno léjes/ → [ɟérno léɟes], while *pierna* and *ley* /pjérna léj/ keep their glides. [ɟ] strikes an English speaker as between his /j/ of *you* and /ž/ of *vision*, which it is. The amount of friction or *rehilamiento* varies from light to rather heavy. After /n/ as in *cónyuge*, *inyección*, the /j/ is so tensed that it is an affricate, [ĵɟ];[6] this variably happens initially, too, under emphasis, so that *¡yo!* reminds an English speaker of *Joe*. In certain dialects (southwest Spain, most of Argentina, adjacent Uruguay and Paraguay), the friction of [ɟ] has intensified even more by shifting to alveopalatal [ž]; and in Buenos Aires, this [ž] variably devoices to [š]. Consequently, a word such as *calle* can be heard as [káʎe káje káɟe káže káše] with progressively greater *rehilamiento*.[7]

A curious development in the *porteño* (Buenos Aires) dialect is that at least some speakers distinguish two kinds of /j/ according to spelling. Words spelled *hi* plus vowel are pronounced with [j] (little or no *rehilamiento*) and those spelled with *ll* or *y* have [ž] or [š]. Hence, *hierro*, *hierba* are not homonyms of *yerro*, *yerba*, as they are elsewhere. It is not clear whether this is a well-rooted phonemic distinction or an attempt to introduce a difference of pronunciation because of a difference in spelling.

Most phonological rules of Spanish apply across word boundaries in fast speech. Glide Strengthening, in that case, seems to depend on the dialect, or even on the speech of each individual (i.e. IDIOLECT). For Castilian, Navarro (1967:151) notes that *voy a morir* can be [bojamorír], with a glide, or [boɟamorír], with a fricative, or even an intermediate [boĵamorír]. Harris (1983:61), though, states that *porteño* Strengthening does not occur over #: *ley* is [léj] and *leyes* is [léžes], but *la ley es* is [laléjes].

3.1.2 Nasal Assimilation.

$$
N \rightarrow \begin{cases}
\text{bilabial [m] /} \underline{\quad} \text{bilabial (p b m)} \\
\text{labiodental [m̩] /} \underline{\quad} \text{labiodental (f)} \\
\text{dental [n̪] /} \underline{\quad} \text{dental (t̪ d̪ θ)} \\
\text{alveolar [n] /} \underline{\quad} \text{alveolar (s n l r̄)} \\
\text{alveopalatal [ñ] /} \underline{\quad} \text{alveopalatal (č)} \\
\text{palatal [ɲ] /} \underline{\quad} \text{palatal (ʎ, ɲ, strengthened /j/)} \\
\text{velar [ŋ] /} \underline{\quad} \text{velar (k, g, x, w̯)}
\end{cases}
$$

(general; categorical in words, variable across word boundaries)

In this formulation, which shows each possible output, the rule looks more formidable than it really is. Expressed simply, nasals ASSIMILATE to, or are pronounced in the same place as, a following consonant.[8] Assimilation always takes place within a word; across word boundaries, it occurs in normal speech styles but may be blocked in slower styles (Harris 1969:8-9, 14-16). Some examples:

[m]: a*m*bos, e*n*viar, co*n*versa; e*n* Perú, e*n* Venezuela, co*n* Manuel
[ɱ]: e*n*friar, é*n*fasis, i*n*fante; e*n* Francia, co*n* Fernando, so*n* fuertes
[n̪]: ca*n*ta, a*n*da*n*do, (co*n*cepto); e*n* Turquía, co*n* David, so*n* dos
[n]: co*n*sta, ho*n*ra; e*n* Suiza, co*n* *n*osotros
[ň]: co*n*cha; e*n* Chile, co*n* Chávez
[ɲ]: i*n*yección, co*n*lleva; e*n* yeso, co*n* llamas
[ŋ]: mo*n*ja, co*n*quista, ho*n*go; e*n* Cuba, e*n* Japón, co*n* Jaime, so*n* gusanos, so*n* huevos

The phonological effect of Nasal Assimilation is to wipe out (neutralize) the nasal distinctions. The phonemes /m n ɲ/ contrast in *cama/cana/caña*, but preconsonantally no contrast is possible since the nasal is pronounced with the following consonant.

3.1.3 Lateral Assimilation.

$$/l/ \rightarrow \left\{ \begin{array}{lll} l̪ & / \underline{\quad} & \text{dental} \\ l & / \underline{\quad} & \text{alveolar} \\ ʎ & / \underline{\quad} & \text{palatal} \end{array} \right\}$$

(general; categorical in words, variable across word boundaries)

Like /n/, /l/ assimilates to a following C, but here only if the consonant is pronounced with the tip or blade of the tongue. Thus, /álto/ → [ál̪to], but in /pálko/ the /l/ stays alveolar since /k/ is velar. English /l/ assimilates to some extent too; the /l/ of *health*, like the /l/ of Span. *alto*, is often dental rather than alveolar.

3.1.4 S-Voicing.

s → z / $\underline{\quad}$ (#)voiced C
(general and regarded as categorical, but details are disputed)

By this rule, /s/ is voiced to [z] when a voiced consonant follows (including strengthened /j w/). Thus, /čísme/ → [čízme], /ísla/ → [ízla], /des+jélo/ → [dezjélo], etc. Like the two preceding rules, this is an assimilation rule, but in voicing rather than point of articulation. Voicing occurs within a word (as in *isla, asno, desde, rasgar, chisme, esbelto*) and across word boundaries in normal fast speech (as in *los dedos, las vacas, las gafas, los maestros, los huecos, las yeguas*).

Although S-Voicing is a universally recognized rule of Spanish phonology, some analysts have questioned its environment and categoricalness. Torreblanca (1978:498-502), for example, carefully examined data from

Spain and America, and while agreeing that /s/ → [z], he found that voicing depends more on articulatory tension than on the nature of the following consonant: [s] dominates when the speaker uses a relatively tense articulation, and [z] when articulation is more relaxed. At any rate, Spanish [s] and [z] are allophones of one phoneme, and contrasts such as Eng. *Sue/zoo, face/phase* are impossible.

3.1.5 S-Aspiration.

$$s \rightarrow h \ (\rightarrow \emptyset) \ / \underline{\hspace{1cm}} \left\{ \begin{array}{c} C \\ \# \\ V \end{array} \right\}$$

(variable and dialectal, but widespread)

This rule changes /s/ into a light aspiration, [h], which may then disappear altogether. Thus, /las číspas/ → [la(h)čí(h)pa(h)]. In one environment, namely, C = /r̄/, /s/ is aspirated in most dialects: *Israel* and (across #) *los reyes*. In the following areas, however, Aspiration occurs before any consonant as well as word-finally: the Caribbean islands and coasts, all of Hispanic South America except the highlands from Bolivia to Colombia, and southern Spain. It seems to be spreading in the latter country; Navarro (1975:187-190) concludes from linguistic atlas data that Castilian [š] is 'weakening' throughout the west, including Madrid. For some speakers the rule is virtually categorical, especially in / $\overline{\hspace{1cm}}$ C. But the typical situation is a variable rule. For example, Obaid (1973:62) estimates that Aspiration occurs in Madrid speech about 50% of the time, and Hammond (1980) more precisely gives the following statistics for Miami Cuban speech:

	/ $\underline{\hspace{1cm}}$ ||	/ $\underline{\hspace{1cm}}$ #	/ $\underline{\hspace{1cm}}$ C
s → h	22%	43%	70%
s →h → ∅	74%	54%	20%

Fontanella de Weinberg 1974 explores in more detail the social variables. Experiments with *porteños* revealed that both sexes and all classes aspirate; but men do so more than women, lower classes more than upper classes, and everyone more in their informal speech. A sample of her results is shown in Figure 3.1.

Poplack 1980 points out another factor in the variation, the functional importance of the /s/ as a grammatical marker. It is deleted most often when it is redundant, i.e. does not uniquely signal a grammatical category. In *las matas se mueren*, plurality is conveyed by two instances of final /s/ and one of final /n/. Not all of these are really needed, but if all are deleted the message changes to *la mata se muere*. She finds a tendency to delete any number of the markers so long as at least one remains. Other investigations have confirmed that Aspiration depends on phonetic environment, social variables, and function.

Figure 3.1 Aspiration in Porteño (Fontanella de Weinberg 1974:50).

	Styles			
Class	A	B	C	D
4	86%	94%	98.5%	100%
3	81.5%	95.5%	95%	98%
2	58.5%	72.5%	83%	98.5%
1	34%	60%	61%	84%

Classes:
4 = high-level executives and business professionals
3 = technicians and university-trained personnel
2 = shop owners and self-employed businessmen
1 = domestics and blue-collar workers

Styles:
A = informal spontaneous conversation
B = story-telling to interviewer
C = oral reading of a passage
D = oral reading of words

Percentages = average that /s/ was pronounced as [s] (i.e. that Aspiration did not apply)

Aspiration before V is much less common, and seemingly less accepted, even in aspirating dialects. Yet it is well attested, especially in common words such as *sí* [hí], *señor, siempre, ser, casa, pasar,* and *nosotros* (Alonso 1967:285, Obaid 1973:63, Resnick 1975:13, Canfield 1981:54, Hammond 1980:12).

Aspiration strongly affects neighboring phonemes, and if the [h] drops entirely, these perturbations are the only traces of the underlying /s/. In Andalusia (Alonso et al. 1950, Zamora-Vicente 1967:319), the [h] opens up a preceding vowel and assimilates to a following consonant, as shown in Figure 3.2. Moreover, this V opening triggers a matching opening of the vowels in preceding syllables: *monótonos* → [mɔnɔ́tɔnɔ], *leches* → [lɛ́čɛ].

Figure 3.2 Effects of aspiration on adjacent phonemes.

On V:
/as/ → æ(h): más, vas, las
/es/ → ɛ(h): mes, les, ves
/is/ → ɪ(h): mis, perdiz
/os/ → ɔ(h): tos, voz, los
/us/ → ʊ(h): sus, luz

On C:
sβ → hβ → ɸɸ: las botas, desván
sð → hð → θθ: los dientes, desde
sɣ → hɣ → xx: desgarro, las garras
sp → hp → pp: obispo, los pasos
st → ht → tt: este, los trenes
sk → hk → kk: tosco, las casas
sn → hn → n̂n: asno, los nombres

Phonetically, then, the difference between singulars and plurals in such dialects may be signaled by close (tense) vs. open (lax) vowels.

3.1.6 Spirantization of /b d g/.

$$\text{b d g} \rightarrow \text{β ð ɣ except /} \left\{ \begin{array}{l} \| \underline{} \\ \text{N} \underline{} \\ \text{/l/} \underline{} \ (=/\text{d/ only}) \end{array} \right\}$$

(general and categorical, but with minor dialectal variation)

The Spanish phonemes /b d g/ have two allophones each, stop and fricative (or spirant). The stops [b d g] are like their English counterparts, although [d] ([d̪]) is dental rather than alveolar (v. 2.1.2). In most varieties of Spanish, the stops occur in three positions: after a pause (i.e. phrase-initially, or word-initially if the word is spoken in isolation), after nasals, and—just in the case of /d/—after /l/.[9] Otherwise, /b d g/ are fricatives, and since 'otherwise' includes most cases (between V, before C, after most C, word-finally), Spanish /b d g/ are really fricatives more often than stops. Thus, /abogádo/ → [aβoɣáðo], /admirába/ → [aðmiráβa], /aberigwád/ → [aβeriɣwáð], etc. Indeed, Danesi 1982 suggests that they are phonemically fricatives, becoming stops just in the designated environments.

The three fricative allophones [β ð ɣ] may give trouble to English speakers. [ð] differs from Eng. /ð/ in *then, mother, bathe* only in being a bit less firmly articulated. [β] is a [b] in which the lips do not close enough to form a full stop, but just enough to compress the airstream for light friction. It resembles Eng. /v/, but is made with the lips alone, not with the upper teeth on the lower lip. [ɣ] is a [g] which likewise does not quite stop the airstream; [ɣ] is to [g] as [x] is to [k], though its friction is typically rather weak.

In normal pronunciation, Spirantization is categorical inside the word, and it occurs across word boundaries too in all but the slowest, most deliberate speech styles (Harris 1969:38-40).[10] Examples of /b d g/ as stops and as fricatives are as follows:

Word-internal:
[b d g]: am*b*os, con*v*ersar; an*d*an*d*o, tol*d*o, humil*d*e; an*g*ustia, meren*gu*e

[β ð ɣ]: Cu*b*a, hue*v*o, cal*v*o, atis*b*e, ha*b*la*b*a, ár*b*ol, a*b*domen, clu*b*, a*b*re; po*d*i*d*o, a*d*mira, tar*d*e, cau*d*al, a*d*quiri*d*o, uste*d*, ar*d*i*d*; ha*g*o, pe*gu*e, ras*g*o, al*g*o, car*g*a, a*g*rio

At the beginning of a speech segment:
[b d g]: ¿*V*as . . . ?, ¡*B*asta!, ¿*D*ónde . . . ?, *D*os y tres son . . . , ¡*G*atito!, Pues, *Gu*illermo . . .

Across word-boundaries in connected speech:
[b d g]: en *V*enecia; con *D*iego, el *d*ía; en *G*recia, con *Gu*illermo, son *g*randes

[β ð ɣ]: el *b*uey, los *b*ueyes, te *v*as a *B*olivia, no *v*en; los *d*ías, le *d*oy, es *d*e ella, hay *d*os *d*ientes; el *g*ato, los *g*atos, de *Gr*ecia, a *Gu*illermo, es *g*rande

A few dialects have stops in other places. To the basic set of environments for stops, /‖ ____ , nasal ____ , and (for /d/) l ____ ,

(a) some speakers in Andean Ecuador, southern Mexico, and western Bolivia add /s ____ , as in *atisbo* ([atízbo] instead of [atízβo]), *desde*, *rasgo*;

(b) some speakers in Cuba, Jalisco, and Costa Rica add liquids, i.e. /r ____ and l ____ (for all three phonemes, not just /d/): tar*de* ([tárde] instead of [tárðe]), cal*v*o, ár*b*ol, al*g*o;

(c) some speakers in Colombia, eastern Bolivia, and Central America between Yucatán and Nicaragua add /l ____ , /r ____ , /s ____ , /j ____ , /w ____ (e.g. *caudal* [kawdál] instead of [kawðál]. This leaves the fricatives mainly just in postvocalic position.

Despite this variation, all dialects of the language vary between stops and fricatives for /b d g/ and all have a Spirantization rule; and in no native dialect is there a phonemic distinction comparable to Eng. *bat* vs. *vat* and *den* vs. *then*.[11]

3.1.7 D-Deletion (or Fricative Deletion).

$$\eth \rightarrow \emptyset \ / \ V \underline{\hspace{1cm}} \left\{ \begin{matrix} V \\ \# \end{matrix} \right\}$$

(widespread but variable)

Except in a few isolated areas (Resnick 1975:82-85), the [ð] produced by Spirantization is so weakly articulated that it variably drops. Several factors affect the rate of deletion (Navarro 1967:99-103): phonetic environment (more deletion when /V́ ____ V), word type (more in everyday words), style (more in casual, informal), speed of articulation (more if faster), and speaker's class and education (more if lower). It is commonest in the suffix -*ado* (*hablado* /abládo/ → [aβláðo] → [aβláo]) and in final position; indeed, *usted* and *Madrid* are normally pronounced without the -*d* in many areas ([u(s)té], [maðrí]).

Fricative Deletion has begun to affect /b g/ too in some dialects. In Chile, for example, Oroz 1966 found examples of [β] deletion in *anduve* [andúe], *cabeza, jabón, joven*, and of [ɣ] deletion in *aguja* [aúxa], *jugar, lagarto, laguna, seguro*. He also notes there a tendency (in 'la lengua vulgar') to weaken preconsonantal [β ð ɣ] to glides (Oroz 1966:133-141):

/b/ → β → w : a*b*domen, a*b*ril, dia*b*lo
/d/ → ð → j : pa*d*re, la*d*rillo, a*d*rede, po*d*rir
/g/ → ɣ → w ~ j : a*g*ricultor, di*g*no, vina*g*re, lá*g*rima

3.1.8 Other consonantal processes: /n r r̄ č f/. In Andalusian, *extremeño*, Leonese, and Caribbean dialects, /n/ is velarized to [ŋ] word-finally, as in

son, pan, hablan, sin (= Eng. *sing*). In relaxed speech styles, this [ŋ] may drop, leaving behind a nasal vowel: *van* /ban/ → [bãŋ] → [bã]. N-Velarization creates alternations in some words: *marrón* [mar̄óŋ mar̄ṍ], *marrones* [mar̄ónes]. It has also been reported preconsonantally, where it then comes into competition with Nasal Assimilation (3.1.2).

The two vibrants are frequently pronounced with a light friction resembling that of the English sibilants /s z š ž/. Because of this resemblance, /r r̄/ are then described as ASSIBILATED. For assibilated /r/, symbolized as [ɹ̌], the tongue approaches the alveolar ridge for a flap, but contact there is incomplete or weak. Its use in Chilean speech has been commented upon by many Hispanic dialectologists, but it can also be heard in many other parts of the Americas and in Spain too (Alonso 1961:123-158, Navarro 1967:117-120), especially at the end of a syllable: *ir* ([iɹ̌]), *dar, por, cortar*. The corresponding assibilated trill, symbolized as [r̄̌], is just as widespread. It can be described as a lengthened [ɹ̌] or as a weak trill with [ž]-like friction: *corro* /kór̄o/ → [kór̄̌o]. Both assibilated vibrants may become voiceless at times: *ir* [iɹ̥̌], *corro* [kór̥̄̌o].

In parts of Puerto Rico and the Dominican Republic, /r̄/ has migrated to the back of the mouth in addition to fricativizing and devoicing. The results vary, so that *corro* can have an alveolar trill [r̄], a French uvular trill [ʀ] or uvular fricative [ʁ], or a voiceless uvular [χ] or velar [x] fricative; Canfield (1981) even found a hybrid [xr̄]. The use of [x] for [r̄] does not result in confusion of *erre* with *jota*, since the latter is aspirated ([h]) in these countries (v. 2.1.3.2); *corro* is [kóxo] and *cojo* is [kóho].

A common fate of /r/ is merger or *igualación* with /l/, usually in syllable-final position (i.e. when / _____ C, / _____ ‖). This Liquid Leveling yields some kind of *r, l*, or intermediate sound for both: flap [ɾ], assibilated [ɹ̌], lateral [l], lateral flap [ɺ], glide [j], or aspirated [h]; and this last can then drop or assimilate just like the [h] of the S-Aspiration rule. In concrete terms, the student who has learned [káɾne] for *carne* may actually hear any of the following: [káɾne káɹ̌ne kálne kájne káhne kánne].

Liquid Leveling occurs in Chile, the Caribbean islands and coasts, Andalusia and a few other areas of Spain. It can create homonyms: *arma* = *alma, mal* = *mar* = *más*. It creates morphological alternations: *sol* and *olor* may end in the same (or no) consonant, but their /l/ and /r/ reemerge in *soles* and *olores*. Likewise, *el* will be [el] in *el ojo* but [er] or [ej] in *el cielo* (Zamora-Vicente 1967:315). *Igualación* tends to coincide geographically with S-Aspiration, N-Velarization, and frequent D-Deletion, giving rise to the term 'weak consonantism' for characterizing such dialects' phonology in general (Canfield 1981:36).

In many Caribbean dialects, northern Chile, Panama, and Andalusia, the affricate /č/ is losing its stop onset and becoming a mere fricative, [š]: *chico* /číko/ → [šíko], *muchacho* /mučáčo/ → [mušášo]. The phoneme /f/ is very widely pronounced as a bilabial fricative, [ɸ], on both sides of the Atlantic: *fuego* /fwégo/ → [ɸwéɣo]. While [f] is made with the upper teeth against the lower lip (=labiodental), [ɸ] is made just with the lips (=bilabial), and the two differ in exactly the same way as [v] and [β].

Sociolinguists are discovering that many of these phonetic processes are variable rules. In Panama, the /č/ → [š] rule correlates to age group, the young applying it more than their elders (Canfield 1981:67). In Mexico City, F-Bilabialization and Assibilation are clear-cut variable rules correlating to sex, class, and age (Perissinotto 1975:100-115).[12] Liquid Leveling varies similarly in Santo Domingo (Jorge-Morel 1974:77-78). Variable rules often indicate changes in progress, and it is quite possible that the articulations now viewed as 'local', 'informal', or even 'nonstandard' will have become the norm within a few more decades.

3.1.9 Vowel Weakening. Under close scrutiny, Spanish vowels turn out to have several allophones. In general, they are somewhat more open when followed by CC, C#, /x/, or /r̄/ than in other environments; consequently, the /e/ and /o/ of *lejos, ves, perra, costa* are not phonetically identical to those of *lleno, ve, pesa, bota*. Moreover, Navarro (1967:44ff.) notes that in rapid speech, the five vowels are more relaxed and less precise in their articulation when they are unstressed.[13]

Yet these variations are subliminal to the nonlinguist, and usually ignored in pedagogy. The two /e/ of *este* or *eje* never differ as much as the English /e/ of *mate* and /ɛ/ of *met*; and unstressed Spanish vowels never reduce to the extent of the English schwa (v. 3.2.8). Navarro, in fact, advises foreign teachers to ignore the slightly weakened allophones of Spanish /a e i o u/ lest their English, French, or German-speaking students equate them with their schwas.

But in Mexico[14] atonic vowels are more noticeably weakened. The results are still not schwas, but several degrees of laxing and devoicing. Perissinotto (1975:26-33) manages to distinguish six degrees, viz. for /e/:

(1) [é]: normal (as described by Navarro) relaxed articulation
(2) [ᵉ]: very weak, but still voiced and carrying a syllabic beat
(3) [ᵉ̌]: short, almost imperceptible
(4) [e̥]: devoiced (whispered), but still syllabic
(5) [é̥]: devoiced and almost imperceptible
(6) Ø: zero, dropped entirely

Ordinarily, an unstressed vowel might reach degrees (1) through (3); an adjacent voiceless consonant (as in *machete, chiquito, plática*) abets the process and sometimes causes devoicing; but it is an adjacent /s/ that promotes the most devoicing: *visitas* /bisítas/ → [bi̥sítas]. Complete deletion is rare except in a handful of words such as *pues, entonces, gracias* [ps entóns ğrass], and Perissinotto believes that non-Mexicans who have reported more rampant deletion misheard one of the other degrees (p. 32). He also notes that this is a variable rule, dependent on social and stylistic factors.

3.1.10 Vowel Gliding.

unstressed   V →   nonsyllabic glide $/ \left\{ \dfrac{}{V} V \right\}$
(ĭ, ŭ)   (j, w)
(general, and almost categorical for high vowels)

Any kind of analysis of Spanish phonology requires a gliding rule in order to account for alternations between the full vowels [i u] and the glides [j w] (v. 2.2.3). For example, *continuar, continuamos, continuó* have [kontinw-] and *continúo, continúan, continúe* have [kontinú-]. The key to Gliding is, of course, stress: if the high vowels /i u/ are unstressed and adjacent to another vowel, they form a diphthong with it by becoming glides, but if stressed, they preserve their syllabicity (i.e. stay vowels). Like most other phonological rules in the language, Gliding occurs across # (word boundaries) in fast speech; note its effects on the conjunctions *y* and *o*:

dos o tres [dósotɾés], siete u ocho [sjétewóčo]
dos y tres [dósitɾés], dos y ocho [dosjóčo], ocho y nueve
[óčojnwéβe]

Whether these glides can then feed into Glide Strengthening and be strengthened to fricatives—e.g. in *cuatro y ocho* [kwátɾojóčo]—is a matter of dispute, or perhaps of different dialects or idiolects. Oroz (1966:58) and Navarro (1967:151) note variable *rehilamiento* of glided *y* between vowels or utterance-initially; but Bowen and Stockwell 1955 and Quilis and Fernández 1975 rule it out.

In fast speech, Gliding occurs in nonhigh ('strong') vowels too. As articulation speeds up, syneresis (v. 2.2.3) applies, and the less open or less stressed vowel loses its syllabicity and ends up crushed against its neighbor.[15] Perissinotto (1975:34-36) recorded the following glidings of nonhigh vowels in Mexican speech:

/ea/ → [ja] : teatro, pasear, real, empleado, le habló
/oa/ → [wa] : toalla, Joaquín, Oaxaca, mexicano adorable
/ae/ → [aj] : cae, trae, mala espina
/eo/ → [jo] : peor, petróleo, vine hoy
/éo/ → [ew] : feo, peleo
/oe/ → [we] : cohete, héroe, soez

Stress is one advantage to the victor in these vocalic battles, but at times the more open vowel overrides, and steals, its neighbor's stress:

océano [éa → eá → já]   país [aí → ái → áj]
baúl [aú → áu → áw]   período [ío → ió → jó]

As an alternative to Gliding, one of the two vowels may be deleted, usually the first one (Perissinotto, p. 37, Dalbor 1980b:183, Boyd-Bowman 1960:153):

la orquesta [loɾkésta]   me imagino [mimaxíno]
ahogarse [oɣáɾse]   tengo uno [teŋgúno]
lo insultó [linsultó]   la unión [lunjón]

The loss is quite generalized for double vowels: *cohorte* = *corte*, *aprehender* = *aprender*.

Pedagogy recognizes syneresis and gliding mainly just when the orthography shows these: *a el* → *al*, *de el* → *del*, and *aún* [aún] in *más aún* vs. *aun* [awn] in *aun más*. Nevertheless, these processes are extremely common in the spoken language throughout the Hispanic world; they increasingly affect even the most formal styles (Navarro accepts [ja] in *cardíaco* and [jo] in *período* as standard now); and in poetry and singing they are often mandatory.

3.2 English rules. Sections 3.2.1 through 3.2.5 describe processes applying to the consonants of English; sections 3.2.6 through 3.2.8 describe processes applying to its vowels. The rules presented here are those with the greatest potential for interference in the pronunciation of Spanish.

3.2.1 Aspiration.

$$/\text{p t č k}/ \rightarrow [\text{p}^h \text{ t}^h \text{ č}^h \text{ k}^h] \Big/ \left\{ \begin{matrix} \# \underline{\quad} \\ \text{V} \underline{\quad} (\left\{ \begin{matrix} \text{G} \\ \text{L} \end{matrix} \right\}) \ \acute{\text{V}} \end{matrix} \right\}$$

(voiceless stops) (aspirated)

(categorical and general)

Voiceless stops in English are exploded with an *h*-like puff of air in certain positions, and are then called ASPIRATED. This occurs basically in syllable-initial position, specifically (1) word-initially (*pick, prick, tick, trick, chick, kick, quick* /kw-/), and (2) before a stressed vowel even across an intervening liquid (/l r/) or glide (/j w/)(*appéar, appláud, retáin, retráin, achíeve, acquíre* /kw/, *accúse* /kj/). Elsewhere, voiceless stops are less aspirated, and especially after /s/ (*spy, stay, score, skill, square*) they are like their Spanish counterparts. Thus, *pie tag quints* [pʰaj tʰæg kʰwĩnts], but *spy stag squints* [spaj stæg skwĩnts].

To understand exactly where the 'puff of air' comes from—and therefore what the student must avoid doing in his Spanish—it may be useful to consider in more detail the difference between the /p/ of *spy* and the /p/ of *pie*.

s[p]y: After the /s/, the lips close to make a stop, holding back the airstream. They separate, release the stop cleanly, and simultaneously the vocal cords begin to vibrate for the vowel.

[pʰ]ie: The lips close to form a stop. They separate, releasing the stop, and the vocal tract assumes position for the vowel. But voicing turns on later, not simultaneously with the release, so that unused air leaks out between the stop's release and the onset of voicing for the vowel. The puff of air is thus a voiceless segment of the vowel; but it is perceived as a release feature of the /p/.

For the English speaker it is as natural to aspirate /p/, say, word-initially, as it is for the Spanish speaker to fricativize his /b/ between vowels; neither is aware of using a different allophone, [pʰ] and [β], in the designated position, and neither can suppress the relevant rule without training and practice. Aspiration is automatic, and the English speaker identifies the [pʰ] of *pie* with the [p] of *spy* as the 'same' sound, in opposition to the /b/ of *buy* which—as a distinct phoneme—is perceived as not the same at all. Yet it must be recognized that aspiration definitely reinforces the voicing contrast of *pie* vs. *buy*; if that clue that English speakers are used to is missing, as in the Spanish /p/ vs. /b/ contrast, then students may not perceive the difference in voicing. In fact, on a dictation test with unfamiliar words, some beginners will write *bata* for a native Spanish speaker's pronunciation of *pata*.

English /t č k/ are aspirated too. Aspiration of /č/ makes it a bit more fricative-sounding than Spanish /č/ (Stockwell and Bowen 1965:66). And of course, English /t/ is furthermore alveolar whereas Spanish /t/ is dental (v. 2.1.2).

3.2.2 Preglottalization.

/p t č k/ → [ʔp ʔt ʔč ʔk] / ____ ||, nasal, or obstruent
(general, but with some variability in application)

Instead of being aspirated, English voiceless stops are PREGLOTTALIZED in the positions shown above (which are roughly 'syllable-final'): the voicing of a preceding vowel is cut off sharply by a glottal stop as the lips or tongue move into position for /p t č k/. Thus, *top tot stock* /tap tat stak/ → [tʰaʔp tʰaʔt staʔk]. As Ladefoged (1982:85) observes, some speakers do this more than others, but Preglottalization is at least a general tendency and a fairly distinctive trait of English articulation. Many speakers proceed to drop [t] once the [ʔ] is inserted, and the [ʔ] can then be considered as standing for the /t/ (i.e. as its allophone): *atmosphere* [ǽʔməsfìr], *satin* [sǽʔn̩], *mountain* [máwnʔn̩], *what kind* [hwɑ̀ʔkʰájnd]. In Cockney, this occurs intervocalically too: *butter* [bʌ́ʔə].

Carried over into Spanish, Preglottalization in syllable-final position yields a perceptible accent because it strengthens the stop quality of /p t č k/, as opposed to their weakening in the same position in Spanish (v. 2.3). As Navarro (1967:87, 97, 140) observes, syllable-final voiceless stops in Spanish tend to become weak voiced fricatives or drop entirely. Note the following contrasts:

| Eng.: | a[ʔ]mosphere | a[ʔ]las | te[ʔk]nical | conce[ʔp]tion |
| Span.: | a[ð]mósfera | a[ð]las | té[ɣ]nico | conce[β]ción |

3.2.3 Flapping.

t, d → ɾ / V̆(r) ____ (#)V̆
(general in the U.S. and Canada, with some stylistic variation)

By this rule, the alveolar stops weaken to a flap in certain environments. Flapping is almost categorical in normal fast pronunciation and leads to many homonyms: *latter* = *ladder, wetting* = *wedding, patted* = *padded* ([lǽɾər wéɾɩŋ pʰǽɾəd]). In slower styles it is somewhat variable and may be overridden for clarification: 'I said *wai*[tʰ]*ed*, not *wa*[d]*ed*.' The [ɾ] is virtually identical to the tapped /r/ of Spanish, and can be used as a basis for acquiring it: *pot o' tea, para ti*.[16]

Flapping is most common between a stressed vowel and an unstressed one: *átom* = *Ádam* = [ǽɾəm], but *atómic* has [tʰ]. As the rule shows, it also occurs (1) even if /r/ precedes (*hearty* = *hardy*), and (2) across #: *còrd of (wóod)* = *còurt of (láw), I lét it* = *I léd it, I húrt it* = *I héard it*.[17] Teachers need to bear in mind that /d/-Flapping in English and /d/-Spirantization in Spanish overlap in /V̇ ____ V and /V̇(r) ____ V. Especially for beginning students, this creates both articulatory and perceptual problems. They may not recognize *todo* in '[ṭóðo]', wondering what is meant by what sounds like 'toe-though'; and in the other direction, their flapped [tʰówɾow] may be heard not as *todo* but as *toro* by Spanish speakers. Two familiar sounds of English, [ð] and [ɾ], will no longer stand for /ð/ and /d/, but must be relearned as /d/ and /r/, respectively.

3.2.4 Palatalization before Yod.

tj dj sj zj → č ǰ š ž / V̇(n) ____ V
(general, but with some stylistic variation)

This rule changes alveolar plus /j/ to an alveopalatal. Old Spanish (more precisely, Vulgar Latin) underwent a similar rule but the modern language lacks it. In English, the alveopalatal has become the norm in some words, and would be represented phonemically in them: *issue, nature, pleasure* /íšu néčər plézər/ < /ɩsju netjər plɛzjər/. In others, the two pronunciations are still vying for ascendancy: *educate* /édjəkèt, éǰəkèt/, *controversial* /kàntrovə́rsjəl, kàntrəvə́ršəl/. Across word-boundaries, the situation conforms to a more straightforward variable rule, depending mainly on style and on speed of speech: *this year* /sj ~ š/, *please you* /zj ~ ž/, *did you* /dj ~ ǰ/, *eat yet* /tj ~ č/.

Palatalization causes special interference in Spanish cognates with unstressed *tu, du, su*. The *u* here is equated with the underlying /ju/ or /jə/ of the English versions, and this /j/ triggers palatalization of the /t d s/ in Spanish *mutual, educar, usual, casual, graduación*. Students may also apply Palatalization to medial /tj dj sj/ in words such as *Asia, gracias, acción, oficial, cordial, televisión, nacional*. Thus, [graǰuašón kʰažuál našonál] may be heard in the classroom for *graduación, casual, nacional*.

3.2.5 L-Velarization.

l → ɫ / (____ $)
(general, but the environment is variable)

The /l/ of Span. *mil, col, tal* is an alveolar lateral, as is the /l/ of Eng. *meal, coal, tall*; in both languages, the tip of the tongue contacts the alveolar ridge and the voiced airstream spills over the side(s) of the tongue. But in Span. *col*, the body of the tongue is high in the mouth, whence a light, clear resonance like that of the high vowel /i/; in Eng. *coal*, the body of the tongue is sunken, with the dorsum (back) tugging back toward the velum, and this yields a dark and somber resonance reminiscent of /u ʊ w/. Phonemically, the symbol /l/ is used for both, but to show detail the 'clear *l*' of Spanish is transcribed [l] and the 'dark *l*' of English can be transcribed [ɫ]: Span. [kól], Eng. [kʰówɫ]. Though the difference (Figure 3.3) may seem minor, acoustically it is very striking, and if darkening—or VELARIZATION, to use the technical term—is carried over into Spanish, *alto* and *calzar* may be heard as *auto* and *causar*.

Figure 3.3. 'Clear' and 'dark' /l/.

Span. [l] (clear) in *col, mil, tal*   Eng. [ɫ] (dark, velarized) in *coal, meal, tall*

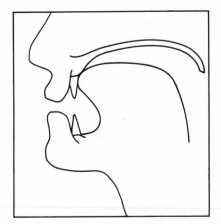 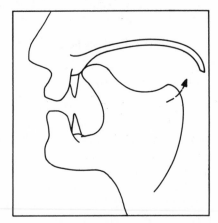

Where Velarization occurs seems to depend on the idiolect. For some speakers, it is strong at the end of a syllable, but otherwise /l/ is clear and Spanish-like. Others apparently velarize syllable-finally and before any back vowel; still others, including this writer, use 'dark /l/' almost everywhere in their English.

3.2.6 Diphthongization.

i e o u → ij ej ow ʉw
(general, although not universal; some variability)

The tense vowels of English tend to be diphthongal, veering off into a palatal glide in the case of the front vowels /i e/ and a labiovelar one in the case of the back vowels /o u/ (v. 2.2.1). It is necessary to say 'tend' because of two sets of exceptions. First, in a few areas of the United States and the British Isles, rather pure, Spanish-like articulations predominate for some or all tense vowels.[18] Second, many speakers who do diphthongize under heavy stress have little or no diphthongization in vowels that are unstressed but not quite reduced (see next rule); for example, in *obey* one may hear a slow, deliberate [owbéj] or a faster, more casual [əbéj], but in between there is [obéj], with a fairly pure /o/ resembling that of Span. *obedece*. Nevertheless, Diphthongization is so general and so marked in contrast with Spanish vowels that for pedagogical purposes it can be considered a categorical rule capable of causing major interference. Thus, *puso*/púso/ becomes [pʰúwsow], and *ves* and *veis* are merged into [béjs].

3.2.7 Vowel Reduction.

V̆ → ə

(general, with some variability)

English vowels are lengthened when stressed (v. 4.1.3)—a feature that can be shown by a colon (V̆:)—whereas unstressed vowels are correspondingly shortened, centralized, and muffled, losing their distinctive resonance. In Spanish, such perturbations are slight, but in English they are so marked that unstressed vowels merge into schwa.[19] In most cases, this rule applies very regularly in normal speech, giving alternations in which a vowel appears as a full vowel when stressed but as [ə] when unstressed (see Figure 3.4). But it does not apply to /i/ before another vowel

Figure 3.4 Vowel reduction in English.

æ → ə : átom, ătómic	aj → ə : invíte, invǐtátion
ɛ → ə : compétitive, compĕtítion	e → ə : fámous, ínfămous
ɪ → ə : oríginal, órĭgin	o → ə : invóke, invŏcátion
ʊ → ə : He cóuld? Hé cŏuld dó it.	u → ə : matúre, matŭrátion
ɑ → ə : biólogy, biŏlógical	i → ə : THÉ movie to see, thĕ móvie

(*various*) or word-finally (*beauty*—but cf. *beautiful*); and there is some stylistic variation in the pronunciation of initial /i/ (*elaborate*), final and initial /o/ (*window, obey*) and initial syllables of 'fancy' words (thus, [æ] in *gastronomy* but [ə] in *astronomy*, as noted by Fidelholz 1975). On the other hand, articles, helping verbs, forms of *be*, pronouns, and short conjunctions reduce so much that they may lose their vowels, and a consonant or two as well.[20]

One may generalize as follows. When a student says a Spanish word slowly and deliberately, he may apply Reduction very little, but as his articulatory speed picks up, he is more likely to reduce the unstressed vowels into some kind of central *uh* vowel. This can be very disruptive, since Spanish preserves a five-way contrast regardless of stress:

pesado ≠ pisado	pasaron ≠ posaron	maleta ≠ muleta
mitad ≠ matad	retina ≠ rutina	piñita ≠ peñita
calor ≠ color	sociedad ≠ suciedad	mercado ≠ marcado

But the worst casualty will be the inflectional system, which depends crucially on differentiating -*o* and -*a*, -*os* and -*as*, -*an* and -*en*, -*a* and -*e*, etc. Thus, *buenos* and *buenas* will be 'fudged' as [bwéjnəs], and *cantaron* and *cantaran* as [kʰəntárən].

3.2.8 Schwa Deletion.

əl ən əm ər → l̩ n̩ m̩ ɚ
(general, but stylistically variable)

By this rule, what might be pronounced as schwa plus a liquid or nasal in slow (but reduced) styles becomes a syllabic *l*, *n*, *m* or retroflex [ɚ], the schwa being dropped or fused with the consonant. Examples:

[əl → l̩]: crad*le*, cast*le*, lab*el*, ca*l*amity, fat*all*y, chann*el*, co*l*ogne
[ən → n̩]: ris*en*, mount*ain*, oc*ean*, ord*i*nal, co*nn*ect, sc*e*nario
[əm → m̩]: pris*m*, chas*m*, leave '*em*
[ər → ɚ]: m*ur*der, lab*or*, f*ir*st, w*or*se

Schwa Deletion often appears in students' rendition of Spanish cognates:

túnel → [túnl̩]	garaje → [gɚáxe]
excelente → [ekslénte]	oportunidad → [opɚtunəðáð]

But it is well attested in beginners' pronunciation of noncognates too:

derecha → [dɚéčə]	sonaba → [sn̩áβə]

3.3 Order of difficulty: Ranking phonological problems.

We have not attempted to describe all the phonological rules of English, but only those which can produce relatively serious mispronunciations if transferred to Spanish. But how serious is serious? To present and practice all the features of Spanish phonology and to drum out all un-Spanish rules of English would leave little time for getting on with grammar, vocabulary, culture, and communication. Clearly, there are some phonological points that are so important that they must be introduced early; others can be deferred a bit, and still others need not be touched upon at all. It is a matter of priorities, and the teacher and text writer will implicitly or explicitly use some kind of decision-making procedure in arranging difficulties in a hierarchy.

One proposal for such a hierarchy comes from Stockwell and Bowen (1965:9-18). Their ranking, from hardest to easiest, has eight 'orders' of problems arranged in three 'magnitudes' of difficulty. These are as follows, with examples that have been covered in Chapters 2 and 3.

Magnitude 1:

(1) An obligatory feature (rule, pattern) of Spanish lacking in English: Spirantization of /b/.

(2) A phoneme or phonemic distinction of Spanish, lacking in English: *r*-sounds, and /k/ vs. /x/.

(3) An obligatory feature of Spanish that merges an English distinction: Spirantization of /d/, which means that [d] and [ð] must be treated as allophones, not as separate phonemes.

Magnitude 2:

(4) Units distinguished in Spanish are obligatorily merged in English: Reduction, which merges into a schwa unstressed vowels that Spanish continues to contrast.

(5) An obligatory pattern of English that Spanish lacks: Flapping, which changes /t/ and /d/ into a flap, whereas Spanish distinguishes all three in *mito, mido, miro*.[21]

(6) An English distinction that has no Spanish counterpart: *sock* with /ɑ/ vs. *sack* with /æ/, with the Spanish /a/ roughly in between.

Magnitude 3:

(7) Shared distinctions: e.g. /p b t d m n s f . . . / word-initially contrast as phonemes.

(8) Shared rules and patterns: /sw-/ must be followed by a vowel in both languages.

As a first approximation to the problem, this hierarchy seems on the right track, and at least vaguely it mirrors actual pedagogical practice. The *r*-sounds and Spirantization are given considerable attention, and usually fairly early; avoidance of Reduction is given some attention; and the fact that Spanish contrasts /p/ and /b/ word-initially is taken for granted and seldom expressly pointed out. Following the Stockwell and Bowen (S&B) criteria, one could proceed to fill in cases such as Spanish Glide Strengthening, English Aspiration, and so on at the proper levels.

Yet S&B admit that their hierarchy alone is insufficient, because other criteria must be applied too. Two of them are 'potential mishearing' and 'functional load'. Applying the former, they note that one might promote the avoidance of Eng. Aspiration to the upper ranks inasmuch as Spanish [p t k] can be misheard as [b d g] by students who still depend on aspiration. As for functional load, this term refers to the relative weight a distinction carries in contrasting minimal pairs: /r/ vs. /r̄/ in Spanish distinguishes many words, but /ɲ/ vs. /nj/ very few; and though the student who uses /nj/ for the *eñe* will have a slight accent, his substitution will not wreak as much havoc as the substitution of *ere* for *erre*. Consequently, the /ɲ/ vs. /nj/ distinction might be demoted from its predicted ranking of '2'. A third criterion might be called representativeness; S-Aspiration in Spanish is difficult to rank in the hierarchy and seems dialectal anyhow, but it is widespread and perhaps deserves more pedagogical attention than it usually receives. Finally, matters of stress and intonation do not fit well in the hierarchy; yet S&B place them high on their agenda of phonological items that are both difficult and important. These will be taken up in the next chapter.

Notes for Chapter 3

1. The advanced linguistics student might prefer a formalization using features, e.g. [+syllabic] → [+nasal] / _____ [+nasal]. This notation has several advantages, and students who know it might try reformulating the rules in this chapter. Yet we will avoid using it since many readers would be unfamiliar with it, and explaining it would take us far afield.

2. As noted in the preceding chapter (v. 2.3), syllable boundaries are fairly clear in Spanish but not so in English. Though we will occasionally refer to positions such as 'end of syllable', any analysis resorting to syllable boundaries should first specify exactly where '$' occurs in phonemic representation, this not always being an obvious given. See Hooper 1976 for an attempt to do this for Spanish and English, and Harris 1983 for a more recent description of Spanish syllable structure.

3. This chapter's description of sociogeographical distribution relies heavily on the work of Zamora-Vicente 1967, Navarro 1967 and 1975, Resnick 1975, and Canfield 1981 for Spanish; and on the work of Kurath and McDavid 1961 and Wells 1982 for English. For more details, the reader is referred to dialect atlases, which record phonetically on base maps the responses elicited from many representative informants by organized teams of dialectologists. For Spanish, these include *Atlas lingüístico de la Península Ibérica, Atlas lingüístico-etnográfico de Andalucía,* Navarro 1948 (for Puerto Rico), and the forthcoming *Atlas lingüístico del español de México* and *Atlas lingüístico-etnográfico de Colombia.*

4. Glide Strengthening of /j/ (chiefly in syllable-initial position) seems to prevail everywhere but in Central America, northernmost Mexico (and adjacent U.S.), and the northwest coasts of South America. In such zones, /j/ is a weak glide in all positions, like the English one, and it even drops when after /í/: *capilla* [kapía], *amarillo, silla,* etc.

5. In the following pairs, the first member has a /j/ or /w/ strengthened because it begins a stem, while the second has a weak glide, though it follows the same consonant.

abyecto, abierto   deshielo, desierto   inyección, vinieron
subyuga, subió   deshueso, desuello   cónyuge, circonio

This complicated picture of near-minimal pairs for [ɟ] and [j], [w̟] and [w], led to spirited debates. For a sample of them, the reader might consult Bowen and Stockwell 1955 vs. Saporta 1956, though bearing in mind that the prevailing theory of that time forbade appealing to morphological information (e.g. 'stem-initial') in phonology.

6. Navarro (1967:128) symbolizes this affricate as 'ŷ'; others have used

'ĵ', the same symbol as for English *Joe*, *age*, though this latter phone is alveopalatal (tongue tip up) while the Spanish affricate is palatal (tongue tip down).

7. Saciuk 1980 manages to distinguish nine degrees of *rehilamiento* for strengthened /j/, in four environments. His data suggest a variable rule, but in general they corroborate others' observations that /j/ is typically an affricate in /‖ _____ , a fricative in /V _____ V, and a semivowel next to C.

8. At least in Castilian, /n/ before /m/ yields a hybrid nasal with simultaneous alveolar and bilabial contacts; Navarro 1967 symbolizes it as [^m_n]. The allophone appearing before /č/ has sometimes been identified with [ɲ], but Harris (1969:9) shows that it is alveopalatal (apex up), not palatal (apex down). There is no agreed-on symbol for an alveopalatal nasal; I have adopted 'ñ' as typographically parallel to š ž č ĵ.

9. The nasal and post-/l/ cases for /d/ as a stop have in common the fact that these sonorants are, by assimilation, dental like the /d/. In a more formal version of the rule, features can show this fact readily (Harris 1969:39-40).

10. But Torreblanca 1980 disagrees (as he does with S-Voicing). After reviewing careful studies, he concludes that stops and fricatives tend to pattern as shown, but there are occasional crossovers in both directions. Jorge-Morel (1974:67) notes the same fact.

11. This is not for want of trying, though. In some sectors of the Hispanic world, earnest teachers have striven to make children distinguish *be de burro* and *ve de vaca* by using a labiodental [v] for the latter, unaware that this sound (and the *b/v* distinction) disappeared from the language centuries ago. According to Boyd-Bowman (1960:54), [v]-loving teachers in the Mexican literacy campaign have only succeeded in adding [v] as yet a third allophone of /b/—there is still no consistent *b/v* distinction.

12. A synopsis of Perissinotto's data for the curious:

f → ɸ: males 70.6% of the time, females 57%; lower, middle, upper classes 78.3%, 60.3%, 53.77%, respectively.

r → ɹ: males 39%, females 89%; lower, middle, upper 54%, 81%, 60%, respectively; youth 73.5%, middle-aged 64.5%, older 31%.

r̄ → ř: males 21%, females 38.5%; lower, middle, upper 18%, 40%, 30%, respectively; youth 36%, middle-aged 34.5%, older never.

13. For these more relaxed unstressed vowels, Navarro and his disciples have used the symbols ҽ ə ! ɔ u̜.

14. According to Canfield 1981, Vowel Weakening also occurs in west and central Bolivia, southwest Colombia, and parts of highland Peru and Ecuador. The phenomenon has best been studied in Mexico, however (see also Lope Blanch 1963).

15. Some analysts perceive an intermediate stage between, say, /e$a/ in *teatro* with hiatus and [ja] with syneresis plus complete gliding. In this middle stage, [ẹa], the /e/ has lost its syllabicity but is still more open than the palatal glide [j] of *viaje* [bjáxe] and *Asia* [ásja]. Yet Boyd-Bowman

(1960:48-50, 153) and Oroz (1966:69) find this very infrequent in normal speech: *te hago* [tjáɣo], *lo hace* [lwáse].

16. This approach to the Spanish /r/ is proposed by Stockwell and Bowen (1965:124); other pairs of theirs are *photo foro, auto oro, motor moro, meadow mero, solder Sara*. Yet [ɾ] for English speakers is firmly a /t/ or /d/ (v. 2.1.3.3) and this fact can interfere with the teacher's attempt to reidentify it as an /r/ for Spanish.

17. There are three other environments for English Flapping we will consign to this note. In /V́n ____ V (*winter, plenty*), /t/ is flapped or even dropped but /d/ (*sandy, bandage*) is not. In /V̆ ____ V̆ (*irritable, variety*), Flapping is somewhat variable. And in /V ____ #V́ (*at eight, let out, that orange*), Flapping is quite common, even though it seems the wrong place for it (note the stress on the *second* vowel).

18. See Kurath and McDavid 1961 and Wells 1982 for details. One teaching assistant who hailed from a nondiphthongizing dialect caused confusion in his Spanish class when he modeled the 'difference' between Eng. *lay, bay, may, say* and Span. *le, ve, me, se*. His students heard no difference, for there was none in his speech. Nevertheless, such dialects are decidedly in the minority.

19. For some speakers, a few vowels reduce instead to [ɨ], which is like [ə] but a bit higher.

20. I *can* go [kæn → kən → kn̩ → ŋ]; see *them* [ðɛm → ðəm → əm]; Harry *would* go [wʊd → wəd → əd → d]; a bag *of* groceries [əv → ə].

21. S&B's examples have been retained except for Order 4, where they used a less familiar example limited to one dialect of English. The distinction between this order and Order 5 is not altogether clear in practice, but from their examples it seems that Order 4 includes rules yielding an un-Spanish phone, whereas Order 5 has rules yielding a phone that Spanish does have, but with different functions.

Exercises for Chapter 3

1. What are the allophones of each of the following Spanish phonemes, and where does each allophone occur?

(1) /j/	(3) /b/	(5) /r̄/
(2) /s/	(4) /d/	(6) /n/

2. Using symbols or articulatory labels, indicate how each of the italicized nasals is pronounced.

(1) e*n*vidia	(6) ga*n*cho	(11) te*n*dencia
(2) i*n*fante	(7) i*n*migrante	(12) ma*n*go
(3) ga*n*so	(8) i*n*yección	(13) e*n* Panamá
(4) fra*n*ja	(9) ba*ñ*ando	(14) e*n* Huelva
(5) e*n*hebrar	(10) co*n*quista	(15) e*n* Valencia

3. Determine whether each italicized occurrence of /b d g/ is a stop or fricative.

(1) om*b*ligo	(6) en*v*ol*v*er	(11) in*d*igno
(2) fe*d*eral	(7) per*d*i*d*	(12) no*v*iazgo
(3) des*v*án	(8) fá*b*rica	(13) o*b*tenga
(4) ries*g*o	(9) igual*d*a*d*	(14) cur*v*a*d*o
(5) a*b*sur*d*o	(10) nin*g*ún	(15) a*d*yacente

4. Repeat the above instructions for the following phrases. Assume that the capital begins a breath-group.

(1) Un *g*rifo, (2) El *g*rifo, (3) Faltan *g*rifos

(4) *D*ámelo, (5) Me *d*a, (6) Él *d*a, (7) Él nos *d*a

(8) *D*ónde, (9) A*d*ónde, (10) Por *d*ónde

(11) *V*einte, (12) Hay *v*einte, (13) Con *v*einte, (14) Los *v*einte

(15) *D*e julio, (16) Los *d*e julio, (17) El *d*e julio

5. How do the English and Spanish articulations of the following differ?

(1) /l/   (2) /e/   (3) /j/   (4) /d/

6. Indicate whether transference of the following English rules will result in (1) an accent (light, heavy), or (2) obliteration of Spanish phonemic distinctions.

(1) Aspiration	(3) Preglottalization	(5) Schwa Deletion
(2) Flapping	(4) Vowel Diph-	(6) Vowel Reduction
	thongization	

7. Given the differences between Spanish and English phonology, what special problems would English speakers have with how Spanish *phonetically* distinguishes *codo, coro, corro*?

8. List some sociolinguistically variable rules of Spanish and identify the general pattern of variation. Which of these, in your experience with native speakers, tend to be stigmatized, despite their actual extent?

9. Take each of the following Spanish words (which are given in phonemic transcription) and retranscribe them phonetically in two ways, using the information from this chapter. First, show how they will be pronounced by native speakers, and then show how an English speaker might render them with interference from his native phonology. Example: *cada* /káda/ → (ntv.) [káða], [káa]; Eng. [kʰárə]

(1) enfermas /enférmas/	(6) verdad /berdád/
(2) yunque /júnke/	(7) selva /sélba/
(3) televisión /telebisjón/	(8) pertenece /pertenése, -θe/
(4) rasgo /r̄ásgo/	(9) casualidad /kaswalidád/
(5) música /músika/	(10) inflado /infládo/

10. Use information from this and the preceding chapter to identify where each of the following pronunciations might be heard. (*¡Ojo!* Some of these are fairly general pronunciations not limited to one or even sever-

al dialects; others may occur in a few fairly specific areas; still others have more than one identifying characteristic that allows you to pinpoint them.)

(1) basta [báhta]

(2) van [baŋ]

(3) pollo [póšo]

(4) desde [dézde̞]

(5) chiquitos [č̆ʲkít^øs]

(6) hornos [ɔ́nnɔ]

(7) café [kaɸé]

(8) jarro [xářo]

(9) jarro [háxo]

(10) hablado [aβláw]

(11) desmayo [dehmážo]

(12) huésped [wéppe]

(13) charco [šálko]

(14) sencillo [še̞n̪θíʎo]

11. The following data are from Andalusian (Zamora-Vicente 1967:291). Explain in terms of rules why the singular is so different from the plural.

	'net'	'bread'	'carnation'	'kiss'
sg.	r̄e	paŋ	klaβé	béso
pl.	r̄éðɛ	pánɛ	klaβélɛ	bésɔ

12. With regard to Nasal Assimilation, Terrell and Salgués (1979:56) state: 'Lo que es obligatorio dentro de una palabra se vuelve "tendencia fuerte" cuando la nasal se encuentra a final de palabra. Por ejemplo, la nasal de *un* se asimila en grupos sintácticos como *un beso, un gato, un chico* casi como si se tratara de una sola palabra.' List other phonological rules that act similarly in Spanish.

13. Obaid (1973:65) observes that vowel syneresis and consonant weakening are currently yielding pronunciations widely at variance with schoolbook Spanish. To cite one of the examples he collected, *Yugoslavia* was [ɟoláβja]. Trace in detail the phonological rules that yield this pronunciation from /jugoslábja/. Obaid emphasizes that such weakenings are widespread and very characteristic of the current vernacular; how do they affect the student's aural comprehension? What, in your opinion, could pedagogy do about this problem?

14. Recently, a textbook writer indicated to prospective users that Spanish pronunciation is very easy for the English speaker. Test this claim by returning to the tables of Spanish phonemes in Chapter 2 and, with information from both chapters, determining how many of these are pronounced as in English. Why, in your opinion, is Spanish regarded as 'easy' to pronounce?

15. Some texts introduce pronunciation at the beginning; others run through the Spanish alphabet in a preliminary lesson but postpone more detailed discussion to later chapters, interspersed with other matters; still others consign pronunciation to an appendix, or dispense with describing it and tell the student to 'listen to your teacher'. Which approach do you prefer, and why?

16. As noted in section 3.3, not every feature of Spanish phonology can or should be commented on in the classroom, so there must be some

'prioritization'. For each of the following, indicate (1) whether the introductory course should cover it (explained, of course, in beginners' terms),
(2) to what extent (i.e. what 'successful mastery' will constitute at this
level), and (3) which version (for those rules with social and/or dialectal
variation). Does S&B's hierarchy match your priorities?

(1) Glide Strengthening   (4) S-Voicing   (7) D-Deletion
(2) Nasal Assimilation   (5) S-Aspiration   (8) Assibilation
(3) Lateral Assimilation (6) Spirantization   (9) Vowel Gliding

17. Choose two of the foregoing rules that you ranked as fairly high,
and explain how you would present them to students. Show, above all,
how you would describe the process, illustrate it, model its effects, drill it,
and reenter it for review.

Chapter 4
Stress and intonation

4.0 Suprasegmentals. Consonants and vowels are called SEGMENTS because they follow from a segmentation of a stretch of speech into discrete phonetic slices. But there is more to the speech signal that just these segments. By vibrating the vocal cords faster or slower, one changes the pitch of a voiced sound, respectively raising or lowering it. By making the vibration more forceful and energetic, one increases its loudness (volume, intensity). These variations in pitch and loudness are termed SUPRASEGMENTALS since they are perceived in addition to, and organized 'on top of', the segments. Alternatively, they can be called by their classical name, PROSODIES.

4.1 Stress. A vowel or the syllable around it that is pronounced more loudly than its neighbors is STRESSED, one that is not especially loud is UNSTRESSED.[1] In phonological transcriptions, stress is shown by an accent mark on the vowel or in front of the syllable; unstressed vowels are usually not marked, although a breve (˘) can be used over them if necessary to draw attention to their lack of stress.

English and Spanish make similar uses of stress, as noted in the following section, but there are two principal differences in their phonetic realization of the stress feature. First, Spanish stress equates to greater loudness, whereas English speakers often reinforce loudness with higher pitch.[2] Carried over into Spanish, this coupling of stress with pitch can greatly disrupt Spanish intonational patterns, which are generally flatter than those of English (v. 4.2). Second, stressed and unstressed vowels in Spanish do not significantly differ in length (quantity) or articulation (quality); lengthening is exceptional and signals strong emphasis (Bull 1965:78, Navarro 1967:200-207). In English, however, stressed vowels are normally lengthened ($\acute{V}$:) while unstressed syllables are correspondingly shortened and reduced to schwa (v. 3.2.7). Transferred to Spanish, this lengthening/shortening effect makes *paró, paré* sound like *p'róou, p'réei* and is a well-known trait of many English and German speakers' pronunciation of Spanish (Navarro ibid).

4.1.1 Stress position. Depending on the language, the position of stress can be fixed or free, predictable or unpredictable. In French, for example, it is always the last full vowel of a word that receives the stress; in Czech, it is the first vowel; in Polish, it is the penultimate (next to last) one. In Spanish and English, however, stress position is freer and less predictable. Thus, in the following sets of words stress position seems contrastive (distinctive). (The accent mark will be used to indicate stress regardless of whether orthography requires it.)

Spanish:	English:
sábana, sabána	súbject, subjéct
término, termíno, terminó	Áugust, augúst
éstas, estás	cónvert, convért
ábra, habrá	ínvalid, inválid
amáran, amarán	rébel, rebél
pápa, papá	cónquer, concúr

But stress position is not totally lawless. In Spanish, most preterites and all futures (*terminó, habrá*) are stressed on the ending; otherwise, verb stress is largely penultimate (*termíno, ábra*). In English, stress depends to some extent on part of speech: noun *súbject*, verb *subjéct*; in fact, it is hard to find minimal pairs for English stress that do not involve different parts of speech. Moreover, certain patterns dominate in each language. In native English words (nonnative ones are more complicated), there is a strong tendency to stress the first stem vowel: *fáther, fátherly, fátherless, fátherlessness.* In Spanish, stress can occur only on one of the last three vowel phonemes of the word,[3] which limits the possibilities to three:

(-V .. V) .. V́ : oxytone (*aguda*): *Panamá, papá, tabú, alemán, españól, honór, bondád*

(-V) .. V́ .. V : paroxytone (*llana*): *sabána, pápa, democrácia, léngua, nómbre, césped, jóven*

-V́ .. V .. V : proparoxytone (*esdrújula*): *sábana, teléfono, páramo, régimen*

Spanish words ending in a vowel are mostly paroxytonic (*híjo, tríbu, paciéncia*) and those ending in a consonant other than inflectional /s/ or /n/ are mostly oxytonic (*imán, olór, tribál, cortés*). Statistically less common are the proparoxytones (*teléfono, análisis, régimen*), followed by oxytones ending in a vowel (*papá, Perú*) and paroxytones ending in a noninflectional consonant (*lápiz, césped, dátil, jóven*). This scale of frequency is recognized in the restriction of the orthographical accent to the less common cases.

As in most other components of language, there is some dialectal variation in stress position. English speakers are aware of nonstandard stressings such as *guítar, hótel, pólice, úmbrella, pérfume*; and with *address, preferable, irrefutable,* and *harass* there is variation even in educated speech. In Spanish, one sometimes hears restressings such as *centígramo, méndigo, síncero, váyamos, fríjol, sútil, cólega* (Flórez 1951: 306-317, Real Academia 1979:84); and the educated vary between *poliglóta* and *políglota, medúla* and *médula* (Navarro 1967:194). The special case of stress shift in syneresis, as in *océano período país → océáno periódo páis,* has already been discussed (v. 3.1.10). On the whole, though, stress position is remarkably stable in both languages.

In both languages, the stress of a word can be increased to emphasize it, and for clarification even an unstressed syllable can be highlighted: *they ímport more than they éxport, estoy refiriéndome a la importación, nó a la éxportación* (Quilis and Fernández 1975:160). In general, though, this seems rather more common in English than in Spanish.[4] Moveover, in both languages certain words are almost never stressed; articles, object pronouns, short prepositions and conjunctions, forms of *be/ser,* relative pronouns, etc. These are phonological CLITICS, words that attach themselves in pronunciation to their stressed neighbors. *Que me lo dé* is therefore a single 'phonological word,' [kemeloðé], just like *contaminé* [kontaminé].

4.1.2 Degrees of stress. In many languages that use stress, a word can have several stressed vowels. Often, however, these will differ in their relative intensity or loudness, so that one stress is subordinated to the other. Standard Spanish has just one case in which the word has more than one stress, the adverb in *-mente.*[5] When this suffix is added to an adjective, it carries the main or PRIMARY word stress, while the adjective's own stress reduces to SECONDARY —a degree of loudness less than primary but still greater than the intensity of any other vowel in the word. For this secondary stress, linguists use a grave accent, reserving the acute for primary:

formál, formàlménte	nítida, nìtidaménte
alégre, alègreménte	felíz, felìzménte

In English, secondary stress is more thoroughly exploited, and it contrasts with unstressed syllables: *gráduàte* (verb), *gráduăte* (noun). In long polysyllables, there is a strong tendency toward alternating among the three degrees:

ˋ ˘ ˊ : kàngaróo, sùperséde, rèprodúce
ˋ ˘ ˊ ˘ : rèferéndum, àutomátic, còmprehénsive
˘ ˋ ˘ ˊ ˘ : appèndicítis, invèstigátion
ˊ ˘ ˋ : réfugèe, álcohòl, récognìze
ˊ ˘ ˋ ˘ : álligàtor, sécretàry, cárburètor
˘ ˊ ˘ ˋ ˘ : refrígeràtor, extérminàting

This pattern of alternation is so entrenched that some students have trouble with the adjacent stresses in *-mente* adverbs, altering *formàlménte* to *fòrmalménte* (Bull 1965:80).

In still longer English words, a third and even fourth degree of stress may be audible, and linguists may then abandon accents and substitute superscript numbers: for primary (^{1}), for secondary (^{2}), for tertiary (^{3}), etc.

r$\overset{2}{\text{e}}$conc$\overset{3}{\text{i}}$li$\overset{1}{\text{a}}$tion	pr$\overset{2}{\text{e}}$stidi$\overset{3}{\text{g}}$it$\overset{1}{\text{a}}$tion	$\overset{2}{\text{a}}$nti-$\overset{3}{\text{i}}$ntell$\overset{1}{\text{e}}$ctual$\overset{4}{\text{i}}$sm
p$\overset{2}{\text{a}}$rall$\overset{1}{\text{e}}$logr$\overset{3}{\text{a}}$m	ch$\overset{2}{\text{o}}$lin$\overset{1}{\text{e}}$ster$\overset{3}{\text{a}}$se	$\overset{2}{\text{a}}$nti-infl$\overset{1}{\text{a}}$tion$\overset{3}{\text{a}}$ry

In both languages, the addition of a derivational suffix frequently alters the stress pattern. Thus, in Spanish:

biólogo, biológico, biología	órgano, orgánico, organizár, organización

Especially in Greco-Latin vocabulary, English is more complicated, thanks to its alternating stresses:

biólogy, bìológical   cómpensàte, compénsatòry, còmpensátion
cátegòry, càtegórical   phótogràph, photógraphy, phòtográphic
éxecùte, èxecútion,   sólid, solídifỳ, solìdificátion
    exécutive

One of the strongest derivational patterns in English is the contrast of compounds (´ `) with phrases (` ´):

a hót-dòg 'sandwich con   a hòt dóg 'perro que tiene calor'
    salchicha'
a Spánish tèacher 'profesor a Spànish téacher 'profesor venido
    de español'   de España'
the máke-ùp 'composición;   to màke úp 'componer; reconciliarse'
    maquillaje'

The student's first task with Spanish stress is to recognize its position in the 'normal' oxytone and paroxytone patterns, and the use of an accent mark to signal other patterns. The floating or unfixed stress position should not be a surprise, since English also has this; but the orthographic accent is sometimes regarded as an optional decoration by speakers of a language with no such mark in its spelling. Many students who have mastered these conventions nevertheless make errors in cognates whose Spanish stress pattern, though transparent in the orthography, contradicts that of English (the asterisks indicate mispronunciations):

indícan → *índican   comuníca → *comúnica
inglés → *íngles 'groins'   circúlan → *círculan
mamá → *máma   difícil → *díficil
melón → *mélon

Moreover, students will have to learn to avoid imposing nonprimary stresses, a problem that is again especially acute in cognates:

refrigeradór → *refrìgeradór   diagnóstico → *dìagnóstico
circulación → *cìrculàci-ón   oportunidád → *òportùnidád

The effect of such distortions is magnified when students lengthen the stressed vowels as in English, yielding Spanish words hammered into the mold of English rhythm.

4.1.3 Stress and rhythm. Languages tend to sort out into two main rhythmic types. One type, called SYLLABLE-TIMED, has a rhythm ticked off by even syllables, each syllable receiving one quick beat called a MORA. The general acoustic effect is a distinctive staccato 'dot-dot-dot-dot-dot'. The other type, STRESS-TIMED, has a rhythm based on stress groups. Syllables are organized into FEET, each foot containing one strongly stressed syllable plus unstressed and lesser stressed satellites. Instead of each syllable taking one mora, each foot occupies about the same measure of time regardless of its number of syllables, and to equalize the feet requires that the unstressed syllables be shortened and squeezed in around the stressed ones. This yields a strikingly galloping effect, 'di-D U M-di-di-D U M-di-D U M.'

English, like other Germanic languages, is stress-timed; Spanish, like most other Romance languages, is syllable-timed. Native speakers hear the difference, though they may not be able to identify precisely what is happening. Spanish strikes the English speaker as fast and machine gun-like; English, to the Spanish speaker, can seem jerky, with alternate drawling and obliteration of syllables. To be sure, some speakers in both languages do speak more rapidly than others, and everyone varies speed according to situation, emotional state, emphasis, rhetorical effect, etc.; but such variations in rate are overridden by the more pervasive difference in the rhythmic organization of syllables. Spanish sounds fast because its stressed syllables—which an English speaker expects to be lengthened—zip past as quickly as the unstressed ones; English sounds uneven because its stressed syllables are held out at the expense of the unstressed ones. The Spanish speaker chants his language in terms of groups of even morae, one per syllable; the English speaker paces his speech in metrical feet, one main stress per foot.

In English, a given foot takes about the same time to pronounce whether it has one or four syllables. For example, in *Lárge dógs wánt méat,* each word = syllable is stressed and constitutes a foot by itself: *DUM DUM DUM DUM.* Adding unstressed syllables to this sequence will not add more feet, *The lárger dógs're wánting some méat: diDUMdi DUMdi DUMdi di DUM.* The examples shown in Figure 4.1 may clarify this point better. For those readers who read music, a very approximate musical notation is provided.[6] As can be seen, increasing the number of

Figure 4.1 English stress-timing as measured feet.

				2/4 allegro
1. The	mán will	grów.		♪ ♩ ♩ ♩
2. The	mán's nòt	grówn it		♪ ♩ ♩ ♩♪
3. The	mán hàsn't	grówn òne		♪ ♩ ♫ ♩♩
4. The	mán còuldn't have	grówn àny		♪ ♩ ♫ ♩♫
5. The	màn's wífe was	grówing it for him		♪ ♫ ♫ ♫♫
6. The	mánager mùst've	grówn fát by	nów.	♪ ♫ ♫ ♫♫ ♩

unstressed syllables complicates the feet (measures), but does not greatly lengthen them; but adding another primary-stressed syllable, e.g. *nów* in the sixth sentence, adds another foot. The overall effect is quite jazz-like, and one teacher of English as a second language, Graham 1978, has demonstrated how 'jazz chants' can be used as a vehicle for English acquisition by speakers of syllable-timed languages.

In Spanish, stressed syllables are louder than unstressed ones, but not much longer. Since each syllable is one mora, increasing the number of syllables (stressed or unstressed) in a sentence proportionally lengthens the time needed for saying it (Quilis and Fernández 1975:161, Dalbor 1980b:243). The only squeezing of syllables is syneresis: *Han ido al teatro* /a ni dǫal tẹa tro/ (v. 2.2.3, 3.1.10). Otherwise, a two-syllable sequence will be *dot-dot* (♪♪) and a six-syllable one will be *dot-dot-dot-dot-dot-dot* (♪♪♪ ♪♪♪), occasionally peaking in word stresses and intonational dips and rises, but still rhythmically even.

The difference between English and Spanish is so marked that using the wrong rhythm in a normal, fluent tempo can hinder the hearer's comprehension and processing of the material being transmitted. The rhythmic difference also impinges on the esthetic side of language. In their traditional forms, Hispanic music and English music are dominated by rhythms that sprint or gallop like their languages. Many carols, hymns, and folk and popular songs are thus distorted in translation: the words can faithfully reflect the original, but they feel out of kilter with the beat and the note values. In poetry, too, the two cultures are accustomed to distinct metrical conventions based on their languages. At least in traditional schemes, lines of Spanish poetry have a determined number of syllables with parallel stress positions, whereas lines of English poetry are organized into symmetrical feet. The difference is clearly brought out by Dalbor (1980b: 242-245), who, among other examples, quotes a Manrique poem along with a translation by Longfellow, shown below. To appreciate the effect, the reader should read both aloud, using the appropriate rhythm of each language.

Recuerde el alma dormida,	O, let the soul her slumbers break,
Avive el seso y despierte	Let thought be quickened, and awake;
Contemplando	Awake to see
Cómo se pasa la vida,	How soon this life is past and gone,
Cómo se viene la muerte	And death comes softly stealing on,
Tan callando.	How silently!

The translation is a good one semantically, but something has been lost from the original by a poet-translator who must conform to his native rhythmic conventions. By saying the two poems with the *opposite* rhythms, the reader will appreciate the effect of a rhythmic 'accent' in a foreign language.

4.2 Intonation. In some languages (e.g. Chinese), each syllable of a word is assigned a certain pitch (or tone), and the pitch scheme becomes an inherent part of the word. But in English and Spanish, pitches are organized into melodies or INTONATIONS that add to the neutral meaning of a word, phrase, or sentence. *Yes* and *sí* alone denote affirmation. When coupled with a falling pitch, they are declarative; but with a rising pitch, the affirmation is questioned. The pitch meanings are not an inherent part of *yes* or *sí*, since exactly the same results obtain with *Mary's going* or *María se va*. In many respects, the two languages make similar uses of intonation, but the similarity can be deceptive. As with rhythm, the transfer of English intonation to Spanish does not quite sound right, and vice-versa.

Contrastive linguists agree that one major difference is that English uses more pitches, and more intonational variations, than Spanish. Generally, the intonation contours of English range over four pitches, whereas those of Spanish range over three; and the four of English are more widely spaced than the three of Spanish (Stockwell and Bowen 1965:25).[7] These pitches cannot be transcribed by musical notes, since 'high pitch', 'low pitch', and so on will be relative to each individual's voice range. Instead of notes for absolute pitch, many linguists prefer numbers for relative pitch. Pitch '2' is one's middle speaking pitch, '1' and '3' are slightly lower and higher, respectively, and '4' is higher still. For the ideal bilingual, '2' will be about the same in the two languages; '1' and '3' will be a bit closer to '2' in Spanish than in English, and '4' will normally occur just in English. (The reader should be careful not to confuse these pitch numbers with stress numbers, which ascend in the opposite direction; see section 4.1.2.)

In addition, the description of intonation requires some indication of whether the voice falls, rises, or stays steady in completing the intonational contour; e.g. '223↓' means 'middle-middle-higher, falling,' and '231↑' means 'middle-higher-low, rising.' Both languages have such TERMINALS, as they are called, but a terminal rise or fall tends to be sharp and abrupt in Spanish, more gradual and trailing off in English (Terrell y Salgués 1979:32).

Many scholars have tried to catalog the basic repertoire of intonational songs in the two languages: Dalbor 1980b, Stockwell and Bowen 1965, Quilis and Fernández 1975, Navarro 1967, etc. The list of examples in Figure 4.2 summarizes and synthesizes the most important and pervasive patterns that have been observed. The reader must bear in mind, though, that some variations are not reflected in these examples. Males and females differ, as do regional dialects (see, for instance, Kvavik 1980 for a study of the features of Mexican intonation). Differences in context, emotional state, and emphasis also affect intonation, sometimes drastically. Moreover, minor dips and rises are conventionally ironed out in intonational analysis, particularly the higher pitches that highlight stressed syllables in English (v. 4.1). Consequently, a '222↓' in Spanish is quite level until dropping at the end, whereas a '222↓' in English actually contains the linguistic equivalents of a singer's appoggiaturas and mordents. Thus, the examples in Figure 4.2 show just the basic melodic lines, which can be modulated by the improvisations of dialects and idiolects.

A cursory examination of the examples reveals that both languages tend to reserve the highest pitch ('4' in English, '3' in Spanish) for emphasis and ore_r: *Figure 4.2* Basic intonations of Spanish and English.

Spanish:	English:
(a) Simple declarative:	
(1)221↓	231↓
Yo/sóy de México.	I'm from Míchigan.
(b) Emphatic, contrastive:	
(1)231↓	241↓
Yo/soy de México (no de Cuba).	I'm from Míchigan (not Ohio).
(c) Information question:	
221↓	2(1)31↓
¿Adónde vás esta nóche?	Where are you/góing tonight?
(d) Yes/no question:	
212↑ (or 222↑)	223↑
¿Y/víste a Bárbara?	And/díd you sèe Bárbara?
(e) Greetings:	
231↓	224↓ or 231↑
Buénos días.	Gòod mórning. Gòod mórning.
(f) Vocatives:[8]	
221↓,1	231,1↑
¿Qué hay de póstre, Mamá?	Whàt's for dessért, Móm?
(g) Listing:	
2,2...2↑, 2↓	2↑, 2↑...2↑, 13↓
Uno, dós, trés, cuátro y cínco.	One, twó, thrée, fóur and/fíve.
(h) Long subject:	
22↑, 21↓	231↑, 231↓
Tódos los documéntos que recogímos fuéron quemádos.	All the dócuments that we gàthered úp were búrned.
(i) Initial adverbial dislocated from predicate:	
22↑, 21↓	231↑, (2)31↓
Miéntras te duchábas, llegó Juán.	While you were tàking a shówer, Jóhn arrìved.
(j) Parenthetical:	
22↑, 22↓, 221↓	231↓, 1↑, 23(2)1↓
Es/ráro, díjo el vencído, que se me agotára la fuérza.	It's stránge, said the lóser, that my stréngth gàve óut.
(k) Tag question:	
221↓, 2↑	231↓, 2↑ = 'I'm unsure'
Son carísimos, ¿nó?	They're vèry expénsive, àren't théy?
	231↓, 31↓ = 'I'm sure'
	They're vèry expénsive, áren't thèy?

Figure 4.2 continued

Figure 4.2 continued

Spanish:	English:
(l) Choice question:	
222↑, 21↓	223↑, 231↓
¿Ló compráste en México, o en España?	Dìd you bùy it in México, or in Spàin?
(m) Command:	
321↓	231↓
Lléne el formulário con bolígrafo.	Fíll out the fòrm with a bállpòint.

contrast, and to reserve rising terminals for yes/no questions. Also, in the most common sentence type, Simple declarative (a), both languages use a more or less sustained middle pitch, although Spanish descends to '1' on the last stressed syllable while English rises to '3' before descending. Differences increase with Information questions (c), Greetings (e), and Parenthetical comment (j), and major ones appear with Vocatives (f), Listing (g), Long subject (h), Initial adverbial (i), Tag questions (k), and Commands (m). In these latter, English uses intonational twists that are quite unmatched in Spanish.

The danger of transferring one's native intonations to a foreign language is not simply one of sounding funny. While the above patterns capture regularities of 'neutral' or 'uncolored' speech, it should be recalled that intonation is altered by one's emotional state or affect. As Bull notes (1965:85), in addition to signaling syntactic information, intonation 'reveals insistence, annoyance, lack of interest, boredom, disgust, urgency, courteousness or curtness, servileness, in short the whole gamut of the speaker's emotional or psychological reaction to what is under consideration or to the person with whom he is speaking.' If really excited, Spanish speakers may resort to a pitch '4,' so that the normal '4' of an English speaker's emphatic/contrastive intonation, once transferred to Spanish, can suggest a strong affective element (anger, indignation, enthusiasm) not at all intended by the foreign speaker of Spanish. Likewise, an English speaker sometimes reduces his normal '231↓' pattern (e.g. Simple declarative (a)) to a near-monotone '221↓' if bored, sleepy, or uninterested; thus, the Spanish speaker's normal '221↓' will convey the same characteristics to him. As another example, consider a combination of the Greeting pattern (e) with Vocative (f): in English, this yields '224↓ + 1↑,' but in Spanish '231↓ + 1.' To the English speaker, the Spanish pattern suggests an 'ingratiating or groveling' attitude (Bull, p. 86), and to the Spanish speaker, the English intonation implies overeagerness or even sarcasm (Dalbor 1980b:233).

It is hard to delineate the boundary between purely linguistic intonations (those signaling syntactic structures) and the more subtle tonal inflections that veer off into nonverbal communication. But it is clear that students who transfer some of their English intonations may unwittingly convey rudeness or superciliousness, causing Spanish speakers to react to them in ways they did not intend. Most texts are silent on intonation, however, as they are on rhythm too; teachers who agree with Stockwell and Bowen (v. 3.3) that proper intonation is crucial from the start may have to devise their own lessons and resources.

Notes for Chapter 4

1. For STRESSED and UNSTRESSED, some use TONIC and ATONIC, or ACCENTED and UNACCENTED. Most English-speaking linguists prefer STRESS for the phonological feature and ACCENT for any written marking of it; a widespread Spanish practice is the use of ACENTO (DE INTENSIDAD) for the former and TILDE for the latter.

2. The reader can verify this tendency by trying to sing the words *sincérity, parálysis,* and *extrémely* with a LOW pitch on the stressed syllable.

3. Note vowel *phonemes,* not vowel letters. The stress in *ventrílocuo* is on the fourth vowel letter from the end, but on the third vowel phoneme, /bentrílokwo/.

4. As noted in Chapter 11, a common alternative to emphatic stress in Spanish is syntactic postposition. Thus, English directly emphasizes *his* in *HÍS home (not yours),* but although Spanish *su* in *su casa* may occasionally be stressed, the version *la casa suya* seems more usual.

5. But Navarro (1967:195) and Harris (1983) perceive some minor secondary stresses in certain dialects and styles of Spanish. Boyd-Bowman (1960:93) perceives them on some speakers' postposed clitics: *¡Vámonòs!, ¡Apúratè!*

6. Figure 4.1 reflects the author's rendition of these sentences; the exact note values of the unstressed syllables would vary a bit from speaker to speaker.

7. The three-pitch analysis of Spanish intonation applies to normal speech. In both languages, certain interjections are a case apart. For instance, Boyd-Bowman (1960:204) notes that Mexican *¿manDE?* (for repetition of a previous utterance) and *¿bueNO?* or *¿diGA?* (upon lifting the telephone receiver) are spoken 'elevando casi una octava el tono de la última sílaba.' Otherwise, in neither language does intonation normally range over a whole octave in this way.

8. VOCATIVES are names or titles used for calling out to others to get their attention; they are added on to the sentence but are not syntactically a part of it. The same intonation is used on tags such as *por favor* and *please.*

Exercises for Chapter 4

1. Students who have not mastered Spanish stress mispronounce verb forms in three ways. First, they may stress the endings (sometimes yield-

ing a different tense): *trabajó, trabajás, trabajá.* Second, they may stress the first stem vowel, as in *trábajo, trábajas, trábaja.* Third, they may say *tràbajár, tràbajámos, tràbajabámos.* Explain as precisely as possible the source of each error pattern.

2. With regard to the foregoing errors, give a comprehensive statement of where stress does occur in Spanish verb morphology.

3. Both Spanish and English nouns tend to keep the same stress position when a plural suffix is added: Eng. *ánimal ánimals, cártridge cártridges, complétion complétions,* Span. *animál animáles, catálogo catálogos, ceréza cerézas.* But the stress of *ínterin* changes to *intérines* in the plural. Why?

4. Comment specifically on the intonational differences shown in Figure 4.2. Can you add any other differences you have noted?

5. How, in general, might an English speaker's intonation sound to a Spanish speaker? What impressions could it give?

6. How does intonation distinguish the three meanings of the following Spanish sequence: /sáka los bolétos tempráno/ (i.e., declarative, question, command)?

7. Spanish has an orthographic system that indicates stress when it does not conform to the usual rules; English, on the other hand, gets by without accent marks. Yet both languages have minimal pairs that contrast stress position. Why are the two cases different? (Hint: why would *término/termíno/terminó* or *sábana/sabána* be confusing without their accents, but not *subject* or *invalid*?)

8. The phonemic representation /komputo/ corresponds to three different Spanish words. Show the difference in meaning according to stress position.

9. Compare English and Spanish stress according to the following considerations:

(1) is it just more force or loudness?
(2) is it distinctive, or fully predictable?
(3) how many degrees of stress are used?
(4) what constraints exist on where it can occur?
(5) does its position change in derived forms of the word?
(6) what effect does it have on the pronunciation of vowels?
(7) what effect does it have on rhythm?

10. Develop a lesson segment on rhythm for a first- or second-year course in Spanish. How would you present Spanish rhythm to English speakers?

11. Morphemes (stems and affixes) have sometimes been classified according to whether they are CONTENT MORPHEMES or FUNCTION MORPHEMES. The former (e.g. *bird, run, -scope*) contain most or all of the semantic substance of a word, while function morphemes (e.g. articles, short prepositions, derivational endings, tense and number endings) have grammatical meaning but not much conceptual meaning in themselves.

Take a fairly long English sentence with both content and function morphemes. Indicate with an accent all syllables with stress. Recall that these are held out while unstressed ones are shortened. Which morphemes—content or function—are thus more phonologically prominent and easier to process auditorily?

Repeat this experiment with a Spanish sentence, perhaps a translation of the English one. Again, what kind of morphemes tend to receive stress somewhere? Given that stressed syllables are not lengthened in Spanish, comment on the ramifications of rhythm for English speakers' impressions of the 'speed' of Spanish, and on their difficulties in processing longish Spanish sentences.

12. In your opinion, at what point in the study of Spanish should intonation patterns be taken up? How much English interference is acceptable at that level without correction from the teacher?

13. Transcribe the following Spanish-English cognates phonemically, indicating stress:

(1) tendencia, tendency
(2) revelación, revelation
(3) reproducción, reproduction
(4) homogeneidad, homogeneity
(5) nacionalidad, nationality
(6) uniforme, uniform
(7) teléfono, telephone
(8) cuestión, question
(9) sinónimo, synonym
(10) arquitectura, architecture
(11) animal, animal
(12) democracia, democracy
(13) inventor, inventor
(14) violín, violin
(15) unanimidad, unanimity

14. Listen to a native speaker of English at the beginning or intermediate level of Spanish study and make a recording of his/her speech (spontaneous or oral reading). Then, carry out an 'error analysis' of this student's pronunciation by describing each problem and its apparent source in English phonology. Distinguish between sporadic errors and fairly consistent ones. You will be drawing on information from all four chapters in this part of the book, and you may want to sort errors out as follows:

(1) basic articulatory errors with Spanish phonemes
(2) failure to master rules of Spanish or to use proper allophones
(3) projection of English phonological patterns or rules onto Spanish phonemes
(4) errors with stress and rhythm
(5) problems with intonation

Part Two: Grammar

Chapter 5
Basic notions
of grammatical description

5.0 The 'grammar' of language. The term GRAMMAR has been used in many ways: for the study of letters (the original Greek sense), for morphology and syntax, for a description or reference work of morphology and syntax, for the entire structural framework of language (thus embracing phonology and semantics as well), and for the proprieties of cultivated usage, as in 'Watch your grammar.' In this book, it will be used mainly in the second sense, morphology and syntax (or MORPHOSYNTAX), i.e. the structure of words and the structure of phrases and sentences.

5.1 Morphology: Morphemes, allomorphs, and rules. In describing morphology, linguists use constructs similar to those of phonology. Just as the basic unit of phonology is the phoneme, that of morphology is the MORPHEME. A morpheme is any minimal form (word or part of a word) with its own meaning, function, and combinatory potential, whether stem (root) or affix (prefix or suffix). Because morphemes are the building blocks of word and phrase formation, they are also called FORMATIVES. Affixed morphemes that express syntactic properties such as person, number, tense, and case are classified as INFLECTIONAL; those that derive a new word from another one are classified as DERIVATIONAL. On the basis of these notions, the morphology of the word *prehistóricos* can be described as follows:

pre + *histór* + *ic* + *o* + *s* : five morphemes (+ = morpheme boundary)
pre- : derivational prefix forming *prehistóricos* from *históricos*, meaning 'before'

75

histor: stem
-ic-: derivational suffix forming an adjective from a noun
-o: inflectional suffix for masculine gender
-s: inflectional suffix for plural number

The stem *histor* can be regarded as a variant form or ALLOMORPH of *historia*. And just as phonological rules derive allophones from phonemes, morphological rules such as the following change morphemes and account for their allomorphs.

/istorja/ → /istor/ / _____ + ik +

Sometimes ALLOMORPHY (alternations in morpheme shape) results from the change of a phoneme or two. In that case, is the linguist dealing with a phonological rule or a morphological one? This question has given rise to several controversies, but one common approach is to use the hybrid term MORPHOPHONEMIC RULE. A Spanish example is the rule governing alternations between the sounds written as *l* and *ll* in the following: *él ~ ellos, aquel ~ aquella, caballo ~ cabalgar, bello ~ beldad, humilde ~ humillar, valle ~ Valderrobles.* The stem-final consonant, which can be represented as Λ, becomes /l/ word-finally or before a consonant (Harris 1983:50):

$$\Lambda \rightarrow l\ /\underline{\hspace{1cm}} \quad \begin{cases} \# \\ C \end{cases}$$

Of course, there is no real phoneme /Λ/ in most varieties of Spanish today; for the *yeísta*, it would be hard to see a palatal lateral behind /el/ and /ejos/. The rule therefore expresses a language-wide regularity in the pronunciation of certain stems, but it is not a normal phonological rule; the Λ here can be called a MORPHOPHONEME that stands for whatever phoneme it is that morphologically alternates with /l/ in such stems.

5.2 Syntax: Word order, constituency, and function. Traditional approaches to grammar devote most of their attention to a description of the morphology, usage, and interrelationships of the various parts of speech or SYNTACTIC CATEGORIES—nouns, pronouns, verbs, etc. For convenience, we will follow this precedent and begin our study of Spanish and English grammar in the same way: verbs are discussed in Chapters 6-7, nouns and their modifiers in Chapter 8, pronominal forms and usage in Chapter 9, and the expressions classified as adverbs, prepositions, and conjunctions in Chapter 10. But an analysis of syntactic categories alone is insufficient; a full account of syntax requires a description of how the categories are combined to form a variety of sentence patterns, and that will be the focus of Chapters 11-13.

Many approaches have arisen in the attempt to characterize syntax. Perhaps the simplest is to represent sentences as left-to-right sequences of word types or categories. Letting N stand for nouns, V for verbs, Adv for adverbs, Aux for auxiliary (helping) verbs, Quant for quantifiers, D for demonstratives (or determiners, as they will be called later), and S for sentences, we can arrive at formulae such as the following:

Emilia corrió.	$S = N + V$
Emilia corrió temprano.	$S = N + V + Adv$
Aquella niña corrió.	$S = D + N + V$
Aquella niña ha corrido.	$S = D + N + Aux + V$
Dos niñas corrieron temprano.	$S = Quant + N + V +$
Aquellas dos niñas han corrido temprano.	Adv
	$S = D + Quant + N +$
	$Aux + V + Adv$

But this procedure is atomistic: since every language is an infinite set of sentences, one could enumerate such sequences forever without obtaining many useful generalizations about syntax. The formulae directly indicate only one useful syntactic fact, namely, word order; for example, Spanish apparently prefers Aux + V over V + Aux. But the formulae say essentially nothing about two other points of interest, sentence structure (constituency) and the functions of the parts. With regard to structure, it should be noted that the units joined together in each sentence string sort out into two parts: N with its companions D and Quant (if present), and V with its companions Aux and Adv (if present). The former part is a NOUN PHRASE, NP; and the latter is a VERB PHRASE, VP. Thus, for all the sentences given above (and infinitely more), one can state the structural generalization that S consists of two parts or constituents, NP and VP, and that NP and VP respectively consist of N and V with their optional companions. But the functions of the parts must also be defined: the NP of the S functions as the SUBJECT of the V, and on that fact rests the difference between *corrió* and *corrieron*, and between *ha* and *han*. The semantics or meaning of the sentence also requires a functional description in that the use of V *correr* in Spanish implies the existence of a subject, i.e. of a runner.

Many French and German linguists (e.g. Tesnière 1959) have concentrated on describing the relationship between syntactic categories and their phrasal companions. In general, these linguists show the relationship as a DEPENDENCY, and use branching diagrams in which the companions (D, Quant, Aux, Adv) are subordinated to their 'head' elements, N and V. A dependency analysis of *Aquellas dos niñas han corrido temprano* is given in Figure 5.1. Variants of this approach are sometimes found in the writings of Spanish grammarians and in certain university courses on *la sintaxis castellana.*

On the other hand, linguists who prefer CASE GRAMMAR (Fillmore 1968) have focused on the function of each sentence part. Each sentence is a 'proposition' consisting of a verb combined with its 'arguments' or units having a 'case' relationship with it. Examples of cases include Agent (= subject with a verb such as *correr*), Object, Instrument, Experiencer,

Time, and Location. The branching diagrams of case grammar explicitly show these functional cases rather than word order or constituency, as illustrated by the analysis shown in Figure 5.2.

Figure 5.1 Syntactic relationships in dependency grammar.

Figure 5.2 Syntactic relationships in case grammar.

Figure 5.3 Syntactic relationships in tagmemics.

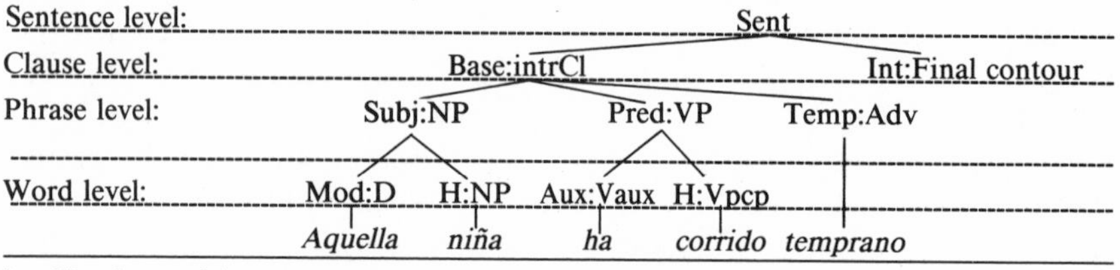

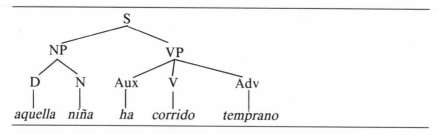

intrCl = intransitive clause: Sent = sentence; Int = intonation; Temp = temporal; Subj = subject; Mod = modifier; H = head; Vaux = auxiliary verb; Vpcp = participle

Figure 5.4 Syntactic relationships in generative transformational grammar.

Linguists who favor TAGMEMICS (Pike 1954-1960, Cook 1969) aim at a direct representation of function, word order, and constituency. Tagmemics postulates five hierarchically arranged levels of grammatical description—sentence, clause, phrase, word, and morpheme; and it analyzes the constructions (SYNTAGMEMES) of each level in terms of two or more TAGMEMES. Each tagmeme is a two-sided unit consisting of (1) a functional 'slot' occupied by (2) a constituent or form class 'filler'. A clause, for example, often consists of the tagmeme 'Subject:noun phrase' (subject filled by noun phrase) followed by the tagmeme 'Predicate:verb phrase' (predicate filled by verb phrase). One tagmemic analysis of the four syntactic levels of *Aquella niña ha corrido temprano* is shown in Figure 5.3. (According to Cook 1969, the functional slot halves of tagmemes need not be indicated in branching diagrams, but they have been retained in Figure 5.3 for the sake of explicitness.)

Although each of the foregoing approaches (and several others) may be found in writings on Spanish and English grammar, the dominant approach to syntax in the United States today (and one that is gaining ground in Europe and Latin America as well) is what is variously called transformational grammar (TG), generative grammar, or to use its full name, GENERATIVE TRANSFORMATIONAL GRAMMAR. Originating with Chomsky (1957, 1965, and subsequent writings), TG resembles the other approaches in some respects. Like dependency grammar, TG represents the structured groupings of sentence parts in terms of branching diagrams; these are called PHRASE MARKERS (since they demarcate phrases), but are commonly known as 'trees'. The trees, however, depict constituency rather than dependency; a tree for NP therefore shows D, Quant, and N branching down from NP rather than D and Quant depending on N. The full phrase marker for the sentence *Aquella niña ha corrido temprano* is shown in Figure 5.4. This phrase marker states that S consists of NP + VP; that the NP in turn has as its constituents D and N; and that the VP consists of Aux + V + Adv.

TG resembles tagmemics in three respects: word order is depicted as a left-to-right sequence, constituent structure is hierarchical, and a kind of structural 'slot' exists at each node or labeled point of the tree. The structural slot of NP, for instance, could be filled equally well by Quant + N, D + Quant + N, or N alone (as with *Emilia*). But unlike tagmemics, TG does not rigorously separate five morphosyntactic levels of analysis, nor does it explicitly label the functions of constituents. The functional message of a tagmeme is assumed in TG to be defined on the basis of constituency: the subject, for instance, is defined as that NP which is DOMINATED by S (i.e. has S above it as the next node).

Unlike other approaches, TG treats sentence structure at two distinct levels, DEEP (or underlying) and SURFACE STRUCTURE. These are somewhat comparable to the phonemic and phonetic levels of phonology. The Spanish word *yodo* may be [ǰóðo] phonetically (on the surface, so to speak), but it is /jódo/ phonemically: [ǰ] and [ð] are respectively allophones of /j/ and /d/ generated by two phonological rules (v. 3.1). Likewise, one could consider the two sentence patterns *Aquella niña ha corrido temprano* (NP + VP) and *Ha corrido temprano aquella niña* (VP + NP) as 'allosentences' of the same basic sentence structure, or in proper terminology, as surface structures of the same deep structure. Both have *aquella niña* as subject, phonological rules changing /j/ and /d/ to [j] and [ð], Spanish syntax has the following TRANSFORMATION for the change in word order. (The arrow means 'may change to'.)

NP VP → VP NP

Transformations account for different surface structures of the same deep structure; another kind of rule in TG, the PHRASE STRUCTURE RULE (PSR), specifies the options available to a speaker in constructing a deep structure. At least for the cases examined so far, the PSRs of Spanish (and of English too) specify that S consists of NP joined with VP; that NP contains D, Quant, and N (D and Quant being optional); and that VP is made up of Aux, V, and Adv (Aux and Adv being optional). These PSRs are conventionally formulated as follows. (The arrows here mean 'consists of, has as its constituents'.)

S → NP VP
NP → (D) (Quant) N
VP → (Aux) V (Adv)

These three rules summarize a great deal of information on the possible sentence structures available to speakers of Spanish or English. They furthermore account for word order in stipulating D + Quant + N, Aux + V + Adv, and NP + VP; any other sequences will be disallowed unless transformations explicitly bring these about. Function, too, may be defined on the basis of the phrase markers. Consequently, TG is a powerful resource for the applied linguist in describing the key facts of syntax—order, constituency, function, and relationships between 'allosentences'; and it is the approach that will be adopted in our discussion of syntax.

5.3 Grammatical and ungrammatical. One more convention requires comment before proceeding to a comparison of Spanish and English grammar. Sometimes it is just as useful to consider ungrammatical or impossible formations as it is to investigate the grammatical ones; otherwise, one might generalize a syntactic statement beyond the real bounds of the language. Ideally, a grammar should not only account for all sentences that are generated (and can be generated) in a language, but it should be so constrained as to exclude the generation of ungrammatical ones. For example, as will be shown later (v. 11.2.3), the transformation that yields *Ha corrido temprano aquella niña* from *Aquella niña ha corrido temprano* can produce other word orders too, so why not broaden the rule to something like 'Scramble constituents in any way you wish'? But this will be erroneous, yielding the following:

*Ha temprano corrido aquella niña.
*Corrido ha niña aquella temprano.
*Temprano aquella niña ha corrido.

The asterisk preceding these examples means 'does not conform to the language', i.e. 'is ungrammatical'. As Chomsky and others have pointed out, the native speaker not only knows what is possible in his language but can also recognize what is not possible. Occasionally, grammaticality depends on the dialect: *¿Qué tú dices?* is common in some regions, but it would bear a decisive asterisk in most others. In fact, there are times when individual idiolects will also differ. But essentially, Chomsky is correct in noting that speakers can distinguish those sentences that conform to their language from those that do not. Certainly, teachers have had abundant practice at this, and they may wonder what is wrong with a textbook rule when students follow it and still produce something that is quite un-Spanish and deserving of an asterisk.

Chapter 6
Verb morphology

6.0 Verb forms and their nomenclature. For the English speaker, the foremost challenge in Spanish morphology is the verb. Whereas the Spanish noun has only two inflectional categories, singular and plural (gender being regarded as derivational for nouns), the verb has 48 distinct simple inflectional forms. ('Inflectional' excludes derived forms in *-ble, -dor*, etc.; 'simple' excludes compound forms; and 'distinct' precludes counting twice identical forms such as *(yo) hacía = (él) hacía*.) A Spanish verb paradigm thus contrasts starkly with the inflectional options of English verbs, which range from one to eight:

1 form: *must*	4 forms: *walk, walks, walked, walking*
2 forms: *can, could*	5 forms: *sing, sings, sang, sung, singing*
3 forms: *put, puts, putting*	8 forms: *be, am, is, are, was, were, been, being*

Spanish verbs have more forms because they are conjugated for more tense and mood categories and for more person and number distinctions. The latter may seen redundant to the English speaker until he understands that Spanish speakers rely on the verb to indicate the subject; that is, the *-s* of *hablas* is not a needless frill of agreement but an indicator of the subject *tú*, which is often dropped.

Linguists, teachers, and text writers in the United States largely agree on what to call English and Spanish tense and mood categories: *drank* is 'past', *bebí* and *bebía* are, respectively, 'preterite' and 'imperfect'. Hispanic scholars who are also L1 speakers of Spanish have not reached such consensus, and the current nomenclatures reflect disagreements between those who retain Latin terminology and those who substitute terms they deem more appropriate for Spanish. Figure 6.1 summarizes the major differences. *He dicho*, for example, has been called 'presente perfecto' and 'presente compuesto', which aptly describe its morphology—the present of *haber* compounded with what is sometimes called the 'perfect' participle (v. 6.3.2). But it is also called 'pretérito perfecto' to suggest that the saying began in the past (*pretérito*), a meaning Bello decided would be even better conveyed by 'antepresente'. Bello also calls *diría* 'pospretérito', *decía* 'copretérito', and *habré dicho* 'antefuturo', again very appropriately in terms of their current meanings (v. 7.1ff.). In this book, it will be useful to retain the prevailing U.S. terms because they are more likely to be familiar to the reader and because other nomenclatures might cause confusion (e.g. *pretérito perfecto* for what is here called 'present perfect', not the preterite perfect *hube dicho*). Nevertheless, teachers should familiarize themselves with the Hispanic terms since these are sometimes adopted by in-Spanish texts.

Figure 6.1 Nomenclatures for Spanish verb forms.

B: Bello 1847/1958	R: Ramsey 1894/1956
RA: Real Academia 1924	SBM: Stockwell, Bowen and
GG: Gili Gaya 1973	Martin 1965
SF: Sallese y Fernández de la	USP: U.S. pedagogical term
Vega 1968	

1. infinitas/nonfinites:
   decír: B, RA, GG, SF infinitivo; SBM, R, USP infinitive
   diciendo: B, RA, GG gerundio; SF gerundio de presente; R present participle; SBM imperfective participle; USP gerund
   diciente: B, GG participio presente; (others omit this category)
   dicho: B participio pasivo; RA and GG participio; SF participio pasivo o pretérito; SBM perfective participle; R, USP past participle
2. modo indicativo/indicative mood:
   digo: presente/present
   decía: B copretérito; RA, GG pretérito imperfecto; SF imperfecto; R, SBM, USP imperfect
   dije: B, SF pretérito; RA pretérito indefinido; GG pretérito perfecto absoluto; R, SBM, USP preterite
   diré: B, SF futuro; RA futuro imperfecto; GG futuro absoluto; R, SBM, USP future
   diría: B pospretérito; RA, SF modo potencial; GG futuro hipotético; R, SBM, USP conditional
   he dicho: B antepresente; RA pretérito perfecto (compuesto); GG pretérito perfecto actual; SF perfecto; R perfect or past indefinite; SBM present anterior; USP present perfect
   había dicho: B antecopretérito; RA pretérito pluscuamperfecto; GG, SF pluscuamperfecto; R pluperfect; SBM imperfect anterior; USP past perfect, pluperfect.
   hube dicho: B, GG antepretérito; RA, SF pretérito anterior; R, USP preterite perfect; SBM preterite anterior
   habré dicho: B, GG antefuturo; RA, SF futuro perfecto; R, USP future perfect; SBM future anterior
   habría dicho: B antepospretérito; RA, SF modo potencial compuesto; GG antefuturo hipotético; R, USP conditional perfect; SBM conditional anterior
3. modo imperativo/imperative mood:
   di, decid
4. modo subjuntivo/subjunctive mood:
   diga: presente/present
   dijera, dijese: B pretérito; RA, GG pretérito imperfecto; SF im-

Figure 6.1 continued

Figure 6.1 continued

B: Bello 1847/1958	R: Ramsey 1894/1956
RA: Real Academia 1924	SBM: Stockwell, Bowen and
GG: Gili Gaya 1973	Martin 1965
SF: Sallese y Fernández de la	USP: U.S. pedagogical term
Vega 1968	

perfecto; R imperfect; SBM, USP past

dijere: B, SF futuro; RA futuro imperfecto; GG futuro hipotético; R future; (SBM, USP omit)

haya dicho: B antepresente; RA, GG pretérito perfecto; SF perfecto; R perfect; SBM present anterior; USP present perfect

hubiera dicho: B antepretérito; RA pretérito pluscuamperfecto; GG, SF pluscuamperfecto; R pluperfect; SBM past anterior; USP past (or plu-)perfect

hubiere dicho: B hipotético; RA, SF futuro perfecto; GG antefuturo hipotético; (others omit)

6.1 Spanish finite verb forms. In the verb form *hablar, habl-* is the verb stem, *-r* is the infinitive suffix, and the connecting *-a-* is the theme (or class) vowel, which identifies the conjugational class (namely, '*-ar* verb' or first conjugation, as opposed to the *-e-* of '*-er* verbs' or second conjugation, and to the *-i-* of '*-ir* verbs' or third conjugation). In conjugating a verb or inflecting it through its morphological categories, one adds to the stem + theme base the appropriate tense, mood, and person/number suffixes.[1] For the 3pl. (third person plural) preterite form of *hablar*, for example, *-ron* is added to the stem and theme vowel: *habl+a+ron*. The same formation is visible in the corresponding form of third conjugation *pedir*: stem plus theme vowel plus *-ron, ped+i+ron. Ped+i+ron*, however, can only be considered an underlying morphological representation; morphophonemic rules must apply both to the stem and to the suffixes, 'raising' the /e/ in the stem to /i/ and diphthongizing the theme vowel /i/ to /je/: *ped+i+ron → pid+ie+ron*. To explain such changes requires further analysis of the suffixes and stems.

6.1.1 Endings as slots for morphemes. A verb form can be analyzed as morphemes allocated to specific positional slots. The English verb has just two slots, one for the stem and one for a single suffix or 'zero' (∅, no suffix): *walk+∅, walk+s, walk+ed*. A Spanish verb form such as *hablaban*, however, consists of four morphemes in distinct slots:

(1)		(2)		(3)		(4)
habl	+	*a*	+	*ba*	+	*n*
STEM		THEME		IMPER-		PERSON/
		VOWEL		FECT		NUMBER

If, in the fourth slot, -*n* is replaced by -*s*, a new form results, *habl+a+ba+s*, which is otherwise the same but for the change to 2sg. If, in the third slot, *ba* is replaced by *ra*, *ría*, or Ø, three other forms are created: *habl+a+ra+n*, *habl+a+ría+n*, *habl+a+Ø+n*.

Note that what is often taught as one ending, -*aban*, actually contains three morphemes. The theme vowel -*a*- identifies the conjugational class; -*ba*- signals imperfect; -*n* is the marker for 3pl. These morphemes, and the whole general setup, are inherited from Latin. But even in Latin the neat sequence of slots was disrupted by irregularities and mergers, and the following disruptions are noteworthy in the modern Spanish verb.

(1) Verbs in -*er* and -*ir* largely converge on the same theme vowel, -*e* (but → *ie* in -*ie+ndo*, -*ie+ron*). Their theme vowels are distinct only in the infinitive, *vosotros* commands, and *nosotros* and *vosotros* present indicatives. In nonstandard dialects, even this much difference disappears, and the two conjugations merge entirely (Sánchez 1982:28).

(2) Theme vowels indicate a mood change if interchanged. Thus, in the subjunctive the characteristic *a* of an -*ar* verb becomes *e* and the *e* of an -*er* (and -*ir*) verb becomes *a*. The present indicatives of *sentir* and *creer* therefore overlap with the present subjunctives of *sentar* and *crear*, and vice versa.

(3) In the preterite, the person/number suffixes change as follows:[2]

1sg.	-*o* → Ø	1pl.	-*mos* = -*mos*
2sg.	-*s* → -*ste*	2pl.	-*is* → -*steis*
3sg.	-*Ø* → -*ó*	3pl.	-*n* → -*ron*

(4) The suffixes of adjacent slots act upon one another at many points in the verb paradigm. Even in Latin, the -*o* ending canceled out the preceding theme vowel in the first conjugation, so that the sequence *am+a+o* was just *amo*, and still is in Spanish. Fusion of adjacent suffixes occurred on a grand scale in the development of Spanish preterites such as *amó*, whose -*ó* merges three originally distinct morphemes:

/am+á+   wi+t/ → /am+á+w+t/ → /am+áw/ → /am+ów/ → /am+ó/
STEM   THEME PAST 3sg.

Similarly, English *drank* fuses *drink+ed* into one form whose underlying morphological stitches are invisible.

It is not necessary to survey each verb formation in detail. All teachers know that the inflections are not just a matter of 'every ending for itself', for there are certain general principles that govern formation. Past subjunctives are neatly described on the basis of *ellos* preterites; most imperatives are present subjunctives; the future is the entire infinitive used as a stem combined with the present indicative of *haber* (*am+a+r + he* → *amaré*, *am+a+r + has* → *amarás*, etc.). The real pedagogical challenge is the infamous irregular verb.

6.1.2 Stem changes: Regular or irregular? Some verbs change a phoneme or two in their stems as they are inflected. English /du/ *do*, for example, becomes /dʌ/ before *-s* and *-ne*, and /dɪ/ before *-d*. Others switch to a wholly different stem, as when *go* becomes *wen-* before *-t* (the same *-t* as in *kept*). Both cases involve stem allomorphs, but the latter is so drastic that it receives the special name of SUPPLETION. Comparable cases in Spanish are *ven- vien- vin-* for *venir* versus the suppletive *s- er- fu-* for *ser* (*s+oy, er+a, fu+i*).

What makes a verb regular or irregular? These labels are used without much precision in texts; some call a verb irregular if it undergoes any kind of change, whether orthographic, morphophonemic, or totally suppletive. Technically, though, REGULAR means 'rule-governed' (Latin *regula*, Span. *regla*) and IRREGULAR 'not rule-governed'. If one adheres to these definitions, then regular verbs should include all those whose allomorphy conforms at least in part to general rules. This will make morphological description analytically and pedagogically neater, and in fact bring many hundreds of so-called irregular verbs within the pale of normalcy.

What follows are ten types of stem and ending changes in Spanish, and the rules governing them. Most of these rules have pedagogical relevance in that the student who learns one rule covering the changes in 50 verbs is better equipped than one who memorizes each verb paradigm individually. On the other hand, it is obvious that when a rule affects only one or two verbs, however generally or predictably, it may be easier just to commit their quirks to memory.

6.1.2.1 Orthographic changing (*c→qu*, etc.).

tocar, toqué	*averiguar, averigüé*
pagar, pagué	*escoger, escoja*
rezar, recé	*distinguir, distingo*
vencer, venzo	*delinquir, delinco*

These are called 'orthographic changing' and the spelling changes are their only oddity. In terms or their pronunciation, there is no stem change at all: /pag+a+r/, /pag+é/, etc. What would be truly irregular would be to have *pagar→pagé* with the stem change of /pag/ to /pax/. Hence, even the greatest aficionados of irregular paradigms write texts that set off orthographic changes from other types.

Unfortunately, no matter how much the teacher or text writer emphasizes the regularity and predictability of spelling changes, students may regard them as anomalous. Part of the problem is that many classes fail to digest Spanish spelling conventions (v. 2.4) thoroughly before the preterite or present subjunctive is encountered. Students thus perceive the *g →* *gu* change in *pagué* as a preterite peculiarity of *pagar* rather than an automatic spelling convention that is language-wide. Moreover, they have learned to depend on the written word, taking that as primary over pronunciation (v. 1.0); what they think should be conjugated is the graphic sequence *PAG* (*pago, page*), not the phonemic sequence /pag/.

6.1.2.2 Orthographic changing (*i*→*y*).

leer, leyendo   *creer, creyó, creyeron*

The change of *i* to *y* is likewise orthographic, though not always recognized as such. Phonetically, the *y* of *-yó* in *creyó* is more fricative ([ɟ]) than the *i* of *-ió* in *comió* ([j]) (v. 3.1.1), but the two phones are allophones of the same phoneme, which Spanish spells with *i* after a consonant and with *y* after a vowel or word-initially. However spelled— *-ió -ieron -iera -iendo,* or *-yó -yeron -yera -yendo*—these endings are phonemically /jó jéron jéra jéndo/. Since the spelling change is predictable, *leer* and *creer* ought to be pulled out of the irregular verb appendices.

6.1.2.3 Glide-high vowel alternations (*i* ∼ *í, u* ∼ *ú*).

variar, varía   *continuar, continúo*

There are about 40 or so such verbs, although most are of rather low frequency. The problem here is a conflict between phonology and orthography. Phonologically, the stems of these verbs end in a high vowel, /i/ or /u/. When the stems are stressed, the last stem vowel receives the stress as usual: /barío barías baría kontinúo kontinúas kontinúa . . . /. When the stress is on a suffix vowel, however, the high vowel becomes a glide according to the Gliding rule (v. 3.1.10): /bariár kontinué/ → [barjár kontinwé]. In contrast, the stems of *estudiar* and *averiguar* end in glides [j w] throughout their paradigms, and these are therefore /estudj/ and /aberigw/; when the stress falls on the last stem vowel of /estudj/, as in *estudio* /estudj+o/, the form must be /estúdj+o/, as opposed to *varío* /barí+o/.

Orthographically, however, there is nothing about the citation forms (infinitives) of *variar* and *estudiar* to suggest different conjugational behavior. The change does not seem to be an underlying /i/ becoming a glide [j], but a /j/ exceptionally becoming [i] as signaled by an accent mark appearing out of nowhere.

6.1.2.4 Stressed diphthongization and raising (*e* → *ie, i,* etc.)

pensar, pienso   *llover, llueve*
contar, cuéntelo   *pedir, piden*

The changes here are Diphthongization in the case of *e* → *ie* and *o* → *ue*, and Raising in that of *e* → *i*.[3] These morphophonemic rules are not predictable from the spelling or phonemic representation of the infinitive form. *Acordar(se)* 'agree, remember' and *acordar* 'harmonize, tune' have identical infinitives, but the former diphthongizes and the latter does not; *defender* and *tentar* diphthongize but the related *ofender* and *intentar* do not; *sentir* has Diphthongization but *rendir* has Raising. Many texts therefore signal these stem changes with the cues (*ue*), (*ie*), (*i*) in vocabulary listings, and students should learn the cues along with the infinitives, just as they learn articles with nouns, as keys to morphology.[4]

The reason why the infinitive form alone is a poor guide to Diphthongization and Raising is that the stem is then unstressed, whereas the changes occur just under stress:

$$\left. \begin{array}{l} o \rightarrow \quad ue \text{ /we/} \\ e \rightarrow \left\{ \begin{array}{l} ie \text{ /je/} \\ i \end{array} \right\} \end{array} \right\} \text{ when stressed}$$

This single rule suffices for all four dozen forms of well over a hundred stem-changing verbs. To apply it, however, requires mastery of the correct stress pattern in Spanish verb forms; students who persist in singing the oxytonic Conjugational Chant of 'haBLÓ, haBLÁS, haBLÁ . . . ' are not using standard forms of *hablar*, and will be ill equipped for stress-cued stem changes.

As with orthographic changes, students should learn that the *e* ~ *ie* and *o* ~ *ue* alternations are not peculiar to verb paradigms but are found throughout the language. Figure 6.2 presents examples of them outside of verb inflection; some of them (e.g. *nueve noventa, siete setenta*) are encountered early enough in most courses to reinforce the same changes in verb forms.[5]

Figure 6.2 Stress-linked stem changes (*ue~o, ie~e*) outside of verb paradigms.

nuéve, novénta	diénte, dentísta
buéno, bondád	caliénte, calentadór
puéblo, población	cién(to), centenár
Venezuéla, venezoláno	tiérra, aterrizár
nuéstro, nosótros	siéte, seteciéntos
cuérpo, corpúdo	diéstro, destréza
cuéllo, collár	fiésta, festívo
vergüénza, vergonzóso	pimiénta, pimentál
fuérza, forzóso	ciélo, celestiál
muérte, mortál	valiénte, valentía
puérto, porténo	ciégo, ceguéra
huésped, hospedár	viéjo, vejéz

6.1.2.5 Unstressed raising (*e* → *i, o* → *u*).

sentir, sintió, sintamos   *dormir, durmieron, durmiendo*

These verbs exhibit raising (*e* → *i, o* → *u*), but unlike the case discussed in 6.1.2.4, just when unstressed. Unstressed Raising is a strange rule whose rationale lies buried in ancient sound changes with triggers that are now obscure:

$$\left.\begin{array}{l} e \rightarrow i \\ o \rightarrow u \end{array}\right\} / \underline{\qquad} \dots \left\{\begin{array}{l} \text{á (i.e. a stressed /a/ in the ending)} \\ \text{j}\hat{\text{V}} \text{ (i.e. a stressed diphthong in the ending)} \end{array}\right.$$

Since Stressed Diphthongization/Raising and Unstressed Raising apply to different forms, a verb can undergo both. *Sentir, dormir, pedir* have *sient-, duerm-, pid-* by Stressed Diphthongization/Raising, and *sint-, durm-, pid-* by Unstressed Raising. Two generalizations could be of use to students. First, Unstressed Raising occurs only in the third conjugation (exception: the *pudiendo* of second conjugation *poder*). Second, virtually all third conjugation verbs whose last stem vowel is /e/ or /o/ (and there are about four dozen of them) undergo both rules. A student who knows this can predict with certainty that a new verb, say *embestir*, will have *embistamos, embistió* by Unstressed Raising, and either *embiesto* or *embisto* (the latter, as it turns out) by Stressed Diphthongization/Raising. There are very few exceptions to these generalizations (e.g. *convergir converjo convergió, sumergir sumerjo sumergió*), and they are rare.

6.1.2.6 Velar extension (*c → zc,* etc.)

conocer, conozco	*venir, vengo*
traducir, traduzca	*salir, salgamos*
caer, caigan	*oír, oiga*

All such verbs have in common the addition of a stem extension containing a velar whenever a back vowel follows:

$$\left.\begin{array}{l} \theta \rightarrow \theta k \\ V \rightarrow Vjg \\ l, n \rightarrow lg, ng \end{array}\right\} / \underline{\qquad} + \left\{\begin{array}{l} a \\ o \end{array}\right.$$

The first change (orthographically *c → zc*[6]) is, like Unstressed Raising, almost entirely predictable, since virtually all the dozens of verbs ending in a vowel plus *c* plus *er* or *ir* undergo it, from the *conocer* and *traducir* of first-year courses to *ennoblecer* and *pacer* at advanced levels. The only exceptions are (1) *hacer* and *decir*, which have their own morphological itineraries, and (2) *mecer* and *cocer* (*mezo, cuezo*), which beginning and intermediate students seldom encounter and in which even some native speakers use *zc* (Boyd-Bowman 1960:170). The *ig* addition is very general for verbs in -vowel *e/i r*, but there are only four candidates for it: *caer, traer, roer, oír.*[7] The *g* addition is automatic for the more high-frequency verbs in -*n/l e/i r* (*salir, venir, tener, poner, valer*), but verbs such as *pulir* bypass it.

6.1.2.7 Yod extension ($u \rightarrow uy$)

construir, construyo, construya, construye
argüir, arguyo, arguyamos, arguyes

All of the 30 or so verbs in *-uir* /uír/ undergo a rule that adds 'yod'—the palatal glide phoneme /j/ spelled *y*—to the stem when a mid or low vowel follows (i.e. whenever *i* does not follow):

$$u \rightarrow uy / \underline{} + \begin{cases} a \\ o \\ e \end{cases}$$

Hence, *construya construyo construye*, but *construir construía construimos*. The actual alternation on the surface is often between [w] and [uɟ] because of Gliding (v. 3.1.10): [konstrwír   konstrúɟo].[8]

6.1.2.8 Yod absorption (*tiñó*, etc.)

bullir, bulló, bulleron   *teñir, tiñó, tiñendo*
reír, rió, rieron   *henchir, hinch(i)ó*

When a stem ends in a palatal (/ʎ ɲ j/), any /j/ beginning the ending is absorbed. Thus, /teɲ+jó/ → (Unstressed Raising) /tiɲ+jó/ → /tiɲó/. This Yod Absorption is not a verb peculiarity; *bull-iendo* = /buj+jendo/ becomes *bull-endo* exactly as *amarill(o)-iento* becomes *amarill-ento*. The /j/ is also absorbed when the stem ends in /i/ arising by Raising from /e/: hence, in *reír* and *freír*, /r̄e+jó   fre+jó/ → *ri-yó fri-yó* → *rió frió*. The alveopalatal /č/ variably triggers the same absorption, according to reference grammars: *henchir   hinch(i)ó*. Despite its generality, Yod Absorption is applicable to only a few verbs in *-llir*, *-ñir*, *-eír*, and *-chir*.

6.1.2.9 Syncope of the theme vowel (*poderé* → *podré*)

poder, podré   *poner, pondré*
salir, saldría   *decir, diría*

Such futures and conditionals are called 'syncopated' because of the dropping (SYNCOPE) of the expected theme vowel in the infinitival base. When Syncope leaves the clusters *nr* and *lr*, a *d* is inserted (*pondré*, *saldré*). The changes *decir-é hacer-é* → *dir-é har-é* are considered syncopations too. Old Spanish vacillated between restoring the dropped vowels and extending Syncope to other verbs; in the modern compromise, Syncope stuck in only a handful of high-frequency verbs of the second and third conjugations.

6.1.2.10 Strong preterites (*hice*, etc.)

saber, supe   *conducir, conduje*
hacer, hizo   *estar, estuvimos*
tener, tuviste   *venir, vinieron*

In Germanic languages such as English, a verb that changes its stem vowel in the past tense (*take took, drink drank, drive drove, get got*) is called STRONG. This label has also been applied to Spanish verbs that have any of the following changes throughout their preterite paradigm (and past subjunctive too, of course):

Vowel change: *hacer hice, poder pude, venir vine*
Consonant change: *traducir traduje, traer traje*
Both: *caber cupe, saber supe, tener tuve, decir dije, querer quise, andar anduve, estar estuve, poner puse*

The general direction is toward a high vowel in the strong preterite stem; in fact, *traer* conformed to this pattern too in Old Spanish, which favored *truje* over modern *traje*.

It cannot be predicted from the infinitive whether a verb will be strong or not: *traer, hacer, andar* are strong, while the nearly identical *caer, nacer, mandar* are not. Yet these verbs are not altogether lawless, for if one knows that a Spanish verb is strong, three facts follow. First, it will preserve that strong stem throughout the preterite, unlike verbs such as *dormir* or *seguir* that undergo a specific Unstressed Raising rule. Second, stress will always be penultimate, yielding *híce hízo* as opposed to *nací, nació*. Third, the suffixes will be those of *-er/-ir* verbs, but with *-e -o* instead of *-í -ió* and—just for strong stems in /x/ (*dij-, traj-, traduj-*)—with *-eron* instead of *-ieron*. (This last quirk historically arose from Yod Absorption; it does not apply to 'weak' preterites such as *rigieron*.)

6.1.2.11 Other changes. Many other changes are partly predictable but analysis of them brings increasingly smaller returns and hence less pedagogical usefulness. *Dar* has preterites that would be unremarkable if its infinitive were only *der* or *dir*. The imperatives *haz, sal, pon, ten, ven, val* have in common the use of naked infinitival stems. There is an interesting pattern in the addition of *-y* to monosyllabic *yo* forms: *soy, voy, doy, estoy*.[9] But with *veo, sé, he hay, quepo*, and most forms of *ser* and *ir*, there is little to do but call a spade a spade: no morphophonemic generalizations are possible with these, and they are truly irregular, just like English *brought, went, was*, and *made*. Languages, after all, are not quite as systematic as teachers, linguists, and language learners might like, and although some irregularities are ironed out over time by analogy to regular formations, high-frequency verbs tend to retain idiosyncratic forms as they are passed down from one generation to the next.

A verb can satisfy the conditions for two or more stem changes. Sometimes the rules will not conflict since they apply to different domains (e.g. one to stressed stems, the other to unstressed ones); other times, they may clash, and then the more irregular pattern seems to win out. Some examples of such verbs follow:

teñir: both kinds of Raising, and Yod Absorption: *teñ-ió* → *tiñ-ió* → *tiñ-ó.*

seguir: both kinds of Raising, and spelling changes: *sigo.*

decir: has *dig-* exactly where *salir* and *conocer* add a velar; obeys both Raisings (*díces, diciéndo*); strong preterite.

tener, venir: strong preterites; Diphthongization except when they satisfy the conditions for Velar Extension (/g/), which blocks the expected diphthongization (but *tiengo* and *viengo* do exist in some nonstandard dialects).

oír: Yod Extension like verbs in *-uir*, except when satisfying the conditions for Velar Extension: thus, *oye* like *construye,* but *oigo oiga* like *caigo caiga.*

yacer: never settled down and ended up on epitaphs; may follow *hacer* (*yago* like *hago*), *salir* (*yazgo* like *salgo*), or *conocer* (*yazco* like *conozco*), if used at all.

The derivational offspring of stem-changing verbs tend to follow their parents' conjugation: *detener detengo detuve.* This may be obvious to the teacher, but as Champion (1979:317) notes, students sometimes fail to see *tener* in *detener, mantener, obtener,* etc., or if they do see it, they may conjugate inconsistently (thus, *detengo* but **detenieron*). Champion gives a comprehensive list of these derivatives, and points out that many of them are of sufficiently high frequency to merit more attention. Perhaps the morphological or etymological relationship is not always obvious to native speakers either, since some derivatives are now treated as regular verbs. *Bendecir, predecir, maldecir* have some of the quirks of *decir,* but are regular in the imperative, participle, and (for some speakers) the future; and derivatives of *ver* seem to swing back and forth between regular and irregular. English behaves similarly; *understand, forgo, forget, overthrow, withdraw, become* follow *stand, go, get, throw, draw, come,* but the past tense of *broadcast* for many is *broadcasted,* unlike *cast* for *cast.*

6.2 English finite verb forms and modals. In contrast with the Spanish verb, English verb morphology is rather paltry. In fact, if the term 'tense' is limited to purely inflectional possibilities, a verb such as *give* has only two real tenses: present *give(s),* past *gave* (*given* being a participle, not a tense). English has no true future or conditional tenses because its *will* and *would* are modal auxiliaries, patterning like *can* and *may* rather than like tense inflections. Thus, whereas an indicative verb may have any of the following simple tense forms in Spanish,

Ella me lo da
         dará
         dio
         daba
         daría

in English there are only two options morphologically, eked out by eight or so possibilities from the modal system:[10]

She gives it to me	She can	give it to me.
gave	could	
	will	
	would	
	should	
	must	
	may	
	might	

Distinguishing tenses from modals makes sense within English grammar; yet functionally, *will* and *would* convey much of the information borne by Spanish tense affixes, and this fact must be taken into consideration in pedagogy (v. 7.2.1 for other meanings of these modals).

However its system is analyzed, it is clear that in all categories the English verb is less inflected for person and number than its Spanish counterpart. *Be* illustrates the maximum differentiation (pres. *am/is/are*, past *was/were*); all other verbs have pasts unmarked for person, and a special person form in the present just in 3sg. (*gives*). In nonstandard English, even this much differentiation breaks down (*I says*, *he don't*). The teacher may direct students' attention to person-number inflection in their native language, but English offers a weak point of departure for taking up Spanish verb forms. In fact, transfer can be negative, since Eng. -*s* represents 3sg. while Span. -*s* represents *tú*. And although English, like Spanish, has strong verbs, irregular verbs, and stem-changing verbs, their morphophonemics is too different to provide much insight into Spanish.

6.3 Nonfinites and compound forms. Many European languages have a set of verb forms called NONFINITES. Unlike the 'finite' forms, which serve as the main verb of a sentence and which are inflected or de-*fined* for tense, person, number, and mood, nonfinites have nominal, adjectival, or adverbial functions and do not show these inflectional categories. The terminology for them is borrowed (like much else) from Latin grammar, and the Latin verb had a host of nonfinites: two distinct infinitives, three participles, four gerunds, a gerundive, and two oddities called supines. Since Spanish and English have a smaller, different set of nonfinites, retention of the elaborate Latin classification may cause confusion: one grammar will call *amando* a gerund, another a participle. Linguistically speaking, it does not matter whether it is called a gerund, form X, the -*ndo* form, or the alpha nonfinite. For our purposes, the prevailing traditional and pedagogical terms will suffice, but with the proviso that they are relative to the system; a Spanish gerund will not necessarily match an English or Latin one.

6.3.1 Infinitives. One nonfinite is the INFINITIVE, which is the conventional citation form of the verb (i.e. how it appears in dictionaries and the form by which the whole paradigm is represented). In Spanish, it is signaled by the suffix -*r* after the theme vowel. In English, it consists of a bare verb stem with no suffixes. (Whether the English infinitive is preceded by the preposition *to* is a matter of syntax, not of morphology; *want to go*, but *should 0 go*.) In both languages, the infinitive form equips the verb for specific syntactic functions, primarily nounlike (nominal) ones, and it patterns rather like subordinate clauses (v. 13.0.2-13.3.4). The infinitive is also the usual form taken by a verb that follows another verb (v. 6.4): *debe ir, should go.*

6.3.2 Gerunds and participles. Spanish has two other nonfinites. The GERUND ends in -*ndo*: *amando* /am+a+ndo/, *comiendo* /kom+e+ndo/ → /kom+je+ndo/. It has an adverbial function in describing the manner, circumstances, or means by which an event took place. It usually refers back to the subject of the main verb, but with an appositive force rather than an attributive (adjectival) one (Keniston 1937:239):

Salió sollozando.
Rompiendo la ventana, logró entrarse.
Los sábados nos divertíamos jugando al tenis.

The PARTICIPLE ends in -*do*: *amado* /am+a+do/, *comido* /kom+e+do/ → /kom+i+do/. Exceptions to this pattern consist of a handful of irregulars inherited from Latin: *abierto, cubierto, dicho, escrito, frito, hecho, impreso, muerto, puesto, roto, resuelto, visto, vuelto.*[11] Unlike the gerund, the participle mainly has an adjectival function, generally with an implied past and/or passive value. Thus, in *Las empobrecidas clases bajas se sentían excluidas de la sociedad, empobrecidas* suggests prior reduction to poverty and *excluidas* suggests 'eran excluidas por alguien' (v. 12.3). But for the English speaker, at least, two groups of -*do* forms lack these meanings. First, there is a sizeable number, illustrated in Figure 6.3, that can be used with no passiveness implied at all; perhaps *aburrido, atrevido,* and so on should be classified as independent adjectives homophonous with verb participles. Second, there are the participles of verbs representing changes of state and body position, as illustrated in Figure 6.4. The student may well wonder whether *está dormido* really signals the same thing as *he's sleeping*, but -*ing* and -*ed* cannot always be equated with -*ndo* and -*do*; in this case, such verbs are intransitive in English and the state is expressed with the progressive, while they are transitive reflexive in Spanish and the state is expressed as resulting from a change upon oneself.

Some grammarians include a fourth nonfinite in Spanish, the form in -*nte*. In Latin, this was a present active participle, contrasting with the past (or perfect) passive one which Spanish inherited as its -*do* form. It is

Figure 6.3 Some *-do* forms with nonpassive and nonpast meanings.

aburrido 'boring'	fingido 'fake'
agradecido 'thankful'	leído 'well-read'
atrevido 'bold'	logrado 'successful'
concurrido 'busy, crowded'	necesitado 'needy'
considerado 'considerate'	ocupado 'busy'
chiflado 'crazy'	parecido 'similar'
desconfiado 'distrustful'	pesado 'heavy'
descreído 'unbelieving'	porfiado 'stubborn'
descuidado 'careless'	presumido 'presumptuous'
desesperado 'hopeless'	sabido 'smart'
divertido 'fun, entertaining'	sacrificado 'self-sacrificing'
entendido 'in the know'	seguido 'continuous, direct'
exagerado 'prone to exaggerating'	

Figure 6.4 Some *-do* forms of reflexives translated by Eng. *-ing* forms.

acostarse: acostado 'lying down'	esconderse: escondido 'hiding'
agacharse: agachado 'stooping, squatting'	inclinarse: inclinado 'leaning, bending'
arrodillarse: arrodillado 'kneeling'	pararse: parado 'standing'
dormirse: dormido 'sleeping'	sentarse: sentado 'sitting'

true that a great many Spanish verbs have *-nte* forms: *amante, influyente, importante, hablante, flotante, volante, conveniente, creciente, preocupante*, etc. But most verbs lack one (**trabajante, *lloviente, *divirtiente, *ordeñante*); some *-nte* forms are now nouns (*estudiante, dirigente, sirviente*) or prepositions (*durante, mediante*); and many retain little connection with their original verbs (*poniente, ocurrente, teniente, corriente, estante*). Such facts suggest that the *-nte* form is outside the verb paradigm and that *-nte* is now derivational, like *-dor, -dero, -tivo* (v. 15.1.1). Given this exclusion (implicit in U.S. pedagogy), the Spanish *-do* form can be called simply *the* participle.

English has a gerund ending in *-ing*, and like the Spanish one it can be used adverbially:

He left sobbing.
Breaking the window, she managed to get in.
On Saturdays we enjoyed ourselves playing tennis.

But it can also be used adjectivally:

The sobbing man left.
The women breaking the window are desperate.

and like a noun (i.e. as subject or object; v. 13.1.1-13.2.1):

Sobbing isn't the answer.
Before breaking the window, try my key.

In these last two functions, it corresponds more to a Spanish adjectival clause and infinitive, respectively: *el hombre que sollozaba, antes de romper la ventana.*

The other English nonfinite regularly ends in *-ed* or *-t* and is then homophonous with the past tense form, but most strong verbs have a distinct form in *-en* and/or with a vowel change: *driven, given, eaten, sung, begun, broken, forgotten,* etc. To distinguish participial *-ed* from past *-ed,* many linguists call the former the *-en* suffix, even for the *-ed* allomorph. In English, this *-en* has a rather consistent past or passive force in contrast with the active or present force of the adjectival *-ing.* A murdering man is carrying out murder while a murdered man is the victim; a falling tree is descending now while a fallen tree has already descended to the ground. Many grammarians therefore call the *-ing* form a gerund in its nominal and adverbial functions, but a present participle in its adjectival function contrasting with the past participle in *-en.*

Since the two languages assign somewhat different functions to their nonfinites, the student must beware of identifying Spanish usage too closely with that of English. Yet there are four constructions in which the two languages converge nicely in their use of gerunds and participles: absolutes, perfects, progressives, and passives.

6.3.3 'Absolutes'. This term is another borrowing from classical grammar. It describes a gerund or participle that presents background information for the main clause and is set off from it. Its subject is normally expressed only if different from that of the main clause (v. 13.2.3):

Estando en huelga los obreros, los jefes intentaron sustituirlos.
(With) the workers being on strike, the bosses tried to replace them.

As illustrated, *with* often accompanies English absolutes and it makes possible the deletion of *being: with the workers on strike.* But while both languages form gerund absolutes, participle absolutes are more common in Spanish than English, which prefers a gerund or an obligatory *with:*

Llegado el dichoso día, . . .	The happy day *having* arrived, . . .
Decidida la ruta, . . .	The route *having been* decided, . . .
	With the route *decided,* . . .

6.3.4 Perfects, progressives, passives. 'Compound' tenses are compounded from a helping verb and a gerund or participle. There are two sets of them, perfect[12] and progressive, that are usually included in traditional paradigms. The perfect consists of *haber/have* + (past) participle, and the progressive of *estar/be* + gerund.

Lo ha bebido.	He has drunk it.
Lo está bebiendo.	He's drinking it.

They can be combined as long as the perfect precedes the progressive:

Lo ha estado bebiendo.	He has been drinking it.
*Lo está habiendo bebido.	*He is having drunk it.

At the beginning levels, Spanish compound tenses tend to be equated with their English counterparts. But their meanings within their respective systems can differ (v. 7.2.2); and the compound forms act more like an integral unit in Spanish, especially the perfects:[13]

¿Lo *han recibido* los hijos?	*Have* the kids *gotten* it?
(*¿Lo han los hijos recibido?)	
Nunca se *ha detenido.*	She *has* never *stopped.*
(*Se ha nunca detenido.)	

Then, too, alternative constructions with *hacer* and *llevar* have conquered some of the domain covered by the English forms:

Hace doce años que vive ahí.	He's been living there (for) twelve years.
Lleva dos días en el hospital.	She's been in the hospital (for) two days.

As for the passive, which in both languages consists of the copula *ser/be* + (past) participle, this is analyzed as a transformation by current linguists, and will be so treated later (v. 12.3).

6.4 Verb + verb and auxiliaries. The inflectional endings on verbs serve mainly to convey tense and mood. But the available sets of endings can only express a subset of the huge number of possible characterizations of an event. For additional distinctions outside the inflectional paradigm, many languages resort to verb + verb combinations. For example, instead of employing a special affix to express potentiality or obligation, as some languages do, English and Spanish deploy a helping verb (AUXILIARY, or Aux): *can/should speak, puede/debe hablar.*[14] To emphasize the fact that verb + verb (or Aux + V) is a kind of secondary conjugation of the main verb, many Spanish grammarians use the term *conjugación perifrástica* or *perífrasis.* In fact, the compound forms described above (v. 6.3.4) are also *perífrasis,* though they traditionally tend to be included in the verb paradigm proper.

In verb + verb, both languages inflect just the first verb; the second stays in one nonfinite form, typically the infinitive (V + V-inf, as in *puede hablar*), but sometimes the gerund (V + V-ger, as in *sigue hablando*) or participle (V + V-pcp, as in *ha hablado*). Therefore, students who know that *hablar* is an infinitive and *poder* is 'can' are presumed to know enough to generate *puedo hablar, puedes hablar, puede hablar,* etc. Yet sometimes students overgeneralize a pattern beyond the limits of either the target or source language, and in this case the constant dictum they hear, 'conjugate those verbs!', leads to *puedes hablas, *quieres hablas, *quería hablaba. As native speakers of English, they would never say *he wants to speaks or *he wanted to spoke, and once this is pointed out to them and they are reminded that Spanish acts the same way, such errors should diminish.

A more difficult problem is the question of which nonfinite form is required, and which relator, if any, is needed for joining the two verbs. To assist the student, almost any reference grammar will present a taxonomy such as the following:

V + V-inf:
deber, hacer, mandar, saber, intentar, querer, desear, permitir, preferir, necesitar, anhelar, esperar, pensar, lograr, conseguir, poder, soler, acostumbrar, decidir, parecer, rehusar, oír, ver, sentir . . .

V + relator + V-inf:
= *a* +: *ir, comenzar, empezar, echar, ponerse, aprender, enseñar, llegar, venir, volver, acostumbrarse, atreverse, tender, obligar, pasar, negarse, invitar . . .*
= *de* +: *terminar, acabar, dejar, haber, deber, gozar, olvidarse, tratar, guardarse . . .*
= *en* +: *convenir, vacilar, insistir, consentir, quedar, tardar . . .*
= *por* +: *acabar, hacer, impacientarse, luchar . . .*
= *que* +: *tener, haber*

V + V-ger:
estar, ir, venir, andar, seguir, ver, oír . . .

V + V-pcp: *haber, estar, ser, quedar . . .*

English has the same four categories and occasionally agrees with Spanish in how it classifies a verb: *deber* and *should* are both V + V-inf, *tender* and *tend* are V + *a/to* + V-inf. More often, the two languages seem to disagree: *saber* requires no relator but *know* takes *how to*; *tener* takes *que* but *must* takes ∅ and *have* takes *to*; *terminar* takes *de* + V-inf while *finish* takes V-ger, etc. Some verbs occur in different patterns according to meaning: *pienso divertirme* ≠ *pienso en divertirme, voy a saltar* ≠ *voy saltando, he renunciado* ≠ *he de renunciar, acabo de afeitarme* ≠ *acabo por afeitarme*. The use of relators in verb + verb is thus difficult to describe, just as it is in verb + object (v. 9.4.1, 10.3.3.2). Teachers can point out that verbs 'of ending' take *de* and those 'of learning or beginning' take *a*, but this takes the student just a short way into a setup that is ultimately arbitrary and verb-specific. In learning that *tratar* takes *de* but its synonym *intentar* does not (while *try* can take either *to* + V-inf or ∅ + V-ger), the student can only memorize what takes which.

With verb + verb, we cross a boundary between the inflectional patterns of verb morphology and the combinatory patterns of syntax. *Intentar, invitar a, decidir, querer, esperar, ver,* and so on can be followed by an infinitive or by a *que*-clause, and many linguists prefer to explain *quiero envolverlo* as derived from a deep structure such as *quiero que lo envuelva.* This connection will be explored later in Chapter 13.

Notes for Chapter 6

1. Both languages have verb prefixes too, but for derivation, never for tense inflection: *oír desoír, tener retener, tell foretell, go undergo.*

2. Outside the standard variety, there are a few other variants in the person-number suffixes: *-nos* for *-mos* (*amábanos*), *-stes* or *-tes* for *-ste* (*amastes, amates*), and a migrating *-n* (*márchesen* for *márchense*). There are also special suffixes for the pronoun *vos* (v. 9.2).

3. Diphthongization applies to /i/ and /u/ also in *adquirir* and *jugar* (O.Span. *jogar*).

4. In nonstandard varieties, the diphthongized or raised vowel has often been extended throughout the paradigm: *aciertar, quiebrar, ñevar* (<*nievar*), *güeler* (=*oler*), *siguir, dicir, pidir* (Boyd-Bowman 1960:168-169, Sánchez 1982:28-29). Likewise, some verbs have jumped categories to or from Diphthongization and Raising: *escuendo* for *escondo, apriendo* for *aprendo, apreto* for *aprieto, colgo* for *cuelgo, frego* for *friego, forzo* for *fuerzo, escrebir* for *escribir* (Boyd-Bowman ibid., Oroz 1966:312, Jorge-Morel 1974: 107).

5. The derivational pattern is not as regular as the inflectional one (v. 15.1.3): *buenísimo* exists alongside *bonísimo, amueblar* alongside *amoblar,* etc.

6. Some students perceive this change as the insertion of a *z* in the stem *cono_c-.* But the *z* is a predictable respelling of *c* for /θ/=/s/ when *e* or *i* does not follow; phonologically, the change is /konoθ-/ → /konoθk-/.

7. There are only four candidates, that is, if the next group in *-uir* is excluded from this vowel *e/i r* case. But at least in Santo Domingo (Jorge-Morel 1974:108), the *-uir* group has been assimilated to it: many speakers say *huigo, distribuigo* for standard *huyo, distribuyo.*

8. When the *u* of *-uir* is part of the digraphs *qu* and *gu,* the verb does not fall into this category: *delinquir delinco, seguir sigo* (but cf. *argüir arguyo*).

9. For *estoy* to be monosyllabic requires the analysis of *estar* as underlying /star/, with the *e* being added by the Epenthesis Rule, as in *snob* → *esnob* (v. 3.0).

10. Some include as modals *used to, ought to, need, dare, be going to, be about to, have to, get to, be supposed to*; but traditionally, modals are limited to those auxiliaries that take a *to*-less infinitive. *Shall* is also a modal but would not normally occur in the example given.

11. Spanish regularized many irregular Latin participles or relegated them to special nooks outside the verb system. Thus, today *tinto, confuso,*

distinto, maldito, incluso are words in their own right, differentiated from (*he*) *teñido, confundido, distinguido, maldecido, incluido.* Outside the standard, there is much more regularization: *ponido* for *puesto, decido* for *dicho, abrido* for *abierto,* etc. (Boyd-Bowman 1960:169).

Derivatives generally retain the irregularities of their primaries: *descrito* like *escrito, compuesto* like *puesto, descubierto* like *cubierto.* But *bendecir* and *corromper* diverge from *decir* and *romper* in having regular participles, and whereas *imprimir* has *impreso, comprimir* has *comprimido.*

12. So-called not for any lack of imperfections, but because in Latin (to which one constantly returns in such matters) the *perfectum* depicted an event as already carried out or 'perfected'; cf. the Spanish *imperfecto,* which still conveys the unperfected aspect (v. 7.1.3).

13. But an object pronoun can break up the combination of perfect auxiliary + participle when the former is infinitivized: *haberse ido.* In Old Spanish, object pronouns were much freer in their position than today: *se había ido, habíase ido, había ídose.*

14. *Can* and *should* are a special kind of Aux called 'modals', as noted in 6.2 and explained in more detail in 7.2.1. For the present, no rigorous distinction is made in the verb + verb construction between an auxiliary + main verb and a main verb + dependent verb complement; see, however, 13.1.2.7 for one criterion that can be applied in defining the difference.

Exercises for Chapter 6

1. The citation form of a verb is the infinitive. Why is this a rather unrevealing form for stem changes? What is the minimum information a text or dictionary-maker could add to this citation form to key the remainder of the conjugation in Spanish?

2. Teachers can address the particular problems of students by determining the sources of their errors, a task called 'error analysis'. Carry out an error analysis of each of the following, focusing especially on whether the student is analogizing incorrectly within the Spanish system or transferring an English pattern.

(1) *comaban
(2) *yo dijo, yo habló
(3) *ella sabes
(4) *venzco (*for* venzo)
(5) *venco (*for* venzo)
(6) *¿has tú comido?
(7) *trato a hacerlo
(8) *tienes a escucharme
(9) *abiertaste, abiertaron
(10) *estaron
(11) *piensaba
(12) *me graduo
(13) *vivemos
(14) *estoy durmiendo
(15) *van trabajar
(16) *(quiere que) dormamos
(17) *nosotros háblamos
(18) *yo habló, tú hablás, ...
(19) *deben terminan
(20) *con mi lápiz estando roto, (decidí escribir con bolígrafo)

3. Some students will render any Eng. -ed form with the imperfect, then later with the preterite, still later with the participle, according to whichever of these is being focused on in the course at a given moment. What mistaken generalization is being made?

4. Traditionally, verb morphology has been treated in terms of 'item-and-paradigm'. In this approach, the grammarian takes an 'item' (an infinitive) and takes it form by form through the entire paradigm in the sequence *yo, tú, él, nosotros, vosotros, ellos*, tense by tense and mood by mood. Some texts still present paradigms in this way for memorization by the student. Other texts are now emphasizing an 'item-and-process' approach, whereby students are given general rules covering stem changes. In your opinion, which specific changes best lend themselves to the latter approach, and why? Which ones might best be learned by rote memorization, à la item-and-paradigm, and why?

5. *Divertir* has the stem allomorphs *divert- diviert- divirt-*; *divergir* keeps *diverg-* (respelled *diverj-*) throughout. Depending on one's definition of 'regularity', is it possible to argue that both are regular?

6. It was pointed out that Diphthongization is not peculiar to verb paradigms but can be found throughout Spanish. Find more examples of this by giving related or derived forms of the following, in which the diphthong 'reverts' to *e* or *o* when unstressed.

Buenos Aires	hierro	nieve	tierno	cuerno
niebla	sueño	fuerte	rueda	invierno
hierba	gobierno	viento	fuente	huevo
estiércol	cuerda	serpiente	cueva	nuevo

7. If you were writing a Spanish text for English speakers, which labels would you use for the various tenses? Would your decision depend on whether the text were in Spanish or English?

8. What value, if any, do you see in getting students to see that the endings -*an*, -*aban*, -*aron* really consist of several morphemes (slots, endings, pieces, parts, or whatever), rather than one? Why?

9. How is the mastery of *conjugación perifrástica* somewhat easier for the student than the normal inflectional conjugation? More difficult? In your opinion, how much should the verb + verb construction be emphasized in the classroom? For example, should *ir a* + V-inf be introduced earlier and the inflected future postponed? Why?

10. The following are some more typical student errors with Spanish verb morphology:

ibamos *for* íbamos	sabo *for* sé	detenieron *for* detuvieron
jugo *for* juego	creiba *for* creía	saliremos *for* saldremos
cubrido *for* cubierto	andé *for* anduve	habemos *for* hemos
volvido *for* vuelto	producí *for* produje	¡sale! *for* ¡sal!

As it turns out, every one of these is also found among native Spanish speakers who have spoken the language all their lives (Boyd-Bowman

1960:168). This fact does not mean that such forms are acceptable to the Real Academia or on the final exams of Introductory Spanish; but it does teach one something about the overall morphological system of the Spanish verb. Not all student errors are committed by native speakers; why would both groups produce forms such as those above?

11. Why, in general, does the Spanish verb give trouble to English speakers? Bear in mind the contrasts between the two grammatical systems.

12. In the study of morphophonemic alternations, three types of changes are often distinguished. In PHONOLOGICAL CONDITIONING, the change depends exclusively on neighboring phonemes and features such as stress. In MORPHOLOGICAL CONDITIONING, the change depends at least in part on grammatical information: the rule for the change must make reference to stipulations such as 'in the present tense' or 'only in verbs'. In LEXICAL CONDITIONING, the change cannot be stated generally because phonological and morphological information alone do not suffice to define where and when the change takes place: certain words (or morphemes) change while others do not, and speakers can only memorize what does and does not undergo the rule.

Review the rules in this chapter for stem changes and ending changes, and classify each one as to whether it is phonologically, morphologically, or lexically conditioned.

Chapter 7
Tense and mood

7.0 Approaches to tense and mood. Although there have been many treatments of tense and mood, one can discern two main trends in them. On the one hand are those scholars who regard each verb category as a constellation of discrete uses and who strive to list all uses of the preterite, of the subjunctive, and so on. The lists vary according to the listmaker. For the Spanish present tense, the RAE (1924:289-290) finds three uses, Michalson and Aires (1981:47-48) four, and Sallese y Fernández de la Vega (1968:118) five. DaSilva and Lovett (1965:4-6) give four uses for the imperfect and two for the preterite, whereas the RAE (1979:466-469) perceives five and three, respectively.

On the other hand are those scholars (e.g. Bello 1847/1958, Ramsey 1894/1956, Gili Gaya 1973, Bull 1965, Stockwell et al. 1965) who have sought a unified description of each category, i.e. one basic, general concept that underlies the particular uses. This concept is necessarily defined on the basis of how the category contrasts with others in the same system, because the meaning of 'present' in a two-tense system must cover more ground than in a five-tense one. Thus, in order to understand such theories, it is necessary to examine the overall system.

7.1 The basic tense system of Spanish and English. One of the most coherent and influential theories of tense is that of Bull (1965: 149-171), who distinguishes SYSTEMIC from NONSYSTEMIC meaning. The former is that meaning each category has within its system, and in general Spanish and English concur here. The latter includes specialized functions it has acquired outside that system by way of extension, and the two languages diverge somewhat in this case.

7.1.1 Systemic meanings. Bull first notes that the tense one chooses for portraying a situation depends on his orientation or perspective: 'as of right now', for example, or 'back then'. Each such orientation can be considered an axis or time-line along which the event being described is to be located in one of three ways: as ANTERIOR to the orientation the speaker adopts, as SIMULTANEOUS with it, or as POSTERIOR to it. The different tenses in the system express these three 'ordered relations' (as Bull calls them) according to different perspectives. The difference of perspective is crucial in Bull's theory: linguistic tenses are not all located on the same axis as points in real time must be.

7.1.1.1 Present perfect, present, future. In using these three, the speaker views matters from his current perspective, the present: these are oriented toward the PRESENT POINT ('now'), which Bull symbolizes as PP. Events (actions, processes, states) that are concurrent with PP appear in the present tense: the present tense therefore represents simultaneity with respect to PP. Events that have been or have begun before PP are anterior with respect to PP, and they are expressed by the present perfect. Those events that are viewed from PP but as posterior to it are expressed by the future tense. These three tenses can be called the 'present system', and their relationship and common PP perspective are depicted by Bull as in Figure 7.1. (For now, at least, we will not concern ourselves with details such as the difference between simple and progressive forms.)

7.1.1.2 Past perfect, past, conditional. When narrating past events, the speaker usually switches his perspective from PP to some RECALLED POINT, RP, a strategy Bull calls BACKSHIFTING. Tenses oriented toward RP indicate

Figure 7.1 The tenses oriented toward the present point (PP).

ANTERIOR =	SIMULTANEOUS =	POSTERIOR =
present perfect	present	future
lo han vendido	*lo venden*	*lo venderán*
	PP	
they've sold it	*they sell it*	*they'll sell it*

Figure 7.2 The tenses oriented toward the recalled point (RP).

ANTERIOR =	SIMULTANEOUS =	POSTERIOR =
past perfect	past (pret./imp.)	conditional
lo habían vendido	*lo vendieron/vendían*	*lo venderían*
	RP	
they'd sold it	*they sold it*	*they would sell it*

how matters stood 'back then' instead of 'right now'. Anteriority is again depicted by a perfect tense, the past perfect in this case, for it shows what had happened before RP. Simultaneity with respect to RP is expressed by the past tense in English and by the preterite or imperfect in Spanish (v. 7.1.3). Finally, posteriority with respect to RP represents what was foreseen or predicted to happen subsequently, i.e. what would happen, and it is expressed by the conditional. Figure 7.2 portrays how Bull summarizes these relationships at RP.

As can be seen by a comparison of Figures 7.1 and 7.2, the two sets of tenses—present system and past system—are parallel, which is precisely the point Bull wishes to make. Present perfect and past perfect express anteriority; present and past (imperfect or preterite) indicate simultaneity with the adopted perspective point; and future and conditional both indicate posteriority. The only difference between the present and past systems is the speaker's point of view, and with 'backshifting' from PP to RP, the tense forms in (a) below systemically shift to those in (b). (The *dice/dijo* and *he says/said* are used here to bring out PP and RP, respectively, as reference points.)

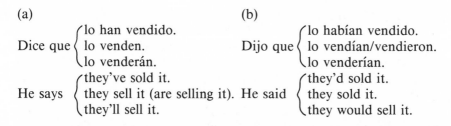

(a)

Dice que $\left\{\begin{array}{l}\text{lo han vendido.}\\ \text{lo venden.}\\ \text{lo venderán.}\end{array}\right.$

He says $\left\{\begin{array}{l}\text{they've sold it.}\\ \text{they sell it (are selling it).}\\ \text{they'll sell it.}\end{array}\right.$

(b)

Dijo que $\left\{\begin{array}{l}\text{lo habían vendido.}\\ \text{lo vendían/vendieron.}\\ \text{lo venderían.}\end{array}\right.$

He said $\left\{\begin{array}{l}\text{they'd sold it.}\\ \text{they sold it.}\\ \text{they would sell it.}\end{array}\right.$

7.1.1.3 Future perfect and conditional perfect. These two tenses are less used than the others because they deal with a complex and quite specialized outlook from PP and RP. Both tenses project forward onto some surmised, expected axis or plane and speculate about anteriority on that axis, i.e. what might have transpired prior to some ANTICIPATED POINT AP. For the future perfect, AP is projected from PP; for the conditional perfect, AP is surmised from the RP point of view. Consequently, both of the following sets of sentences strongly imply a 'by then, by that time' AP, and both express anteriority with respect to that AP.

(a)
Dice que lo habrán vendido.
He says they will have sold it.

(b)
Dijo que lo habrían vendido.
He said they would've sold it.

7.1.1.4 Summary of the tense system. Figure 7.3 depicts the overall system that defines the eight basic tenses that Bull investigated. There are four axes, two major ones (those of PP and RP) and two minor ones (those of AP projected from the other two). Note that it is the system that deter-

Figure 7.3 The overall tense system in Bull's analysis.

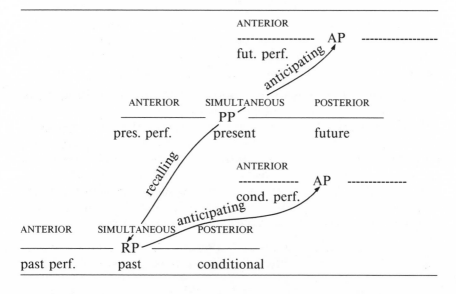

mines the tense distinctions: a present perfect such as *lo han vendido* is meaningless in itself except (1) in reference to a perspective (PP), and (2) in contrast with other relationships (anteriority vs. simultaneity or posteriority, and anteriority with respect to PP vs. anteriority with respect to RP and AP). Moreover, Bull's analysis postulates that tense categories correspond to a speaker's discourse strategies: in adopting conditional as opposed to future, the speaker shifts back to another plane, and in adopting conditional perfect he shifts beyond to some hypothesized plane. Tense, then, is a matter of what the speaker wishes to say, how he chooses to express it, and the point of view he selects; it is not, strictly speaking, e-quatable with real-world time. As Bull (1965:157) states it,

> A system based on four axes of orientations (with three ordered relations to each) cannot be synchronized with the three notions of calendar time: past, present, and future or yesterday, today, and tomorrow. The traditional approach that the tense system is a time construct has led textbook writers (and teachers) to believe that the functions of tense systems can be defined by relating them to adverbs of time. The preterite, for example, is associated with *ayer* (*lo vendimos ayer*), the present with *hoy* (*lo vendemos hoy*), and the future with *mañana* (*lo venderemos mañana*). This association ... can only lead to confusion and contradictions in a pedagogical explanation of the functions of tense systems.

In fact, with *hoy* one can say *vendemos* or *hemos vendido* or *vendimos* or *vendíamos* or *venderemos* or *venderíamos* or *habríamos vendido*, depending on his perspective; and with *mañana*, he could say *vendemos, venderemos, venderíamos, habremos vendido*. As Gili Gaya (1973:157) points out, it is even possible to use the preterite for an event that is technically still in the future, as when a traveler whose train is approaching the station says *Ya llegué* before actually arriving. Time is beyond human control, but tense is adapted to human viewpoints and is set up for manipulation by humans in humanly edited discourse.

7.1.2 Nonsystemic extensions. Language stretches to conform to its users' needs, and just as the literal denotation of a word expands to cover figurative meanings, the systemic or basic meaning of a tense can spread to express other characterizations of events. The resulting nonsystemic meanings are not necessarily minor in importance, but are less related to contrasts among the primary ordering relationships on Bull's four axes. Bull does not enumerate all nonsystemic functions; perhaps that is as difficult a task as listing all the connotations of a word. But the following selection includes the common ones taken up in pedagogy.

7.1.2.1 Historical and Anticipatory Present. The present extends back into the past and forward into the yet-to-come, and speakers of both languages exploit this lack of fixed boundaries. For the so-called Historical Present, one interrupts a narrative in past tense with a switch to the present: RP becomes PP. According to Silva-Corvalán (1983:778), who has extensively researched this strategy in Spanish narratives, the speaker presents the events 'as if they were occurring before us.'

In the Anticipatory Present there is a forward shift, with the present tense covering future time. The rationale for this is variously analyzed as (1) lending 'more vivacity and color to the statement' (Ramsey 1956:337), (2) indicating 'intención presente de realizar una acción futura' (Gili Gaya 1973:156), and (3) combining the currency of the present with future reference to express intended 'subsequence' (Stockwell et al. 1965:148-152). Nevertheless, it is not always clear whether a speaker means for his *salimos mañana* to be construed differently from *saldremos mañana* or, for that matter, from the periphrastic *vamos a salir mañana*; some observers, in fact, believe that the inflectional future is yielding to the Anticipatory Present and the *ir a* construction in many dialects for all characterizations of posteriority (Kany 1945/1951:152).[1]

7.1.2.2 Probability and speculation. With *Ya serán las dos y todos estarán en casa*, the speaker intends simultaneity at PP, not posteriority. The same is true of *Ya serían las dos y todos estarían en casa* when the perspective has been shifted to RP. Systemically, the future and conditional speculate about the future, and nonsystemically that speculation is applied to situations concurrent with PP and RP as well. English more often uses an adverb of probability (*surely, probably, allegedly*) or a main verb of supposition or speculation (*I guess, suppose, reckon*, or in questions, *Do you think . . . ?*); but it is not true that English never adopts the nonsystemic future. After a knock on the door, one can say *Who will that be?* (like Span. *¿Quién será?*), and on seeing an approaching vehicle, he may say *That'll be our bus now* (*Será nuestro autobús*). The difference between the two languages is not grammatical but pragmatic (v. 16.0): English speakers do not exploit this communicative strategy quite as much as Spanish speakers.

7.1.2.3 Conditionals and hypotheticals. In its systemic meaning, the conditional is the backshift of the future; it expresses posteriority with respect to RP, i.e. what the future looked like at some recalled point. But in both languages, the distance between RP and PP can be psychological rather than temporal, and by extension the conditional has come to be used for posteriority with respect to some hypothetical situation—what consequences might ensue if a certain RP existed or, with anteriority highlighted, had existed:

¿Se comportaría así?   Would she behave that way?
¿Se habría comportado así?   Would she have behaved that way?

If the hypothetical condition or premise (PROTASIS) is explicitly stated, its verb will be in the past subjunctive.[2]

¿Se comportaría así *si*   Would she behave that way *if*
tuviera la oportunidad?   *she had the chance*?

This conditional construction is traditionally called 'contrary to fact'. It is essentially atemporal, and for that reason some grammarians in Spain and Latin America have preferred to call the conditional a mood (*el modo potencial*) rather than a tense.

In both languages, the conditional and past subjunctive have been adapted for another function, the softening of a request or suggestion. The rationale seems to be that speakers are suggesting what might be the case *if* they were to ask more directly:

Quería/Quisiera un poco más.   I'd like some more.
¿Podría Ud. ayudarme?   Could you help me?

The *could* in the foregoing sentence stands for *would could* 'would be able': since English modals do not combine, the conditional of *can* is not distinct from its past. Modals have their own nonsystemic functions (v. 7.2.1), and these can cause interference when students take up the Spanish tense system.

7.1.3 Two aspects of one tense: Preterite and imperfect. With the possible exception of the subjunctive, no topic in Spanish morphology has aroused more pedagogical and linguistic discussion than the preterite/imperfect distinction. Perhaps no single analysis (including those to be taken up below) has captured it in a way that covers all cases, accounts for native speakers' intuitions, and satisfies the needs of floundering students. Yet it is true some treatments have been worse than others. The following illustrates a popular but particularly unsatisfactory one.[3]

IMPERFECT	PRETERITE
(1) tells what was happening	(1) records, reports, narrates
(2) recalls what used to happen	(2) with certain verbs, causes
(3) describes a physical, mental, emotional state in the past	a change in meaning
(4) tells time in the past	
(5) describes the background and sets the stage upon which another action occurred	

The defects are manifold here. First, this treatment represents the two categories as arbitrary groupings of independent uses: five different imperfects, two different preterites; and the fact that 'recording' ends up as preterite rather than imperfect seems as capricious as the classification of tomatoes as vegetables rather than fruits. Second, it visually suggests that the preterite is the less used of the two, so that when students must guess, imperfect looks like the safer bet; in actuality, the preterite is much more frequent. Third, it is extremely difficult to apply, because its vagueness in specific contexts robs it of any criterial value. If students wish to convey their *I slept all day*, should they opt for 'what was happening', 'describes physical state', 'describes background', or 'records, reports'? All these seem applicable, and conflicting; thus, students are baffled when their teacher recommends *Dormí todo el día* over *Dormía todo el día*.

Fourth, it is wrong even when it is clear, for counterexamples are easy to find:

Llovió a cántaros ayer ('what was happening', but preterite)
Viví allí hasta mudarme ('used to', but preterite)
Estuvimos cansados ('physical and mental state', but preterite)
Juanito rompió unos platos y a María se le cayó la cafetera; luego entró horrorizada Mamá ('background' for Mom's entry, but preterite)
La foto no está bien porque Abuelita masticaba chicle y Jorge bostezaba y Papá se sonaba la nariz. ('recording, reporting, narrating', but imperfect)

One understands the zeal of some writers to make grammatical explanations as succinct as possible; reducing a point to 'use X here, Y there' injunctions avoids quasiphilosophical discussions, makes the point at least appear manageable, and allows the writer to get on with the *lectura* on Machu Picchu. But in this case, short-cuts are doomed to failure. A few students who believe everything in a text may fervently memorize the table of seven uses sorted into two piles, but they soon learn that their best efforts contradict actual usage. Other students become totally confused and eventually merge the two categories into one, even melding their forms in a conjugation such as *yo vendí, tú vendías*, and the hybrid **él vendío*. The facts that (1) this approach has failed with several generations of students and (2) it must recognize some verbs (the 'meaning-changers') as beyond the pale, suggest that something is fundamentally wrong with it.

With the preterite/imperfect distinction, one must begin with two important facts. First, these are not really separate tenses, despite the convenience of calling them that, but categories that represent different ASPECTS of the same past tense. From this follows the second fact: both can be used in the same RP context, with a contrast in meaning:

A las siete miraron/miraban la luna.
Hernando siempre asistió/asistía a sus clases.
Ese coche costó/costaba $10.000.
Pilar fue/era rebelde.

'Recording, reporting, narrating, backgrounding' and so on are not aspects, but communicative functions of language; in carrying out any of these, the Spanish speaker can choose between preterite and imperfect and even combine them for different characterizations of the event:

María rió cuando Pablo salió.
María rió cuando Pablo salía.
María reía cuando Pablo salió.
María reía cuando Pablo salía.

ASPECT refers to (1) the nature of the event being described (e.g. instantaneous and point-like vs. enduring or recurring) and (2) which part of the event is being depicted at a recalled point (beginning vs. middle vs. end). English does not consistently make such distinctions, and in order to develop an awareness of them, teacher and students may need to delay taking up preterite/imperfect and first reflect on what they mean in English when they use the past tense.[4] As an example, let us consider the form *rained* in English. In *It rained yesterday*, the speaker confines an event of some duration to a limited period, assigning it a beginning and an end; in *The clouds gathered and suddenly it rained*, he focuses only on the beginning (= 'it began to rain'); in *As it rained, I noticed some leaking*, he recalls a moment in the middle of the downpour; and in *Where I grew up it rained every day*, he describes a recurrent, indefinitely repeated event, a series of rainings. All these different events can be expressed by *rained*, but in Spanish the first two will be *llovió* and the second two *llovía*.

Most grammarians and linguists[5] who have explained preterite/imperfect in terms of aspect agree that the imperfect situates one at some recalled point in the middle of an event or a series of events that, at RP, was fairly open-ended and unbounded. For a single event, this middle aspect can be depicted as follows:

(1) _____ – – – –|– – – – – – _____ (A las ocho, me bañaba.)
              RP

For a series of recurring or habitual events, middleness is as follows:

(2) ⌒ ⌒ ⌒ ⌒|⌒ ⌒ ⌒ (De niño, me bañaba cada noche.)
              RP

The preterite, on the other hand, can express an occurrence from the viewpoint of either RP or PP, and it handles all aspects but middleness. At a recalled point, it can indicate that the event ended (concluded, culminated) then:

(3) _____ – – – – →|_____ (A las ocho, me caí.)
              RP

or that it began (broke out, came into existence) then:

(4) _____|– – – – – →_____ (A las ocho, llovió a cántaros.)
              RP

With respect to the present point, the preterite can indicate that the event simply happened (was done, completed) before PP:

(5a)_____⊢—⊣_____PP_____ (Estudié con Juan.)

or that it lasted or recurred for some interval; but, unlike the imperfect in cases (1) and (2), the preterite depicts that interval as now terminated or discontinued from the PP viewpoint:

(5b)⊢—————————⊣_____PP_____ (Viví ahí por ocho años.)

or

_____ꙨꙨꙨꙨꙨꙨꙨ_____PP_____ (Me bañé cada día)

This aspect-based explanation fits most cases quite well. But consensus among modern analysts evaporates when they try to specify when the preterite refers to the beginning and when to the end, and why. On the one hand, Bull and Gili Gaya concur that 'beginning' vs. 'end' depends on the nature of the event itself, i.e. the kind of verb. Some verbs represent both the onset of a state of affairs and the resulting state; once begun, that state is understood as continuing indefinitely unless expressly terminated. Thus, *ver* is to catch sight of (= beginning, onset) and to keep on seeing (=continuing state); *pensar* is both to take thought and to continue in reflection; *caminar* and *correr* are to commence putting one foot in front of the other and to continue this process. Such verbs are called NONCYCLIC by Bull, *imperfectivos* by Gili Gaya. Other verbs express the culmination, ending, or 'perfecting' of an event; this event will not then continue unless one repeats a 'cycle' by starting over. For example, *caerse* is to lose balance and to hit the ground; falling thereupon ends, and one does not say *se cayó* until that end is reached. Unlike seeing, thinking, or walking, to continue falling requires that one go through the cycle of getting back up and falling all over again. Verbs like *caerse* are called CYCLIC by Bull, *perfectivos* by Gili Gaya.

In this theory, the preterite expresses at RP the beginning of noncyclic (imperfective) verbs, but the end of cyclic (perfective) ones. And of course, the imperfect of any kind of verb will depict the middle:

Cuando dio las cinco, (RP = 5:00)
- Juan corría (middle of running, case (1))
- Juan corrió (beginning, 'broke out running,' case (4))
- Juan se caía (middle of falling, case (1))
- Juan se cayó (end, 'hit the ground,' case (3))

The Bull-Gili Gaya analysis can be shown succinctly as in the diagram in Figure 7.4.

Guitart (1978), however, argues that the meaning of the preterite, though always contrasting with the middleness of the imperfect, does not

Figure 7.4 Imperfect as middle aspect, and preterite as beginning or end.

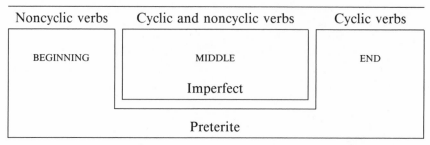

Noncyclic verbs	Cyclic and noncyclic verbs	Cyclic verbs
BEGINNING	MIDDLE Imperfect	END
	Preterite	

reduce so neatly to beginning vs. end in all cases, nor are all verbs obviously either cyclic or noncyclic. He thus expands the classification as follows.

(a) Cyclic events: *pasar*
   En ese momento pasó (vs. pasaba) un coche.

The preterite here means 'occurred before PP', and 'that is all it means' in contrast with the imperfect (Guitart 1978:137). If one infers that the car's passing did terminate, the tense ending alone does not necessarily imply this.

(b) Noncyclic events: *hablar, caminar, correr*
   El presidente habló (vs. hablaba) por televisión.
   El hombre corrió (vs. corría) hacia el avión.

Again, the event took place before PP; this event could conceivably have gone on indefinitely, but it may have ended. The preterite of a noncyclic verb does not really say whether it continued or ended.

(c) States: *ser, estar*
   Pedro fue (vs. era) comunista.

The preterite here suggests that Pedro was once a communist (at some RP) but no longer is (at PP). For noncyclic verbs such as (b) above, this is not necessarily the case.

(d) State-egressives: *costar, tener que*
   El libro costó (vs. costaba) $4.
   Tuve (vs. Tenía) que ir al aeropuerto.

By this term, Guitart means states that can either continue in effect or come climactically to an end (i.e. 'egress'). *Costaba $4* expresses a latent state of potential, 'the book was for sale for $4', whereas *Costó $4* has a dynamic, completive meaning, 'it was bought for $4.' *Tenía que ir al aeropuerto* likewise describes a state in effect, while *Tuve que ir al aeropuerto* means that the state of obligation ended or egressed with my actually going there.

(e) State-ingressives: *gustar*
Me gustó (vs. gustaba) el lugar.

Guitart's state-ingressives signify in the preterite that a state came into effect (ingressed rather than egressed); unlike noncyclic verbs (b), with which Bull grouped these, state-ingressives are understood as continuing once begun. In some contexts, *ser* and *estar* belong to this category rather than to (c); for example, in *Fue una experiencia inolvidable*, the speaker focuses on the coming-into-effect of his perception that the experience was unforgettable *and still is* unforgettable at PP; *Fue comunista* in (c), however, implies 'not true anymore at PP.'

Not all verbs fit precisely into this reanalysis either,[6] and Guitart must admit reversals of polarity with some adverbials. *Fueron enemigos* implies they are no longer enemies, hence case (c); yet *Desde aquel día fueron enemigos* suggests case (e). *Me gustó ese cuadro* is ingressive, hence case (e); *Me gustó ese cuadro hasta aquel día*, however, is (d).

The meaning of the preterite is thus rather broad, and its exact thrust depends on the verb and the sentential context. In contrast, the meaning of the imperfect is quite specific. For Guitart, not only does it highlight middleness (as Bull and Gili Gaya stated), but it hints that in the middle of one event 'some other situation took place or was taking place' (Guitart 1978:154). So strong is this implication that Guitart notes that one would seldom say just *El hombre corría hacia el avión* in isolation, but would go on to mention 'at least one other experience or situation that took place or was taking place over the same stretch of time' (Guitart 1978:141). He therefore approves of Bello's term for the imperfect, *copretérito* (v. 6.0), which so clearly brings out the notion of accompaniment.

Whatever their theory of preterite meanings, observers who explain the two pasts in terms of aspect are quite agreed that 'meaning-changing' verbs do not change their meaning in any remarkable way. Most (if not all) of such verbs are noncyclic states, egressive (like *costar*) or ingressive (like *gustar*). Therefore *sabía, conocía, tenía* express the middle of continuing states already begun and in effect; *supe, conocí, tuve* refer to the beginning or 'ingression' of these states—the start of knowledge, familiarity, possession. *Podía* and *quería* + verb indicate the middle of the state of ability or desire, a latent potentiality or attraction; *pude* and *quise* emphasize culmination (state-egression), with the latent state being put to the test and fulfilled. English sometimes changes verbs to convey the same senses, but not necessarily; contrary to the traditional rule that *sabía* is 'knew' and *supe* is 'found out', one very good translation of *Después de pensarlo bien, supe el motivo* would be 'after thinking it through, I *knew* the motive.' The fact that English translation sometimes changes should have no bearing at all on the Spanish grammatical system and its regularity; by the same reasoning, Spanish *hijo* would be an irregular meaning-changing noun because its translation in the feminine changes 'son' to 'daughter'.

7.2 The contributions of auxiliaries. It was noted in the previous chapter (v. 6.2-6.4) that many tense-like meanings are conveyed by the use of helping or auxiliary verbs (Aux) with the main verb. Hence, in addition to choosing from various morphological possibilities of the type V+tns (verb with a tense ending), one has at his disposal a rich 'periphrastic' system of Aux + V. A syntactic criterion for which of the various V + V combinations (v. 6.4) are truly Aux + V will be discussed later (v. 13.1.2.7); for now, however, it is sufficient to accept the dominant view in English and Spanish linguistics that the following, at least, are to be classified as Aux rather than as main verbs in their own right.

English: modals (*can, may, will, shall, must,* perhaps *ought to* and *used to,* and their morphological pasts), *have* (in the perfect), *be* (in the progressive)

Spanish: *poder, soler, deber, haber* (in the perfect), *estar* (in the progressive)

7.2.1 Meanings of modals. One obvious problem in mastering the Spanish equivalents of English modals is that the former are fully conjugated in the same categories as other verbs. English modals, in contrast, are defective in that they are uncombinable in the standard variety (**he should can do it* for *debe poder hacerlo*), uninflected for person (*he may,* not **he mays*), and severely limited in tense options. *Must* has no past form at all, and the morphological pasts of the others—(*can*) *could,* (*may*) *might,* (*will*) *would,* (*shall*) *should*—are often not semantically past or related to the Bullian RP (cf. *Tomorrow he could/should/might change his mind.*); and since modals do not combine, there is no distinct way of conveying 'posteriority' (future and conditional)—**will can go, *would may go.* Consequently, the Spanish tense distinctions for verbs such as *deber* cannot be grasped through English *should, ought to,* or *must* (Keniston 1937:199ff):

Debes ⎫
Deberás ⎪
Debías ⎬ intentarlo, Luis.
Debiste ⎪
Deberías ⎭

The difficulty is compounded by the fact that English speakers partly remedy their modals' defectiveness by borrowing from the perfect conjugation for backshifting to RP: *you should have tried it* corresponding to *debiste intentarlo.* Ideally in pedagogy, a lesson or two might well be devoted to directing students' attention to their modals and to the finer distinctions exploited by Spanish speakers.

Some English modals are pedagogically matched not with a Spanish Aux but with a tense category. Thus, *shall go* and *will go* are said to represent 'future tense' corresponding to *iré* and *irá,* and *should go* and *would go* are said to represent 'conditional tense' corresponding to *iría*. Strictly speaking (i.e. in terms of morphological systems), the modals are Aux, not tenses, but it is true that they can supply tense-like information. The problem is that English modals have additional nonsystemic meanings that are frequently ignored when modals are treated as functionally tense-like. Systemically, *will* and *would* occupy positions on Bull's axes corresponding, respectively, to the Spanish future (PP posteriority) and conditional (RP posteriority). Nonsystemically, however, they also convey (1) willingness (*Will/Would you shut the door?*) or (2) habitual occurrence at PP and RP (*Everyday he'll/he'd come in here with his tie undone to show he's just one of the guys*). Willingness is conveyed in Spanish by *querer*, and since habitual occurrence is simultaneity, it is expressed by the present (PP) or imperfect (RP) of Spanish, not by its future and conditional. *Shall* and *should* are a case apart; in current American English (the British differ on this point), neither one represents true posteriority (in Bull's sense) at all. Note, in fact, the striking contrast in meaning in *Shall we sit down?* vs. *Will we sit down?*, and in *Should they sit down?* vs. *Would they sit down? Should* expresses mild obligation and pairs off with *deber* rather than with the Spanish conditional; *shall* indicates (1) prescribed procedures in constitutional language (*Each person shall have one vote*) or (2) first-person offers and requests for approval (*Shall I tell it to you?*). This second *shall* corresponds more to the simple present in Spanish (*¿Te lo digo?*), which in this context Gili Gaya (1973:156) analyzes as an application of the Anticipatory Present. Hence, textwriters should exercise caution in explaining the Spanish future and conditional in terms of *will* and *would*, and avoid confusing students by tossing in *shall* and *should*.

In passing, one might note that the imperative, which is typically used in response to offers such as *Shall I tell it to you?* and *¿Te lo digo?*, does not fit readily into the basic tense system. For want of a better pigeonhole, some grammarians have called it a mood; others describe it in terms of an imperative transformation, a precedent we will follow later (v. 12.4).

7.2.2 'Secondary' modifications: Perfect and progressive. According to Bull, *he hablado* contrasts with *hablo* as anterior to PP vs. simultaneous with PP, and with the preterite as anterior to PP vs. simultaneous with RP. Stockwell et al. (1965:157) describe the present perfect as indicative of 'relevant anteriority', emphasizing that an event began in the relatively recent past and continues to be in effect or to impinge in some way on PP. (For past perfect and future perfect, one adjusts PP to RP and AP.) In both languages, this 'relevance' depends on the nature of the verb. It can represent a state that began in the past and continues into the present:

Hemos estado muy contentos en esta casa.

or a series of events that has continued right up through the present (= 'so far'):

Ya te lo he dicho mil veces.

or one event that ended but with abiding repercussions in the present:

El huracán ha destruido su casa.

As for the progressive, both languages generally use this to characterize events as ongoing, in progress (whence the name). But they relate this shared meaning to those of the simple tenses quite differently. In Spanish, the simple present can convey at least four verb aspects:

(1) occurring now at PP (middle): *¡Mamá! El bebé llora.*
(2) recurring generally, though not necessarily at PP: *El sol sale a las siete. Juana se lava con Jabondelux. Trabajo en una oficina. Truena mucho en las montañas.*
(3) about to happen (anticipatory, 7.1.2.1): *Se van mañana a las ocho.*
(4) occurs and is completed during observation (= end): (Witness describing a scene as it unfolds—) *El tren entra en la estación; se detiene; salen algunos pasajeros; se les revisa el equipaje.*

With so many possibilities for one tense, Spanish resorts to its progressive to zero in on the first one and to exclude the others. The progressive is thus optional in Spanish; in the context of the example given for (1), *El bebé está llorando* means roughly the same thing as *El bebé llora*,[7] but it excludes from consideration the possibility of senses (2), (3), (4). Backshifted, the imperfect progressive does the same for the simple imperfect, which otherwise can have meanings (1), (2), or (3), (but not (4), which is allocated to the preterite).

In English too, the simple present potentially has all four meanings, but the first—'occurring at PP'—is permitted only with stative verbs such as *be* or *know*. For a process or action verb such as *die* or *fall*, the simple present is *not* used for meaning (1) at all, but the progressive is used instead. Thus, for meaning (1) the English speaker says *I know it* (state) but *I'm dying* (process), not **I'm knowing it* or **I die*; and the equivalent of the first Spanish example is *The baby's crying*, not *The baby cries* (=meaning (2), perhaps (4)). Also unlike the Spanish set-up, English allows meaning (3) to be expressed by either the simple present or the progressive: *They leave tomorrow at eight, They're leaving tomorrow at eight.*

Hence, Spanish uses its progressive as an alternate way of expressing meaning (1), whereas English uses its progressive as an alternate way of expressing meaning (4) and as a form *contrasting* with the simple present for meanings (1) vs. (2), at least for nonstatives. This difference can be diagrammed as in Figure 7.5.

The (partial) optionality of the progressive is to some extent true of the perfect also, which is why Stockwell et al. call both of them 'secondary modifications' (1965:139). That is, just as Spanish *está llorando* can also be handled by *llora*, and English *he's leaving tomorrow* by *he leaves to-*

Figure 7.5 The progressive in relation to the simple present.

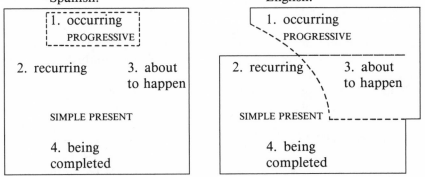

morrow, the perfect lends precision and explicitness but need not be used when 'relevant anteriority' is already clear from context (e.g. because of adverbs and relators), as illustrated in:

Antes que hubieran cenado = Antes que cenaran
Before they'd eaten supper = Before they ate supper

When and if secondary modifications are used, there are as many of them available as there are corresponding simple tenses; in other words, Spanish has more perfects and progressives than English, thanks to its richer tense and aspect system. Perhaps to reduce this burden, some textwriters ignore or discard as literary the preterite perfect and the preterite progressive. Yet both are decidedly in use, and if they are less frequent than other compound forms, it is because the meaning of preterite combined with those of perfect and progressive yields a fairly specialized characterization of an event, and one that accompanying adverbs and relators may make redundant. English *I had finished it* usually describes a situation resulting from some previous event (current relevance for RP), and *I was finishing it* tends to express middle aspect. Hence the probable Spanish equivalents are compound imperfects, *Lo había terminado* and *Lo estaba terminando*. But it is quite possible to emphasize the immediately prior termination of the event:

Cuando hube terminado, me eché una siesta.

and the termination of an ongoing one:

Estuviste jugando bien hasta que tropezaste.

7.3 Mood: Indicative vs. subjunctive. Most references to 'tense categories' and to 'tense systems' so far have applied only to what is called the 'indicative' system. It sometimes dismays students to learn, after what seems to be the light at the end of the tunnel in a rapid succession of Spanish tense forms, that there is a second set of tenses. Their text then names the tenses covered up to that point as 'indicatives', the new set as 'subjunctives', and both as 'modes' or 'moods'. All these terms seem quite mystifying to the student, as are many other terms inherited from ancient grammatical traditions. On taking up the study of Spanish, most students have heard of and can identify 'present tense' and perhaps 'infinitives'; the subjunctive, however, is frequently new to them, and this category is not easily explained.

Some texts point out to students that English also has a subjunctive, as illustrated by the following sentences:

It's urgent that he $\begin{cases} \text{come (*comes)} \\ \text{be on time (*is on time)} \end{cases}$

The English subjunctive may also contrast with indicative forms:

I insist that he drive/drives very carefully.
I suggest that she sign up/is signing up today.
If Frank was/were guilty, . . .

These subjunctives and mood contrasts compare quite well to certain Spanish usages, but they are nevertheless a poor pedagogical point of departure. They are relics, and of little help to students who seldom use them and are unsure of them when they hear or read them. The English subjunctive is moribund, and current usage relies more on modals and infinitival constructions (v. 13.1.2) to convey the nuances expressed by the Spanish subjunctive:

Sugiero que se matricula.	I suggest that she's signing up.
Sugiero que se matricule.	I suggest $\begin{cases} \text{for her to sign up.} \\ \text{that she should sign up.} \end{cases}$

Consequently, students must approach the Spanish subjunctive on its own terms as a grammatical category for which there is essentially no direct English equivalent in English grammar.

7.3.1 The tense system in the subjunctive. The subjunctive is a second tense system, or better, the same system as in the indicative but shifted to another mode or kind of perspective, from the 'creo que . . .' to the 'dudo que . . .' of human perception. Potentially, any proposition that is believed might also be denied, so that for every indicative form there should be a corresponding subjunctive. Actually, the subjunctive system is less elaborate, thanks to two neutralizations. First, posteriority (future for PP, conditional for RP) is not distinguished from simultaneity (present for PP, past for RP): the *vienen* and *vendrán* of *Creo que vienen* vs. *Creo que vendrán* are both *vengan* in the subjunctive—*Dudo que vengan*. Old Spanish had a future subjunctive in -*are*, -*iere* that has largely fallen into disuse; in the modern language, the so-called present subjunctive handles both posteriority and simultaneity. Second, Spanish has never distinguished aspect (preterite/imperfect) in its subjunctive; there are two sets of past subjunctive forms (-*ara* -*iera* and -*ase* -*iese*), but these do not stand for any tense or aspect distinction.[8] Since a form such as *viniera* neutralizes the distinction between *venía* and *vino*, and the one between these and *vendría* as well, the term 'imperfect subjunctive' for it is definitely imperfect; 'past subjunctive' is descriptively more correct. Hence, the ten systemic categories of the indicative are reduced to only four in the subjunctive, as shown in Figure 7.6.

Figure 7.6 Correspondence of tenses between the indicative and the subjunctive.

Tenses	Indicative	Subjunctive
present	(1) vienen	(1) vengan
future	(2) vendrán	
present perfect	(3) han venido	(2) hayan venido
future perfect	(4) habrán venido	
imperfect preterite conditional	(5) venían (6) vinieron (7) vendrían	(3) vinieran (viniesen)
past perfect (imp.) past perfect (pret.) conditional perfect	(8) habían venido (9) hubieron venido (10) habrían venido	(4) hubieran (hubiesen) venido

In imitation of Latin grammar, some scholars have handed down a principle of 'sequence' or 'agreement' of tenses (*concordantia temporum* in Latin), whereby a main verb on Bull's present (PP) axis may introduce any tense in the subordinate clause, but one on the recalled (RP) axis requires that the subordinated verb's tense be of its own system; i.e. 'past' takes 'past.' In the list of forms in Figure 7.6, *Creo que* . . . could introduce options (1) through (10) in the indicative, and *Dudo que* . . . could introduce (1) through (4) in the subjunctive; but *Creía* (*Creí, Creería*) *que* . . . would be limited to taking (5) through (10) in the indicative, and *Dudaba* (*Dudé, Dudaría*) *que* . . . would be limited to (3) and (4) in the subjunctive. Some English scholars have also promoted a version of this principle. But in reality, native speakers do not care for *concordantia temporum*, and they run roughshod over it; perhaps they always have, outside of Latinist circles. According to Gili Gaya (1973:175, 290-293) and Studerus (1979:333-335), modern speakers select the appropriate tense according to the meaning they wish to convey, not according to strict tense-matching. Gili Gaya tries to compromise by reinstating *concordantia* for the subjunctive while giving it up for the indicative; but

Studerus quotes convincing examples of nonagreement in the subjunctive as well, e.g. *Propuso que se fabrique heno en la parte norte de Puerto Rico.* He interprets this as meaning that the speaker sees the event as still unrealized at PP and the unfulfilled proposal as still pending. Gili Gaya notwithstanding, such sentences are now abundant in both the spoken and written versions of the language on both sides of the Atlantic. Knowledgeable teachers might spare their students a foray into the intricacies of *concordantia temporum* and focus on the more important question of the meaning of mood.

7.3.2 The meaning of mood: Theories and approaches. As with treatments of tense categories, two approaches to mood can be distinguished. Some scholars itemize all discernible uses of the subjunctive, and correlate the selection of each use to the choice of verb or relator in the main clause. Others seek in mood contrasts one or two common denominators that subsume the various surface usages; in other words, the subjunctive will have one or two basic meanings, not several discrete ones, and the selection of mood by a speaker will depend on the meaning he wishes to convey, not on main clause cues. The first approach is described in 7.3.2.1, and the other in several theoretical versions in the following sections.

7.3.2.1 The subjunctive as a set of uses conditioned by the main clause. Ramsey (1894/1956:415-457) determined that the use of the Spanish subjunctive is governed by verbs and relators that sort out into the following classes:[9]

command	emotion, feeling	exception
demand, request	impersonal expression	concession
proposal, suggestion	denial, doubt	temporal clause
desire	indefinite relative	of futurity
permission	negative result	imperative
approval, preference	supposition	exclamatory wishes
prohibition, hindrance	proviso	conditions of
		implied negation

Bergen 1978 brought together all such taxonomies he could find and arrived at a total of 34 'separate rules' for the Spanish subjunctive.

Aside from the psychological question of whether 34 rules for one mood can be memorized and applied, and the philosophical question of why such a catch-all category would develop in an otherwise systematic language, this approach is objectionable because it misleads students into thinking that mood selection is entirely dictated by the choice of main verb or conjunction; if they learn enough cases of '*pedir* and *para que* take subjunctive', '*saber* and *porque* take indicative', etc., they will be ready for the fill-in-the-blanks. However, (1) there are too many subjunctive-takers to commit to memory, (2) subjunctive-takers need not take the subjunctive (*Ordenó que hicieran cola, Ordenó que tenían que hacer cola*), and (3) a large number of contexts allow either mood, with a difference in meaning (*Gritó que saltaban/saltaran*). This approach remains popular in some quarters today, but the doubt and uncertainty it engenders in students often last well into the advanced levels of language study.

7.3.2.2 The subjunctive as conveying unreality. Gili Gaya (1973:131-143) focuses on mood in noun clauses, as in *Niego que sean honrados*. On some pages, he follows the traditional approach of cataloging uses, but eventually he reaches a generalization by concluding that most uses reflect just two categories: the (classical) *subjuntivo* of doubt and uncertainty and the *optativo* of necessity and desire. Then he generalizes one step further: both suggest unreality in contrast with the indicative, which expresses reality. That is, both *dudo que* and *deseo que* introduce propositions whose reality at PP is unguaranteed and unrealized. But there is another kind of subjunctive that does not conform to the real/unreal principle: that which follows emotional reactions such as *temo, me alegro, me gusta, espero*, and *es sorprendente*, regardless of whether the situation being reacted to is actual or hypothetical, real or unreal. For example, in *Temo que nos vean* the speaker fears a situation that may or may not come to pass, whereas in *Siento que estés descontenta* he reacts to a situation he apparently grants as an observed reality. For Gili Gaya, the subjunctive of emotional reaction is a special case that overrides the normal contrast; he speculates that it arose through analogy from the reaction-to-something-uncertain case (*Temo que nos vean*), or alternatively, it may follow from the fact that emotion is a subjective state that has 'realidad interna, pero no fuera de nosotros' (Gili Gaya 1973:137)—i.e. emotional reactions are not really real.

7.3.2.3 The subjunctive as a signal of unexperienced events and the influencing of behavior. Bull (1972:174-197) agrees with Gili Gaya that a limited number of principles accounts for mood usage, and that emotional reaction ('psychological response') is one of them. But he points out that some verbs can be used either to express psychological responses (with the subjunctive) or to make reasonable predictions (with the indicative). For example, *temer* with the indicative as in *Temo que ha llegado* expresses no fear at all, but politely says 'creo que . . . '; and *esperar* with the indicative in *Espero que estarán allí* indicates a prediction rather than a hope. Clearly, then, it will be difficult or impossible for students to commit to memory classifications such as the one in 7.3.2.1; verbs such as *temer* and *estar* do not inherently 'take' the subjunctive, but are used with or without it according to whether the speaker intends to express emotional reactions.

Bull's second principle for the subjunctive is similar to Gili Gaya's reality/unreality distinction. The indicative suggests that an event or entity has been experienced and found to be real, whereas the subjunctive suggests that it is unexperienced (anticipated but uncertain, yet to be encountered, unproven). This principle underlies mood contrasts in many noun clauses (*Sé que saldrá* vs. *Dudo que salga*), relative clauses (*Busco un gato que no tiene/tenga pulgas*), and adverbial clauses (*Vamos después que regresan/regresen*). Some expressions (*sin que, para que*) always introduce subjunctives, not because of grammatical requirements but because of their meaning, which is 'as yet unexperienced'; others (*cuando, hasta que, mientras*) can introduce experienced or unexperienced events; with still others, some speakers have generalized one mood while others preserve a contrast (Bull 1972:179-180). An example of this last case is the sentence frame *Se sentaron antes que (llegó/llegara) Jorge*, in which many speakers assume that at RP George's eventual arrival was not a guaranteed certainty and should therefore be expressed by *llegara*; others accept *llegó* if George is known (at PP) to have arrived eventually (his arrival did take place), but they would prefer *llegara* otherwise.

In developing his third principle, Bull notes that one key to the subjunctive is that it SUBJOINS one event to another in a causal way. Cause-and-effect is expressed equally well in *Se abre el grifo y sale el agua* and *Se abre el grifo para que salga el agua*, but the former just joins (links) cause with effect while the latter subjoins or subordinates the effect to the cause, making one dependent on the other. When a verb of communicating introduces a subjoined verb, the indicative will be used in reporting an event while the subjunctive will be used for the special cause-and-effect of attempting to influence behavior. Thus, *Oigo que te vas* merely reports; *Mando que te vayas* aims at the effect of getting the addressee to do something. Verbs such as *decir* can convey either situation, and Bull notes an orderly progression in the quoting of a direct command and the subjoining of an indirect one:

Reporting an event:	Relaying a command:
(1) Papá: ¡Se va!	(1) Papá: ¡Váyase!
(2) Papá dice—¡se va!	(2) Papá dice—¡váyase!
(3) Papá dice que se va.	(3) Papá dice que se vaya.

Yet the principle of influencing behavior is not entirely distinct from that of unreality and nonexperience. At the moment that an attempt is made to affect someone's actions, the implied command is as yet unfulfilled, and one has no guarantee that the desired event will ever materialize. The noun clause of *Mando que regresen* or of *Dice que se vaya* thus expresses a proposition that, for now (at PP), is as unreal as that of *Dudan que regresen* or *Me escondo para que se vaya*.[10]

Jelinski 1977 largely accepts Bull's theory, but he tries to conflate psychological response with influencing behavior as one category, cause-and-effect. With the latter, one attempts to cause some effect, and with the former one describes a fact that causes an effect. But Zlotchew 1977 disagrees, and points out how emotional reactions are both structurally and semantically distinct from other cause-and-effect patterns. Stockwell et al. (1965:241-261) have much the same theory as Bull, but syntactically they believe it advisable to distinguish four patterns: sentences (1) of uncertainty (*dudo que*...), (2) of necessity (*es necesario que*... , *quiero que*...), (3) with unknown or unidentifiable antecedents (*busco un gato que*...), and (4) with adverbial clauses containing events yet to occur or be confirmed (*para que*... , *antes que*...).

7.3.2.4 The subjunctive as optative-dubitative vs. attitude. The pages of the journal *Hispania* were the forum for a lively debate which sharpened linguistic definitions of the parameters of mood usage. It began with Lozano 1972, who elaborated on Gili Gaya's distinction by positing two features governing subjunctive usage, [+optative] and [+dubitative]. Optative expressions are epitomized by *querer*, but include any implicit or explicit command; in fact, for Lozano the emotional reaction expressions such as *es importante que*... and *me gusta que*... are optative too in expressing a speaker's wishes. Dubitative expressions are epitomized by *dudar*, but include any expression of doubt, from strong *negar* to weak *quizás*. Lozano further includes as dubitative those adjective and adverbial clauses of unrealized (unexperienced) entities and events, as well as contrary-to-fact conditional sentences with *si*. He denies that optative and dubitative can be merged into a single principle for the subjunctive, inasmuch as a negated [+optative] expression still takes subjunctive (*no quiero que*...) whereas a negated [+dubitative] one cues a switch to the indicative (*no dudo que*...); that is, there must be two distinct subjunctives. He then proceeds to classify main-clause expressions according to subtypes of optative and dubitative and to illustrate how mood selection in syntax follows from the choice of features; e.g. *llámalo antes de* [+dub] *yo* EMPEZAR → *Llámalo antes de que que yo* EMPIECE (Lozano 1972:84).

Bolinger 1974 replies that Lozano has unnecessarily split asunder what traditional grammarians regarded as one subjunctive. If optative and dubitative main verbs were really distinct, then combining them with one subjunctive clause should be a ZEUGMA (i.e. a nonsensical conjoining[11]); but in the following, Bolinger combines a dubitative, optative, and for good measure, an emotional reaction, with no strangeness at all:

> Es posible, tal vez necesario, pero sin embargo deplorable, que él sea nuestro representante.

He further observes that many expressions can be followed by the subjunctive without clearly belonging to either of Lozano's categories: *es interesante que*... , *es típicamente profesorial que*... , *no tiene ninguna importancia que*...

Bolinger therefore advocates a return to the 'traditional' view that the subjunctive is a single mood conveying a single meaning in its contrast with the indicative. The selection of one over the other does not automatically follow from some syntactic feature but is controlled by the speaker: the indicative shows that the speaker is communicating 'intelligence' (information alone) while the subjunctive conveys an expression of 'attitude' toward information. Even in those cases where one mood is supposedly required, as in Lozano's negated dubitatives, there is some freedom of choice; Bolinger (1974:465), in fact, unearths a subjunctive with affirmative *creo que* . . . :

Creo, señor Gordon, que la prensa de su país no esté bien informada correctamente respecto al Dr. Fidel Castro.

This state of affairs does not make pedagogy easy, but Bolinger believes there is an English clue that can assist students, namely, in whether a 'performative' expression such as *I'm afraid, I assure you, I'm sorry*, or *it's probable* can be used. If a performative can be placed after a clause, then the equivalent Spanish clause will have the indicative; if it cannot, then the clause will have a subjunctive:

He's coming, I think.	Creo que viene.
*He's coming, I don't think.	No creo que venga.
You've broken it, I fear.	Temo que lo has roto.
*You've broken it, I'm sorry.	Siento que lo hayas roto.
I bought a house which has 10 rooms, I assure you.	Compré una casa que tiene 10 cuartos.
*I need a house which has 10 rooms, I assure you.	Necesito una casa que tenga 10 cuartos.

Lozano 1975 counters by noting that Bolinger's theory is not the 'traditional' one at all and by claiming that his optative/dubitative distinction has been misunderstood. He proceeds to explicate these notions more fully and to sort out troublesome cases into a finer classification. As for the speaker's freedom of choice, there is certainly little freedom after *mandar* and *para que*, and certain syntactic constraints limit one's choice even further.

In his 1976 rebuttal, Bolinger reiterates his point that dubitative and optative are just manifestations of speaker attitude. He also repeats his assertion that knowledge of which mood is used for what and where is more than knowledge of Lozano's classifications; for example, how would the latter (or a speaker using them) anticipate a novel but perfectly normal subjunctive in *Yace en la mente de Dios que el hombre obedezca a Sus mandamientos* (1976:44)? Also, Bolinger continues to find counterexamples with subjunctives after affirmative *parece que, estoy seguro que, supongo que*, revealing some degree of choice. If some choices are statistically infrequent or improbable (e.g. the combination of a main verb of commanding with a clause conveying the reporting of intelligence, *Mando que te vas*), this is because of semantic incompatibility, not some arbitrary syntactic feature that compels one to follow up with the right mood after selecting a certain main verb. 'A grammar that creeps along a sentence from left to right and attempts to determine everything on one side from what has already occurred on the other is a fun thing to make up as an exercise in guesswork, but is not true to life' (Bolinger 1976:48).

7.3.2.5 The subjunctive as a marker of presupposition. What Bolinger described as 'speaker attitude' is today described in terms of PRESUPPOSITION. Whenever one makes a statement, he asserts some material but presupposes or assumes as givens other pieces of information. For example, in both *The teacher criticized Jan for cheating* and *The teacher accused Jan of cheating*, the speaker asserts that the teacher openly blamed Jan for having cheated, but his presuppositions are different: with *criticized*, he evaluates the proposition and assumes Jan did indeed cheat, whereas with *accused* he makes no such presupposition but leaves the question open. Many current linguists[12] see in such presuppositional differences the key for understanding mood. That mood contrasts are almost exclusively found in subordinated (Bull's 'subjoined') clauses is highly significant in that placing a proposition in a subordinate clause allows one to set up a syntactic environment in which he can hold it up for comment, appraisal, and inference in the main clause.

Goldin 1974 perceives two distinct patterns in the presuppositional content of the Spanish subjunctive. First, this mood accompanies expressions of emotional reaction because the speaker is then EVALUATING an assumed proposition rather than asserting it. The point of *Me alegro de que vengas* is not that the hearer is coming, which is simply presupposed, but that the speaker finds this news satisfying. Goldin notes that emotionality is not the source of the mood choice, for one can also evaluate something quite unemotionally, as in *Es lógico que tengan la culpa* or Bolinger's *es típicamente profesorial que . . .*

Second, the subjunctive portrays shadings of truth value. Goldin distinguishes three stances a speaker can take in this regard. POSITIVE PRESUPPOSITION is the assumption that the subordinated proposition is true, exists, has happened, has been observed, is certain; NEGATIVE PRESUPPOSITION is the opposite, ranging from denial to hedged reservation; and INDEFINITE PRESUPPOSITION is a suspension of speaker belief one way or the other (the proposition is not necessarily false, but is not concluded to be true either). According to Goldin, then, the indicative conveys positive presupposition (*Es verdad que se van*), while the subjunctive conveys negative (*Es dudoso que se vayan*) or indefinite (*Es posible que se vayan*) presupposition. But with *si*-clauses the system shifts: here, the indicative takes care of both positive (*Esquiamos si nieva*) and indefinite presupposition (*Esquiaremos si nieva*), so that the subjunctive can be reserved just for the negative presupposition of contrary-to-fact (*Esquiaríamos si nevara*).

Goldin believes that it is pedagogically feckless, and linguistically unrealistic, to force mood selection into either/or decisions based on sentential context alone. Like Bolinger, he holds that native speakers do not select mood solely on the basis of conjunctions or main verbs. The speaker's presuppositions may not be clear from the rest of the sentence, so that to choose between moods students should begin with how they, as speakers of a sentence, wish their assumptions to be understood.

Terrell and Hooper 1974 develop a more complex presuppositional theory. In their interpretation, to assert something is to introduce or report it as confirmed, believed, or inferred, whether strongly (*it's certain that . . . , I know that . . .*) or weakly (*it seems that . . . , I gather that . . .*). To presuppose something is to take it for granted and proceed to comment on it. The proposition *She dances* is asserted in *It's obvious that she dances*, presupposed in *It's great that she dances*, and neither asserted nor presupposed in *It's not certain that she dances*. As shown in the following schema, Terrell and Hooper discern two subcases in each of these three, giving six approaches a speaker can take to a proposition:

Asserted:
- (1) by the speaker: *me parece que, sé que, es cierto que*
- (2) by others: *cuentan que, contesta que, se cree que*

Presupposed:
- (3) in the learning of a proposition: *se da cuenta de que, aprende que*
- (4) for commentary: *me alegro de que, es lástima que, es interesante que*

Neither:
- (5) it's doubted: *duda que, niega que, no creo que*
- (6) it's willed: *manda que, quiere que, pido que*

The indicative covers the first three categories, and the subjunctive the last three.

Like others, Terrell and Hooper illustrate their theory by focusing on sentence frames permitting contrasts. *Dice que viene*, for instance, reports another person's assertion (2), while *Dice que venga* relays a command (6), which neither asserts nor presupposes that anyone is necessarily coming at all. And like Goldin, they advocate a departure from the pedagogical practice of filling in blanks with mood forms according to memorized cues in the main clause—which, in *Dice que (viene/venga)*, is impossible anyhow. Instead, students should receive practice in actively manipulating the presuppositional and assertive sides of self-expression; for example, the teacher could introduce a clause such as *Mañana nos visitarán* and invite students to react to it by doubting it, commenting on it, asserting it, wishing it, and so on.

Bergen (1978a:211) strives to reduce all rules, categories, features, and uses of the subjunctive to one principle: 'whereas the indicative denotes that the speaker (or actor) of the higher clause regards his proposition . . . as an objective fact, the subjunctive expresses a subjective reservation on the part of the speaker (or actor) concerning the reality of that proposition.' Others (recall Gili Gaya) saw this principle as explicating most mood contrasts, but Bergen perceives it in all of them and proceeds to use it in explaining a host of interesting examples. There is one problem, however, when the speaker is expressing his attitude toward a proposition that, on the surface at least, is not subordinated, as with *tal vez* + subjunctive in a main clause or even commands. These, for Bergen, are analogous to *es posible que* or *mando que* + subordinated clause, and he posits for them an implicit higher level 'performative' clause: *Te digo que, Te mando que . . .*

Bell 1980 reviews his predecessors and eclectically assembles his own theory of mood. He holds that the subjunctive is used for (1) commenting on a fact, with the presupposition that the hearer may already know the fact but expects a reaction to it, (2) subjective reservations (doubt, noncommitment) about truth value, (3) unrealized or unexperienced entities and events (à la Bull), and (4) indirect commands. Although all these have their roots in speaker presupposition, Bell doubts they can be merged into a single principle, as Bergen attempted to do.

7.3.3 Summary of mood usage. Most of the scholars mentioned in the preceding sections have claimed some pedagogical value for their theories, in that the special principles they posit reflect the factors and options native speakers take into account in deciding between moods. The same factors must be mastered by students if they are to use mood in a native-like manner. The decision making implicit in six of these accounts of mood usage can be represented in terms of flow charts such as those in Figure 7.7, and the reader might wish to use these summaries in comparing the approaches and in evaluating their potential usefulness to students.[13]

Following Gili Gaya, many analysts have viewed the use of the subjunctive with emotional (psychological, evaluative) reactions as a bit wayward, given the more pervasive reality/unreality (or whatever) contrast found elsewhere; this shows up in 'reaction', 'response', 'comment', appearing as separate decisions preceding the others in the flow charts. Interestingly, it also seems a less stable principle in actual (as opposed to prescribed) usage. Lantolf 1977, for example, asked Puerto Rican informants to complete sentences with either of two verb forms, one indicative and one subjunctive. Some of his results are given in Figure 7.8, where the percentages reveal the use of indicative forms after the indicated main clause stimulus. Teachers' eyebrows might rise at the sprinkling of indicatives after *piden que* or *quiero que*, but these are negligible next to the relative surge of indicatives after cues of emotional reaction such as *qué bueno que, se sorprendió de que,* and *se alegró de que.* For Goldin (1974:300), such data suggest that the system is gravitating toward the single contrast of positive versus negative presupposition; Bull (1965:192) likewise infers that psychological responses are beginning to conform to the contrast of experienced/unexperienced, so that the subjunctive is not automatic after *alegrarse* or *temer* but reflects one's perception of the reality of what is being reacted to.

Figure 7.7 Six theories interpreted as decisions speakers make in using mood.

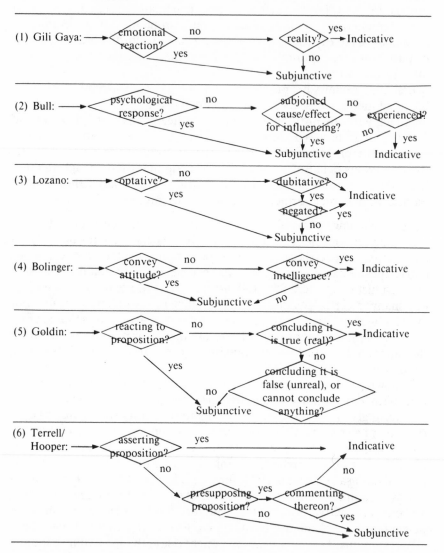

In summary, modern observers have tended toward the position that mood selection in Spanish has less to do with infallible mood-triggers than with the speaker's attitude toward a proposition he places in any subordinated clause. Consequently, the widespread pedagogical practice of filling in blanks according to sentential context is as unrealistic for understanding mood as it is for understanding the two past tenses; as Terrell and Hooper pointed out, students must learn that native speakers actively ex-

Figure 7.8 Puerto Ricans' use of the indicative after selected main-clause cues (Lantolf 1977).

(1) *Piden que* . . .	10%	(8) *¡Qué bueno que* . . .	54%
(2) *Sugiero que* . . .	7%	(9) *Es bueno que* . . .	15%
(3) *Quiero que* . . .	1%	(10) *Se sorprendió de*	
(4) *Es necesario que* . . .	0%	*que* . . .	34%
(5) *Espero que* . . .	1%	(11) *Se alegró de que* . . .	38%
(6) *Es posible que* . . .	14%	(12) *Siempre me sorprende*	
(7) *¡Qué ridículo que* . . .	7%	*el hecho de que* . . .	18%

ploit the contrast in order to convey different meanings. As long as selection is made to depend solely on the rest of the sentence, students cannot be blamed for wondering why Spanish has such apparently useless machinery when the context suffices entirely.

Notes for Chapter 7

1. Many scholars have offered their impressions of the 'overuse' or 'underuse' of certain tense categories in various Spanish dialects. For a more precise, data-based approach to this question, one should consult the thorough study of tense usage by Moreno de Alba (1978), who calculated the statistical frequency of each tense (and of the systemic and nonsystemic applications of each tense) in a sampling of Mexican Spanish.

2. Historically, the English verb forms in the protasis of conditionals are past subjunctives, as they still are in Standard Spanish. But with the decline of the English subjunctive (v. 7.3), few contrasts remain between past indicative and past subjunctive. Educated speakers may still distinguish them in *If she were a thief, she'd tell us* (= contrary-to-fact) vs. *If she was a thief, she'll tell us* (= granting this as quite possible); but the folk have generalized *was* in both, completing the merger.

In Spanish, too, there have been shifts away from the classical standard, and many speakers have generalized one form for both parts of conditional sentences (Bull 1965:161, Kany 1945/1951:159, Gili Gaya 1973:321):

Si yo lo tenía, se lo daba. ⎫
Si yo lo tendría, se lo daría. ⎬ = Si yo lo tuviera, se lo daría.
Si yo lo tuviera, se lo diera. ⎭

3. This description comes from Da Silva and Lovett (1965:4-6). They eventually proceed to a generalization, but this itemized list of uses is representative of what many students recall as the explanation they received.

4. This, in fact, is the strategy adopted by LaMadrid et al. (1974a), who spend parts of three lessons on 'the nature of events' before finally introducing preterite/imperfect.

5. E.g. Gili Gaya (1973:157-162), Ramsey (1894/1956:317-328), Stockwell et al. (1965:136-139), the Real Academia (1924:291), Bull (1965:152-153, 166-170).

6. For example, Guitart has trouble with *quedar(se)* because it 'partitions' or expresses interruption in states that then resume or yield to new ones. In *Irma se quedó dormida viendo televisión*, there is state-ingression, but in *La puerta estaba abierta y así se quedó* it expresses continuation.

7. King and Suñer (1980) disagree. After analyzing numerous examples of the Spanish progressive, they conclude that it not only focuses on the meaning 'occuring now, at PP', but depicts the event as 'unfolding before the speaker's eyes'.

8. The original past subjunctive was the *-se* one; the *-ra* form was a past perfect (pluperfect) indicative displaced by the rise of *había* + past participle. Yet, as Kany (1945/1951:170-174) notes, the *-ra* form survives as a pluperfect among some Spaniards and Americans, at least in cultivated usage. He also notes the lingering use of the future subjunctive in some regions (p. 185), and Jorge-Morel (1974:131) confirms it among upper-class Dominicans: *Si fuere necesario, lo visitaré*. But for Guanajuato, Mexico, Boyd-Bowman (1960:227) finds the more typical situation of *-re* 'en el estilo literario o retórico, en oraciones, proclamaciones y casos parecidos; sentido como arcaísmo, el futuro de subjuntivo sirve para prestar al lenguaje burocrático un tono de solemnidad.' Following common usage, we will equate *-ra* with *-se*, and ignore *-re*.

9. But eventually, Ramsey (1956:465ff.) concludes with inductive generalizations that still compare favorably. Bello took a similar approach, beginning with subjunctive takers (1849/1958:166-168) and arriving at a generalized meaning (p. 220). Textwriters who have followed these two giants of Spanish grammar have not always picked up on their generalizations.

10. Bull encounters problems in applying his theory to *si* clauses. The conditional clause of *Deberás usar botas si llueve* seems just as 'subjoined' as the one in *Deberás usar botas con tal que llueva*, but the two differ in mood. Bull (1972:184-185) is forced to conclude that *que* subjoins but *si* does not. Bello's explanation for the difference is that *si* introduces 'una premisa que se supone alegada o concedida, y de que se saca lógicamente una consecuencia' (1849/1958:220).

11. An English example of zeugma is the oddity in *After breakfast I brush my teeth and hair*, which joins two distinct kinds of brushing.

12. But this is not really a recent discovery. Although he did not use the term *presupposition*, Keniston (1937:163) was on the same track in observing that the subjunctive often introduces 'an approach toward the action or state as an assumption rather than as a fact.'

13. In summarizing the theories in this way, I have borrowed an idea from M. Suñer (personal note), who has had some success in interpreting Goldin's theory with flowcharts for English-speaking students.

Exercises for Chapter 7

1. In each of the following, indicate what other simple tense and mood forms could occur in the same context as the italicized one, and explain the change of meaning.

(1) Es muy dudoso que *viniera* Luis.

(2) Hoy se *cierran* las escuelas.

(3) Ayer a las ocho *ponían* la tele.

(4) Sugirió que María *comprara* tallarines.

(5) Si *llueve, pasaremos* el tiempo jugando a los naipes.

(6) Salen de modo que no *llegan* tarde.

(7) Dijo que te *callarías.*

2. How much transfer value does the English subjunctive have for acquiring Spanish? When it is used, does it conform to much the same principles?

3. Why are progressives and perfects generally postponed in first-year texts? To what extent can the student get along without them in Spanish? Why?

4. It was pointed out that when a Spanish auxiliary verb such as *deber* corresponds to an English modal, the tense distinctions of the former may be difficult to understand. Take the forms *puedo podré podía pude podría* and contrast them with those of *can* and *be able to.* How would you explain them to English speakers?

5. Many Spanish texts utilize fill-in-the-blank exercises for practicing preterite vs. imperfect and indicative vs. subjunctive. To what extent is this either/or approach possible? Can you suggest alternative exercises that might develop more expressive ability with these distinctions?

6. Take a passage from a written or recorded oral narrative in Spanish, and analyze the usage of preterite and imperfect (and present, if it appears), explaining the writer's or speaker's apparent point in selecting each.

7. In traditional approaches, one category of subjunctive usage is 'impersonal expressions'; modern analysts do not distinguish this from other categories. Which expressions are meant? Why can they be merged with other principles?

8. The following examples are from the Spanish newspaper *El País (Internacional).* Explain the italicized subjunctives.

(1) (From an interview with president Siles Zuazo of Bolivia, 13/II/1984:7):

pregunta: ¿Qué le parece que España *haya* firmado esa declaración?

respuesta: Creo que la presencia de España es una evolución . . . muy positiva.

(2) (From an editorial on the French attitude toward Spanish entry in the Common Market, ibid., p. 8):

Que el presidente Mitterand lo *haya* proclamado ahora en una ocasión particularmente solemne tiene aún más valor si se recuerda que no siempre ha sido tal su actitud.

(3) (Comment by the leader of the Guatemalan Christian Democrats on the military regime's decision to hold elections, 9/VII/1984:2):

No hay que pensar que el Ejército se ha vuelto demócrata porque el Espíritu Santo le *haya* pasado por encima. Ha tomado una decisión estratégica . . . reversible.

9. Summarize the uses of the Spanish conditional and future. Which are systemic? Which nonsystemic ones might be interpreted as extensions of the basic meaning? To what extent do these tenses match the English modals *will, would, shall, should*?

10. What mergers of indicative categories occur in passing to the subjunctive? What advantage is there in calling the 'imperfect' subjunctive simply 'past'?

11. Which uses (applications, principles) of the subjunctive do English speakers seem to have the most trouble with? Least? Which ones are prescribed in some grammars but not consistently adopted by native speakers in current usage?

12. In your experience as student or teacher, what tense and aspect errors do beginning and intermediate students of Spanish tend to make? Which categories do they overuse, and underuse? Which errors reflect a transfer of the English system? (Alternatively, you might turn this into a research project and carry out an error analysis of a recorded sample of a student's Spanish.)

13. Draw up a plan for your 'ideal' textbook by indicating the sequence in which Spanish verb categories (tenses, aspects, moods, periphrastic formations) should be taken up. To guide your thoughts, consider the following questions:

(1) How would you rank all these in order of difficulty in (1) morphology and (2) meaning and usage?

(2) How would you rank their systemic and nonsystemic functions (from most to least basic)?

(3) How would you rank them in order of communicative need (from indispensable and frequent to optional or uncommon)?

(4) How would you need to sequence them because of interrelatedness in morphology and meaning? (That is, all agree that preterites must precede past subjunctives because of morphological reasons, and that the conditional—though morphologically related to the future—often pairs off with past subjunctives.)

(5) What other points of morphology and syntax must be covered before a given verb category makes its appearance? (That is, obviously relative and noun clauses must be explained along with or before the use of mood in them.)

Combine these rankings into a sequence that seems as balanced as possible to you. Compare your results with those of your classmates and defend your decisions.

14. With regard to your 'ideal' setup in number 13, would you alter this for second-year and third-year courses? Why? What new considerations might then apply? At what point should the overall system (as in Figures 7.3, 7.5, and 7.6) be presented as a whole?

15. This chapter has treated mood in some depth in order to present a variety of ideas on explaining mood contrasts to students who seldom use them in their English. Apply this information now by studying the following examples of the two moods and addressing the following points:

(1) To what extent do the textbook explanations you are most familiar with cover these?

(2) How well do the theories discussed in this chapter account for them?

Whether by synthesizing others' theories or by developing your own point of departure, try to describe how you understand Spanish mood contrasts and how you would explain them to students. Compare your ideas with those of your classmates.

Indicative only (or usually):
(1) El sol sale/salió/saldrá/saldría/salía a las seis.
(2) (Recuerdo, sé, me doy cuenta de) que no sabes mi número.
(3) (Consta, es verdad, es obvio, es evidente, es seguro, estoy seguro de) que se muere.
(4) (Ven, oyen, observan, notan, perciben, comprenden) que es algo difícil.
(5) (Declaro, afirmo, supongo) que no lo merecen.
(6) (Salimos, saldremos) si hace buen tiempo.
(7) (Esta es la mujer que) denunció el robo.
(8) (Volvieron porque, ya que, puesto que) les dolían los pies.
(9) (Volviste después que, cuando, en cuanto) surgieron problemas.
(10) (Me dijo que) llovió, llovería.

Subjunctive only (or usually):
(1) (Puede, es (im)posible, es (im)probable, es (in)concebible) que jueguen.
(2) (No es verdad, no es cierto, no es evidente, no es) que lo sepan.
(3) (Rechazo, dudo, es dudoso) que la paguen.
(4) (Prohibo, impido, me opongo a, no es lícito) que Ud. lo estacione aquí.
(5) (Mando, exijo, ruego, pido, quiero, prefiero, se permite) que lo hagas así.
(6) (Necesito, es necesario, es importante, conviene, es regla general) que asistan.

(7) (Me gusta, nos sorprende, me alegro, celebro, estoy contento de) que os caséis.

(8) (Es un milagro, es triste, es desdeñable, es típico) que se hayan escapado.

(9) (Cruzan la calle antes que, sin que, con tal que, a menos que, para que) los vea el policía.

(10) (Saldríamos si, salían como si) hiciera buen tiempo.

(11) Ojalá que no llueva/lloviera.

Both, in contrast:

(1) (Dijo, escribió, murmuró, hizo señas de) que firmaban/firmaran el contrato.

(2) (Insisto, advierto, propongo, sugiero) que no comen/coman productos lácteos.

(3) (Sospecho, temo, siento) que se van/vayan. Espero que se irán/vayan.

(4) (El ateísta no cree, no sabe, no está convencido de) que hay/haya un ser supremo.

(5) (Confío en, no es dudoso) que se ha/haya resuelto el problema.

(6) (Es necesario confesar, es lógico) que lo ha/haya estrangulado.

(7) Se trata de que todos son/sean respetados.

(8) (Te dejaré el libro que, cuando, como, donde) quieres/quieras.

(9) (Vienen aunque, siempre que) nieva/nieve.

(10) No fallas porque eres/seas incapaz (sino por la pereza).

(11) (Dijo que vendrían en cuanto, después que, cuando) se acabó/acabara la fiesta.

(12) Por muy difícil que parece/parezca el asunto, vamos a solucionarlo.

(13) Luis va cortando los árboles de modo que caen/caigan lindamente.

(14) Quizás tiene/tenga razón.

(*Feel free to add examples of other instances.*)

Chapter 8
Noun phrase syntax and morphology

8.0 Nouns and noun phrases. A noun together with its adjacent modifiers, if any, constitutes a NOUN PHRASE, NP. Since pronouns (v. 9.0) and noun clauses (v. 13.0.1-13.1.3) occur in the same positions and with the same functions, linguists generalize and call these NPs too. NPs are conspicuous in grammar because of their functional relationships with verbs and because of phenomena such as agreement holding inside them.

8.1 Functions of noun phrases with verbs. NPs have five main roles in the syntax of both Spanish and English: SUBJECT (Subj), DIRECT OBJECT (DO), INDIRECT OBJECT (IO), PREDICATE ELEMENT (PredE), and OBJECT OF A PREPOSITION (Obj of Prep, or OP). These are illustrated in Figure 8.1. Of the

Figure 8.1 Subject (Subj), direct object (DO), indirect object (IO), predicate element (PredE), and object of a preposition (OP).

Subj:
El caballo comenzó a correr.   *The horse* started to run.
DO:
Ayer vimos *el caballo*.   Yesterday we saw *the horse*.
IO:
(*Le*)[1] di heno *al caballo*.   I gave *the horse* hay.
PredE:
El animal más bello es *el caballo*.   The most beautiful animal is *the horse*.
OP:
Pasaron por detrás d*el caballo*.   They passed behind *the horse*.

---

five, PredE—the traditional 'predicate nominative' (v. 11.1.2.2)—and OP (v. 10.2.3) are rather straightforward; PredE follows a copula (verb of being) and OP is always governed by a preposition. The other functions, however, are more elusive and harder to define to students. Those with prior grammatical training in English may have a kind of feel for them that can help when they undertake the study of Spanish. But many students today lack such a background, and the burden of explaining Subj, DO, and IO falls on the Spanish teacher. Describing these notions of general grammar adequately will inevitably deflect valuable classtime from practice with Spanish grammar in particular; yet the teacher who economizes by offering oversimplified definitions may find students even more confused.

8.1.1 Subject and direct object. Suppose that we follow traditional grammar and instruct students that Subj is the doer or agent, that entity that acts upon the verb and carries out the event. This works for most verbs of action, as in *Luisa saltó* or *Luisa me abrazó*, but what is to be done with the following?

$$
\text{Luisa}
\begin{cases}
\text{padece una enfermedad grave} \\
\text{ve un letrero} \\
\text{recibe cartas} \\
\text{está sin empleo} \\
\text{se parece a mi tía} \\
\text{huele a cebolla}
\end{cases}
$$

In these sentences, Luisa does nothing, carries out nothing, acts upon nothing; she is, in fact, quite passive. If we analogize from actors and actions and use 'agent' for explicating subjecthood in general, it is only as an approximation.

As for DO, the traditional definition that this is the NP that 'receives' the action is literally in trouble with the receiving Subj of *recibir* and runs aground elsewhere too:

$$
\text{Jorge}
\begin{cases}
\text{oyó} \\
\text{admiró} \\
\text{comprendió} \\
\text{grabó} \\
\text{recordó} \\
\text{comentó}
\end{cases}
\text{a Jruschov.}
$$

Here, Khruschev received nothing from Jorge, was not acted upon in any clear sense, and may never have been directly affected by Jorge's behavior. *A Jruschov* merely completes directly (whence the Spanish term *complemento directo*), in a purely syntactic sense, the grammatical constituent beginning with the verb, i.e. the verb phrase (VP) of the sentence.

As a second approach, one might appeal to syntactic characteristics, telling students that (1) Subj precedes the verb and DO follows it, (2) Subj is the NP a verb *must* have while DO is optional, and (3) Subj is the NP the verb agrees with. Of these, only (3) is reliable; but it is entirely circular since verbs agree with Subj NPs because these are Subj. The other two work fairly well in English but not in Spanish. In English, Subj precedes the verb (unless rearranged by transformations, v. 12.1-12.4), but Spanish word order is freer (v. 11.2.2); word order is thus unreliable for Subj and DO in *A Sergio lo odian todos sus vecinos*. As for optionality, it is true that English permits *John ate the custard* and *John ate*, but not just **Ate* or **Ate the custard*, so Subj is the required NP and DO is the optional one. But Spanish surface structure requires neither: *Juan comió el flan, Juan* *comió, Comió, Comió el flan.* Of course, the last two sentences have an 'understood' or underlying Subj—*Juan*, or *él*—that is deleted after leaving its trace on the verb ending. But meteorological *hacer* and existential *haber* take DO but not Subj (v. 11.1.1), and *llover* and *tronar* normally take neither. In these cases, Spanish uses its third singular verb form not out of agreement with any underlying Subj but because this is the unmarked, semantically most neutral form (Suñer 1982:182); *-o, -s, -mos, -n* convey more specific person and number information. Hence, Subj is optional in Spanish; English, on the other hand, requires Subj even in these cases, adopting an *it* with no reference and no meaning: *It's hot, It rained, It thundered* (v. 9.1.2).

Subj and DO are real notions of grammar and crucial ones for agreement, pronominalization, use of personal *a*, and word order. Yet they do not convey any single meanings consistent with all verbs. Fortunately, the Subj and Obj specifications of most Spanish verbs resemble those of their English counterparts, so that if the student knows that the Subj of *sow* or *plant* is not the seed or the field but the sower, he can transfer this same knowledge to how *sembrar* is constructed. That, in fact, is implicit whenever *sembrar* or any other verb is given in a vocabulary list with an English gloss and the student is thereupon expected to be able to use it. In the next three sections, however, we see less agreement.

8.1.2 Indirect object or involved entity. The IO in English is any entity to which or for which the Subj 'verbs' the DO. This entity need not be a person or even animate: *I gave my fullest attention to John/to the puppy/to the dahlias/to philosophy/to the issue at hand.* A grammatical test for it is that the *to* or *for* can be deleted, whereupon the IO flips over the DO: *I gave John/the puppy/the dahlias/philosophy/the issue at hand my fullest attention.* By this test, the last NP in *I mailed the letter to Africa* is not IO (**I mailed Africa the letter*), but the one in *I mailed the letter to Alfred* is (*I mailed Alfred the letter*).[2]

But English criteria again fail us in Spanish. *A* accompanies many DO nouns (v. 11.2.3) and all IO nouns, so the presence of a 'to' in front of NP does not uniquely signal IO in Spanish. Also, there is no IO-DO inversion rule: the transformation *(le) di la cerveza a Juan → *(le) di Juan la cerveza* is impossible. But the main difference is that the IO is used with a much broader meaning in Spanish, not being restricted just to giving-to or doing-for. It represents a generalized interest in, participation in, or effect from the Subj + verb (DO) event or relationship. Consequently, Bull (1965:258) finds pedagogical value in renaming it the INVOLVED ENTITY. The specific role of the involvement depends on the nature of the event— i.e. on the verb—and the most common possibilities are illustrated below (see also Goldin 1972, Davis 1969, Real Academia 1979:205 for other examples).

$$\text{Elena le}\begin{cases}\text{dio/mandó/ escribió/mostró una carta } a\\\quad\textit{Juan.}\\\text{hizo/cocinó/preparó la comida } a \textit{ Juan.}\\\text{quitó/exigió/escondió/robó la llave } a \textit{ Juan.}\\\text{puso/echó otra sábana } a \textit{ Juan.}\\\text{notó/observó cierto desdén } a \textit{ Juan.}\\\text{apuntó/cambió/revisó el número}\\\quad a \textit{ Juan.}\end{cases}$$

'...to John'
'...for John'
'...from John'
'...on John'
'...in John'
'...of John,
John's'

Many texts do not explain to students this generalized meaning of loose involvement or prepare them for understanding and using the un-English IOs of *Le tiene miedo a Juan, Le queda muy ajustado a Juan, Le saqué provecho a Juan, Le quieren algo a Juan*, etc. Most do, however, note at least the corollary case of involvement as possessor:

$$\text{Elena le}\begin{cases}\text{lavó el pelo } a \textit{ Juan}\\\text{amarró los pies } a \textit{ Juan}\\\text{admiró la estrategia } a \textit{ Juan}\\\text{levantó las piernas } a \textit{ Juan}\end{cases}$$

'...washed John's hair'
'...bound John's feet'
'...admired John's strategy'
'...raised John's legs'

That such IOs are nevertheless not equivalent to possessive *de* phrases is cogently argued by Kliffer 1979, who, like Bull, insists that casting an NP as IO rather than as object of *de, para, por*, etc. more strongly involves the entity in the event.[3]

With such broadness of meaning and multiplicity of specific roles, the Spanish IO is occasionally ambiguous: *Elena le compró la moto a Juan* can express a purchase from John, or for his benefit. Fortunately, the ambiguity is more potential than real in most contexts.

8.1.3 Variation between direct and indirect objects. In Spanish, both kinds of verbal Obj can be marked by *a*, and the distinction is observed in pronouns only in the third person nonreflexive, and is shaky even there (v. 9.1.3, 9.2, 9.4.1). Hence, DO and IO contrast most distinctly just when both simultaneously accompany the same verb, as in the following VPs:

aconsejar(les) la buena conducta a los niños
enseñar(les) la biología a los alumnos
reñir(le) el descuido a la mecanógrafa

Cuervo (1948:338) observes that when these verbs are used only with the *a*-phrases (i.e. for the meanings 'advise the children', 'teach the pupils', 'fuss at the typist'), it is unclear whether *a* + NP stays IO or becomes DO. In fact, even in *loísta* zones, one can hear both *aconsejarlos, enseñarlos, reñirla* and *aconsejarles, enseñarles, reñirle*. To these three variable-object verbs can be added a host of others: *ayudar, cansar, llamar, honrar, aventajar, escuchar, obligar, estorbar, convencer, pegar, hacer* and *ver* + V-inf (*hacer sufrir a alguien*, v. 13.1.2.5), and most verbs of emotional reaction (*sorprender, preocupar, inquietar, molestar, temer, alentar, alegrar*, etc.). Is this a kind of free variation—either Obj is permissible with no semantic difference—or will the Spanish speaker mean something different in choosing *aconsejarlos* over *aconsejarles* and *ayudarlo* over *ayudarle*?

García and Otheguy (1977) insist on the latter interpretation. Returning to a case where objects contrast, *Yo le di una carta a Juan*, they postulate that Subj is the most active and potent participant, DO is the least, and IO falls in between, being less active than Subj but more potent than DO. When there is one Obj, they perceive the same contrast: the speaker's strategy will be to use *verlo, ayudarlo, aconsejarlo* for an inactive Obj, *verle, ayudarle, aconsejarle* for a more active or potent one.

To test this hypothesis, they gave native speakers from six countries (Spain, Ecuador, Mexico, Argentina, Colombia, Cuba) a questionnaire in which *le, lo*, or *la* was to be placed in blanks accompanying forms of *ayudar, llamar, distraer, ver salir*. They found that the incidence of *le* rose when Subj was inanimate and relatively less potent; i.e. *le distrajo* was more likely for the Subj *el ruido* than for the Subj *Luisa*. The incidence of *le* also rose a bit when the referent was clearly a male, a finding they ingeniously harmonized with their theory.[4]

If this theory is carefully constrained, it could have merit. In a different experiment, Hurst (1951) limited the objects to feminine humans (to bypass the *loísmo/leísmo* problem, v. 9.2.2). She found that choices between IO and DO were affected by two main factors. First, the more forceful, physical, or dynamic the event, the greater the preference was for DO with single-Obj verbs; thus, the incidence of DO rose higher with *irritar* 'physically irritate (e.g. the skin)' and *sorprender* 'show up unexpectedly' than for the same verbs meaning 'irk' and 'amaze'. Second, the incidence of IO shot up when the Subj was nonhuman. Both findings mesh with the García-Otheguy theory, but Hurst carefully states them as tendential, not absolute. That is, potency scales affect the role selection of NPs, but do not completely dictate it. As we saw earlier, Subj is not necessarily active or potent, and IO—though always expressing some kind of involvement in Bull's sense—can be passive, remote, and impotent (Keniston 1937:62). This is particularly evident in the construction of *gustar*, a verb that takes IO, not DO, regardless of how actively or passively one likes something, and its Subj is typically inactive. The García-Otheguy principle is to some extent constrained by another basic fact of the language: NP roles are often determined by the verb, as shown in the next section.

8.1.4 Different construction, 'reverse' construction. English and Spanish do not always agree on how to cast the NPs accompanying their verbs (i.e. on the verb's construction with NPs, or *régimen*, as it is called in Spanish grammar):

wait *for the bus* (OP)   esperar *el autobús* (DO)
look *for a book* (OP)   buscar *un libro* (DO)
look *at the stoplight* (OP)   mirar *el semáforo* (DO)
answer, ask, write *Dad* (DO)   contestar, preguntar,
                                     escribir*le a Papá* (IO)

ask { *a friend* (DO) *for money* (OP)   pedir*le dinero* (DO)
    { *for money* (OP) *from a friend* (OP)   *a un amigo* (IO)

Part of the problem is that certain verbs in both languages require special prepositions in order to join up with an Obj NP (v. 10.4.2). But more generally, each verb seems to impose its own special grammatical *régimen*. Searching and waiting do not require OP in English for semantic reasons, for alongside *wait for* and *look for* there are the synonyms *await* and *seek*, which take DO. And in giving, the presenter and the beneficiary are not irrevocably Subj and IO, since alongside *Fulano le da algo a Zutano* one can say *Zulano recibe algo de Fulano* for the same event.

All texts take up this problem at least in REVERSE CONSTRUCTION, by which is meant any case in which English and Spanish verbs have exactly opposite *régimen*. The prototype is *like/gustar*, and in dealing with *Mary* (Subj) *likes oranges* (DO) vs. *A María le* (IO) *gustan las naranjas* (Subj), different writers have proposed different learning strategies. One of the least conventional is that of LaMadrid et al. (1974a:350ff.), who introduce *gustar* only after preparing a cognitive grounding for it. First, they have students consider their English verb *disgust*, with which the displeased person appears as Obj and the unpleasant entity as Subj: *Mangos disgust Mary*. Spanish *disgustar* is similar, though the Obj is specifically IO: *Los mangos le disgustan a María. Dis-* is a negative prefix, as in *displease, distrust, disobey*; hence the opposite of *disgust* should be **gust*. Of course, English has no such verb in reality (aside from *gusting winds*), but one can get used to thinking in terms of it with a little imagination and practice: *Mangos disgust Mary but oranges 'gust' her a lot*. Spanish definitely has 'gust', it takes IO like *disgustar*, and presumably students are now ready for *Las naranjas le gustan a María* or *A María le gustan las naranjas* (for word order, v. 11.2.3, 11.3.1).

Unfortunately, there are other reverse construction verbs, as shown in Figure 8.2, and inventing a one-time crutch for *gustar* takes the student no farther than this verb alone. The real problem here is not a lexical gap where *gust* should be in English, but the fact that many states and emotional reactions gravitate toward the pattern Subj + verb + IO in Spanish whereas English actually allows several options, as illustrated in Figure 8.2. One option corresponding to *gustar, please*, is much closer to it syntactically than *like*, and if students must use an English bridge in mastering *gustar, Oranges are pleasing to me* might be preferable over *Oranges gust me*. Similarly, although *importar* can be translated as *care about* and *parecer* as *think of*, *matter* and *seem* are closer syntactically.

Figure 8.2 Some reverse-construction verbs and their English equivalents.

Spanish:	English:
CAER	
Te cae bien ese suéter.	That sweater looks good on you.
	You look good in that sweater.
COSTAR	
Eso me costó muchísimo.	I had a lot of trouble with that.
	That was really hard for me.
DOLER	
Le duelen las encías.	His gums hurt (him), are hurting (him).
	He has sore gums.
ENCANTAR	
Nos encanta este tiempo.	We love this weather.
	We're delighted with this weather.
	We find this weather delightful.
	This weather delights us.
FALTAR	
Te faltan tres botones.	You're missing three buttons.
	You lack three buttons.
	Three buttons are missing (on your . . .)
GUSTAR	
Les gusta el queso francés.	They like French cheese.
	French cheese pleases/is pleasing to them.
IMPORTAR	
Tú me importas, hijito.	I care about you, son.
	You matter to me, son.
	You're important to me, son.
INTERESAR	
Le interesan los retratos.	Portraits interest her.
	She's interested in portraits.
	She finds portraits interesting.
MOLESTAR	
Les molesta la humedad.	Wetness bothers them.
	They find wetness bothersome.
	They're bothered by wetness.
QUEDAR	
Nos queda sólo uno.	We've only got one left.
	Only one is left for us.
	Only one remains to us.
	We're left with just one.

Nor is a language that can recast *dar* as *recibir* stuck with reverse construction in these matters:

A Juan le gusta el drama. Juan gusta del drama.
A Juan le faltan recursos. Juan carece de recursos.
A Juan le hace falta un estudio avanzado. Juan necesita un estudio avanzado.

Especially versatile are verbs of emotional reaction and their reflexives (v. 9.3.7):

A Juan le aburre el arte. Juan se aburre del arte.
A Juan le interesa el comercio. Juan se interesa en/por el comercio.
A Juan le enfadó su novia. Juan se enfadó con su novia.

The converse patterns are not always synonymous, but grammatically one does have some choice in verb construction for the casting of NPs. The choices need not be grasped by the beginner, for whom a thorough mastery of an almost formulaic *me gusta(n)* is laudable enough in active language. But at higher levels, the student must see that in both languages, the speaker has alternative modes of expression, each triggering syntactic concomitants.

8.2 Noun morphology. The main or 'head' element of NP is the noun (N), and it shows two main properties or SYNTACTIC FEATURES with which inflected modifiers agree: number and gender. Both are fundamental in morphology, and both tie in with how humans perceive and organize nature.

8.2.1 Number and the count/mass distinction. In most languages of Europe and western Asia, the noun is inflected for number. The ancestor of many of these languages, Proto-Indo-European, made a three-way distinction among SINGULAR (one of something), DUAL (two of something, a pair), and PLURAL (three or more). Some of its daughter languages retained this arrangement, but in the historical processes leading to Spanish (and other Romance languages) and to English (and other Germanic languages), it was reduced to just two terms, SINGULAR (one of something) and PLURAL (two or more).

It seems a universal tendency (Greenberg 1963:94) in languages with a number distinction that the UNMARKED form (the plain, unadorned one) serves for the singular while the MARKED one (the one with something added) represents the plural. Thus, in both Spanish and English, the singular ending is Ø (nothing, no suffix) but the plural has a suffix—or suffixes, for the plural morpheme has allomorphs:

Spanish		English	
-es / $\left.\begin{array}{c} C \\ G \end{array}\right\}$ ____ (color-*es*)		-əz / sibilant _____	(bush-*es*)[5]
-s / V ____ (taza-*s*)		-s / voiceless _____	(hat-*s*, cup-*s*)
		-z / voiced _____	(dog-*s*, row-*s*, pin-*s*)

This comparison illustrates a recurrent theme in contrastive analysis: superficially, one notes a close convergence that could facilitate the language-learner's task, but with further scrutiny, differences appear that make the similarity dissipate like a mist. Here, both languages use alveolar sibilants to represent the plural and sometimes insert a vowel in front of them, resemblances that are reinforced by the same spelling for the sibilants (*s*) and for the inserted vowel (*e*). Yet the sibilant is [s] in Spanish but most often [z] in English; the inserted vowels (respectively [e] and [ə]) are different; and the insertion occurs in a different place (after sibilants [č ǰ š ž s z] in English, after all consonants and glides in Spanish; hence, Eng. *color*[z], *ray*[z], but Span. *color*[es], *rey*[es]). As Stockwell et al. (1965:46) observe, such differences of detail can rob the apparent convergence of useful transfer value.

In at least four other particulars, the pluralization patterns of the two languages seem more alike than they really are. First, a few nouns have a Ø plural suffix (i.e. the sibilant ending is dropped or silent), so that the singular and plural are homonyms. In English these are unpredictable from the sound or spelling: *these sheep*Ø (but *these heaps*), *these deer*Ø (but *these steers*). But in Spanish the deletion is predictable: /s/ drops after any unstressed vowel plus *s*:

$$s \rightarrow \emptyset \: / \: \ldots \breve{V}s+ \underline{\quad} \#$$

Hence, *el/los lunes, el/los miércoles, el/los análisis, el/los atlas, la/las caries, el/los paraguas, el/los cumpleaños* (but because of the final stress, *compás compases*). The deletion also occurs regularly after -$\breve{V}t$ (*el/los déficit, superávit*) and with family names (*los Montano*).[6]

Second, some words have not settled into the normal patterns. In English, these include (1) a few irregular Germanic plurals (*man men, foot feet*) and (2) learnèd Latin or Greek words that variably retain their classical plurals (*antennae~antennas, cacti~cactuses, curriculums~curricula*, etc.) The loanwords that vary in Spanish are recent ones from English and French ending in a consonant: *clubs~clubes, zigzags~zigzagues, gánsters~gánsteres*.

Third, in both languages some nouns are always plural, and in this regard *scissors* and *tongs* converge nicely with *tijeras* and *tenazas*. But *pliers* and *pants* are plural whereas Spanish has *un alicate* vs. *dos alicates* and (for many speakers) *un pantalón* vs. *dos pantalones*. *Clothes* is plural, *ropa* is singular; *vacation* and *funeral* contrast with *vacations* and *funerals* but Spanish speakers often generalize the plurals *vacaciones* and *funerales*; the number for nouns in -*ics* (*acoustics, tactics, genetics, politics*) is variously treated in English while -*ica* is straightforwardly singular in Spanish. *People* has no overt plural suffix but it is plural nonetheless (*these people are . . .*),[7] but *gente* is singular, although *gentes* can be used for particular individuals or groups.

Fourth, in both languages some nouns are ordinarily not pluralized at all because they are mass nouns. In our environment, some entities occur as individual units with physical boundaries delineating them from the rest of the world: *carrot, car, pen, island, animal, planet.* These are COUNT NOUNS, because their referents are discrete and stable enough to be counted in quantity: *one carrot, two cars, three pens . . .* In languages with a singular/plural distinction, all count nouns can be pluralized. But other entities occur not as self-contained things that can be counted, but as shapeless substance or abstraction: *water, soil, peace, air, gravitation.* The nouns referring to these are MASS NOUNS, and they contrast with count nouns, as shown in Figure 8.3.

Figure 8.3 Grammatical differences between count and mass nouns.

	Count noun (*car, carro*)	Mass noun (*air, aire*)
(1) pluralized?	yes	no
(2) countable?	yes	no
(3) occur with *a(n), un*?	yes	no
(4) occur with *some* [sm̩], *much, un poco de*?	no	yes

But it is necessary to qualify somewhat the generalization that mass nouns are uncountable. One can indeed count them, indirectly, by imposing form or measure on them, as in *a cup of water, two cubic feet of air, three bars of soap.* Expressions such as *a bar of* are called COUNTERS and they can contrast interlingually: *three bars of soap, tres panes de jabón* (see Stockwell et al. 1965:82ff. for other examples). Also, one can pluralize mass nouns not to indicate exemplars of a count entity but servings (*two milks, please*) or types (*sugars* and *salts* in chemistry) of the substance. More limited is a third practice of pluralizing mass nouns for metaphorical senses: *take the waters* or *hacer las paces.*

The count/mass distinction is not an obvious one when extended to things that are not readily classifiable as either discrete units or shapeless substance. *Egg* is a count noun when the egg is bounded by a shell or emptied into a single puddle, but smeared or scrambled it becomes a mass noun, as in *You've got egg (*an egg) on your chin. Rock* and *stone* can denote a substance (building material) or a discrete piece of it (something to throw). And when looking at rice, does one see a mass of white substance (as with flour) or a pile of small things (as with peas)? The grammatical solutions to such quandaries can be arbitrary, and two languages may not arrive at exactly the same classification. English and Spanish happen to agree that *egg/huevo* and *stone/piedra* can be count or mass, and that *rice/ arroz* should be mass, but there are many cases where they diverge, as shown in Figure 8.4. If there is any general tendency here, it is that Spanish more readily 'countifies' than English (Stockwell et al., ibid.). Thus, the English speaker may resist pluralizing a Spanish noun which, from his

Figure 8.4 Differences in mass/count classification of nouns.

(a) Eng. mass noun vs. Span. count noun	
(a piece of) furniture	mueble, -s
(a slice of) toast	tostado, -s
(a bolt of) lightning	rayo, -s
(an item of) news	noticia, -s
(a piece of) candy	dulce, -s
	bombón, -es
(a bit of) advice	consejo, -s
(a piece of) equipment	equipo, -s
(a piece of) junk	porquería, -s

(b) Eng. mass noun vs. Span. mass or count noun	
(a piece of) clothing	ropa(s)
(a point of) information	información(es)
(a piece of) luggage	equipaje(s)
(a stick of) chalk	tiza(s)
(a stick of) gum	chicle(s)
(an act of) stupidity	estupidez(es)
(a round of) applause	aplauso(s)
(an item of) business	negocio(s)
(a bout of) diarrhea	diarrea(s)

perspective, is obviously mass; and since dictionaries do not identify the countness of nouns, the student will obtain little help there. But with gender, dictionaries are much more informative.

8.2.2 Gender. The rationale for a gender distinction resembles that for count/mass, but it tends to be more salient to biological language users. Just as in nature there are many entities which are easily classifiable as count or mass, some entities are clearly of either male or female sex. This is the origin of the masculine/feminine distinction in Spanish (*el muchacho, la muchacha*) and in English (*the boy . . . he, the girl . . . she*)— or more generally, in Indo-European.

But like count/mass, gender becomes blurred when extended to the large realm of sexless things. In Proto-Indo-European, the distinction became grammaticalized and all nouns—sexed or sexless—came to be classified as MASCULINE, FEMININE, or NEUTER ('neither'), frequently with great arbitrariness. Latin inherited this setup, but as it passed on to Spanish, the neuter dropped out ('neuter' *lo, esto*, etc. evolving in a different direction, v. 8.4.2). This was just as well, since the Latin neuter included some obviously sexed creatures and its masculine and feminine already swarmed with sexless things and abstractions. English went a step further by dropping the gender distinction entirely except for obviously sexed referents; something that is sexually neither a *he* nor a *she* is an *it*.[8]

In Spanish it is almost impossible to use a noun without marking its gender, thanks to the required agreement of its modifiers. Spanish speakers therefore get abundant practice with gender from infancy onward and the decision to say *la sal es blanca* instead of **el sal es blanco* takes no more conscious effort than for an adult English speaker to say *he thought* instead of **he thinked*. But masculine and feminine seem unfathomable to English speakers, especially for things. Why are *lecho asiento idioma rostro* masculine but their synonyms *cama silla lengua cara* feminine? Is it *el* or *la mar*, *el* or *la fin*?[9]

Fortunately, gender is partly predictable. One clue is orthographic/phonemic, namely, how the noun ends. Expanding on the traditional rule of thumb that -*o* signals masculines (usually) and -*a* feminines (usually), Bull (1965:109) offers the statistics in Figure 8.5 for the gender of nouns

Figure 8.5 Bull's statistics on gender classification according to noun ending.

-n	(not counting -*ción*, -*sión*): 96.3% M	-l:	96.6% M
-o:	99.7% M	-a:	98.9% F
-r:	99.2% M	-d:	97% F
-s	(not counting -*tis*, -*sis*): 92.7% M	-*ción*, -*sión*: 100% F	-*sis*, -*tis*: 99.2% F
-e:	89.2% M		

ending in -*n*, -*o*, -*r*, -*s*, -*e*, -*l*, -*a*, and -*d*. Nouns in -*z* 'show no significant statistical pattern' (Bull, 1965:108)—are as likely to be feminine as masculine,[10] and although Bull gives statistics for -*b*, -*c*, -*ch*, -*i*, -*m*, -*t*, -*y*, etc., such nouns are too few to justify pedagogical rules for them. One can therefore memorize an acronym such as NORSEL (LaMadrid et al. 1974:104) or LONERS (Briscoe et al. 1978:2) for the masculines. Bergen 1978 builds on this treatment and adds refinements for details.

But a general headcount does not take into account relative frequency. About 99% of the nouns in -*o* and -*a* are respectively masculine and feminine, but the tiny 1% or so of each class with the 'wrong' gender includes everyday words that are likely to be encountered early by the student. *Día* and *mano* come to mind quickly; Figure 8.6 lists other exceptions to a NORSEL rule. Obviously, the student who guesses that his first 100 words in -*l* will be 96.6% masculine will not make 3.4 and only 3.4 mistakes, for his first sampling of nouns is not that of the lexicographer. As a further complication, he will run across several homonymous pairs with different genders, as shown in Figure 8.7.

The other criterion for gender is meaning. To be sure, there are many masculine/feminine pairs with no consistent semantic underpinnings, as

Figure 8.6 Common exceptions to the NORSEL rule.

-n	= F:	armazón, imagen, opinión, región, religión, razón, sartén, virgen
-o	= F:	mano, moto, foto, polio
-r	= F:	flor, labor, mujer
-s	= F:	diabetes, res, sintaxis, tos, caries
-e	= F:	calle, carne, clase, costumbre, fuente, ingle, leche, llave, muerte, noche, nube, sangre, superficie, tarde
-l	= F:	cárcel, col, piel, sal, señal, vocal
-a	= M:	clima, delta, día, drama, mapa, planeta, poema, problema, programa, síntoma, sistema, tema, tranvía
-d	= M:	ardid, ataúd, césped

Figure 8.7 Masculine/feminine homonyms.

el canal 'canal, channel'; la canal 'gutter'
el capital 'money'; la capital 'capital city'
el cólera 'cholera'; la cólera 'anger, rage'
el coma 'coma'; la coma 'comma'
el cometa 'comet'; la cometa 'kite'
el corte 'cut'; la corte 'court'
el cura 'priest'; la cura 'cure'
el doblez 'crease'; la doblez 'duplicity'
el frente 'front'; la frente 'forehead'
el mañana 'tomorrow'; la mañana 'morning'
el orden 'order, arrangement'; la orden 'order, command'
el Papa 'Pope'; la papa 'potato'
el parte 'communiqué'; la parte 'part'
el pendiente 'pendant'; la pendiente 'slope, grade'
el radio 'radius; radium'; la radio 'radio'

in *el mango/la manga* and the others shown in Figure 8.8 (see also Boyd-Bowman 1960:104). But meaning can help nonetheless. Names of rivers, trees, ships, days, and months are masculine as if in apposition to *río*, *árbol*, *barco*, *día*, *mes*; especially noteworthy is the pattern of *el árbol/la fruta* in *naranjo/naranja*, *avellano/avellana*, *peral/pera*, *nogal/nuez*, etc. And of course, nouns referring to persons tend toward sex gender, and at this point the Spanish system comes into sharp focus by matching masculine/feminine with male/female. There are four main morphological patterns:

(1) *Different roots:* el padre/la madre, el hombre/la mujer, el yerno/la nuera

(2) *Common roots with idiosyncratic derivational suffixes:* el actor/la actriz, el rey/la reina, el poeta/la poetisa, el héroe/la heroína

Figure 8.8. Pairs in *-o/-a* differing idiosyncratically in meaning.

---

el barco 'ship'; la barca 'small boat'
el brazo 'arm'; la braza 'fathom'
el cargo 'position, job'; la carga 'cargo, load, charge'
el cesto 'basket'; la cesta 'large basket'
el cuchillo 'knife'; la cuchilla 'cleaver'
el fruto 'fruit (metaphorical)'; la fruta 'fruit (for eating)'
el huerto 'orchard'; la huerta 'vegetable garden; irrigated land'
el huevo 'egg'; la hueva 'roe, spawn'
el hoyo 'hole, dent'; la hoya 'pit'
el jarro 'jug'; la jarra 'jar'
el leño 'timber'; la leña 'firewood'
el mango 'handle; mango'; la manga 'sleeve; hose'
el marco 'frame(work)'; la marca 'mark, brand'
el partido 'party; match, game'; la partida 'departure; certificate'
el puerto 'port'; la puerta 'door'
el río 'river'; la ría 'inlet, estuary'
el velo 'veil'; la vela 'sail; candle'

---

(3) *Same word, with gender assigned according to the referent's sex:* el/
    la idiota, el/la homicida, el/la acróbata, el/la pianista, el/la artista,
    el/la testigo, el/la joven, el/la mártir, el/la modelo, el/la belga, el/la
    cantante, el/la reo, el/la amante, el/la estudiante (*But:* la gente, per-
    sona, víctima, criatura)
(4) *Same stem, with a femininizing* -a *added to the masculine (and re-
    placing its* -e *or* -o): el abuelo/la abuela, el hijo/la hija, el viudo/la
    viuda, el monje/la monja, el señor/la señora, el francés/la francesa,
    el español/la española, el profesor/la profesora, el huésped/la
    huéspeda, el autor/la autora.

Especially in ranks or roles that women have only entered fairly recently, there is some uncertainty about which of these last two patterns should
be applied. Some speakers follow *el/la testigo* and *el/la amante* (pattern
(3)) and say *la jefe, la presidente, la médico*; others follow *el monje/la
monja* and *el abuelo/la abuela* (pattern (4)) and say *la jefa, la presidenta, la
médica.* Part of this uncertainty comes from conflict with competing patterns in which the masculine represents a person (traditionally a male
with no female counterpart) and the feminine has been preempted for
something else. Among the patterns listed by Bergen 1980 are the following:

(1) *M = male worker, F = his wife:* el corregidor/la corregidora, el
    molinero/la molinera, el general/la generala

(2) *M = male worker, F = his profession or field*: el físico/la física, el químico/la química, el músico/la música, el gramático/la gramática, el lógico/la lógica, el matemático/la matemática

(3) *M = male worker, F = collective noun*: el policía/la policía, el escolta/la escolta, el guardia/la guardia

One may well hesitate to call a female musician *la música* 'the music' or a female chemist *la química* 'the chemical/chemistry'.

Comparable to the ambiguous area between count and mass is EPICENE gender: human nouns and pronouns that refer to neither sex in particular but to either or both together. In English there have been at least four treatment of epicenes: words such as *parent, driver, child, professor, who, anyone, nobody, neither* can be referred to (1) by *he/his/him* (traditionally prescribed), (2) by *he or she/his or her/him or her* (currently increasing but stylistically unwieldy), (3) by *s/he* (*precioso* but unpronounceable), and (4) by singular *they/their/them* (stigmatized, but convenient, widespread, and endowed with a long pedigree in the language's history). In Spanish, the English-speaking student must realize, whatever his, his or her, s/his, or their stance on 'sexism' in language, that it is the masculine gender that always handles epicene reference. In *Necesito otro consejero* or *¿Hay profesores arriba?*, the speaker may be referring to males only or to males plus females or to anyone regardless of sex; likewise, *los padres, los hijos, los españoles*, and pronouns such as *nosotros* and *ellos*. From one point of view, then, the so-called 'masculine' gender should be renamed 'non-feminine' to signal that this category does not mean 'males' but instead, 'not exclusively females'.[11]

Spanish differentiates the sexes of the higher or more familiar animals according to human patterns, as does English too to some extent: *gato/gata, perro/perra, gallo/gallina, pato/pata, vaca/toro, carnero/oveja, zorro/zorra, león/leona, tigre/tigresa, mono/mona, ganso/gansa, puerco (cerdo)/puerca*; cf. Eng. *lion/lioness, fox/vixen, stallion/mare, tiger/tigress*. In both languages, the epicene treatment of M + F = M prevails for the species: *lion + lioness = lions, león + leona = leones*. In some cases, the species name is distinct: *buck + doe = deer, stallion + mare = horses, gallo + gallina = pollos, toro + vaca = reses*; or it may be the feminine term: *drake + duck = ducks, carnero + oveja = ovejas*.

Wilder or less familiar animals arbitrarily end up in one or the other gender in Spanish: *el chimpancé, el rinoceronte, el canguro, el delfín, el elefante, la jirafa, la liebre, la cebra, la ballena, la comadreja*. If the sexes must be distinguished, *macho* and *hembra* are added, giving rise to a curious pattern of (mis)agreement: *el chimpancé hembra, la jirafa macho*. Lower animals and plants are undifferentiated entirely, as though—aside from biologists and gardeners—no one really cared about the sex of these (cf. English *it* here): *el mosquito, la mosca, el sapo, la rana, el gusano, la culebra, la abeja, el lagarto, el acebo*.

One complication of the gender system in Spanish is what could be called the 'transvestite' *el*, which is *la* in disguise. Even though the noun stays feminine, *la* becomes *el* if the noun begins with /á-/. All texts bring this out for *el agua*, but the pattern is general: *el álgebra, aula, acta, hacha, ala, ave, hambre, alma, arma*. Historically, this *el* is not the masculine *el* at all, but a relic of the earlier feminine form *ela*, which contracted to *el'* in these cases but to *'la* in all others (including those nouns with initial unstressed /a/, as in *la acera, habilidad, atmósfera*). *Una* became *un'* in exactly the same environment (*un aula, ala, arma*). But students are confused because they learn *el* as a marker of masculinity: *el agua* should be masculine, like *el día*. (Native speakers are sometimes confused too, and perhaps this is why *el arte* wound up as masculine in the singular.) The rule is now a very strange one, since it does not apply in front of an adjective beginning with /á-/ (*el agua agria, la agria agua*), nor to names of letters (*la a, la hache*).

8.3 Modifiers in the noun phrase. As defined earlier, NP is (1) a noun plus any modifiers accompanying it, or (2) any constituents that can substitute for it or occur in the same syntactic slots. The former kind of NP—one based on a noun—is sometimes called a NOMINAL or LEXICAL NP when it must be distinguished from the latter or nounless NP. In the following sections, the system of constituents that can make up NP is investigated in terms of English and Spanish phrase structure rules (v. 5.2); subsequently, the morphology and usage of the inflected noun modifiers in NP are discussed.

8.3.1 Noun phrase constituents. For English, the following phrase structure rule presents most of the possibilities available for the construction of NP.

$$
NP \rightarrow \left\{
\begin{array}{ll}
(D) & (Quant)\ (Adj)^n\ N\ (PP) \\
NP & (C\ NP)^n \\
NP & S \\
Pro & \\
S & \\
\end{array}
\right\}
$$

The abbreviating symbols summarize a great deal of information. The first line indicates that NP can consist of a left-to-right sequence of the following elements: an optional determiner D (= articles, demonstratives, preposed possessives); an optional quantifier *Quant* (=*two, five, many, each*, etc.); any number of adjectives, Adj^n (the raised n = choosable any number of times); a noun N; and an optional prepositional phrase, *PP*. Only N is necessary in this lineup (but v. 8.4); the other constituents are optional and arranged in the order shown if any of them appear. The second line then states that the NP can alternatively be COMPOUND, one NP conjoined with any number of other NPs by conjunctions (C). The third line represents an NP modified by a relative (adjectival) clause, which is simply a sentence *S* attributive to D + N, D + Adj + N, or whatever (v. 13.3.1 for relative clause formation). The fourth line is for pronouns, and the fifth is for embedded sentences that act like NP, the traditional 'noun clauses'; e.g. *that you want this* in *That you want this surprises me* (v. 13.1).

For Spanish, the PSR for NP is similar:[12]

$$\text{NP} \rightarrow \left\{ \begin{array}{ll} \text{(D)} & \text{(Quant) (Adj) N (Adj)}^n \text{ (PP)} \\ \text{NP} & \text{(C NP)}^n \\ \text{NP} & \text{S} \\ \text{Pro} & \\ \text{S} & \end{array} \right\}$$

The only obvious difference is that the Spanish NP has two normal positions for its adjectives; this fact will be taken up later in a discussion of word order (v. 11.3.2). There are other differences as well that cannot be shown in these generalized formulas, and the following sections concentrate on three of them: possessives, articles and demonstratives, and agreement.

8.3.2 Possession and other noun-to-noun relationships. English speakers have available two means of expressing possession inside NP: (1) with a possessive NP in the determiner (D) slot, and (2) with a postposed NP introduced by *of* in the PP slot. These are illustrated in Figure 8.9 by means of phrase markers based on the PSR for NP given in the preceding section.

Figure 8.9 Two ways of expressing possession: possessive determiner and possessive prepositional phrase.

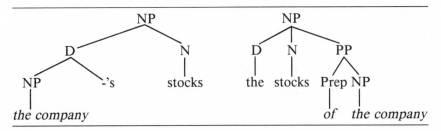

Spanish has the former option (preposed, in D) only when the possessor is pronominal, in which case *yo* + poss. → *mi, nosotros/-as* + poss. → *nuestro*, etc. Since English pronouns also form possessive determiners (*I* + poss. → *my, we* + poss. → *our*, etc.) these forms give little trouble for the most part. But in the third person, the male/female and singular/plural distinctions of the corresponding pronouns are neutralized in Spanish: *él ella ellos ellas usted ustedes* + poss. → *su*. Many students are slow to accept this neutralization, for their English experience seems to demand at least a distinction between *su* for the singular possessors *él ella usted* and *sus* for the plural ones. Instead of using the PP alternatives *de él, de usted, de ellos,* etc. for clarification as Spanish speakers do, they attempt to use *su casa,* *su casas for 'his, her, your house(s)' and **sus casa, sus casas* for 'their, your house(s)'. This error is quite common even for students who have otherwise mastered agreement. (For the long-form possessives, v. 8.4.1 and 11.3.2.)

When the possessor is a noun or nominal NP instead of a pronoun, Spanish requires that it be placed in the PP slot: *las acciones de la compañía.* Beginning students readily grasp this pattern because it is an option in English too, but in active performance they occasionally forget that it is the only possibility in Spanish in this case. Fortunately, errors such as **la compañía(s) acciones* need not be corrected too many times before students get the point. Another difference is that Spanish optionally uses the postposed pattern even for pronominal possessors, contrary to English usage: *las acciones de usted/él,* **the stocks of you/him.* The two languages thus contrast as follows: in English, a possessive nominal NP can occur as either D or PP but a pronominal one occurs as D, whereas in Spanish a possessive nominal NP occurs as PP but a pronominal one occurs as either D or PP.

When leading off a PP after the head noun, *of* and *de* do not indicate possession alone, but more broadly modification of the head noun by a second NP. Specific relationships can be expressed by more specific prepositions in English, while Spanish tends toward *de* with any NP that identifies the head noun:

the girl *with* the green eyes	la chica *de* los ojos verdes
the man *with* the guitar	el hombre *de* la guitarra
the woman *from* Denmark	la mujer *de* Dinamarca
the statue *in* the park	la estatua *del* parque
the best hotel *in* Malaga	el mejor hotel *de* Málaga

For locative relationships with some other preposition, Spanish adopts a relative clause, which is an alternative in English too:

the guest (who's) at the door	el invitado que está a la puerta
the book (that's) under the table	el libro que está debajo de la mesa

But it is not the case that *de* is the only NP-to-N connector in Spanish. *Con* and *sin* appear when accompaniment and its lack are meant literally: *arroz con pollo, café con/sin leche, frascos con/sin fecha. Para* is freely used when the PP indicates purpose: *cartas para ti, cajas para cigarros, ropa para caballeros.* Abstract nouns are constructed with special prepositions: *interés en la política, afición a los deportes, enojo con su novia, repudio a drogadictos, invitación a una fiesta, habilidad en los idiomas, fe en Cristo, semejanza a la poesía, derecho a libertad de cultos, remedio contra amibas,* etc. To a certain extent, such NPs recreate VP structure—

Dios ama al hombre, el amor de Dios al hombre—and some analysts posit a transformation for converting VP structure to a complex NP. A French-like use of *a* for manner has also entered the language: *un juguete a pilas, asesinato a patadas.* Even with clearly identifying PPs, the textbook rule that stipulates *de* is too strong: a Spanish newspaper recently quoted average figures for 'alquiler de piso *de* 3 ó 4 habitaciones' on one page but for 'alquiler de piso *con* dos habitaciones' on the next. Prepositional usage is very difficult to pin down, either descriptively or pedagogically, and it often enters the realm of idiom (v. 10. 4).

A major source of interference in learning Spanish is the fact that nonpossessive N_1 *of* N_2 relationships in English may be changed to $N_2 N_1$; the stress pattern is then either the compounding Ǹ Ń or the phrasal Ǹ Ń (v. 4.1.2):[13]

> the bottom of the lake → the láke bòttom
> a leg of a chair → a cháir lèg
> a watch of gold → a gòld wátch
> a house of brick → a brìck hóuse
> the economy of the world → the wòrld ecónomy

There is no theoretical limit to how many English nouns can be piled up in this way: the following example shows four.

> a manufacturer of screws of furniture of metal
> → a metal furniture screw manufacturer

This pattern is highly productive in English, but severely limited in Spanish. Even when N + N occurs, it is the second noun that modifies the first, exactly the reverse of English usage: *esposa modelo model wife, caso límite borderline case, lengua madre mother language.* Otherwise, English $N_2 + N_1$ corresponds to N_1 Prep N_2 in Spanish:

bookshelf, estante para libros	color TV, televisión en colores
tea cup, taza para té	six-cylinder engine, motor de seis
gold watch, reloj de oro	cilindros
winter clothes, ropa de invierno	bus station, estación de autobuses
orange juice, jugo de naranja	data banks, bancos de datos
physics book, libro de física	noodle soup, sopa de fideos
sodium chloride, cloruro de	tomato seeds, semillas de tomate
sodio	history files, archivos de historia

Alternatively, an adjective can be used in Spanish:

> world problems, problemas del mundo~problemas mundiales

The same difference appears when the modifying noun is a nominalized verb, which will be a gerund in English but an infinitive in Spanish (v. 6.3.2):

> sewing machine, máquina de coser writing table, mesa de escribir

8.3.3 Articles, demonstratives, and other determiners. Traditionally, words such as *a(n)* and *the* are classified as ARTICLES, *this* and *that* as DEMONSTRATIVES, *my your their* as possessives, and premodifiers like *such* and *no* are left in a taxonomic limbo. But the syntax of both English and Spanish treats all these as varieties of one category 'determining' the noun's reference, and it assigns them to the same syntactic slot. To capture this generalization, many linguists today call them DETERMINERS.

The nonpossessive determiners match up fairly well in the two languages:

the: el, la, los, las   such (a): tal, -es
a, an: un, una   (a) certain: cierto, -a, -os, -as
some [sm̩]: unos, unas   no, (not . . .) any: ningún(o), -a
this, these: este, -a, -os, -as   some [sʌm]: algún(o), -a, -os, -as

that, those: $\begin{cases} \text{ese, -a, -os, -as} \\ \text{aquel, -lla, -llos, -llas} \end{cases}$

The convergence here is much closer than between either system and, say, Russian. Nevertheless, students must revise their English system of spatial orientation for 'that'. They have little trouble grasping that *ese* (with *ahí*) refers to something at an intermediate distance, often near the addressee, and that *aquel* (with *allí, allá*) refers to something further away, more remote from speaker and addressee, 'over there, over yonder'; *yonder*, in fact, is a relic of a similar distinction English once had in *this (here)*, *that (there)*, *yon (yonder)*. But in active manipulation of the system, students tend to make errors such as *aquel lápiz que tienes*, or to confuse *ese* and *este*, which differ in a mere /t/. In some dialects of Spanish, too, the system is unstable in that *ese* and *ahí* are encroaching on the range of *aquel* and *allí*.

The articles differ in some ways, too, though not in their basic functions, which are two. First, a speaker adopts the indefinite article to introduce a singular count noun[14] into conversation or discourse for the first time: *I saw a horse.* This article is related to *one*—obviously so in Spanish, but etymologically *a(n)* was once an unstressed allomorph of *one* in English, too—and it selects one member out of a class for comment. *Vi un caballo afuera* means 'of all horses I might discuss, I am selecting one I saw outside and will proceed to tell you about it.' After this initial introduction, the speaker switches to definite reference (a definite pronoun or definite determiner) to keep listeners focused on this entity, i.e. to maintain what Bull (1965:216) calls 'common focus' or what Alonso (1974:158) calls 'lo consabido en la esfera de atención.' Hence, *Vi un caballo afuera. El caballo se comía tus petunias, Mamá.* If the speaker instead follows up on the first sentence by saying *Un caballo se comía tus petunias, Mamá*, the listener infers that the speaker has introduced yet another horse, or has his narrative confused.

A second function of articles is to indicate GENERIC REFERENCE, all members of a group in general: *A cat has four legs, The cat has four legs, Un gato tiene cuatro patas, El gato tiene cuatro patas.* All of these signify that cats in general, any and all of them, have four legs—not this cat, that cat, or a particular cat I am focusing on to discuss as an individual, but the entire set of domestic felines.

People communicating with one another take short-cuts in establishing and maintaining reference. Given a shared culture, situation, and focus of attention, speaker and hearer sometimes proceed to definite reference without explicitly presenting the entity first with an indefinite article. Our planet has one sun and one moon; such referents are called *el sol* and *la luna*, and it is unnecessary to back up and introduce them as *un sol, una luna.* Likewise, in certain contexts one can strike up a conversation about *el presidente, el bebé, el techo, el tren, la sala, el tomacorriente, el mitin, el inodoro*, etc. and the referents of these NPs will be perfectly clear on first mention because they are uniquely conspicuous in the context.

Where Spanish and English differ is mainly in four fairly circumscribed areas in which one language uses an article and the other dispenses with it.

(1) Vi al señor/general/profesor López en la Calle Kennedy.
I saw (*the) Mister/General/Professor Lopez on (*the) Kennedy Street.

Both languages use a definite article for established reference in *Vi al general en la calle, I saw the general on the street*; but when the name of the person or street is added appositively, English drops the article. In vocatives, however, in which one addresses a person instead of referring to him, both languages omit the article: *¡General López! General Lopez!*

(2) Lo terminarán el lunes. They'll finish it (on) Monday.

Both languages tend to use the definite article for specific dates that are modified: *Lo terminarán el último lunes del mes, They'll finish it (on) the last Monday of the month.* English drops it otherwise, and also when the modifier is *next* or *last* with reference to the present point: *next Monday* (but in a narrative, *on the next Monday*). Spanish retains the article for all such dates, as well as in time-telling (*son las tres, a las tres*).

(3) Me gustan las papas. I like potatoes.
El hombre es mortal. Man is mortal.
Los hombres son mortales. Men are mortal.

As noted earlier, both languages can express genericity with their articles. But in English a competing pattern with ∅ (no determiner) has won out with many nouns (Quirk et al. 1972:147). The Spanish construction is consistent, and the English speaker has only to learn that generic reference regularly requires the article in Spanish. The Spanish-speaking student of English has a harder time with an apparent grammatical anarchy:

THE TIGER *has four legs* = generic, or particular.
But THE MAN *has two legs* = particular only.
TIGER *has four legs* = proper name (otherwise ungrammatical)
But MAN *has two legs* = generic.

(4) Jorge salió sin abrigo. George left without a coat.
¿Tiene hijo tu prima? Does your cousin have a child?
Luisa suele llevar sombrero. Louise generally wears a hat.
Mauricio es arquitecto. Maurice is an architect.
Anda buscando novio. She's searching around for a boyfriend.
Moza bonita no paga. A pretty girl doesn't (have to) pay.

Here it is Spanish which, to the student, is peculiarly dropping articles. But *un* still retains its numerical value of 'one,' and the message in all these examples is that the speaker is not selecting one and only one entity from a group, but referring indefinitely to unquantified membership in the group denoted by the 'naked' (undetermined) noun. Omission of *un* signifies that the noun is being used for its sense alone, without reference to a particular individual (Suñer 1982:219). The real force of *sin abrigo* might be paraphrased as 'coatlessness', that of *tiene hijo* as 'parenthood', that of *es arquitecto* as 'membership in the architectural profession'. Sometimes Spanish has a contrast between $\emptyset$ and *un*: *Yo no tengo hermano* is 'I have no sibling(s)' whereas *Yo no tengo un hermano* can mean 'I don't have one sibling, but several.' Likewise, *¿Sabes que Juan ha comprado automóvil?* implies the status of car ownership, while *¿Sabes que Juan ha comprado un automóvil?* introduces a particular car, and just one, into the conversation (Alonso 1974:136-37). If there is any reason why English does use *a(n)* here despite the lack of individualization, it is because nongeneric singular count nouns are not used in that language without some kind of determiner: **George left without coat, *John has bought car.*[15]

In summary, both languages assign articles the same basic communicative functions, and users of both languages may bypass the initial step of indefinite reference. They differ primarily in certain omissions of articles, i.e. in the use of the naked noun construction $\emptyset$ +N. The problem becomes more confused than it really is only when the student is led into adjusting Spanish grammar to English through the addition of ad hoc amendment rules to English grammar ('DO use the article here, DON'T use it there'). As Bull (1965:221-22) expresses it, 'the student . . . is taught to project English patterns onto Spanish except when he is told not to. He operates, consequently, with a set of exceptions to his English intuition rather than with a clear understanding of how the Spaniard organizes reality. Moreover, the number of rules needed to define the Spanish exceptions to English patterns exceeds the number needed to describe the entire Spanish system.' In the treatment of articles, it is easy to lose sight of the forest in itemizing the location of each tree.

8.3.4 Agreement and its morphology. Within the NP, the gender and number features of the head noun spread to its inflected modifiers. Bull (1965:105) has described this as a process of 'matching': one says *la otra hija morena* because the ends of the modifiers take on the *-a* of the noun, thereby matching it. But the value of matching dwindles in *aquel pobre país destruido*, and very little is gained by a change in terminology alone. The traditional term AGREEMENT is as good as any other.

The difference between English and Spanish is not in absence versus presence of agreement, but in its extent. In English, only a few determiners agree, and then just in number: *this nail these nails, a nail some nails.* In Spanish, agreement in number and gender is carried out over everything in the NP except the PP:

D　Quant　Adj　N　Adj　PP

Ideally, a modifier will have four inflectional forms corresponding to the four categories of the noun: masc. sg., masc. pl., fem. sg., fem. pl. This morphological parallelism is exact for an adjective like *alto, -os, -a, -as* (like *abuelo, -os, abuela, -as*) or *hablador, -es, -a, -as* (like *profesor, -es, profesora, -as*). But it breaks down in four cases.

(1) The masc. sg. of the articles and demonstratives is irregular: *el, los, la, las*; *este, -os, -a, -as*; *ese, -os, -a, -as*; *aquel, -llos, -lla, -llas*.[16] The expected 'matching' forms in *-o, lo esto eso aquello*, are preempted for the neuter (v. 8.4.2).

(2) Most numerical quantifiers (cardinal numbers) agree semantically with plural nouns without showing it morphologically: *cuatro* (*cuatras) *cuerdas*. Only *uno* and *-cientos* have overt gender and number agreement.

(3) Adjectives, and those possessive determiners (*mi, nuestro*) and noncardinal quantifiers (*segundo, mucho*) that act like them morphologically, conform to two basic patterns, 'four-form' and 'two-form'. First, they have four forms if their masc. sg. (the citation form in vocabularies and dictionaries) ends in *-o: alto/nuestro/mucho, -a, -os, -as*. Second, they have only two (singular/plural, with no gender marking) if their masc. sg. ends IN ANY OTHER WAY, as illustrated here:

mi, mis	árabe, árabes	cortés, corteses	indígena, indígenas
su, sus	libre, libres	mejor, mejores	agrícola, agrícolas
hindú, hindúes	verde, verdes	azul, azules	maya, mayas
cursi, cursis	probable,	joven, jóvenes	realista, realistas
israelí, -íes	probables	común,	alerta, alertas
	feliz, felices	comunes	

Yet many adjectives that should have two forms since they end in 'any other way' are accorded four forms. These include adjectives of nationality, ethnicity, religious affiliation, etc. ending in a consonant (*español, francés, musulmán, andaluz -es, -a, -as*) and many adjectives in *-or, -ón,*

-*ote*, -*án* (*conservador, trabajador, chillón, holgazán*, -*es*, -*a*, -*as*). But there are exceptions: *superior, mayor*, and *provenzal* have the expected two forms, unlike *conservador* and *español*.

(4) A limited number of adjectives and quantifiers apocopate prenominally: *un* (and in compounds: *veintiún, ciento un*), *primer, tercer, ningún, buen, mal, algún, postrer*.[17] Two-form modifiers are gender-blind in apocopation: *gran, cualquier*. Formerly, *ciento~cien* was explained in the same way—*hay ciento* but *cien árboles*; but many speakers say *hay cien* and count with *cien*, restricting *ciento* to the compound numbers 101-199. The Real Academia (1979:237-38) deplores this development but recognizes that it is too widespread to eradicate.

8.4 NP without N. The PSRs presented in section 8.3.1 provide for optional modifiers with an obligatory noun. Thus, as the DO of *ver*, one could say *Veo unos cerdos, Veo aquellos cerdos hambrientos, Veo los felices cerdos gordos, Veo cinco cerdos de Ramón*, or simply *Veo cerdos*. D, Adj, Quant, and PP are grammatically optional elements arranged around the head noun *cerdos*. Yet there are two cases in which the modifiers can appear with no head, as discussed in the following sections.

8.4.1 Nominalization and pronominalization. Sometimes the missing noun head is understood from the context, and modifiers show agreement with it; many linguists therefore assume that the noun is present in deep structure but deleted in surface structure for communicative economy. The remainder of the NP is then said to be NOMINALIZED. The following sentences illustrate nominalizations, with the deleted head nouns indicated in parentheses.

I bought *eight bottles* and John bought *six* (bottles), so now there're *too many* (bottles).

Yo compré *ocho botellas* y Juan compró *seis* (botellas), de modo que ahora hay *demasiadas* (botellas).

As shown, with most quantifiers the rest of the NP stays intact. Otherwise, nominalization can be complicated, especially in English, when the lineup is one of the following.

(1) Article (N). In this case, nominalization is *pro*nominalization, inasmuch as a definite article is replaced by a third-person pronoun when the noun is dropped:

I fixed *the* (washer) → I fixed *it*.
Arreglé *la* (lavadora) →*La* arreglé.

The connection between definite articles and third-person pronouns is obvious in Spanish, and Bull (1965:248) believes there is still pedagogical value in presenting pronominalization as noun deletion and pronouns as article 'residuals' of NP: *Arreglé la lavadora→Arreglé la ∅ →La arreglé*. (Of course, morphological adjustments are needed in Bull's analysis for

Arreglé el motor→*Arreglé el Ø*→*Lo arreglé.*)

For singular indefinite reference, English uses *one* and Spanish *uno* (recall the relation between 'a' and 'one'):

I fixed *a* (washer) → I fixed *one*.
Arreglé *una* (lavadora) → Arreglé *una*.

For the indefinite plural, nominalization leaves *some* and *unos*; for the negative indefinite determiner *no* and *ningun(o)*, it leaves *none* and *ninguno*:

I have *some* (brothers) → I have *some*.
I have *no* (brother(s)) → I have *none*.
Tengo *unos* (hermanos) → Tengo *unos*.
No tengo *ningún* (hermano) → No tengo *ninguno*.

(2) Possessive (N). Possessive determiners become pronominal or 'long-form' possessives in nominalization:

My (house) cost me a lot. → *Mine* cost me a lot.
Mi (casa) me costó mucho. → *La mía* me costó mucho.[18]

When the possessor is not a personal pronoun, both languages just drop the noun; but the difference between a preposed possessor in English and a postposed one in Spanish (v. 8.3.2) yields strikingly different patterns, despite the shared rule of noun deletion:

John's (house) is beige. → *John's* is beige.
La (casa) *de Juan* es beige. → *La de Juan* es beige.

Nominalization with a postposed possessor is impossible in English unless *one(s)* is inserted; but a Spanish-like pattern exists with *that* or *those*:

The (stocks) *of the company.* → $\begin{cases} *The\ of\ the\ company. \\ The\ ones\ of\ the\ company. \\ Those\ of\ the\ company. \end{cases}$

Las (acciones) *de la compañía.* → *Las de la compañía.*

(3) Demonstrative (N). Spanish again just drops the noun, leaving a pronominal demonstrative on which an accent may be written (it is no longer required, however). English follows suit for plurals, but inserts *one* for singulars (and plurals, too, in some dialects):

this tool → *this one*　　　　*these* tools → *these* (*these ones*)
esta herramienta → *ésta*　　*estas* herramientas → *éstas*

(4) Other structures: D Adj (N), D (N) Adj, D (N) PP, D (N) S. When the noun is modified by an adjective, PP, or relative clause, Spanish once more deletes the noun, whereas English replaces it with *one(s)*:

el (pájaro) *verde* → *el verde*　　*las* (estatuas) *del parque* →
　　　　　　　　　　　　　　　　　　　　las del parque

the green (bird) → *the green one*	*the* (statues) *in the park* → *the ones in the park*
un (libro) *rojo* → *uno rojo* *a red* (book) → *a red one*	*la* (niña) *que te vio* → *la que te vio* *the* (girl) *that saw you* → *the one that saw you*

There are a few nominalized adjectives in English that conform to the Spanish pattern: *the rich, the poor, the former, the latter, the powerful.* These might serve as illustrations of what happens in Spanish, but nominalization with *one(s)* is far more common today, and that is the pattern from which interference must be anticipated.[19]

One more case remains to be discussed, namely, what happens when the dropped noun has no determiners or modifiers at all in its NP (i.e. when it is naked). Spanish, as usual, simply drops the deemphasized noun (and with it, the vacated NP node of a phrase marker). This yields a construction that is quite puzzling to English speakers, whose language prohibits the complete elimination of the NP but has no one replacement for it.

A: ¿Venden Uds. carburadores?	A: Do you sell carburetors?
B: No, no vendemos (carburadores) → No, no vendemos.	B: No, ⎰*we don't sell. ⎱ we don't sell any/them/those.

A: ¿Tienes harina?	A: Have you got flour?
B: Sí, tengo (harina) → Sí, tengo.	B: Yes, ⎰*I've got. ⎱ I've got some/it/that.

Surface structures such as *No vendemos* and *Sí, tengo* can hardly be described as nominalizations, for nothing remains of the NP to call 'nominalized'; yet the same Spanish process of noun deletion is occurring here as in the other cases. Perhaps the term 'nominalization' is unsuitable in general as a characterization of the Spanish structures examined throughout this section. As an alternative approach, Agard (1984:111-112) has proposed a principle of 'noun throw-away' to explain not only the dropping of nouns from Spanish NPs, but also the dropping of deemphasized subjects (*¿Se va José? Sí, se va.*).

8.4.2 The Spanish neuter. The so-called 'neuter' is another case in which NP modifiers are present without any overt noun. The forms *ello lo esto eso aquello* are described as neuter because they derive etymologically from Latin neuters, not because they agree with neuter nouns or refer to sexless inanimates; Spanish has no neuter nouns, since all the neuter = sexless nouns of Latin were reassigned to masculine or feminine.[20] Simply put, Spanish neuters are used when there is no gender-determining noun, whether explicit or 'understood' (underlying but deleted), with which they might agree, and they have come to represent general concepts, preceding ideas, unnamed qualities or events, and indefinite extents of determination. English equivalents vary because English does not exploit this option systematically:

Lo mismo les sucedió a ellos.	*The same (thing)* happened to them.
Debes tomar *lo bueno* con *lo malo.*	You should take *the good (part, aspect, point)* with *the bad.*
¿Has oído *eso del instituto*?	Have you heard about *that matter of (the news about) the institute*?

Syntactically, neuter NPs resemble nominalized determiners, possessives, phrases, and clauses, but they have no understood or namable noun which can be regarded as deleted. Neuters thus contrast with nominalizations in ways for which there is no consistent equivalent in English:

Lo mío no es *lo tuyo.* (*La mía* no es *la tuya* = mi bicicleta, casa, filosofía, etc.)

Esto me molesta. (*Este* me molesta = este tipo, aparato, curso, etc.)

Prefiero *lo más fácil.* (Prefiero *el más fácil* = el método, plan, ejercicio, etc.)

¿Qué es *eso*? (¿Qué es *ésa*? = 'name or define that kind of *comida, falda, moneda*')

Lo de Alejandro nos fascina. (*La de Alejandro* = la novia, la madre, la obra . . .)

Lo que mencionaste me extraña. (*El que mencionaste* = el cuento, el chico, el criterio)

Otheguy (1978:241-257) suggests that the semantic contrast between *el~la* and *lo* involves DISCRETENESS. With *el*, the speaker assigns clear, distinct, well-delineated boundaries ('delineated' by a noun he has in mind), whereas *lo* suggests nondiscreteness. He uses examples such as the following to illustrate this point:

Alcánzame ese diccionario. A ver, aquí está $\left\{ \begin{array}{l} \text{la que} \\ \text{lo que} \end{array} \right\}$ quiere decir *serendipity*.

Carlos tiene una mujer ambiciosa, por $\left\{ \begin{array}{l} \text{la que} \\ \text{lo que} \end{array} \right\}$ hace los más grandes sacrificios.

The only hint of a comparable English distinction is in *this* vs. *this one*, *that* vs. *that one*, because *this* and *that* with no nominalizing *one* are rather neuter in the Spanish sense:

This is impossible. (*This one* is impossible. = this step, recipe, exercise . . .)

I don't believe *that*. (. . . *that one* = that hypothesis, anecdote, report . . .)

Perhaps because of the nebulousness or 'nondiscreteness' of *lo*, it has acquired the function of expressing extent or degree of adjective or adverb modification. The *lo* remains nounless, yet the adjective agrees with a later noun:

No sabes
- lo eficaz de nuestra enseñanza.
- lo bien que se ha construido este puente.
- lo cansadas que estamos nosotras.
- lo torpes que son esos tipos.

This *lo* + Adj/Adv + *de/que* corresponds somewhat to English *how* + Adj/Adv + clause, at least functionally, but the agreement of the adjective (but not *lo*) with a noun strikes students as decidedly odd.

The neuter equivalents of the pronouns (or nominalized 'residuals') *él lo* and *ella la* are, of course, *ello lo*:

A: ¡Manuel se ha casado!
B: No lo sabía. Pero no hablemos de ello.

English *it* can be used similarly for unnamed concepts, matters, propositions, and so on; but Spanish *lo* can also be used as a kind of 'pro-adjective' with copulas, and *it* is not so used.

A: La novia de Alfonso no es muy linda.
B: Sí, pero él cree que lo es.

(Cf. English *Yes, but he thinks that she is.*)

With nominalizations and neuters, one crosses an unclear boundary between nouns and pronouns. The latter will be discussed in the next chapter.

Notes for Chapter 8

1. The parenthesized *le* with NP IO is optional in some dialects, regarded as redundant in others, but heavily favored in many (v. 9.4.1).

2. In fact, this is one way the English IO is described in transformational grammar: *John lent Harry* (IO) *twelve dollars* (DO) and *Mary made us* (IO) *some paella* (DO) are respectively derived from *John lent twelve dollars to Harry* and *Mary made some paella for us* by means of an IO Movement transformation (also called Dative Shift). But this analysis encounters problems. First, the proposed underlying version of *The car cost Ed $7000* is ungrammatical: **The car cost $7000 to Ed*. Second, there are many verbs with which the transformation mysteriously does not apply:

He told that lie to Ed. → He told Ed that lie.
He said that lie to Ed. → *He said Ed that lie.
He taught everything to Ed. → He taught Ed everything.
He explained everything to Ed. → *He explained Ed everything.

Such verbs are stumbling blocks to Spanish students of English, who often generate **Explain me that* on the basis of their *Explícame eso*.

3. Of special interest in Kliffer's analysis are contrasts such as *levanto la mano* vs. *me lavo la mano*. For him, the former suggests doing some-

thing with the hand while the latter (with its *me* contrasting with *te, le,* and other possible IOs) suggests doing it to one's hand. *Me levanto la mano* combines both meanings, as when a paralytic forces his hand up.

4. 'A male is generally viewed as stronger, more active, and socially higher than a woman would be. He is thus at least potentially more active than a woman would be' (p. 75). The verification of this claim, it should be noted, lies outside the bounds of linguistics.

5. The [əz] allomorph (as in *bushes, judges, buses, watches*) is pronounced by some with a higher mid vowel, [ɨ].

6. But *los Habsburgos, los Borbones.* The order-loving Real Academia (1979:189) is distressed by this, finding the 0 plural on most family names an 'impropiedad', but it is forced by current usage to accept it.

7. Other English collective nouns (*the family, the government*) vacillate between singular because of morphology, and plural because of meaning; in Spanish, grammatical number always takes precedence over semantic plurality.

8. Cases like *the ship . . . she* are relics, and so rare they have little transfer value.

9. The answer is 'both' here. Nouns such as *margen, fin, cutis, análisis* have vacillated in gender, and still vary dialectally. Jorge-Morán finds variation in Santo Domingo on the gender of *azúcar, calambre, calor, hambre, mar, radio, reuma, sartén,* as does Cárdenas (1967:71-75) in Jalisco, Mexico.

10. But according to Wonderly 1983, 61% of the nouns in -*z* are feminine; specifically, -*az* = 17% F, -*ez* = 84% F, -*iz* = 50% F, -*oz* = 35% F, -*uz* = 14% F.

11. In technical terms, the so-called masculine is UNMARKED and the feminine is MARKED. Prado 1982 develops this point more fully, noting that in addition to epicene reference, it is the masculine that handles loanwords (*el bar, el show*), infinitives (*el deber, el atardecer*), compounds (*el cuentagotas*), nominalized adverbials and interjections (*el sí, el más allá*), nonagreeing participles (*ha comprado*), and other words without a clear gender assignment. Moreover, the augmentatives of feminines become masculines, except in speaking of females: *la sala → el salón, la silla → el sillón* (but *la mujer → la mujerona*). Prado also investigated unmarked/marked relationships in the Spanish tense system, pronouns, syntax, and phonology.

12. For brevity, we will consign the following possibilities to this note:

Quant Quant: two more stamps, dos timbres más
Quant D: all the pages, todas las páginas
Pro modifier: I myself, yo mismo.

We also ignore here, and defer for later discussion, certain modifiers that can precede the whole NP (*even, just, only, aun, hasta, sólo,* v. 10.2.3), appositives (*el general Gómez,* v. 11.1.3), and modifiers of adjectives (the *muy* and PP of *muy orgulloso de su familia,* v. 11.1.2.3), so as to keep our rule for NP within bounds. See Hadlich (1971:ch. 6), Stockwell et al. (1965:ch. 4), and Stiehm (1978:413) for attempts to specify a fuller NP schema for Spanish.

13. In English N + N, some teachers label the first N as an 'adjective'. This may be an apt description of its function when its stress is secondary—*a gòld wátch*, like *a nèw wátch*—but not when it is primary, as in *a wríst wàtch*, for in this case the stress indicates compounding. It must be noted that not all N *of* N combinations in English can change to N +N: *a man of courage*, **a courage man*; *the island of Cuba*, **the Cuba island*; *a glass of water* ≠ *a water glass*. This peculiarity can be quite frustrating to Spanish-speaking students of English.

14. For brevity, we focus on this case here. The fuller system in both languages is basically as follows for establishing initial focus on a noun:

singular count: *a(n), un(a)*: *I saw a horse, Vi un caballo.*

plural count: Ø ~ *some, unos*: *I saw (some) horses, Vi (unos) caballos.*

mass: Ø in Spanish, Ø ~ *some* in English: *I saw (some) sand, Vi arena.*

These differences do not matter once definite reference takes over: *the horse, the horses, the sand; el caballo, los caballos, la arena.*

15. But in the plural English parallels Spanish: *they have children*, with Ø determiner, has exactly the same thrust as *tienen hijos.*

16. In some nonstandard dialects, *el* and *la* both become *l'* before a vowel: *l'amigo, l'amiga* (cf. French *l'ami, l'amie*). Sánchez (1982:32) notes this as the usual practice in Chicano speech.

17. Apocope applied to the feminine also in the Golden Age, and still does in some nonstandard dialects on both sides of the Atlantic (Kany 1945/1951:30-31).

18. Actually, *la mía* should be considered more directly a nominalization of *la casa mía* (v. 11.3.2 for a discussion of *mi casa* vs. *la casa mía*).

19. But these English forms are not true nominalizations; they have specialized meanings and probably should be considered as a class of true nouns. Note the following contrasts:

The rich get away with everything.

But: You eat the diet desserts and I'll eat the rich ones. (* . . . the rich.)

The former was sick, but the latter was malingering.

But: The present head of the council is Alice; the former one was John (*the former was John).

20. Latin had three genders, as in *iste leo* (M), *ista mulier* (F), *istud nomen* (N). All Latin neuters were reassigned to masculine or feminine; neuter *nomen* thus became masculine *nombre* in Spanish, whence modern *este león* (M), *esta mujer* (F), *este nombre* (M). The neuter determiner *istud* > *esto* was displaced from the system and acquired a new niche for itself in which it never modifies any noun.

Exercises for Chapter 8

1. Error Analysis: account for the source of each student error:

(1) *los animals	(10) *los unos que oí
(2) *los atlases	(11) *busco por mi libro
(3) *esto cuchillo	(12) *es mi biología libro
(4) *la arroz	(13) *Lucía es una doctor
(5) *tal un caso	(14) *cientas unas páginas
(6) *la gente lo quieren	(15) *ciencia nos ayudará
(7) *me gusto legumbres	(16) *conocí a señora Pardo
(8) *carros franceses	(17) ?? el sofá es un pedazo de mueble
(9) *Marías informe	

2. Why might the IOs in the following sentences give trouble to English speakers?

(1) Pedro siempre le viene a Carmen con quejas.

(2) A ese autor no le estoy de acuerdo con las opiniones.

(3) Me le han robado la muñeca a mi hija.

(4) ¿Te examino la oreja?

(5) Le hacía ruido el estómago y le picaba la nariz.

(6) Nos comienzan las clases mañana.

(7) Le impusiste demasiados deberes a la alumna.

(8) ¿Le abrochaste la cremallera a tu hija?

(9) La criada le pasó el dedo a la mesa.

What is the meaning of the Spanish IO in these and other sentences, and how does it differ from English IO usage?

3. It was pointed out in section 8.1.4 that English and Spanish do not agree on the roles in which NPs are cast with *ask/pedir*. The following verbs also differ. Identify their difference in construction; e.g. X *asks* Y *for* Z, X *pide* Z *a* Y.

(1) wait; esperar	(9) listen; escuchar
(2) thank; agradecer	(10) marry; casar(se)
(3) look; buscar, mirar	(11) have enough; bastar
(4) ask; preguntar	(12) fit; quedar bien
(5) hold; caber	(13) hurt; doler
(6) answer; contestar	(14) need; hacer falta
(7) pay; pagar	(15) provide, supply; proporcionar,
(8) resemble; parecerse	suministrar

Can you add to this list?

4. Given cases such as those in question 3, *gustar* and other reverse-construction verbs, the variation between DO and IO, and cases such as *pegar* + IO vs. *golpear* + DO for 'hit' (Fish 1967), what do 'subjecthood' and 'objecthood' mean, and what determines whether an NP will function as Subj, DO, or IO?

5. Some texts inform the student that *gustar* is used only in the third person—presumably to suppress any urge to transfer the English *I like*,

you like, we like patterns. How true is this? Can you imagine a Spanish context with second- or first-person forms of *gustar*?

6. How predictable is the gender of each of the following nouns?

(1) barril	(5) virtud	(9) cometa	(13) unión
(2) honor	(6) profeta	(10) cliente	(14) Amazonas
(3) calle	(7) apendicitis	(11) sucursal	(15) calambre
(4) nariz	(8) víctima	(12) alarma	(16) examen

7. It was pointed out that the gender of trees, days, and some fruits can be explained in terms of apposition to an understood *árbol, día, fruta*. What are the understood appositives for the following (or are there any understood ones)? Would the connection be pedagogically useful, or just a matter of etymology?

(1) la consonante, fricativa	(6) el jerez
(2) la catedral	(7) la capital (e.g. Santiago)
(3) el dos	(8) la central (e.g. del sindicato)
(4) la diagonal	(9) la efe
(5) la divisoria	

8. The usual rule for the allomorphs of the Spanish plural morpheme stipulates -*s* after a vowel, -*es* after a consonant. After a stressed vowel, however, there is no universal consensus; some say *rubí-s*, some *rubí-es*, some *rubí-ses*. Make a corpus of a dozen or so such vowel-final oxytone nouns and compare (1) the plural you prefer, (2) the one a(nother) native speaker you know chooses, and (3) what reference grammars such as that of the Real Academia recommend.

9. For the feminine of *marrón*, some native speakers say *marrona* while others use the same form as for the masculine: *una chaqueta marrona* ~ *una chaqueta marrón*. Why would there be variation here, but not with *azul, gris*, or *negro/negra*?

10. In what ways do Spanish and English agree, and disagree, on the expression of possession within the NP?

11. In what ways do the two languages differ in their use of ∅ + noun, i.e. of naked nouns?

12. Consider the following PARTITIVE expressions:

un millón de datos	*más de ocho* dramas	*un sinfín de* quehaceres
un poco de azúcar	*un par de* señoras	*una cantidad de* gente
dos litros de agua	*algunos de* los muebles	*tres quintos de* la población

How should they be accounted for in the PSR for a Spanish NP? In your opinion, are the underlined counters and partitives unit items that, despite the *de*, modify the noun as quantifiers, or do they subordinate the noun so that the latter is in a PP following a head noun *millón, par, poco*, etc.? Does English treat equivalent phrases in the same way? (In answering, consider syntactic evidence such as verb agreement—does *un millón de datos* take a singular or plural verb? Dialect evidence is also pertinent;

Boyd-Bowman (1960:157) and Kany (1945/1951: 148) found *un poco de pan* but *una poca de agua* in some regions.)

13. English speakers have little trouble understanding NPs such as *taza para café, libro de arte, cosecha de maíz, producción de acero*, etc.; the problem comes in actively generating NPs of their own in which one noun modifies another. What sources of interference then appear?

14. N + N combinations in Spanish are beginning to appear more often, at least in journalistic and technical writing: *avión espía, fecha límite, misiles mar-tierra, coche-bomba, ciudad dormitorio, punto clave, padre-dios, casa-refugio*. As shown, hyphenation varies; pluralization does too, as witnessed in one newspaper that discussed *buques-hospital* but *coches-bombas*. Examine samples of current Hispanic writing, and see how many such N + N combinations you find and whether there is any pattern in punctuation and pluralization.

15. In most texts, demonstrative pronouns, possessive pronouns, relatives such as *el que*, and nominalized adjectives are presented separately. What motivation is there for treating all of them—perhaps together with the neuters—in a single lesson on nominalization? How would you explain them to English-speaking students?

16. Consider the following premodifiers (preposed elements of the NP) and determine which sequences of them in NPs are grammatical and which are ungrammatical; then revise the NP → D Quant Adj N rule so as to reflect more precisely the cooccurrence possibilities. Do not hesitate to break down the categories of D, Quant, and so on if your analysis reflects the need for finer distinctions or subcategories.

mucho(s)	primero(s)	propio(s)	demás
alguno(s)	cierto(s)	sendos	el, los
otro(s)	tal(es)	cada	un(os)
todo(s)	diez	bastante(s)	este, -os

17. According to Wonder (1981), there are problems with analyzing nominalization as simply the deletion of a deep-structure (underlying) noun, as in *los pájaros verdes → los verdes*. One is that there are apparently *two* degrees of nominalization in D + Adj, as shown by the following pairs. Specify, as clearly as possible, what the difference is.

(1) Juan es el verdadero rico. Juan es el verdaderamente rico.

(2) Aquel eterno quejumbroso nos molesta. Aquel eternamente quejumbroso nos molesta.

(3) Entre los convidados se contaban dos autores españoles y un americano.
Entre los convidados se contaban dos autores españoles y uno americano.

(4) Fue hecho por algún descuidado. Fue hecho por alguno descuidado.

18. Pilleux y Urrutia (1982:78-79) define IOs as 'aquellas FN [frases

nominales, NP] que nombran a los seres . . . en que se cumple o termina la acción del verbo transitivo ejercida ya sobre el complemento directo.' How reliable is this definition, given IOs such as the following?

$$A\ Juan\ le \begin{cases} \text{parece bien la obra.} \\ \text{es difícil el esquí acuático.} \\ \text{corresponde/pertenece gran honor.} \\ \text{conviene la cita.} \\ \text{escuece el codo.} \\ \text{basta el surtido.} \\ \text{toca ducharse ahora.} \end{cases}$$

Chapter 9
Pronouns

9.0 Pronouns as proforms. A PRONOUN is a word that refers back to or substitutes for some designated NP*, and is so-called because in classical grammar it was regarded as standing 'for a noun' (Lat. *pro nomen*). There are also PRO-VERBS (the *do* in *She hesitates more than I do*), PROADVERBS (the *allí* in *No se ve nada allí*), and PROADJECTIVES (the *lo* in *¿Rico? Sí, lo es*), and all of these are sometimes called PROFORMS. The main substitute words or proforms, though, are pronouns, and they are traditionally classified as follows:

personal, which show person (1,2,3) and are definite (like *el, este*): *I, she; yo, ella*
indefinite, which do not distinguish person: *someone, nothing; alguien, nada*
interrogative, for questioning NPs: *who, what; quién, qué*
possessive: *mine, ours; mío, nuestro*
demonstrative, which are deictic (pointing): *this, those; éste, ésos*
relative, which introduce relative clauses: *that, who; que*
quantifying: *few, some, several; pocos, algunos, varios*

Many of these are just nominalized determiners (v. 8.4.1): *ese aparato →* *ése, mi casa → la mía, algunos escollos → algunos*. Others are best treated along with the syntactic processes in which they play a role: interrogatives with questioning (v. 12.1.2), relatives with relativization (v. 13.3.1). This chapter will focus on reflexive and nonreflexive personal pronouns, which form their own cohesive systems.

9.1 Nonreflexive pronouns. As can be seen in Figure 9.1, the English and Spanish systems of personal pronouns are based on the same čategories of number, gender, person, and case.[1] Nevertheless, they differ in so many particulars that Spanish pronouns can offer as big a challenge to English speakers as Spanish verbs; and since many texts proceed quickly from one set (e.g. DO forms) to the next (IO and OP forms), students are often confused well into their second or third year of study. Among the differences are the following.

9.1.1 Person. In Spanish, the three persons are not exactly speaker/addressee/all others, because the referentially second-person *usted* has grammatically third-person forms. The reason for this is its etymology from the third-person phrase *vuestra merced* (v. 9.2). English pronouns are not person-ambiguous, with the exception of 'personal' vs. 'impersonal' *you* (v. 9.3.9); and many students have difficulty in accepting that *lo, la,* and *le* can refer to the addressee as well as to third persons.

Figure 9.1 Nonreflexive personal pronouns.

English (standard system):					Spanish (maximal system):			
Subj	Obj			Person and number	Subj	OP	IO	DO
	OP	IO	DO					
I		*me*		1sg.	*yo*	*mí*	*me*	
you				2sg.	*tú*	*ti*	*te*	
					usted		*le (se)*	*lo/la*
he/she/it	*him/her/it*			3sg.	*él/ella/ello*			
we	*us*			1pl.	*nosotros/-as*		*nos*	
you				2pl.	*vosotros/-as*		*os*	
					ustedes		*les (se)*	*los/las*
they	*them*			3pl.	*ellos/-as*			

9.1.2 Gender. Both languages distinguish masculine from feminine in the 3sg., but otherwise English lacks gender distinctions in pronouns while Spanish seems inconsistent. The Subj/OP form *nosotros* is distinct from *nosotras*, but the DO/IO form *nos* applies to both genders; the Subj/OP form *ustedes* does not distinguish gender while its DO form does (*los* vs. *las*); and *yo* and *tú* show no gender distinction at all, nor does any pronoun in the IO form.

Contrasting with masc. *he* and fem. *she*, English has an *it*, or actually several *its*. First, there is the dummy proform inserted into Subj position because English requires some kind of Subj, not because this *it* stands for any real referent (v. 11.1.1). Spanish grammar has no such requirement, and this *it* is unmatched:

It's 68 degrees outside.	Hace veinte grados afuera.
It's obvious it'll snow.	Está claro que va a nevar.

Next is the *it* which is 'neuter' in the Spanish sense of standing for a general concept with no implied noun (v. 8.4.2). Here Spanish has Subj/OP *ello* and DO *lo*, though *ello* is rare as a Subj, especially in Spanish America (Cárdenas 1967:139).

He was snoring; did it bother you?	Estaba roncando; ¿te molestaba (ello)?
He was snoring; I'm going to complain about it.	Estaba roncando; me voy a quejar de ello.
He was snoring; I heard it.	Estaba roncando; lo oí.

Third is the *it* referring to an inanimate noun. This one is neuter = 'thing' in English but not neuter = 'unnamed' in Spanish. The Spanish noun will be either masculine or feminine, and one chooses between *él* and *ella, lo* and *la*, for it. Yet this *it* is likewise seldom expressed in Spanish as a Subj:

$$
\text{I need my pencil;} \left\{ \begin{array}{l} \text{where is it?} \\ \text{have you seen it?} \\ \text{are you writing with it?} \end{array} \right.
$$

$$
\text{Necesito mi lápiz;} \left\{ \begin{array}{l} \text{¿dónde está?} \\ \text{¿lo has visto?} \\ \text{¿escribes con él?} \end{array} \right.
$$

Pedagogically, a good (if not infallible) rule of thumb would be not to translate Subj *it* into Spanish.

9.1.3 Case. Neither language distinguishes Subj, DO, IO, and OP throughout. English, in fact, merges the last three into one all-purpose Obj form, but this form is consistently distinguished from the Subj form (except with *you*). Spanish distinguishes DO and IO in the third person but not otherwise, while OP is merged with the Subj forms except for the special OP forms *mí, ti*, and reflexive *sí* (with *con* allomorphs *-migo, -tigo, -sigo*). Spanish DO/IO distinctions such as *lo sirvo* 'I serve up some masculine thing' vs. *le sirvo* 'I serve him (something)' will pose special problems to speakers whose language makes no DO/IO contrast morphologically, and who, in fact, see no IO at all in *I serve him*. Moreover, there are certain Spanish relators that seem prepositional but take Subj, not OP, forms: *según tú, excepto tú, como yo, entre tú y yo*. Neither language provides a special form for a fifth case or function, the PredE (v. 8.1, 11.1.2.2) with a copula: in this case, all but the most formal styles of English use Obj forms with a nonagreeing *be*, whereas Spanish adopts the Subj forms with an agreeing *ser*: *it's me, it's them* vs. *soy yo, son ellos*.

Because of these differences, no translation approach to the target system can be successful. For *her* there are 6 translation equivalents (*la, le, se, ella, su, sus*) and for *you* there are 17 (*tú, te, ti, -tigo, vosotros, vosotras, os, usted, ustedes, lo, los, la, las, le, les, se, -sigo*), 8 of which represent other pronouns too. Students who persist in matching target with source forms soon confuse *nos* with *nosotros, lo* with *le* and *él, me* with *mí* and *yo*. Those who do manage to keep the various forms straight commonly meet their *coup de grâce* when introduced to the *le(s) → se* change; the nonreflexive system thereupon collapses into the reflexive one (v. 9.3.1). There is also the inevitable problem of dialect variation.

9.2 Variation in the pronoun system. Old and Middle English had a number distinction in the second person: sg. *thou*, pl. *ye*. This later shifted to sg. *thou* for an intimate or talking-down relationship vs. *you* for both polite singular address and all plural address, like French *tu/vous*. Eventually, *you* won out and *thou* perished, leaving a neutralization of singular/plural in a language that otherwise distinguishes number rather consistently. As a partial remedy, the folk have developed special plural forms that vary regionally: *y'all* (*you-all*), *y'uns* (*you-ones*), *you-guys*, *youse*, etc.

Spanish second-person pronouns exhibit variation that also originated in systemic change. Old Spanish had *tú* vs. *vos* with the same values as Fr. *tu/vous* and Eng. *thou/you*, namely *tú* for singular intimate address and *vos* for plural or for singular polite. Then *-otros* was added to *vos* to earmark its plural sense, like the *all* of Southern U.S. *y(ou)all*; this spread to *nos* as well, giving a *nosotros* parallel to *vosotros*. Gradually, the politeness of singular *vos* and plural *vosotros* diminished, and they joined *tú* in expressing intimate or talking-down relationships (v. 16.1.1 for more on the social basis of this). As a new polite second-person expression, the elegant phrase *vuestra merced(es)* 'your grace(s)' arose, and this contracted to *usted(es)*. It still betrays its etymology in its third-person verb and pronoun forms (cf. Eng. *your honor/grace has, is, does* vs. *you have, are, do*).

These changes, coupled with equally great social changes, left the following variations in the modern language:

(1) *Vosotros* fell out of use in America and most of Andalusia. In these areas it is now literary or biblical, rather like Eng. *ye*, and *ustedes* serves as the plural of both *tú* and *usted*.

(2) With the waning of *vosotros*, the corresponding *vuestra* of *vuestra merced* was replaced by *su*. The resulting *sumercé(d)* survives in several corners today (Kany 1945/1951:427). At least for some Colombians, it has represented greater familiarity than *tú*, especially in family relations, but it currently seems to be on the wane (Uber 1985:390).

(3) When *vos* descended to the level of *tú*, it displaced it in many areas. The resulting *voseo* is especially common today in the South American cone (i.e. Argentina, Chile, and Uruguay). Its morphology is a hybrid of *tú* and *vos(otros)* remnants:

Subj, OP: *vos*   IO, DO: *te*   Poss.: *tu, tuyo*

So are its verb forms, which come in three main sets:[2]

(a) *vos habláis, coméis* ~ *comís, pedís, sois*
(b) *vos hablás, comés, pedís, sos*
(c) *vos hablas, comes, pides, eres*

Many native teachers of Spanish have followed Bello (1847/1958:89, note) in condemning *vos* and inculcating the 'standard' *tú*. But at least in Argentina the *voseo* remains well rooted, appearing at times even in the written language. It is even possible to claim that for some, the pro-*tú* campaign has merely yielded a three-term system: *vos* for intimate compatriots, *tú* for intimate foreigners, and *usted* otherwise.

The Spanish pronoun system varies in the third person DO and IO forms too. As we saw earlier (v. 8.1.3), there is not much difference in how Spanish marks NP IOs and human DOs, and in the pronoun system the distinction is not marked in most forms (*me, nos, te, os, se* = IO and DO). Given such SYNCRETISM or convergence in marking, great pressure is exerted on the sole point where a distinction was inherited between *dativo* (IO) and *acusativo* (DO), namely, *le(s)* vs. *lo(s)* and *la(s)*.

Already by the sixteenth century (Kany 1945/1951:102), this lonely contrast was eroding among some Castilians, who were using *le(s)* for DO instead of IO. The eventual compromise favored by grammarians in Spain was to reserve *la(s)* for feminine DO and *lo(s)* for masculine inanimate DO, and to allow *le(s)* for all else (i.e. masculine human DO and all IO). This practice is today known as *leísmo*, as opposed to the historical *loísmo* basically retained in America (i.e. *lo(s)* for masculine DO, human or inanimate, vs. *le(s)* for IO only). But, as with *seseo* and *yeísmo* (v. 2.1.4), it is an overgeneralization to label Spain as *leísta* and America as *loísta*. In Spain, *loísmo* survives in many areas, and the continuing fluctuations have yielded at least five different *pronombrismos* in that country, as Gili Gaya (1973) counts them. These are shown in Figure 9.2. (System 1 is *loísmo*, System 2 is *leísmo*, and System 3 is called *laísmo*; System 4 reserves *lo* for the DO form of neuter *ello* only, and System 5 eliminates *le* altogether.)

Figure 9.2 Five *pronombrismos* in Spain.

System:	1	2	3	4	5
DO:					
(a) masc. hum. (Al hombre) ____ veo	lo	le	le	le	lo
(b) masc. inanim. (El coche) ____ veo	lo	lo	lo	le	lo
(c) fem. (A la mujer) ____ veo.	la	la	la	la	la
IO:					
(d) masc. (Al hombre) ____ daré uno.	le	le	le	le	lo
(e) fem. (A la mujer) ____ daré uno.	le	le	la	la	la

Nor is Spanish America purely *loísta*. Verbs with one object *(ayudar, asustar,* etc.) vary between taking *dativo* and *acusativo*, as noted earlier (v. 8.1.3). Kany (ibid.) quotes from several writers who alternate between *le* and *lo* for the DO of the same verb in the same paragraph. Opinion is divided on the reasons for this. Perhaps the distinction between DO and IO is simply neutralized with single-Obj verbs, so that one uses either or both interchangeably in a kind of free variation. Alternatively, perhaps native *loísmo* is contaminated by imitative flourishes of (presumed) peninsular *leísmo*. Or perhaps *le ayudo* and *lo ayudo* depict different degrees of Obj involvement or potency, as García and Otheguy maintained (v. 8.1.3).[3] For whatever reason, the *leísmo/loísmo* situation in current Spanish is fluid and impossible to describe with precision.

There is more variation. In Argentina (and other places), the *de* of compound prepositions fuses with a pronoun Obj to yield a pseudopossessive:

delante de mí → *delante mío, alrededor de ella* → *alrededor suyo.* On both sides of the Atlantic, many speakers abandon the special OP forms *mí, ti, sí* and generalize the Subj pattern: *para yo, por tú, a él (mismo)* like *para nosotros, por ustedes. Nosotras* is not used by the women of many areas (Boyd-Bowman 1960:154). When one goes on to include still other variants (Kany 1945/1951: 92-127) and to uncover the ebullient cauldron of reflexives (v. 9.3), the Spanish pronoun system swells with formidable complexity. Yet in the classroom Spanish synthesized for U.S. consumption, much of this variation is swept aside in favor of a system that is rather artificial, and even the most exacting descriptive linguists can suggest no practical pedagogical alternative. The system given as *the* system in Figure 9.1 is quite complex as it is, and proves a big enough challenge without introducing all fluctuations and alternatives. If students master it, they will be equipped for expressing themselves adequately, and for understanding the pronouns of native speakers—of most of them, that is, and most of the time.

9.3 Reflexives. In English, all reflexive pronouns end in *-self* or *-selves*, so that for each Obj pronoun there is a contrasting reflexive counterpart: *me* vs. *myself, you* vs. *yourself(-ves), her* vs. *herself, them* vs. *themselves*, etc. In Spanish, the contrast is marked only in the third person (including Ud. and Uds.): *le(s) lo(s) la(s)* vs. *se*, and in the standard language, *a él(ella Ud. ellos Uds...)* vs. *a sí (consigo)*. Reflexive morphology, at least, is clear in the two languages.

But the meanings and usage of the reflexive are more elusive. REFLEXIVE is etymologically 'bending back', and in its most literal sense it describes a case in which the Obj refers back to the Subj: *(John saw John)* → *John saw himself.* Here, Subj and DO are referentially identical, for John verbs John and not someone else. But the reflexive has extruded itself into other patterns with other meanings, not just in Spanish but in English and other European languages too. For example, in all of the following the Subj is not literally acting upon itself, despite the italicized reflexive morpheme:

Spanish: *Se* construyó otro puente. 'Another bridge was built.' (lit. 'another bridge built itself.')
French: Ça *se* voit. 'That's apparent.' (lit. 'that sees itself.')
German: Die Tür öffnete *sich.* 'The door opened.' (lit. 'the door opened itself.')
Russian: Kak píshet*sya* éto? 'How is that written?' (lit. 'how does that write-self?')
Latin: It*ur.* 'One goes' (lit. 'goes-self')
English: No opportunity presented *itself.*

Bull (1965:265-73) has proposed that these semantic evolutions are quite natural. If one can say, by way of contrast,

Yo no vestí a Manuel; él se vistió.

then why not

Yo no paré el motor; se paró.

and, one step further,

Yo no rompí ese vaso; se rompió.

and finally, a long ways from where we started,

Yo no pude viajar por el Maghreb fácilmente, pero otros dicen que se viaja por allá sin problema alguno.

In other words, regardless of whether a Subj can logically act upon itself or not, the reflexive has become a marker that, in varying degrees, deemphasizes personal agency from without. The various usages of *se*, according to Bull, will thus lie on a continuum.[4]

Other analysts, however, have been more taxonomic, sorting out uses of *se* into semantically and grammatically distinct classes. The following classification synthesizes these classifications for expository purposes, but the reader should bear in mind that not all grammarians would distinguish all these categories, for some (if not all) can be grouped around one central principle.

9.3.1 Pseudo-reflexive or 'spurious' *se*.

Les di la llave. → (Les la di →) Se la di.

Le and *les* change to *se* when followed by another pronoun beginning with *l*. This rule is a strange one, and ill-informed commentators have sometimes attributed it to a 'cambio eufónico' so as to avoid the 'cacofonía' of two occurrences of /l/ in adjacent syllables. This reasoning is dubious, for no one otherwise regards the same sequence in *paralelo*, *aleluya*, *darle lo mejor*, *le lastimó*, *vale la pena*, etc. as cacophonous, nor has the language ever tried to purge itself of it. In reality, this *se* comes from a medieval *ge* that had the same Latin source as *le*; *ge* was pronounced [že], then [še]. When /š/ disappeared from the phonemic inventory of Spanish (usually evolving into modern /x/), [še] crossed paths with [se] and the two merged into *se*. In short, pseudo-*se* has nothing to do with the other uses of *se*. Nevertheless, it can cause severe problems when students overgeneralize the *le* → *se* rule to produce **se gusta*, **se duele la cabeza*, **se di una llave*, etc.

9.3.2 True reflexive *se*.

Ella se vio en el espejo.	She saw herself in the mirror.
El gerente se disparó.	The manager shot himself.
Olga se compró una blusa.	Olga bought herself a blouse.

Here the reflexive has its original meaning, namely, that the DO or IO is the same entity as the Subj. In both languages, it contrasts with non-reflexives:

Ella la vio en el espejo.	She saw her (someone else) in the mirror.
El gerente le disparó.	The manager shot him (someone else).
Olga(-Luisa) le compró a Olga(-María) una blusa.	Olga (Louise) bought another Olga (Mary) a blouse.

The two languages thus correspond rather well here. Of course, since the concept of IO is broader in Spanish (v. 8.1.2), Spanish may use a reflexive IO where English does not: hence, corresponding to nonreflexive *Mamá le lavó la cara a su hija* and *Tomás le puso/quitó una chaqueta a su hija*, Spanish has:

Mamá se lavó la cara.	Mom washed her (own) face.
Tomás se puso/quitó una chaqueta.	Tom put on/took off his/a jacket.

The two languages diverge with certain verbs that allow omission of the reflexive Obj in English. It is as though English optionally deletes the reflexive if it is understood,[5] whereas Spanish prefers a reflexive Obj whenever a transitive verb's action is not carried out on some other entity:

$$
\text{Pedro}
\begin{cases}
\text{se lavó.} \\
\text{se vistió.} \\
\text{se afeitó.} \\
\text{se bañó.}
\end{cases}
\qquad
\text{Peter}
\begin{cases}
\text{washed (himself), washed up.} \\
\text{dressed (himself), got dressed.} \\
\text{shaved (himself).} \\
\text{bathed (himself), took a bath.}
\end{cases}
$$

Spanish thus contrasts *se lavó* with *lo lavó*, while English contrasts *washed* Ø with *washed him*.

A criterion for the true reflexive in Spanish is the possibility of emphasis with *a sí mismo* (*a mí mismo*, etc.). For example, one can say *ella se vio/lavó a sí misma* but not **ella se atrevió a sí misma*, indicating that *lavarse* and *verse* are true reflexives (whether or not English uses *-self*), while *atreverse* belongs to some other category.

9.3.3 Reciprocal *se*.

Lucía y Joaquín se miraron. Lucy and Joaquin looked at each other.

When the referents of a plural Subj carry out something on each other, not each upon itself, the construction is called RECIPROCAL. English uses *each other* or *one another*, and like the reflexive *-self* forms, these can be omitted from some verbs: *they agreed (with each other), they fought (one another), we argued (with each other), you got married (to each other)*. Spanish applies its reflexive system to the reciprocal, but the reciprocal emphasizer is not *a sí mismo* but *uno a otro*, whose *a* represents IO or DO. (If the verb requires a different preposition, *a* is replaced accordingly: *se alejaron uno de otro*.) Colloquially, *entre ellos* is also used (Roldán 1973:203). Without emphasizers, a plural reflexive can be ambiguous outside of context: *todos se miraron* could be 'everyone looked at himself/herself' or 'everyone looked at each other'.[6]

9.3.4 Lexical or inherent *se*.

Ella se quejó de la calidad del paño (*a sí misma).	She complained (*herself) of the cloth's quality.

Quejarse is 'inherently' reflexive in that a speaker who selects *quejar* automatically deploys it with a reflexive morpheme. Other such verbs include *arrepentirse, resentirse, obstinarse, abstenerse, atreverse, jactarse,* and *atenerse*. The *se* is reflexive in that it agrees with the Subj (*yo me quejo, tú te quejas,* etc.), but it is essentially meaningless since it contrasts neither with $\emptyset$ (no Obj) nor with *lo(s), la(s), le(s),* or some other Obj. It is lexically a part of the verb and denotes no real reflexivity. English parallels exist but are few and uncommon: *avail oneself, pride oneself, perjure oneself.*

9.3.5 Meaning-changing and/or inchoative *se*.

Ella bebió el café.	She drank the coffee.
Ella se bebió el café.	She drank down (up) the coffee.
Ellos durmieron.	They slept.
Ellos se durmieron.	They fell asleep.

The verbs of this category are a mixed lot, but they agree in (1) contrasting with nonreflexive versions of the same verb (unlike lexical reflexives) and (2) failing the *a sí mismo* test for true reflexivity (**ella se bebió el café a sí misma*). In terms of English translation equivalents (a poor criterion, to be sure, but one that students apply), the *se* subtly shifts the verb's meaning. In *irse, reírse, olvidarse, temerse, entrarse, morirse, merecerse, beberse, comerse,* etc. it intensifies the action or state rather like English particles such as *up, down, out, away* (v. 11.1.2.4). For Bello (1847/ 1958:246-48) and Ramsey (1894/1956:380), what is intensified is specifically the involvement or affect of the Subj. Bello's glossings are illustrative:

> *me temo*: indicates 'el interés de la persona que habla'
> *se lo bebió*: indicates 'la buena disposición, el apetito, la decidida voluntad'
> *te lo sabes*: indicates 'la presunción de saberlo todo'
> *estáte tranquilo*: indicates 'permanecer voluntariamente'
> *te entraste*: indicates 'cierto conato o fuerza con que se vence algún estorbo'

Gili Gaya (1973:127) finds in these senses a more or less normal reflexive IO: since the IO represents a broad involvement (v. 8.1.2-8.1.3), the reflexive IO in *el perro se comió toda la ración* suggests that the dog both initiated (as Subj) and participated (as IO) in the event. Roldán (1971b:21) adds that this reflexive IO can suggest that the Subj is 'keeping at' a state, which is her interpretation of examples such as *Luis se quedó en casa* and *Luis se estuvo en casa*. Neither rationale suffices, though: *dormirse* has no necessary subject involvement or keeping-atness, and it and *comerse* cannot have true reflexive IOs (**se durmió a sí mismo*, **se lo comió a sí mismo* vs. *se lo puso a sí mismo*); on the other hand, no reflexive appears in *Juan viajó por toda Europa*, even though John presumably initiated, participated in, and 'kept at' his travels.

Roldán recognizes this problem and introduces a second explanation: some meaning-changing reflexives have the *se* to indicate not a reflexive NP but, instead, INCHOATIVE ASPECT, i.e. the initiation of a process whereby the Subj enters a new state. This meaning certainly holds for *dormirse* 'fall asleep' in contrast with *dormir* 'sleep'. Moreover, she notes an important property of inchoative reflexives, namely, that their state—once entered—is expressed by *estar* + participle:

Process:	State:
Se durmió. 'She fell asleep'	Está dormida. 'She's asleep, sleeping'
Se agachó. 'She squatted'	Está agachada. 'She's squatting'
Se murió. 'She died'	Está muerta. 'She's dead'
Se casó. 'She got married'	Está casada. 'She's married'
Se calló. 'She shut up'	Está callada. 'She's quiet'
Se enteró. 'She found out'	Está enterada. 'She's aware'

Roldán expands her inchoative *se* category to include many verbs from other reflexive types as well because of the same contrast:

Se arrepintió. 'She repented'	Está arrepentida. 'She's sorry'
Se enojó. 'She got angry'	Está enojada. 'She's angry'
Se cerró. 'It closed'	Está cerrada. 'It's closed'
Se resintió. 'She resented'	Está resentida. 'She's resentful'

Pedagogically, her observation would be especially useful in explaining to students why the participle is used with *estar* instead of the gerund as in English: *she's sitting* = *está sentada* (≠ *está sentándose*), *she's standing* = *está parada* (≠ *está parándose*).

Yet there remain many verbs whose reflexives convey other meanings. In the following list, for example, the semantic change seems idiomatic, and the two verbs may even be allocated to different grammatical patterns (e.g. *le quedan dos* but *se quedan en su habitación*).

quedar 'be left, be'	quedarse 'stay, remain'
poner 'put; turn on'	ponerse 'begin'

salir 'go out, leave'	salirse 'leak, overflow'
marchar 'march'	marcharse 'go away'
saltar 'jump'	saltarse 'skip (something)'
sentir 'regret; sense'	sentirse 'feel (+ Adj)'
escurrir 'wring out'	escurrirse 'slip'
fijar 'attach, drive in'	fijarse 'notice, pay attention to'
llevar 'carry'	llevarse con 'get along with'
pasar 'pass, spend'	pasarse 'go bad, spoil'
sonar 'ring, sound'	sonarse 'blow one's nose'

A definitive characterization of 'meaning-changing' *se* has yet to be made, and it remains a catch-all category for uses that do not fit elsewhere.

9.3.6 Intransitive or decausative *se.*

Ella se detuvo en el andén.	She stopped on the platform.
El aluminio se ha fundido.	The aluminum has melted.
Los vasos se rompen.	Glasses break.
El barco se hundirá.	The boat will sink.
El conejito se movió.	The bunny moved.
Las fronteras se extienden hasta el mar.	The boundaries extend down to the sea.
Se volcó el vino.	The wine spilled.

Many English verbs can be used transitively (with DO) or intransitively (without DO) with the special semantic contrast of 'X caused Y to VERB' vs. 'Y VERBed (all by itself)': *Joe stopped her* 'caused her to stop' vs. *She stopped.* The Spanish counterparts to such verbs often take *se* for the intransitive or 'decausative' sense.[7] The foregoing examples illustrate the intransitive-decausative meaning in contrast to the following transitives:

José la detuvo en el andén.	Joe stopped her on the platform.
El incendio ha fundido el aluminio.	The fire has melted (down) the aluminum.
Emilia rompe los vasos.	Emily breaks glasses.
El pirata hundirá el barco.	The pirate will sink the boat.
La niña movió el conejito.	The girl moved the bunny.
El dictador extiende las fronteras hasta el mar.	The dictator is extending the boundaries down to the sea.
Papá volcó el vino.	Dad spilled the wine.

At first glance, the intransitive/transitive contrast resembles that between *se lavó* 'he washed (himself)' and *la lavó* 'he washed her': Spanish seems to use a reflexive when the Subj acts upon itself while English optionally deletes its reflexive. But the analogy quickly collapses. In English there is no reflexive optionally deleted from *the aluminum has melted* (cf. **the aluminum has melted itself*); likewise, in Spanish *a sí mismo* can be added to *se lavó* but not to *se ha fundido* (*por sí mismo* could indeed be used, but for the quite different meaning of 'all by itself'). Note the following additional examples of the nonreflexivity of intransitive *se*:

$$\text{Guillermo} \begin{cases} \text{se arrodilló} \\ \text{se inclinó} \\ \text{se acostó} \\ \text{se enfermó} \\ \text{se estremeció} \end{cases} (\text{*a sí mismo}).$$

$$\text{Las cajas} \begin{cases} \text{se rompieron} \\ \text{se empaparon} \\ \text{se aplastaron} \\ \text{se enfriaron} \\ \text{se agotaron} \end{cases} (\text{*a sí mismas}).$$

On the other hand, certain verbs with *se* have a dual potential here: (1) they can be intransitive-decausative, in which case the event happened by itself (and *a sí mismo* is excluded), or (2) they can be interpreted as true reflexives, in which case the Subj caused the event to happen to itself (and *a sí mismo* can be added). As one informant put it, 'depende de la intención.'

(1) El perro se mojó.	The dog got wet.
(2) El perro se mojó (a sí mismo).	The dog got himself wet, wetted himself.
(1) Pilar se lastimó.	Pilar got hurt.
(2) Pilar se lastimó (a sí misma).	Pilar hurt herself.
(1) Él se llama 'Zorro'.	His name is Zorro.
(2) Él se llama 'Zorro' (a sí mismo).	He calls himself Zorro.
(1) El robot se descompuso.	The robot broke down.
(2) El robot se descompuso (a sí mismo).	The robot shut itself down.

As Ramsey (1894/1956:377-81) noted, the obvious pedagogical generalization is that Spanish adds *se* to a transitive verb where English just intransitivizes it by omitting a DO. Consequently, it would be helpful to language learners if dictionaries and vocabularies avoided one-word English glosses and distinguished *detenerse* and *detener*, *moverse* and *mover*, etc. as 'to stop' vs. 'to stop someone', 'to move' vs. 'to move something', with some indication of the (in)transitivity of the English gloss.

Like all generalizations, Ramsey's equation of Spanish V vs. V-*se* with English V-tr vs. V-intr has certain holes in it (as he himself was quick to point out). One is that English sometimes adopts distinct verbs for the contrast:

apagar (tr), apagarse (intr)	turn off/out (tr), go off/out (intr)
acostar (tr), acostarse (intr)	put to bed (tr), go to bed (intr)
encargar (tr), encargarse (intr)	put in charge (tr), take charge (intr)
criar (tr), criarse (intr)	bring up, rear (tr), grow up, be raised (intr)
acercar (tr), acercarse (intr)	draw up, pull up (tr), approach (intr)
sentar (tr), sentarse (intr)	seat (tr), sit down (intr)
reunir (tr), reunirse (intr)	bring together (tr), meet (intr) (but gather = tr/intr)
equivocar (tr), equivocarse (intr)	confuse, mix up (tr), be wrong (intr)
desatar (tr), desatarse (intr)	untie (tr), come untied (intr)
atascar (tr), atascarse (intr)	obstruct (tr), get stuck (intr)

Verbs of becoming (which Roldán would call inchoative) fall into the same pattern:

El café me pone nervioso. (tr)	Coffee *makes* me nervous.
Yo me pongo nervioso. (intr)	I *get* nervous.
La hicieron ejecutiva. (tr)	They *made* her an executive.
Se hizo ejecutiva. (intr)	She *became* an executive.
Lo convertí en un garaje. (tr)	I *changed* it into a garage.
Se convirtió en un garaje. (intr)	It *turned* into a garage.
La pastilla la enfermó. (tr)	The pill *made* her sick.
Ella se enfermó. (intr)	She *got* sick.

The other problem is that Spanish is not entirely consistent either, for not all transitive verbs require *se* for intransitivity. Given the analogy '*lo cerré* is to *se cerró* as *I shut* (tr) *it* is to *it shut* (intr)', one would expect *lo terminé* for 'I finished it' vs. *se terminó* for 'it ended'; but Spanish does not require *se* for the intransitive of *terminar: el curso terminó*. Other verbs like *terminar* include:

parar (tr, intr) 'stop'	enmudecer (tr) 'silence', (intr) 'get quiet'
tocar (tr, intr) 'play'	
mejorar (tr, intr) 'improve'	subir (tr) 'carry up, raise', (intr) 'go up, rise'
cambiar (tr, intr) 'change'	
empezar (tr, intr) 'begin, start'	bajar (tr) 'lower', (intr) 'go down'
engordar (tr) 'fatten, make fat,' (intr) 'get fat'	

9.3.7 Reflexive *se* of emotional reaction.

Se alegra mucho de esto.   She's very happy about this.

The verbs in this group form a large set, as illustrated here:

aburrir(se)	desesperar(se)	espantar(se)
alegrar(se)	desilusionar(se)	extrañar(se)
animar(se)	divertir(se)	inquietar(se)
asombrar(se)	enfadar(se)	interesar(se)
asustar(se)	enfurecer(se)	irritar(se)
calmar(se)	enojar(se)	molestar(se)
confundir(se)	entristecer(se)	ofender(se)
conmover(se)	entusiasmar(se)	preocupar(se)
deprimir(se)		sorprender(se)

When nonreflexive, the cause(r) of the emotional reaction is cast as the verb's Subj, and the reactor or experiencer is cast as Obj (IO or DO, v. 8.1.3):

Esto les aburre.   This bores them.
Yo la sorprendí.   I surprised her.
Tú lo enojaste.   You made him mad.

When reflexive, such verbs have the reactor/experiencer as Subj and the cause of the reaction is expressed (if at all) by a PP (which can be preposition + NP or preposition + noun clause, v. 10.4.2, 13.2.1):

Ellos se aburrieron (de la tele).   They got bored (with TV).
Ella se sorprendió (de que   She was surprised (that you were
  llegaras).   coming).
Él se enojó (de la condición).   He was angry (at the condition).

This category resembles the inchoative one in certain respects (cf. *se preocupó* vs. *está preocupado* like *se durmió* vs. *está dormido*), and also the intransitive one. In fact, *calmar* 'calm someone down' is to *calmarse* 'calm down' as *hundir* is to *hundirse*. And like the intransitives, reflexives of emotional reaction are not true reflexives: to say **se alegró/ preocupó/deprimió a sí mismo* is rather peculiar, experientially if not grammatically. Babcock (1970), however, sets them aside as a special category because of what she sees as a unique contrast in them: *se sorprendió* suggests a state of surprise while *yo la sorprendí* suggests an action. Obviously, this is not true of intransitive *se*, since both *se hundió* and *yo lo hundí* are processes; but whether it is true even of all emotional-reaction verbs is doubtful. Depending on the context, *se enoja* can indicate the condition of anger (state: 'he's mad') but also the speaker's inchoative entry into that state (process: 'he's getting mad'). However analyzed, the verbs in this group form a conspicuous set in Spanish and their systematic reflexive/nonreflexive contrasts merit pedagogical attention.

9.3.8 Causative *se*.

Juan se operó anoche.   John had an operation last night.

The verbs in this group are relatively few: *operarse, bautizarse, hacerse (un traje), retratarse, vacunarse, cortarse (el pelo)*, and some others. *Se* with them indicates that the Subj caused something to be done for or upon himself. Since these verbs are transitive, they can, of course, occur nonreflexively too: *el médico lo/le operó anoche*. They may or may not be ambiguous between causative and true reflexive senses: in a culture where self-baptism is not recognized, *Juanito se bautizará* is semantically clear, but in *la enfermera se vacunará* the nurse may vaccinate herself or have herself vaccinated.

9.3.9 Passive and impersonal *se*.

Se cierra la puerta a las ocho.   The door is closed at eight, one
                                  closes the door at eight.
Se habla español aquí.   Spanish is spoken here, one speaks/
                                  you speak Spanish here.

This category is likewise hard to separate from the intransitive one. Whereas Eng. *close* can be transitive or intransitive (*I close the door, the door closes*), in Spanish one does not usually say *la puerta cierra* but *se cierra la puerta* or *la puerta se cierra*, which may be intransitive ('it closes'), passive ('it is/gets closed'), or impersonal ('one closes/you close it')—or even true reflexive when said of automatic doors with their own action-initiating mechanisms. Perhaps *se cierra* has the single meaning of 'no external causer' embracing all these senses, as Bull's continuum theory would predict. But in some contexts, *se cierra la puerta* or *la puerta se cierra* is equivalent to *la puerta es cerrada (por Juan, por el viento)*, and 'passive/impersonal' *se* is often recognized as a distinct category.

Or as two categories: Perlmutter (1971), Contreras (1974), and others distinguish passive from impersonal on the basis of at least five syntactic differences. First, many speakers see *se cerró la puerta* as so passive in its force that they add an agent phrase: *se cerró la puerta por el guarda* = *la puerta fue cerrada por el guarda*. This agent phrase never appears when the sentence is meant impersonally, as in **se cierra la puerta por nosotros antes de entrar*. Second, impersonal *se* is distinct from passives, for it can be added to true passives: *se es juzgado por la posteridad*. Third, passive *se* obviously accompanies transitive verbs only (intransitives cannot be passivized, *fui venido), in which case it converges with intransitive *se*:

Se cerraron las puertas.   The doors were closed, the doors
                              closed.

But impersonal *se* accompanies any kind of verb, transitive or intransitive, that admits a human subject (*se llueve is odd for the same reason as *ella llueve):

Se está muy cómodo aquí.	One is very comfortable here.
Se vivía bien en aquel entonces.	One/They lived well back then.
¿Se puede entrar?	Can one enter?
¡No se fuma!	No smoking!
Se caminó todo el día.	People walked all day.
Como se vive, se muere.	One dies as one lives, you die as you live.

Fourth, with passive *se* the NP is the Subj of the verb, which accordingly agrees with it, and this Subj precedes or follows the verb like any other Subj (cf. *Juan comió ~ Comió Juan*, v. 11.2.2-11.3.1):

Se organizarán *las fiestas* así.⎫	The festivals will be organized this
Las fiestas se organizarán así.⎭	way.

But with impersonal *se*, the verb stays in the third singular; the NP occupies a DO position after the verb, or if it is preposed, it requires a pronominal copy (cf. *Juan comió las nueces ~ Las nueces las comió Juan*, v. 11.2.2-11.3.1):

Se organizará *las fiestas* así. ⎫	One/you/they will organize the
Las fiestas se *las* organizará así.⎭	festivals this way.

And fifth, when the NP in a passive *se* + V + NP is deemphasized, it drops like any other Spanish Subj (cf. *¿Cómo juega Luis? → ¿Cómo juega?*):

¿Cómo se .define *esa palabra* con precisión? → ¿Cómo se define con precisión?

But the deemphasized NP of impersonal *se* + V + NP becomes a DO pronoun (cf. *¿Cómo haces el café? → ¿Cómo lo haces?*):

¿Cómo se define *esa palabra* con precisión? → ¿Cómo se *la* define con precisión?

Nevertheless, granting the syntactic differences between the two, often there is little real difference in meaning, and some native speakers may wonder why *¿Cómo se define esta palabra?* is regarded as ambiguous. One should note that in English, too, there is more structural than semantic difference between *How is this defined?* and *How does one define this?*, for both downplay the personal identity of the agent.

In pedagogy, it might be useful to give some attention to how English renders impersonal subjects, since the lack of a single good equivalent for *se* can hinder mastery of it. Formal English prefers *one* whereas spoken English tends toward *you, people,* or *they.* Students are not generally aware of the impersonal functions of these, although they are distinct from the personal ones. (Note the ambiguity in *How do you get good grades?* If *you* is construed as personal, 'tú, Ud.', the question may be answered *I study a lot*; if taken impersonally, *you = one*, it is answered *You study a lot.*) But *one* and *you* are mostly restricted to generic or habitual characterizations of events and procedures; they are not used for particular, single events. Thus, *se revisa las llantas cada día* can be aptly translated *one checks/you check the tires every day* since it deals with generalized behavior, not a one-time event; but for *se revisó las llantas ayer, one checked the tires yesterday* is strange and *you checked the tires yesterday* would be interpreted as personal *you*. In this case, English speakers must resort to a Subj such as *people* or *someone*, or to a passive (*the tires were checked*), which obscures the distinction between *se revisó las llantas* and *se revisaron las llantas*, such as it is.

The impersonal *se* coexists with a more direct equivalent of impersonal *one, uno*: *es que no se tiene suficiente cuidado, es que uno no tiene suficiente cuidado*. But as Roldán (1971b:26) and Perlmutter (1971:36-37) note, *se* and *uno* are not entirely interchangeable. One difference is that a female speaker can use a feminine *una*, with agreement throughout the sentence:

Una está satisfecha consigo misma.   *Se está satisfecha consigo misma.

Another is that only *se* is used when the verb's Subj is implicitly many people indefinitely; *uno* particularizes (for obvious etymological reasons) and is incompatible with that sense:

*A las cinco uno empezó a llegar.   A las cinco se empezó a llegar.

Third, *uno* counts as a genuine NP, occurring in any NP slot, while *se* represents only an impersonal Subj, and even then it does not occupy a Subj slot: *no se habla, uno no habla*. Hence, only *uno* can be used for an impersonal Obj (IO, DO, OP):

Le deprimen a uno las noticas.   *Se deprimen (a sí) las noticias.

With so many *se*'s, it seems impersonal and passive *se* might be confused not only with each other but with the other types as well. This is sometimes the case: *¿Se mató la gallina?* might ask if the chicken killed itself or if the chicken was or got killed or if someone killed the chicken. Here, though, the intended meaning is probably not true reflexive, since chickens normally do not engage in suicide. But especially with humans, who do unto others and do unto themselves, the distinction must often be marked. For example, with *matar + tirano* one would want to separate the true reflexive sense from the passive and/or impersonal one, and he does this by employing *a* before the NP for the latter—demonstrating, once again, that the NP is the DO in that case:[8]

Nunca se matará el tirano.   The tyrant will never kill himself.
Nunca se matará al tirano.   One/People will never kill the tyrant,
                              the tyrant will never be killed.

If a female DO in this construction is pronominalized, it becomes *la*: *se critica a la reina* → *se la critica*. For males, even *loísta* grammarians have recommended *le*: *se critica al tirano* → *se le critica*. However, the use of *lo* here—*se lo critica*— is well attested (Roldán 1971b:25).

It should be borne in mind that a given reflexive verb may belong to several of the preceding categories, depending on context and meaning. *Verse* in *se ven en el espejo* is a true reflexive, or reciprocal; in *se ven muy cansados* it serves as a copula and perhaps is 'meaning-changing'; in *se ven muchas películas extranjeras* it is passive. *Vestirse* is a true reflexive in *se vistió (a sí misma)* 'she got dressed', in opposition to *lo vistió* or *vistió a su hijo*; but *vestirse* could also be considered an inchoative meaning-changer in opposition to the *vestir* meaning 'wear' (*vistió una camiseta nomás*) with the same contrast as in *dormirse* vs. *dormir*: and in *se vistió de luto en el pueblo* it is impersonal.

9.3.10 The so-called 'unplanned occurrence'. Spanish has an IO that expresses general involvement or interest in an occurrence or state (v. 8.1.2), and it has a *se* which variously reflexivizes, intensifies, inchoativizes, passivizes, or intransitivizes the verb. When the two are used together, sentences such as the following result:

El caudillo se murió (+ a nosotros) → El caudillo se nos murió.
El peine se cayó (+a mí) → El peine se me cayó.
Se pagó el dinero (+a ti) → Se te pagó el dinero.
Se olvidó la respuesta (+a mí) → Se me olvidó la respuesta.
Se perdieron las llaves (+a Uds.) → Se les perdieron las llaves.
Se armó un lío (+a ella) → Se le armó un lío.

Consequently, the IO in a reflexive construction is no more a special category of usage than it is in any other verb phrase: cf. *es difícil (+a mí)* → *me es difícil, pagan bien (+a él)* → *le pagan bien, fue dado (+a ella)* → *le fue dado.*

Yet *se + IO + V* has been singled out as quite distinct by many U.S. text writers, who see in it the expression of accidents, unplanned events, and escape from responsibility (*sic* in Mujica 1982:35). Interestingly, the Real Academia, Gili Gaya, and other Hispanic authorities have seen nothing of the sort in this construction, nor have they set it up as a special category. In reality, many cases could not possibly be construed thus: *se te pagó* would usually suggest a deliberate compliance with responsibility, and *el caudillo se nos murió* would not necessarily imply a dodging of responsibility (nor would the nonreflexive *el caudillo murió* normally be taken as a planned death).

With *yo olvidé la respuesta* vs. *se me olvidó la respuesta*, it is true that the former spotlights the speaker as Subj and proceeds to comment on what he did, while the latter casts him as an 'involved entity'. But subjecthood does not always entail willful agency or deliberate causation

(v. 8.1.1), and with both statements the hearer could hold the speaker responsible for a faulty memory. Neither version, in itself, necessarily implies *sin querer, por casualidad,* or *con intención.* If the forgetting was planned, i.e. was something the speaker *did,* then *yo olvidé la respuesta* is preferable, but it would be dangerous to generalize from this unlikely case (how many forgettings are planned?) to the host of other such constructions, and this in fact would obscure the real basis of *se* + IO + V.

It is even more dangerous to introduce notions such as 'responsibility' and 'avoidance of responsibility,' for these convey a juridical, ethical, and moral sense more than a grammatical one. Students studying a foreign culture have lamentable stereotypes of it, and to explain the frequency of *se* + IO + V in terms of cultural mores can reinforce the very misimpressions teachers are trying to correct. Indeed, one student who read his text's 'avoidance of responsibility' presentation of this construction proceeded to explicate it to his classmates on the basis of the fatalism, indolence, and lack of initiative that supposedly characterize Hispanics.

'Unplanned occurrence' is the tenth category of recognized *se* uses. It can be abolished, not only because of its dubious reasoning but because the other nine suffice entirely, and they offer a big enough challenge as they stand.

9.3.11 Summary. *Se* is multifaceted in modern Spanish, perhaps more so than any other morpheme. Its functions are varied and complex, and presumably for that reason, many first-year texts focus on its reflexive meaning, postponing (if taking up at all) the nonreflexive ones to final chapters on passives or grammatical miscellanea. But if a text's organization is predicated on a prioritization reflecting the relative frequency of items studied, nonreflexive *se* deserves more, and earlier, attention. It is certainly more common than the true passive (v. 12.3), and is quite likely more common than the true reflexive as well. Moreover, even those teachers who are adept at scaling down their Spanish in accordance with what students have covered so far find it difficult and painfully artificial to circumlocute around *¿Cómo se dice/escribe/puede... ?, ¿Qué se hace con... ?, ¿Dónde se ve/habla/oye... ?, ¿A qué hora se abre/cierra/ come... ?,* and so forth.

9.4 The syntax of pronouns. Aside from the meaning and morphology of pronouns, their syntax confuses many lower-level students. This is because Spanish pronoun forms differ very strikingly from their English counterparts in their sentence positions and in how they double up and combine with one another.

9.4.1 Pronominalizing with clitics. PRONOMINALIZATION is the process whereby nominal or lexical NPs are changed into pronouns.[9] In English, this process does not greatly affect word order, for pronouns obey much the same placement rules as nominal NPs.[10]

$$\left\{\begin{array}{c}\text{Mary}\\\text{She}\end{array}\right\} \text{gave} \left\{\begin{array}{c}\text{her phone number}\\\text{it}\end{array}\right\} \text{to} \left\{\begin{array}{c}\text{the man who asked her out.}\\\text{him}\end{array}\right\}$$

In Spanish, though, word order depends on which kind of pronoun is used. Traditionally, two sets have been distinguished syntactically, the Subj and OP forms vs. the DO and IO forms:

(1) yo, mí, tú, ti, Ud., él, ella, ello, nosotros, nosotras, vosotros, vosotras, Uds., ellos, ellas, sí

(2) me, te, le, lo, la, nos, os, los, les, las, se (*all types*)

The two go by different names, respectively *disjunctive* and *conjunctive*, *strong* and *weak*, *stressed* (*tonic*) and *unstressed* (*atonic*), *emphatic* and *clitic*; but all these labels really encapsulate the same points. The first set is stressed and forms constituents that can be separated (disjoined) from the verb and moved: *ellos saben, saben ellos*. The second set is stressless and always joined phonetically to the verb, 'leaning on' (Greek *enklítikos*) it. Usually, they occur as a kind of prefix on the verb (PROCLITIC), but are suffixed (ENCLITIC) to infinitives, gerunds, and affirmative commands: proclitic *se va*, enclitic *váyase*. Following the currently prevailing usage, we will call the second set CLITICS.

In English, one emphasizes or contrasts a pronoun by stressing it: *Hé introduced her to you, He introduced hér to you, He introduced her to yóu.* Spanish handles emphasis and contrast differently since the clitics are atonic: **Té la presentó, *Te lá presentó*. The procedure is to take the basic clitic + V 'nucleus' (v. 11.2) and add forms from Set 1 to it:

Te la presentó.   He introduced her to you (neutral).

$$\left.\begin{array}{l}\textit{Él}\text{ te la presentó.}\\\text{Te la presentó }\textit{él.}\end{array}\right\}$$ Hé introduced her to you.

$$\left.\begin{array}{l}A\ \textit{ti}\text{ te la presentó.}\\\text{Te la presentó }a\ ti.\end{array}\right\}$$ He introduced her to yóu.

An emphatic *a*-phrase can be used for DO as well as for IO:

¿Me escogiste *a mí*? (DO)
¿Me lo quieres dar *a mí*? (IO)

Yet the clitic + V + *a*-phrase construction has become so strongly associated with the IO pattern that many speakers today prefer the IO clitic even when the *a*-phrase is a nominal NP rather than a mere emphasizer. For such speakers, *Di los dulces a mi amigo* is awkward or even ungrammatical, and the so-called 'redundant' construction with a clitic, *Le di los dulces a mi amigo*, has become the norm for IO expression. Many current texts so teach it.

We have already remarked (v. 9.2, 8.1.3) on the syncretism of IO and DO marking in Spanish. Given *a* + NP, it is not always apparent what kind of clitic pronominalization should yield. Indeed, since *a* + NP also represents adverbial prepositional phrases of location, movement, and so on, there are actually three possible pronominalizations:

(1) IO: hablar *a Clara*, hablar*le*
(2) DO: llevar *a Clara*, llevar*la*
(3) OP: regresar *a Clara*, regresar *a ella*

The DO case can be ascertained by passivization (v. 12.3): one says *Clara fue llevada* but not **Clara fue hablada* or **Clara fue regresada*, so in pronominalization *a Clara* will be treated as a DO with *llevar*. This leaves us with the problem of disentangling IO (as with *hablar*) from OP (as with *regresar*), which is not as straightforward. There are many cases in which Spanish speakers treat *a* + NP as IO even though, to English speakers at least, it seems to have a locative adverbial force suggesting OP:

Se acercaba *a nosotros*, Se *nos* (IO) acercaba.
El artículo se antepone *al sustantivo*, El artículo se *le* (IO) antepone.
La información no llega *a los exiliados*, La información no *les* (IO) llega.
La fama vino *al general* muy temprano, La fama *le* (IO) vino muy temprano.

9.4.2 Sequences of clitics. When pronominalization yields two or more clitics with one verb, they form a phonetically melded (AGGLUTINATED) clump with it. If they are clitics of the second verb in V + V, they optionally move to the first verb by a process called 'Clitic Promotion', although as Suñer 1974 points out, they must be promoted together; *querían mostrármelo* → *me lo querían mostrar* (not **lo querían mostrarme*).

What determines which of two clitics precedes the other in this 'clump'? The traditionally consecrated rule in U.S. pedagogy is 'IO before DO': *me* (IO) *lo* (DO) *querían mostrar*, not **lo me querían mostrar*. It works often enough for its credentials to seem impeccable, but they are peccable nonetheless. Aside from the students' problem of having to keep IO and DO straight (no mean task in Spanish, as has been shown), scholars of the language have repeatedly pointed out that the IO-DO rule does not always work. Over a century ago, Bello (1847/1958:293) noted that, regardless of function, *te* and *os* precede *me* and *nos*, and that the latter precede *le(s)*, *lo(s)*, *la(s)*: *me le humillé*, *te les aficionaste*, *te me recomendaron*, *te me acerqué*, *te nos rendiste*[11]—all of which contradict IO-DO order. More succinctly, the RAE (1924:218) gave the lineup as *se* + second person + first + third, with no comments on an IO precedence over DO.

Nevertheless, the IO-DO rule enjoyed such favor in the United States that Holtan (1960) felt compelled to show its inadequacies anew in *Hispania*. He observed that in *nos le reunimos* 'we joined him', the reflexive DO precedes the IO and that the predicted ordering **le nos reunimos* is flatly ungrammatical. Furthermore, the traditional rule cannot handle what happens with *two* IOs, which is quite possible: ¡*no me* (IO) *le* (IO) *calientes la oreja a la muchacha!* (cf. **no le me . . .*).

In order both to account for the permissible sequences and to exclude the ungrammatical ones, Perlmutter (1971:45) proposed a SURFACE-STRUCTURE-CONSTRAINT (SSC) that acts like a filter in allowing only certain combinations of clitics to surface from the underlying syntax. This SSC was not at all revolutionary, since it just reformulated the RAE's earlier analysis of *se* + 2 + 1 + 3:

se	te	me	l-
	os	nos	

Note that only one slot or box is available for all clitics beginning with *l-*; if two of them are generated (*le lo, les la*, etc.), a convention can be posited such that *le(s)* travels to the *se* box—a descriptively neat (if non-etymological) way of handling 'pseudo-*se*'. Moreover, there is only one box for *se*, regardless of whether it is reflexive, pseudo, impersonal, lexical, or whatever; if the syntax generates two *se*'s, the SSC runs out of room and the sentence cannot pass. Thus, the following are correctly rejected as ungrammatical.[12]

*Se se arrepiente pronto for 'one repents soon'
*Se se baña por la mañana for 'one bathes in the morning'
*Se se lo puso for 'he put it on (himself) for her' or 'someone put it on him'
*Se se los dio for 'they were given to him'

Hence, the SSC has considerable pedagogical value; it covers more ground than the IO-DO rule and students can memorize and apply it with relative ease. Still, at least four amendments have been proposed for it. First, Perlmutter himself grants that some speakers have combined the SSC with a preference for IO before DO; for such speakers, if IO pronominalization results in the contradiction of either, then the IO does not become a clitic. Thus, while *María te* (DO) *me* (IO) *recomendó* 'Mary recommended you to me' is acceptable to other speakers, these prefer *María te recomendó a mí*. On the other hand, the traditionally predicted **me* (IO) *te* (DO) *recomendó* is universally ungrammatical in standard Spanish, and the SSC correctly excludes it.

Second, as Szabo (1974) and Perlmutter both point out, there is a strong tendency to place reflexive clitics (not just *se*) before nonreflexive ones. For 'I exerted myself for your sake', **me te esforcé* is blocked by the SSC, but *te me esforcé* is also rejected by some speakers as awkward at best.

Third, Suñer (1974) notes a maximum of three clitics with any one verb; i.e. not all four slots in the SSC grid may be occupied simultaneously. It is hard to construct an example in which four clitics might arise in the first place, but Suñer tries to push the grammar to its limits. Consider *se te mandó flores para mí* '(some)one sent flowers to you for me'; if *flores* is pronominalized as DO *las, para mí* is expressed by a clitic IO *me*, and both enter the existing lineup, the result should be *se te me las mandó*—and Suñer finds this an unacceptable sentence. And fourth, Dinnsen 1972 believes that the SSC is further subject to a condition that an IO of benefit or interest must precede an IO of giving-to; he thus rules out *te me regalaron flores* for *they gave me* (IO of giving-to) *flowers for you* (IO of benefit), although this conforms to the SSC.

If these details seem overwhelming and make the shaky IO-DO rule look attractive by comparison, the reader should bear in mind that the syntax of a language has more generative potential than its speakers ever really put to use. For example, both Spanish and English grammar permit one to join sentences (S) with conjunctions (C): SCS, SCSCS, SCSCSCS, SCSCSCSCS, and so on (v. 11.1.2); theoretically, the grammar thus allows the creation of an infinite number of infinite sentences. The fact that no one ever speaks infinitely, and with finite attention spans and lifetimes, no one *can*, is a matter of human 'performance', not of grammar. As a second example, note that English grammar allows one sentence to be embedded as a relative clause inside another sentence (v. 13.3.1):

The man is outside. + The gardener saw the man.
→ The man *the gardener saw* is outside.

Reapplying exactly the same rule, one obtains the following, which is still grammatical but harder to understand:

(?) The man the gardener *the nurse helped* saw is outside.

And again,

(??) The man the gardener the nurse *the doctor insisted on* helped saw is outside.

A hearer (or reader) has increasing trouble processing such 'nested' embeddings as they accumulate. But this problem has to do with short-term memory, not with English grammar (which allows one to go on forever at this, if so inclined).

Likewise, in Spanish each individual DO and IO has full grammatical permission to become a clitic, but processing them grows harder as they stack up, and ambiguity increases as well:

Me presentó.
(?) *Te me* presentó.
(??) *Te me le* presentó.
(???) *Se te me le* presentó.

It is therefore possible that the add-ons to the SSC have less to do with Spanish grammar than with intelligibility, clarity, and processing. But to prove the issue one way or the other would require more data, and unfortunately (for the linguist), Spanish speakers just do not go around saying things like *se te me le presentó*, whether because of grammar, stylistics, semantics, or situational need. The SSC does account for all grammatical sequences; and although it does not exclude a few unacceptable, marginally acceptable, or unprocessable ones, it handles all cases that students themselves would normally encounter.

Notes for Chapter 9

* This traditional definition is technically true only of 'anaphoric' pronouns. 'Deictic' pronouns such as *yo* and *tú* point directly to something in the speech situation instead of pointing back to something in discourse.

1. CASE refers to inflectional differentiation of forms according to their functions as Subj, DO, etc. Hispanic grammarians have often retained the Latin case names *nominativo, dativo, acusativo* respectively for *sujeto, complemento indirecto*, and *complemento directo*.

2. Dialect (a) is mainly western Argentina, Chile, Panama, northwestern Venezuela, and southern Peru. Dialect (b) is eastern Argentina, Uruguay, western Colombia, coastal Ecuador, El Salvador, and the Andean zone of Venezuela. Dialect (c) is Bolivia, the Ecuadoran mountains, Paraguay, and Áncash (Peru). *Voseo* is very strong in the ríoplatense area and generally weaker elsewhere or consigned to lower-class or rural usage. See Zamora Vicente 1967 and Resnick 1975 for more details.

The *vos* forms of tense categories other than the exemplified ones tend to be like those of *tú* elsewhere. In Argentina, however, there are the special imperative forms *hablá, comé, pedí*.

3. García and Otheguy readily admit that, their theory notwithstanding, there was more *leísmo* in Spain than in America. The overall incidences of *le* usage with single-object verbs in their study were 73% for the Spaniards, 41% for the Ecuadorans, 38% for the Mexicans, 29% for the Colombians, 27% and 22% for Cubans (two groups), and 13% for the Argentinians.

4. Babcock 1970 also sees all reflexives as interconnected. For her, *se* indicates what was called 'middle voice' in classical grammar ('middle' between active and passive and between transitive and intransitive). In particular, *se* incorporates the Subj into the predicate and identifies it with some element (implicit or explicit) therein, downplaying external agency. Babcock presents a fascinating set of data and her theory of *se* as a voice marker is insightful; but to explain her model here would take us too far afield. Readers with some advanced theoretical training might profitably consult her analysis in attempting to develop their own theory of the reflexive.

5. Clearly, the condition 'if understood' is imprecise, and for Spanish students of English it is not obvious why the reflexive can be 'dropped' (and usually is) in *Peter washed himself* but not in *Peter kicked himself*. According to Haiman (1983:803), the difference is that *wash* is an 'introverted' verb whose transitivity is interpreted as internalized if not explicitly directed outward toward a DO, whereas *kick* is fundamentally 'extroverted'. This is not necessarily true: in *Peter washed and Carol dried*, Peter is probably washing dishes, not himself; and at any rate, this theory begs the question of defining 'introversion' in verbs.

Spanish has a similar problem in that many speakers currently favor *despertar* over *despertarse*, reducing the contrast *lo despiertan/se despiertan* to *lo despiertan/despiertan*. One must conclude that it is not true that either language automatically deploys a reflexive morpheme when the Subj logically 'verbs' itself.

6. For Roldán (1973:206), the syntactic derivation of reciprocals is roughly as follows: *Juan respeta a Pablo y Pablo respeta a Juan* → *Juan y Pablo respetan a Pablo y Juan* → *Juan y Pablo se respetan*.

7. Aid (1973:80-108) argues for DECAUSATIVE as the more precise term for this *se*. In pairs such as *Rosa apagó el cigarrillo* vs. *El cigarrillo se apagó*, and *La serpiente asustó a Eva* vs. *Eva se asustó*, Aid sees *se* as a kind of verb inflection signifying 'removal of external cause'. She is able to accommodate meaning-changing and passive *se* into the same account by distinguishing the effects of what she calls '*se*-focus' on verbs of action vs. process vs. state.

8. *Nunca se matará al tirano* does double-duty for the impersonal and passive since the expected *Nunca se matará el tirano* for passive *se* is preempted for the true reflexive.

9. Whether pronominalization is a transformation (as early transformationalists assumed) or simply a way of describing a discourse strategy for avoiding repetition, is still debated among linguists. At least in pedagogy, though, it is a widely used conversion technique for drilling pronouns.

10. Nevertheless, some find the pronominalized version of *Mary gave John her number*, namely, *She gave him it*, awkward at best.

11. Bello personally preferred avoiding some of these combinations; for example, instead of *te me recomendaron* for 'they recommended me to you' (or ambiguously, ' . . . you to me'), he proposed *me recomendaron a ti*. Yet he cited abundant literary attestation for such combinations and admitted that they were well entrenched.

12. This restriction against *se se* is not a global one against two *se* in the same sentence; as long as they belong to different clitic blocks, there can be two of them, as in *Hoy día se* (impers.) *prefiere bañarse* (reflex.) *por la mañana*.

Exercises for Chapter 9

1. Error analysis:

(1) *Se gusta.	(5) *Les la ofreció.	(9) *Se lavas.
(2) *Me gusto.	(6) *Nos tenemos dos.	(10) *Es yo. *Es mí.
(3) *Dio me $4.	(7) *Lo hice como te.	(11) *Es para tú.
(4) *Escribí a le.	(8) *Tú lo me diste.	(12) *Vi mi mismo.

2. One fairly common error in first-year classes is exemplified by *Lo está aquí, *Lo parece gris, *Se lo gusta. What is the problem here, and how can teachers obviate it?

3. Many teachers have firm opinions about whether vosotros should be taken up, practiced actively, and used in class. Text writers therefore find themselves in the quandary of damned if they do present and use it, and damned if they do not. Moreover, in questions to the student some writers alternate between tú and usted, presumably to practice both equally. Almost none introduces vos, despite its widespread use. What policy do you think writers should adopt toward tú, vosotros, usted(es), and vos? As a teacher, what ground rules would you establish in the classroom on address (1) between students and yourself and (2) among students? What is the rationale for your preference?

4. In what ways is the Spanish system portrayed in Figure 9.1 rather artificial? As a teacher, what would your policy be toward adhering to it exclusively, and why?

5. If you were designing, writing, and teaching from your own 'ideal' text, how would you take up and present the Spanish IO? Address the following and outline your presentation and sequencing. (For some of these points you might wish to review 8.0-8.1.4.)

   (1) meanings and functions of IO
   (2) IO pronoun forms
   (3) time (if any) intervening between the presentation of DO and IO forms, and between these and 'double object' combinations (se lo, me las, etc.)
   (4) the emphasizers a él, a mí, etc.
   (5) the 'redundant construction,' e.g. le escribí a Miguel
   (6) reverse-construction verbs and others taking IO rather than DO

6. In teaching reflexive verbs, one sometimes tells students that acostarse is really 'put oneself to bed', llamarse 'call oneself', sentarse 'seat oneself', detenerse 'stop oneself', etc. Why could this be misleading, both in terms of the Spanish system and the English one? That is, are these true reflexives? What test can be used for true reflexives?

7. Enfadarse, acercarse, alegrarse, bañarse are usually introduced as reflexive verbs in vocabularies, and the student learns them as inherent reflexives like quejarse. Why is this treatment misleading? What can teachers and text writers do in order to ensure that students perceive reflexive/nonreflexive contrasts where they exist?

8. Classify each of the following reflexive verbs according to the taxonomy presented in section 9.3. (Assume that none is being used impersonally, passively, or with 'pseudo-*se*'.) What criteria do you apply in classifying them? In which cases is the classification unclear or ambiguous?

agotarse	desquitarse	equivocarse	negarse
apoyarse	divertirse	estremecerse	oponerse
arrepentirse	echarse	fiarse	pasarse de Adj.
avergonzarse	emborracharse	imaginarse	pasearse
burlarse	empeñarse	imponerse	peinarse
calmarse	encargarse	llamarse	resquebrajarse
darse 'exist'	encontrarse	mantenerse	refugiarse
deshacerse	enderezarse	meterse	reunirse
desplazarse	enemistarse	mudarse	tragarse
			vengarse

9. What meaning (if any) does the third-person clitic have in *me las arreglo* 'I get by', *no le hace* 'it doesn't matter', and *ándale*? How is it similar to 'inherent' *se*?

10. What generalization can be made about reflexive and nonreflexive versions of 'verbs of emotional reaction'? About the *estar* + participle pattern for many reflexives?

11. Do you agree or disagree with this chapter's criticism (9.3.10) of the traditional category of 'reflexives of unplanned occurrence'? Discuss your reasoning with your classmates.

12. The following sentences come from the international edition of *El País* (28-V-1984, 25-II-1985). Explain the uses of the italicized occurrences of *se*.
(1) 'O *se* destruyen las ciudades o *se* las transforma desde sus símbolos.'
(2) 'La ambición de no ser quien *se* es es bastante común.'

13. Explain the (potential) ambiguity of each of the following:
(1) Se la preparó.
(2) Se ha mojado.
(3) Se cerrará la taquilla.
(4) Los herejes se mataron.
(5) Se debe lavar el pelo.
(6) No se lo podrá comprar.
(7) No se bebió la leche.
(8) Ellos se aburrieron.
(9) Se lo pondrá después.
(10) Se mataron las reses.

14. Explain the differences in meaning within each of the following sets of sentences.
(1) Se lavó a Emiliano.
Se lavó Emiliano.
Lo lavó Emiliano.
(2) Se engañará a la maestra.
Se engañará la maestra.
(3) Se ve en el espejo.
Se ve muy linda hoy.
Se ve una diferencia.
(4) Se hizo unos medicamentos.
Se hicieron unos medicamentos.
Se hicieron médicos.
Se los/les hizo médicos.
(5) Él vistió a Manolito.
Él vistió el uniforme.
Él se vistió.

15. Draw up a lesson plan on intransitive, inchoative, impersonal, and passive *se* (although they need not be called by those terms), and show how you would present, illustrate, and drill them. (If you prefer, you can adopt some version of Bull's continuum theory for them.)

16. The following exchange illustrates a common student problem in the first year of language study. Why is the student's error not due to interference from English? What is the reason for it? (T = teacher, S = student)

T: ¿Escribe Ud. con lápiz o con bolígrafo?
S: Escribe Ud. con bolígrafo.

17. The following additional teacher-student exchanges show other typical problems once Obj pronouns have been taken up. Explain the students' problems.

(1) T: ¿Qué ropa se ha puesto Ud. hoy?
     S: He puesto una camisa y un pantalón.
(2) T: ¿A quién se lo dije?
     S: Ud. dijo a Juan.
(3) T: ¿A quién se lo dije?
     S: Juan se lo dijo.
(4) T: ¿Ud. les presta su dinero a sus amigos y a sus familiares?
     S: No, yo nunca pres-, presto uhh . . . , presto mi dinero a mis amigos y a mis familiares.
(5) T: ¿Quieres que te lo dé?
     S: Sí, quiero que te lo dé.
(6) T: ¿Se habla allí portugués?
     S: No, no hablo portugués.
     T: No, escuche: ¿se habla portugués en Brasil?
     S: ¡Ah! No, no ME hablo portugués en Brasil.
(7) T: ¿Cómo se llama Ud.?
     S: Me llamo es Susana.

18. Babcock 1970 considers clitics to be verb affixes (generally prefixes) representing on the verb information about Obj NPs just as person-number endings do about Subj NPs. She also regards many of the *se*-types as affixes for voice or intransitivity, comparable to the affix *-aba* for imperfect aspect. What is your assessment of this analysis, and what evidence (pro and con) is there for treating clitics as verb affixes rather than as true pronouns?

19. Though all teachers must correct and supplement their texts somewhat, it is inconvenient (and confusing to students) to revamp everything according to one's own theories of the language. Despite their own preferences, teachers must 'live with' some textbook inadequacies. Assume you are using a text containing the 'IO-DO' rule for clitic placement. As we saw, this rule fails in some cases, and even the SSC (which works more often) does not cover all data. After having evaluated the two, would it be worth it in your opinion to correct the text for your students? Why or why not?

20. Many texts and reference works give lists of verbs that take certain prepositions. Why is the syntax of 'verbs taking *a*' unclear from a mere vocabulary entry? Consider the following in answering this question, using the tests discussed in 9.4.1. (Alternatively, turn this into a project by testing native speakers' pronominalizations of sentences containing these.)

acceder a NP	corresponder a NP	preceder a NP
acercarse a NP	dedicarse a NP	referirse a NP
adelantarse a NP	dirigirse a NP	restar X a NP
adorar a NP	ganar a NP	someterse a NP
adaptarse a NP	llegar a NP	sustituirse a NP
añadir X a NP	oponerse a NP	unirse a NP
contribuir a NP	parecerse a NP	

Chapter 10
Adverbs, prepositions, and conjunctions

10.0 Problems with the uninflected words. In describing Greek and Latin grammar, classical scholars dealt at length with those parts of speech that offered challenging and complex inflectional paradigms: verbs, nouns, adjectives, and pronouns. Most other words were consigned with little comment to three other categories. These were (1) the class standing 'at the verb' (Lat. *ad-verbium*), (2) the class 'positioned before' others (*praepositio*), and (3) the class signaling a 'joining together' (*con-junctio*). With rare exceptions, modern grammarians, linguists, and text writers have retained this preference for studying the 'major' categories of V, N, Adj, and Pro, to the relative neglect of what are still called ADVERBS, PREPOSITIONS, and CONJUNCTIONS.

It is understandable why these last three categories have been overshadowed by the others. They are fewer in number, apparently simple in morphology, and comparatively mundane in their meanings and grammatical roles. Consequently, aside from notes on *por/para, pero/sino*, and mood contrasts after certain conjunctions, these parts of speech are largely presented as mere vocabulary items in Spanish pedagogy. However, student errors such as the following suggest the need for more attention to the uninflected parts of speech.

*¡Estás tarde!
*Paré el coche porque del tráfico.
*Mi amiga nos esperaba afuera el restaurante.
*Escuchamos la radio mientras estudiando.
*Miró la tele en lunes.
*Es difícil a romper.

When a source/target difference is not explicitly noted and students lack sufficient experience to infer it for themselves, they automatically assume positive transfer value. Given the usual matching in vocabularies of *tarde, porque, afuera, mientras, en, a*, respectively, with *late, because, outside, while, on/in, to/at*, with no further comment from text or teacher, it is natural for students to generate the foregoing sentences on the basis of the grammar of the English glosses. Corrected in piecemeal fashion, such errors are bound to continue because the problem is as much grammatical as it is lexical. In fact, in order to master the usage of Spanish adverbs, prepositions, and conjunctions, students require at least four kinds of information about them: lexical, categorial, semantic, and grammatical.

(1) Lexical. Spanish speakers do not say *because*, but *porque*; they do not say *while*, but *mientras*. This much is obvious in a vocabulary list, but

little else is. Moreover, there are systematic lexical relationships in both languages that are obscured when new vocabulary is presented as *palabras sueltas*. For example, Span. *por* is to *porque* as *para* is to *para que*, but this connection is lost when all four words are presented separately in terms of Eng. *for, because,* and *in order that.*

(2) Categorial. The way in which words are CATEGORIZED (classified) is crucial for their syntactic behavior, but it is not obvious from meaning alone. For indicating exterior location, English adopts *outside* as a noun, adverb, or preposition; Spanish, however, sets up *afuera* and *fuera* as adverbs, and *fuera de* as a preposition. Unfortunately, many students have only a sketchy idea (if any at all) about categories or parts of speech in their own language, and injunctions such as 'Do not use *afuera* as a preposition' may add to their confusion instead of eliminating it.

(3) Semantic. Both *por* and *para* can translate Eng. *for*, while *a* can convey both *to* and *at*. But *por* and *para* are no more synonymous for the Spanish speaker than *to* and *at* are for the English speaker. Such words reflect conceptualizations that are relative to the semantic organization of their language, and the concepts they represent cannot easily be conveyed by one-word glosses in another language.

(4) Grammatical. Many uses of *a* and *por* have little to do with their primary meanings. They have become GRAMMATICALIZED or grammatically fixed in certain constructions as markers of syntactic relationship and function (i.e. as FUNCTORS). In pedagogy as well as in linguistic analysis, such words cannot be explained apart from the constructions in which they are embedded.

The following sections explore these four kinds of information, with special emphasis on the problems that three rather neglected parts of speech pose in pedagogy.

10.1 Lexical relationships. It is often useful to retain the tripartite division among *adverbium, praepositio,* and *conjunctio.* But in reality, adverbs, prepositions, and conjunctions are syntactically related, and this relationship is recognized in the lexical system of each language. In order to clarify the relationship, it may be useful to turn first to verbs and adjectives. A verb can be subcategorized according to the Obj or complement it governs. Four possibilities for a verb such as *creer* are (1) no Obj, (2) an Obj NP (pronoun or nominal NP), (3) a noun clause complement, or (4) an infinitival complement. Case (1) is traditionally described as intransitive and case (2) as transitive; cases (3) and (4) are variously analyzed (v. 13.1.2).

(1) V + ∅   *Ella cree.*
(2) V + Obj NP   *Ella cree nuestro cuento.*
(3) V + clause   *Ella cree que lo ha explicado bien.*
(4) V + VP-inf   *Ella cree haberlo explicado bien.*

An adjective such as *contento* has similar possibilities, although it requires a connecting *con* or *de* to form a phrase with its Obj:

(1) Adj + Ø   *Está contenta.*
(2) Adj + *con* + Obj NP   *Está contenta con su regalo.*
(3) Adj + *de* + clause   *Está contenta de que todos la respeten.*
(4) Adj + *de* + VP-inf   *Está contenta de haberlo entendido.*

Now, consider the word *después*, whose category we will provisionally represent as X. It occurs in the same four patterns.

(1) X + Ø   *Saliste después.*
(2) X + *de* + Obj NP   *Saliste después de la primera función.*
(3) X + (*de*) + clause   *Saliste después (de) que terminaron.*
(4) X + *de* + VP-inf   *Saliste después de comer.*

Traditional grammar does not assign verbs or adjectives to wholly distinct categories according to their transitivity or complements, but that is exactly how it has treated X-words. Used 'intransitively', *después* is called an adverb (Adv); used with an Obj NP or infinitive, it becomes a preposition (Prep); and used with a *que* clause, it is renamed a subordinating conjunction (C-subord). Occasionally, prepositions and conjunctions are grouped together as RELATORS, but there is syntactic and lexical justification for recognizing a higher relationship among all three as ADVERBIALS (Advl).[1]

The ways in which this relationship is reflected in the lexical set-up of Spanish and English are shown in Figure 10.1. For locative Advl, it can be seen that Spanish employs the base form (e.g. *encima*) as an Adv and adds *de* for the corresponding Prep (*encima de*). English sometimes behaves in the same way (*ahead, ahead of*), but often categorizes one form for both functions (*behind*). With nonlocatives there is less lexical consistency, but the general Spanish pattern is the use of the base form as Adv (*después*), plus *de* for the Prep (*después de*), plus *de que* or just *que*[2] for C-subord (*después (de) que*). English may use one form for all three (*before*), derive Adv or Prep from C (*because, because of*) or derive Adv from the Prep/C form (*after, afterwards*). Both languages have a few lexical gaps filled in by expressions verging on idioms (*por eso* corresponding to *por* and *porque*) or by suppletive forms (*mientras* and *durante, while* and *during*).

The Spanish system is the neater one overall, and the triplet pattern of X, X *de*, X (*de*) *que* for Adv, Prep, and C (Keniston 1937:245) deserves more pedagogical emphasis. Moreover, since labels such as 'adverb' may have little meaning for students, teachers may have to devise more in-Spanish drills that manipulate, for instance, *por eso* vs. *por el tráfico* vs. *porque había tráfico, después* vs. *después de la fiesta* vs. *después de celebrar* vs. *después que celebraron*. Inductively or deductively, students must learn which Advls stand alone and which ones introduce NP, infinitives, or clauses.

Figure 10.1 Adverbial systems.

(a) Locatives—adverb vs. preposition

Span.	Eng.
1. debajo, abajo	underneath, below
debajo de	under, below
2. detrás, atrás	behind, in back
detrás de	behind, in back of
3. enfrente	in front
enfrente de	in front of
4. (a)fuera	outside
fuera de	outside (of)
5. (a) dentro	inside
dentro de	inside (of)
6. al lado	on/to the side
al lado de	beside, next to
7. encima	above, overhead, on top
encima de	above, over, on top of
8. lejos	far, far away
lejos de	far from
9. (de) cerca	nearby, close
cerca de	near, close to
10. más allá, allende	beyond
más allá de	beyond
11. arriba	up, above
arriba de	up, on top of
12. (a)delante	ahead, in front
delante de	ahead of, in front of

(b) Nonlocatives—adverb vs. preposition vs. conjunction

Span.	Eng.
1. antes	before(hand)
antes de	before
antes que	before
2. después	afterwards
después de	after
después que	after
3. luego	then, afterwards
luego de	after
luego que	after
4. (por eso)	so, therefore, hence
por	for, because of
porque	because

Figure 10.1 continued

Figure 10.1 continued

5. (para eso)	(for that purpose)
para	for, to
para que	so that, in order that
6. además	besides, in addition
además de	besides, in addition to
además de que	besides the fact that
7. conforme	accordingly
conforme a, según	according to
según (que)	as, according to how
8. (hasta entonces)	(until then)
hasta	until
hasta que	until
9. (sin eso)	(without it)
sin	without
sin que	without
10. mientras (tanto)	meanwhile
durante	during
mientras	while

10.2 Bases for categorial classification. In general, one discerns three approaches to a TAXONOMY or classification of Advl types. These are (1) classification by meaning, (2) classification by formation, and (3) classification by position and function.

10.2.1 Classification by meaning. Advls tend to sort out into a limited set of semantic groups, and some scholars have classified them as follows.

manner: (Adv) *bien, despacio, contentamente, gratis . . .*
        (Prep) *con, de, mediante, conforme a . . .*
        (C) *de modo que, como . . .*

time: (Adv) *entonces, siempre, ayer, antaño, antes . . .*
        (Prep) *durante, antes de, por . . .*
        (C) *cuando, hasta que, siempre que, en cuanto . . .*

place: (Adv) *allí, afuera, arriba, acá . . .*
        (Prep) *en, a, detrás de, junto a . . .*
        (C) *donde*

reason: (Adv) *adrede, por eso, por lo tanto . . .*
        (Prep) *para, por, a causa de . . .*
        (C) *así que, porque, puesto que . . .*

extent: (Adv) *tanto, mucho, demasiado . . .*
        (Prep) *por, hasta . . .*
        (C) *tanto que, más . . . más . . . , . . .*

Such semantic taxonomies are adopted in some pedagogical presentations under the assumption that common denominators of meaning make it easier to learn Advls by sets. Syntactically, a semantic taxonomy underlies the formation of information questions, in which *cuándo* corresponds to Advls of time, *dónde* to Advls of place, and so on (v. 12.1.2).

10.2.2 Classification by formation. In this approach, a distinction is made between SIMPLE (consisting of a single morpheme) and DERIVED (formed from several morphemes).

10.2.2.1 Adverbs. Spanish has a fairly limited set of simple Advs; *bien, nunca, siempre, ya, quizás, gratis, tarde,* etc.; Keniston (1937:250-53) offers an exhaustive listing of them. For the most part, their English equivalents tend to be simple as well: *well, never, always,* etc.

Derived Advs are more abundant in both languages. Those formed off Adj usually have *-mente* in Spanish corresponding to *-ly* in English. The suffix *-mente* is specifically added to the feminine Adj form, betraying its origin as a feminine noun.[3] When the feminine is not morphologically distinct, as with two-form Adj (v. 8.3.4), the feminineness fails to show on the surface, a situation many students try to rectify by overgeneralizing *-a-mente*: **felizamente, *alegramente.* Other Advs have arisen from the joining of Prep with Adv, Adj, or N: *aparte, adentro, abajo, afuera, anoche, apenas, ahora, despacio (de+espacio), encima.* Similarly formed but written as separate words are the adverbial expressions discussed later in 10.4.1: *de repente, a propósito, en fin, en seguida, de paso, en vano,* etc. Another pattern is a compound of N + Adv: *cuesta arriba, río abajo* (v. 15.1.2).

It is not obvious whether such morpheme combinations with Advl functions should be analyzed as phrases or as single Adv. The spaces between words in the written language seem too arbitrary to be relied on criterially, inasmuch as both *encima* and *en seguida* are pronounced as single words, as are *aparte* and *a propósito, despacio* and *de repente,* etc. In fact, there is good reason to consider an Advl such as *a propósito* as LEXICALIZED or fixed as one lexical unit: if it were truly Prep + NP, one would expect possibilities such as *a tu propósito nuevo, a propósitos abstractos, al propósito reciente,* and so on, but these are semantically odd.

10.2.2.2 Prepositions. Reference grammars typically present the following list of simple Preps:

a	de	entre	mediante	según
ante	desde	excepto	para	sin
bajo	durante	hacia	por	so
con	en	hasta	salvo	sobre
contra				tras

The derived Preps are often called 'compound', or in Spanish, *frases prepositivas* (Gili Gaya 1973:247), a term that must be distinguished from *frase preposicional* or PREPOSITIONAL PHRASE (which is Prep + Obj, v. 10.2.3). The compound Preps are an open-ended class, for Spanish has several formulae for creating expressions that link NP to the rest of a sentence.

Adv + *de* (v. 10.1): *alrededor de, cerca de, además de . . .*

Adj + *a*: *conforme a, junto a, contrario a . . .*

N + *a*: *cara a, respecto a, frente a, rumbo a . . .*

Prep + Prep: *de a, para con*

Prep + N + Prep: *a causa de, a diferencia de, a petición de, a consecuencia de, a lo largo de, a prueba de, al lado de, a la vuelta de, en razón a/de, en calidad de, de acuerdo con/a, en torno a, a la derecha de, al norte de, a cambio de, a base de (en base a), en lugar de, . . .*

English forms compound prepositional relators too, although they do not always coincide in their formation with the Spanish types: *in place of, apart from, as to, in view of, by means of, in addition to, up through, with respect to,* etc.

10.2.2.3 Conjunctions. In their formation, conjunctions can be sorted into four groups. The simple ones are a small set:

ni 'nor'	como 'as, how'	pues 'for, because'
o, u 'or'	cuando 'when'	que 'because, than, as, that'
y, e 'and'	donde 'where'	si 'if, whether'
pero sino } 'but'	mientras 'while'	según 'according to how'

A second group is called CORRELATIVE: these Cs are made up of two parts, each preceding one of the conjoined constituents (or CONJUNCTS):

apenas . . . cuando . . .	'scarcely . . . when . . .'
(cuanto) más . . . (tanto) más . . .	'the more . . . the more . . .'
ni . . . ni . . .	'neither . . . nor . . .'
o . . . o . . .	'either . . . or . . .'
ora . . . ora . . .	'now . . . now . . .'
tanto . . . como . . .	'both . . . and . . .'
ya . . . ya . . .	'sometimes . . . sometimes . . .'

A third group is variously formed off other words with which they may retain only a tenuous semantic connection; most can be considered as lexicalized units.

a medida que 'as'	por cuanto 'in that'
a menos que 'unless'	por muy/más/mucho que 'however
así que 'so, thus'	much that'

aunque 'although, even if'	por si 'in case'
como si 'as if'	puesto que 'as, since, because'
de modo/manera que 'so (that)'	siempre que 'whenever; provided
en cuanto 'as soon as'	that'
en tanto que 'inasmuch as'	ya que 'since, because'

The fourth group is formed specifically from Prep (simple or compound) + *que*:

a fin (de) que 'so, in order that'	hasta que 'until'
a pesar (de) que 'in spite of'	luego (de) que 'after'
antes (de) que 'before'	para que 'so (that), in order that'
conque 'so'	porque 'because'
con tal (de) que 'provided'	salvo que 'except that'
desde que 'ever since'	sin que 'without'

This Prep + *que* group is a special one in Spanish in that these relators allow their clause to reduce to VP-inf under certain conditions and other Advls traditionally called conjunctions do not. For example, *antes de que vayas* can become *antes de ir*, whereas *mientras vayas, si vas, aunque vayas*, and *siempre que vayas* never permit this infinitivization: **mientras ir, *si ir, *aun(que) ir, *siempre ir*. English relators, on the other hand, rather freely allow this kind of reduction (although to gerunds, not usually infinitives): *before going*, but also *while going, if going, although going*, etc. This difference, as noted in Whitley (1986b), will be described in more detail in the discussion of clause types (v. 13.2.1).

Except in this last case of Prep + *que*, classification by formation generally has more analytical importance than pedagogical usefulness. Both languages have all these subtypes of Advl, although not always in equivalent Advls; and students do not need to know that *a diferencia de* is 'compound' and *tanto . . . como . . .* is 'correlative' in order to use them.

Problems arise mainly when one language has an Advl with no direct equivalent in the other, or when one language has a multiple categorization of one Advl for which the other provides different forms. Examples of the former case include *sin que* (Eng. *without* is Prep with no C equivalent) and *a pesar de que* (which must be rendered by something like 'in spite of the fact that'); examples of the latter include *until* = Prep/C (Spanish distinguishes *hasta* from *hasta que*) and *late* = Adv/Adj (Spanish *tarde* is Adv only—*llegué tarde, *estoy tarde*). *Según* illustrates both problems, inasmuch as it is doubly categorized as Prep and C, unlike the Eng. Prep *according to*, which has no C equivalent (except perhaps *according to how*).

10.2.3 Classification by position and function: The adverbial phrase. Linguists often define constituent types and categories by means of syntactic position and function. One definition of NP, for example, might be that class of constituents that can occur in such sentence frames as *Vi ___ ayer, ___ no me sorprende,* and *Tengo confianza en ___ .* Likewise, the determiner in the NP could be defined in terms of what could occur in an environment such as ___ *cliente que atendiste ayer.*

Many Advls may be categorized and subcategorized in similar fashion in terms of whether they can be used (and how they are constructed) in a sentence. One useful notion in this respect is what is called the *complemento circunstancial* in Spanish grammar. This constituent, like the *complemento directo* (DO) and *complemento indirecto* (IO), is a complement of the verb and occurs with it in the VP. It generally expresses 'el lugar, modo, tiempo, medio, causa o instrumento de la acción verbal' (Gili Gaya 1973:70). As an analog to the constituent class NP for what serves as Subj, DO, IO, and PredE (v. 8.0), the term ADVERBIAL PHRASE (AdvlP) will be used here as a syntactic characterization of what functions as *complemento circunstancial.*

A defining sentence frame for AdvlP might be the following: *Elena investigó eso ___ .* Many Advs qualify for this slot: *Elena investigó eso despacio, contentamente, bien, pronto . . .* Such Advs modify the verb in the same way that Adjs modify a noun; in fact, parallelisms between NPs such as *una respuesta directa* and VPs such as *respondió directamente* have motivated some linguists to posit linguistic models that specify analogous syntactic structure for all major phrase types.

But not all Advs would be categorized as elements of AdvlP. Certain of them need not occur 'at the verb' or in VP. One group (*quizás, además, desgraciadamente, en cambio . . .*) typically provides discourse linkage between sentences and/or indicates the speaker's attitude toward his proposition. Such words have been called SENTENCE ADVERBIALS rather than VP adverbials. A second group is comprised of modifiers of modifiers, morphemes that qualify the intensity or degree of modification. These have been called INTENSIFIERS (Int) or DEGREE WORDS (Deg), and include *muy, más, menos, tan, algo, poco, bastante, extremadamente, sumamente* in Spanish, and *very, more, less, that, so, somewhat* (and colloquial *kind of, sort of*), *not very, rather, extremely,* and *highly* in English. While some of these could occur in the AdvlP slot of VP to indicate extent (*Elena investigó eso bastante, más, poco*), they may also precede and modify the nonverbal categories Adj and Adv:

Se siente muy incómoda.	She feels very uncomfortable.
Lo realizaste bastante bien.	You carried it out rather well.
Es algo aburrido.	It's kind of boring.

A third group of Advs that cannot be categorized solely as elements of AdvlP is made up of words that can modify virtually any constituent type—V and VP but also N and NP, Adj, Adv, Prep, D, Quant, S . . . They include the following:

sólo, tan solo, solamente	only, just
hasta, aun, incluso	even
por lo menos, al menos	at least
especialmente, sobre todo	especially, above all
también	also, too
casi, por poco	almost
nomás	just

Keniston (1937:246) called these 'distinguishing adverbs'; Suñer (1982:234) calls them 'focus attractors'. As the unsettled nomenclature suggests, these are hard to pin down syntactically and semantically. Syntactically, *solamente* can be applied to many constituent types: *solamente la madre, solamente dos, solamente escribió su nombre de pila*; moreover, it is rather free-floating in its position: *Solamente tengo dos, Tengo solamente dos, Tengo dos solamente*. Semantically, it does not convey any 'circumstantial' information (Gila Gaya's 'place, way, time, means, cause, instrument'), but signals the speaker's focus on a constituent and indicates that the real turns out to be less than the expected. A definitive analysis of such properties has yet to be made, and ultimately the focus atttractors might be grouped together with determiners, quantifiers, and intensifiers as a class that specifies or delimits modification, reference, and focus.[4]

Besides certain Advs, NPs can be used in AdvlP to present the 'circumstances' of the verb event. In both languages, however, most NPs in AdvlP must be governed by Prep, with which they form a PREPOSITIONAL PHRASE, PP. Since PPs freely occur in our sample sentence frame, they too can be classified as members of AdvlP: *Elena investigó eso con su hermano, por tres años, antes de su graduación, de acuerdo con nuestros criterios* . . . But in addition to NP, the Obj of Prep may be Adv or even some other PP:

PP = Prep + NP *desde aquel día, since that day*
PP = Prep + Adv *desde abajo, from underneath*
PP = Prep + PP *desde antes de la revolución, since before the revolution*

Nevertheless, not all Preps are subcategorized to occur in this last (Prep + PP) construction, and sometimes the two languages differ in this respect: Spanish freely uses PP as the Obj of *por* (*por encima de la mesa, por detrás del taller*), whereas Eng. *through* and *for* do not combine in this way. Likewise, both languages permit a few intensifiers before PP, but these seldom match. For example, Int + PP occurs in *Estamos muy por debajo de los demás países* and *He went right through the chute*, but unlike Span. *muy*, Eng. *very* happens not to occur before PP (**We're very under the other countries, *He went very through the chute*).

Although Prep is usually needed for NP functioning as *complemento circunstancial*, there is a prominent group of NPs in both languages that can serve in AdvlP without a governing relator. These include words and phrases such as *hoy, ayer, el viernes, cada mes, todos los días, la semana pasada*, and *el año que viene*, and their double functions as *complementos circunstanciales* and as Subj or Obj are illustrated in Figure 10.2. The two languages coincide rather well in what NPs they categorize for AdvlP with one notable exception, dates and days of the week. These take an optional Prep (*on*) in English, but Ø in Spanish.

Figure 10.2 Adverbial and nonadverbial NPs.

As *complemento circunstancial*:	As subject or object:
(1) No se esquía *hoy*.	*Hoy* (Subj) es lunes.
There's no skiing *today*.	*Today* (Subj) is Monday.
(2) La vimos *la semana pasada*.	*La semana pasada* (Subj) fue un
We saw her *last week*.	horror.
	Last week (Subj) was awful.
(3) Cumplirá 20 años *el jueves*.	Prefiero *el jueves* (DO).
He'll be 20 years old (on)	I prefer *Monday* (DO).
Monday.	
(4) Pesó *70 kilos*.	Consumieron *70 kilos* (DO).
He weighed *70 kilos*.	They consumed *70 kilos* (DO).

In order to occur in the AdvlP slot, conjunctions are constructed with a clause (sentence, S):*Elena investigó eso cuando era candidata, puesto que le gustaba la ciencia, como si se tratara de su futuro profesional. Cuando, puesto que, como si*, and most of the other traditional Cs are said to 'subordinate' their clause to the VP, and they are called SUBORDINATING CONJUNCTIONS (C-subord). The following Cs, however, do not subordinate one clause to VP to provide circumstantial information, but instead connect two elements with roughly equal importance; *y ~ e, o ~ u, ni, pero, sino que*, and the correlatives *ni ... ni ... , tanto ... como ...*, etc. These have been called COORDINATING CONJUNCTIONS (C-coord), and they connect not only clauses but almost any constituents of the same syntactic type, thereby forming COMPOUND structures such as the following (v. 11.1.1, 13.0):

NP C-coord NP *tanto tu cuñada como mi nieto*
VP C-coord VP *descubrió el desorden y se enfureció*
Adj C-coord Adj *difícil pero interesante*
S C-coord S *Jorge puso la mesa e Isabel lavó los vasos*

In summary, the options available to Spanish and English speakers in forming the *complemento circunstancial* of VP can be expressed by the following PSRs.

$$\text{AdvlP} \rightarrow \text{(Int)} \left\{ \begin{array}{l} \text{Adv} \\ \text{PP} \\ \text{NP} \\ \text{C-subord S} \end{array} \right\}$$

$$\text{PP} \rightarrow \text{Prep} \left\{ \begin{array}{l} \text{Adv} \\ \text{PP} \\ \text{NP} \end{array} \right\}$$

Alternatively, given the systematic lexical relationships among Advls (v. 10.1), the analyst could disregard the classical distinction of Adv, Prep, and C, and state simply that AdvlP consists of Advl with or without Obj complements. This approach is cogently argued for Spanish and its Romance sisters by Agard (1984:63-73), who considers Adv, Prep, and C (or at least C-subord) to be subcategories of one general 'Adverb' category, just as transitive and intransitive verbs are treated as subcategories of one. This analysis, and its relationship to verb classification, is summarized in Figure 10.3, and it makes possible a merger of the preceding two PSRs into one simplified one that furthermore brings out the intimate connection among Advls in Spanish.

$$\text{AdvlP} \rightarrow \text{(Int)} \left\{ \begin{array}{l} \text{Adv}\left(\left\{ \begin{array}{l} \text{NP} \\ \text{S} \end{array} \right\} \right) \\ \text{NP} \end{array} \right\}$$

Figure 10.3 Adverbs, prepositions, and conjunctions as subcategories of Adverb.

	Verbs:	Adverbs:
(1) transitive: takes Obj	*descubrir, conocer*	*para(que), con, como*
(2) optional transitive: may take Obj	*creer, estudiar*	*después* (*de, que*)
(3) intransitive: stands alone without Obj	*andar, morir*	*bien, despacio*

10.3 Semantic problems. If asked for a spontaneous definition of *pájaro*, a Spanish speaker probably would not hesitate in offering something like 'pues, es un animalito que tiene plumas y dos alas y puede volar.' Asked what *de, pero,* or *si* means, on the other hand, he might be at a loss. This is because unlike words such as *pájaro*, Advls often have abstract senses or logical functions that become precise only when they are employed in specific constructions. When meaning is thus tied to, and relative to, the construction, interlingual glosses may be quite misleading. For example, *in that* as a gloss for *por cuanto* can wrongly suggest to students the meaning 'en eso', since the conjunctive functions of Eng. *in that* are not apparent outside a sentential context; and *that* for *que* can wrongly suggest a demonstrative rather than any of the various grammatical functions both words have as relators. Dictionaries and vocabulary lists could offer more useful information to language learners by always illustrating relators in context.

Most pedagogical materials address at least the problems posed by the Spanish equivalents of Eng. *but, so, to, in, from, for,* and *by,* and these are discussed below.

10.3.1 'But'. The territory covered by *but* is divided among three distinct Spanish relators and their synonyms. *Menos* (with *salvo*) expresses exception to or subtraction from a generalization: *everyone but Edward, todos menos Eduardo. Pero* (with *mas*) adds an opposed consideration, 'but on the other hand, yet, however'. *Sino* (+ *que* before S) cancels what precedes and replaces it with what the speaker regards as the true state of affairs, 'but instead, but on the contrary'. The fact that *pero* and *sino* (*que*) can contrast in the same context undermines the value of fill-in-the-blank exercises:

No enseña música, $\left\{ \begin{array}{l} \text{pero} \\ \text{sino que} \end{array} \right\}$ toca el violín.

10.3.2 'So'. English *so* has a variety of functions allocated to several distinct morphemes in Spanish:

(1) intensifier: He's *so* dumb. Es *tan* bruto.
(2) proform of manner: And he *so* did it. Y *así* lo hizo.
(3) proform of predicate Adj or N (PredE): He's witty and *so* is she. Él es gracioso y ella *lo* es también.
(4) proform of a proposition: Is it too late? I think *so.* ¿Ya es tarde? Creo *que sí.*
(5) conjunction: She ate too much, *so* she's sick. Comió demasiado, *así que* está enferma.

As a true C (case 5), *so* and its variant *so that* express (1) logically inferred or generally experienced consequence, or (2) hoped-for consequence or purpose. Spanish distinguishes these two by mood and by relator (although *de modo/manera que* can be used for both):

She fell down, *so* (*that*) she got hurt.	Se cayó, *así que* se lastimó. (also: *conque, de ahí que, de modo que*)
She fell down *so* (*that*) everyone would notice her.	Se cayó *para que* todos se fijaran en ella. (also: *a fin que, de modo que*)

10.3.3 'To, in, from'. Compound Preps (v. 10.2.2.2) generally have more precise meanings and a lower frequency of usage than the simple ones. In fact, in view of the lengthy itemizations of discrete senses for each simple Prep that are given in some grammars and texts—'usos de *a,* usos de *de,* usos de *por* . . . ' (RAE 1979:438-443)—it is a valid question whether each Prep has one specifiable meaning. However, once certain idiomatic expressions and grammaticalized functions (v. 10.4) are set aside, many Preps can be analyzed as having at least one basic primary sense that underlies the various uses.

For example, *a*, *en*, and *de* form an interesting system in Spanish that is often obscured when they are learned by way of English glosses. To grasp this system, one should first imagine how location might be depicted. In the following diagrams, (a) represents enclosure within a three-dimensional space, (b) surface contact (e.g. with a two-dimensional wall or table top), and (c) adjacency (as opposed to enclosure or contact).

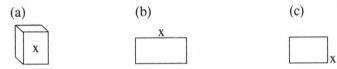

Now, we can describe object *x* as (1) already located in one of these positions, and not altering that position, (2) approaching and entering that position, or (3) leaving that position. We will call these three modes 'location', 'direction', and 'origin'. Three positions times three modes will yield nine possibilities,

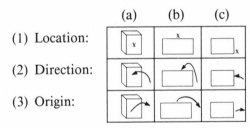

	(a)	(b)	(c)
(1) Location:			
(2) Direction:			
(3) Origin:			

which is, in fact, the English system:

	(a)	(b)	(c)
(1) Location:	*in*	*on*	*at*
(2) Direction:	*into*	*onto*	*to*
(3) Origin:	*out of*	*off(of)*	*from*

The basic Spanish system is less differentiated in that three simple terms can cover all nine possibilities (though, of course, more specific terms— *sobre*, *junto a*, *dentro de*, etc.—can be substituted for clarification):

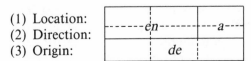

(1) Location:
(2) Direction:
(3) Origin:

It is hard to convey the Spanish concepts in words. *De* represents generalized origin, regardless of whether it is origin from within, from next to, or from the surface of. *A* means unenclosed position at some point; whether this is static location (*está a la puerta*) or movement into that position (*vino a la puerta*) depends on the verb. *En* is roughly some kind of containment, whether by a two-dimensional surface (*está en el techo/la mesa/la pared*) or by a three-dimensional space (*está en la casa/el aire/el lago*)—and, as with *a*, location and direction are distinguished by the verb (*está en la mesa, lo puse en la mesa*). It is not the case that *a* has two meanings, 'to' and 'at', or that *en* has four or *de* has three; these are their English translations, which are beside the point for non-English systems. Some students are surprised that *en* is *in* and *on* and *into* and *onto* (and even *at*, as with *en la escuela*), but each Spanish Prep reflects its value within its own system, and until students grasp that system, prepositions will seem more baffling than they actually are.[5]

10.3.4 'For' and 'by'. As with *a en de*, English glosses are not helpful with *por* and *para*; both can be translated by *for* and *by*, and by other relators as well. Instead of listing many uses for *por* and for *para*, many linguists have sought to find one general underlying meaning for each, as was done above for *a en de*. In a manner of speaking, one looks for one 'use-eme' behind the various superficial 'allo-uses'.

One of the best explanations of *por/para* is that of Bull (1965: ch. 22), which is paraphrased here. Again, it is helpful first to depict their basic meanings graphically, as follows (the line represents movement):

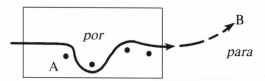

Por emphasizes passage through A, with respect to A, among the parts of A, whereas *para* indicates passage toward some goal B. These abstract meanings become more concrete (like those of other prepositions) in specific sentential contexts.

(1) Location.
El humo se extendió por/para el dormitorio.
La familia salió por/para el jardín.
Cruzamos por/para el puente.
Venga Ud. por/para acá.

Por very generally conveys extension or movement over an area or by a point, whether through, across, past, down, up, out, or along it. This vagueness allows a Spanish speaker to modify *aquí* ('this specific point') to *por acá* ('around here'). The movement-through can be in an area already defined by some other PP: *pasó por debajo de/encima de/delante de la estación*. *Para* indicates a goal of the movement, contrasting thereby not only with *por* but also with *hacia* (toward B but not necessarily with B as a goal), *hasta* (arrival at B, with emphasis on B as endpoint), and *a* (assuming a position at B, not necessarily with B as endpoint or goal).

(2) Time.
   Se quedaron en casa por/para la Semana Santa.
   Háganlo por/para la tarde.

With *por*, 'passage-through' time becomes duration; with *para*, goal is again emphasized, either in the sense of purpose or deadline.

(3) Persons and things.
   Compré los zapatos por/para mi mujer.

Many texts explain *por* here in terms of 'reason,' supposedly in contrast with 'purpose'. Unfortunately, the English word *reason* covers both the *por qué* and the *para qué* of an event or situation, and it is therefore useless as a criterion for distinguishing the two. *Para* again denotes goal; with persons and things, it specifically means purpose, the result one aims for or the benefactor one hopes to satisfy if and when the event is fulfilled. *Por* more generally covers any prior or existing considerations other than goal which have influenced the event or its agents from its conception or during its implementation. These considerations can be almost anything contrasting with purpose: factors, sake, means, behalf, agency, request, cause, explanation, etc. Thus, in the above example, *para* suggests that the purchase was intended for my wife while *por* could mean in her place (she couldn't make it to the store), or on her behalf (she asked me); *por $25* would indicate what I exchanged in buying the shoes, *por un simple estratagema* the means I used, *por vanidad* my motive, *por estar cerca de la zapatería* the explanation, and so on.

(4) Abstract grounds for judgment.
   Por/para su edad, Ramona cose con destreza.

Por here means 'given her age as a cause for reaching a judgment', i.e. 'because of her age, on account of her age'. *Para* again denotes goal, but 'goal' interpreted as standard of judgment—gauged against what one expects for someone of her age, Ramona sews skillfully.

Por is much less specific in all these cases than *para*, and another way of looking at their contrast is *para* for goal and *por* for the rest. When greater precision is required, *por* can be replaced by specialized alternatives: *durante, por medio de* or *mediante, en vez de, con motivo de, a causa de, a lo largo de, a través de*, etc.

10.3.5 Abstract relationships. The meaning of a relator becomes more elusive when it is pressed into use for conveying relationships more abstract than location, time, goal, and so on. For example, the basic meaning of *con* is accompaniment (*fuimos con Maripili*), but *con* also conveys manner (*se lo expliqué con paciencia = pacientemente*) or means (*todo es posible con la mordida*). *Sobre* indicates an upper position, whether in contact ('on') or not ('over, above'); but it also expresses topicality (*habló sobre la política*). *De* denotes origin, as noted earlier, but also composition (*es de plástico*), reason (*loco de alegría*), capacity (*trabaja de joyero*), time (*trabaja de noche*), ownership (*es de Miguel*), topicality (*habló de política*), and much else. *Por* and *con* can contrast in locative contexts, but both may express means (*los estafó con/por un simple truco*), as may *a* (*escribir a máquina*). The semantic extensions of English prepositions are just as problematic.

With sufficient abstraction, the semanticist can uncover generalized senses that accommodate such extensions; Bull (1965:275-290) does this with a more far-reaching analysis of *a, en, de, por*, etc. In fact, with a little reflection even the layperson can perceive how 'origin' becomes 'composition' or 'possession', and how 'accompaniment' evolves into 'means'. But in trying to account for why 'manner' is *a* in *a caballo* (. . . *pie, gatas*), *con* in *con furia* (. . . *cariño, los ojos abiertos*), *de* in *de mala gana* (. . . *memoria, canto*), *por* in *por fuerza* (. . . *la mano, escrito*), and *en* in *en broma* (. . . *grande, voz alta*), explanation becomes a posteriori rationalization that is useless for the language learner, and we eventually throw up our hands and cry 'idiom!'

10.4 Lexically or grammatically fixed usage. One approach to the problem of 'idiomatic' Advls consists in determining the extent to which a native speaker has a real choice in using one relator over another. Certainly in the sentence frame *María se fue _____ la plaza*, the speaker has a choice among *para, por, hacia*, and several other Preps, and he selects the Prep that best conveys his intended meaning. He has less latitude in *María se fue _____ buena gana*, however, for in this case it is conventional to use *de*, and *de* only. *De buena gana* is a true idiom or lexicalized unit, and the use of *de* can be described as 'lexically fixed'. In the sentence *María se fue llena _____ esperanza*, *de* is likewise the only choice but for a different reason: here, the use of *de* is 'grammatically fixed' in that it is the grammar of Adj + complement, not the lexical properties of *esperanza*, that requires the link *de*. *De* is a functor in this case, having no real meaning except the indication of grammatical relationship.

10.4.1 Relators that introduce adverbial idioms. Spanish and English concur in some of their adverbial idioms, i.e. 'concur' in beginning them with Preps that often match elsewhere:

murieron *de* hambre, died *of/from* hunger
están *en* huelga, are *on* strike

cuatro *al* menos, four *at* least
en efecto, *in* fact
dejarlo *en* paz, leave him *in* peace

está *a* $100 el kilo, it's *at*
$100 a kilo
salimos *a* las dos, we left *at* two
se abre *con* facilidad, opens
with ease

manejó *a* 100 km. por hora, drove
at 100 km. per hour

But often they have lexically fixed Preps that are different, and in pedagogy one can do little more than arrange the idioms by sets for memorization:

a: a la larga, al contado, a medias, a sus anchas, a propósito, a continuación, a máquina, al revés, al contrario, a oscuras, a gatas, a menudo . . .

de: de rodillas, de vez en cuando, de repente, de nuevo, de acuerdo, de buena gana, de paso, de vuelta, de prisa, de canto . . .

en: en seguida, en cambio, en punto, en principio, en todo caso, en regla, en suma, en vano, en grande . . .

por: por supuesto, por lo general, por lo pronto, por tanto, por casualidad, por fin, por favor, por poco, por si acaso . . .

The reason that 'immediately' is expressed in Spanish by /ensegída/ is a lexical matter rather than a grammatical one; to ask why this unit begins with *en-* is like asking why *aclarar* begins with *a-* or *perjudicar* begins with *per-*.

10.4.2 Relators that are functors. Relators are fixed by grammatical usage in structures such as the following.

Vi ＿＿＿ Felipe anteayer. (=a)
La madre ＿＿＿ Felipe se ha enfermado. (=de)
El caballo me fue regalado ＿＿＿ Felipe. (=por)
Yo sé ＿＿＿ Felipe te quiere mucho. (=que)

A, de, por, and *que* here are functors, grammatical markers with little if any semantic substance in themselves. The 'personal' *a* signals DO (v. 8.1.3, 11.2.3); *de* marks the modification of one NP by another (v. 8.3.2); *por* identifies the agent or underlying Subj of a passive (v. 12.3); and *que* is a complementizer that introduces noun clauses (v. 13.1.1). English adopts similar functors in three of these patterns: *the mother of Philip* (or better, *Philip's mother*), *was given by Philip*, *I know that Philip loves you*; but it is meaningless to ask for an equivalent of personal *a* in a language that requires no syntactic marker of its DO.

Preps can also be analyzed as mere functors in the construction of Adj with complement NPs. Whatever the English equivalent, most Spanish Adjs take *de*: *harto de* NP, *libre de* NP, *lleno de* NP, *cubierto de* NP, *digno de* NP. Where English has Adj + *to* + V referring to a noun understood as the Obj of the verb (*that book is hard to read* = *it is hard to read that book*), Spanish uses Adj + *de* + V (v. 13.1.1): *ese libro es difícil de leer*. But there are enough idiosyncratic usages to suspect some lexical (adjective-specific) determination of the functor as well: *contento con, lento en, primero en, necesario para, equivalente a, paciente con, aficionado a, acorde con.*

Perhaps the hardest use of Prep to master is as a link between verbs and Obj NPs. For example, in *La leyenda de don Juan influyó en la cultura europea*, the PP *en la cultura europea* is not a freely added *complemento circunstancial* or AdvlP of location, but a constituent that completes a VP with *influir* much like the DO of *tener* or the IO of *gustar*. For that reason, the complement PP *en* + NP of *influir* is sometimes called the verb's OBLIQUE OBJECT instead of an adverbial phrase. The reason for *en* is both grammatical and lexical: being an intransitive verb in Spanish, *influir* is grammatically blocked from taking a DO NP; a Prep is required by the grammar if NP follows, but the particular Prep is dictated by the verb. As Klein (1984:417) expresses this fact, 'the determination of which preposition is linked to a given verb is essentially arbitrary, and must be learned as a lexical fact about that verb'. A good dictionary will in fact indicate that *influir* takes *en, quejarse* takes *de, interesarse* takes *en* or *por*, and so on.

English has its own arbitrary classification of transitive and intransitive verbs, with the latter dictating special Preps as in Spanish; but the classifications differ, as shown in Figure 10.4.[6] Interference of English with Spanish in V + NP vs. V + Prep + NP often endures right up into the advanced levels of study: **pido por agua, *depende en su opinión, *influyó la cultura europea*, etc.

Notes for Chapter 10

1. Aid (1973) takes into account parallels such as those just observed among adverbials, verbs, and adjectives, and argues for grouping all three into one supercategory with similar constructional properties.

2. The *de* of *de que* is grammatically optional, but for their own idiolects many speakers have decided preferences for or against it. One speaker consulted about this usage laughed at what he called the *dequeísmo* of some of his friends.

3. I.e. *-mente* from *la mente* 'mind'. The Romance languages agree in pointing back to the ablative case form *mente* of Latin *mēns* 'mind' for adverbializing adjectives. Thus, the ancestor of *contentamente* might have been something like *mente contentā* or *contentā mente* 'with or by a contented mind'. Adj + *mente* still acts like a phrasal Adj + N (i.e. NP) combination in that (1) it has a double stress (v. 4.1.2) which is rare in single words in Spanish, and (2) when conjoined to other *-mente* adjectives, it becomes Adj C Adj N: *armoniosa y alegremente*, like *una armoniosa y alegre melodía*.

4. Such, in fact, is the thrust of certain kinds of generative grammar that allow every constituent type (NP, VP, etc.) to have a 'Specifier' node for all modifiers that specify focus in this way.

Figure 10.4 Verb + (Prep) + NP in Spanish and English.

(a) Span. = V + NP, Eng. = V + Prep + NP:

anhelar; long for	escuchar; listen to	operar; operate on
aprobar; approve of	esperar; wait for/on	padecer; suffer from
atropellar; run over	impedirle X a Y; keep Y	pagar; pay for
buscar; look for	from X	pedir; ask for
cobrar; charge for	interferir; interfere with	presidir; preside over
enfocar; focus on	lograr; succeed in/with	solicitar; apply for
	mirar; look at	tratar; deal with

(b) Span. = V + Prep + NP, Eng. = V + NP:

abogar por; advocate	disponer de; have available
abusar de; abuse, misuse	divertirse en; enjoy
acabar con; destroy, eliminate	enfrentarse a/con; confront
acordarse de; remember	entrar en/a; enter
asistir a; attend	exceder de; exceed
cambiar de (ropa); change	influir en; influence
coger de; grab	parecerse a; resemble
confiar en; trust	presionar sobre; pressure
dar a; face	renunciar a; give up
dar en; hit	reparar en; notice
desconfiar de; distrust	salir de; leave
disfrutar/gozar de; enjoy	tirar de; pull

(c) Span. and Eng. = V + Prep + NP (but not necessarily with equivalent Prep):

aburrirse de[7]; be bored with	empeñarse en; insist on
acusar de; accuse of	esforzarse por; strive for
adelantarse a; get ahead of	interesarse en/por; be
apostar por; bet on	interested in
apoyarse en; lean on	librarse de; get out/free of
aumentar en; increase by	luchar por: fight for
basar/estribar en; base on	oler a; smell of/like
consistir en; consist of/in	pensar en; think about
contar con; rely on	prepararse para, disponerse a;
convenir en; agree on	get ready for
convertir en; change into	prescindir de; do without
culpar X de Y: blame X for Y,	salir a; take after
blame Y on X	servir de; serve as
cumplir con; comply with	soñar con; dream of
dar/topar con; run into	sustituir (a) X por Y;
depender de; depend on	replace X with Y, substi-
deshacerse de; get rid of	tute Y for X
dividir entre; divide by	tropezar con; run across
dudar en; hesitate in/with	votar por; vote for

---

5. One exception to our analysis of *en* vs. *a* appears with verbs of movement. In *Sofía se fue a Venezuela*, it is not the case that she went up to the shores or frontiers of Venezuela and no further. *A* here supplants the expected *en*, as it does also in the Americanism *entrar a* for *entrar en*.

6. Figure 10.4 excludes cases of Eng. V + Prep + NP in which the so-called preposition is actually a PARTICLE (v. 11.1.2.4). Prepositions must be 'preposed' to the NP they govern, whereas particles can float around what is actually the verb's DO: *rely on the radio* is thus V + Prep + NP, whereas *turn on the radio* = *turn the radio on* is V + Prt + NP.

7. Most other reflexive verbs of emotional reaction (v. 9.3.7) take *de* like *aburrirse: sorprenderse de, alegrarse de*, etc.

Exercises for Chapter 10

1. Error Analysis:

(1) *probablamente	(10) *Terminó sin mí ayudándolo
(2) *antes de leyendo	(11) *Tanto Julio como Luis se
(3) *Están a trabajo	matriculó
(4) *Nos visitaste ayudarnos	(12) *Ponlo debajo el escritorio
(5) *Ella está detrás de	(13) *A la escuela aprenden mucho
(6) *Este regalo es por ti	(14) *No te confío 'I don't trust you'
(7) *El vidrio es fácil romper	(15) *Depende en la clavija
(8) *Saliste la habitación	(16) *Ella trabaja tan programadora
(9) *Buscaban para su papel	tan puede ganar más dinero

2. How would you present and practice distinctions such as *cerca* vs. *cerca de*, and *antes* vs. *antes de* vs. *antes que*?

3. Why in Spanish does one say *Papá está en casa/la playa/la oficina* for *Dad is at home/the beach/the office*?

4. Note the following statements from teachers and then the Spanish sentences the students subsequently encounter. Why is there an apparent contradiction (and why is it only apparent)?

(1) 'With *mirar*, don't translate the *at* of *look at*.' (*Miraron a su mamá*.)

(2) 'With *pagar*, don't translate the *for* of *pay for*.' (*Pagaron $80 por la llanta*.)

(3) 'With *pedir*, don't translate the *for* of *ask for*.' (*Les pedí un vaso de agua para Lucía*.)

(4) 'With days of the week, don't translate *on*.' (*Insisten en el domingo próximo para el coloquio*.)

(5) 'Use *para*, never *por*, for purpose.' (*Van por pan*.)

5. The following Spanish sentences differ in various ways from their English equivalents. Describe the differences and predict student problems with *sustituir* and *reemplazar*:

(1) El vaso reemplazó/se sustituyó a la copa. The glass replaced the goblet.

(2) Juan reemplazó/sustituyó la copa por el vaso. John replaced the goblet with the glass, John substituted the glass for the goblet.

6. Spanish and English distinguish an adverb from its corresponding adjective with a suffix: *-mente, -ly*. How then does one account for the following?

(1) Hablaron muy fuerte. (. . . rápido, claro)
(2) Charlan mucho. (. . . poco, bastante, demasiado)
(3) Compran barato y cobran caro.

7. In many areas (Kany 1945/1951:363-64, Keniston 1937:264-65), *donde* and *cuando* are being used as prepositions: *Me alojé donde el director, Se refugió donde su querida, Los edificios se arruinaron cuando las invasiones.* Why do you think these two conjunctions have acquired these functions?

8. As the RAE (1979:435) puts a point made in section 10.3, relators 'dicen muy poco a la mente del que las oye o lee, fuera de una vaga idea de relación que solo el contexto puede precisar.' What are the 'ideas' of *a*, *de*, *por*, and *para*, and how do they become more precise in context? Give examples of other relators whose roles are best understood in context.

9. It was noted (10.2.3) that adverbs may occupy intensifier slots in adjective and adverbial phrases. Both languages also permit certain NPs of extent to function as intensifiers: *diez veces mejor, ten times better* (NP + Adj); *veinte años después, twenty years later* (NP + Adv). Note that in these the NP indicates the degree of the adjectival or adverbial quality just like *muy, algo*, etc. But the two languages do not entirely agree on the construction of Int + Adj or Int + Advl when Int = NP. Study the following examples, and comment on how Spanish would convey the same message. Try to arrive at a general description about the use of NP for Int in Spanish.

Int = Adv: This table is *very* old/*quite* high/*too* long.
Int = NP: This table is *twenty years* old/*two feet* high/*five feet* long.

10. The following sampling of expressions with *de* and *a* is based on Dowdle (1967). Classify the samples as follows, using information from this chapter and your own intuitions and evidence:

(a) follows from the primary (basic) meanings of *de* or *a*; not idiomatic
(b) unrelated to these basic meanings, but based on some other general principle or pattern of the language
(c) unpredictable, inexplicable; a fixed usage that is lexicalized as an idiom

de	*a*
(1) aprenderlo de memoria	(1) prefieren hacerlo a la española
(2) pintarlo de amarillo	(2) avanzaron a tientas
(3) dejó \$3 de propina	(3) se debe cocinar a fuego lento
(4) se lo dieron de comer	(4) hueles a vino
(5) trabajan de día	(5) lo logró a duras penas
(6) había más de ocho	(6) prefieren tejerlo a mano
(7) no se hará de esta manera	(7) quieren estar a sus anchas
(8) cinco metros de diámetro	(8) más vale no hacerlo a medias

(9) obró de acuerdo con el pacto

(10) te resulta fácil como de costumbre

(11) lo cogió del mango

(12) lo había aprendido de joven

(13) es de esperar

(14) lo pagaré de aquí a diez meses

(15) muy fácil de leer

(16) me hirió y de yapa/pilón me insultó

(17) son de Bilbao

(9) progresan paso a paso

(10) a un lado está el campeón

(11) al día siguiente se levantaron cansados

(12) está a doce pesos la docena

(13) se lo puso al revés

(14) se lo prestó a largo plazo

(15) se vende al aire libre

(16) no vire/gire a la izquierda

(17) se dirigió al auditorio

Chapter 11
Word order and constituency

11.0 Rules of syntax. The previous chapters have followed traditional grammar in treating each of the major parts of speech. The present and following chapters turn to how these syntactic categories join to form sentences and how sentence structure is altered for various communicative functions. As explained in Chapter 5 (v. 5.2), we are adopting the descriptive framework of transformational grammar or TG, which analyzes grammatical structure at two levels, deep and surface. One set of rules, the phrase structure rules (PSRs), specify the underlying sentence patterns of deep structure by describing the constituents of sentence (S), then the possible configurations of elements that make up those constituents, and so on until the phrase marker has branched into the terminal nodes onto which words are inserted according to their syntactic category (N, V, Adj, etc.). Another set of rules, transformations, may then convert these deep structures into various surface structures. The student of linguistics should understand that different linguists have different interpretations of the nature and function of PSRs and transformations, but since the primary goal here is a parallel description of Spanish and English that has applications for language teaching, we will forgo in-depth discussion of theoretical issues.

11.1 Phrase structure rules. The PSR S → NP VP (v. 5.2) is read aloud as 'a sentence consists of a noun phrase joined with a verb phrase', 'expand S as NP VP', or 'rewrite S as its constituents NP and VP'. Through the use of parentheses for elements that are optionally present and of curved braces ({}) for alternative 'expansions' of structures of the same type, one PSR can abbreviate many options a speaker has in constructing a sentence. In addition, the PSRs specify a particular word order: S is NP followed by VP, and the sequence VP NP for S will be disallowed (defined as ungrammatical) unless later transformations expressly create this by altering deep structure order.

Some English and Spanish PSRs have already been developed in previous chapters in the description of nouns and their modifiers, of adverbial types, and so on. The following sections explore English and Spanish PSRs more extensively.

11.1.1 Sentences. In English, a Subj NP is obligatory for sentence structure. Even when there is no 'logical' or referentially real Subj of the verb, something occupies the initial NP node of S, as with the *it* of *It snowed* (v. 9.1.2). There are some apparent counterexamples whose surface structures do lack an overt Subj: e.g. *Get out of here!* and *Want an apple?* Yet these have an understood Subj *you*, and they are equivalent to the fuller structures *You get out of here!* and *Do you want an apple?* It can be assumed that the understood *you* is present in deep structure, and that transformations delete it later.[1] The generalization about an obligatory Subj for deep structure can thus be retained for English:

(1E) S → NP VP

But in Spanish, the initial NP must be regarded as optional. In sentences such as *Vas/Van/Vamos a la playa hoy*, verb agreement points to an understood Subj in deep structure. Therefore Hadlich (1971:63-66) and others treat these surface structures as derived from *Tú vas/Ellos van/ Nosotros vamos a la playa hoy:* a Spanish transformation called Subject Pronoun Deletion optionally drops the Subj after the verb is made to agree with it. On the other hand, sentences such as *Llovió/Tronó/ Amaneció a las ocho* have no Subj, explicit or understood, meaningful or dummy, even in deep structure; the verb is 3sg. not because of agreement but because this is the unmarked form (v. 8.1.1). Hence, in the generalized PSR for Spanish, parentheses are placed around the NP to show that it is not required for all sentences:[2]

(1S) S → (NP) VP

Sentences with *there is* and *hay* require comment. In standard Spanish, *haber* is an impersonal (subjectless) verb like *llover* and *tronar*; it does not agree with an NP, and the NP asserted as existing is its DO, as revealed by pronominalization: *¿Hay tazas en la mesa? Sí, las hay (*ellas hay).*[3] In standard English, however, *there is* agrees with the following NP, which is therefore its Subj. English transformationalists account for this by deriving *There are five bugs in my soup* from *Five bugs are in my soup;* after subject-verb agreement applies, the Subj flips over the *be* and the *There*-Insertion transformation fills in the vacated Subj node with *there*.[4]

Both languages also have compound sentences, which consist of other sentences joined by coordinating conjunctions (v. 10.2.3, 13.0). This is customarily shown by the notation S (C S)^n, meaning that one can generate S plus any number (^{n}) of C S sequences: S C S, S C S C S, S C S C S C S ad infinitum. This option of compounding can be incorporated into the earlier rules for S as follows, with curved braces for 'or':

(1E') S → $\begin{Bmatrix} \text{NP VP} \\ \text{S (C S)}^n \end{Bmatrix}$ (1S') S → $\begin{Bmatrix} \text{(NP) VP} \\ \text{S (C S)}^n \end{Bmatrix}$

11.1.2 Phrases. Additional PSRs are now needed for stating the internal structure of NP and VP, and of the phrases that in turn occur inside these.

11.1.2.1 Noun phrases. The PSRs for NP have already been presented (v. 8.3.1), but are repeated here as (2E) and (2S):

$$
\text{(2E)} \quad \text{NP} \rightarrow
\begin{cases}
\text{(D)(Quant)(Adj)}^n \text{ N (PP)} & \text{e.g. } \textit{the two big themes of the debate} \\
\text{NP (C NP)}^n & \text{e.g. } \textit{the trees and the flowers and} \ldots \\
\text{NP S} & \text{e.g. } \textit{those citizens } \text{WHO VOTED} \\
\text{Pro} & \text{e.g. } \textit{she} \\
\text{S} & \text{e.g. } \textit{that you work so hard} \ldots
\end{cases}
$$

$$
\text{(2S)} \quad \text{NP} \rightarrow
\begin{cases}
\text{(D)(Quant)(Adj) N (Adj)}^n\text{(PP)} & \text{e.g. } \textit{los dos grandes temas sociológicos de la discusión} \\
\text{NP (C NP)}^n & \text{e.g. } \textit{los árboles y las flores y} \ldots \\
\text{NP S} & \text{e.g. } \textit{esos ciudadanos } \text{QUE VOTARON} \\
\text{Pro} & \text{e.g. } \textit{ella} \\
\text{S} & \text{e.g. } \textit{el que trabajes tanto} \ldots
\end{cases}
$$

When NP is NP + S (NP with a relative clause) or just S (a noun clause), special transformations adjust the structure in ways to be described in Chapter 13.

11.1.2.2 Verb phrases. A VP has as its head constituent a verb (V), optionally preceded by auxiliaries (Aux). At the end of the VP are located the various *complementos circunstanciales* described in Chapter 10 as AdvlP. Independently of the AdvlPs, the V may have with it a special prepositional phrase (PP) that expresses noncircumstantial information: an IO, as in *les gusta a los bailarines* (v. 8.1.2), or a verb complement (NP Obj with a verb-specified preposition, v. 10.4.2): *influyó en los bailarines, confío en los bailarines, disponemos de varios bailarines.*

The presence of other constituents in VP depends on the verb's subcategory. Transitive verbs may take or must take a DO: *comer* + NP, *destruir* + NP, *mover* + NP. Intransitive verbs do not take a DO: **caer* + NP, **amanecer* + NP, **morir* + NP. A third subcategory, linking or COPU-LATIVE verbs (or just COPULAS), take special elements traditionally called 'predicate nominative, predicate adjective, predicate adverb', all of which can be called PREDICATE ELEMENTS (PredE). The following sentences illustrate copulas + PredE (italicized):

Jorge fue/se hizo *ingeniero*.	George was/became *an engineer*.
Ana se puso/pareció/se volvió *pálida*.	Ann got/seemed/turned *pale*.
Juan está/se encuentra/se queda *ahí*.	John is/stays/remains *there*.
El problema salió/resultó *complicado*.	The problem ended up/turned out *complicated*.

The generalized PSR for VP in (3) takes into account the constituents that depend on verb subcategorization. Then rule (4) specifies the possibilities for PredE.

$$(3)\ VP \rightarrow (Aux) \left\{ \begin{array}{l} V\text{-intr} \\ V\text{-tr (NP)} \\ V\text{-cop PredE} \end{array} \right\} (PP)\ (AdvlP)^n$$

$$(4)\ PredE \rightarrow \left\{ \begin{array}{l} NP \\ Adj \\ AdvlP \end{array} \right\}$$

11.1.2.3 Adverbial and adjective phrases. Rule (3) indicates that a VP may contain any number, $(AdvlP)^n$, of adverbial phrases. The PSRs for AdvlP developed in Chapter 10 (v. 10.2.3) are repeated here:

$$(5)\ AdvlP \rightarrow (Int) \left\{ \begin{array}{l} Adv \\ PP \\ NP \\ C\text{-subord S} \end{array} \right\}$$

$$(6)\ PP \rightarrow Prep \left\{ \begin{array}{l} Adv \\ NP \\ PP \end{array} \right\}$$

Also in Chapter 10 (v. 10.1, 10.2.3), it was observed that adjectives may be preceded by intensifiers, as in *muy alto* and *very tall*, and that they may be followed by two kinds of complements: PP, as in *seguro de la verdad* and *sure of the truth*, and a clause or sentence, as in *seguro (de) que todo saldrá bien, sure that everything will turn out well*. Hence, like the N of NP, the V of VP, and the adverbials of AdvlP, Adj can be the head of a phrase, AdjP. Moreover, AdjP can be compound like NP and S: *una niñita triste y decepcionada.* 'Adj' in rules (2) and (4) should therefore be replaced by 'AdjP', for which the following rules specify internal structure:

$$(7)\ AdjP \rightarrow \left\{ \begin{array}{l} (Int)\ Adj\ (PP)\ (S) \\ AdjP\ (C\ AdjP)^n \end{array} \right\}$$

11.1.2.4 Other details of phrase structure. Rules (1) through (7) account for most of the deep structures of English and Spanish, but there remain several other details that should be accounted for in a fuller analysis, either by building them into the PSRs or by describing them as transformational derivatives of other structures. Among them are the following.

(1) As noted earlier (v. 10.2.3), some Advls are not really part of the VP but sentence modifiers providing discourse linkage (*sin embargo, por eso*) or an indication of the speaker's attitude toward the whole proposition (*desgraciadamente, probablemente, en realidad*). One way of providing

for such constituents would be to revise the rule for S to something like S → (AdvlP) NP VP.

(2) Both languages allow one DO per V (V + NP, though NP may, of course, be compound) but in Spanish there can be more than one IO (v. 9.4.2); perhaps rule (3) should be revised to allow two or more PP after V, at least in its Spanish version. Moreover, when pronominalized, the Spanish IO and DO become clitics adhering to the verb (v. 9.4), and some transformationalists have proposed a Clitic node in deep structure to accommodate these. Rule (3) might thus be revised to begin as follows for Spanish: VP → (Clitic) Aux . . .

(3) In many generative analyses, the tense and mood morphemes are placed under Aux (not on V) in deep structure as constituents distinct from the verb stem. One reason for this is that some transformations manipulate these morphemes separately, as when Passivization attaches them to the inserted *ser* or *be* (v. 12.3). Aside from this tense-in-Aux treatment, some allowance must be made for more than one Aux per VP. Spanish allows virtually any combination of auxiliaries as long as the perfect precedes the progressive; standard English allows at most one modal plus perfect plus progressive:[5]

*Puede haber esta-*do haciéndolo.	He *may have be-*en doing it.
Debe poder hacerlo.	*He *should can* do it.

In addition, some Advs can take up residence in or next to Aux in both languages: *Ella siempre ha pensado en sus hijos, She has always thought about her children.* For these and other reasons, Aux structure has yet to be worked out with the precision one might like.

(4) Like S, NP, and AdjP, the VP may be compound. Yet many linguists prefer to treat sentences like *Mercedes abrió el sobre y leyó el telegrama* as derived from an underlying compound sentence, *Mercedes abrió el sobre y Mercedes leyó el telegrama.* That is, VP C VP is analyzed as NP VP C NP VP in deep structure.

(5) Finally, in its version of the VP rule, English requires accommodation for its PARTICLES. Particles (Prt) are words such as *up, down, out, in, back, through, over,* that can occur on either side of the DO. As shown below, these are distinct from true adverbs and prepositions, which do not jump around in this way.

V Prt NP: He found *out* the answer. → He found the answer *out.*
V Prep NP: He flew *out* the window. → *He flew the window *out.*
   PP
V NP Adv: He found the answer *fast.* → ??He found *fast* the answer.

V + Prt is semantically and lexically one unit, a so-called TWO-WORD VERB: *find out* has nothing to do with outness, but denotes 'discover'. Spanish lacks two-word verbs and the particle category, so students must learn that idioms such as *throw up, ring up, fill up, sign up, set up, make up, put up, take up* will not be verb + *arriba*, nor will *turn up/down/on/off/over/around/in/out* be *volver* or *girar* + particle.

11.1.3 NP complements and appositives. In most of the phrase structures surveyed so far, one constituent is the main one, the HEAD, while others are subordinated to it as qualifiers, objects, modifiers, intensifiers, etc. But there are certain elements that are equated to others rather than subordinated to them. One such case includes the AdjP and NP that complement an existing Subj or Obj without being a part of it, as shown in the following examples (the arrows indicate the complementation):

Ya tenemos *terminado* el proyecto.

Ella se llama *María Pilar*, pero la llamamos *Maripili*.

Ellos vivían *felices* en su nueva casa.

Consideran *un capataz* a Juan.

Lo eligieron *presidente de la junta*.

Subject and object complements are used in both languages, and they could be analyzed as PredE, with the rationale that *Ella se llama María Pilar* sets up the same syntactic relation as *Ella es María Pilar*. Yet Stockwell, Bowen, and Martin (1965:245) prefer deriving at least some of these complements from subordinated clauses: *Consideran que Juan es un capataz → Consideran ser un capataz a Juan → Consideran un capataz a Juan.*

Another case is APPOSITION, in which two constituents of the same type are juxtaposed and equated:

NP=NP: *El comandante González* lo ordenó.
       Acabo de leer *un libro interesante, Viajes por el Alto Aragón.*
Adj=Adj: Fue muy *raro, extraño.*
VP=VP: Luego *endóselo, fírmelo en el reverso.*

An APPOSITIVE names, reformulates, or exemplifies its companion (Quirk et al. 1972:628, Gila Gaya 1973:210), functions that can be made more explicit with expressions such as *es decir, precisamente, especialmente, o sea*, e.g., *i.e., vgr.* As with adjective clauses (v. 13.3.3), there may be a contrast between restrictive and nonrestrictive appositives:

My friend Peter helped us. ≠ My friend, Peter, helped us.

But the distinction between them—and between both and titles (*la doctora Ramírez*)—is not always very clear, and the various types may lie on a continuum.

Quirk et al. (1973:874ff.) include in the appositive category those structures in which an abstract noun introduces a complement noun clause:

The fact that the court can decree this right has nothing to do with our decision. (Likewise, *the belief/hypothesis/news/hope that...*) Spanish has a similar construction equating a N with a following noun clause, but the two must be joined by *de*: *El hecho de que el tribunal pueda decretar este derecho no tiene nada que ver con nuestra decisión.* (Likewise, *la creencia/hipótesis/noticia/esperanza de que...*) The *de* effectively differentiates the appositive noun clause from a modifying relative clause: *la noticia que publicaste* (relative) vs. *la noticia de que publicaste* (appositive); and it also appears whenever the appositive is an infinitive or noun: *la satisfacción de verte, el riesgo de confusión.* It must be distinguished from the *de* that introduces a PP identifying (often possessively) the head noun (v. 8.3.2): *la costumbre de la siesta* equates 'custom' and 'nap' whereas *la costumbre de la gente* is possessive (*la costumbre de la corrida* could be ambiguous). English phrases such as *the problem of land-reform, the satisfaction of seeing you, the city of Los Angeles* show a similar appositional *of.*

There is no agreed-on analysis for all these appositives. One might provide for them directly in the PSRs, or derive them from other constructions. Hadlich (1971: 145, 158) takes the latter course, assuming that appositive NPs come from relative clauses containing an explicit marker of the equating function of apposition, namely a copula:

Madrid, que *es* la capital de España → Madrid, la capital de España
el hecho que *es* de que lo tengas → el hecho de que lo tengas

11.1.4 Summary. Although the deep structures of several constructions, and therefore their PSRs, are still unclear, the PSRs established in 11.1.1-11.1.2 suffice to generate a multitude of different syntactic structures. For example, one can form the structure shown in Figure 11.1 by following the indicated PSRs; this structure is defined as grammatical (insofar as syntax is concerned) since each branching or constituent specification conforms to options permitted by the PSRs, and it is the framework for both of the following sentences and for a great many others in the two languages.

Ese payaso reventó doce globos con su larga aguja.
That clown burst twelve balloons with his long needle.

Not only do Spanish and English share the same constituent structure in these two sentences, but their phrase structures in general coincide impressively. Perhaps this is why most Spanish courses dwell far more on morphology than on syntax, taking basic word order and constituency for granted. Spanish nouns, pronouns, and verbs are inflected differently from their English counterparts, but NPs and VPs largely have the same functions and positions in the two languages, and are built up out of similar configurations of similar elements. The English-speaking student of Spanish is blessed in this regard; his friend in a Japanese class is confront-

Figure 11.1 A sample phrase marker and the phrase structure rules that specify it.

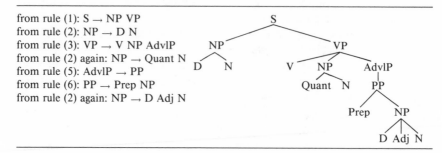

from rule (1): S → NP VP
from rule (2): NP → D N
from rule (3): VP → V NP AdvlP
from rule (2) again: NP → Quant N
from rule (5): AdvlP → PP
from rule (6): PP → Prep NP
from rule (2) again: NP → D Adj N

ed with a much more formidable syntactic challenge—the Japanese VP, for example, is generally (AdvlP) (NP) V (Aux), exactly the reverse of Spanish and English VPs.

Yet there are differences. Some of them lie in the PSRs themselves: as opposed to English, Spanish has an optional Subj NP in its S, a double Adj position in its NP, and no Prt in its VP. Other differences are due to constructional quirks of particular words, as with 'reverse construction' verbs (v. 8.1.4). Many more differences arise when transformations alter, often very drastically, the basic word order generated by PSRs, and English and Spanish surface structures then diverge in ways that may cause severe problems in language learning.

11.2 From deep to surface structure. Both languages have deep structures consisting of NP + VP, with VP in turn consisting of V and its Aux, PredE, Obj NPs, and various Advls. But in passing to the surface level, Spanish syntax undergoes several transformational reorganizations with no counterparts in English. A pronominal Subj is deleted unless emphatic, contrastive, or clarifying; only the verb ending then signifies the underlying Subj. Pronominal Objs become clitics phonetically attached to the verb. Finally, NPs (if they are still intact in the surface structure) can be moved out of their deep structure positions and repositioned. The result is a structure consisting of nucleus and satellites.

11.2.1 The nucleus. The NUCLEUS consists of verb + ending (*cant-an*), clitics + verb + ending (*lo cant-an*), or clitics + Aux + ending + verb (*lo pued-en cantar*). Only this much is obligatory in surface structure, and it is pivotal for the rest. Thus, *Yo lo vi ayer a las cuatro* is a complete sentence, but so is the bare nucleus *Lo vi*; in just two syllables the Spanish speaker

Figure 11.2 The internal structure of the Spanish sentential nucleus.

(no)	(se)	(te) (os)	(me) (nos)	(l-)	verb stem	tense/mood suffixes	person/number suffixes

gives a complete sentence indicating 'I + see + past + him/it' and a good deal of aspectual information besides. The ordering within this nucleus, shown in Figure 11.2, is quite fixed (v. 9.4.2 for the clitic sequence).

Of course, the clitics move to the other side of the verb in affirmative commands and with gerunds and infinitives; if the latter nonfinites follow another V, one has a choice of positions, with clitics optionally marching leftward and upward through the phrase marker (v. 13.1.2.8): *Está intentando hacerlo → Está intentándolo hacer → Lo está intentando hacer*. Old Spanish permitted freer clitic placement, but the nucleus eventually congealed in its modern form.

For the English speaker, there are three main features of the Spanish sentential nucleus that pose major problems. First, with a deleted Subj and pronominalized Obj, the basic—and English-like—order 'Subj verb Obj' (SVO) becomes 'Obj verb Subj' (OVS): the Obj is now a kind of prefix, and the Subj is incorporated into the verb suffix. Listening for, and processing, Obj information before a verb stem and Subj information after it can be quite difficult for speakers of a firmly SVO language.

Second, a great deal of information is packed into a rapid flurry of unstressed monosyllabic clitics and a largely unstressed set of short verb suffixes. English speakers are not accustomed to communicating or hearing so much information in phonetically inconspicuous syllables; they therefore tend to register incomprehension in exchanges such as *¿Se lo doy? Sí, démelo*. But within a normal context (one in which the referent of *lo* has been introduced or is obvious from the setting), these stripped-down nuclei are entirely sufficient for the Spanish speaker.

Third, everything in the nucleus is pronounced as one word, with a single stress somewhere in the verb. A form such as [noseloðaɾán] *no se lo darán* is a glued-together or AGGLUTINATIVE series of morphemes. With Syneresis and Vowel Gliding (v. 2.2.3, 3.1.10), the morphemes blend further:

se le olvidó → [seljolβiðó]
te la ha anunciado → [telanunsjáðo]
no os he hecho → [noséčo]
me la hirió → [melajɾjó]
se ha ahorcado → [sjawɾkáðo]

The student expects three distinct, phonologically prominent words for Subj, verb, and Obj, but hears only a verb with assorted consonants and vowels affixed to it.

11.2.2 Satellites. Constituents outside the nucleus can be called SATELLITES because they are grammatically optional elements governed by the verb nucleus and pivoting around it in surface structure. They may occur to the left, to the right, or not at all.

¿A María se lo han dado *los jueces?*
¿Los jueces se lo han dado *a María?*
¿Se lo han dado *los jueces a María?*
¿Se lo han dado *a María los jueces?*
¿Se lo han dado?

Being stressed in their own right, satellite NPs and Advls are more audible than the incorporated elements of the nucleus, but their free-floating position contradicts the patterns English speakers rely on to process sentential relationships. Students hear the prominent words—NP, Advl, V—and often reconstruct meaning on the basis of English word order without paying attention to the relationships defined in the rapidly passing nucleus; consequently, *A nosotros nos ayudaron los policías* is misinterpreted as 'We helped the police officers.' The task ahead of the student is to learn to anticipate satellite transpositions, and to grasp what these transpositions mean.

11.2.3 Transposed satellites and 'personal' *a*. Languages with a highly developed inflectional system tend to have a relatively free word order. Latin, for instance, had five different cases for its nouns, each designating a different kind of syntactic relationship to other elements in the sentence. If there was one basic, unmarked word order, it was Subj Obj verb or SOV; this was the most neutral and ordinary way of constructing a sentence, and presumably the deep structure configuration generated by the PSRs. But several permutations were possible because the case endings clearly indexed NPs for who was doing what to whom. Thus, 'Paul saw Julia' was ordinarily *Paulus Juliam vidit*, but for special effects this could be transformed to *Juliam Paulus vidit*, *Vidit Juliam Paulus*, *Vidit Paulus Juliam*, and so on. No matter how the words were scrambled out of their deep structure position, the *-us* of *Paulus* and the *-am* of *Juliam* signaled Subj and DO, respectively.

English nouns, on the other hand, are inflected only for number (v. 8.2.1); the rich and Latin-like case system of Old English has been lost. The language therefore depends on word order to indicate function, and the deep-structure configuration of SVO tends to be preserved in surface structure. One can say just *Paul saw Julia*, and the so-called 'dislocated' variant *Julia, Paul saw* (with a sharp intonational set-off); otherwise, permutations reverse Subj and Obj roles (*Julia saw Paul*) or yield an ungrammatical sequence (**Saw Paul Julia*).

Spanish, like English, is classified as SVO—as long as we understand 'V' to be the whole nucleus and 'O' to be an uncliticized Obj NP. SVO is the usual ordering (Meyer 1972) as well as the one that best qualifies for the deep structure (Suñer 1982). But even though Spanish also has lost its noun case system, its transformations can shift the satellites around in surface structure, and in this respect Spanish resembles its Latin parent more than it does English.

Gili Gaya (1972:81ff.) sorted out the possibilities into three grammatical and three ungrammatical orders, as shown below. Note that all of these are declaratives, not questions.

SVO Mi padre compró una casa. OVS *Una casa compró mi padre.
VOS Compró una casa mi padre. SOV *Mi padre una casa compró.
VSO Compró mi padre una casa. OSV *Una casa mi padre compró.

He notes that although poets may resort to the starred orders for metrical or stylistic effects (English poets have aspired to similar grammar-warping rights), these are now strained (*hipérbaton*) or entirely ungrammatical. He generalizes to state that the verb must occupy the first or second syntactic slot in the modern language (Gila Gaya 1973:88); and the Real Academia concurs (1979:399).

Meyer 1972 demonstrates that this analysis overgeneralizes, and she meticulously notes details Gila Gaya passed over. First, OVS is indeed possible in Spanish if the Obj NP is definite and a clitic copy of it is added to the nucleus:[6]

*Un coche se ha comprado José.
*El coche se ha comprado José.
El coche se *lo* ha comprado José.

Second, for VSO the Subj is preferably indefinite (v. 11.3.1):

*Se ha comido el niño la manzana.
Se ha comido un niño la manzana.

Third, a definite Subj NP is usually sentence-initial, although this SVO can shift to VOS to emphasize the Subj:

Se ha comido la manzana *Paco.*

For subordinated clauses, her data reveal a strong tendency toward VSO, although SVO occurs occasionally to contrast the Subj:

Si tuviera María el libro,⎫
Si *María* tuviera el libro,⎭ me lo daría.

It is in yes/no questions that Meyer finds the most variety. SOV and OSV are still excluded, VSO is most common (regardless of the subject's definiteness), but SVO, VOS, and OVS also occur:

VSO ¿Se comió Eva la manzana? SVO ¿Eva se comió la manzana?
VOS ¿Se comió la manzana Eva? OVS ¿La manzana se *la* comió
                                          Eva?

Nevertheless, this task of listing allowed, disallowed, and allowed-but-constrained orders eventually runs up against language variation. Meyer (1972:192-193) relied on one informant for her data and suspected that further studies would turn up dialectal and idiolectal variation. In fact, such is the case, and some details of Meyer's and Gila Gaya's analyses do not hold for all speakers.[7] There is stylistic variation too, since OSV—which Meyer excludes and Gili Gaya regards as poetic—occasionally appears in journalistic usage, which is decidedly unpoetic. Given this variation, it makes sense to proceed on a fairly general level of analysis, leaving details to be filled in for particular dialects and styles.[8]

Agard (1984:105) notes that Spanish is not the only Romance language to allow permutations of the underlying SVO order; Portuguese, Italian, and Rumanian also rearrange Subj and Obj around the verb. How to account for this is somewhat under dispute at present; some current transformationalists prefer to posit a generalized 'move alpha' transformation in which any 'alpha' (read 'any designated constituent') may move anywhere in the sentence subject to language-specific restrictions. Obviously, those restrictions are much more severe in English than they are in Spanish or its Romance sisters. Other grammarians prefer to describe each particular movement as a transformation, and this is the approach Agard takes. For Spanish, he requires three rules that are grammatically optional in that the speaker has the 'option' of applying them or bypassing them in the generation of a sentence. These rules are SUBJECT POSTPOSING (SVO → VSO), SUBJECT EXTRAPOSING (SVO → VOS), and OBJECT PREPOSING, which must be accompanied by Subject Postposing (SVO → VSO → OVS). Figure 11.3 illustrates the application of the three transformations.

Figure 11.3 Agard's analysis of the transformations for verb-satellite permutations.

SVO	*Juan Ramón recibió el premio.*	no transformations applied; surface order preserves underlying order.
SVO→VSO	*Recibió Juan Ramón el premio.*	application of Subject Postposing.
SVO→VOS	*Recibió el premio Juan Ramón.*	application of Subject Extraposing.
SVO→OVS	*El premio lo recibió Juan Ramón.*	application of Subject Postposing plus Object Preposing.

But whatever the transposings are called and however they are described transformationally, how is it that Spanish has more surface word orders than English when neither marks its NPs for case? Despite having lost the Latin case-endings, Spanish still has resources that speakers rely on in determining the underlying function of transposed NPs. First, NP V NP is unambiguous: this corresponds to the deep structure ordering and it receives the interpretation of SVO (OVS being impossible without a clitic copy of Obj). Second, the verb ending agrees with the Subj, so that the Subj need not stay in one slot that uniquely announces its subjecthood. However the string *Juan + vio + los árboles* is rearranged, *vio* indicates a 3sg. Subj, and of the two NPs only *Juan* qualifies. Of course, this clue fails with two NPs of the same person and number, as in *Juan + vio + el árbol* and *los monjes + vieron + los árboles* or Gili Gaya's *mi padre + compró + una casa.* When these constituents are permuted, neither the unmarked SVO order nor the verb ending is helpful; but semantics comes to the rescue here, since humans see and sell things but trees and houses do not.

In addition, Spanish has its rather distinctive 'personal *a*.' The traditional rule for it, as the name suggests, is that *a* is inserted before all human DOs—with two exceptions. First, *a* does not accompany *tener* 'to have', although it may follow *tener* 'to hold'; likewise (in some versions of the rule) *querer* 'want' vs. 'love'. Second, *a* may be used with nonhuman DOs if these are 'anthropomorphized' or 'personified', as in the metaphorical *La Luna admiró al Sol.*

Spanish speakers have no need of a preposition to remind them of which NPs represent real or adopted members of their species. Actually, *a* is primarily used to mark the DO so that it will not be confused with the Subj in a language with movable satellites. As noted above, there is no ambiguity in any permutation of *Juan + vio + el árbol*; but consider what happens when unmarked word order, verb ending, and semantics do not help, as in *Vio + Juan + Pedro* (=VSO? VOS?). Function is unclear here, since either person would be capable of seeing or being seen, and the Spanish solution is to insert *a* as a kind of DO case-marking:

Juan vio a Pedro.
Vio a Pedro Juan.
Vio Juan a Pedro.
A Pedro lo vio Juan.

Likewise, in *invitarán + los padres* it would not be clear in surface structure whether the NP is DO (with an understood Subj *ellos* or *Uds.* shown by the verb ending), or a postposed Subj. *A* before the DO will clarify function, so that *Invitarán los padres* is interpreted as 'the parents will do the inviting' and *Invitarán a los padres* as 'they'll invite the parents'.

Contrary to the traditional rule, *a* is also fairly common with nonhuman (but unpersonified) DOs whenever these might be confused with Subj. In any permutation of *El gato comerá las gallinas*, the verb ending will match *el gato* only; of course, in *Los gatos comerán las gallinas* the verb ending is unhelpful, but the constituents are in SVO order, and we know that cats normally eat chickens, not vice versa. But with dogs chasing cats, chickens seeing cows, and any two animate entities with roughly equal potency or likelihood of acting as Subj, *a* may be needed, especially once the SVO order is altered.

Los perros persiguen (a) los gatos. → Persiguen a los gatos los perros.
Las gallinas vieron (a) las vacas. → Vieron a las vacas las gallinas.

Nor should we limit *a* to animates. Ramsey (1956:43) gathered examples of *a* before inanimates:

El bullicio siguió al silencio.
Alcanzó al vapor el yate.

And Gili Gaya (1973:84) noted that while the following need no *a* thanks to their SVO order,

La amistad dominó el interés de todos.
El arenal desvió la corriente.

permutation could cause confusion—friendship dominating interest or vice versa, sandbar pushing aside current or vice versa—unless *a* is inserted:

Dominó la amistad al interés de todos.
Desvió a la corriente el arenal.

As for the subrule for *querer* and *tener*, Fish (1967:81) observes that the lost child wailing *¡Quiero a mi mamá!* is expressing his urgent desire, not commenting on his filial affections; and Miles and Arciniegas 1983 find abundant cases with *tener a* for 'have', not 'hold':

Tenía, a su lado, a Magda López.
Yo no tengo a nadie.
Tenía a otro consigo.
Aquí tiene a su nena, señor.
Hay varios estados . . . que tienen al español como idioma oficial.
Teniendo a tu marido, bastante médico tienes.

The problem with *a* is that it mainly differentiates DO from Subj, yet—unlike the Latin accusative case ending—it is not obligatorily used with all DOs, and it may appear even when there is no danger of confusion. As Miles and Arciniegas (1983:85-86) point out, the use of *a* is governed by 'several interlocking components, with considerable latitude for alternate choices'; indeed, native speakers are not always sure whether to use it. They do not specify these 'interlocking components', but the literature attests to at least four of them.

First, undoubtedly *a* has spread to almost all human DOs: **Ellos ven Raúl* is plainly ungrammatical, even though the objecthood of *Raúl* is clear here and in any permutation.

Second, *a* has also spread to certain verbs whose Obj may be totally inanimate, e.g. *renunciar* (*Renuncié al puesto*), *seguir, preceder, comparar, distinguir, unir, separar, afectar, acompañar, reemplazar*. Fish (1967:83) lists such verbs, and adds examples such as the following:

El segundo surco tocaba al primero.
Cuide que la carga contrapese al agua.
Cada una de estas rectas corta a la otra.

Third, *a* is avoided (but not categorically) with indefinite or naked nouns, even if human. The traditional subrule for *querer* and *tener* belongs here, but these two are not at all unique:

¿Tienes hermanos?	Se busca secretaria.
Quiero médico.	Hay que escoger otro capitán.

Fish (1967) explains this as a playing down of individuality; the speaker has no interest in the personal distinctiveness of the DO's referent. His best example of the particularizing effect of *a* is the following: *No tengo padres pero sí tengo a mi hermana que me educa.*

Fourth, *a* raises the status and enhances the functional role of the DO. According to Fish, nonhumans can be upgraded in status, though this does not necessarily yield an anthropomorphic metaphor:

Ahuyentó a una mosca de su cerveza.
Ve al lobo, y abandonando sus ovejas, huye.

And humans can be downgraded, even if definite:

¡Llame el chofer!
Dejó su niña en la puerta y huyó.
Perdimos tres hombres y una metralladora.

Teachers and texts can point out the basic tendencies in the use of *a*: where it is required, where it is an option, and where it tends not to be used. In this respect, *a* resembles other grammatical matters such as the subjunctive or the indefinite article. By contrast, the simpler traditional rule seems attractive. But that rule, in the words of Miles and Arciniegas (1983:84), is only a 'myth': 'the observant student, leaving the classroom and confronted with Spanish in the real world, must sooner or later be puzzled by usage that clearly contradicts what he has been taught.'

11.3 The meaning of Spanish word order. Thus far, this chapter has considered word order from a purely grammatical point of view. There are PSRs that generate a set of basic sequences, and transformations that rearrange these sequences. As a result, a speaker has several options in encoding his message: there are several points at which he can choose either X + Y or Y + X. But often the selection of one ordering over the other will signal a different way of presenting information. This is particularly true in the case of nucleus with satellites, nouns with determiners and quantifiers, and nouns with adjectives.

11.3.1 Nucleus with satellites. What is the difference between *A María le dio el premio Juan, Juan le dio el premio a María*, and other such permutations? None, grammatically; in each case, *Juan* is the Subj, *le . . . a*

María the IO, and *el premio* the DO, and all these variants would be analyzed as surface structures formed off the same deep structure. But each rearrangement subtly alters the force or thrust of the sentence. As Ramsey (1894/1956:660) puts it, 'in general, any change from the natural order attracts attention.' Of course, 'nature' does not govern the human conventions of word order, but if 'natural' were replaced by 'unmarked' in this statement, modern linguists would agree with Ramsey. A change in word order reflects a change in how the speaker is presenting his information and what he wants the hearer to pay attention to.

In order to develop this idea further, it should be noted that we have so far been using SUBJECT in its grammatical sense, which is hard to define (v. 8.1.1). At least for most action verbs, the grammatical Subj is loosely the agent or doer of the verb. But SUBJECT also means 'theme, topic,' and it is not by accident that grammarians came to use the same word for both. In *Lidia me trató con desdén*, the NP *Lidia* is both the subject=agent of the verb and the subject=topic of the statement. The VP *me trató con desdén* comments on this topic and makes a predication about it, whence the traditional term PREDICATE. Thus, on the grid of NP + VP or grammatical subject + grammatical predicate, the speaker superimposes a presentational schema of TOPIC + COMMENT, or THEME + RHEME as they are also called. But sometimes other constituents are topicalized, necessitating the shift of the subject=agent out of its customary theme position to make room. Even within the fixed word order of English, we have already seen the dislocation OSV, as in *John, I can't stand but Mary's okay*. But Spanish uses transposition to alter thematic structure on a much grander scale.

As the Real Academia (1979:395) describes unmarked SVO order, 'el sujeto representa de ordinario el término conocido, la continuidad del discurso.' If it is some other constituent which is the given, familiar term carried over from previous discourse, then it moves into this favored thematic position and the Subj moves out of it. That is, in clause-initial position the speaker singles out some topic presumably familiar to the hearer, a step Stiehm 1978 calls 'paradigmatic focus' since the speaker is selecting from a 'paradigm' of possible themes. The speaker then proceeds to comment on this theme, presenting or affirming new information about it. Since sentence intonation (v. 4.2) highlights constituents toward the end with rising or falling terminals, key elements of the rheme will gravitate toward that position of 'syntagmatic focus.' Thus, a topicalized Obj or Advl will tend to move to the front, and a Subj which is not the real topic but a part of the comment will move to the end where it can be focused on.

The rationale for transformed word order becomes clearer when one moves beyond the consideration of single sentences isolated from context. Consider a speaker who, in the course of a conversation about a dinner party and the subsequent clean-up, asks *¿Qué hicieron Margarita y*

Susana? The topic is established, and the new information will be what these two individuals did. The hearer, who knows only what Susana did, answers *Pues, Susana lavó los platos.* But if the question is *¿Quién lavó los platos?*, washing the plates becomes the topic and the point of departure for a comment, and the subject=agent becomes the new information to be focused on; the hearer may now respond with OVS, *Pues, los platos los lavó Susana.* As an alternative strategy, speakers may stick to SVO and highlight the subject with unusually elevated intonation and stress and perhaps slower tempo: *Pues, SUSANA lavó los platos.* This phonological highlighting is the NORMAL procedure in English, as illustrated here:

'What did Margaret and Susan do?' 'Well, Sùsan washed the plátes.'
'Who washed the plates?' 'Well, SUSAN washed the plates.'

The difference between the two languages here is a tendential one: English occasionally dislocates to show a changed thematic structure, but more commonly it uses a phonological procedure, whereas Spanish can use the latter but more often adopts a change in word order.

Meyer (1972:187) seeks to explain each word order in terms of discourse. The reason for the constraint against *OSV and *SOV follows from the nature of topicality: if Subj remains in front of the verb and Obj is preposed and topicalized, the sentence will be starting out with two topics, which does not conform to normal discourse procedure. VOS in declaratives focuses strongly on the postposed Subj, as if in answer to 'Who did X?' In questions, ¿VSO? is normal, but ¿SVO? and ¿VOS? are used to highlight the Subj; ¿SVO?, Meyer (1972:188-189) believes, gives more emphasis to an already stated NP, sometimes with disbelief. ¿OVS? is used for topicalizing Obj.

¿VSO? ¿Se comió Eva la manzana?   ¿SVO? *¿Eva* se comió la manzana?

¿VOS? ¿Se comió la manzana Eva?   ¿OVS? ¿La manzana se la comió Eva?

Suñer 1982 explores in greater depth the underlying theme-rheme structure of Spanish sentences. The theme or topic is PRESUPPOSED as already presented or taken for granted; the rheme or comment is material which is ASSERTED about the theme, with special focus on its last constituent. Like others, she posits that in the unmarked case, a neutral declarative sentence, the Subj is the theme and the predicate VP the rheme, as shown in Figure 11.4 for the sentence *Mis hijas* (theme) *están en la Florida con sus abuelos* (rheme). But the theme is not always old information; in answer to another speaker's observation *Se te ve muy cansada*, the whole sentence in Figure 11.4 would be new information, whereas in answer to *¿Dónde están las niñas que no las oigo?*, just the focused PP *con sus abuelas* would be new information (Suñer 1982:5).

Figure 11.4 Grammatical structure and thematic structure.

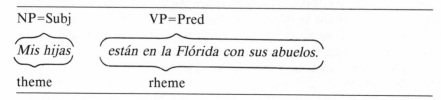

Suñer notes two special conditions that affect thematic structure and therefore word order. First, in PRESENTATIONAL SENTENCES, the speaker introduces a referent into the discourse, and this NP will be rheme (asserted), not theme (presupposed). Consequently, the presented NP moves rightward into the rheme if it is not already there in deep structure (i.e. if it is a Subj rather than a VP constituent), as shown in Figure 11.5 for the change *Un elefante apareció en el jardín → En el jardín apareció un elefante*. This latter presentational sentence would answer a question such as *¿Qué viste en el jardín?*, because the locative AdvlP becomes the theme (the questioner broached it and the answerer presupposes it) and the elephant is presented in the focus position of the rheme, though it remains the grammatical Subj. When the presented noun is naked (an unmodified, undetermined common noun), this transposition is obligatory under normal intonation because the noun is being presented for the first time and cannot be presupposed. Suñer (1982:208-264) calls this requirement the 'Naked Noun Constraint':[9]

(Dirección falta.) → Falta dirección.
(Abogados vivían allí.) → Allí vivían abogados.
(Niños juegan en el parque.) → En el parque juegan niños.

Presentational sentences thus favor Subject Postposing, and require it when the Subj is a naked noun.

However, Suñer notes that the Naked Noun Constraint can be overridden and the Subj can stay in its initial position provided that it is being strongly contrasted with a previously mentioned element. A contrasted element carries heavier stress and heightened intonation, and even though the speaker is presenting it for the first time, he is presupposing its

Figure 11.5 Syntactic permutation for showing the thematic structure of presentational sentences.

NP=Subj   VP=Pred

Un elefante apareció en el jardín. → *En el jardín apareció un elefante.*

                                      theme   rheme

differentiation from some topic or assertion that has been broached already. Suñer (1982:229-240) illustrates the consequences of contrast on the placement of naked nouns by means of exchanges such as the following:

(1) A: Surgió gas, ¿no?
     B: No, PETRÓLEO surgió.

(2) A: ¿Surgió petróleo?
     B: PETRÓLEO no surgió, pero sí agua.

Note that, although B's responses have the naked noun *petróleo*, it has not been postposed. This is because A's questions introduce 'something coming up' into the discourse; the particular substance A had in mind, however, is different from the one B has in mind, and B proceeds to correct this. In (2), *petróleo* leads off B's response because, despite its nakedness, it is thematic or old information broached by A; in (1) *petróleo* can begin B's response because, although new information, it is part of the established theme of 'something coming up'. B's use of phonological heightening on *petróleo* instead of syntactic postposition emphasizes its contrast with *gas* in (1) and with *agua* in (2).

To account for how speakers alter the basic Subj=theme + VP=rheme sequence by moving satellites, Suñer requires two transformations. One is Subject Postposing, which highlights this NP by moving it into the focus of the rheme; the other is Topicalization (what Agard called Preposing, v. 11.2.3), which moves VP elements to the front of the sentence when these are treated as the topic of assertion rather than as a part of the assertion. The two combine with her principle of contrasting to create several discourse possibilities, as illustrated in the following sentences (Suñer 1982:259-260).

(3) A: ¿Por qué estás tan contenta?
     B: El petróleo surge a carradas.

(4) A: ¿Surgió petróleo?
     B: Petróleo no surgió.

(5) A: ¿Qué pasó?
     B: Surgió petróleo.

(6) A: ¿Surgió agua?
     B: No, surgió petróleo.

(7) A: ¿Surgió agua?
     B: No, PETRÓLEO surgió.

In (3), the *petróleo* in B's response is new information but serves as B's topic for a comment; there is no contrasting. In (4), B's *petróleo* is the theme and old information (since A broached it); there is a contrasting of predicates. In (5), B's response is presentational; the whole sentence is a rheme and new information, and the Subj is postposed. Finally, in both (6) and (7) B's responses have *surgió* as the theme and *petróleo* as the rheme; in the usual case, (6), *petróleo* is postposed, but in heightening the contrast with the theme *agua* in (7) the speaker chooses to emphasize *petróleo* phonologically instead of postposing it.

Given her theory of word order in Spanish, Suñer (1982:317) believes that ' "free" word order is not so free after all. Different word orders convey different functional perspectives: Subject-verb does not carry the same information as verb-subject.'

11.3.2 Nouns with determiners and quantifiers. In both languages, determiners and quantifiers regularly precede their head nouns. In English, this sequence is quite fixed, but Spanish allows certain postposings:[10]

mi casa → la casa mía
este tipo → el tipo este
cualquier obrero → un obrero cualquiera
no hay ningún motivo → no hay motivo alguno[11]

For Gili Gaya (1973:220), postposition of a possessive is simply the automatic consequence of the use of *el* or *un* before the noun; there being only one determiner slot, the possessive is displaced when the D node is already occupied by an article. As Stiehm (1978:414) adds, some such postposings must be regarded as grammatically automatic anyway: (*ese tu hijo*) → *ese hijo tuyo*, (*tres más viajeros*) → *tres viajeros más*, (*nuestros varios parientes*) → *varios parientes nuestros*. But a 'grammatically automatic' postposition rule fails to explain why *la casa mía* exists alongside *mi casa*; both are grammatical, both are definite, both have the same possessor. As for postposed demonstratives (*el tipo este*), these have sometimes been described as disparaging or connoting contempt; but that interpretation is inaccurate, since preposed demonstratives may suggest disparagement at times too, and postposed ones do not always suggest it (Keniston 1937:103). The analyst is left with the problem of explaining why postposing occurs at all in such cases as *mi casa* → *la casa mía* and *este tipo* → *el tipo este*, in which there is a choice rather than a purely grammatical requirement.

The RAE (1979:43) explains that postposing premodifiers of N depends on 'matices afectivos'; this explanation begs for an explanation, but it does suggest that postposing is not merely a matter of grammar. More precisely, Ramsey (1894/1956:112) states that postposing expresses emphasis or contrast; Fish (1961:707) and Stiehm (1978:414ff.) agree. *Mi casa* is fairly neutral or unmarked, whereas *la casa mía* emphasizes the possessor, often in explicit or implicit contrast, as in English *MY house, not YOURS*.[12] Postposing *cualquier(a)* and *ningún(o)* (→*alguno*) gives these a more sweeping characterization of reference; and postposing demonstratives gives them a stronger deictic (pointing) force, which may or may not be disparaging. The basic principle underlying the observations of Ramsey, Fish, and Stiehm seems to be that such modifiers have greater strength and prominence when postposed than when they stay in their unmarked or neutral position before the N.

11.3.3 Nouns with adjectives. In English the Adj regularly precedes its head N, as stipulated by the NP rules presented earlier (v. 11.1.2.1). But if it is actually an AdjP with a dependent PP or S, it moves over the N. Adjectival participles act similarly.

a kind woman but *a woman kind to everyone*
an independent people but *a people so independent that they reject help.*
a laughing clown but *a clown laughing at his audience*

In the Spanish PSR for NP, however, we recognized that Adjs occur more systematically in pre-position[13] and postposition, often with a difference in meaning. This difference has often been commented upon in Hispanic grammar and linguistics in a kind of running dialog periodically impinging on pedagogy; indeed, if the question of word order is ever broached in a textbook, it is in this case.

Bello (1847/1958:34ff.) and the Real Academia grammar (1924:192-194) that built on his work dwelled on few examples to make their point that a preposed Adj characterizes the entire group delimited by the noun, and indicates some natural property of it. It is 'explicativo' in just elaborating on a trait that logically follows from the noun's meaning. The postposed Adj restricts the noun's referential scope; it is 'especificativo' in specifying some members of the group and excluding others. Thus, in Bello's oft-quoted examples, the Adj in *las mansas ovejas* brings out the presumed inherent tameness of sheep and adds essentially nothing; but in *los animales mansos* it selects gentle animals from the group of *animales* and excludes wilder ones.

Ramsey (1956:665-668) accepted the Bello explanation, but in contrasting Spanish with the English of his readers he added two new observations. First, postposition sometimes corresponds to the use of emphatic or contrastive stress in English: *vivos colores* 'bright cólors' vs. *colores vivos* 'BRIGHT colors.' This is insightful, and true (at least in this case). Second, some Adjs appear to be fixed in one position semantically, having one sense in Adj + N and a distinct one in N + Adj, as illustrated in Figure 11.6. Many writers picked up on Ramsey's meaning-changers and adopted some form of his list in their texts. Some of the distinctions may be correctly stated: *cierto, nuevo, simple*, and *varios* do have a kind of determiner force when preposed like other determiners, but when postposed they add descriptive meanings to the noun or attribute characteristics to it. Yet *antiguo, puro, propio*, and *grande* do not completely conform to Ramsey's rules:

los antiguos templos egipcios 'the ancient (*not* former) Egyptian temples'

más vale tener libros propios que libros ajenos 'it's better to have one's own (*not* suitable) books than someone else's'

anhelaba la pura agua de los manantiales 'she yearned for the pure (*not* mere) water of springs'

el paro es el otro gran problema de la economía 'unemployment's the other big (*not necessarily* great) problem of the economy'

Figure 11.6 Adjectives that are said to change meaning in Adj + N vs. N + Adj (based on Ramsey 1956:667).

---

1. antiguo:
   el antiguo presidente   'the former president'
   el presidente antiguo   'the ancient (very old) president'
2. cierto:
   ciertas fórmulas   'certain formulas'
   fórmulas ciertas   'true formulas'
3. grande:
   una gran reina   'a great, grand queen'
   una reina grande   'a large, big queen'
4. medio:
   media manzana   'half an apple'
   la manzana media   'the average apple'
   la clase media   'the middle class'
5. mismo:
   el mismo portavoz   'the same spokesman'
   el portavoz mismo   'the spokesman himself'
6. nuevo:
   se ha puesto una nueva blusa   'she's put on a new (different) blouse'
   se ha puesto una camisa nueva   'she's put on a brand-new blouse'
7. pobre:
   la pobre hijita   'the poor (pitiful) daughter'
   la hijita pobre   'the poor (not rich) daughter'
8. propio:
   lee sus propios libros   'he reads his own books'
   lee libros propios   'he reads suitable books'
9. puro:
   ¡Es pura agua!   'It's merely (just) water!'
   ¡Es agua pura!   'It's pure water!'
10. simple:
    un simple caso de confusión   'a mere case of confusion'
    un caso simple de confusión   'a simple case of confusion'
11. varios:
    Hay varios solicitantes.   'There're several applicants.'
    Hay solicitantes varios.   'There're all kinds of applicants'

Nevertheless, the effort to sort out Adjs into one position or the other by laying down rules snowballed in pedagogy. By the sixties, DaSilva and Lovett had the system as neatly regulated as possible for the student. The following were said to 'regularly' follow their nouns (Da Silva and Lovett 1965:161):

(1) Adj of nationality, religion: *los perfumes franceses*
(2) Adj of color and shape: *una mesa blanca, una mesa redonda*
(3) Adj referring to 'branches of learning, classifications, or scientific terminology': *un estudio psicológico, ácido acético*
(4) Adj modified by Adv (Int): *una canción muy triste*
(5) participles used as Adj: *una figura arrodillada*

Despite the wide and continuing appeal of these prescriptions, they are quite wrong since all five groups can be preposed as well as postposed.[14] Even if they are interpreted as mere statistical projections (e.g. *psicológico* is more likely to occur after than before), there is no explanation of why this is so. And at any rate, unless the Adj clearly fits one of these five categories (and *rápido, lleno, fácil, preocupante, manso*, etc. ad lib. do not), the student is at a total loss.

Bull (1965:226ff.) abandoned the rule-and-subrule approach and developed Bello's *explicativo/especificativo* distinction into a general theory of the 'mathematical' organization and presentation of entities. Pre-position signifies totality (the whole set), meaning (with a plural noun) the description of all the noun's referents, or (with a singular noun) reference to one unique entity. Thus, *los pequeños arbustos* implies that conversation has been about a certain group of shrubs all of which are small, and *el pequeño arbusto* suggests that conversation has dwelled on a single shrub which happens to be small. Postposition, on the other hand, signifies partitiveness (subset)—a group (plural) or individual (singular) selected from a larger group defined by the noun; *los arbustos pequeños* and *el arbusto pequeño* select the small shrubs and one small shrub, respectively, from the shrubs being discussed. One of Bull's clearest examples is *los blancos cabellos de don Hugo* vs. *los cabellos blancos de don Hugo*; in the former the speaker presupposes that Hugo's entire head is white, but in the latter he implies that only some hairs are white, and he singles these out for some comment. Likewise, *su linda mujer* assumes monogamy and *su mujer linda* suggests polygamy (Bull 1965:227).

Sometimes, according to Bull, only one option is open: *el famoso autor de Don Quijote* rather than *el autor famoso de Don Quijote*, as the latter would imply another, less famous author. (In fact, there was one—the Fernández de Avellaneda whose usurpations so galled Cervantes.) As for Adjs which (supposedly) must follow their nouns, Bull states that this is because of their partitive meaning, not because of some word-specific idiosyncrasy: in *hombres españoles, problemas astronómicos*, and *naciones republicanas*, 'all men cannot be Spanish, all problems cannot be astronomical, and all nations are not republican' (Bull 1965:227). It should be noted that in Bull's 'mathematical organization' the speaker need not be mathematically accurate or even honest. *'Las hermosas mujeres de Tehuantepec* sustains a legend, but does not describe all of the facts. *Las gloriosas tradiciones de nuestra república* may well be a politician's little white lie' (Bull 1965:228).

Cressey 1969 accepted the basic thrust of Bull's theory but suggested that both analytically and pedagogically a simpler approach was to be found in relative clauses. In some transformational analyses, Adjs in the NP are derived from relative clauses: *the blue box* is not generated by the PSRs, but transformed from *the box which is blue* (v. 13.3.4). For Cressey, postposed adjectives in Spanish come from restrictive relatives because both specify one or some entities from a group; and preposed adjectives come from nonrestrictive relatives, because both attribute something to all members of a designated set. Hence, *Los hombres que son valientes* (=some men) *nunca huyen* → *Los hombres valientes nunca huyen; Los araucanos, que son valientes* (=all Araucans), *nunca huyen* → *Los valientes araucanos nunca huyen.* For pedagogy, Cressey (1969:880) suggests question-and-answer drills with the following format:

(1) T: ¿Lee Ud. libros que son aburridos?
    S: No, no leo libros aburridos.

(2) T: Nuestra banda, que es malísima, tocará esta tarde,
       ¿verdad?
    S: Sí, nuestra malísima banda tocará esta tarde.

Moody 1971 agreed with Bull and accepted Cressey's comparison with relatives, but he expressed doubts about Cressey's pedagogical application. Many students do not consciously grasp the restrictive/nonrestrictive distinction in their own language, and to teach this first in English before proceeding to Spanish can take the class far afield from the problem at hand, which after all is a matter of Spanish grammar alone.

Gili Gaya (1973:216-219) opposed the growing trend toward devising rules for Adj position. The principles are tendential, not rigid, and the mainstream Bello-to-Bull theory works only for NPs with definite determiners (*el, este, su*, etc.). With undetermined or indefinite nouns, it fails. In the following, for example, there is little or no explicative/specifying or totality/partitive contrast in meaning:

Blancas nubes/Nubes blancas asomaban en el horizonte.
Valiosos cuadros/Cuadros valiosos adornaban el salón.
Esperamos *tiempos mejores/mejores tiempos.*

For Gili Gaya, the distinction is one of esthetics or pragmatics more than logic or mathematics. A preposed Adj often suggests subjectivity, an affective quality 'synthesized' with the referent, whereas a postposed one has a more objective thrust in 'analyzing' or setting off a quality from the referent itself. But this tendency (not rule) can be overridden by (1) prosodic factors: rhythm, melody, stress group, word length (short Adj before longer N, and vice versa); (2) frozen idioms (*idea fija*, not *fija idea*); (3) arbitrary assignment to one position (*la mera opinión*); and (4) differentiation of senses by position (as with Ramsey, but Gili Gaya concedes only *cierto, pobre, simple, triste,* and *nuevo*).

Fish 1961 also criticized attempts to lay down rules, but in his zeal to correct the 'persistent effort to cram all embarrassing cases into the Procrustean bed of the restrictive' (Fish 1961:701), he perhaps erred in the opposite direction, an atomistic rundown of the semantic nuances of each Adj. Instead of one generalization, he finds at least eight different principles at work:

Postposed for:
(1) Restrictive modification (Bello, Bull): *el gato doméstico, los ángulos adyacentes*
(2) Pictorial effect: *el aire claro y suave*
(3) Affiliation: *el espútnic ruso*
(4) Explanatory comment: *su Mallorca natal, el Dios poderoso* (Bello, Bull, and Cressey cannot account for this case)

Preposed for:
(1) Affective comment: *la triste noticia de su fallecimiento*
(2) Impressionistic comment: *un ser de extrañas costumbres*
(3) Attitude or evaluation: *la desastrosa política del gobierno*
(4) Moral-esthetic judgment: *unas bellas muchachas luciendo sus esbeltas figuras*

Fish thus offers a rich corpus of data, but in the end he sets up several Adj classes, each with its own special philosophy.

Other analysts have agreed with Fish and Gili Gaya that the Bello-to-Bull theory is at best incomplete, but they have continued the search for one principle that, both pedagogically and descriptively, accounts for Adj position. The theory that many tend to accept today has to do with the relative contribution an Adj makes to the information presented by the NP. Stockwell et al. (1965:89) express this point as follows after surveying other theories:

Another way of looking at the same distinction [i.e. pre- and postposition] might be termed the 'relative informativeness' of the noun and adjective. In *un famoso héroe*, the order suggests that we expect heroes to be well known, but in *un héroe famoso* we are differentiating the hero who is famous from others who have not been acclaimed. The item in final position carries more information.

Bolinger 1972 interprets 'more information' as 'greater semantic weight'. To some extent, as Ramsey had observed, the English NP receives contrastive stress to signal semantic weight: *ricos hombres* 'rich MEN' vs. *hombres ricos* 'RICH men'; but Bolinger finds a better parallel in the English VP, where certain Advs can be placed before or after the verb. He offers the following parallels between the Spanish NP and the English VP:

Tenía ricos ornamentos.	It was richly ornamented.
Tenía ornamentos ricos.	It was ornamented richly.
Sufrió terribles daños.	It was terribly damaged.
Sufrió daños terribles.	It was damaged terribly.

In both cases, the last element in the phrase carries more semantic weight, reflecting the speaker's center of interest and informational focus.

The reason Bolinger offers for this property is based on how noun modifiers combine to delimit the set of entities (referents) that their head noun could stand for. As the Spanish NP unfolds from left to right, each successive element narrows down the reference one step further, a process Bolinger calls LINEAR MODIFICATION. Take, for example, the NP *las grandes repúblicas democráticas europeas*. Here, the determiner leads as usual to signal definiteness, often as a carryover from previous discourse. The speaker then proceeds to broach the greatness associated with the republics he has in mind; subsequently, he subclassifies the great republics by limiting these to the democratic ones; finally, he closes the linear modification by adding his most informative element, *europeas*, to indicate that the great democracies he has in mind are specifically those of Europe. A different sequencing would deliver a different organization of information and a different referential specification of *repúblicas*.

Terker 1985 uses well-documented examples to show that Bolinger's theory seems to work more successfully than its predecessors, and he urges that it be more widely used in pedagogy. He notes, however, four special cases that must be borne in mind whenever one develops a Spanish NP by linear modification.

(1) Preposing will signal more, not less, semantic weight if the Adj has a heightened intonation. Thus, *su GALLARDA contribución* is much more emphatic than *su contribución gallarda*, and a strong contrast is felt in *yo hablo de las HERMOSAS casas y no de las feas*. (Recall Suñer's similar observation on contrasted nouns such as *petróleo* at the sentential level.)

(2) Conjoined adjectives have equal weight regardless of ordering: *usos militares o civiles* = *usos civiles o militares*.

(3) The greater the determiner force of a modifier (as opposed to descriptive or attributive functions), the earlier it appears in the NP. Thus articles, the determiners par excellence, always come first; and although both *único* and *posible* could precede or follow a noun, *único* precedes if both are preposed because of its stronger force in determining reference: *la única posible solución*, **la posible única solución*. For the same reason, so-called 'meaning-changing' adjectives will precede the noun when they determine reference like an article (*ciertas fórmulas*, like *unas fórmulas*),

but follow it when they give important descriptive information (*fórmulas ciertas*, like *fórmulas fiables*).

(4) Complex AdjP (Adj + PP, Adj + S) must be postposed, this being a grammatical requirement overriding the constituents' relative informativeness:

las rutas *difíciles*   las rutas *difíciles de ascender*
las *difíciles* rutas   *las difíciles de ascender* rutas

Unlike Gili Gaya, Terkel notes that it is modifier complexity and not mere length that matters here: one can say *una mujer distinguida* or *una distinguida mujer*, even though the modifier has twice the syllables of the head noun.

According to Bolinger (1972:94), the problem with the Bello-to-Bull theory is not that restrictiveness (partitiveness, or whatever) plays no role at all, but that it is only a partial explanation that seizes on just one use of the pervasive principle of informativeness; i.e. it amounts to 'labeling a principle by one of its applications'. The following examples show why this is so.

(1a) Juan es el buen médico de Jipijapa.
(1b) Juan es el médico bueno de Jipijapa.
(2a) Juan es un buen médico.
(2b) Juan es un médico bueno.

Bull is correct in suggesting that *el buen médico* in (1a) refers to one unique Jipijapa doctor, whereas *el médico bueno* in (1b) selects one doctor, the GOOD one, from all Jipijapa doctors. But as Gili Gaya noted, this 'mathematical' interpretation vanishes in (2). The key lies in the obvious difference in determiners. Definite determiners, as in (1), after all 'define' reference by singling out from a universe of possible referents the one(s) the speaker has focused on (v. 8.3.3). A postposed and thus more informative Adj will proceed further with the defining of reference begun by *el/la*; hence, *el médico bueno* has Bull's partitive or Bello's specifying sense. A preposed adjective has less informational value, and therefore it will not define the reference any more than the plain determiner would; hence, both *el médico* and *el buen médico* indicate a unique individual for whom the hearer presumably requires no further specification. When reference is indefinite, as in the second pair of sentences, a postposed Adj has little defining or differentiating value for singling out the one from the many; but it continues to have more semantic weight in that position than when preposed. In other words, quite apart from the partitiveness imposed by the determiner, in both of the (a) sentences Adj + N highlights Juan as doctor and deemphasizes any specialness about his goodness, while in both of the (b) sentences N + Adj suggests that Juan, as a doctor, is a GOOD one. Bull's theory holds for one case; Bolinger's apparently covers both cases with one generalization.

11.3.4 Summary and generalization. Bolinger believed that his principle of semantic weight, as part of a general strategy of linear modification, applies to other areas of Spanish syntax as well. One may generalize as follows: whenever the syntax allows both X + Y and Y + X as grammatically equivalent options (whether by PSR or by transformation), Y will carry more information in the order X + Y than in Y + X (provided, as Suñer and Terkel pointed out, that neither element is phonologically highlighted for emphatic contrast). Adjectives conform to this principle, as already noted. Demonstratives, possessives, and quantifiers conform too, since they have a more forceful thrust when postposed.

At the sentential level, informativeness translates into thematic structure: the rheme presents important information about the theme. Both *Juan quiere la leche* and *A Juan le gusta la leche* use Juan as a point of departure, i.e. as a topic already established by discourse (perhaps by a preceding *¿Qué quiere Juan?* or *¿Qué le gusta a Juan?*) or presupposed as the hearer's center of interest. What Juan wants or likes is then presented as the rheme. But in *La leche la quiere Juan, Quiere la leche Juan, La leche le gusta a Juan,* and *Le gusta la leche a Juan,* Juan is postposed so as to occupy the sentence's center stage of attention ('rhematic focus'). Here, *Juan* is higher in informational value, asserted rather than presupposed; the speaker takes 'wanting milk' or 'liking milk' as thematic, and focuses on Juan as if to answer questions such as *¿Quién quiere la leche?* or *¿A quién le gusta la leche?* Just like modifiers in the NP, satellites in the S move into positions reflecting the speaker's center of interest.

In their initial year or so of Spanish study, students will not be very sensitive to how sentence structure is edited so as to present information effectively. In fact, although they constantly highlight or downplay information in English, largely through phonological means, they have little awareness of doing so since high school grammars of English no more touch upon *rich MAN* vs. *RICH man,* or *HE came with his date* vs. *He came with HIS date,* than their Spanish texts explain NP + VP vs. VP + NP, D + N vs. N + D, or (except for 'great' vs. 'big' for *grande*) Adj + N vs. N + Adj. Moody's criticism of Cressey is therefore quite apt: there *are* analogs in English, but they involve subtleties the students use masterfully but unconsciously, and to use them as springboards for Spanish word order will require tangents on English syntax first. Whether such tangents are cost-effective or not, given the goal of acquiring Spanish grammar, is a matter the teacher must evaluate. But the variability of Spanish word order requires some comment in any course, particularly when texts proceed to use sentences such as *A ellos les interesan los bomberos* without explanation and students misinterpret them, or when students answer questions with sentences that are grammatical but that would seem informational non sequiturs for the native Spanish speaker.

Notes for Chapter 11

1. Specifically, Subj *you* is deleted by the Imperative Transformation (v. 12.4) in *Get out of here!*, and by Ellipsis in *Want an apple?* ELLIPSIS drops elements that are understood from context (*You want an apple?* → *Want an apple?* → *Apple?*); it is difficult to formulate precisely because a transformation cannot foresee what will be obvious to speaker and hearer from contextual cues outside the grammar itself.

2. Suñer 1982 concurs. On the other hand, Pilleux y Urrutia (1982:80-82) argue that the deep structure Subj of *llover, tronar,* and *anochecer* is 'El Allí' and that *haber* + DO (see next paragraph) is underlyingly Subj + *existir.* The only reason they offer for some kind of obligatory Subj is that 'su presencia en la estructura profunda se da como supuesta.' They do not footnote the *suponedor* of this *supuesto.*

3. In some nonstandard dialects, *haber* agrees with the NP: *Habían varios restaurantes típicos.* Jorge-Morel (1974:127-131) finds this agreement widespread in Santo Domingo, even in the first plural: *Aquí habemos muchos enfermos* 'there are lots of sick among us'; and Kany notes its extensive use in other countries, including Spain (1951:212-217). Even so, the NP with which *haber* agrees is still its Obj in deep structure since it is pronominalized with Obj pronouns.

Compare this situation with the reverse one in English, where agreement (*There are several restaurants*) is standard and nonagreement (*There's several restaurants*) is regarded as nonstandard, although it is widespread in colloquial styles.

4. This *there* is a dummy element like the *it* of *It's raining,* having no reference or meaning. Note the contrast with locative *there* 'in that place' in *There're several cars there.* The inversion with *there* is a relic of an earlier Germanic flipflop rule that is preserved in a few other structures, e.g. *Never had she seen such an assembly* and *Out came four more giraffes.* See Quirk et al. (1972:948-950) for details.

5. But in Black and Southern dialects of the United States, and in Scottish dialects in Britain, some double modals are possible: *He might should do it.* Old English had this option generally, but most dialects today are limited to one modal per clause, which makes it difficult to explain Aux tense forms and combinations in Spanish (v. 7.2.1).

6. Meyer calls this leftward movement of the Obj 'dislocation' and punctuates it with a comma: *El coche, se lo ha comprado José.* I am omitting her comma, however, because standard orthography does not require it and because the pause and intonational break it is meant to convey are not nearly as wrenching (if present at all) as in the truly dislocated OSV of English mentioned earlier: *Júlia, Paul saw* or *The cár, Joe bought.*

7. I have heard and read many sentences such as *Una muestra del problema la ofreció el estudioso danés,* in contradiction of Meyer's constraint against OVS with indefinite Obj. The informants I have

questioned agree that (1) SVO is most frequent but not unique, (2) OVS is common but generally requires a clitic copy of Obj, and (3) VSO is possible but not quite as common. On VOS they disagreed: some accepted it readily, others only when an appropriate context led up to it, but one Colombian only winced and said '¡No! Nunca diría eso a menos que sea interrogativo.' Further research on this matter is greatly needed; traditional dialectology has tended to ignore syntax in favor of phonology and vocabulary.

8. The English transformation of IO Movement can illustrate the same point. We have noted earlier (v. 8.1.2) that *He gave the book to Mary* can change to *He gave Mary the book*. Yet when the DO is a pronoun, native speakers' judgments go awry. Asked about *He gave Mary it* or—with the IO pronominalized as well—*He gave her it*, some accept IO Movement, some reject it, and some accept it (perhaps marginally) only if the IO is strongly stressed. For a description of the language as a whole, IO Movement cannot be categorically prohibited with pronouns, but the transformation must be tagged as variable in its output.

9. Suñer notes that the Passive Transformation (v. 12.3) can have the same effect of postposing a presented NP: (*Guerrilleros implantaron la bomba*) → *La bomba fue implantada por guerrilleros.*

10. The postposing of numbers (*el día quince, Carlos cinco, el siglo veinte*) is generally regarded as converting them to ordinals, in which role they then assume the same responsibilities as postposed adjectives (Gili Gaya 1973:220). Fish (1961:708), however, notes a complication in the contrast *por primera vez* vs. *por vez primera*, which to him suggests 'beginning of a series' vs. 'after a long delay'.

11. Postposed *alguno* is an exception to the rule that negation spreads lexically to all indefinites (v. 12.2).

12. Again, Spanish can adopt this phonological contrasting too, but *MI casa* is not as common as *la casa mía.*

13. In trying to render the Spanish terminology *anteposición/posposición*, the Anglo linguist has trouble. There is no word *anteposition* in English, and *preposition* is preempted for adverbial relators governing NP. For the noun of *preposed*, I will adopt *pre-position.*

14. E.g. against case (a) the following quote from *El País* (*edición internacional*, 9-IV-1984:22): 'Siempre metido en sus oficinas de *la barcelonesa calle* Provenzal, ... desde allí maneja sus múltiples negocios.'

Exercises for Chapter 11

1. Consider the following sentences and determine whether 'personal' *a* is impossible, possible, or required in the blank. Then generate permutations of the SVO order and repeat the procedure.
   (1) El entusiasmo vence _____ la dificultad.
   (2) El tren atropelló _____ un camión.
   (3) La casa sostenía _____ el árbol.

(4) Alicia buscará ___ un médico.
(5) El niño acarició ___ el perrito.
(6) El complemento precede ___ el verbo.
(7) El médico tiene ___ una enfermera.
(8) La cocinera mató ___ el gallo.
(9) Estas tribus adoran ___ los misioneros.
(10) Necesitamos ___ un jefe bilingüe.
(11) Los mercaderes vendían ___ los esclavos.
(12) La economía afectará ___ la natalidad.
(13) El pato mató ___ la gallina.
(14) La palabrería sustituye ___ la acción.

2. Evaluate the traditional rule for the use of 'personal' *a*. How effectively and successfully do students apply it in your experience? How accurate is the rule? How would you, as a teacher, present it?

3. How similar are Spanish and English in their basic deep structure patterns? In their surface structures?

4. In what ways are copulas different from other verbs in the constituents that accompany them?

5. Draw tree diagrams (phrase markers) to show the deep structure constituency of each of the following. Use the PSRs described in this chapter as a guide for what is a part of what. When an 'understood' constituent has been deleted or the word order has been transposed, restore the sentence to its deep structure configuration.

(1) Las jóvenes acataron a sus mayores.
(2) Los veinte obreros fatigados salieron de la fábrica.
(3) Permaneceremos allí cuatro días pero visitaremos a varios amigos.
(4) Juan cantaba una canción obscena y Luisa le pegó.
(5) Entró en el cuarto una mujer de ochenta años.
(6) Puedes ofrecer(le) ese aparato al basurero esta tarde.
(7) Su hija ha sido la directora de las sucursales extranjeras.
(8) El carro ese lo compró un cliente perspicaz.
(9) Llamó a la policía la pobre víctima sueca.
(10) En nuestra clase hay veinte estudiantes de primer año.

6. How do the units of the Spanish nucleus differ from those in the satellites? Why do these surface constituents cause trouble to English-speaking students?

7. List all two-word verbs you can think of formed off *turn*, and contrast them with their Spanish equivalents (e.g. *turn in* 'entregar; acostarse'). Why do these structures cause interference in Spanish?

8. Explain the difference in how information is being presented in each of the following pairs. To clarify your explanation, give examples of the questions or discourse lead-ups that might precede each statement.

(1) Esta tarde salgo para Caracas. Salgo para Caracas esta tarde.
(2) Acudieron a verlo ocho turistas ingleses. Ocho turistas ingleses acudieron a verlo.

(3) María es una magnífica representante. María es una representante magnífica.

(4) Juan escribió el capítulo once. El capítulo once lo escribió Juan.

(5) Mi colección ya no sirve para nada. La colección mía ya no sirve para nada.

(6) Una jirafa grande apareció en la calle. En la calle apareció una jirafa grande.

(7) Hay que reemplazar los quebradizos ladrillos del puente viejo. Hay que reemplazar los ladrillos quebradizos del viejo puente.

9. Construct a Spanish sentence of a nucleus plus two to three satellites. Make a list of all possible permutations, including some less used ones and even some that Gili Gaya and others might exclude altogether. Now, make a list of Spanish questions that might elicit different presentations of the material in the sentence. Scramble the two lists, and then have native speakers match questions with preferred answers. Do your 'judges' agree? Are there any permutations left over which they reject totally?

10. Draw up a lesson on Spanish adjectival position based (to some extent) on one or more of the theories described in this chapter. Give special attention to (1) how you would explain the meaning of position, (2) how you would illustrate it, (3) the exercises and drills you would use to drive the point(s) home and develop them into a skill. Explain also the extent to which you would expect active mastery.

11. Both English and Spanish can highlight information phonologically and syntactically. How do they differ on their relative use of the two mediums?

12. Most texts touch upon adjectival position in some way, but otherwise bypass most questions of word order. Consider the following solutions and choose the one you prefer.

(1) Describe to students the 'normal' SVO order in Spanish, and assume that they will eventually pick up alternative orders on their own through exposure.

(2) Describe 'normal' SVO order, but also (perhaps later) comment explicitly on alternative orders and their communicative functions.

Defend the position you prefer. If you choose (1), address the question of whether the syntax of dialogs, readings, and exercises should be controlled to SVO (and if so, until what point in language study); if you choose (2), indicate when permutations should be introduced, how they should be explained, and the level of mastery expected.

13. How do *there is* and *haber* differ syntactically? *Rain* and *llover*?

14. Review the section on appositives, studying the examples and adding others that occur to you. Try to determine where *de/of* is needed in each language.

15. Silva-Corvalán 1982 urges that there be more analysis of Spanish word order in large samples of discourse. She has launched such an inves-

tigation with Mexican-American informants in Los Angeles. As an interviewer, she asked stimulating questions, and then recorded the free conversation as it proceeded from there. Subsequently, she analyzed the rate of deletion of subjects and the incidence of pre- and postposition of subjects when they were not deleted. Some of her statistics are reproduced below. Discuss them, identifying the relative strength of each variable in its effect on deletion and placement. Given that the variables interact and that each represents a discourse TENDENCY rather than a categorical grammatical rule, how would you interpret the implications of her study for pedagogy?

Definitions of terms: SAME REFERENCE means that the Subj is the same as in (is carried over from) the preceding clause; SWITCH REFERENCE is when the speaker introduces a new Subj. PERSON-AMBIGUOUS describes a verb form such as *hacía* which, by itself, could be 1sg. or 3sg.; PERSON-UNAMBIGUOUS is one such as *hizo*, which can only be 3sg.; CONTEXTUALLY UNAMBIGUOUS is a form such as *hacía* which may be clearly *yo* since the speaker has been talking about himself. ARGUMENTS are Subj, DO, IO satellite NPs—i.e. not deleted and not cliticized; *Juan vio a Alicia* has two arguments, *Juan la vio* one, *la vio* none. Silva-Corvalán excluded from analysis impersonal verbs, nonfinites, exclamations, questions, and relative clauses because these have special properties with regard to Subj.

(a) Deletion of Subj:
(1) Same reference: 75% deleted
    Switch reference: 47% deleted
(2) Person-ambiguous: 31% deleted
    Contextually unamb.:   61% deleted
    Unambiguous: 62% deleted

(b) Placement of Subj when not deleted:
(1) Same reference: 74% preverbal
    Switch reference: 53% preverbal
(2) Person-ambiguous: 64% preverbal
    Contextually unamb.:   79% preverbal
    Unambiguous: 54% preverbal
(3) Sub=old information: 61% preverbal
    Subj=new information: 36% preverbal
(4) Preposed Advl: 15% preverbal
    Postposed Advl: 64% preverbal
(5) One argument: 46% preverbal
    Two-three arguments: 64% preverbal
    (With the *post*verbal-subject remainder of the two-three argument case, she finds the orders OVS, VSO, VOS almost exactly equal in occurrence.)

Chapter 12
Questions, negations, passives, and commands

12.0 Simple affirmative active declarative sentences. The sentence patterns surveyed so far have largely been 'simple affirmative active declarative', or SAAD for short. An example of a SAAD sentence is *Los líderes de Occidente se reunirán mañana en Bruselas.* It is SIMPLE in not containing any internal clauses; there is only one verb with its associated NPs and Advls (sometimes grouped together as the verb's 'arguments'). It is AFFIRMATIVE as opposed to negative: no negative morphemes occur in it. It is ACTIVE as opposed to the passive sentence *Los líderes serán reunidos por el primer ministro.* It is DECLARATIVE in asserting information, not asking a question or giving a command that would overtly require a hearer's response.

SAAD structure can be altered by means of transformations that rearrange constituents, delete 'understood' elements, and introduce functors. Though preserving the underlying relationships of the sentence constituents as these are defined in deep structure by the PSRs, transformations edit the surface configuration and specify alternative patterns. Many of the processes studied earlier for SAAD sentences can be regarded as transformational: Nominalization (v. 8.4.1), Agreement (v. 8.1.1, 11.2.1), Clitic Movement (v. 9.4.1, 11.2.1, 13.1.2.8), *A*-insertion and the rules for preposing and postposing (v. 11.2-11.3.3), etc. In addition, linguists have tended to regard non-SAAD constructions as derived from the more basic SAAD structure. Specifically, questions, negations, passives, and commands are described as transformationally modified derivatives (or TRANSFORMS) of the more basic sentence types defined by the PSRs.[1] Teachers should recognize that this treatment accords with the typical pedagogical approach whereby students first learn structures such as *Juan conoce a Mercedes* and then the rules for changing this to *¿Conoce Juan a Mercedes?*, to *Mercedes es conocida por Juan*, and so on.

12.1 Questions. English and Spanish have several kinds of questions, and their transformations for them are similar in their broad outlines but different in certain details. The three most important question types are tag questions, *yes/no* questions, and information questions.

12.1.1 Tag and *yes/no* questions. In TAG QUESTIONS, a 'tag' is added to the end of a declarative sentence to elicit agreement with the assertion. In English, the tag begins with a negated form of the first auxiliary (Aux) or the copula *be*, or a positive one if the sentence is negative to begin with; if there is no Aux and no *be*, *do* is used in the tag. The Aux, *be*, or *do* is then followed by a pronominal version of the Subj:

The women will oppose this, *won't they?*
The women won't oppose this, *will they?*
You are sick, *aren't you?*
You aren't sick, *are you?*
Joe won the match, *didn't he?*
Joe didn't win the match, *did he?*

Spanish more simply adds *¿verdad?* or, after affirmatives only, *¿no?*:

Las mujeres van a oponerse, *¿no/verdad?*
Las mujeres no van a oponerse, *¿verdad?*

A second kind, the YES/NO QUESTION, requests 'yes' or 'no' for an answer, as the name suggests. In English, the transformation for this type (called simply the Question Transformation) again depends on the kind of VP that is present: the first Aux (if there is one) is inverted over the Subj; if there is a form of *be* but no Aux, then *be* is inverted; if neither is present, the Aux *do* is inserted and inverted, taking with it the tense/number/person ending of the main verb. In all three cases, a contracted *not* → *-n't* (v. 12.2) is carried with the fronted verb form. Finally, the sentence is most commonly given a rising terminal intonation (v. 4.2).[2] Thus,

Mary will/won't come. → Will/Won't Mary come?
Mary was/wasn't a nurse. → Was/Wasn't Mary a nurse?
Mary left (=*leave* + past) the room. → (Mary *do* + past leave the room) → Did Mary leave the room?

Spanish can form a *yes/no* question similarly by inversion plus rising intonation: *¿Salió María del cuarto?* But there are three key differences. First, no dummy Aux *do* is inserted, to the frustration of literalist students who press *hacer* into this function (*¿Hizo María salir?*). Second, the inversion is optional, reflecting a strategy for presenting information (v. 11.2-11.3) more than a syntactic device for creating questions. Rising intonation suffices, so that *¿María salió del cuarto?* coexists with *¿Salió María del cuarto?* English, too, can omit the inversion step, but this yields an ECHO QUESTION: *Mary left the room?* echoes, with an incredulous or 'I didn't quite catch that' tone, the same statement asserted or implied just before. Uninverted questions may or may not be echo questions in Spanish. Third, if inversion does occur in Spanish, the whole verb nucleus moves, often with an Obj or PredE. This contrasts strikingly with the English practice of inverting only Aux or *be*:

Hasn't Larry eaten it? *¿No lo ha comido* Lorenzo?
Is Larry that tall? *¿Es tan alto* Lorenzo?

Students who have not learned to treat the nucleus as one agglutinated quasi-word may mistakenly generate *¿*Ha Lorenzo lo comido?* or *¿*No lo ha Lorenzo comido?*

12.1.2 Information (WH-) questions. A third question type has been called the INFORMATION QUESTION or WH- question, because it asks for specified information (not just 'yes' or 'no') signaled by words usually beginning with *wh-* in English. As a Spanish counterpart, Stockwell et al. (1965:221) propose 'K/D- question' since the phonemes /k/ and /d/ begin Spanish WH- words, or K/D words, whereas Suñer (1982:263) is satisfied with 'QU- question' and 'QU- word' for Spanish. We will retain here the traditional term, INTERROGATIVE, for the WH-, K/D, or QU- word.

The basic transformation for information questions has two steps: first, there is Subj-verb inversion (Subj-Aux in English, Subj-nucleus in Spanish) as in *yes/no-* questions;[3] next, the interrogative is moved from its deep structure position (as DO, IO, Subj, or whatever) to the front of the sentence. These two movements are shown in the following derivations.

$$
\text{John has eaten} \left\{ \begin{array}{l} \textit{what} \\ \textit{where} \ ? \\ \textit{how} \end{array} \right. \rightarrow \textit{Has} \text{ John eaten} \left\{ \begin{array}{l} \textit{what} \\ \textit{where} \ ? \\ \textit{how} \end{array} \right. \rightarrow
$$

$$
\left. \begin{array}{l} \textit{What} \\ \textit{Where} \\ \textit{How} \end{array} \right\} \text{ has John eaten?}
$$

$$
\text{Juan ha comido} \left\{ \begin{array}{l} \textit{qué} \\ \textit{dónde} \ ? \\ \textit{cómo} \end{array} \right. \rightarrow \text{¿Ha comido Juan} \left\{ \begin{array}{l} \textit{qué} \\ \textit{dónde} \ ? \\ \textit{cómo} \end{array} \right. \rightarrow
$$

$$
\left. \begin{array}{l} \textit{Qué} \\ \textit{Dónde} \\ \textit{Cómo} \end{array} \right\} \text{ ha comido Juan?}
$$

As the next examples show, (1) an interrogative modifying a noun takes the whole NP with it and (2) an interrogative can be fronted even if it originates in a subordinated noun clause deeper in the sentence:

You think (that) the thieves stole *which jewels*? →
Which jewels do you think (that) the thieves stole?
Ud. supone que los ladrones robaron *qué joyas*? →
¿*Qué joyas* supone Ud. que robaron los ladrones?

The two languages differ in how they treat interrogatives in a PP. In English, an interrogative OP optionally carries the preposition with it to the front of the sentence; in Spanish, the whole PP must be fronted:

You talked *to who(m)*? → *Who(m)* did you talk *to*? ~
To whom did you talk?
You spoke *about what*? → *What* did you speak *about*? ~
About what did you speak?

He came *from where?* → *Where* did he come *from?* ~
From where did he come?
Le hablaste *a quién?* → *¿A quién* le hablaste?
Hablaste *de qué?* → *¿De qué* hablaste?
Vino *de dónde?* → *¿De dónde* vino?

Whatever prescriptive ideas a teacher may have about 'stranded prepositions', this is currently the more common construction in English, and the
one that will occur to students when they translate: *¿Qué mano escribes
con?*, *¿Qué hablaste de?*

Interrogatives are often treated as a small set of vocabulary items: *qué,
quién, cuál, cómo, cuándo, cuánto, dónde* are respectively equated with
what, who, which, how, when, how much, where, and—except for comments on *qué/cuál* usage—the matter is then closed. But interrogatives
represent signals for the hearer to fill in missing information in the speaker's proposition, so that in principle *any* constituent can be questioned; in
other words, there may be a questioning strategy for every possible slot or
function. The traditional 'canon' of matched interrogatives does not
cover all strategies, and ignores how they are tied to their respective languages. One gap in this canon is the questioning of VP, illustrated below.[4]
Note that either the full VP or an embedded VP can be questioned:

Lydia *decided to escape.* → Lydia *did what?* → *What* did Lydia *do?*
Lydia decided *to escape.* → Lydia decided *to do what?* →
What did Lydia decide *to do?*
Lidia *decidió escaparse.* → Lidia *hizo qué?* → *¿Qué hizo* Lidia?
Lidia decidió *escaparse.* → Lidia decidió *hacer qué?* →
¿Qué decidió *hacer* Lidia?

Another gap concerns how adjectival information is elicited. The canon
provides *which* = *qué/cuál,* but just as common are a variety of expressions based on the formula *what* + N + *of:*

Lydia wants *a (Adj) car.* → *What kind/color/model/size . . . of car* does
Lydia want?
Lidia quiere *un carro (Adj).* → *¿Qué clase/color/modelo/tamaño . . . de
carro* quiere Lidia?

Continuing this probing for other interrogatives, one eventually adds
many other expressions to the inventory: *de qué manera, cada cuánto,
hasta qué hora, a qué hora, cuánto* (adverbial), to cite a few.

In at least two places, there are holes in the Spanish system due to the
obsolescence of two of its interrogatives. First, both languages can question a predicate possessive, i.e. one in the PredE position following a
copula: *This book is yours* → *Whose is this book?*, *Este libro es tuyo* →
¿De quién es este libro? However, prenominal possessives (determiners)
can be questioned in English but not directly in Spanish. The older lan-

guage had *cúyo* corresponding to the set *mi, tu, su, nuestro*, but in modern standard Spanish it is necessary to switch to some structure in which the PP *de quién* can be generated:

Your book got ruined. → *Whose* book got ruined?

Tu libro se ha estropeado. → $\begin{cases} (¿\textit{Cúyo} \text{ libro se ha estropeado?}) \\ ¿\textit{De quién es} \text{ el libro } \textit{que se ha} \\ \qquad \textit{estropeado?} \\ ¿\text{El libro } \textit{de quién} \text{ se ha estropeado?} \end{cases}$

Second, virtually all texts equate *how* and *cómo*, but this is misleading, even aside from the *¿cómo?* 'what?' for failure to understand. *How* in English actually covers three syntactic slots. One is adverbials of manner, and a second is certain PredE Adj and Adv; in both cases, *cómo* matches up rather well (though *qué tal* is used too):

How did you arrive? *¿Cómo* llegaste?
How are you/do you feel? *¿Cómo/qué tal* estás/te sientes?

But a third, and seldom mentioned, function of Eng. *how* is to represent the category of Intensifier (v. 10.2.3), which modifies an adjective or adverb and expresses the extent or degree to which it is true:

Eng.: *very/rather/somewhat/not very/too/that, so, as* . . . tall
Span.: *muy/bastante/algo/poco/demasiado/tan* . . . alto

With a regular interrogative for this category, the English speaker freely generates questions with *how* + Adj and *how* + Adv: *how tall, how tired, how true, how fast, how big, how dangerous, how regularly, how wide; how much/many* belongs to the same series. *Cuán* originally served the same function in Spanish, but it has been following *cúyo* into oblivion.[5] In its stead, *qué tan* is widely used from Mexico to the South American cone, and *cómo de* has appeared on both sides of the Atlantic:

How tall is the table? $\begin{cases} (¿\textit{Cuán alta} \text{ es la mesa?}) \\ ¿\textit{Qué tan alta} \text{ es la mesa?} \\ ¿\textit{Cómo} \text{ es } \textit{de alta} \text{ la mesa?} \sim ¿\textit{Cómo de alta} \\ \qquad \text{es la mesa?} \end{cases}$

Neither, however, is used as universally or as freely as Eng. *how* (Whitley 1986a). The demise of *cuán* has not been fully remedied and the language is in flux in finding a substitute.

The gap can be avoided by means of other questioning strategies. When *how* + Adv broadly represents extent in time, place, or degree, Spanish may adopt adverbial *cuánto* or an expression indicating endpoint:

How long did he sleep? *¿Cuánto* durmió?
How far did she run? *¿Cuánto* corrió?
How long did you stay? *¿Hasta cuándo* permaneció Ud.?

Expressions indicating endpoint may accompany adjectives and participles too:

How involved is he?   ¿*Hasta qué punto* está *involucrado*?

In some sentence types, *cuánto* is used with a verb of measurement:

How far away is the capital? ¿*Cuánto dista* la capital?
How important is this? ¿*Cuánto importa* esto?
How tall is she? ¿*Cuánto mide* ella?

But as shown by Whitley (1986a), the most widespread strategy, aside from *qué tan*, is to switch from Adj or Adv to *qué* + N, which then requires syntactic adjustments for the resulting NP:

How often does she come? ¿*Con qué frecuencia* viene?
How tall is she? ¿*Qué altura/estatura* tiene? ¿*De qué altura* es?
How fast does it go? ¿*Qué velocidad* alcanza?
How important is this? ¿*Qué importancia* tiene esto?
How far away is the capital? ¿*A qué distancia* está la capital?
How big/long/wide/thick is it? ¿*Qué tamaño/largo/ancho/grosor* tiene?
(¿*De qué . . .* es?)

English also uses a nominalized construction, but it is not always the more common or idiomatic one. Thus, *What is its height/weight/width?* matches *How tall/heavy/wide is it?*, but one will seldom say *What is its difficulty/coldness/stability?* for *How hard/cold/stable is it?* The student therefore has two problems: (1) to switch from intensifier interrogation to nominal structures in Spanish, and (2) to master noun equivalents of the Adj and Adv. Most introductory and intermediate texts do not address the problem at all, even though *how* + Adj/Adv is very frequent in English, causes errors in Spanish, and represents an important question type. Perhaps *qué tan* deserves more attention as a way out of the problem.

12.2 Negating and disagreeing. Like the Question Transformation, the Negative Transformation in English depends on what is present in the VP. A sentence-negating *not* (allomorph -*n't*) is moved into the sentence and placed to the right of the first Aux, or *be* if there is no Aux; if neither is present, the dummy Aux *do* is inserted, taking the tense morpheme from the main verb:

NOT Louise should have left. → Louise should *not* have left.
NOT Louise is over there. → Louise is *not* over there.
NOT Louise knows it. → Louise *does not* know it.

Once again, Spanish lacks *do* insertion. Regardless of the type of verb, *no* is placed at the beginning of the entire verb nucleus:

NO Luisa lo sabe. → Luisa *no* lo sabe.

But if some other negative element is already in place before the verb in Spanish, or before or after it in English, the sentence-negator *not/no* does not appear:

Louise should *never* have left. Luisa *nunca* debió salir.
Nobody knows it. *Nadie* lo sabe.

The contrast in the conditions for omitting *not/no*—a negative *before* the verb in Spanish vs. one *before or after* it in English—is a key one. Spanish requires that one negative precede the verb nucleus, so that the transposition (Subject Postposing, v. 11.2.3) of *Nadie lo sabe* must be accompanied by *no*-Insertion: *No lo sabe nadie.* Furthermore, the negation must spread rightward to all subsequent indefinites: *No tengo algo* → *No tengo nada.* This MULTIPLE NEGATION is not foreign to English speakers, who hear it and may use it in nonstandard speech: *I don't have nothing.* Formerly, it was proper in standard English too, but grammarians stamped it out with the reasoning that language must behave like logic and algebra: $(-x)(-y) = +xy$, or two negatives yield a positive. Consequently, educated students are programmed to avoid multiple negation by changing *some* (*-body, -one, -thing, -where*) to *any* (*-body, -one, -thing, -where*), not *no* (*-body, -one, -thing, -where*). That is, they are familiar with multiple negation, but whenever they think about what they are saying they eschew it, so that a teacher's attempt to explain *Yo nunca le dije nada* (*a nadie tampoco*) in terms of *I never said nothing* (*to nobody neither*) will meet with a mental block as students extend their English constraint to their Spanish.

There is more to the subject of negation once we pass from isolated sentences to connected discourse. In a typical interaction, speaker A offers new information to B by asserting the proposition *P* or its negation *not P* (formulaically $-P$). B may then indicate his agreement (+) or disagreement (−) with either kind of proposition, which yields four options: 'I agree with *P*' = $+(P)$, 'I agree with *not P*' = $+(-P)$, 'I disagree with *P*' = $-(P)$, and 'I disagree with *not P*' = $-(-P)$. Spanish and English both have these four, but sometimes with different morphemes:

(1) P → +(P):
   A: John sells tires. A: Juan vende llantas.
   B: ⎰Yes, he sells them. B: Sí, las vende.
      ⎱Yes, he does.

(2) P → −(P):
   A: John sells tires. A: Juan vende llantas.
   B: ⎰No, he doesn't sell them. B: No, no las vende.
      ⎱No, he doesn't.

(3) −P → +(−P):
   A: John doesn't sell tires. A: Juan no vende llantas.
   B: ⎰No, he doesn't sell them. B: No, no las vende.
      ⎱No, he doesn't.

(4) −P → −(−P):
    A: John doesn't sell tires.   A: Juan no vende llantas.
    B:⎧Yes, he DOES sell them.   B: Sí, sí las vende.
      ⎩Yes, he DOES.

When this last case ((4), −(−P)) is touched on in pedagogy, it is typically as a mere lexical matter; as one text put it in a vocabulary list, *sí = indeed*. But *indeed* is a poor rendition, and since vocabularies are at the extreme of linguistic decontextualization, the real contextual function of *sí* and *do(es)* is difficult to explain in them. In normal English, speaker B corrects A's negative proposition by reversing *do(es)n't* to its emphatic affirmative counterpart *do(es)*; Spanish does exactly the same thing in reversing *no* to its affirmative counterpart *sí*.

As another case, consider what happens when speaker B asserts that A's proposition *P* or −*P* is also true (+) or not true (−) of himself or of some other entity besides the one in A's assertion:

(5) P → +(P)
    A: John sells tires.   A: Juan vende llantas.
    B:⎧And I sell them too.   B:⎧Y yo las vendo también.
      ⎨And I do too.   ⎩Y yo también.
      ⎩Me too.

(6) P → −(P)
    A: John sells tires.   A: Juan vende llantas.
    B:⎧But I DON'T sell them. B:⎧Pero yo no las vendo.
      ⎨But I DON'T.   ⎩Pero yo no.
      ⎩Not me.

(7) −P → +(−P)
    A: John doesn't sell tires.   A: Juan no vende llantas.
    B:⎧I don't sell them either. B:⎧Yo no las vendo tampoco.
      ⎨I don't either.   ⎩Yo tampoco.
      ⎨Neither do I.
      ⎩Me neither.

(8) −P → −(−P)
    A: John doesn't sell tires.   A: Juan no vende llantas.
    B:⎧But I DO sell them.   B:⎧Pero yo sí las vendo.
      ⎩But I DO.   ⎩Pero yo sí.

In addition to the *do/sí* problem, here the student encounters *tampoco* for both *either* and *neither* and the problem of pronominal case (*I, me*). Colloquial English discards the subjective/objective distinction when no verb is present, so that both *I see them too* and *He saw me too* reduce to *Me too*. Spanish meticulously observes the distinction between *Yo también/ tampoco* and *A mí también/tampoco*, but its usage will be hard to master until students learn how grammar carries across sentences.

In a few cases, students may be unprepared for the extent to which a negative morpheme semantically affects what follows it (i.e. its SCOPE). For example, in the following pair of sentences the two languages agree that a negative before Aux + V applies to the Aux; i.e. the meaning of *not have to* is 'not obligated' = 'one may or may not, as he pleases':

Tengo que hacerlo hoy.　　　=　I have to do it today.
No tengo que hacerlo hoy.　=　I *don't have to* do it today.

But now consider the negation of *haber que*, which is also an Aux of obligation and is often glossed as 'one must, has (got) to, it's necessary'. When *no* precedes *haber que* + V, it is the V (the main verb) that is negated: *no hay que* + V is thus 'it is necessary NOT to V'. Eng. *must* works the same way, but *have to* does not:

No hay que sembrarlo en el invierno.
$$\begin{cases} = \text{One } \textit{must not} \text{ sow it in the winter.} \\ \neq \text{One } \textit{doesn't have to} \text{ sow it in the winter.} \end{cases}$$

In introductory classes, the 'must not' meaning of *no hay que* is seldom pointed out to students, but one can imagine many situations in which students, on their own at last among Spanish speakers, could fatally misinterpret *no hay que* as 'it's not required, so I may do as I choose'.

12.3 Passive and related structures. In a sentence such as *Mike killed the chickens*, the NP *the chickens* occupies a sentence position indicating not only DO but also the highlighting of asserted information (v. 11.3.1). Suppose that we wish to preserve the respective Subj and DO roles of *Mike* and *the chickens* but highlight *Mike* in the rheme. In English, it is not possible just to exchange the two NPs, because *The chickens killed Mike* puts *Mike* under the spotlight but also makes it the DO. How then can the DO be fronted for topicalization and the Subj postposed, without reversing or confusing deep structure functions?

The answer is the Passive Transformation, which yields *The chickens were killed by Mike*. This is a fairly complicated rule that can be stated in four steps:

Initial string of morphemes:	Mike kill+past the chickens.

(1) Move the deep structure Subj NP to the end of the clause and make it the Obj of the Prep *by*, with which it forms a PP called an AGENT PHRASE:　Ø kill+past the chickens *by Mike.*

(2) Front the deep structure Obj NP to the vacated Subj position:　*The chickens* kill+past by Mike.

(3) Insert the passive Aux *be* before the verb, giving it the
latter's tense ending and making
it agree with the new Subj:

The chickens *be+past+3pl*
kill– by Mike.

(4) Change the main verb to its participle form:

The chickens be+past+3pl
kill+ppcp by Mike.

Subsequently, the morphology of the language supplies the forms *were* and *killed* for *be+past+3pl* and *kill+ppcp*. The net effect of all this is to move Subj and Obj but to mark clearly with *be* and the past participle morpheme the fact that the new surface Subj is not the underlying one. This rule precedes Question Formation, for its output can be questioned: *Were the chickens killed by Mike? By whom were the chickens killed?*

In addition to moving the deep structure Subj and Obj into rheme and theme positions, respectively, the English passive is used for downplaying the identity of an underlying Subj, i.e. for when a speaker cannot or will not identify it. In this case, the sentence must be passivized; a subjectless sentence is generally impossible (but see commands, 12.4), so something must move into the Subj slot. Hence, *(unidentified NP) killed the chickens* becomes *The chickens were killed*, an 'agentless passive'. An alternative passive Aux in this construction is *get* (*The chickens got killed*), although it occurs in full passives as well, especially in colloquial English (*The chickens got killed by a truck*). Thus, English actually has two passive constructions.[6]

The Spanish Passive Transformation parallels the English one.

Initial string of morphemes: Miguel mata+pret. las gallinas.

---

(1) Move the Subj NP to the end of
the clause and give it the Prep
por:

∅ mata+pret. las gallinas *por Miguel.*

(2) Front the deep structure DO (uncliticized, and without personal
a) to the vacated Subj position:

Las gallinas mata+pret. por Miguel.

(3) Insert the passive Aux *ser* before
the verb, giving it the tense/mood
morphemes of that verb, and making it agree with the new Subj:

Las gallinas *se+pret.+3pl* mata- por Miguel.

(4) Change the main verb to its participial form, which, being morphologically an Adj here, must agree

| with the new Subj (unlike the participle in the perfect construction): | Las gallinas se+pret.+ 3pl *mata+ppcp+fpl* por Miguel. |

Subsequently, the morphology of the language supplies the forms *fueron* and *matadas* for *se+pret.+3pl* and *mata+ppcp+fpl*. In this way, *Miguel mató las gallinas* becomes *Las gallinas fueron matadas por Miguel.*[7]

Despite their similarity, the Spanish passive is less frequent than its English counterpart because the language has less need of it (Keniston 1937:207, RAE 1979:379). One reason is that the Spanish speaker can rearrange an active sentence from SVO to VSO, VOS, OVS to highlight constituents directly (v. Chapter 11), without the gymnastics of passivization: *Mató Miguel las gallinas, Las gallinas las mató Miguel*, etc. Another reason is that one can deemphasize or leave unidentified a Spanish Subj by just omitting it (*Miguel mató las gallinas →Mató las gallinas*) or by adopting the impersonal *se* construction for further deemphasis of a Subj (*Se mató las gallinas*, v. 9.3.9).

There is a purely grammatical difference, too. In the description of the English passive, it was said that the 'Obj' moves into the vacated Subj position; no distinction was made between DO and IO, or between these and OP, for in fact English allows all these objects to become a passive Subj:

I gave *some money* (DO) *to George* (IO). →
{ *Some money* was given to George by me.
  George was given some money by me.

The teacher { delved into / talked about / went over } *the crisis* (OP). →

The crisis was { delved into / talked about / gone over } by the teacher.

Moreover, certain verb idioms consisting of V + NP + Prep with an Obj NP allow either NP to be passivized (Quirk et al. 1972:848-849):[8]

Jessica took *good care* of *the cats*. →
{ *Good care* was taken of the cats by Jessica.
  The cats were taken good care of by Jessica.

Spanish, however, allows only the DO to be fronted, never IO or OP. The semantically closest equivalent to English IO and OP passivization is the impersonal *se* construction:

Se le dio dinero a Jorge~A Jorge se le dio dinero 'George was given some money',
Se habló de la crisis 'the crisis was talked about'.

In both languages, the past or passive participle (ppcp) can be used adjectivally: *boiled/baked/fried potatoes* like *raw/small/dirty potatoes*, *papas cocidas/asadas/fritas* like *papas crudas/pequeñas/sucias*. Many linguists explain these adjectival participles in the NP by deriving them from passivized relative clauses (v. 13.3): *potatoes that were fried (by X) → potatoes fried (by X) → fried potatoes*. However attractive this treatment may be in a descriptive analysis, it would have little pedagogical utility but for its explanation of two facts. First, such participles tend to retain the force of a passive: *papas fritas* implies 'papas que fueron fritas por alguien' (*papas crudas* has no such implication). Second, adjectival participles can surface with dependent VP constituents, including a passivized Subj or agent phrase: *las papas fritas ayer con cuidado por tu mamá*. On the other hand, it should be borne in mind that there are many morphologically participial Adjs that have no passive thrust at all (*divertido, pesado, considerado*, etc. v. 6.3.2).

Once the participle acquires an adjectival function, it becomes ambiguous with copulas. In English, the surface structure NP *be* V-ppcp can be understood in two ways. For example, *The dishes were washed* can convey a passive, meaning an action in the past with a deemphasized Subj, or it can describe a state, meaning that the dishes were clean, not dirty, as the result of having been washed previously. The terms TRUE PASSIVE and PASSIVE OF RESULTING STATE, respectively, are traditionally used to distinguish the two. Spanish contrasts them overtly by using *ser* as the Aux of a true passive but *estar* as the copula of a resulting state:[9]

$$\text{los platos} \begin{Bmatrix} \text{estaban/estuvieron} \\ \text{eran/fueron} \end{Bmatrix} \text{lavados} \quad \text{'the dishes were washed'}$$

The *ser/estar* contrast, combined with that of preterite/imperfect, yields four potentially distinct messages for the Spanish speaker. For the English speaker, who uses *The dishes were washed* with no awareness of finer distinctions, the Spanish options seem subtle and overdifferentiated. In fact, still other shades of meaning are possible in Spanish through the use of other copulas or intransitive verbs: *La ley es/va/queda/resulta firmada por el presidente*. Such variants (and recall *get/be* in English too) call into question whether there is one Passive Transformation.

But in a way, the Spanish setup is underdifferentiated. In adopting the following solution:

ser + V-ppcp = true passive
estar + V-ppcp = resultant changed state

Spanish forgoes the possibility of maintaining the contrast of normal states vs. changed ones, i.e. the usual *ser/estar* contrast with Adj (v. 15.4.2). Thus, in *Fueron casados* it is unclear whether the speaker is referring to a passivized event ('alguien los casó') or to a civil state regarded as the former norm for two people ('no fueron solteros sino casados'). English *They were married* is, of course, just as ambiguous.

12.4 Commands. The IMPERATIVE is sometimes considered a third mood for lack of a better pigeonhole for it (v. 7.2.1). If it is a mood, it is a defective one in that it lacks a *yo* form and overlaps morphologically with other categories (with the subjunctive in Spanish, with the infinitive in English). It is not even clear which forms should be called imperative. If the net is cast widely enough, a Spanish verb such as *salir* can be assigned the following imperatives:[10]

. . .	nosotros: salgamos, vamos a salir
tú: sal	vosotros: salid
Ud.: salga	Uds.: salgan
él/ella: que salga	ellos/ellas: que salgan

All but the *tú* and *vosotros* forms are subjunctives, and under negation they all emerge as subjunctives: *no salgas/salga/salgamos/salgáis/salgan.* The subjunctive connection and the *que* of the 'indirect commands' (*que salga/salgan*) suggest a noun clause (v. 13.1-13.1.2.7) following an understood verb of wishing or ordering, and teachers and linguists alike sometimes explain imperatives in that way: (*yo mando/propongo/quiero que) salgan.*

Having cast our net widely for Spanish, we are entitled to do likewise for English, catching a rather motley school of fish:

. . .	we: let's leave
you: leave	you: leave
he/she: let him/her leave, have him/her leave	they: let them leave, have them leave

The second-person commands are easiest to describe. In Spanish, what is called the Imperative Transformation deletes the Subj unless it is emphatic, in which case it is postposed; also, unless there is a *no* or other negative before the nucleus, clitics are suffixed to the imperative verb. In English, Obj pronouns are left undisturbed, but subject *you*, if not dropped, precedes an affirmative command and follows the *don't* of a negative one:

despiértalo (tú)	(you) wake him up
no lo despiertes (tú)	don't (you) wake him up

Nosotros commands behave like the second-person ones: *despertémoslo (nosotros), no lo despertemos (nosotros)*; the indirect commands, though, preserve the normal clitics-before-verb arrangement of any *que*-clause: *que (no) lo despierte ella.* The English equivalents are harder to describe. The negative of *let's wake him up* is *let's not wake him up* for some, *don't let's wake him up* for others, and there is the emphatic affirmative *let's ús wake him up*, which becomes bizarre when one thinks about it (*let us us wake?*). In the third person, *let them not wake him up* seems a bit old-fashioned, while *don't let them wake him up* seems more a second-person command, 'no permitas tú que lo despierten'.

The Imperative Transformation follows the Passive one, so that passivized structures can be commanded: *be guided by my advice*, and the *sé tú amado* of the RAE's traditional paradigm (1924:69). (But as pointed out earlier, the Spanish passive or impersonal reflexive is more frequent than the true passive, and it yields command forms such as *véase, hágase, consúltese, agréguese, échese*, etc.) There is also the matter of morphological tidying-up operations: *levantémos-nos* → *levantémonos, levantad-os* → *levantaos*. For students, however, the biggest problem is clitic placement. A rule that postposes clitics with affirmatives and preposes them for negatives seems capricious, and its origins lie in leveled out variations from the older language rather than in logic or reason. It makes just as little sense as the preposing of English Subj *you* in affirmatives and its postposing in negatives.

Notes for Chapter 12

1. The deep structure of some of these constructions is disputed. For questions such as *¿Está allí Juan?*, the usual analysis has been to posit a deep structure suggesting the questioning of the proposition *Juan está allí*, namely, '*Q Juan está allí* (Q is an abstract morpheme signaling interrogation). For a negative such as *Juan no está allí*, the deep structure is typically represented as *Neg Juan está allí* or *No Juan está allí*, i.e. 'it is not the case that *Juan está allí*'. These analyses require that our PSR for sentence (v. 11.1.1) be modified to something like the following:

S → (Q) (Neg) NP VP

Imperatives and passives are more recalcitrant, and some linguists do not accept their derivation from SAAD-type structures.

In this and the following chapter, readers with advanced linguistic preparation will perceive that our model of description does not conform to certain recent proposals in generative grammar, as expressed by Chomsky 1981 and 1982, among others. The general effect of these proposals has been to simplify the description of transformations, to restrict their 'power' (ability to alter structure), and to make possible a broader understanding of universal properties of movement and deletion rules. While these proposals hold great promise, they rely on certain key theories (e.g. 'Binding' and 'X-Bar Syntax') that are difficult to explain in an introductory or applied linguistics work such as this one. We will therefore present transformations more or less in their older format, which—though not as useful to the advanced linguist as the newer one—is a bit easier for beginners. Those with advanced training and a more theoretical orientation might wish to reformulate the PSRs and transformations in this book in line with current proposals or alternative models.

2. A falling intonation is not unusual, however, and is indeed quite likely to occur when several such questions are asked in close succession. (Cf. David P. Harris, 'The Intonation of English "Yes-No" Questions: Two Studies Compared and Synthesized,' *TESOL Quarterly*, 5 (June 1971), 123-127.)

3. At least it is true that Spanish more regularly inverts with information questions than with *yes/no* questions. Yet inversion here is still not obligatory: *¿Cómo los gobernadores han podido resolverlo?* (Cf. Eng. **How the governors have been able to solve it?*) When the Subj is a pronoun, most dialects do invert, but even here some speakers say *¿Qué tú dices?* instead of *¿Qué dices tú?* This seems to be confined to Caribbean dialects (Suñer 1982:323, Kany 1945/1951:125, Jorge-Morán 1974:122).

4. More precisely, with VP questioning one must distinguish processes caused by the Subj from those noncausally undergone by it. For a sentence such as *John died* or *Juan murió*, VP questioning yields *What happened to John?* and *¿Qué le pasó a Juan?*, not *What did John do?* or *¿Qué hizo Juan?*

5. *Cuán* is not completely dead, but simply rare in the spoken language. As demonstrated by Whitley (1986a), many native speakers still regard it as an elegant way of questioning intensifiers, although they seldom use it.

6. Alert readers may see a contradiction here. It was assumed earlier (v. 11.1.1) that Eng. PSRs require a deep structure Subj, yet here we see surface structure passives with no *by NP* representing an underlying Subj. Some linguists have proposed the deep structure *Someone killed the chickens* for *The chickens were killed* (positing a transformation that deletes *by someone* after the application of the Passive); but the agent of death could just as well be some*thing* (a truck, disease, earthquake, contaminated feed), and to circumvent this problem others propose the Subj 'PRO', a proform unspecified as to humanness. Alternatively, one might allow the Subj to be 'empty' in deep structure.

7. The use of *de* instead of *por* with the agent, as in *Es amado de todos*, has been steadily declining, and the ingeniously contrived traditional rules for it are no longer valid, much less useful for students. See Suñer 1981 for a critique of the *por/de* rules for passives.

Our statement of the Spanish passive transformation implies that personal *a* is 'dropped' and a clitic reverts to its nonclitic form before the DO becomes the passive's Subj. Such is the thrust of pedagogical examples and exercises in which students convert *María vio a Ernesto* to *Ernesto fue visto por María*, and *María los vio* to *Ellos/Uds. fueron vistos por María*. Actually, in generative grammar it makes more sense to assume that the rules inserting *a* and cliticizing objects are later transformations, applying *after* passivization; in other words, when the Passive Transformation applies to NP V NP, the second NP does not 'yet' have *a* or a clitic form.

8. Likewise, *lose/keep track of, make fun of, take advantage of, keep pace with, pay attention to, make use of*. Other syntactically comparable constructions do not allow these special passives: *They lost the labels off their luggage* → **Their luggage was lost the labels off*. Likewise, not all OPs can be passivized: *They flew through the air* → **The air was flown through by them*. Fortunately, though, English speakers do not need to know which OPs in Spanish undergo passivization, but simply the fact that NONE of them does.

9. We should note that it is erroneous to use *por* + NP to cue true passives, as is common in many fill-in-the-blank exercises; the agent phrase could just as well accompany *estar* + V-ppcp for what Bull (1965:292) calls 'maintenance of resulting state'. In other words, either copula could occur in blanks such as the following:

El vaso _____ roto.   El camino _____ bloqueado por las tropas.

There is no agreement on the transformation(s) for the passive of resulting state. Hadlich (1971:191-192), who does try a transformational approach, notes the consistency of the meaning of *estar* + V-ppcp with that of *estar* + Adj, namely, 'result of change', and opts for a solution in which V-ppcp is underlyingly a clausal PredE. His deep structure for *Los platos están lavados* is roughly as follows:

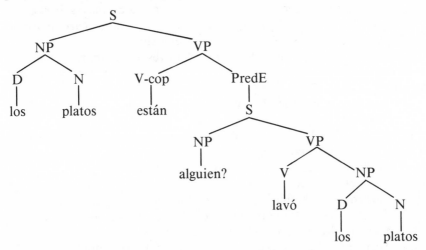

Paraphrased, this represents something like 'the dishes are in a changed state such that someone washed them'. Specified transformations then passivize the clause under PredE and reduce it to a participial VP. Alternatively, Hadlich notes that the embedded clause in deep structure might be some kind of reflexive *se* construction before reduction to a participle; this approach would have the advantage of handling cases such as the following too (v. types of reflexives, 9.3):

Se lavaron los platos (passive *se*) → los platos están lavados
Se cerraron las puertas (intrans. *se*) → las puertas están cerradas
Las mujeres se arrodillaron (inchoative *se*) → las mujeres están
  arrodilladas
Se aburrieron los hombres (emotional reaction *se*) → los hombres están
  aburridos

10. Terrell y Salgués (1979:176) cast their net and come up with the following categories:

(1) direct command: *tráigamelo*
(2) indirect command: *que me lo traiga*
(3) exhortative command: *traigámoslo*
(4) transmitted command: *le dije que me lo trajera*
(5) attenuated command: *preferiría que me lo trajera*

To which one perhaps could add the first-person invitation to a command, *¿Te lo traigo?* The point, however, of their proposal is that there is
no imperative mood; commands are simply uses of the subjunctive.

Exercises for Chapter 12

1. Error analysis:

(1) *¿Ha Juan salido?
(2) *¿Son Vicente y su papá
    altos?
(3) *Cristina no quiere algo.
(4) *¿Cómo largo es el sofá?
(5) *¿Qué hablasteis sobre?
(6) *¿De quién toalla usaste?
(7) *Pedro está no caminando.
(8) *No tú hazlo.
(9) *Carmina no hace saberlo.
(10) *No estudiantes participarían
    en esto.

2. In what ways are the following student responses inappropriate or
even ungrammatical? What special usages of Spanish are being misunderstood?

(1) Teacher: ¿Qué hace Ud. por la mañana?
    Student: Hago estudiar.
(2) Teacher: Si Ud. fuera jefe de alguna empresa, ¿qué clase de
             secretaria buscaría?
    Student: Buscaría clase media de secretaria.
(3) Teacher: Yo prefiero las películas cómicas. ¿Y Ud.?
    Student: Mí también. ¿No? ¿Me también?
(4) Teacher: ¿Qué tal le parece nuestro equipo este año?
    Student: Me parece un equipo de fútbol.
(5) Teacher: ¿Qué les pasó a las víctimas del terremoto?
    Student: Les pasó fueron llevadas al hospital.
(6) Teacher: ¿A quién se lo dio Ud.?
    Student: Se lo di yo.
(7) Teacher: ¿Cuánto mide Ud.?
    Student: Mido cosas como muebles.
(8) Teacher: ¿Se llamó a la abogada?
    Student: Sí, ella se llamó abogada.

3. Draw up a lesson plan to explain the use and placement of *no* and *sí*.

4. How would you, as a teacher, explain to students the ways in which *how* + Adj/Adv is conveyed in Spanish? Would you emphasize (1) *cómo de* and/or *qué tan*, (2) *qué* + noun, (3) both, or (4) neither (i.e. avoid this point of usage)?

5. Indicate the ways in which English and Spanish differ on each of the following points:

(1) inversion in questions
(2) formation and use of the passive
(3) meanings of copula + past participle in surface structure
(4) formation of commands

6. Why do English speakers have trouble finding suitable equivalents for *anybody, anything, anywhere, ever,* and *either* in a Spanish dictionary?

7. Draw up an exercise in which students practice a wide range of interrogative expressions by forming information questions to elicit designated constituents of declarative sentences. For example,

Se lo regalé A BEATRIZ → *¿A quién se lo regalaste?*
La estación está MUY LEJOS. → *¿A qué distancia está la estación?*

8. The Spanish Passive Transformation can be used to distinguish cases of *a* + DO from *a* + IO and *a* + adverbial OP (v. 8.1.3, 9.4.1, 10.2.3). Use it to discern DOs in the following:

(1) La revolución ha reemplazado a las urnas.
(2) Las lluvias invernales siguen a la sequía.
(3) Su renta per cápita corresponde a su rango demográfico.
(4) Las ventanas dan al patio.
(5) El ejecutivo renunció al puesto.
(6) Tú no has contestado a Luis.
(7) Tú no has escuchado a Luis.
(8) Los perros olían al reo.
(9) Los perros olían a orina.
(10) Miguel asistió a clase.
(11) La moza sirvió a don Marcos.

9. The Passive also distinguishes verb + DO from verb + PredE or adverbial NP. Which of the following are thereby true DOs?

(1) Lupe fue *una ingeniera famosa*.
(2) Lupe midió *el perímetro*.
(3) Lupe midió *158 centímetros*.
(4) Lupe llamó *el perrito*.
(5) Lupe lo llamó '*Perrito*'.
(6) Lupe pasó *dos días allí*.
(7) Lupe se quedó allí *dos días*.

10. Transformations apply in a particular order, rather like cooking instructions or the commands of computer programs. The ordering can be ascertained by taking the transformations known to have applied in the

generation of a certain sentence, and trying them out in different sequences until the right output results. For the following sentence, for example, the indicated transformations have applied, though not in the stated order; determine their proper sequence in Spanish, from the first to apply to the deep structure to the last to apply before the surface structure.

Surface Structure: ⌃ ¿Por quién no fue envuelto ningún paquete?

> Negation
> Question Inversion
> Fronting of Interrogative
> Passive

Deep Structure: Q NO quién envolvió algún paquete

11. A common transformation we have not discussed is 'Gapping'. Following are examples of it; study them and then state as precisely as possible how the rule operates. How is it similar to Nominalization (v. 8.4.1) in operation and in function?

Ella defendió a Leopoldo y yo defendí a Ramiro. →
Ella defendió a Leopoldo y yo a Ramiro.

Mercedes quiere tomar vino y su hermano quiere tomar cerveza. →
Mercedes quiere tomar vino y su hermano cerveza.

12. 'Indirect commands', as in *que se calle Tomás*, are often treated as third-person imperatives, but they are not so limited: *y que te calles tú también*. Like other scholars, Carnicer (1977:51-53) regards them as ellipses of a fuller *mando (digo, quiero . . .) que se calle/te calles*; the *que*, in other words, is not an imperative morpheme but the subordinating conjunction or complementizer of a noun clause (v. 13.1.2) following a verb of communication. He likewise believes that sentences such as the following are ellipses of fuller sentences containing something like *yo te digo . . .* or *tú me preguntas . . .* :

Que sí.   Que sí quieres arroz.   ¿Que ya vienen?
Que no.es así.   ¿Que por qué hago esto?   Que eso no se dice.

Carnicer judges *que*, from its many uses, as 'este gozne fundamental del castellano.' How would you explain to English speakers this 'gozne', insofar as English *that* is not used identically?

13. Because of their connection to the Passive Transformation, past participles have sometimes been called passive participles (v. 6.3.2). But even aside from nonpassive adjectives such as *pesado* 'heavy' and *divertido* 'fun, amusing', there are many cases of the Spanish participle that are not truly passive, as illustrated here. Study them, noting that participles would not be used in the English equivalents and that the Passive Transformation in no way underlies these uses:

Los contrabandistas chilenos *huidos a Argentina* no quieren rendirse.

El dinero *salido del país* valdría unos dos millones de dólares.

El portavoz reveló un accidente *ocurrido a diez kilómetros de la capital.*

Participó mucha gente en los debates *habidos aquí sobre el aborto.*
Ese terrorista, *fallecido en 1977,* sigue inspirando a la juventud.
No piensan volver los ciudadanos *recién venidos de las islas.*
El país se ha atenido a la estrategia de un general *nacido en 1902.*
In the last example, the English participle *born* could be used in the same way:
The country has adhered to the strategy of a general *born in 1903.*
But something is still different, as one discovers by replacing *nacido* and *born* with their participial antonyms *muerto* and *died.*

If a name helps, Bello (1847/1958:152) called these cases 'deponentes' (after a similar Latin category). What, exactly, does Spanish allow here that English grammar prohibits? Can you describe transformationally 'deponent' formation in Spanish? How does (in)transitivity bear on the question? Does the Spanish usage have anything to do with the use of the participles of reflexives, as in *se durmió → está dormido* (v. 9.3.5)?

Chapter 13
Complex sentences

13.0 Compound vs. complex sentences. At several points in the phrase structure rules examined in Chapter 11, the symbol S for 'sentence' appeared inside another S or inside some constituent of another S. Thus, S may contain S, or put in different terms, sentences may be combined to form longer sentences. This syntactic property is a universal one, found in all languages, although how the combining takes place structurally depends on the grammar of each language to some extent. In many languages, including Spanish and English, there are two distinct types of sentence combinations, compound and complex.

A COMPOUND SENTENCE consists of two or more sentences (or CLAUSES) connected by coordinating conjunctions (v. 10.2.3, 11.1.1). It results from the application of the PSR S → S (C S)^n, i.e. 'S may consist of one S combined with the sequence C + S any number of times.' An example is [*Tú saliste*] *y* [*la criada te vio*], whose coordinated or compound S C S structure is given by phrase marker (a) in Figure 13.1. (Note the introduction of two linguistic conventions here: square brackets can be used to enclose and highlight constituents, internal clauses in this case; and in the trees of Figure 13.1 the triangles abbreviate internal details of constituents.)

A COMPLEX SENTENCE also contains two or more clauses, but instead of being loosely or additively joined as in compound S, one is built into the other. The larger S is then called the MAIN CLAUSE, PRINCIPAL CLAUSE, or MATRIX; the inner one is variously described as EMBEDDED IN, SUBORDINATED TO, DEPENDENT ON, or a COMPLEMENT OF some constituent of the main clause. Consequently, whereas a coordinated clause plays no grammatical role in its compound mate, a subordinated clause carries out a syntactic function within the main clause, generally acting like a noun, adjective, or adverbial.

13.0.1 Types of embedded clauses. Some embedded clauses function like nouns or NP as the Subj or Obj in the main clause. These are called NOUN CLAUSES, and are generated by the PSR NP → S, i.e. 'NP can consist of S alone'. This rule specifies the structure in tree (b) of Figure 13.1 for *Yo sé* [*que la criada te vio*]. Note that the bracketed material in this example is itself a sentence (*la criada* = NP, *te vio* = VP, and NP + VP = S), and that it carries out the same NP function (namely, Obj) in the main clause as the final NPs of *Yo sé los números* and *Yo sé la identidad de la testigo*. The *que* that introduces the noun clause *que la criada te vio* is a functor (v. 10.4.2) whose only meaning is to mark the subordination of the noun clause; it is called a COMPLEMENTIZER.

Figure 13.1 Types of clauses.

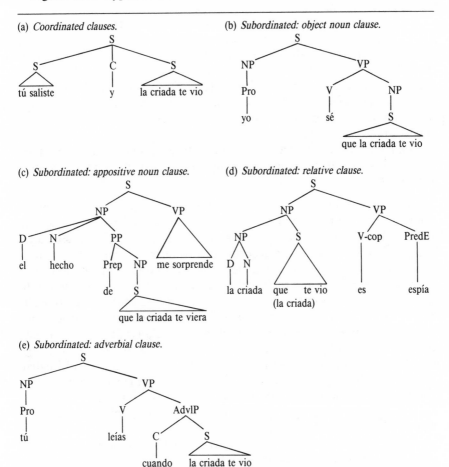

(a) *Coordinated clauses.*

(b) *Subordinated: object noun clause.*

(c) *Subordinated: appositive noun clause.*

(d) *Subordinated: relative clause.*

(e) *Subordinated: adverbial clause.*

A noun clause may also serve as an appositive (v. 11.1.3) to some noun in the matrix. An example of an appositive noun clause is found in *El hecho de [que la criada te viera] me sorprende*, shown in tree (c) of Figure 13.1. In this case, the bracketed clause is equated with *hecho* in the same way that *Lima* is equated with *ciudad* in *la ciudad de Lima*.

Instead of being equated appositively with N, an embedded clause may modify NP like an adjective, in which case it is called a RELATIVE or ADJEC-TIVE CLAUSE. A relative clause conforms to the PSR NP → NP S, i.e. 'NP may consist of some other NP (e.g. D + N) combined with a modifying S'. Tree (d) in Figure 13.1 shows the structure of a sentence containing a relative clause, *La criada [que te vio] es espía. Que te vio* defines which *criada* is meant, exactly like the Adj in *la criada risueña, la criada traviesa,* and *la criada susodicha*. The *que* that introduces a relative or adjective clause is termed a RELATIVE PRONOUN, not a complementizer, since it has a meaning or at least a referent: *que* = *ella*, i.e. *la criada*.

Another possibility is for the embedded clause to be governed by a relator (Prep or C-subord), and thereby carry out an adverbial function in the matrix VP. It is then called an ADVERBIAL or CIRCUMSTANTIAL CLAUSE and is represented in the AdvlP or *complemento circunstancial*. The structure of a sentence containing an adverbial clause, *Tú leías [cuando la criada te vio]*, is given in (e) of Figure 13.1. Note that the bracketed clause has the same function and position as the Adv in *Tú leías entonces* or the PP in *Tú leías durante la misa*.

Finally, as will be shown later, comparative sentences can be analyzed as complex too, although pedagogically they are usually treated as simple sentences.

13.0.2 Reduced clauses. Whereas the clauses of compound sentences tend to preserve their own internal structure, subordinated clauses are tightly integrated into the matrix, and certain syntactic processes alter their internal configuration according to what is present in the matrix. Above all, they may REDUCE to simpler constructions in which the verb is untensed (nonfinite) and the Subj has been either dropped or raised into the matrix. For example, another way of saying *La criada afirma [que ella te ha visto]* is *La criada afirma [haberte visto]*; and one means of accounting for this relationship is to posit that the noun clause *que ella te ha visto* has been reduced to the infinitival phrase *haberte visto*. In general, a large number of the infinitival and gerundial phrases of Spanish and English may be explained as reduced noun clauses. Many linguists see the reduction as transformational: certain rules convert deep structure clauses to surface phrases. Others see *que* and the infinitival morpheme as alternative complementizers of a noun clause in deep structure. Both approaches are valid, and both provide insight into a variety of structures often consigned to lists of *usos del infinitivo*.[1]

13.1 Noun clauses. Noun clauses function as Subj, as discussed in section 13.1.1, or as the verb's DO, as discussed in section 13.1.2. (But see also the use of noun clauses as OP, discussed in 13.2.1.)

13.1.1 As subjects. Suppose one wishes to comment on the proposition *John smokes cigars* by making it the Subj of the VP *bothers Henry*. The resulting sentence is *[John smokes cigars] bothers Henry*, but this is not yet an acceptable English surface structure. The embedded clause *John smokes cigars* must be fitted out with complementizers (COMP) to show its subordination. English permits three distinct COMPs for Subj noun clauses:

that NP VP: [*that* John smokes cigars] bothers Henry
for NP to VP: [*for* John *to* smoke cigars] bothers Henry
NP-possessive VP-ing: [John*'s* smok*ing* cigars] bothers Henry

A clause with *that* or *for . . . to . . .* has the special property that it can be uprooted and moved to the end of the matrix sentence, whereupon *it* is inserted into the vacated matrix Subj position. The transformation for this process is called EXTRAPOSITION.

[that John smokes cigars] bothers Henry→ *it* bothers Henry [that John smokes cigars]

[for John to smoke cigars] bothers Henry → *it* bothers Henry [for John to smoke cigars]

On the other hand, *for . . . to . . .* shares with poss.-*ing* the property of introducing clauses that are untensed or nonfinite: infinitivized and gerundized clauses exclude the expression of tense and modals (**for John to smoked, *John's woulding smoke*). They also share the possibility of losing their Subj, whereupon *for* NP *to* VP becomes just *to* VP, and NP-poss VP-*ing* becomes VP-*ing*. This reduction to a subjectless infinitive or gerund occurs in two cases. First, the Subj NP (*for* NP or NP-poss.) can drop when it is referentially identical to some other NP in the main clause, a condition called EQUI-NP:

[for *Henry* to smoke cigars] bothers *Henry* → [to smoke cigars] bothers
Henry (+ *Extrap.* → it bothers Henry [to smoke cigars])

[*Henry*'s smoking cigars] bothers *Henry* → [smoking cigars] bothers
Henry

Second, no Subj NP appears in surface structure when the clause is understood as referentially IMPERSONAL. Whether there is a real underlying Subj (*someone, people*) or some generalized proform ('PRO') is debated; we will use 'X' for it here.[2]

[for X to smoke cigars] is expensive → [to smoke cigars] is expensive
(+ *Extrap.* → it is expensive [to smoke cigars])

[X's smoking cigars] is expensive → [smoking cigars] is expensive

(It is understood here that this sentence contains the gerund *smoking*, not the homonymous participle; cf. *Smoking* (ger.) *cigars is expensive* vs. *Smoking* (pcp.) *cigars are smelly*.)

As we will see with object clauses, yet another variant is NP *to* VP, with the *for* dropped. Thus, English actually has the following set of complementizers in surface structure:

(1) Full clause, tensed: that NP VP (*that* Henry smokes cigars)
(2) Infinitive (untensed): for NP to VP (*for* Henry *to* smoke cigars)
                         NP to VP (Henry *to* smoke cigars)
                         to VP (*to* smoke cigars)
(3) Gerund (untensed): NP-poss VP-*ing* (Henry*'s* smok*ing* cigars)
                         VP-*ing* (smok*ing* cigars)

The commonest complementizer for Spanish noun clauses is *que*, with its alternate *el que*. (*El hecho de que* has a similar function, but is properly analyzed as an appositive structure.) *(El) que* NP VP resembles *that* NP VP, but it allows mood contrasts according to how the speaker views the proposition (v. 7.3.2). Subject noun clauses may be extraposed in Spanish as in English; but it should be recalled (v. 11.2.3—11.3.1) that Spanish can apply Extraposition to any Subj NP, whether nominal, pronominal, or clausal, in order to show a different presentation of information.

[(el) que Juan fume cigarros] le molesta a Enrique → le molesta a Enrique [que Juan fume cigarros]. (*but cf. also*: Juan viene → Viene Juan)

Like English, Spanish uses its infinitival morpheme as a second clausal complementizer. Unlike English, however, Spanish allows *el* to precede its infinitive (like its *que* clause), postposes or extraposes the infinitival Subj if this is expressed at all,[3] and has no equivalent of Eng. *for* in this construction:

[(el) fumar cigarros Juan] le molesta a Enrique

Given Equi-NP, the Subj drops as in English:

[(el) fumar cigarros Enrique] le molesta a Enrique → [(el) fumar cigarros] le molesta a Enrique → le molesta a Enrique [fumar cigarros]

The condition of Impersonal X, or as Gili Gaya (1973:189) calls it, 'sujeto indeterminado', has the same effect:

[(el) fumar cigarros X] es costoso. → es costoso [fumar cigarros]

Spanish has no noun clause COMP corresponding to Eng. NP-poss VP-*ing*, for its gerund is specialized for adverbial functions (v. 6.3.2). Thus, our inventory for Spanish includes the following:

(1) Full clause (tensed): que NP VP (*que* Enrique fume cigarros)
    el que NP VP (*el que* Enrique fume cigarros)
(2) Infinitive (untensed): VP-inf (fum*ar* cigarros)
    el VP-inf (*el* fum*ar* cigarros)
    el VP-inf NP (*el* fum*ar* cigarros Enrique)

To say that each language has several COMP options is not to claim that these are completely interchangeable. They clearly are not; for one thing, we have already seen that the infinitive and gerund versions are untensed, excluding tense and mood morphemes in Spanish and tense and modal morphemes in English. Spann 1984 furthermore shows that the English gerund complementizer is much more nounlike than the other two in how it passes certain syntactic tests for nominal (nonclausal) NPs. Applying the same tests to Spanish data, she reveals that *el* + COMP is used in exactly the same contexts in which English prefers its gerund. She therefore proposes (Spann 1984:228) that the usual equation of English gerunds with Spanish infinitives be revised as shown in Figure 13.2 for noun clauses as subjects.

Figure 13.2 Spann's (1984) correlations for subject noun clauses and their reductions.

English:		Spanish:
that + tensed clause	=	*que* + tensed clause
That Julia stays at home is absurd.		*Que Julia se quede en casa es absurdo.*
subjectless infinitive	=	subjectless infinitive
To stay at home is absurd.		*Quedarse en casa es absurdo.*
NP-poss and gerund	=	*el que* + tensed clause
Julia's staying at home is absurd.		*El que Julia se quede en casa es absurdo.*
subjectless gerund	=	*el* + subjectless infinitive
Staying at home is absurd.		*El quedarse en casa es absurdo.*

Before proceeding to object noun clauses, we will comment on a transformation commonly called '*Tough*-Movement.' Given the following lineup (resulting from infinitival reduction plus Extraposition):

([to V NP] is tough) → *it* is tough [to V NP]

English allows the following change:

NP is tough [to V _____]

For example, *It is tough to play a French horn* → *A French horn is tough to play.* The trigger for the transformation is the presence of an Adj such as *tough* that evaluates the infinitivized clause: *hard, easy, (im)possible, convenient, expensive,* etc. The transformation is also possible when the NP is an Obj of Prep in its clause: *It is hard to play arpeggios on a French horn* → *A French horn is hard to play arpeggios on.* Spanish has an analog of *Tough*-Movement, but it differs from its English equivalent in that (1) *de* must be inserted between the Adj and the clause, and (2) it is impossible with NPs governed by Prep except for personal *a*:

Es $\left\{ \begin{array}{l} \text{fácil} \\ \text{difícil} \\ \text{imposible} \end{array} \right\}$ [tocar la trompa] →

$$\text{La trompa es} \left\{ \begin{array}{l} \text{fácil} \\ \text{difícil} \\ \text{imposible} \end{array} \right\} de \text{ [tocar]}$$

Es difícil [oír bien a esa profesora] → Esa profesora es difícil de [oír bien]

Es difícil [trabajar para esa profesora] → *Esa profesora es difícil de [trabajar para]

Es difícil [tocar arpegios con la trompa] → *La trompa es difícil de [tocar arpegios con]

13.1.2 As objects. Two facts stand out in the analysis of noun clauses used as verbal Obj. First, with its object clauses English allows the deletion of *that* whereas standard Spanish seldom drops *que* outside of telegraphic or direct-quote usage: *I say that he'll do it → I say he'll do it, Digo que lo hará → *Digo lo hará*. Second, with object clauses COMP selection is typically dictated by the governing verb in the matrix sentence. One verb in one language may allow two or more options while its semantic equivalent in the other language requires different ones and under different conditions. Consequently, generalizations of the type illustrated in Figure 13.2 are difficult here. Some contrastive analysts have attempted comprehensive taxonomies of source and target language verbs according to their complementizers (see, for example, Stockwell et al. 1965); we will limit ourselves to a handful of cases illustrating the main problems English speakers face in Spanish with noun clauses as objects.

13.1.2.1 With *creer* vs. *believe*. *Creer* is constructed with an object *que* clause that, under Equi-NP, optionally reduces to a subjectless infinitive:

Marta cree [que Luisa lo ha logrado]

Marta cree [que (Marta) lo ha logrado] → Marta cree [haberlo logrado]

Believe also takes a *that* clause, but reduction to an infinitive is possible regardless of Equi-NP. The Subj of the infinitive is moved up into the main clause by a transformation called 'Raising', becoming the DO of *believe* in surface structure:

Martha believes [that Louise has achieved it] →

Martha believes *Louise* [_____ to have achieved it]

Martha believes [that she (Martha) has achieved it] →

Martha believes *herself* [_____ to have achieved it]

That the raised NP Subj of the infinitive becomes the DO of *believe* is proved by two facts. First, under Equi-NP the result is a reflexive, *herself*, as shown here. Second, the raised NP can subsequently be passivized like any other Obj: *Louise is believed to have achieved it by Martha.*

13.1.2.2 With *decir* vs. *say, tell*. *Decir* introduces a full *que* clause whose verb is subjunctive if relaying a command, indicative if relaying an asserted fact (v. 7.3.2). Only in the latter case can the clause reduce, and only under Equi-NP; the result is a subjectless infinitive, as with *creer*.

Command: Juan dice [que Uds. tengan cuidado]
Assertion: Juan dice [que Uds. tienen cuidado]
Juan dice [que (Juan) tiene cuidado] → Juan dice [tener cuidado]

Say and *tell* operate differently. An object clause reporting an asserted fact is cast as *that* NP VP; one relaying a command is cast as *for* NP *to* VP in the case of *say*, and (with *for* deleted) as NP *to* VP with *tell*. In this last case, the NP Subj of the infinitive is raised to become the Obj of *tell* (as with *believe*):

Command: John says [for you to be careful]
John tells [you to be careful] → John tells *you* [____ to be careful]
Assertion: John says [that you are careful]
John tells us [that you are careful]

Reduction to a subjectless infinitive occurs with *say* for Impersonal X, never for Equi-NP, and then only for commands.[4]

John says [to be careful]

Clearly, then, the student will have to learn (1) that the difference between assertive *that* NP VP and imperative (*for*) NP *to* VP corresponds in Spanish to a mood difference in full clauses, and (2) that the reduced versions *John says to be careful* and *Juan dice tener cuidado* are far from the matches they seem to be in surface structure.

13.1.2.3 With *preferir, querer, intentar* vs. *prefer, want, try*. These Spanish verbs are the prototypes for most pedagogical statements on expressions that indicate an attempt to 'influence behavior' (v. 7.3.2.3). When clausal Subjs are distinct (no Equi-NP), the noun clause is a full *que* clause in the subjunctive; no reduction is then possible. When there is Equi-NP, however, reduction must occur, and the result is a subjectless infinitive:

Prefiero [que lo haga Laura]
(Prefiero [que lo haga yo]) → Prefiero [hacerlo]
Quiero [que Daniel se vaya]
(Daniel quiere [que Daniel se vaya]) → Daniel quiere [irse]
Intento [que no lleguen tarde]
(Intento [que yo no llegue tarde]) → Intento [no llegar tarde]

Their English equivalents are idiosyncratic in their complementation. *Prefer* can take all three complementizer types, regardless of Equi-NP. Whether or not the noun clause Subj is retained in reduction under Equi-NP depends on its emphasis:

I prefer [that Laura do it]	I prefer [that Í do it]
I prefer [for Laura to do it]	I prefer [for ME to do it] =
I prefer [Laura's doing it]	I prefer [to do it]
	I prefer [MY doing it]. =
	I prefer [doing it]

Impersonal X can also promote reduction; I *prefer* [*doing it this way*] is thus ambiguous, since the gerund's Subj could be the speaker or someone else. *Want*, on the other hand, allows just NP *to* VP, which obligatorily reduces to *to* VP under Equi-NP; it never takes a *that* clause, though its synonym *desire* may:

I want [Daniel to go away]
(Daniel wants [Daniel to go away]) → Daniel wants [to go away]
I desire [that Daniel go away]

Like *want*, *try* cannot take a *that* clause; unlike *want*, it can be used *only* for Equi-NP, and it occurs just with a subjectless infinitive:

*I try [(for) them not to arrive late]
(I try [me not to arrive late]) → I try [not to arrive late]

Pedagogically, there are few problems with the *preferir/querer/intentar* class as long as these verbs are followed by infinitives under Equi-NP. Otherwise, students must essentially block transfer from English complement types here, and acquire a different but systematic Spanish pattern of full *que* clauses.

13.1.2.4 With mandar, rogar, impedir vs. order, beg, prevent. *Mandar* and *rogar* are followed by a noun clause in the subjunctive, which optionally reduces to an infinitive whose Subj is raised to become a matrix IO:

Jaime (les) mandó/rogó [que ellos derribaran el muro.] →
Jaime les mandó/rogó [derribar el muro] *a ellos.*

Unlike the Spanish verbs in 13.1.2.3 (*preferir*, etc.), these two have optional reduction of their clauses, with no Equi-NP between clausal Subjs (*Jaime* ≠ *ellos*). As Hadlich (1971:167) notes, however, Equi-NP typically does hold between the noun clause's Subj and the main clause's IO, as shown in Figure 13.3; that is, the one to whom an order is given is intended to carry it out. Nevertheless, the Impersonal X option exists too, as in *Mandó derribar el muro*, and in this case there is no overt IO in the main clause and no explicit Subj for the infinitive. With these verbs, then, reduction optionally applies without the requirement of Equi-NP between anything in the sentence.

Figure 13.3 The relation between clausal subject and the IO of *mandar.*

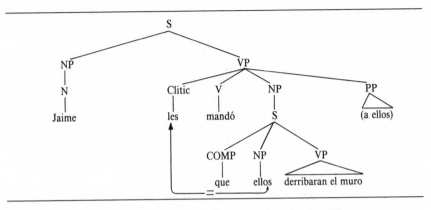

The syntax of *order* and *beg* depends on stylistic level. In rather formal English, one can use a *that* clause with them, but without an accompanying IO:

James ordered/begged (*them) [that they tear down the wall]

More commonly, they take (*for*) NP *to* VP; if the *for* is absent, the infinitive's Subj is raised into the main clause to become its DO (as with *believe* and *tell*), not its IO as in Spanish:

James ordered [them to tear down the wall] → James ordered
them [_____ to tear down the wall] (+*Passive* → They were ordered [to tear down the wall] by James +*Extraposition* → They were ordered by James [to tear down the wall])
James begged [(for) them to tear down the wall] → James begged
them [_____ to tear down the wall]

The Impersonal X option allowed by *mandar* and *rogar* is excluded by *order* and *beg*. **He ordered to tear down the wall* is ungrammatical, and *He begged to tear down the wall* has an Equi-NP interpretation.
Impedir follows *mandar* and *rogar* exactly:

Carlos (les) impidió [que los vecinos vinieran] = Carlos les impidió [venir] a los vecinos.

But *keep* and *prevent* take neither a *that* clause nor an infinitive, but instead NP *from* VP-*ing*, with the NP being raised to become their DO:

Charles kept/prevented [the neighbors from coming] →

Charles kept/prevented *the neighbors* [_____ from coming]
(+*Passive* → The neighbors were kept/prevented [from coming] by Charles.)

13.1.2.5 With *hacer* vs. *make, have.* These verbs join up with others to form CAUSATIVES. Causatives indicate that an agent causes or brings about some event. Spanish provides clear evidence of a relationship to the verb + Obj clause construction, in that it allows either *hacer* [que S] or *hacer* [VP-inf]: *Hice que corriera el caballo, Hice correr el caballo.* English *have* and *make*, however, never take *that* clauses: *have* is constructed with NP (*to*) VP (the *to* usually being dropped), and *make* with NP VP (no *for*, no *to*), as in *I had the horse (to) run, I made the horse run.* But English allows many verbs to be directly (i.e. lexically) transitivized with no causative helper: *I made the horse trot = I trotted the horse.*

Like *mandar, hacer* does not require Equi-NP for its complement's reduction to an infinitive. But its analysis poses special problems, because the postposed NP of *hacer* + V functions as the Obj of *hacer* in surface structure but is interpreted as representing either the Subj or the DO of the infinitivized verb:

Hice [que corriera *el caballo* (Subj)] → Hice correr *el caballo.*
Hice [que X construyera *la casa* (DO)] → Hice construir *la casa.*

This creates potential ambiguity: *Hice matar a Juan* could correspond either to *Hice que Juan* (Subj) *matara* or to *Hice que X matara a Juan* (DO). These cases are distinguished in English by the use of another causative formula, *have* + V-ppcp: *I made/had John kill* vs. *I had John killed, I made/had the horse run* vs. *I had the house built.* The use of the past participle here in English suggests an underlying passive, and this supposition is strengthened by the fact that *by* + NP can appear with it. In other words, the NP in the middle of this English causative functions as both the DO of *have* and the Subj of a passive: *I had John* (←DO/Subj→) *killed by an assassin, I had the house* (←DO/Subj→) *built by Hernandez and Sons.* The NP at the end of the Spanish causative shows the same double orientation: we see the personal *a* of a DO in *Hice matar a Juan* 'I had John killed' but a passive's agent phrase in *Hice construir la casa por Hernández e Hijos.*

Contreras 1979 notes these and other problems in the analysis of the causative, among them the pronominalization of objects. In surface structure, *hacer* + V acts as one agglutinated unit with limited accommodations for clitics. Whatever their function in a full noun clause, in reduction to an infinitive the clause's NPs must become the DO or (if the DO node is already occupied) IO of *hacer* + V. The following examples are illustrative, though native speakers vary somewhat in their usage:[5]

Hice [que *él* (Subj) corriera] → $\begin{cases} \text{*Hice correr}lo \\ Lo \text{ hice correr} \sim Le \text{ hice correr} \end{cases}$

$$\text{Hice [que } \textit{él} \text{ (Subj) } \textit{la} \text{ (DO) construyera]} \rightarrow \begin{cases} *\textit{Lo} \text{ hice construir}\textit{la} \\ *\text{Hice construír}\textit{sela} \\ \textit{Le} \text{ hice construir}\textit{la} \\ \textit{Se la} \text{ hice construir} \end{cases}$$

13.1.2.6 With *ver* vs. *see*. Verbs of sensory perception take as complements full clauses, infinitives, or even in Spanish, gerunds. In both languages the untensed complements resemble those of causatives in word order and in the fate of the subordinated clause's Subj:

Vieron [que *Alicia* (Subj) cantaba]
Vieron [cantar *Alicia* (Subj)] → Vieron [cantar] *a Alicia* (DO), *La* vieron cantar.
Vieron [cantando *Alicia* (Subj)] → Vieron [cantando] *a Alicia* (DO), *La* vieron cantando
They saw [that *Alice* (Subj) was singing]
They saw [*Alice* sing] → They saw *Alice* (DO) sing, They saw *her* sing
They saw [*Alice* singing] → They saw *Alice* (DO) singing, They saw *her* singing.

The three complements are not wholly synonymous, for there is a quasi-aspectual difference between the infinitive and gerund reminiscent of that between preterite and imperfect. *La vieron cantar* and *They saw her sing* suggest completion of the song (recital, performance), whereas *La vieron cantando* and *They saw her singing* indicate that she was viewed in the middle of her performance.

The preceding comparisons have been piecemeal, verb by verb, and —we must note—they are more useful to the teacher for understanding interference errors than to the student for grasping Spanish syntax. In fact, the student who proceeds by alternately transferring and then amending his English verb grammar for Spanish verbs will probably conclude that Spanish usage is utterly chaotic. He learns, for example, that *querer* takes infinitives just for Equi-NP, unlike his *want* NP *to* VP, but then discovers that *mandar* and *decir* do allow something like NP *to* VP, except that *le dijo hablarlo bien* is a far cry from *le mandó hablarlo bien*. He finds that *impedir* and *preferir* never take gerund complements, but *ver* peculiarly does; that *intentar* allows a clause for which there is no direct English equivalent; and so on until frustration sets in. What the student must understand is that each language's complement patterns fall into a few major groups, that these groups are not the same, and that the real goal is not to convert English patterns to Spanish patterns but to acquire the latter on their own terms. However their English counterparts fall into English patterns, most Spanish verbs with object clauses follow the types described above, and generally the affiliation proceeds along semantic lines. *Gritar*, for instance, is a verb of communication and predictably uses the same patterns as *decir*; *afirmar* and *dudar* are like *creer*, *necesitar* is like *querer*, *forzar* is like *mandar,* and *oír* is like *ver.* One who knows the prototype cases thoroughly can predict the behavior of many others in the language.

13.1.2.7 *Querer* + V vs. *poder* + V. Not all sequences of V + V are related to or derived from V + noun clause. Hadlich (1971:58) has shown how *querer* and *poder* differ in this respect. One can ask *¿Qué quiere Marisa?* and get the answer *Quiere considerar el porvenir. Querer* is transitive and *qué* elicits NP; thus, *Quiere considerar el porvenir* is syntactically V + NP, a fact captured by analyzing the infinitive as a kind of reduced noun clause, as in Figure 13.4. But in *Marisa puede considerar el porvenir, poder* is intransitive (**¿Qué puede Marisa?*), cannot take a DO NP, and therefore cannot take Obj noun clauses either. Thus, the underlying structure of *poder* + V is distinct from that of *querer* + V. Figure 13.5 shows two possible analyses of *poder* + V, the second of which (*poder* = Aux) is preferred by Hadlich.

Figure 13.4 V + V from V + noun clause.

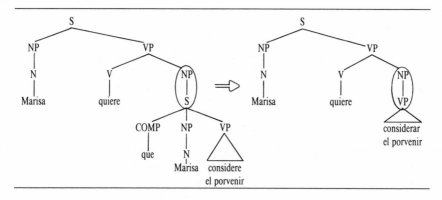

Figure 13.5 V + V not derived from V + noun clause.

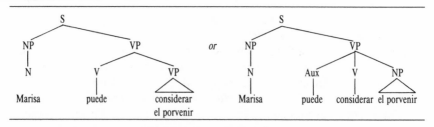

13.1.2.8 Clitic promotion. Clitic pronouns (v. 9.4.1) normally precede a conjugated (tensed) verb, but are alternatively suffixed to a gerund or infinitive accompanying a conjugated verb: *tengo que relatárselo ~ se lo tengo que relatar, estoy lavándolo ~ lo estoy lavando.* In explaining this double option for V + V, one assumes that the clitic originates next to the verb whose Obj it is in deep structure, and advances to the left by a transformation called CLITIC PROMOTION (or Clitic Movement) (v. 9.4.2):

Puede haber estado haciendo*lo* → Puede haber*lo* estado haciendo _____
→ *Lo* puede haber _____ estado haciendo.

Once a noun clause has reduced to an infinitive complement, the doors to Clitic Promotion are opened on a grand scale. This transformation cannot occur as long as *que* stands in the way and (unlike the case with *tener que* + V-inf), the *que* clause is tensed. But with infinitivization, a clitic can move leftward and upward through the syntactic tree, carrying along with it any higher clitics it collects on the way. The process is illustrated in Figure 13.6.

Figure 13.6 Clitic promotion after a noun clause reduces to an infinitival VP.

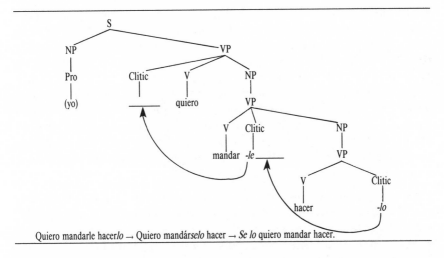

Quiero mandarle hacer*lo* → Quiero mandár*selo* hacer → *Se lo* quiero mandar hacer.

Several observers (e.g. Roldán 1974, Bordelois 1978, Contreras 1979) have found subtle constraints on this verb-to-verb romp, but the more pressing pedagogical problem is a psycholinguistic one. It will be recalled (v. 11.2) that English speakers have trouble processing objects before their verbs: *se lo escribo* as opposed to the *I write it to him* (*her*, etc.) they are accustomed to. When Clitic Promotion follows on the heels of clausal reduction, students' problems multiply: the Obj pronouns hop leftward and upward from branch to branch until they come to rest in front of a verb with which they have no connection. Since each English verb keeps its own pronouns, and in the postposed Obj position, 'him it want-I order do' often elicits a blank look from someone who still thinks in terms of 'I want to order him to do it'.

13.1.3 Noun clauses that are questions.

Interrogative noun clauses are often called embedded or INDIRECT questions. For an embedded yes/no question, English adopts *whether* or *if* as the COMP, and Spanish uses *si* (or *que si*). For an information question, both languages move the interrogative expression to the front of its clause, as in direct questions (v. 12.1.2). Unlike direct questions, indirect questions in English lack inversion and *do*-Insertion:

$$\text{Queremos saber} \left\{ \begin{array}{l} [\text{¿Llegará Ana?}] \\ [\text{¿Dónde/Qué comiste?}] \end{array} \right\} \rightarrow$$

$$\text{Queremos saber} \left\{ \begin{array}{l} [\text{si llegará Ana}] \\ [\text{dónde/qué comiste}] \end{array} \right\}$$

$$\text{We want to know} \left\{ \begin{array}{l} [\textit{Will} \text{ Ann arrive?}] \\ [\text{Where/What } \textit{did} \text{ you eat?}] \end{array} \right\} \rightarrow$$

$$\text{We want to know} \left\{ \begin{array}{l} [\text{whether/if Ann } \textit{will} \text{ arrive}] \\ [\text{where/what you } \textit{ate}] \end{array} \right\}$$

The indirect question can be the Obj of Prep: *Se le interrogó acerca de si conociera al testigo, She was asked about whether she knew the witness.* And, like any other noun clauses, indirect questions may appear as infinitives given Equi-NP, and they then suggest a sense of obligation: *Queremos saber si matricularnos (o no)* (= *Queremos saber si debemos matricularnos*), *Queremos saber qué hacer / cuándo regresar / a quién acudir*, etc. The reduced indirect question *qué hacer* must be distinguished from the *que hacer* of *hay mucho que hacer*, which is a reduced RELATIVE clause (v. 13.3.4); and the COMP *si* 'whether' must be distinguished from the *si* for conditional 'if' because the latter does not permit reduction, as will be shown in section 13.2.2.

13.2 Adverbial clauses.

Adverbial clauses supply locative, temporal, causal, and other circumstantial information in the matrix. Traditionally, they are treated as C (i.e. C-subord) + S. But at least in Spanish, there is strong evidence that those so-called subordinating conjunctions that are formed off prepositions comprise a distinct group in their syntactic behavior.

13.2.1 Preposition + clause.

Many Spanish relators for adverbial clauses are formed off Prep (v. 10.1): *después de, después (de) que*. The *que* in *después que* is merely the COMP for any Spanish noun clause, and if *veo que llovió* is V + clausal NP, then *después que llovió* is Prep + clausal NP too. By this analysis, the structure of the PP *después (de) que llovió* is comparable to that of the PP *después de la lluvia*; it is a difference between the OP being a nominal NP and the OP being a clausal NP, as shown in Figure 13.7.

Just as noun clauses reduce to untensed constructions as DO of the verb, they do so as OP, becoming infinitive phrases in Spanish but gerund

Figure 13.7 Adverbial clauses as noun-clause objects of prepositions.

phrases in English. As with verbs, Equi-NP is the usual condition for this reduction:

Elena suele leer *después de* [*que (Elena) se acuesta*] →
Elena suele leer *después de* [*acostarse*]
Helen usually reads *after* [*she (Helen) goes to bed*] →
Helen usually reads *after* [*going to bed*]

The same reduction occurs with those verbs that specify particular prepositions (v. 10.4.2) for their NP Obj or complements, whether these are nouns or noun clauses: *oponerse a (que* S), *invitar a (que* S), *confiar en (que* S), *quejarse de (que* S), as illustrated here:[6]

Nos oponemos a {
la venta de armas
[que el gobierno venda armas]
[vender armas]

We're opposed to {
the sale of weapons
[the government('s) selling weapons]
[*that the government sell weapons]
[selling weapons]
[*sell weapons]
}

That is, the Obj of *a* in *oponerse a* can be a nominal NP (*la venta de armas*), an unreduced noun clause (*que el gobierno venda armas*), or a noun clause reduced to VP-inf under Equi-NP (*vender armas*). The Obj of *to* in Eng. *opposed to*, however, can take a nominal NP (*the sale of weapons*), NP-poss VP-*ing* (*the government's selling weapons*), or, under Equi-NP or Impersonal X, the reduced subjectless gerund VP-*ing* (*selling weapons*). English does not permit the Spanish options of a full clause or VP-inf, nor does Spanish permit the English option of a gerund construction.

This difference is reflected in the pedagogical generalization that Spanish Prep + VP-inf is matched by English Prep + VP-ger, i.e. 'use an infinitive, not a gerund, after prepositions in Spanish'. While this generalization is largely correct, usage is more complex in that different Preps may cue different COMP or conditions for reduction. *After* takes either a clause (but without COMP) or a subjectless gerund, the latter under Equi-NP and optionally then:

The government increases R and D after $\begin{cases} \text{[*that it sells weapons]} \\ \text{[it sells weapons]} \\ \text{[selling weapons]} \\ \text{[the agency sells weapons]} \\ \text{[*the agency's selling weapons]} \end{cases}$

The *to* of purpose (Span. *a* or *para*) differs from both *after* and the *to* of *opposed to*: it does not take NP-poss VP-*ing* or the reduced VP-*ing*, but falls into the *for* NP *to* VP COMP pattern which, under Equi-NP, must reduce to *to* VP. Consequently, the following contrasts between the two languages involve a distinct pattern.

They're coming $\begin{cases} \text{[for the government to sell them weapons]} \\ \text{[*to that the government sell them weapons]} \\ \text{[*to selling us weapons]} \\ \text{[to sell us weapons]} \end{cases}$

Vienen a/para $\begin{cases} \text{[que el gobierno les venda armas]} \\ \text{[vendernos armas]} \end{cases}$

As shown by Whitley (1986b), the Spanish end of the pedagogical generalization is just as complicated with regard to the need for Equi-NP in the reduction of a *que* clause to VP-inf after Prep. *Para* permits reduction just under Equi-NP, and in fact requires it then:

Los recojo para $\begin{cases} \text{[que José los vacíe después]} \\ \text{[*vaciarlos José después]} \\ \text{[*que yo los vacíe después]} \\ \text{[vaciarlos después]} \end{cases}$

Antes de requires reduction under Equi-NP like *para*, but permits it optionally when there is no Equi-NP:

Antonio compra su boleto antes de $\begin{cases} \text{[*que él salga]} \\ \text{[salir]} \\ \text{[que salga Julia]} \\ \text{[salir Julia]} \end{cases}$

Finally, *después de* and *por* allow optional reduction of their clausal OPs, with or without Equi-NP:

Inés toma un café después de $\begin{cases} \text{[que termina los quehaceres]} \\ \text{[terminar los quehaceres]} \\ \text{[que termina la criada los} \\ \quad \text{quehaceres]} \\ \text{[terminar la criada los quehaceres]} \end{cases}$

Juan ha renunciado por $\begin{cases} \text{[que es terco]} \\ \text{[ser terco]} \\ \text{[que su jefe es terco]} \\ \text{[ser terco su jefe]} \end{cases}$

In summary, the prepositions of both languages impose much the same idiosyncratic conditions on the reduction of their Obj clauses as do verbs; and they fall into distinct groups in this respect like *decir, querer, mandar*, and so on.

13.2.2 Subordinating conjunction + clause. Other adverbial clauses are introduced by relators that are not based on Prep. These include *si, cuando, como si, en cuanto*, etc. (v. 10.2.2.3, 10.2.3). A clause such as *si pasan por acá* or *cuando hayan terminado* cannot be analyzed as Prep + noun clause; not only are *si* and *cuando* not prepositional, but their clauses lack the COMP *que* of *después que, porque, para que*, etc. The difference between the prepositional and nonprepositional group is not just a matter of etymology. As demonstrated by Whitley (1986b), Spanish permits the reduction of adverbial clauses if and only if these consist of Prep + noun clause; when the adverbial clause is introduced by a true (nonprepositional) subordinating conjunction, reduction is impossible even under Equi-NP:

Háganlo $\begin{cases} \text{si pasan por acá (*si pasar por acá)} \\ \text{como si lo disfrutaran (*como si disfrutarlo)} \\ \text{como quieran (*como querer)} \\ \text{cuando hayan terminado (*cuando haber terminado)} \\ \text{mientras se bañen (*mientras bañarse)} \end{cases}$

English, however, allows reduction to gerunds and even participles after many of its equivalent conjunctions as long as Equi-NP exists.[7]

Do it $\begin{cases} \text{if you pass this way, if passing this way.} \\ \text{as if you enjoyed it, as if enjoying it} \\ \text{as you desire, as desired} \\ \text{when you've finished, when finished} \\ \text{while you bathe, while bathing} \end{cases}$

Consequently, *si* + clause is C-subord + S, whereas *porque* + clause is Prep + noun clause, as represented in Figure 13.8. Since Prep + noun clause allows reduction and C-subord + S does not, there is good reason to pull *porque, después que, para que*, and so on out of the 'conjunction' lists of most Spanish textbooks.

Figure 13.8 Conjunction (C-subord) + clause vs. preposition (Prep) + clause.

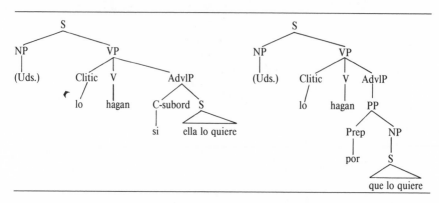

13.2.3 'Obligatorily reduced' adverbial clauses.

Certain infinitive and gerund constructions with adverbial functions lack the expected full clause counterparts. If, for example, *al llegar* and *(up)on arriving* are treated as derived from *al que* + S and *(up)on* + S, then their reduction must be made obligatory; **al que llegó*, unlike *después que llegó*, must not surface in its underlying form. Conditional *de*, as in *Habríamos llegado de no habernos detenido en el mercado*, would be treated similarly, or perhaps it is the 'missing' reduction of the conditional *si* clause. For Hadlich (1971:183-185) and Ozete (1983:77-82), adverbial gerunds and the absolute construction (v. 6.3.3) are also surface structure fragments of underlying clauses. Permitting 'S' alone (with no relator) to be one of the options for Advl in a PSR, they would assign a deep structure such as that in Figure 13.9 to *Visitando mi esposa a su madre, aproveché la ocasión*, positing an obligatory reduction transformation for it.

Linguists are not agreed on whether all infinitives and gerunds should be derived from clauses by a reduction transformation (see note 1). But it is indisputable that a strong connection exists in both languages between clauses, infinitives, and gerunds, whether as Obj of verbs or of prepositions, and whether used as nouns or as adverbials. At the introductory level, the intricacies of the connection will elude most students, for they are still wrestling with the structure of main clauses and have assimilated little syntactic complexity so far. But by the intermediate and advanced levels, they are using, hearing, and reading more complex sentences, and just as they encounter both *impide que coman* and *impide comer*, but not **impide comiendo*, they must now cope with both *antes que coman* and *antes de comer*, and they find their **antes de comiendo* consistently marked wrong. The reason for what is and what is not possible in adverbial clauses is fundamentally the same as for the behavior of noun clauses as DO of verbs, and students might profit from an overall view of what is happening.

Figure 13.9 'Absolute' phrases as sentence adverbials.

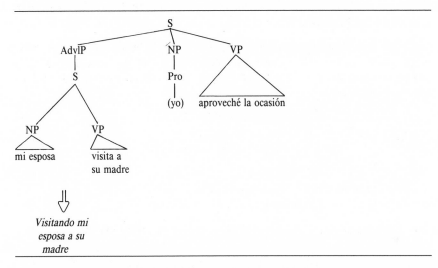

13.3 Relative or adjective clauses. A relative clause is a sentence embedded inside NP, modifying that NP's head noun like an adjective. The modified head noun or NP is called the ANTECEDENT, and some NP inside the relative clause refers to it and may be said to match it. The usual deep structure given to an NP containing a relative clause is shown in Figure 13.10. In that phrase marker, NP_1 (the antecedent) and NP_2 (in the adjective clause) match referentially. NP_2 is thereupon RELATIVIZED (changed to a RELATIVE PRONOUN) and moved leftward to the same position as the COMP of a noun clause:

the man [I saw *the man*] → the man [I saw *whom*] →

the man [*whom* I saw ____]

Fronted relative pronouns obey the same constraints as fronted interrogatives (v. 12.1.2). In particular, a Prep governing the relative pronoun

Figure 13.10 Underlying structure of NP containing a relative clause.

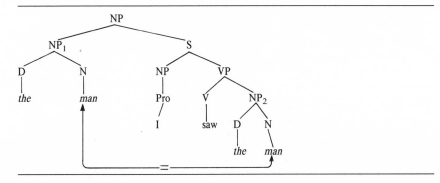

must be fronted with it in Spanish (*el hombre con quien hablé*) while in English it can be left behind (*the man with whom I spoke* ~ *the man who(m) I spoke with*).

13.3.1 Relativization according to NP type. Both languages have a variety of relativizations. We begin our survey of them by considering what happens when the relativized NP is a thing,[8] originating as Subj, DO, or OP in its clause:

I have the book
⎰ [*the book* describes climate]
⎱ [Cervantes wrote *the book*]
  [you kept leaves in *the book*]

Tengo el libro
⎰ [*el libro* describe el clima]
⎱ [Cervantes escribió *el libro*]
  [guardaste hojas en *el libro*]

The Relativization Transformation yields the following surface structures:

I have the book
⎰ [which/that describes climate]
⎱ [which/that/∅ Cervantes wrote]
  [which/that/∅ you kept leaves in], [in which you kept leaves]

Tengo el libro
⎰ [que describe el clima]
⎱ [que escribió Cervantes]
  [en que guardaste hojas]

Note that in English, nonhuman NPs generally become either *which* or *that*, but just *which* in case a governing Prep is fronted with the relative. Moreover, the relative is often deleted in English (∅) as long as no Prep has been fronted and it is followed by some other NP (i.e. the clausal Subj): *I have the book ∅ Cervantes wrote*, but not **I have the book ∅ describes climate* or **I have the book in ∅ you kept leaves*. By contrast, Spanish usage is simpler: *que* is used for things and is never deleted. (Recall the similar difference on the deletability of the COMP *that/que* (v. 13.1.2).

Next, consider what happens if the NP is a person:

This is the woman
⎰ [*the woman* wears boots]
⎱ [you should hear *the woman*]
  [they sent $50 to *the woman*]
  [I can rely on *the woman*]
  [*the woman*'s face has enchanted me]

Esta es la mujer
⎰ [*la mujer* usa botas]
⎱ [deberías oír a *la mujer*]
  [le mandaron $50 dólares a *la mujer*]
  [puedo contar con *la mujer*]
  [la cara de *la mujer* me ha encantado]

Relativization yields many possibilities here:

This is the woman
{
[who/that wears boots]
[who/whom/that/∅ you should hear]
[to whom they sent $50], [who/whom/that/∅ they sent $50 to]
[on whom I can rely], [who/whom/that/∅ I can rely on]
[whose face has enchanted me]
}

Esta es la mujer
{
[que usa botas]
[que/a quien deberías oír]
[a quien le mandaron $50]
[con quien puedo contar]
[cuya cara me ha encantado]
}

The English relative pronouns for humans are *who(m)*, ∅, *that*, but never *which*. Conditions on deletability and Prep fronting are as for nonhumans, but a complication is introduced by the *who/whom* distinction, which is observed in formal styles but seldom in most colloquial ones. In Spanish, *que* is used for clausal Subj, and alongside *a quien* for DO. Both languages also have a possessive relative, *whose* and the four-form *cuyo*, and it can also be used for nonhuman antecedents: *a river whose water is polluted, un río cuya agua está contaminada*.

Both languages permit Extraposition for relative clauses, as for noun clauses (v. 13.1.2):

I saw a woman [who knows you well] last night →

I saw a woman ⎯⎯ last night [who knows you well]
Vi a una mujer [que te conoce bien] anoche →

Vi a una mujer ⎯⎯ anoche [que te conoce bien]

When the relativized NP is OP, many Spanish texts and grammars still prescribe *que* for nonhumans, *quien* for humans after short prepositions (*a, con, de, en*), and *el cual* after long prepositions—and after short ones, too, if a genderized relative removes ambiguity of antecedents: *la hija del señor* A LA CUAL *le escribiste*. But current usage is strongly at variance with this treatment; *el que* is being generalized regardless of the Prep and the antecedent's humanness, making for a much neater rule:

la mujer *con la que* puedo contar
el cantante *al que* me refiero
los futbolistas *en los que* pensábamos
las llaves *con las que* se abre esta puerta

Ozete 1981 verified this trend by tallying the frequency of each relative in six periodicals. He found that although *que* and *quien* did occasionally appear after Prep, the forms of *el que* were much more common, even after short *de* and *a*. With understatement, he concluded that 'from the myriad of opinions surrounding relatives as objects of a preposition, a reconsideration of their use is in order' (Ozete 1981:89).

There are other points, too, where the rules need reconsideration. Kany (1945:132-133) notes and documents several other cases, two of which we note here. First, many speakers have extended the *que* for DO to IO: *esa mujer que le faltan los dientes*. Second, *cuyo* has faced stiff competition in the spoken language from *que su* for centuries: *esa mujer que su papá se ha muerto*. (Cf. nonstandard English *the child that I asked his parents to come see me*.)

Additional vistas open up for relativized NPs of time, manner, and place. With these one can adopt the usual relative pronouns or switch to adverbial interrogatives (minus their accents in Spanish):

We bought the house [Bolívar had slept *in the house*] →

We bought the house $\begin{cases} [\textit{where}/\text{in which Bolívar had slept}] \\ [\text{that/which/∅ Bolívar had slept in}] \end{cases}$

Compramos la casa [Bolívar había dormido *en la casa*] →
    Compramos la casa [*donde*/en la que había dormido Bolívar]

13.3.2 Relative clauses without antecedents ('headless'). Some relative clauses lack an overt noun antecedent. A Spanish example is [*Quien no trabaja*] *no come*, in which *quien no trabaja* is a 'headless' relative.[9] An alternative to *quien* here is *el que*, which was described earlier as a nominalization (v. 8.4.1), as in the following case:

¿Ves a aquellos dos hombres? Pues, *el que* (=el hombre que) se ha licenciado está a la derecha.

But this analysis is less appropriate for *El que no trabaja no come* when uttered with no previous mention of any masculine noun; *hombre* is not necessarily the antecedent the speaker has in mind, if any noun is. It is therefore possible to enumerate four distinct *el que* in Spanish: (1) the *el que* resulting from nominalization, (2) the *el que* for *quien* in headless relatives, (3) the *el que* allomorph of the relative *que* after Prep (as observed by Ozete), and (4) the *el que* serving as a noun clause complementizer (v. 13.1.1).

In English, *he who* has been prescribed in traditional grammar for headless relatives—*He who doesn't work doesn't eat*—but current usage favors *those who, anyone that, whoever* (but for true nominalizations, *the one who/that* is usual).

13.3.3 Nonrestrictive relative clauses. Relative clauses commonly restrict the reference of their antecedent. In *The brown shoes which are dirty are Veronica's*, the speaker selects from an understood set of brown shoes just those that were dirty and asserts that those, and only those, belong to Veronica. Contrast this with the following sentence, where commas indicate a slight pause and a broken off, interrupted intonation (v. 4.2): *The brown shoes, which are dirty, are Veronica's*. Here the speaker implies that all of the brown shoes under consideration are dirty; rather than restricting reference to a subset of the whole, the relative clause merely makes a parenthetical observation, 'all the brown shoes are Veronica's (and they happen to be dirty)'.

This contrast between restrictive and nonrestrictive resembles that between preposed and postposed adjectives in Spanish, as in *los zapatos sucios* vs. *los sucios zapatos*. Cressey 1969 noted this and proposed that it be emphasized more in pedagogy (v. 11.3.2). *Los zapatos marrones que están sucios son de Verónica* thus implies 'los zapatos marrones sucios', whereas nonrestrictive *Los zapatos marrones, que están sucios, son de Verónica* implies 'los sucios zapatos marrones'.

In English, the nonrestrictive relative pronouns are *who(m), which, whose*, but never *that* or ∅: **The brown shoes, that are dirty, are Veronica's*, **The brown shoes, you messed up, are Veronica's*. In Spanish, there is again a difference between prescribed and actual usage; whereas some recommend *quien, cuyo, el que*, and above all *el cual*, many educated speakers use *que* too: *La mujer alta, quien/la cual/la que/que acaba de recibirse, se va mañana*. Ozete (1981) has chronicled the use of all of these in periodicals, and has again noted the predominance of *el que* after Prep: *La mujer alta, de la que hablamos ayer, se va mañana*.

13.3.4 Reduced relative clauses: Infinitives and participles. English noun clauses can take the COMPs *that* and *for . . . to . . .*: *It bothers Henry [that John smokes cigars], It bothers Henry [for John to smoke cigars]*. Interestingly, relatives can be clausal or infinitival as well: *Jane has a lot of work [that Paul should do], Jane has a lot of work [for Paul to do]*. Moreover, the Subj element *for* NP drops from relative clauses under the same conditions as from noun clauses:

Equi-NP: Jane has a lot of work [*for Jane* to do] → Jane has a lot of work [to do]

Impersonal X: There's a lot of work [*for X* to do] → There's a lot of work [to do]

The connection between (*for* NP) *to* VP after a noun and full relative clauses is clinched by the occasional appearance of relative pronouns in the former structure (Quirk et al. 1972:879):

Chez Nous is a good place $\begin{cases} \text{[to eat (at)]} \\ \text{[at } which \text{ to eat]} \end{cases}$

Spanish also has an infinitival relative, and it always begins with a relative pronoun or relative adverb;

> Juana tiene mucho trabajo [*que* hacer]
> Chez Nous es un buen lugar [*donde* comer]

But it is used only for Equi-NP and Impersonal X. For the equivalent of *Jane has a lot of work for Paul to do,* Spanish retains a full relative clause, as it does with most noun clauses that lack Equi-NP:

> *Juana tiene mucho trabajo [que Pablo hacer, que hacer Pablo]
> Juana tiene mucho trabajo [que deberá hacer Pablo]

Infinitival relatives in both languages convey a special sense of obligation, advisability, or suitability, suggesting that something should or may or can be carried out in (on, with) the antecedent. Consequently, many grammarians and linguists (e.g. Bello 1847/1958:339, Ramsey 1894/1956:353, Drake et al. 1982, Klein 1984) see *que* VP-inf. after a noun as the reduced version of a relative clause containing *poder* or *deber*. (Compare the similar thrust of 'obligation' in reduced indirect questions, v. 13.1.3) Where the two languages differ is in constraints on usage.[10] First, as noted above, Spanish uses its infinitival relative only with Equi-NP or for Impersonal X; a distinct Subj NP equivalent to Eng. *for* NP cannot be expressed. Second, the antecedent in Spanish must be interpretable as DO, IO, or OP of the infinitive; unlike English, which also allows a Subj interpretation, Spanish otherwise requires a full clause. In fact, the English construction can be ambiguous between Subj and Obj functions, and even between adjective and noun clause functions; *You need someone to teach,* for example, can be (1) a reduced relative with the antecedent as Subj ('te hace falta alguien que pueda enseñar'), (2) a reduced relative whose antecedent is the Obj ('te hace falta alguien a quien (le) enseñes'), or (3) a reduced noun clause ('te hace falta que alguien enseñe'). The Spanish constructions, being more restricted, are generally clearer. These differences are summarized in Figure 13.11.

Another difference is that in Spanish, *para* can replace *que*: *Juana tiene mucho trabajo que hacer, Juana tiene mucho trabajo para hacer.* Drake et

Figure 13.11 Infinitival relatives.

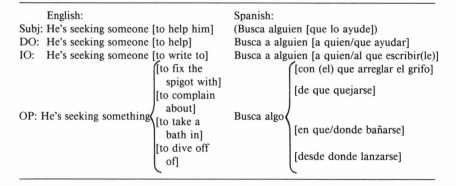

English:	Spanish:
Subj: He's seeking someone [to help him]	(Busca alguien [que lo ayude])
DO: He's seeking someone [to help]	Busca a alguien [a quien/que ayudar]
IO: He's seeking someone [to write to]	Busca a alguien [a quien/al que escribir(le)]
OP: He's seeking something { [to fix the spigot with] [to complain about] [to take a bath in] [to dive off of]	Busca algo { [con (el) que arreglar el grifo] [de que quejarse] [en que/donde bañarse] [desde donde lanzarse]

al. 1982 noted this equivalence, as well as the occurrence of other Preps conveying different shades of meaning:

En esta tienda
hay muchos libros

para vender	('availability for sale')
por vender	('remaining to be sold')
sin vender	(nonperformance, i.e. 'unsold')
a vender	('regularly sold')

They also observe that NP *a* VP-inf, disdained in some quarters as a Gallicism, has caught hold in Spanish and is spreading rapidly, sometimes displacing *para* or *que* (Drake et al. 1982:82): *un ejemplo a imitar, libros a consultar, mensualidades a abonar, métodos a seguir.*[11]

Although we have so far used 'reduction' for the infinitival relative just illustrated, the term RELATIVE REDUCTION has been applied more broadly in transformational grammar to any process that shrinks a full clause down to briefer modifiers of the head noun. Relative reduction in this sense can be described generally as follows (Hadlich 1971:142):

D N [rel. pron. copula R] → D N [R]

i.e. the relative pronoun and copula drop, leaving the remainder of the clause ('R') as a direct modifier of the noun. We have already seen how this treatment accounts for participial phrases in the NP (v. 12.3):

las papas [*que fueron* fritas por Mamá] → las papas fritas por Mamá

and for certain appositives as well (v. 11.1.3):

mi gran amigo, [*quien es* Pedro,] → mi gran amigo Pedro

But some linguists[12] also derive the Adj and PP of a NP from reduced relatives:

la actriz [*que es* $\begin{Bmatrix} \text{más popular} \\ \text{de Sevilla} \end{Bmatrix}$] → la actriz $\begin{Bmatrix} \text{más popular} \\ \text{de Sevilla} \end{Bmatrix}$

Our survey of relative clauses in this section warrants at least three observations on their usual pedagogical treatment. First, the typical presentation focuses very narrowly on pronoun and mood selection in full clauses; other aspects of formation and usage (especially reduction) tend to be ignored. Second, the rules laid down for even these restricted areas do not reflect current usage. Third, instead of encouraging students to form relative clauses actively, most texts overemphasize the purely passive procedure of filling in the blanks: *el hombre _____ vi es el director.* The result is often a student who can insert relative pronouns into someone else's sentences but who hesitates to adopt relative clauses (full or reduced) in his own speech. The text's rules, accurate or not, are soon forgotten because relative clause formation does not become a part of the student's own communicative repertoire.

13.4 Comparative sentences. There is little agreement on the underlying structure of comparative sentences, or even on a definition of what kinds of structures are comparatives. In general, though, all comparatives establish a comparison between the degree or amount of one thing and that of another, the latter being syntactically subordinated to the former by a special set of morphemes.

13.4.1 Patterns and forms. It is customary to distinguish three major kinds of comparison, namely, EQUALITY (*as . . . as . . .*), SUPERIORITY (*more than*), and INFERIORITY (*less than*), though the last two are often conflated as INEQUALITY because of the similarity of their formation.

Equality: Juan está *tan* nervioso *como* Pilar.
          John's *as* nervous *as* Pilar.

Inequality
Superiority: Juan está *más* nervioso *que* Pilar.
          John's *more* nervous *than* Pilar.
Inferiority: Juan está *menos* nervioso *que* Pilar.
          John's *less* nervous *than* Pilar.

At least in these examples, Spanish and English agree nicely; the only problem for the student is that *as* is *tan* in one place, *como* in another. With one exception, *tan* can precede any Adj or Adv: *tan rápido, tan alto, tan ridículo, tan silenciosamente*. That exception is *mucho(s)*, for in this case the expected **tan mucho(s)* becomes *tanto(s)*. In terms of morphology, *tan* is often presented as an apocopation (shortening) of *tanto*, but in terms of the inner structure of Spanish, it is *tan* which is the basic morpheme for comparisons of equality, and in just one case this intensifier (v. 10.2.3) contracts or fuses with its Adj or Adv. That is, *tanto* does not just mean 'tan mucho', but acts and patterns as if it were underlyingly *tan mucho*.

The morphemes signaling inequality require some attention. As has often been pointed out before in this book, much of our grammatical terminology comes from classical grammar. Latin, for instance, had three degrees of comparison that were named POSITIVE, COMPARATIVE, and SUPERLATIVE. Standard English distinguishes the same three, so the inherited terminology is appropriate for its system:

Positive: Comparative: (for two) Superlative: (for three or more)
beautiful more/less beautiful   most/least beautiful

The same distinction came to be applied to Spanish; after all, Spanish descended from Latin and presumably has all three. The comparative is obvious: one places *más/menos* before the adjective or adverb, giving *más/menos bonito*. But *más/menos* are also 'most/least'; where, then, is the superlative?

Some look to etymology and give as the superlative the *-ísimo* form, since it comes from the Latin superlative suffix *-issimus*. Yet *-ísimo* no longer implies comparison, but just intensifies the modifier like *muy* and *re(quete)-*; it corresponds to English *very, real(ly), extremely* and not to the usual sense of *most*. Other grammarians have decided that Spanish adds the definite article to *más/menos* to distinguish its superlatives from its comparatives: *bonito, más bonito, el más bonito*. This is a misanalysis, for the definite article occurs in *el más bonito* simply to convey definiteness or uniqueness, and it can just as well accompany the comparative:

Pilar es *la más bonita* { de las dos. / de las tres. }   Pilar is *the* { more beautiful of the two. / most beautiful of the three. }

In short, there is no comparative/superlative distinction at all in modern Spanish, and the class time often spent on this artifice ought to be devoted to weightier matters.

In addition to using comparative intensifiers (*more, most, less, least, más, menos*) with the Adj or Adv, both languages have inherited some inflected comparatives, ending in *-er/-est* in English and *-r/-s* in Spanish:

young, younger, youngest	(joven), menor
old, older, oldest	(viejo), mayor
good/well, better, best	bueno/bien, mejor
bad, worse, worst	mal(o), peor
much, more, most	mucho, más
little, less, least	poco, menos

This type is very limited in Spanish, and unpredictable to boot; one must memorize that the comparative of *bueno* can be either *más bueno* or *mejor* (RAE 1979:418), but not **buenor*. *Mayor* and *menor* actually lack a positive, for they sometimes (not always) replace *más viejo* and *más joven* and other times signal relative importance, seriousness, rank, or size (rather like Eng. *greater* and *lesser*). The fact that one can say *niños de 10 años y niños más mayores* suggests that *mayor* and *menor* are not true comparatives in themselves. The *-er/-est* forms of English, on the other hand, are freely applied to one- and two-syllable adjectives: *taller* and *prettier* are normal, *politer* alternates with *more polite*, and *beautifuler* is replaced by *more beautiful*.

We will note in passing certain other patterns that are sometimes called comparatives, since they are built up with similar elements:

No se aceptará el texto *tal como* está.   The text *as it is* won't be accepted.

El tocadiscos está descompuesto *así como creías*.	The record-player is broken *just as you thought*.
Juan está *tan nervioso que le* tiemblan las manos.	John is *so nervous that his* hands are trembling.
Ese edificio fue diseñado por *el mismo arquitecto que el de al* lado.	That building was designed by *the same architect as the* one next door.
Estos electrodomésticos son *iguales que esos*.	These appliances are *the same as those*.
(Cuanto) más te esfuerzas, *(tanto) menos consigues hacer.*	*The more you try, the less* you manage to do.
Es *demasiado joven como para* ayudar.	He's *too young to help*.

Despite their rather high frequency, these constructions have attracted less interest than the analysis of the traditionally recognized ones, which are sketched in 13.4.2.

13.4.2 The structure of comparative sentences. At first glance, comparatives such as *Yo tengo más hijos que tú* and *Ella es tan alta como una casa* seem simple, not complex. Yet they imply a comparison between two propositions, the second embedded in the first: *Yo tengo hijos + tú tienes hijos, ella es alta + una casa es alta*. In fact, full-clause alternatives are grammatical, if a bit unwieldy: *Yo tengo más hijos que tú tienes (hijos)*, *Ella es tan alta como es (alta) una casa*. Hence, comparatives have been treated as reductions of fuller complex sentences by some grammarians, traditional (RAE 1979:545) as well as transformational (Hadlich 1971:177). The latter have posited transformations that prune out of the subordinated comparative clause those constituents that are identical (aside from agreement) to their counterparts in the main clause, as shown here:

Yo *tengo* más *hijos* [que tú *tienes hijos*] → Yo tengo más hijos [que

tú _____ _____]

Teachers might well wonder whether such a treatment has any practical application in pedagogy. It does have at least one merit, namely in explaining the pronoun form that follows the *que* or *como*:

Ella tiene $\begin{Bmatrix} más \\ tantos \end{Bmatrix}$ hijos $\begin{Bmatrix} que \\ como \end{Bmatrix}$ *yo* tengo hijos. →

... $\begin{Bmatrix} que \\ como \end{Bmatrix}$ *yo* (Subj)

Ella te ama a ti $\begin{Bmatrix} más que \\ tanto como \end{Bmatrix}$ *me* ama a mí. →

... $\begin{Bmatrix} que \\ como \end{Bmatrix}$ *a mí* (Obj).

English speakers commonly neutralize this distinction; despite their English teachers' threats and entreaties, they use Obj forms once the comparative clause is reduced:

She has $\begin{Bmatrix} \text{more} \\ \text{as many} \end{Bmatrix}$ children $\begin{Bmatrix} \text{than} \\ \text{as} \end{Bmatrix}$ *I* have (children). →

... $\begin{Bmatrix} \text{than} \\ \text{as} \end{Bmatrix}$ *me.*

She loves you $\begin{Bmatrix} \text{more than} \\ \text{as much as} \end{Bmatrix}$ she loves *me.* →

... $\begin{Bmatrix} \text{than} \\ \text{as} \end{Bmatrix}$ *me.*

The merger of *I* with *me* occurs elsewhere too (*me too*, v. 12.2), and it can cause problems when the forms must be distinguished, as in Spanish.

Not all comparative sentences can be analyzed as combinations of two clauses. Sometimes *more than* and *less than* establish a direct relationship between two quantities instead of two propositions (Quirk et al. 1972:767). Such is the case with *I have more than five children*, which is usually not construed as 'I have more (toys, clothes) than five children have'. Here, *more than five* simply verbalizes the quantity that mathematicians symbolize by '>5', i.e., 'six or more'. Spanish distinguishes two cases in this regard, *más de* when *more than* means '>', and a negated *más que* to signify '=' (i.e. neither *more than* '≯', nor *less than* '≮', but *exactly, only, merely, just*):

Tengo *más de* cinco hijos.   I have more than five children.
No tengo *más que* cinco hijos.   I only have five children, I don't have
  but five.

The two can contrast (Ramsey 1894/1956:143): *No necesito más que dos* is 'I only need two, exactly two' while *No necesito más de dos* is 'I need ≯ 2, i.e. ≤2, two or fewer, two at the most'.

There is a third comparative construction, illustrated in the next example, that is more complicated. Note that unlike the first kind of comparative we examined, as in *Yo tengo más hijos que tú (tienes hijos)*, this one has clauses containing different verbs:

Siempre *compras* más alimentos de los que *necesitas.*
You always *buy* more food than you *need.*

The Spanish version, with its *más de*, strongly suggests a connection with the *Tengo más de cinco hijos* type. This connection stands out even more clearly in the fuller versions:

Siempre compras más alimentos de *los alimentos* [*que necesitas*]
You always buy more food than *the food* [*that you need*]

The italicized constituents following the comparative connector (*de*, *than*) are not comparative clauses at all, but NPs containing a relative clause. For both languages, the general pattern is as follows:

There is a quantity of *x* such that the quantity >
the quantity of *x* [that NP VP]

In pruning down this elaborate logical schema, English deletes the second *x* (*the food*) and the relative pronoun (*that*): *more food than the food that you need → more food than you need*. (Alternatively, it converts both to *what*, as in *more food than what you need*.) Spanish deletes the second *x* (*los alimentos*) but retains the rest intact as a nominalization; and since this pattern emphasizes the mathematical '>' relation, *más de* is used instead of *más que*: *más alimentos de los alimentos que necesitas → más alimentos de los _____ que necesitas.*[13]

In both languages, this same construction can handle extent or degree instead of quantity. In that case, *x* in the formula represents no real noun at all, and Spanish uses its neuter as in other cases when there is no noun (v. 8.4.2): *Es más cómico de lo que piensas.* English, however, keeps the same patterns: *He's funnier than you think, He's funnier than what you think.*

13.5 Complex sentences: General summary. This chapter has surveyed an area of syntax that has attracted much recent linguistic attention: complex sentences and the processes operating in them. Many problems remain in their description, but we have penetrated the subject enough to show the major hurdles that students of Spanish encounter when they progress beyond short simple sentences and try to use one clause (or clausal fragment) inside another as they do in their English.

Subordinated clauses act like nouns, adjectives, and adverbials in their matrix sentences or as complements to comparatives and other constituents. Their deep structures in the two languages are quite similar, and if all embedded propositions were uttered in their full clausal forms, as in the tree structures given in Figure 13.1 at the beginning of this chapter, then interlingual mastery of complex sentences might be a relatively simple affair. But some economy and flexibility are gained when repeated elements are dropped and when tense/mood information is dispensed with, and the grammar of each language stipulates how clauses may be whittled down to abbreviated fragments and how processes such as Clitic Movement, *Tough*-Movement, and Extraposition may rearrange surface configurations. These stipulations differ interlingually, and may depend on particular verbs and relators. Thus, it will not be obvious to students why a certain lineup in one language allows (or requires) infinitivization of the verb and the deletion of a NP, why an analogous line-up does not, why two superficially identical reductions mean quite different things, or why a change necessitates a grammatical morpheme (*que, para, a, de, that, to, for, of*) in one language but not the other. What we have broadly termed 'reduction' makes communication easier and more flexible for native speakers of a language, but unfortunately at a rather high price for foreign language students.

Notes for Chapter 13

1. As established by works such as Chomsky 1965 and Jacobs and Rosenbaum 1968, the dominant theory of clauses, infinitives, and gerunds has been that a surface structure such as *Tom wants to do it* comes from something like *Tom wants [Tom do it]* via transformations that 're-duce' the noun clause by infinitivizing the verb and dropping its Subj. One advantage of this analysis is that it explicitly accounts for why *to do it*, which has no overt Subj of its own, is understood as having *Tom* as its Subj, not the speaker, the addressee, Miriam, or whatever. The superficially similar *Tom says [to do it]* is different, for someone else is understood as Subj of *do it* in this case, and it would be derived from a different deep structure. Moreover, in Spanish it is hard to avoid treating infinitives as a kind of reduced clause: one says *Tomás quiere [que Laura lo haga]*, but instead of *Tomás quiere [que Tomás lo haga]* one says *Tomás quiere hacerlo*. Traditional grammarians also saw such infinitives as clausal reductions, specifically as 'elipsis' (Bello 1847/1958:339) or 'oraciones incorporadas' (RAE 1971:487), and transformationalists followed suit (Hadlich 1971, Contreras 1979, Pilleux y Urrutia 1982).

Yet the machinery of clause-to-infinitive reduction transformations is not as well oiled as it ought to be, and alert readers will note later in this chapter several apparent 'mysteries' in why reduction sometimes applies and sometimes does not. Consequently, some recent transformationalist proposals (e.g. Chomsky 1981, 1982) treat infinitives as underived. The deep structure of *Tom wants to do it* would be simply *Tom wants [PRO to do it]*: the brackets enclose a clause with no tense or mood, and its Subj PRO is a kind of silent pronoun (or ANAPHOR) whose reference depends on which element in the main clause is defined as 'controlling' it.

In this book we will retain the earlier approach because, despite its manifest problems, it is better elaborated, corresponds to traditional approaches, and underlies many pedagogical treatments. However, in keeping with the applied nature of this book, we must pass over many details and mop-up operations a fuller analysis would require, leaving the term 'reduction' very ill defined. Readers with a theoretical orientation might interpret 'reduction' as shorthand for any nonfinite complement structurally less than a full clause, and reanalyze the data in line with current proposals.

2. As indicated in the preceding note, subjectless infinitives and gerunds are currently analyzed as having the Subj 'PRO'. In the Equi-NP interpretation, PRO is controlled by another NP; in the Impersonal X in-

terpretation, it is uncontrolled and therefore unspecified as to reference.

3. *El* + VP-inf + Subj NP is uncommon in the spoken language as a subject noun clause, and some of my informants felt it to be awkward or even ungrammatical. But it does appear in the literary language (Ramsey 1894/1956: 345, Gili Gaya 1973:189).

4. Oddly, though, the passive version of *say* NP *to* VP does indicate an assertion (*Mary is said to be careful*).

5. Usage is unsettled on pronominalization with causatives and verbs of observation. Bello (1847/1958:338) insisted that *hacer* and *ver* + VP-inf act like 'simples verbos' that take IO and DO like one-word verbs; but then he waffled and decided that the DO of *hacer* and *ver* is the infinitive, so that any NP Obj must be IO, not DO. I submitted the matter to a group of native speakers from various countries and the ensuing debate was fiery, even among *loístas* from the same dialect area. There was agreement that the sentences I have starred are ungrammatical, but little on other matters. More research is needed on this usage.

6. But perhaps V + PP should be analyzed differently when the PP is a verb-stipulated complement (as with *oponerse a*) rather than a freely added adverbial. (This difference was provided for in the PSRs, v. 11.1.2.2). The following pair of sentences shows an interesting contrast between the two cases:

Me intereso por que el país progrese más.	'I'm interested in the country progressing more'
Me intereso porque el país progresa más.	'I'm interested because the country is progressing more'

7. What actually seems to be happening in English here is a reduction of conjunction + *be* + gerund/participle, for the nonfinite forms are possible only when *be* could occur: *if (you are) passing this way, when (they are) finished*; note the ungrammaticality of **Do it when eaten* for *Do it when you have eaten.*

8. The case of nonhuman animates—i.e. animals—is unsettled in both languages. Usually, animals are handled as things (*the dog which has its head stuck in the fence*) except when they have a personal identity to the speaker (*the dog who has her head stuck in the fence*).

9. Suñer (1982:43) favors the term 'headless relatives' for such constructions, but perhaps an apter term is that of Quirk et al. (1972:737), 'nominal relative clause,' because it emphasizes that such clauses serve as noun clauses but consist of a mere relative clause.

10. My observations here are based on the judgments of available native speakers; standard grammars seldom discuss these constructions.

11. The Drake et al. (1982) study is recommended as one of the few to have tackled infinitival relatives, but readers should be wary in using it since the authors were not always sensitive to constituency. For example,

the following examples of theirs validly show the relative-like use of Prep. + VP-inf after an antecedent; note that the antecedent is interpreted as the Obj of the infinitive, just as with *que* + VP-inf:

Quiero pizza para llevar. (=pienso llevar la pizza (DO))
El niño tiene pan para comer. (=podrá comer el pan (DO))
Hay temas a escoger. (=uno puede escoger los temas (DO))

Yet the authors also mix in with these several constructions having very different syntactic relationships:

No tiene el interés para doctorarse. (≠*Se doctorará el interés)
Tiene una tendencia a exagerar. (≠ Exagera la tendencia)

—and even some cases in which the NP and PP have nothing at all to do with each other except as fortuitously juxtaposed constituents:

Cantaban chistes (DO) para pasar el rato (Advl)
Salió el sol (Subj) para ocultarse en seguida (Advl)

12. For English, see Jacobs and Rosenbaum (1968:204ff.); for Spanish, see Pilleux y Urrutia (1982:54, 99).

13. Nevertheless, as Ramsey (1894/1956:142) noted, 'in colloquial practice *que* alone is used', and this yields a construction much closer to the English one than the *más del que* prescribed for the standard language.

Exercises for Chapter 13

1. Error Analysis:
   (1) *Estudias más que me.
   (2) *Tan músico, Casals tenía talento.
   (3) *Después de viajando me siento cansado.
   (4) *Escribiendo es difícil.
   (5) *Necesito Luis hacerlo.
   (6) *Teresa dijo te estudiar.
   (7) *El tema que hablaste sobre me interesó.
   (8) *La asignatura preferimos es la historia.
   (9) *Queda una cosa para Hernán a hacer.
   (10) *La chica quien vino es mi sobrina.

2. Following is a list of paired sentences that are related to one another syntactically. On the basis of the analysis of embedded clauses and infinitives presented in this chapter, identify which of the listed transformational processes account(s) for the relationship in each pair.

Clause Reduction	Raising (of embedded Subj to matrix Obj)
Clitic Promotion	Relativization
Extraposition	*Tough*-Movement

   (1) Es imposible ver Neptuno sin telescopio.
       Neptuno es imposible de ver sin telescopio.
   (2) Nos mandaron que los siguiéramos.
       Nos mandaron seguirlos.
   (3) Afirman que no pueden resolver la crisis.

Afirman no poder resolver la crisis.
(4) Que tengas la culpa es probable.
Es probable que tengas la culpa.
(5) Intentan ayudarme.
Me intentan ayudar.
(6) Juan es el hombre, yo conozco bien al hombre.
Juan es el hombre que yo conozco bien.
(7) Hizo que todos obedecieran.
Les hizo obedecer a todos.

3. Identify whether each embedded clause in the following is (1) a noun clause, (2) an adjective/relative clause, or (3) an adverbial clause introduced by a true conjunction. If it is a noun clause, indicate its function (Subj, DO, or OP), and whether it has been moved (extraposed).
(1) Es lógico que el general haya mentido.
(2) Me preguntó si cabrían otras dos sillas.
(3) Te lo preguntaré si no nos avisa Tomás.
(4) Te lo preguntaré después de que Pilar nos deje.
(5) Quieren que nos esforcemos más.
(6) Los médicos con los que nos reunimos ayer van a cambiar de idea.
(7) No llevaba paraguas cuando empezó a llover.
(8) El que ese tipo se enamore de ti no debe influir en tu decisión.

4. Under the assumption that clausal fragments and infinitivized VPs originate as full clauses, describe the underlying syntax of the italicized constituents in the following sentences. (You may use a rough paraphrase or may draw phrase markers.)
(1) Luisa quiere *cambiar su dinero.*
(2) Manuel dice *tener razón.*
(3) No puede encontrar una herramienta *con la que aflojar la tuerca.*
(4) Les prohibimos *salir del teatro.*
(5) Encendió la luz *para ver mejor.*
(6) Juana escribió más poemas *que tú.*
(7) No sé *si obedecerle o no.*
(8) Los edificios *construidos por el gobierno* se desplomaron en seguida.
(9) Aquel barrio es un buen lugar *donde criar a los niños.*
(10) *Este modelo de carro* es muy fácil *de manejar.*

5. The following English sentences are ambiguous; how does Spanish distinguish the senses?
(1) She has more than three students.
(2) Visiting relatives can be boring.
(3) We need someone to help.

6. Why is Spanish grammar usually assigned a superlative category? What evidence suggests that it lacks one?

7. In section 13.1.2, we noted that some Spanish verbs can have full clauses as objects, and that these clauses may or may not, must or must

not, reduce. Study the behavior of each of the following and contrast it with that of its English equivalent, as was done for *creer* vs. *believe*, *mandar* vs. *order*, etc.

afirmar	exigir	enseñar a	conseguir
odiar	lamentar	aconsejar	causar
dar por sentado	recordar	evitar	alegrarse de
esperar	temer	esforzarse por	prohibir
gritar	animar a	acostumbrarse a	consentir en

8. Also in 13.1.2 we saw that *poder* + V and *querer* + V are structurally different in that the former's infinitive is not derived from a noun clause. Each of the following can also appear with an infinitive; decide whether it is like *poder* or like *querer*.

volver a	lograr	dejar de	decidir	prometer
tender a	comenzar a	necesitar	confiar en	saber
acabar de	pensar	deber	soler	anhelar a

9. Combine the following sentence pairs according to the model, thereby producing indirect questions in (i) and nominalized relative clauses in (ii). (Alternatively, submit this exercise to native speakers and elicit their responses.)

    (i) *Model:* Se les preguntó eso. [¿Cuándo iban a volver?] → Se les preguntó cuándo iban a volver.

  (1) Quiero saber eso. [¿Por qué trabajas tanto?]
  (2) Me pregunto eso. [¿Cada cuánto se baña?]
  (3) Me pregunto eso. [¿En qué insistirán?]
  (4) Pienso en eso. [¿En qué insistirán?]
  (5) Pienso en eso. [¿De dónde provinieron?]
  (6) Se trata de eso. [¿De qué se compone esa aleación?]
  (7) Pienso en eso. [¿De qué se compone esa aleación?]
  (8) Fíjate en eso. [¿Por cuáles asuntos disputamos?]

  (ii) *Model:* Me ayudó él. [Él conducía una camioneta.] → Me ayudó el que conducía una camioneta.

  (9) Se presentó él. [Él había servido de testigo.]
 (10) Fíjate en ella. [Ella viste tejanos amarillos.]
 (11) Se presentó él. [Confías tanto en él.]
 (12) Depende de ella. [Te casas con ella.]
 (13) Me refiero a ellos. [Confías tanto en ellos.]
 (14) No hay que contar con ellos. [Trabajamos para ellos.]
 (15) Se parece mucho a él. [Tropezaste con él.]

What happens when there is a clash or stacking up of prepositions governing the clause and prepositions inside, and moved to the front of, the clause? In other words, how does Spanish handle (as in (12)) 'it depends on the one you're getting married to'?

10. In addition to occurring as Subj, DO, and OP (i.e. after a relator) in a main clause, noun clauses may occur in the PredE slot, in which case Pilleux y Urrutia 1982 calls them 'atributos'. For example, *El problema es*

[*que los votantes lo rechazarán*] and *Mi anhelo era* [*que todos dejaran de contaminar el ambiente*]. Find or create more examples of PredE noun clauses, and examine (1) their mood and (2) their possibilities for reduction to infinitives. Do they operate like other noun clauses in these respects?

11. Review Clitic Promotion (v. 13.1.2.8). Then determine whether each italicized clitic can be moved to the left of the conjugated verb. Do any restrictions appear?

(1) Tienen que hacer*lo*.
(2) Hay que hacer*lo*.
(3) ¿Tu espejo? Sí, lo vi romper*se*.
(4) Espero poder hacer*lo*.
(5) Renuncian a hacer*lo*.
(6) Muero por hacer*lo*.
(7) Le hice leer*lo*.
(8) Lo/le hice suicidar*se*.
(9) La vi matar*lo*.
(10) La oyeron mencionar*me*.
(11) Me oyeron mencionar*la*.
(12) Deseo volver a ver*lo*.
(13) Creo poder hacer*lo*.
(14) Quisiera no ver*lo* jamás.
(15) Ella me parece saber*lo*.
(16) Te hice pegar*lo*. ('I made you glue it')
(17) Te hice pegar*le*. ('I made you hit him')
(18) Insisto en mandarte hacer*lo*.

12. In what respects are the following like the causative construction? (1) *No se dejó persuadir*. (2) *Mandó subir el paquete*.

13. Prepare a lesson on how you would teach students to discriminate in Spanish among the following messages in English.

(1) I had her (to) steal a book.
(2) I had her book stolen.
(3) I had stolen her book.
(4) I had her book to steal.
(5) I had her stolen book.
(6) I had to steal her book.

14. One matter not discussed in the section on comparatives is the behavior of indefinites in them. Study the following pairs of sentences and state how English and Spanish differ.

(1) It matters more to me than to anybody.
   Me importa a mí más que a nadie.
(2) She seems to practice more than anyone.
   Parece practicar más que nadie.
(3) He knows more than any expert.
   Sabe más que ningún experto.
(4) They dug in more than ever.
   Se empeñaron más que nunca.

Does the Spanish negative in these have anything to do with the negative in the following?

(5) Antes que resuelvas nada, consúltalo con la almohada.

15. Review (v. 13.3.4) the discussion of 'relative reduction' that yields a noun modifier 'R' from a relative clause containing a copula. Take several English and Spanish pairs that conform to 'rel. pron. + copula + R', e.g. *the key that was lost*, *la llave que fue perdida*; then reduce the rela-

tives, and state where and how the two languages sometimes part company on forming modifiers in this way (e.g. *la llave perdida*, but in English *the key lost → the lost key*).

16. Many of the phenomena mentioned in this chapter are not often discussed in pedagogy. 'Grammar' amounts to morphology (e.g. verb endings), 'usage' (e.g. relative pronoun distinctions), parts of speech (e.g. prepositions vs. conjunctions), and occasional remarks on word order (e.g. adjective position). Although students may be given a list of 'usos del infinitivo', the great differences between English and Spanish infinitival constructions and their relationships to clauses are seldom explained in detail, even though interference in this area appears early and abundantly. In this respect, Klein 1984 is especially critical of pedagogical grammars; he notes that texts continue to treat *para, a, que*, and so on as lexical matters (*para = for, a = to* . . . , like *árbol = tree*) instead of markers of clauses and their reductions.

The following sentences illustrate the problem. For each, indicate the proper Spanish equivalent(s) and the probable errors students will make if they translate literally. Show, too, something of the deep structures of the sentences.

(1) *For Mark, to lie* would be incredible.
For Mark to lie would be incredible.
It would be incredible *for Mark to lie.*
It would be hard *for Mark to lie.*

(2) I see a tendency in Mark *to lie.*
I promise *Mark to lie.*
I want *Mark to lie.*
I prefer *for Mark to lie.*
I prefer *to lie for Mark.*

(3) It is hard *to read* ('reading is hard')
It is hard *to read* ('that thing is hard to read')
The library is a good place *to read/for reading.*

(4) Mariluz has a strong desire *to help her friends.*
Mariluz came *to help her friends.*
Mariluz came *for her friends to help her.*
Mariluz is believed *to help her friends.*
Mariluz is addicted *to helping her friends.*
Mariluz is the friend *to help.*

(5) It's necessary *to install more lights.* ('installing more lights is necessary')
It's necessary *to install more lights.* ('this thing is necessary for the installation of more lights')

The crux of the problem is that Spanish treats reduced clauses differently from English but students do not see any embedded clauses—full or reduced—in such sentences. Few would advocate that students first be introduced to transformational grammar and its tree diagrams, PSRs, and transformations to perceive the underlying structures that result in different surface structures; what, then, is a practical pedagogical strategy? Should students INDUCE the grammar of embedded clauses and their fragments by absorbing it through trial and error, or is there some more direct approach that teachers and texts could adopt that would facilitate syntactic discussion without turning a Spanish course into a linguistics course? What, as teacher, would you do?

Part Three: Beyond grammar

Chapter 14
Introduction to the study of words and usage

14.0 What it means to know a word. In addition to the phonology and grammar of their language, native speakers know its vocabulary or LEXICON. They learn and store each word as an item subject to the rules and categories of their language, and each LEXICAL ENTRY contains all the information needed for using the word appropriately and accurately. For many readers, 'lexical entry' will suggest what is recorded in a dictionary: syntactic category and subcategory (e.g. 'transitive verb'), morphological quirks, pronunciation, and meaning(s). But the contents of a native speaker's lexical entry are much richer than dictionaries can portray, inasmuch as meaning and usage tie in with the wealth of experiences that people have had, individually and collectively, in using language in sociocultural contexts and in a universe whose properties are apprehended in certain ways by human beings.

14.1 An example: The meaning of *compadre*. The depths of knowledge that must be ascribed to lexical entries can be illustrated by Spanish *compadre*. García-Pelayo y Gross (1983) gives it a definition that reads in part as follows:

> COMPADRE m. Padrino del niño respecto de los padres y la madrina de éste. (SINÓN. V. *Padrino*). || *Fam.* Amigo o conocido.

This definition is accurate and precise, but it presupposes much more information than it states. It relies crucially on the knowledge of what *padrino*, *niño*, *padres*, and *madrina* mean, and interpreting it requires complex linguistic skills and cognitive abilities, three of which are described here.

314 / 14 Introduction to the study of words and usage

(1) *Padre* has several senses in Spanish (duly listed under PADRE by this dictionary writer), but it is rightly assumed that the reader will scan the context of *los padres* and select the meaning 'parents', not 'priests', 'ancestors', nor even 'fathers'. It is also assumed that the reader has sufficient biological and cultural knowledge to infer the connection between *padres* and *niño*.

(2) Definite articles—*el niño, los padres, la madrina*—suggest that reference is already established and uniquely defined; it is indeed uniquely defined, but by the background situation, not by the dictionary writer.

(3) *Respecto de* implies a 'vis-à-vis' relationship between *padrino* and *padres*, and between *padrino* and *madrina*. This relationship will be taken for granted by readers from a Hispanic culture, but it is not obvious in the definition itself.

To proceed further in our semantic analysis, we must pick up the reference 'véase Padrino'. García-Pelayo y Gross defines *padrino* in turn as follows:

PADRINO m. El que asiste a otro para recibir el bautismo, en el casamiento, en un desafío, certamen, etc. . . . || *Fig.* El que favorece y ayuda a otro en la vida . . . (SINÓN. Protector.)

The key word here is *bautismo* 'baptism', for this ceremony primarily establishes a link between the *padrino* and *el niño* and secondarily among *padrino, el niño, los padres*, and *la madrina*. García-Pelayo y Gross assumes that the reader is in a particular social milieu based on the customs of Roman Catholic—and particularly traditional Hispanic Roman Catholic—religious practices. *Bautismo* and the roles it defines for its participants would be enigmatic to nonbaptizing societies, and almost so for those Protestants who recognize a different kind of baptism. Even to those North Americans who likewise practice infant baptism and recognize roles for certain adults in the ceremony, the 'sponsor' or 'godparent' does not assume the network of responsibilities and family ties to which the *padrino* commits himself. The *compadre/padrino* has a special status in the Hispanic world that is taken for granted in Spanish dictionaries but fully appreciated by Spanish speakers.

Other points of information that native speakers can fill in with *compadre/padrino* include the following.

(1) The referent of *compadre/padrino* is an adult. (*¡Hola compadre!* would not be directed to a four-year-old by an adult, even for the sense of 'amigo o conocido'.)

(2) Assuming the role of *compadre* initiates a life-long state and relationship called *compadrazgo*, and the two words are both morphologically and semantically linked.

(3) The child becomes the *ahijado* of the compadre, and the latter commits himself to helping provide for him. He becomes literally the 'co-parent', *con-padre*, of that child.

(4) He therefore becomes an extended family member in traditional Hispanic culture, related to the parents as *compadre* and to the child as *padrino*.

(5) The *compadre* is coupled with a *comadre/madrina*, whose coresponsibility for the child can be just as great, although with implicitly distinct roles. (The two also have a different *fama*, as witnessed by the secondary meanings of 'friend or acquaintance' for *compadre* vs. 'gossipy woman' for *comadre*.)

(6) One is not a *compadre* when standing as *padrino* in duels or contests (the dictionary's '*desafíos, certámenes*'); in fact, this kind of *padrino* strikes modern Spanish speakers as archaic, quaint, and perhaps barbaric.

(7) In certain situations and usage levels that the dictionary writer vaguely labels as 'fam(iliar)' and 'fig(urativo)', *compadre* and *padrino* assume meanings other than those defined by the baptismal ceremony. Spanish speakers, however, will recognize that these secondary usages ('friend or acquaintance', 'protector') are not entirely distinct from the primary ones, but flow from them as natural extensions given the cultural significance one has as *compadre* with other adults and as *padrino* to children.

Finally, it must be added that the references to *sinón(imo)* imply a systematic organization of concepts in one's lexicon. By synonymy, *compadre* is connected with *padrino*; by antonymy, with *ahijado*; by taxonomy (classification by category and member), with *padre, abuelo, suegro, tío,* etc. as *parientes*. We must conclude that the lexicon is as much a thesaurus and an encyclopedia as it is a dictionary, and that knowledge of any word entered into it implies knowledge of a culture, of a society, and of a world.

14.2 The ranges of usage and meaning. As the preceding example showed, the study of words and usage is complicated and rather open-ended. It has been addressed by scholars of LEXICOGRAPHY (dictionary compilation), SEMANTICS (word meaning), and SEMIOTICS or SEMIOLOGY (meanings of communicative symbols in general), as well as by grammarians, critics of literary texts, philosophers, psychologists, anthropologists, and specialists in information theory, speech communication, and reading. There have been numerous theories on the subject, and it would be impossible here to sketch even briefly the rich traditions of scholarship in Europe and the Americas. For applied linguistics, though, the approach of Stockwell, Bowen, and Martin (1965:265-281) offers a practical point of departure. In their analysis, the use of a word is held to 'range' over a set of grammatical, referential, and situational contexts, and they discern seven major ranges where the words from two languages are used differently.

(1) SYNTACTIC RANGE, the domain of constructions in which a word appears. Syntactic classification or part of speech is one aspect of this range:

Eng. *down* can be a noun, verb, adverb, particle, preposition, or even adjective (*the computer is down*), while Span. *abajo* is an adverb only. But Eng. *want* and Span. *querer*, although of the same part of speech, also differ in syntactic range in permitting distinct complement structures (v. 13.1.2.3). Likewise, pairs such as *ask* and *pedir*, and *like* and *gustar*, have a different *régimen* in how they are constructed with NPs (v. 8.1.4).

(2) MORPHOLOGICAL RANGE, the inflectional and derivational potential of a word. *Aburrir* and *bore* have different tense potentials and different derivational patterns (*aburrido* vs. *boring*, *aburrimiento* vs. *boredom*). The word *compadre* examined in 14.1 likewise has a derivative *compadrazgo* whereas Eng. *godfather* has no such form.

(3) GRAMMATICAL RANGE, the particularly grammatical functions a morpheme has. In this respect, *se*, *a*, and *hacer*, respectively, do not match up with *-self* (v. 9.3), *to* (v. 11.2.3), and *do* (v. 12.1-12.2). Since such grammatical functions are relative to the syntactic system, dictionaries cannot easily present them. As Stockwell, Bowen, and Martin (1965:269) put it, 'when the meaning of *a* or *se* is indicated in a list, it necessarily applies only to certain contexts, which are usually not specified, and is basically fallacious.'

(4) COOCCURRENCE RANGE, the typical or conventional expressions (COLLOCATIONS) formed when a word combines with others. Eng. *take* cooccurs with *a trip*, *a train*, *a friend*, *a look*, *a walk*, *an oath*, but Spanish prefers *hacer un viaje*, *tomar un tren*, *llevar a un amigo*, *echar una ojeada*, *dar un paseo*, *prestar juramento*. Ignorance of a language's collocations is often a major factor in the lack of an 'idiomatic' flavor in student Spanish.

(5) DENOTATIVE RANGE, the semantic 'space' or conceptual area(s) covered by the basic meaning of a word. SBM note that *abrigo*, though often equated with *overcoat*, actually denotes more broadly 'protection or shelter from', and this general sense is useful for understanding derivatives such as *abrigar*, *desabrigar*, *abrigado*, and *al abrigo de*. Frequently, a word ranges over several concepts and is then called a POLYSEME; and a polysemous word often corresponds to several distinct words in another language, as with the Eng. *work* subsuming both *trabajo* and *obra* in Spanish. Derivatives may distinguish the polyseme's senses: *volar* 'fly' has the noun *vuelo* 'flight' whereas *volar* 'explode, blow up' has *voladura* 'explosion'.

(6) CONNOTATIVE RANGE, the secondary meanings associated with a concept. These reflect the special values and experiences of individuals with the concept within their culture. For example, a lexicographer ignores a great deal of connotative difference in equating *maid* with *criada*, *honest* with *honesto*, and *guts* with *entrañas*. As already shown in 14.1, *compadre* has a set of warmer and more favorable connotations in Hispanic culture than *godfather* does in English; in fact, the latter sometimes connotes a sinister character in North American culture.

(7) CIRCUMSTANTIAL RANGE, the special behavior a word or expression cues in certain contexts. *Yield* and *one way* often match *ceder* and *una manera*, but in the context of traffic control they cue what is conveyed in Spanish by *preferencia* (*prioridad*) and *dirección única* (or *sentido único*). Likewise, in offering someone something the English speaker resorts to *Here you are* or *Here's (NP)*, while one carries out this ritual in Spanish typically with *Aquí tiene(s) (NP)* or *¡Toma!*.

Much of what Stockwell, Bowen, and Martin (1965) regard as syntactic and grammatical range has already been explored in this book, and the following two chapters turn to the information they would place in the other ranges. Of special concern will be two points that follow from their approach. First, any time that one uses English words to gloss Spanish words, this is 'only because some part of their ranges in some way or other overlaps with some part of some range of the Spanish items, but they are rarely if ever wholly equivalent' (Stockwell, Bowen, and Martin 1965:281). Unfortunately, students are seldom warned of this incongruence, and each time they learn a Spanish word and proceed to use it as they have used its English equivalent, they unwittingly open seven doors to possible linguistic error (i.e. the seven 'ranges'). Second, since much of a word's range must be understood within the experiences, culture, and society of native speakers, foreign language learners are essentially being asked to acquire more than just new phonemes, phrase structures, and lexical labels; they are involved in a profound transmutation of their inner thought and being, and some will hold back, retreat to English norms, and resist changes in how they conceptualize the universe.

Chapter 15
Words and their meanings

15.0 The lexicon. The term LEXICON is used in linguistics for the set of words a speaker knows and for the larger communal set available to the speech community as a whole. Strictly speaking, the two are not identical; an adult speaker may have a personal vocabulary of around 60,000 words, many of them known passively (receptively) but seldom used actively (expressively), whereas the language of his community, as encoded in dictionaries, has several times that number.[1]

There are several reasons for the difference, as one learns by skimming through an unabridged dictionary and comparing its lexical stock with his own. Many of the words are archaic, appearing only in poetry or in period literature (e.g. words for types of armor in a story about knights or for clothing fashions in Golden Age drama); some are restricted to certain dialects (e.g. Eng. *brolly*, Span. *choclo*); and still others belong to the specialized terminology, or argot, of various fields and subcultures (v. 16.1.3).

Specialists in lexicography pool their experiences to record any and all words that appear in print (words appearing in speech are, of course, harder to monitor). But despite their strenuous efforts to keep up with the communal lexicon, it is impossible to give an exhaustive listing because new words (NEOLOGISMS) are constantly arising. Borrowing is one productive source of neologisms, and though purists may mount their chargers in combat against *tipiar, el chip, el test, el chequeo, el lonche*, etc., languages do not exist in a vacuum; borrowing has always been a simple, direct way of enriching the vocabulary in both English and Spanish.[2] Moreover, native speakers create neologisms within their language by using existing morphemes and morphological rules. Americans who refer to the *pre-Reaganite* era or Nicaraguans who condemn *neosomocistas* are utilizing the resources of their languages to create perfectly intelligible words (at least within their respective societies) that may or may not enter the dictionaries. By studying the patterns of word formation, or DERIVATIONAL MORPHOLOGY, one can get a glimpse of how the lexicon continues to grow.

15.1 Derivational morphology. There are two main ways by which English and Spanish derive new words in their lexicons: (1) through the addition of affixes to stems, and (2) by COMPOUNDING (combining stems). Like other Romance languages, Spanish has an abundance of derivational affixes; and like its Germanic sisters, English makes frequent use of compounding.

15.1.1 Affixes. The affixed morphemes that derive new words may be classified by their position in the word. Those that precede the stem are

PREFIXES; those that follow it are SUFFIXES. The latter are more numerous in English and Spanish, and when several of them are added to one stem, they line up in an order that reflects derivational stages, with the purely inflectional ones (number, tense, etc.) coming last of all. Thus, *personalidades* is morphologically *persona* + *al* + *idad* + *es*, i.e. the inflected plural (*-es*) form of the noun *personalidad*, which is derived from the adjective *personal* formed off the noun *persona*, which here serves as the stem or derivational base of the whole. This structure can also be shown as follows, with brackets enclosing each successive layer of derivation:[3]

[[[*persona*]*al*]*idad*]*es*].

A second way of classifying derivational morphemes is by their relative productivity. Some morphemes are rather frozen, i.e. little used in new formations. The Latin prefix *ob-*, for instance, appears in Eng. *obscene* and Span. *obsceno* but in neither language is it likely to be used in many current neologisms. At the other extreme, Span. *des-* and *-ero*, and Eng. *un-* and *-able*, are freely used to produce new words. If one describes his hammer-wielding friend as a *martillero* or a difficult nail as *unhammerable*, hearers will not have to ask what either word means in these contexts, nor will they be especially shocked on not finding it in a dictionary. Between these two extremes are countless degrees of productivity, and the two languages may not always agree on the value they assign to otherwise comparable affixes: Eng. *un-* is more productive than Span. *in-*, but Spanish uses diminutives, both singly and serially (*chico, chiquito, chiquitico*, . . .), far more than English.

A third way of classifying derivational morphemes is in terms of their function. Many serve primarily to adapt a word for use in a different syntactic category (part of speech):

Adj → N: Span. (arid)*ez*, (alt)*ura*, (alt)*eza*, (alt)*itud*, (cert)*idumbre*, (posibil)*idad* (allomorphs *-tad*, *-dad*, *-edad*); Eng. (good)*ness*, (similar)*ity*, (wid)*th*, (heigh)*t*, (likeli)*hood*.

V → N:[4] Span. (observa)*ción* (allomorphs *-ión*, *-sión*), (par)*o*, (para)*da*, (cort)*e*, (corta)*dura*, (vir)*aje*, (mud)*anza*, (empuj)*ón*, (casa)*miento* (allomorph *-mento*), (emplea)*dor*, (emplea)*do*, (cerra)*zón*, (presta)-*tario*, (prepara)*tivos*, (canta)*nte*, infinitive (*parecer, poder, bienestar*); Eng. (observa)*tion*, (bore)*dom*, (paint)*ing*, (pay)*ment*, (revers)*al*, (paint)*er*, (employ)*ee*, (disinfect)*ant*, (cover)*age*, ∅ suffix (*work*)

N → Adj: Span. (nacion)*al*, (lluvi)*oso*, (republic)*ano*, (guerr)*ero*, (art)-*ístico*, (estudiant)*il*, (esperanz)*ado*, (pacienz)*udo*, (vin)*ícola*, (mujer)-*iego*, (fronter)*izo*, (di)*ario*, (telefón)*ico*; Eng. (nation)*al*, (ruin)*ous*, (sugar)*y*, (care)*ful*, (world)*ly*, (burden)*some*, (fool)*ish*, (republic)*an*, (atom)*ic* (allomorph *-ical*), ∅ suffix (*gold* watch, *student* life).

V → Adj:[4] Span. (convenie)*nte*, (resbala)*dizo*, (diverti)*do*, (conta)*ble*, (llor)*ón*, (trabaja)*dor*, (exclama)*torio*, (deriva)*tivo*, (hace)*dero*; Eng. (expect)*ant*, (exclama)*tory*, (work)*ing*, (work)*able*, (tire)*d*, (deriva)-*tive*

N or Adj → V: Span. (civil)*izar*, (traicion)*ar*, *en*(ajen)*ar* (allomorph *em*-), *a*(clar)*ar*, (humed)*ecer*, *en*(roj)*ecer*, (telefon)*ear*, (clas)*ificar*; Eng. (civil)*ize*, (hard)*en*, (simpl)*ify*, ∅ suffix (*wet, book, garden*)

Adj → Adv: Span. (rápida)*mente*, ∅ suffix (*rápido*); Eng. (rapid)*ly*, ∅ suffix (*fast*)

Students cannot predict the particular morpheme combinations that have already been fixed within the Spanish lexicon. They might study derivational morphology in order to perceive *cortar* in *corte* and *cortadura* (which, however, are not synonymous), but they should not try to create *cortanza or *cortación on their own as they create new sentences. That is, pedagogy cannot treat word formation like sentence formation. Spanish-speaking students of English must likewise cope with unpredictable formations like -*ment* for *pay* vs. -*al* for *reverse* and -*ation* for *observe*, all for the same nominalizing (V → N) function.

Fortunately, some patterns are shared by the two languages, and many texts exploit the similarity of -*oso* to -*ous*, -*ción* to -*tion*, -*izar* to -*ize*, and so on (v. 15.2). One option not extensively shared is the one symbolized by '∅' in the preceding list. English often transforms part of speech with no overt derivational suffix. There may be a slight morphophonemic change (nouns *shelf*, *use* /jus/, *bath* /bæθ/ vs. verbs *shelve*, *use* /juz/, *bathe* /beð/), but more often not (*book* → *to book*, *gold* (N) vs. *gold* (Adj) *watch*). In Spanish, the similarity of N and Adj inflection does allow some direct crossover between these two categories (as with *hablador, médico, hueco, vacío, vecino, enemigo, santo, malentendido, realista*); otherwise, categorial changes require the addition of derivational suffixes.

In changing syntactic category, some morphemes affect meaning also. Among the nominalizers, -*ción* and -*tion* create abstract nouns of action or countable instances thereof, -*dor* and -*er* express verbal subject, and -*do* and -*ee* indicate verbal object. The following derivational morphemes more drastically affect meaning, with or without a change in part of speech:

(1) opposite, negative, lack: Span. *in*(útil, -cumplir, -coloro), *des*(hacer, -honesto, -empleo), *no* (violencia, -especialista); Eng. *un*(happy, -employed, -do), *dis*(honest, -assemble), (harm)*less*, *non*(toxic, -violence), *de*(frost), *mis*(understand).

(2) feminine (v. 8.2.2): Span. (doctor)*a*, (abad)*esa*, (act)*riz*; Eng. (lion)-*ess*, (wait)*ress*, (major)*ette*.

(3) diminutive and/or endearment: Span. (carr)*ito*, (carr)*illo*, (carr)-*ico* (allomorphs -*cito*, -*cillo*, -*cico*); Eng. (dadd)*y*, (hors)*ie*, (pig)*let*, (kitchen)*ette*.

(4) affiliation, origin, language: Span. (itali)*ano*, (franc)*és*, (panam)-*eño*, (canad)*iense*, (marroqu)*í*, (manch)*ego*, (britán)*ico*, (santander)*ino*, (crist)*iano*, (húngar)*o*; Eng. (Puerto Ric)*an*, (Span)*iard*, (Span)*ish*, (Christ)*ian*, (Chin)*ese*.
(5) doctrine, lifestyle, follower thereof: Span. (capital)*ismo*, (capital)-*ista*[5]; Eng. (capital)*ism*, (capital)*ist*.
(6) fractional part (sometimes ordinal): Span. (quinz)*avo*, (cent)-*ésimo*; Eng. (fifteen)*th*.
(7) degree: Span. (roj)*izo*, (blanc)*uzco*, *sub- sobre-semi*(desarrollado), (grand)*ísimo*, *re- requete*(bueno); Eng. (redd)-*ish*, *under- over- semi*(developed).

Spanish has more resources in this category than English:

(8) augmentative, pejorative: (sill)*ón*, (mujer)*ona*, (libr)*ote*, (cas)-*ucha*, (perr)*azo*.
(9) area for the purpose of: (manzan)*ar*, (naranj)*al*, (desembarca)-*dero*.
(10) associated person, receptacle, outlet: (escud)*ero*, (joy)*ero*, (malet)-*ero*, (azucar)*ero*, (bañ-, gasolin)*era*, (partid)*ario*.
(11) associated store or occupation: (zapat)*ería*
(12) blow to or with: (pal)*iza*, (cod)*azo*, (puñ-, nalg)*ada*.
(13) collective set: (profesor-, tecl)*ado*, (muebl-~mobl)*aje*, (mobili)-*ario*, (doc)*ena*, (alam)*eda*

15.1.2 Compounding. While Spanish has more derivational suffixes than English, English makes more derivational use of compounding. There are just four main compounding patterns in modern Spanish; the first two are fairly productive for technical terms and products, but otherwise compounding is relatively uncommon.

(1) N + N = N (v. 8.3.2): *grupo control, lengua madre, factor precio, estado-nación, fecha tope ~ fecha límite.*
(2) V + N-*s* = N: *cuentagotas, tocadiscos, lavaplatos, salvavidas, lanzacohetes, paraguas, cumpleaños.*
(3) N-*i* + Adj = Adj: *boquiabierto, barbiesposo, pelirrojo.*
(4) N + Adv = Adv: *patas arriba, cuesta abajo, río abajo*

English has many more patterns, most of them very productive. Whether written as one word or two, with a hyphen or without, they tend to have the distinctive stress pattern 'primary-secondary' (v. 4.1.2); see also Quirk et al. 1972 for more on compounding types):

(1) Adj + N = N: *fathead, paleface, loudmouth, longwall*
(2) Adj + N-*ed* = Adj: *thickheaded, red-faced, long-lived, three-toed*
(3) N + Adj = Adj: *taxfree, dustproof, carsick, brick-red, diamond-hard*

(4) V + N = N: *pickpocket, scarecrow, drawbridge*
(5) N + V-*ing* = N/Adj: *airconditioning, bookkeeping, story-telling, meat-eating*
(6) V-*ing* + N = N: *washing machine, swimming pool, chewing gum, spending money, baking powder*
(7) N + V-*er* = N: *biology teacher, gate-crasher, babysitter, songwriter*
(8) N + N = N: *toothache, coffee pot, book review, table leg, tax cut, applesauce, birth control, workbench*
(9) V + Particle = N: *make-up, set-up, workout, hangover, turnout, turnover*
(10) Particle + V = N/V: *outbreak, upset, income, outcome, outgo, overhang, input*
(11) Advl or Particle + N = Advl/N/Adj: *uphill, downtown, throughway, indoor, outlaw*

To the English-speaking student, whose personal lexicon includes hosts of compounds plus the resources for creating more ad libitum, the uncompounded Spanish equivalents for these concepts may seem maddeningly unpredictable. Even where Spanish has resorted to a kind of compounding by combining classical roots—*oleoducto, autodidacto, antropófago*—these will seldom be recognized as English-like compounds. In working on vocabulary development, it may be necessary for the student to grasp enough about compounding in his native language to recognize nontransferable patterns.

15.1.3 Morphophonemics: Phonology in the lexicon. Adding a derivational suffix may trigger changes in the stem's pronunciation. These MORPHOPHONEMIC changes (v. 5.1) are also found in inflection; the pairs *viejo vejez* and *nueve noventa* show the same diphthongization under stress as the verb forms *pienso pensar* and *puedo poder* (v. 6.1.2.4). Yet processes that apply rather consistently in inflection weaken somewhat in derivation, so that some forms will undergo a rule that others bypass, and for no apparent reason. Consequently, there is a gamut of types ranging from rule-governed and predictable to one-of-a-kind irregularities, as illustrated here. (For a more exhaustive listing, see Saporta 1959.)

(1) Very predictable. Adjectives in -*ble* change to -*bil*- with derivational affixes; *posible posibil+idad posibil+itar, amable amabil+ísimo amabil+idad.* Also, nouns in -*en* change to -*in*-: *origen origin+al, examen examin+ar.*

(2) Almost predictable. The final unstressed vowel of a word drops (usually) when a vowel-initial suffix is added: *hijo hij+ito, feo afe+ar, base bás+ico bas+ar, católico catolic+ismo, día di+ario.* (If this leaves the sequence /-Cj+i-/, then the postconsonantal /j/ drops too: *copia* /kopja/ *cop+ista, sucio suc+ísimo.*) But the stem-final vowel fails to drop in *golpe golpe+ar, álgebra algebra+ico, espíritu espiritu+al.*

(3) Common, but with many exceptions (vacillations, subconditions). Stem-final /k/ becomes /θ/~/s/ before a derivational suffix beginning with a front vowel, /i e/: *médico medic+ina, eléctrico electric+idad, magnífico magnific+encia.* But it stays /k/ with diminutives, *-ísimo, -ero,* and *-e*; *poco poqu+ito poqu+ísimo, vaca vaqu+ero, arranc(ar) arranqu+e.* Oddly, *-ense* induces the change but *-eño* does not: *costarric+ense, puertorriqu+eño.* Diphthongization illustrates the same problem: *diestro destr+eza* but *a+diestr+ar* (in which the *ie* is unstressed), *viejo vej+ez* but *a+viej+ar* and *viej+ísimo, bueno bon+dad* but *buen+ísimo~bon+ísimo.* Diphthongization fails to apply in *el costo* from *costar* (*ue*), and the diphthong is kept (despite its stresslessness) in *encuesta encuest+ar, presupuesto presupuest+ar, muestra muestr+eo.*

(4) Idiosyncratic or isolated changes. The verbs and nouns in the following pairs are related to each other in exactly the same way as those in *observar observación* and *prohibir prohibición*; but they show different allomorphs of the stem, unlike /obserb+a+/ and /proib+i/, and the rules needed for their allomorphy seem word-specific quirks:

dirigir /dirix-/, *dirección* /direk-/
construir /konstru(j)-/, *construcción* /konstruk-/
conceder /konθed-/, *concesión* /konθes-/
conseguir /konseg-/, *consecución* /konseku-/

oír /o-/, *audición* /awd-/
nadar /nad-/, *natación* /nat-/
devolver /debolb-/, *devolución* /debolu-/
recoger /r̄ekox-/, *recolección* /r̄ekolek-/

Similar problems are posed by the stem changes in noun-adjective pairs such as *leche lácteo, padre paternal, reflejo reflexivo.*

Linguists have debated the extent to which native speakers exploit or even perceive these phonological relationships in the lexicon. For some analysts (e.g. Harris 1969), *leche* and *lácteo* have a common base morphophonemically like *cariño* and *cariñoso, puerto* and *porteño,* and they posit phonological rules to derive them from the same stem. Others acknowledge a semantic relationship between *leche* and *lácteo,* but see no more of a common stem in them (or the need for rules to explain a difference in pronunciation) than in *corazón* and *cardíaco, perro* and *canino, bosque* and *silvestre,* or for that matter English *milk* and *lactic.* In the classroom, of course, matters are different: it is admirable if students infer useful morphophonemic patterns within Spanish, but what is more often expected of them is some degree of ability to recognize the meaning of *lácteo* and *dirección,* not because of morphophonemic rules that derive their consonants and vowels from those of *leche* and *dirigir,* but because of their 'cognate' resemblance to English *lactic* and *direction.*

15.2 Cognates: True friends, or false? In descriptive (as opposed to applied) linguistics, the term COGNATE is used with a very specific meaning. A word W_x from Language X and a word W_y from Language Y are termed 'cognates' if and only if they have been inherited from the same ancestor language of X and Y. They are not true cognates, in this sense, if their resemblance is merely a coincidence, or if X borrowed its word from Y, or Y from X, or both borrowed their words from yet a third language Z. Some examples of each case may illustrate the distinction.

(1) INHERITANCE. (Span. < Latin < Indo-European; Eng. < Germanic < Indo-European):
   madre/mother, me/me, es/is, seis/six, mente/mind, nombre/name, yugo/yoke, diente/tooth, seguir/see, oveja/ewe, vivo/quick, estar/stand, joven/young, ver/wit(ness), lengua/tongue.

(2) COINCIDENCE. *haber/have, mucho/much, otro/other, o/or.*

(3) BORROWING.
   (a) (Eng. → Span.): *estándar, boicot, sandwich, mitin, láser, líder, túnel, biftec (bife, bistec), software*
   (b) (Span. → Eng.): *ranch, vista, canyon, patio, vanilla, cigar, cockroach;* (via Span. from Arabic): *algebra, alcohol, guitar, hazard;* (and via Spanish from Amer. Ind. languages): *tomato, tobacco, potato, chocolate.*
   (c) (Both from Latin): *aplicación/application, rápido/rapid, exacto/exact, actor, animal;* (both from French): *hotel, control, menú/menu, garaje/garage, silueta/silhouette, turno/turn, tren/train;* (both from Italian) *piano, soprano, tráfico/traffic, banco/bank;* (both from Greek) *mapa/map, diploma, planeta/planet, bio-, auto-, fis-/phys-, -grafía/-graphy;* (Span. inherited from Latin, Eng. borrowed from Latin or French) *valle/valley, razón/reason, sol/sol(ar), fiesta/feast.*

But these distinctions involve too much etymologizing for language learners. In fact, true cognates (category 1) are often pedagogically useless because during the 5,000 years or so since the breakup of Indo-European, meaning and pronunciation have changed too drastically (as with *seguir/see, vivo/quick*) for the relationship to be transparent to the nonlinguist. It is usually category 3, which contains no cognates at all for the linguist, that teachers and text-writers refer to as 'cognates', and we will accede to this usage henceforth.

Cognates are touted as hosts of words for free, meaning that they require little effort to master (aside from pronunciation, spelling, 'morphological range', part of speech, gender, stem changes, etc.). To a certain extent, this claim is true. Having developed in the same general region and culture, the two languages exchanged many words, borrowed extensively from French, were flooded by Greco-Latin roots, and today participate in a linguistic Common Market for scientific and technological neologisms. Furthermore, the student soon learns that there is a good chance that his words in -*nce*, -*nt*, -*ity*, -*tor*, -*ic(al)*, -*ist*, -*ment*, -*tion*, -*ize* can become acceptable currency in Spanish if amended to -*ncia*, -*nte*, -*idad*, -*dor*, -*ico*, -*ista*, -*mento*, -*ción*, -*izar*, and with -*al*, -*ble*, and -*sis* even less effort seems necessary.

But, for several reasons, cognates are as much a bane as a boon. First, they are phonetically seductive, inviting transference of a source-language pronunciation (v. 2.4). Second, they can differ in their stylistic level of usage: *aumento, socorro, denunciar* are rather ordinary Spanish words whose English cognates *augment, succor, denounce* are 'fancy' and absent from some speakers' vernaculars. Vice-versa, some Spanish words are rarer than their English counterparts, and the reading passage that avoids *cómodo, exigir, parecido, unir*, and *por fin* for the English-like *confortable, demandar, similar, conectar*, and *finalmente* may seem unnatural and unauthentic.

Third, students overgeneralize cognate derivational patterns, creating 'Spanglish' words that do not exist:

abortion → *aborción (aborto)   vaccination → *vaccinación
portable → *portable (portátil)   (vacunación)
procrastinate → *procrastinar   serious → *serioso (serio)
   (aplazar)   protective → *protectivo (protector)
deterioration → *deterioración   visitor → *visitor (visitante)
   (deterioro)

Fourth, the two lexicons are replete with items that resemble each other in spelling and in etymology, but not in meaning. These have been called 'false friends' or 'false cognates' (*false* = 'treacherous'; all of these 'cognates' are *false* = 'fake' for the linguist). The classic example is *embarazada* ≠ *embarrassed*; following is a list of several others.

fábrica ≠ fabric	reunir ≠ reunite	firmar ≠ firm (up)
avisar ≠ advise	dormitorio ≠ dormitory	largo ≠ large
actual ≠ actual	desgracia ≠ disgrace	colegio ≠ college
éxito ≠ exit	idioma ≠ idiom	decepción ≠ deception

Almost as 'false' are those cognates whose common Spanish meanings are carried by the English words just in restricted contexts; their usual English senses, and therefore the ones that come to students' minds, do not match at all.

tabla ≠ table 'mesa'	cuestión ≠ question 'pregunta'
realizar ≠ realize 'darse cuenta'	respecto ≠ respect 'respeto, -ar'
oficio ≠ office 'oficina, despacho'	signo ≠ sign 'señal, letrero;
polo ≠ pole 'poste'	firma'
argumento ≠ argument 'rencilla'	suceder ≠ succeed 'tener éxito'
	tarifa ≠ tariff 'arancel'

Conversely, the usual English meaning may be a possible one in Spanish in certain contexts, but the Spanish cognate has other meanings that English speakers cannot anticipate:

extremo: (extreme), end

formación: (formation), training

gracia: (grace), wit, humor

raro: (rare), strange

compromiso: (compromise), commitment, appointment

tipo: (type), rate; guy

15.3 Dialect differences in vocabulary. Regional differences in Spanish phonology and grammar have been discussed elsewhere in this book. Lexically, there are many differences such as the following:

'car': auto, carro, coche

'grass': hierba, césped, pasto

'ticket': boleto, billete, tiquete

'potato': patata, papa

'peas': guisantes, arvejas, chícharos

'kitchen sink': fregadero, pila, lavaplatos, lavadero

'bus': autobús, ómnibus, camión, chiva, colectivo, guagua

'corn': maíz, choclo

'sidewalk': acera, banqueta, vereda

'throw away': arrojar, tirar, botar

'stamp': estampilla, sello, timbre

'city block': manzana, cuadra

'little boy': chico, chino, mozo, chamaco, pelado, pibe, cabro, patojo, cipote

Besides assigning different words to the same meaning, dialects may end up with different meanings for the same word. *Provocar* means 'be appealing' in Colombia, 'cause to fight' in most other areas; *pararse, liviano, barranca* are 'stop, lewd, ravine' in Spain but 'stand up, lightweight, cliff' to many Spanish Americans. And of course, *coger* is innocently 'catch' in many countries but an obscene synonym of *joder* in others.

The so-called standard word or meaning sometimes coexists with a regional one, perhaps distinguished as formal vs. colloquial. Other times the term that Spaniards, at least, might regard as standard is known elsewhere just as a book word, if at all. Etymologically, distinctive local terms derive from a variety of sources (see Kany 1945/1951 and Zamora Vicente 1967, among others):

(1) Older terms now archaic or marginal in Spain: *frazada* for *manta, lindo* for *bonito, fundo* for *finca, taita* for *papá, recibirse* for *licenciarse, prieto* for *oscuro, agora* for *ahora, ñudo* for *nudo.*

(2) Nautical argot generalized by seafaring colonists: *jalar ~ halar* for *tirar de, arribar* for *llegar, amarrar* for *atar.*

(3) Neologisms using native morphemes and patterns: *dar una caminata* for *dar un paseo, arriba de* for *encima de, carniar* for *matar reses.*

(4) Borrowings from Indian languages: (Nahuatl) *pulque, cacahuete, chile, tamal;* (Pipil) *cipote* 'niño', *peche* 'delgado'; (Quechua) *pon-*

cho, vicuña, alpaca; (Caribbean, especially Arawakan) *yuca, jején, tiburón, cacique, barbacoa, ají, papagayo.*
(5) Borrowings from languages of immigrants: (Italian) *chao, pibe*; (African languages) *ñame, marimba, bongó.*
(6) Anglicisms from 'el coloso del norte': *lonche* for *merienda, suiche* for *interruptor, asistir* for *ayudar, chequear* for *revisar* or *comprobar, zípper* for *cremallera, queque* for *torta.*

Marrone (1974) notes that many differences have arisen in Spanish as new styles and products diffused through different societies before academies could come up with a single standardized term that all might accept. She interviewed students from each Spanish-speaking country and compiled their answers for 43 items, among them the following (for which just six countries' usages will be given here):

'ballpoint': (Arg.) *biro(me)*, (Col.) *lapicero*, (Cuba) *bolígrafo*, (Mex.) *pluma*, (Peru) *estilográfica*, (Spain) *bolígrafo ~ párker*
'folder': (Arg., Cuba, Spain) *carpeta*, (Col.) *folder*, (Mex. and Peru) *cartapacio*
'faucet' (Arg.) *canilla*, (Col., Cuba) *llave*, (Mex.) *bitoque ~ llave*, (Peru) *caño*, (Spain) *grifo ~ pila.*
'lightbulb': (Arg.) *lamparita*, (Col.) *bombilla ~ foco*, (Mex.) *foco*, (Cuba, Peru, Spain) *bombilla.*
'closet': (Arg.) *placar(d)*, (Col., Cuba, Mex., Peru) *clóset*, (Spain) *armario*
'pickup truck': (Arg., Peru) *picap ~ camioneta*, (Col., Mex.) *camioneta*, (Cuba) *pisicorre*, (Spain) *camioneta ~ furgoneta*

For 'bra', she found almost a dozen terms, and for 'panties', sixteen.
The degree of dialect divergence in Spanish lexicography is disputed. Those who assert their cultural autonomy may emphasize and even exaggerate the differences; those who favor international *hispanidad* interpret diversity as a communal wealth of resources accessible to all; those with strong beliefs about *casticidad* condemn local terms as *vulgarismos* that the 'educated' avoid. But it must be borne in mind that the overwhelming bulk of Spanish vocabulary is held in common; unless the topic is uniquely one of local color, Spanish speakers from different countries (or valleys or provinces or *patrias chicas*) really have little trouble understanding one another. Moreover, many regionalisms soon achieve broader currency through international communications, so that the dialectalness of a term may be a matter of more-or-less rather than of here-but-never-there.
English dialects vary lexically too, both between the U.S. and U.K. (*elevator/lift, wrench/spanner, can/tin*, etc.) and within the U.S. (*faucet/spigot, pail/bucket, quarter till/of/to*; see Kurath 1949); so students are seldom surprised by similar variation in Spanish. Yet they sometimes demand to know which term is 'proper' or 'standard' Spanish, or (more to

the point) which term they are expected to learn. Text writers confront the same problem; some set out to adhere to one major country's usage (particularly Mexico's or Spain's), while others mix-and-match or introduce several terms together: *coche + carro, papa + patata, computadora + ordenador*, etc.). Spanish and English are international languages used by diverse societies and cultures and, unlike French, they are not defined by the cultural dominance of any one center; it is unreasonable to expect lexical uniformity in either, although pedagogy would certainly be simpler if that condition existed.

15.4 Different lexicons, different meanings. Laypersons—and that includes most students—expect different languages to have different phonologies and grammars, but they tend to believe that their lexical organizations are identical. This is because a word denotes a concept, and monolinguals have had very little experience with other conceptualizations that follow from a different perspective, culture, and lifestyle; they naturally assume that the things they see in the world are the same ones seen in other cultures, merely with different labels. Most foreign language materials do little to dispel this assumption, introducing target words with source glosses as if they matched exactly. If one gloss is given, as in *la cena: dinner*, students proceed to adopt *cena* in all contexts where they have heretofore used *dinner*, just exchanging one name for another for the same Anglophone concept. If several glosses are given, as in the following bilingual dictionary entry,

grade: el grado; la clase; la calidad; la pendiente; la nota; a nivel

many students will construe the multiple equivalents as synonyms and arbitrarily select one of them in translating their English thoughts; as one student wrote in her composition, *La maestra me dio la pendiente 'A'*. Even if students realize that Eng. *grade* is a polyseme covering several distinct concepts (*grade* of an incline ≠ *grade* for class work), dictionaries seldom clarify which Spanish word corresponds to which meaning, nor do they offer sentence-length examples that would allow users to infer this.

15.4.1 Differences in denotation and connotation. Precise one-to-one matching exists for a few concepts, e.g. common everyday objects, universally perceived physical characteristics, and internationally fixed measurements and technical terms: *broom = escoba, hand = mano, red = rojo, big = grande, liter = litro, electricity = electricidad, lithium = litio.* But even if two languages agree on the basic senses or DENOTATIONS of such words, they may differ strikingly in their CONNOTATIONS, the secondary, subjective nuances carried by them. Some connotations tend to be universal because of common psychological, biological, and ecological elements shared by all human beings; 'mother', for example, conjures up pleasurably warm associations throughout the world (Osgood 1963). But others depend on the culture of a society. For instance, the denotations of *bar-*

gaining and *regateo* are close enough, but the images, affect, interpersonal value, and situational appropriateness evoked by the two are quite different. Likewise, *church* and *home* do not evoke quite the same visual images as *iglesia* and *hogar*, and *honor* and *pull* are evaluated differently in English-speaking societies from the way that *honor* and *enchufe/palanca* are evaluated in Hispanic ones. In fact, returning to one of the supposed one-to-one matches, one could say that the Spaniard's *litro* cannot be what a liter is in a society that still regards it as a bothersome, alien conversion from quarts and gallons.

Yet not even denotations match in much of the Spanish and English lexicons. Some linguists and philosophers have considered thought as essentially amorphous and unstructured in itself; by demarcating word-sized 'concepts,' it is language which imposes cognitive structuring on this amorphous 'substance' (to use Saussure's terminology, 1915/1959:111-113). To the extent that their lexical setups differ, speakers of different languages may be led to think, perceive, relate, and reason differently (Whorf 1956).

One graphic way of showing different lexical structure is with series of linear correspondences (Stockwell, Bowen, and Martin 1965:274-275). Whereas some words match up rather well, as shown in (a) of Figure 15.1, others show multiple correspondences in which different senses are distinguished by different words, as shown in (b). The correspondences ultimately become complicated zigzags, as depicted by (c); and in numerous cases they seem to march right across the lexicon with no end in sight, as shown in (d). To impose some control on such dauntingly limitless vistas, many analysts from linguistics and anthropology have focused on specific SEMANTIC FIELDS, conceptual systems which are fairly well delimited and self-contained. One ready-made one is kinship terminology, which has been investigated systematically in many languages and subjected to contrastive analysis; in pedagogy, too, kinship words are often presented together as a semantic field. Other cases include color terms, prepositions of location (v. 10.3.3), clothing terms, and the adult/young and male/female distinctions for humans and animals.

When the target language uses one word for concepts that the source language distinguishes lexically, students can sometimes perceive a common denominator that is the real meaning of the target word.[6] For example, although the referents of *reloj* and *dedo* are respectively divided into *clocks* and *watches*, and *fingers* and *toes*, in English, they actually represent more general concepts that English speakers may know (but seldom verbalize) as *timepiece* and *digit*. When it is the target language that makes a lexical distinction that is missing in the source language, the students' task is quite different, and they might initially assume synonymy, as pointed out earlier. If the distinction is clear and concrete, as with *rincón/esquina* or *pie/pata*, teachers can demonstrate it with pictures, pointings, descriptive glosses ('inside/outside corner'), or set injunctions

Figure 15.1 Lexical correspondences between English and Spanish.

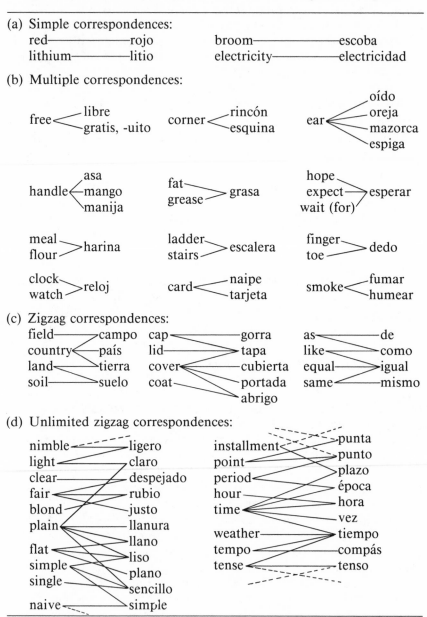

('use *pie* for people and mountains, *pata* for animals and furniture—in most cases, that is'). After some practice, students should be able to make such distinctions correctly. This is not to say that they fully accept it yet, for their English-based 'common sense' may still suggest that the distinction is semantically picky, a useless nicety stipulated by a weird language.

When semantic distinctions are more abstract, neither glosses nor brief injunctions (much less pictures) ensure consistently correct usage. Students can be taught to amend their *I'm coming* to *Ya voy*, but the real problem with *ir* vs. *venir* is that one must learn to adhere to his own perspective on movement—movement toward self vs. movement away—and avoid the English practice of taking the addressee's perspective. For *saber/conocer*, students can depend on glosses or syntactic cues in some cases (*Conozco a Elena*, not **Sé a Elena*), but the two verbs contrast in many others (*¿Sabes/Conoces esta sinfonía de Manuel de Falla?*), and the two kinds of knowing will not be immediately obvious to students, nor will they fully exploit the contrast. Similar problems are posed by *dejar/salir, tomar/llevar, igual/mismo, pedir/preguntar, sentir/sentirse*, and so on. The contrast between Eng. *make* and *do* can be just as difficult an abstraction for the Spanish speaker (Hagerty and Bowen 1973), who uses *hacer* for both. But the most conspicuous case of an abstract distinction is *ser* vs. *estar*, and even the briefest text will usually give these two verbs special attention.

15.4.2 Verbs of being: *ser* vs. *estar*. Spanish has a variety of verbs translatable as Eng. *be*: *ser, estar, haber, hacer, tener, quedar, sentar, verse, salir, resultar, hallarse, encontrarse* . . . Pedagogy in the United States, however, has traditionally narrowed down the focus to the *ser/estar* contrast. Most studies thereof proceed from an analysis of three sorts of data: cases in which only *ser* appears, those in which only *estar* appears, and those in which both appear in contrast. Examples of each case follow.[7]

Set 1: ser:
(1a) Ya es tarde: son las cinco.
(1b) Hoy es lunes.
     Ella es abogada.
     Ese es el vagón de primera clase.
(1c) Tres más cuatro son siete.

(1d) Es $\begin{cases} \text{de España, español} \\ \text{de María, suyo} \\ \text{de plástico} \\ \text{de mucho interés} \end{cases}$

(1e) ¿Cuál es la fecha? Es el doce.
(1f) Es que no lo saben.
     Puede ser que estén equivocados.
     ¡Esto no será!

Set 2: estar:
(2a) Está corriendo.

(2b) La finca está $\begin{cases} \text{al norte.} \\ \text{a 10 km. de aquí.} \\ \text{cerca del río.} \\ \text{en otra parte.} \end{cases}$

(2c) Ella está $\begin{cases} \text{sin empleo} \\ \text{en su tercer año} \end{cases}$

(2d) Está bien. Está en vigor.

(2e) Está $\begin{cases} \text{de prisa, de acuerdo, de luto} \\ \text{de vacaciones, de moda, de viaje} \\ \text{de cónsul} \\ \text{de sobra, de turno} \end{cases}$

(2f) ¿A cuánto estamos? Estamos a doce.

(2g) ¿Está el gerente? No, no está.

Set 3: ser vs. estar:

(3a) Son/están para verlo mejor.

(3b) La casa fue/estuvo destruida.

(3c) El banquete⎫
     La sinfonía⎭ es/está en otro cuarto.

(3d) Mi casa es/está en Almería.
     Allí es/está Bogotá.

(3e) ¿Cómo es/está? Es/está $\begin{cases} \text{agrio, verde, jugoso} \\ \text{ciego, enfermo, borracho} \\ \text{malo, loco, listo, vivo, seguro, limpio} \\ \text{pobre, rico, antipático} \\ \text{grande, sabroso, caro, bajo} \end{cases}$

(3f) ¡Qué hombre es/está!

There is little controversy about the first two sets. *Estar* forms progressives (2a) and locates, whether literally (2b) or figuratively (2c).[8] *Ser* conveys most other relationships: time-telling (1a), identifying or equating (1b), (1c), presenting origin/possession/purpose/make-up (1d), etc. In a few cases (particularly (2d), (2e)), the reason for copula selection seems obscure, and though some analysts try to explain these uses in terms of other categories or principles, others call them idioms. The expression of dates allows either copula, though in different constructions; this can be explained as alternative strategies (equation in (1e), location in a series in (2f)) for the same message. Except with *estar* 'be in, present' as in (2g) and with *ser* as a verb of existence as in (1f), there always seems to be some kind of predicate element conditioning selection, and the two copulas are virtually in complementary distribution (Stockwell, Bowen and Martin 1965:170).

But this is not true in Set 3, where they occur with the same PredE and contrast semantically. (3a) is perhaps just a superficial convergence of *ser para* for purpose and the (idiom?) *estar para* 'be about to'. (3b) contrasts a passivized event with the state resulting therefrom (v. 12.3). For (3c) one must bear in mind that certain nouns represent either things or events; as things, they are located with *estar*, and as events, with *ser* (whence 'take place'). Similarly, some nouns indicate objects or places, and in (3d) a speaker can either equate the nouns with the locations

(*Bogotá = allí*) or locate them there (*Bogotá está allí*). So far, again, there is little controversy.

Disputes begin when the PredE is an adjective (3e), its question word (*cómo*), or certain adjectivalized nouns (*hombre* in (3f)). Two main approaches will be examined here: one that can be called 'traditional' and the other based on the overlapping views of Navas Ruiz (1963) and William Bull (1965).[9]

The traditional explanation was laid down by the earlier grammars of the RAE (1924: 172-173), although perhaps it should be traced back to a comment from Bello (1847/1958:200). With adjectives, *ser* supposedly denotes permanent qualities while *estar* indicates transitory or accidental conditions. As worked out in many U.S. texts, this dichotomy has blossomed into the following five-part treatment:

(1) *ser*: permanence, inherence, characteristic or innate quality, natural state, essence
(2) *estar*: temporariness, accidental condition, transience, semblance of being, subjective judgment
(3) Exceptions to the above
(4) Memorizable cases: *ser* + nationality, *ser* + affiliation, etc.
(5) Distinguishing polysemous adjectives' senses, i.e. adjectives that 'change meaning' according to the copula:[10]

es/está alto 'is tall/high'   es/está listo 'is clever/ready'
es/está bueno 'is good/well'   es/está verde 'is green/unripe'
es/está callado 'is taciturn/quiet' es/está malo 'is bad/sick'
es/está cierto 'is true/assured' es/está seguro 'is reliable/protected'

This approach persists in many quarters today, and in view of several generations of confused students and of critical linguists and teachers, its durability through various revolutions in methodology is a tribute to inertia in certain matters of pedagogical substance. The criticisms are directed at three fundamental inadequacies. First, the notions offered as criteria for copula selection are too vague for students to apply because they are questions of metaphysics, not of communication (Navas Ruiz 1963). Is a judgment of width natural or subjective? Are paper's whiteness, nature's variety, and humans' goodness essential or accidental? Are wealth, poverty, age, and psychological disposition temporary or permanent? What *are* essences, conditions, qualities, and semblances in the first place? As Bull (1965:295) observes, 'modern science cannot, with certainty, determine what is an inherent characteristic, and the difference between a quality and a condition becomes, in many instances, a subject for philosophical debate.' Naturally, there is nothing wrong with a debate on human essences in a philosophy class, but few Spanish classes have the time to indulge in one.

Second, it wrongly depicts copula selection as automatically cued by the referent (the entity being referred to): snow must be described as *es blanca*, a citizen as *es francés*, and a person as either *es lista* if clever or *está lista* if ready. Yet Gili Gaya (1973:60-65) notes that one can say both *el chico es alto* and *el chico está alto* for tallness rather than height, and both *la nieve es blanca* and *la nieve está blanca* for snow's whiteness. Bull (1965:293-294) adds that a person's cleverness can be expressed as either *es lista* or *está lista*; Navas Ruiz (1969:165-66) finds many other counterexamples, including *está muy francesa*. We can only conclude that with adjectives the choice of copula is not automatic, but depends on what the speaker chooses to convey.

Third, to the extent that the traditional approach's notions are clear at all, they work in some cases, seem forced in others, and are flatly contradicted by many others (Gili Gaya, 1973:60-65). Virtually every generalization about human behavior has its exceptions, but those which this approach must concede are numerous and glaring. Some of Navas Ruiz's observations are pertinent in this respect:

> *Ella es protestante*, although religious affiliation is neither innate nor necessarily permanent.
> *La casa es azul*, although blueness is not inherent when the house must be painted that color.
> *Es español*, although having Spanish citizenship is not a 'quality'.
> *¡Qué fría está la nieve!* although snow's coldness *is* a quality, and a cold one by definition.
> *Está muerto*, although death is permanent (and a natural state to boot).

Bull (1965:295) adds that 'there are few states more temporary than being young and none more permanent than being old, yet the Spaniard expresses both with either *ser* or *estar*.' It is the theory with such holes in it that is anomalous, not its accumulating exceptions; and to continue to use it, in Bull's strong words, is 'to perpetuate a fraud on the students' (Bull 1965:295).

For Bull, the real key to *ser* vs. *estar* is NORM. Attributes that one regards as normal for an entity are expressed with *ser*, while deviations or changes from the norm are signaled with *estar*. *Estar* accompanies *muerto* because death represents a change from the original condition in which one is remembered; its permanence, innateness, or semblance of being are issues that grammarians cannot resolve and that students cannot apply. *Es viejo* indicates how one generally visualizes a certain individual; *está viejo* indicates a change in how the person strikes the speaker after an interval. The grass of a region can be *es verde* or *está verde* regardless of 'ripeness'; it may normally be green, or 'greened up' by a post-drought shower. *Es triste/enfermo/borracho* suggests that the speaker regards a person as typically gloomy, prone to sickness, given to drunkenness; *está triste/*

enfermo/borracho implies that these are aberrations from the person's usual behavior or physical condition.

Four points are crucial for understanding Bull's theory. First, 'change' can simply be a greater degree of some attribute than usual, not necessarily a switch to the polar opposite. In *¡Qué altas están aquellas montañas!* or *Luisa no sabe lo bonita que está*, the speaker may be suggesting that the observed mountains are especially high for him (in comparison with others) and that Louise is especially good-looking today, rather than implying that a lot of mountain-building occurred overnight or that Louise was formerly hideous. Second, norms are subjective and relative to the individual's own perceptions, expectations, reasoning, and generalization from prior experience. One person may describe carrots as *son ricas*, whereas another who hated them until trying them with a special marinade might say *están ricas*. In fact, a single individual can choose between different perspectives on the same observation. On being introduced to carbon steel, he could form a norm from the evidence of this first contact and declare *Este acero es muy duro*, or he could compare it to his existing norm for metals or for ferrous metals that seemed relatively malleable, and say *Este acero está muy duro*. Third, norms can be revised and adjusted, as when one describes an obese friend who lost weight as *está flaco*, and then later—with the friend's new weight stabilizing and seeming normal now—as *es flaco*.[11] And fourth, sometimes change is so constant, two opposing states so equally likely, and conditions so variable, that there is no real norm at all, as in *está verde* for a stoplight, *está cerrada* for a door, or *está despejado* for a changing sky.

Although Bull's theory works to a large extent, sometimes the norm/deviation distinction becomes rather fuzzy and even seems to disappear.[12] Gili Gaya (1973:63) observes that the contrast blurs when the aspectual force of the preterite or present perfect imposes a termination of a state and therefore a change: 'toda persona de lengua española siente de un modo más o menos confuso que una frase como *esta señora ha sido elegante en otro tiempo* presenta muy atenuado el matiz que la separa de *esta señora ha estado elegante en otro tiempo*. Entre *la reunión fue muy lucida* y *la reunión estuvo muy lucida* apenas si notamos la diferencia.' For Gili Gaya, then, any theory of *ser/estar* must eventually be tied to verbal aspect.

The most ample treatment to date (202 pages) has been that of Navas Ruiz (1963). He compares *ser* and *estar* with other copulas (*seguir, ir, ponerse, resultar, parecer, quedar*, etc.), examines contrasts in copula usage with all kinds of adjectives, and surveys almost two dozen theories, discarding all of them. He agrees with Bull that *estar* implies change, and that copula selection depends on the native speaker's point of view (p. 148) rather than on laws of grammar or metaphysics. He rejects, however, the description of *ser* + Adj as 'norm' because some uses of *estar* portray seemingly normal states: *la nieve de allí siempre está blanquísima; las camas están limpias; la biblioteca está llena de libros.* His own generalization is as follows. *Ser* sets up a relationship between an entity and an attribute that linguists might call unmarked or neutral; it is 'un verbo enteramente gramaticalizado cuya función atributiva es señalar la mera relación' (Navas Ruiz 1963:147). It does little else but 'aportar unos caracteres verbales' to the attribute, allowing a VP to be built up around the Adj. Depending on the specific attribute and entity, this relationship may become classification, definition, identification, or expression of norm, but *ser* does not denote any of these in and of itself; the only particular note it contributes is abstraction from the vicissitudes of time or of time duration—it is essentially *atemporal* (Navas Ruiz 1963:171, 193). *Estar*, on the other hand, never imposes identity between subject and attribute, but establishes the possession of the attribute during an indefinite period of time; it is therefore *temporal* (in the sense of 'contingent upon time', not of 'temporary'). Since relating a subject to an attribute in time brings up possible cessation, result, initiation, intermittence, interruption, resumption of a quality, or a shift in viewpoint, *estar* naturally implies mutability (i.e. Bull's change or deviation):

> Cuando un individuo afirma: *la nieve es blanca,* no se trata de que objetivamente la nieve no pueda ponerse sucia, sino que él, subjetivamente, en aquel momento de su aserto, la ve así, blanca y sin posibilidad de no serlo. . . . Cuando un individuo, por el contrario, afirma: *la nieve está blanca,* la ve como susceptible de cambio desde su punto de mira subjetivo, bien porque pueda ensuciarse o bien porque pueda estar menos blanca. (Navas Ruiz 1963:147)

It is quite possible that the *ser/estar* distinction poses special problems for the English speaker not because it is immeasurably more complicated than other abstractions and abstract distinctions based on the speaker's viewpoint, but because many text writers have not presented it in terms that are clear, applicable, and correct. Fortunately, many newer texts have adopted some version of the Bull and Navas Ruiz theories, and future generations of students may find the use of the two main copulas in Spanish easier than their predecessors.

15.5 Idioms. Some economy is gained in language by expressing new meanings through combinations of old words instead of neologisms. These are IDIOMS, phrases whose meaning is not the sum of the meanings of their parts. For example, although *meter la pata* and *tomarle el pelo* can mean literally 'stick in the paw' and 'take one's hair', in many contexts they bear the special meanings of 'blow it' and 'pull one's leg'; the same observation applies to these two English expressions, which also have both literal and idiomatic meanings. Like *meter la pata* and *tomarle el pelo,* many idioms are fossilized metaphors:[13]

dar en el clavo	echar sapos y culebras	meter la nariz
dar gato por liebre	estar en la luna	pedirle peras al olmo
echar flores	estirar la pata	ser cabeza de turco
	hablar hasta por los codos	

Like proverbs (v. 16.2), metaphorical idioms evolve from the collective cultural experiences of a people, some of which are shared with other cultures. Thus, English speakers will recognize some Spanish idioms as similar to their own: *dar en el clavo* should be clear to those who also regard 'hitting the nail on the head' as a measure of accuracy. Other idioms will make sense in a suitable context, although they will seem unusual when their metaphor is not a salient image in English speakers' culture or a familiar vehicle of meaning in their linguistic experience; such is the case with *pedirle peras al olmo*. Still other idioms are firmly embedded in their respective cultures: *echar sapos y culebras* may seem bizarre to someone whose culture somehow associated obscenity with blueness (*swear a blue streak*) rather than with medievally demonic toads and snakes. We can also cite the vivid contrast of the following Venezuelan reinforcers of *nunca* (Gómez de Ivashevsky 1969:227-228) with the English speaker's *when hell freezes over*:

cuando la rana eche pelos	cuando el chato eche nariz
cuando el gallo ponga	cuando San Juan agache el dedo

Some expressions are treated as idioms simply because their construction is fixed. In *Lo mató a sangre fría* there is no particular semantic or syntactic reason for the use of *a*; it does not have its literal meaning(s), is not required by the transitivity of *matar* or the nature of *sangre*, and does not reflect the speaker's choice of this preposition over *de, con, hacia*, etc. for a PP with a distinct message. *A sangre fría* is a set expression, and *a* is an integral part of it, just like the *in* of the corresponding English *in cold blood*.

Other expressions seem idiomatic not because their meaning or construction is totally arbitrary but because their usual sense is more specific than grammar alone might predict. For example, in both languages the combining of 'give' with 'hand' in a sentence opens up a wide range of potential meanings, including the literal (if unlikely) one of presenting a disconnected limb. But English has specifically narrowed down *give a hand* to (1) assistance and (2) applause, whereas Spanish has settled on handshaking for *dar la mano* and a manual application of paint for *dar una mano*. The narrowed senses are both logical in their own way and might be inferred from context, but they are not predictable from 'give' + 'hand' alone, nor do they match.

In pedagogy, IDIOM is a slippery term that is often applied to locutions whose meaning would be crystal clear to native speakers. In English, for example, the meanings of *housebroken* and *house-warming* are so specialized that they can be regarded as idiomatic, as opposed to *housekeeper* and *house keys*, which native English speakers would find more transparent; using the same patterns, one can say *storekeeper* and *store keys*, whereas *storebroken* seems rather strange. To the Spanish speaker, however, any such compound could be a semantic puzzle. Likewise, *get* + Particle (*in, out, through, over, under, up, down*) makes perfect sense to an English speaker, for whom *get* is an all-purpose verb of attainment, whether of things or of states, postures, and locations; but for the Spanish speaker, who uses *obtener* or *conseguir* for the attainment of things but distinct verbs of movement or becoming otherwise, two-word verbs based on *get* will seem unfathomable and therefore idiomatic.

Conversely, many Spanish collocations have been labeled as idioms just because they strike English speakers as strange when analyzed in terms of English equivalents. As Kirshner (1951:88) put it, the student approaches his language-learning task with the premise that 'Spanish is crazy and unpredictable whereas English is a model of clarity'; any Spanish expression that is different is therefore weird, and relegated to the idiom section of the vocabulary. Yet many such idioms belong to systematic, even productive patterns, and they make perfect lexical and grammatical sense to one who exploits them regularly. *Hacer* in *hace frío/ viento/falta/tiempo que* is impersonal, but otherwise not far off its basic Spanish meaning of 'producir, causar, componer' (RAE 1956:693); it will seem more idiomatic than it is to those who have grown up using some different verb in such contexts.

Likewise, the vast series of collocations with *tener* (... *frío, calor, razón, gracia, cuidado, ganas, miedo, hambre, prisa, X años, X centímetros de largo* ...) is quite systematic in that the verb relates one noun to another in an attributive, nonclassificatory manner. One should note that English uses its *have* in exactly the same way: *have a suspicion, a fever, a dread, a mind to, a hankering, a point, a grudge, patience*, etc. But English speakers happen not to adopt this specific pattern when an NP strikes them as cold, humorous, careful, or of a certain age or size. Hence, *tener paciencia* never appears in idiom lists for English speakers while *tener X años* and *tener cuidado* always do, although they are all cast out of the same mold and are not really idiomatic for Spanish speakers. As DiPietro (1971:130) notes, 'a student is not likely to notice that *tener años* is an idiom in Spanish, meaning 'to be X years of age', if he speaks a language with a comparable expression, such as Italian *aver anni.*' Idioms do exist, but some are less idiomatic than others.

Notes for Chapter 15

1. I have seen estimates of adult vocabulary size ranging from a low of 26,000 words to a high of almost 100,000; I arbitrarily choose 60,000 here as the midpoint of this range. But all such estimates of vocabulary size are risky conjectures, and the ambitious lexicographer who attempted the daunting task of actually counting how many words an adult informant knows would confront several major problems. One is that the lexicon is not static, but steadily changes over one's lifetime with continued education and new experiences. Another problem is the lack of agreement on what constitutes the 'words' to be counted. Should the hosts of proper names and their derivatives be included? Do *más allá* 'beyond', *apañarse* 'get by', and *año luz* 'light year' count as single words or as phrases? Are *yo* and *me*, *él* and *ella*, *amar* and *amante* six distinct words or inflected variants of three? Do pairs such as *el frente* 'front' and *la frente* 'forehead', *gracioso* 'witty' and *gracioso* 'comic character', *cuándo* 'when?' and *cuando* 'when', and *auto* and *automóvil* 'car' constitute single or double lexical entries? Many thousands of items would be affected by one's answer to such questions.

2. Borrowings into Spanish can often be acknowledged as 'naturalized' when their orthography is adapted and when they spin off derivatives: *leader* → *líder liderar*, *clone* → *clon clonar clonación*. Sometimes the borrowing is masked as LOAN TRANSLATION: *luna de miel, ultraligeros, videocintas, anticuerpos, agujero negro*, and *bebé probeta* are based on Eng. *honeymoon, ultralights, videotapes, antibodies, black hole*, and *testtube baby*, but their English morphemes were replaced with Spanish ones.

3. This bracketed representation is equivalent to a tree structure showing internal constituency as in syntax:

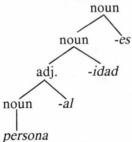

4. Affixes deriving Spanish nouns and adjectives from verbs are generally preceded by some form of the verb's theme vowel (v. 6.1): *observación/repetición, observatorio/dormitorio, cantante/creciente, casamiento/crecimiento, resbaladizo/bebedizo*, etc. Sometimes, however, Spanish retained an irregular derivative from Latin that lacked the theme vowel: *digerir, confundir* → *digestión* (**digerición*), *confusión* (**confundición*).

5. But -*ismo* and -*ista* are currently broadening their meaning and function. *Nerviosismo* is just a noun equivalent of *nervioso*, 'condition of being *nervioso*', not a doctrine; and people who, because of their work, are called *telefonistas, socorristas, oficinistas, electricistas, futbolistas* have no defining -*isms* as groups.

6. This is not to imply that when language X has one word corresponding to two or three in language Y, X necessarily has 'one concept' for these. Neither linguists nor psychologists can really define the concepts of anyone's mind, and it is debatable whether the Spanish speaker has only one concept in *esperar* where the English speaker sees the distinct ones of *waiting, hoping*, and *expecting*. After all, *espero que . . .* may be distinguished from *espero a que . . .*, and the derivatives *la esperanza* and *la espera* are distinct. Vice-versa, although *dull* covers the ground of both *deslustrado* and *desfilado*, English distinguishes the two concepts or senses in the antonyms *bright* or *shiny* for *dull* 'deslustrado' and *sharp* for *dull* 'desfilado' (Stockwell, Bowen, and Martin 1965:273).

7. It will be assumed, in these contrasts, that the surface structures are roughly comparable. Thus, we will ignore a pair such as ¿*Es el gerente?* vs. ¿*Está el gerente?*, whose word orders are alike but not their structures (respectively, copula + PredE vs. copula + Subj).

8. More precisely, as noted by Bull (1965:174), *estar* locates definite NPs and *haber* handles indefinite ones. Thus, ¿*Están ahí los hombres/tus hijas/los González/esos médicos?* vs. ¿*Hay ahí un hombre/suficiente harina/algunos ganchos/veinte médicos?* According to Suñer (1982:324), this *estar* = definite and *haber* = indefinite dichotomy works '95%' of the time, and is therefore of pedagogical value; but it is not foolproof. She offers examples such as the following to suggest that either the Bull theory should be revised, or 'definiteness' should be redefined (Suñer 1982:190):

unique superlative: *Allí había el diamante más grande del mundo.*
identifying relative clause: *Luego hay la otra chica que no ha hecho su tesis.*
identifying PP: *Siempre hay la tendencia a la inercia, ¿no?*
reference back to previous statement: ¿*Hay el sistema ese en tu país?*
listing alternatives: ¿*Cómo voy al centro? Pues, hay el colectivo, y el subte . . .*
locating something indefinite but thematic: *Una pecera de cristal estaba sobre una mesita.*

For Suñer, the function of *haber* is to assert a NP's existence and to introduce it into discourse; that of *estar* is to locate a NP whose existence is taken for granted (presupposed), which usually (but not always) implies definiteness.

9. Most other contributions to the question fall in between. DaSilva (1982:141-147) concedes the inaccuracy of the traditional approach but tries to salvage it, with increasing obfuscation. Ramsey (1894/1956:307-15) starts with a traditional classification but arrives at a Bull-like

generalization (p. 310): 'frequently the use of *estar* implies that the state is different from the normal or expected.' Stockwell, Bowen, and Martin (1965:171) begin with 'classification' for *ser* vs. 'comment' for *estar*, but then decide to follow Bull. Gili Gaya (1973:60-65) concurs with Bull in criticizing the earlier approach, and he explains *ser* and *estar* as respectively showing 'imperfective state' and 'perfective state' ('perfective' in resulting from the previous completion of a process); but he accedes to the traditionalists in retaining 'meaning-changers'. For a fuller critical account of various proposals, see Navas Ruiz (1963).

10. The list of putative meaning-changers with *ser* and *estar* varies according to the analyst; these come from Ramsey (1956). Zierer (1974:18-32) generates an immense list of them distributed among 18 different categories.

11. This example comes from Bull's *Visual Grammar of Spanish* (1972). Although I have tried not to recommend any particular pedagogical materials in this book, this is one resource that deserves endorsement. *VGS* is an excellent series of colorful posters whose pictures and stories pinpoint grammatical and lexical distinctions. It proves the maxim that a picture is worth a thousand words, and it ought to be used more widely than it is.

12. We do not always bear this 'fuzziness' of semantic distinctions in mind when we ask for either-or choices from students. In English, *up the street* contrasts very strongly with *down the street*—until one gives directions on a level street, in which case either can be used with no difference. Likewise, the *ser/estar* contrast is stronger in some contexts than in others.

13. Word formation can be based on metaphor too: *empantanado* and *bogged down* could refer literally to being in a *pantano/bog*, but both carry the additional meaning of 'stuck, unable to proceed'.

Exercises for Chapter 15

1. Divide the following words into their component morphemes. For example, *nerviosismo* = *nervi(o)+os(o)+ismo*, *aclarado* = *a+clar(o) +a+do*. As in these examples, you may use pluses for the morpheme boundaries, and parenthesize sounds/letters that are dropped in derivation. (Alternatively, you may use the bracketing method illustrated in section 15.1.1:[[[*nervi(o)*]*os(o)*]*ismo*].)

(1) incomodidad	(8) rítmicamente
(2) lluviosa	(9) enredadera
(3) sentimiento	(10) enloquecido
(4) descompusieron	(11) veintiseisavos
(5) enojadizo	(12) invencible
(6) ajusticiar	(13) brillantez
(7) retención	(14) asociaciones

(15) maniataron
(16) apesadumbrado
(17) hacedero
(18) sobreviviente
(19) descuidado

(20) trabajadoras
(21) realidad
(22) estadounidense
(23) desembarcadero
(24) ininterrumpidamente

2. (a) What rules are given in texts for the use of the diminutive forms -ito -ico -illo as opposed to the allomorphs -cito -cico -cillo? How 'fixed' are these rules? Can both sets sometimes be used on the same noun?

(b) -illo is labeled as a diminutive suffix; to what extent does -illo mean 'smaller version', given the rather specialized meanings of nouns such as the following?

ventanilla	planilla	tornillo	pasillo
camilla	vainilla	casilla	bocadillo
mantequilla	guerrilla	barbilla	tortilla
bombilla	cerilla	gatillo	bastardillas

(c) What is the semantic effect of the diminutive ending in *ahorita*, *calientito*, and *verdecito*?

3. In your opinion, to what extent—and at what level—should students control Spanish derivational morphemes and patterns of word formation? In particular, which derivational morphemes are productive enough to warrant attention in pedagogy?

4. Some foreign language methodologists argue that the early lessons of a course should make maximal use of cognates, and that major lexical development should be postponed so as to allow more initial concentration on mastering morphology and sentence structure. Others reject this reasoning. Both groups have a point; what is your view, and why? To what extent should readings avoid new or unrecognizable vocabulary items, or gloss them in English? In general, what do you believe should be important in any policy of 'vocabulary control'?

5. Many Latinate words in English do not have the cognates the student might expect in Spanish: *procrastinar, *expectar. The reverse situation exists too, in Latinate Spanish words with no English counterparts. English often has the morphemes that make up such words, but not the words themselves. Following are some examples; can you think of others? To what extent would these give students trouble?

ambicionar	flexibilizar	tremendista	autoproclamación
colisionar	profundizar	posibilitar	problemática (noun)

6. (a) The following list gives more examples of 'amigos falsos', at least for some senses. For each one, give (1) the English word(s) closest to it in meaning and (2) the English word closest to it in appearance and presumably a source of possible error. For example, *facultad*: school, college (≠ faculty 'profesorado')

bombero	soportar	trampolín	asistir
ducha	desplazar(se)	patrón	renta, -able
paso	pretender	armar	quieto

recordar	jubilación	hacienda	sano
constipado	sujetar	pariente	retirar
sopa	ropa	librería	traslación
atender	manifestación	anticipar	intervención
ingenio	intentar	editor	contesta

(b) *Discusión* and *discutir* are usually equated with *discussion* and *discuss*; how true is this matching? That is, if we are discussing, then *¿estamos discutiendo?*

(c) How might the native English speaker, bathed in current American culture, misinterpret the following sentence? *Los jueces integraron el nuevo comité estatal.*

(d) The following headline appeared in *El País* (27-II-1984, *edición internacional*):
ESPAÑA RESISTIRÍA EL CIERRE DEL ESTRECHO DE ORMUZ
The article then reported that Spain had built up oil reserves in case of any cutoff in supply from the Persian Gulf; there was no mention of Spanish intervention in the event of war in the Strait of Hormuz. What is the real meaning of *resistir*, and how might English speakers misinterpret the headline?

7. Construct zigzag diagrams (as in Figure 15.1) for denotative lexical correspondences between English and Spanish, using each of the following as a point of departure.

miss (V)	put (V)	smooth (Adj)	take	thick
add	throw	ease (N)	soft	little
fit (V)	meet	agree	last (Adj)	hole

8. *Back* in English can be used as a verb, adverb, particle, noun, or adjective. How would its concept(s) be conveyed in Spanish?

9. *Desarrollar(se)* is 'develop' and *revelar* is 'reveal'. Yet, on finishing a roll of film, what is the difference between *desarrollar la película* vs. *revelar la película*?

10. *Water supply* translates as *abastecimiento de agua*, and a student who knows the words for 'water' and 'supply' (and, of course, the grammar of noun + noun modification in Spanish) could perhaps generate this term. But *sewage system and water treatment* is typically *alcantarillado y depuración de aguas*, which students probably could not generate on their own. Is this example a case of 'idiom' or of something else?

11. It was pointed out that idioms may or not be idiomatic for native speakers. The following are often treated as idiomatic in U.S. pedagogy; indicate whether you regard each as truly idiomatic in Spanish, and why (not).

trabar amistad	querer decir	hoy día	morder(se) la lengua
por si acaso	tal vez	a todo correr	desde luego

hacer +: mella en, agua, aguas, caso, cola, falta, calor, -se con, juego (con), papel, hincapié

dar +: a la calle, por supuesto, a conocer/entender, -le ganas, a luz, una
    vuelta, las gracias, contra (una pared), una ojeada
tener +: que ver con, hambre, ganas, remedio, cuidado con/de, en
    cuenta, razón
poner +: huevos, la mesa, en marcha, -le al día, por las nubes, en
    ridículo, -se de acuerdo
echar +: al correo, la llave, la culpa, de menos, rayos, mano a/de, a
    perder
llevar +: a cabo, libros, la cuenta, dos años de casado (hospitalizado), el
    compás

12. Many Spanish nouns have adjectival equivalents (often derivatives of the same stem) which their English counterparts lack. In fact, at least in certain technical styles, such adjectives are rather freely created.

televisión, un programa *televisivo* (television, a television program)
banco, una red *bancaria* (bank, a bank network)
Navidad, fiesta *navideña* (Christmas, a Christmas party)
carbón, producción *carbonífera* (coal, coal production)
presupuesto, problemas *presupuestarios* (budget, budget problems)
labor, movimiento *laboral* (labor, labor movement)
teléfono, conversación *telefónica* (telephone, telephone conversation)
policía, archivos *policíacos* (police, police files)
frontera, pueblos *fronterizos* (border, border towns)

Can you think of a syntactic reason for this difference?

13. Onomatopoeia differs from one language to another almost as much as normal lexical items. See how many English/Spanish contrasts in sound effects you can collect. For example, *bang—pum, woof/bowwow—guau-guau.*

14. (a) What criticisms have been leveled at the traditional presentation of *ser/estar*? Where are the two copulas almost in 'complementary distribution', and where do they contrast? How would you explain and illustrate the distinction to students?

(b) The reason for copula selection is sometimes elusive. For example, one says *estoy seguro de que lloverá mañana*, not *soy seguro . . .* Can the presence of *estar* in this construction be rationalized (i.e. made to conform to the usual basis for copula usage), or is this a fixed collocation or idiom? What other uses of *ser* and *estar* pose special problems?

(c) Try to determine the usage of Eng. *make* vs. *do*. First, generate a list of examples for each verb; then, in each example, substitute one verb for the other and ascertain whether this results in (1) oddness or ungrammaticality, (2) an acceptable version synonymous with the original, or (3) an acceptable version with a different meaning. Use your observations to develop a general account of *make/do* usage in English. (Note: the point of this exercise is not so much to arrive at an authoritative analysis of English verbs as to learn how contrasts such as *ser/estar* are investigated.)

15. It was pointed out that words often form fairly self-contained sets or 'semantic fields'. One such area, sensation, was investigated by Lindstrom (1980:722), and the following chart summarizes some of her work. Fill in the remaining entries, and then determine what contrasts, if any, would exist with the corresponding English field. To what extent might such classifications or listings be useful to students, and at what level?

Sense	Part of body	Action	Perception	Stimulus	Modifiers
1. *la vista*	*ojos*	*mirar*	*ver*	*color, forma, apariencia, aspecto*	*claro, oscuro, rojo brillante, chillón, ciego, . . .*
2. *el olfato* . . .		. . .	. . .	. . .	. . .
3. *el oído* . . .		. . .	. . .	. . .	. . .
4. *el tacto* . . .		. . .	. . .	. . .	. . .
5. *el gusto* . . .		. . .	. . .	. . .	. . .

16. Choose some other semantic field and organize its terms in similar fashion.

17. In oral proficiency testing, it is a common observation that a nonnative speaker being examined may talk smoothly and confidently in describing or narrating until he comes up against something whose Spanish name he does not know or has forgotten. One of three things may then happen: his communication comes to a grinding (and painful) halt, or he plugs in his native English word (perhaps semi-Hispanized), or he freely circumlocutes in Spanish around the gap and proceeds with his story. According to the Educational Testing Service (1982), a few lexical gaps are not necessarily damaging to the evaluation, and a successful circumlocution can even be a plus. Why would circumlocuting and paraphrasing be a valued skill that would not necessarily detract from a high performance level? How could teachers promote its development in students?

18. The automobile culture has developed since the importation of Spanish into the New World, and terminology varies regionally today. (Recall the Mamone (1974) study.) See how many Spanish equivalents you can find for the following, perhaps by comparing native speaking informants.

(1) 'drive'
(2) 'turn around/at an intersection/a curve'
(3) 'pass (overtake) another vehicle'
(4) major parts of a car (e.g. 'hood', 'gear shift', 'clutch', 'steering wheel')
(5) types of vehicles: 'car', 'truck', 'station wagon,' 'pickup', 'truck', 'van', 'bus'.

19. Steel (1975) offers a tentative checklist for lexical variation between Spain and America. The following list is based on his work. Ask

some native speakers their normal word for the item (if they do not speak English, elicit it with a definition, picture, or description), and check their usage against Steel's observations. After their first response, probe to see if they know the other term (and when and whether they might use it) or any other variants. You might add other items that occur to you, including the examples used in this chapter.

  (1) 'take, grab': Amer. *agarrar*, Sp. *coger*
  (2) 'pepper' (Capsicum): Amer. *ají*, Sp. *pimiento*
  (3) 'tie': Amer. *amarrar*, Sp. *atar*
  (4) 'pineapple': Amer. *ananás*, Sp. *piña*
  (5) 'narrow': Amer. *angosto*, Sp. *estrecho*
  (6) 'hurry up': Amer. *apurarse*, Sp. *darse prisa*
  (7) 'peas': Amer. *arvejas*, Sp. *chícharos*
  (8) 'bucket': Amer. *balde*, Sp. *cubo*
  (9) 'baby': Amer. *bebé*, Sp. *nene*
(10) 'ticket': Amer. *boleto*, Sp. *billete*
(11) 'throw away': Amer. *botar*, Sp. *tirar*
(12) 'earrings': Amer. *caravanas/aretes*, Sp. *pendientes*
(13) 'P.O. box': Amer. *casilla*, Sp. *apartado*
(14) 'ID card': Amer. *cédula*, Sp. *carnet*
(15) 'of course': Amer. *¡cómo no!*, Sp. *¡claro!*
(16) 'block': Amer. *cuadra*, Sp. *manzana*
(17) 'cream': Amer. *crema*, Sp. *nata*
(18) 'lock': Amer. *chapa*, Sp. *cerradura*
(19) 'peach': Amer. *durazno*, Sp. *melocotón*
(20) 'a stay': Amer. *estadía*, Sp. *estancia*
(21) 'stamp': Amer. *estampilla*, Sp. *sello*
(22) 'thin': Amer. *flaco*, Sp. *delgado*
(23) 'lazy': Amer. *flojo*, Sp. *perezoso*
(24) 'drizzle': Amer. *garúa*, Sp. *llovizna*
(25) 'lightweight': Amer. *liviano*, Sp. *ligero*
(26) 'pretty': Amer. *lindo*, Sp. *bonito*
(27) 'tire': Amer. *llanta*, Sp. *cubierta/neumático*
(28) 'peanut': Amer. *maní*, Sp. *cacahuete*
(29) 'socks': Amer. *medias*, Sp. *calcetines*
(30) 'money': Amer. *plata*, Sp. *dinero*
(31) 'chat': Amer. *plática*, Sp. *charla*
(32) 'bus stop': Amer. *paradero*, Sp. *parada*
(33) 'bedroom': Amer. *recámara*, Sp. *dormitorio*
(34) 'shanty town': Amer. *barriada/callampa/villa miseria*, Sp. *chabolas*
(35) 'refrigerator': Amer. *refrigerador(a)*, Sp. *nevera*
(36) 'can': Amer. *tarro*, Sp. *lata*
(37) 'sidewalk': Amer. *vereda*, Sp. *acera*
(38) 'turn around': Amer. *voltearse*, Sp. *volverse*

Chapter 16
Language knowledge and language use

16.0 Linguistic and communicative competence. Chomsky (1965:3-9) has introduced the term LINGUISTIC COMPETENCE for the knowledge native speakers have of their language: of its phonemes and phonological rules, its grammatical patterns, its lexical and semantic systems, and so on. This knowledge is not conscious awareness, for without special training native speakers cannot explicitly describe question transformations, the pronunciations of vowels, the use of the articles, or the placement of adverbs. In fact, to ask most Spanish speakers '¿Cómo se colocan las palabras en la oración?' would be about as fruitful as to ask '¿Cómo se resta?' or '¿Cómo se atan los cordones?' Yet they correctly and efficiently use their language's word order, just as they quickly carry out subtractions or tie their shoelaces, all with an unconscious but thorough command of what might take linguists, mathematicians, and motor physiologists several tomes to describe fully.

Many linguists today are emphasizing that although linguistic competence is fundamental and vast, native speakers know and use much more in their communication. For one thing, they approach communication with a knowledge of their world and culture that cannot always be disentangled from knowledge of language: to know the meanings of *entender*, *vaca* vs. *toro*, and *hostia* is to share with other speakers a certain understanding of practical epistemology, of zoology, and of religious rites. Moreover, native speakers constantly monitor how their message is being received, and their sentences reflect a situational editing and organizing of material as much as interacting rules of grammar. Their speech is molded by their emotional states, premises, outlooks, beliefs, cultural norms, and perception of consensus and social status; and they follow linguistic etiquettes prescribed by their societies. Expanding the scope still further, the observer notes that speakers accompany their verbal messages with nonverbal ones—gestures, eye contact, posture, facial expressions, use of speaking distance and body contact, and so on; these can differ from one culture to another as much as morphemes and phrase structures. Thus, it is hard to impose boundaries between language, on the one hand, and nonverbal communication, sociocultural background, and world knowledge, on the other. Linguistic competence is one part (though a big one, to be sure) of a broader COMMUNICATIVE COMPETENCE.

One aspect of communicative competence is PRAGMATICS, the effect of context on what is said and how it is construed. It is impossible to study language in isolation of context because pragmatics impinges on the innermost parts of grammar. The following are examples of points at which pragmatic effects have already appeared in this book:

(1) Word order (v. 11.3) reflects how information is being presented in a given situation.

(2) Pronominalization (v. 9.4.1), nominalization (v. 8.4.1), and subject dropping (v. 11.2) are adopted when a noun is obvious from the linguistic or physical context.

(3) Demonstratives and articles (v. 8.3.3) show how a speaker is tagging nouns for reference in a given context.

(4) Mood (v. 7.3.2) conveys the speaker's assumptions about truth or reality, or his assumptions about the hearer's assumptions.

(5) *Ser/estar* (v. 15.4.2) indicates how the speaker feels about the normalness of a characteristic in his experience.

Even phonology ties in with pragmatics. Intonation, for example, is highly sensitive to the speaker's beliefs and communication strategy, as shown by the following examples (based on Lakoff 1971:333; the numbers signal pitch, 3 being highest; v. 4.2).

John called Mary a real lady, and then

(a) she inSÚLted him.

(b) SHÉ insulted HÍM.

In (a), the speaker implies that John paid Mary a compliment, whereupon she inexplicably turned on him; in (b), he implies that *real lady* was taken as a sexist put-down, so that her insulting of John was in justifiable retaliation. This example shows that it is the whole background culture, and not just the physical microcontext of the speaker and hearer, which affects interpretation; in a society less sensitive to the putative sexism of certain labels, the thrust of (b) would be quite obscure. At this point, then the linguist must join up with the sociologist and the anthropologist in explaining the behavior of a language user.

16.1 The pragmatics of the speaker-hearer relation. The most conspicuous element in the social context of speech is the hearer, and the speaker must make certain assumptions about that hearer and about the 'ego-alter' relationship, as it is sometimes called. From those assumptions follow several linguistic decisions, among them (1) forms of address and reference, (2) stylistic levels of pronunciation and grammar, and (3) types of vocabulary to be used.

16.1.1 Address and reference, and *tú* vs. *usted*. In most texts, *tú* and *usted* are respectively described as 'informal, intimate, familiar' vs. 'formal, polite'. These labels are convenient, but they have little meaning for someone who is unfamiliar with the norms of informality and politeness in Hispanic societies, and in specific concrete situations they may be unreliable. Any English-speaker easily appreciates that speaking to one's lover is intimate while speaking to royalty should be formal and polite. But what about speaking to an animal, a police officer, a waiter, a secretary, a young aunt, an elderly aunt, a kindly deliveryman, a fellow student with whom there is no intimacy, a well-known village priest, another driver, a distant cousin, God, a friendly teacher, a *criada* near one's own age, or the dear old *señora* with whom one lodges? How does one address audiences and exhort them to vote, adopt modern farming methods, buy a car, or oppose insidious threats to the community? In such cases, it is unclear whether a 'formal' or 'intimate' pronoun should be used, and in fact these labels could cue exactly the wrong choice.

The pragmatic basis of *tú/usted* is the social relationship between the speaker and the addressee. Older English had a similar distinction between *thou* and *you*, but the latter was eventually generalized (v. 9.2.1). In Modern English, the only comparable distinction is in VOCATIVES, the sentence tags for calling out to people and getting their attention. In *Are you going, John?*, the vocative *John* signals a *tú*-like relationship; in *Are you going, Mr. (Dr., Pres.) Smith?*, the more formal vocative suggests *usted*. In fact, a useful rule of thumb is to use *tú* if 'you' would be addressed with a given name and *usted* if a title or title + last name would be used. But this is not infallible, given social differences between cultures. In the United States, a clergyman and adult parishioner, a professor and student, or a plumber and homeowner may proceed quickly to reciprocal or nonreciprocal use of given names, whereas all three relationships tend to be more formal in Spanish.

Brown and Gilman (1960) abandoned the problematic notions of familiarity and formality and took a fresh approach to describing the 'T/V' phenomenon (so named for French *tu/vous*) in European languages. After analyzing results from questionnaires and comparing a variety of specific DYADS (two-person relationships), they concluded that the main bases for T/V are POWER and SOLIDARITY. With 'power', the person who is superior (in rank, age, experience, position, social advantage) gives T and receives V, a nonreciprocal (asymmetric) usage. With 'solidarity', two people use reciprocal T for expressing ingroupness, mutual attraction, or commonality of beliefs, backgrounds, position, goals, status, and affiliation; otherwise they adopt mutual V (e.g. for business relationships). The power basis dominated in the Middle Ages, but the trend more recently has been toward solidarity; the main remnant of power in T/V today is that the more 'powerful' person in the dyad is the one who signals the switch from mutual V to mutual T (*tuteo*) in recognition of solidarity having developed (as in English, 'Just call me John'). Figure 16.1 summarizes these observations.

Brown and Gilman note that the social relationships behind T/V are fluid or dynamic, because a mutual V ⟵⟶ V can shift to T ⟵⟶ T and vice-versa, whether permanently or for transient attitudes. Thus, two drivers can change from a businesslike V to an angry shouting match with T; two acquaintances on T-terms can show estrangement or ironic detachment with V; and an employer and employee on V-terms for conducting office business may change to T when gossiping about mutual acquaintances or community affairs.

Figure 16.1 Brown and Gilman's analysis of T-forms (*tú*) and V-forms (*usted*).

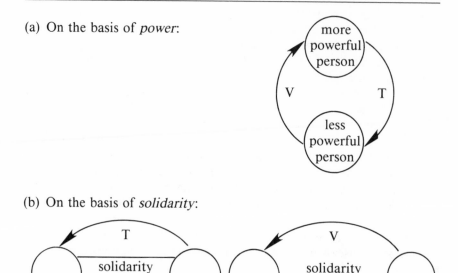

(a) On the basis of *power*:

(b) On the basis of *solidarity*:

This analysis must be regarded as a general tendency, not an absolute social law, since different societies and different individuals do not define 'solidarity' in exactly the same way. Brown and Gilman themselves observed sharp differences in how the French and Germans used family ties in establishing a T-relationship. Since Hispanic societies are even more diverse and heterogeneous than those of France and Germany, one would expect more variation there —which, in fact, is the case. At one extreme, Hispanics of the U.S. southwest have generalized *tú* at the expense of *usted* (Sánchez 1982:30); at the other, among some Central and South Americans *usted* has been generalized even for affectionate address (Kany 1945/1951:92ff.). In between lie countless variations. Lambert and Tucker 1976 found that Puerto Ricans, for instance, apply 'power' and 'solidarity' according to their own individual experiences, whereas middle-class children in Bogotá have more fixed norms as a group: reciprocal T within the family, and reciprocal V outside it (but nonreciprocal, power-based T ⟷ V with much older people), and reciprocal T with peers (but V ⟷ V among boys).

The teacher grants that there is dialectal, social, and idiolectal variation in *tú/usted* (as there is also in English vocative usage), but in the classroom one must generalize, and the notions of 'power' and 'solidarity' are as useful generalizations as any. Nevertheless, students should be cautioned that the exact application of such principles will really become clear only through personal experience in particular native-speaking societies.

16.1.2 Style and style shifting. The relationship between two speakers is not defined in a sociolinguistic void, for it depends on their situation. In all the T/V languages, a judge and a lawyer might use mutual T at a soccer game and over their beers, but in the courtroom they will switch to mutual V, regardless of their solidarity outside that situation. But more than pronominal selection is affected by changes of situation; one's phonology, grammar, and lexicon also shift. Linguists describe these contextual levels of language as a scale of STYLES (or REGISTERS) that range from relatively formal to quite casual. At the formal extreme lies 'literary' standard usage, with occasional florid and hypercorrect flourishes; at the casual extreme are found slang and ellipsis. In between is a continuum of semiformal, colloquial, and semicasual levels. One changes styles of speech much as he changes styles of clothing, and the ability to shift styles appropriately is a crucial marker of communicative competence.

We have already seen this stylistic differentiation in phonology: the application of variable rules increases or decreases according to the kind of speech used in a given setting (v. 3.0-3.2). Thus Argentines aspirate /s/ more when speaking casually (e.g. at home and about family concerns) than when delivering a prepared address to a large audience. In grammar, too, different speech levels appear in that the more formal the style, the longer and more complex the sentences and the more standardized the morphology. In the lexicon, words such as *proferir, perjudicial, procurar* are more formal than the plainer *decir, dañino, lograr,* and *crisma, mamá, jorobar* are more colloquial than *cabeza, madre, molestar.* Seizing on such differences, Lombardi and Peters (1981:143-144) show how sentences can be 'translated' from style to style:

	Formal:	Colloquial:	'Vulgar':
(a)	¡Tenga la bondad de callarse!	¡Cállate!	¡Cierra ese pico!
(b)	Ella está en estado interesante.	Ella está encinta.	Ella está preñada.
(c)	Pasó a mejor vida el rico.	Se murió el ricachón.	Estiró la pata el platudo.
(d)	¡Qué vida tan pobre!	¡Qué vida tan perra!	¡Qué vida tan jodida!

The products of foreign language pedagogy tend to be quite monostylistic, steeped in an essentially formal, even literary, register of language. Proceeding abroad, they soon encounter, and are expected to respond to , *¿Quiay?,' Tá bravo, Pal reffriao nomá,* and so on for what they learned as *Buenos días, Está enfadado,* and *Solamente para el resfriado.* Moreover, they are generally unaware that a change from *Buenos días* to *¿Quiay?* may be just as strong a signal as the change from *usted* to *tú.* In the same way, Hispanic students of English learn *Could you not find them?* and *I must leave,* but instead hear (and fail to pick up on) *Couldncha findem?* and *Gotta split.* Until nonnative speakers round out their stylistic repertoires, their language will seem relentlessly formal, sounding stilted and standoffish in casual situations; and they may be insensitive to social messages being conveyed by the speech around them.

Style is sometimes used in a second sense, namely, for the special characteristics and conventions of cultivated exposition. This is the 'style' of literary, journalistic, and essay writing. It is hard to lay down useful generalizations for it, because it is learned through imitation of native models, not by following rules. It combines verbal mannerism, a feel for rhythmic cadences, attention to precise formulation, a degree of lexical and syntactic refinement, and what Stockwell et al. (1965:276-277) call the native 'mold of thought'; but it is too elusive and subtle to be pinned down by any of these notions or subjected to contrastive analysis. Some of the contrasting Spanish/English examples of Stockwell et al. illustrate the problem.

(1) Se salvó oportunamente al refugiarse detrás de una columna.

(1) He saved himself in the nick of time by ducking behind a post.

(2) Estuvieron trabajando toda la mañana con abnegada y sacrificada labor.

(2) They spent the whole morning working without thought for themselves.

(3) Los policías tuvieron que realizar varios disparos para detener a los prófugos.

(3) The police had to fire several shots in order to stop the escapees.

It would probably not occur to the native English speaker to say or write *con abnegada y sacrificada labor.* Thinking in English and then attempting a Spanish translation, he might resort instead to *sin pensamiento para sí mismos,* which is bizarre. Correcting this to *sin pensar en sí mismos* improves it, but it still is not as 'sofisticado' (as one informant put it) as the Spanish idiom. Unless he assimilates this kind of stylistics to some extent, the student's Spanish will sound wooden and plain, or hot off the translation machine. And since people are judged by their language, a student who may project considerable sophistication in his English may come across as lifeless and unrefined in Spanish.

16.1.3 Words of group identity: Argot and slang. As noted in the previous chapter (v. 15.0), a large number of words recorded in dictionaries belong to the special jargon or ARGOT of particular fields and subcultures. Consequently, the average Spanish or English speaker is unlikely to use terms such as the following without some degree of experience in the indicated fields. (See Duden 1963 for a reference collection of certain argots.)

retorta/retort (chemistry)
isobara/isobar (meteorology)
umbela/umbel (botany)
escarificador/harrow (farming)
positrón/positron (physics)
subrutina/subroutine (computers)
asíntotas/asymptotes (geometry)
escoria/slag (mining)
amortizar/amortize (economics)
fonema/phoneme (linguistics)
barrena/auger (carpentry)

médula oblonga/medulla
 oblongata (anatomy)
doble bemol/double flat (music)
año-luz/light-year (astronomy)
devolución de revés/backhand
 (tennis)
muestreo aleatorio/random
 sample (statistics)
sobreseimiento/stay (law)
estribor/starboard (sailing)

The learning of such words is often regarded as a simple matter of semantic need: in most realms of life speakers can get along without knowing of legal stays, but if they ever study law or are affected by a stay, then they will pick up *sobreseimiento* and other 'legalese' terms as needed. Yet there is another side to argot, a social one. Just as speakers change their pronouns, vocatives, and styles in response to one another's status, they adopt vocabularies that identify shared experience in the various endeavors of life. To use legalese appropriately can mark the speaker as conversant with the legal profession, perhaps belonging to it; and it can either signal solidarity with a hearer of like status or exclude one that is not 'in the know' about such matters. In other words, one function of argot is to establish group identity by demarcating an in-group from the out-group, and one's control of the jargon indicates which group he identifies with.

In this social respect, argot resembles slang. Slang is more colloquial than professional argot, but both are used to define grouphood. Some expressions offered by Lombardi and Peters (1981:156-164, 289-294) include the following:

(1) Student slang: *profe* 'profesor', *cole* 'colegio', *mili* 'servicio militar', *materia jodida* 'clase aburrida'
(2) underworld *caló*: *afufar* 'escaparse', *birlar* 'robar', *tasquera* 'pelea'
(3) the *lunfardo* of the Buenos Aires underclass: *morfar* 'comer', *aceitar* 'sobornar', *macanear* 'mentir'

To some extent, too, many usages of the chicanos may be considered slang as much as dialect: e.g. *borlo* 'fiesta', *birria* 'cerveza', *gabachado* 'asimilado a los gringos', *tecolote* 'policía', *migra* 'agente de inmigración', and the abundant derivatives of *chingar* 'joder'.

Argot and slang are generally not considered a problem in pedagogy. Terms such as *sobreseimiento* and *profe* are unlikely to appear in texts addressed to a general audience except as glossed terms in a reading. They may be needed (and presumably will then be acquired) during extended stays in Hispanic societies, but they have low priority in most classrooms. On the other hand, argot is gaining importance with the rise of specialized courses such as *Español Comercial*, *Español para Médicos*, and *Español para Policías*, and many teachers who find themselves in charge of generating such courses might appreciate greater access to professional lexicons.

16.2 Proverbs and other cultural allusions.

In our cosmopolitan-oriented culture, folk wisdom as expressed in the proverb has lost much of its meaning, and, even more, its prestige. Hispanic culture is still close to the land, its characteristic wisdom is still legal tender among the educated, and the proverb is a key to understanding the people. Tell students that they are going to learn some of the most common proverbs, first to learn more vocabulary and patterns, and second to get to understand Spanish-speaking people better. (LaMadrid et al. 1974b:121)

The foregoing statement is a bit too sweeping, since many English speakers still use proverbs or understand them even if they seldom use them. Moreover, there are plenty of urbanized Hispanics who, like their equally 'cosmopolitan' Anglophone counterparts, retain little proverbial folk wisdom.[1] Certainly, there are few walking *refraneros* like Sancho Panza with us today. But it is true that Spanish speakers as a whole tend to use more proverbs, and to use them more often, than most modern English speakers.

It is also true that proverbs may help students to understand Spanish speakers and their culture to some extent. This is because such sayings are verbal repositories of the collective experiences and traditions of a people. By appealing to proverbs, a speaker does several things: (1) he identifies himself with his society's values, (2) he establishes consensus rather than staking out ideological independence, and (3) he economizes by forgoing a discussion of the ins and outs of an issue and appealing to a time-tested generalization. For example, an allusion to *A bird in hand is worth two in the bush* or to *Más vale pájaro en mano que cien volando* relates an issue to conventional wisdom, assumes agreement and a shared perspective on life, and reduces a lengthy exposition on risk-taking to one short sentence. In this example, the two languages converge on the same hunting metaphor; in *A big frog in a small pond* and *En tierra de ciegos el tuerto es rey*, their images differ but they make the same point. But cultural outlooks can contrast, and proverbial wisdom with them. English speakers are often exhorted to speak out and speak up, for *The squeaky wheel gets the grease*; Spanish speakers, however, learn that *Por la boca muere el pez* and that *En boca cerrada no entran moscas*. Here, Spanish culture seems more akin to that of Japan, where one grows up on *Deru kugi wa utareru* ('the nail that sticks out gets hit'). Yet cultures are multifaceted and they register opposing philosophies, so that no single proverb conveys the entire communal wisdom. The speaker who sighs in resignation after saying *Más vale pájaro en mano que cien volando* can be rebutted by the rejoinder *Pero quien no se aventura no pasará la mar.*

The sociocultural context of communication seeps into language in many other places. The traveler attempting to use his second language in conversations with his hosts is soon hit with a barrage of allusions to folklore, history, literature, popular heroes and antiheroes, current fads and trends, placenames, isms, and sports teams. There will be references to domestic products, jokes about local affairs, euphemisms and innuendo, appraisals of the sociopolitical scene, and much else, and the foreigner will fail to get the point. His dictionary, no matter how inclusive it may be, will not explain references such as the following:

tan gracioso como Cantinflas	the Truman surprise in '48
esos etarras de Euskadi	he talks like a Cosell
Guadalupe me ha oído	the IRS ignores IRAs
¿ganó el Real Madrid?	the patience of a Job
¡ni la CEE ni la OTAN!	an Archie Bunker mentality

Also, the traveler may have an excellent command of grammar and vocabulary but not the slightest understanding of local terms for foods, drinks, flora and fauna, room accommodations, weights and measures, medications, film types, clothing sizes, currency, landmarks, banking procedures, and so on; and knowing these for one country does not guarantee success in the next. Thus the Spanish scholar Ramón Carnicer (1977:99-120) relates how, on his first trip to Mexico, he was struck not only by the expected dialect differences, but also by references to *la mordida* ('bribe'), *salaciones* (bad luck brought on through salt), *balaceras* (gunfights in the streets), *loncherías* ('fast-food restaurants'), *licuados, mole, tequila, Zona Rosa,* etc.

When Spanish language syllabi are already so full that final chapters cannot be covered, teachers might understandably argue that it is one thing to introduce an occasional proverb or cultural capsule but quite another to cover soccer teams, political parties, commercial products, and the ephemeral 'celebs' and fashions of the countries whose language is being studied. Knowing a language requires knowing something about its speakers' culture, but for the student some details of native speaker life can be regarded as relatively marginal. With the speech acts discussed below, however, sociocultural information pervades the structure of conversation itself, and the native speaker may not excuse ignorance in this area so readily.

16.3 Speech acts and their verbal lubricants. Speakers use special verbal rituals and procedures to conduct SPEECH ACTS, i.e. linguistic business such as requests, proposals, acknowledgments, introductions, etc. In any given speech act, certain words and phrases are intended, and understood, as having a special pragmatic meaning cuing a certain behavior in the particular context. A good example from English is *Can you pass the salt?*, which in an appropriate dining context does not inquire into the addressee's salt-passing capacity but instead implies (1) 'there's a salt shaker near you', (2) 'I want it', and (3) 'give it to me.' The response to this ostensible yes/no question is not *Yes I can*, but the carrying out of the implicit command, often with the verbal accompaniment of *Here you are* (which is pragmatically specialized itself, ≠ 'You are here').

As another example, the short phrase *Cash or charge?* is pragmatically interesting in three ways. First, it presupposes familiarity with the purchasing options that prevail in U.S. culture; *charge*, even when well defined in a bilingual dictionary, would have little meaning for a traveler from a society that prefers cash for everything. Second, this phrase is ELLIPTICAL, whittled down from the fuller version *Are you going to pay with cash, or are you going to charge your purchases?* By ellipsis, a sentence is abbreviated to a formula that is understandable only because native speakers readily fill in the missing information from their knowledge of the first point, i.e. what customarily transpires in a given situation. Third, this is superficially a choice question, grammatically akin to *Coffee or tea?*, (< *Would you prefer coffee, or tea?*), but in this situation the cashier is not giving an either/or choice but only asking how the customer wishes to pay. The unmentioned option *By check*—or even more elliptically, *Check*—is therefore an acceptable response, IN THIS SITUATION. Otherwise, choice questions exclude unmentioned options; if a hostess offers *Coffee or tea?* the answer *Tequila with a worm* would be odd, perhaps a social gaffe. Formulas such as *Cash or charge?* are part of a linguistic etiquette that encodes a vast knowledge about expected behavior in a culture, and they lubricate and expedite our interpersonal transactions.

Similar pragmatic formulas are, of course, used in Spanish. A native speaker may begin an encounter with *Hola, ¿qué hay?* If the hearer is unfamiliar with Spanish pragmatics, he may interpret this as a rather strange question—*¿Qué hay DÓNDE?* But it has the force of a greeting, like Eng. *How's it going?* or *How are you?* (themselves pragmatically specialized). If one asks *¿Sabe Ud. la fecha?*, this will be construed as a request for the date (and presupposed but not stated, *today's* date), not an inquiry into the hearer's mastery of calendar systems. If the addressee does not know, he may answer *Lo siento, no sé*, with the *lo siento* signifying merely the inability to comply with the request, not regret, commiseration, or an apology for stupidity. The special situation of letter writing abounds with pragmatic expressions—*estimado señor, su seguro seguidor, queda suyo afectísimo*—which are neither meant nor taken at face value. Likewise, on hearing a salesclerk announce *A sus órdenes*, a customer recognizes that he is not entitled to start issuing any *órdenes* that come to mind—

¡Salte!, *¡Quite los maniquíes!*, etc.; in fact, even the semantically germane order *Véndame este traje* would be pragmatically blunt or clumsy. And after being introduced to a new person, one may say *Mucho gusto* or *Para servirle*, regardless of how much pleasure or willingness to serve is felt. These formulas conventionally supplant responses such as *Me alegro de que nuestro mutuo amigo nos haya presentado*, which makes sense but is not the usual etiquette.

These examples are but the tip of the iceberg. Among the communicative functions in which pragmatists have discovered specialized usages are the following:[2]

(1) inviting, requesting (and complying or declining)
(2) excusing, apologizing, thanking (and responding to these)
(3) sympathizing, complimenting, congratulating (and acknowledging these)
(4) narrating, expounding
(5) arguing, criticizing, debating, objecting, counseling
(6) agreeing, disagreeing, indicating 'yes, I follow'
(7) initiating and concluding conversation, interrupting, turn-taking
(8) hesitating, hedging, qualifying
(9) expressing affect (anger, shock, dismay, relief, etc.)
(10) greeting, leave-taking, addressing with vocatives
(11) promising (bets, contracts, etc.)
(12) rituals: parliamentary procedure, ceremonies, introducing guest speakers, prayers
(13) transacting business (telephone calls, purchases, bartering)
(14) phatic communion (speech for establishing or maintaining contact, as in chit-chat about the weather or about each other's families)

One learns the customary verbal procedures for such speech acts through lifelong experiences with his language in a variety of sociocultural settings. Hence it is debatable how much can be, or should be, taken up in a sterile classroom that is psychologically and physically distant from the culture and the people being studied. Most texts introduce such *fórmulas de cortesía* as *gracias, hola, por favor*, and *adiós*, but there is little consensus on what else should be covered. In fact, there are few resource materials that teachers and text writers could consult for learning what to present and how. Lindstrom (1980:719) notes this gap and proposes that dictionaries identify the specific pragmatic functions of certain words—e.g. the use of *nomás, a ver, o sea* as 'filler words' with the meaning of 'keeping the lines of communication open'. Receptively, students can misinterpret such signals, as Lindstrom learned when a student 'deciphered the repetitive *o sea*'s of her professor as appeals to the prophet Hosea'. Expressively, students who fail to use such expressions may miscue their interlocutors, making for awkward or even painful conversations.

Some of the formulas that one language uses with pragmatic force have ready equivalents in the other, and they can be loosely equated in pedagogy: *oye/oiga* = *hey, eh(ste)* = *uh, ¿y (qué)?* = *so (what)?, eso es* = *that's it, felicitaciones* = *congratulations.* Others may match in ordinary speech, but certain situations may call for more florid variants in either or both languages. Thus, students are taught that *thanks, I'm sorry,* and *please* are, respectively, *gracias, lo siento,* and *por favor;* but Spanish speakers sometimes prefer *es favor que me hace* (e.g. 'thank you' in response to a compliment), *dispense Ud.* (e.g. 'I'm sorry' in apology for lateness), and *sírvase (tenga la bondad de, me hace el favor de* . . .). There may be a difference in emotive content or forcefulness too: *¡Dios mío!* and other invocations of holy figures are not as strong in Spanish as their literal English equivalents. Likewise, the common taboo words can be mild imprecations in one language but disastrously shocking in the other.

In other cases, the verbal conventions of two languages may differ strongly or signal very different behaviors. The English speaker's *excuse me* covers at least three situations that Spanish distinguishes with *¿cómo?* (failure to comprehend), *perdón/perdone* (after committing a social offence), and *con permiso* (in anticipation of inconvenience). Clearly, it would be boorish to say *con permiso* after stepping on another's foot. Sometimes, too, a literal translation of pragmatic formulas can be quite misleading. The traveler approaching a shopkeeper's open door may hear *¡Pase Ud.!* or *¡Siga!* and wrongly infer that he is unwelcome and has been bidden to pass on by without entering. Often a verbal convention will seem mysterious to the nonnative speaker because it entails procedures in a local culture which are obvious to everyone but him. For example, on showing a postal clerk a package to be mailed, the tourist may be told *Hay que revisarlo* and be dismissed; to the English speaker, this seems a brusque nonsequitur (even when he knows that *revisar* is 'check,' not 'revise'); yet to locals it obviously implies 'así que suba Ud. esa escalera y siga a la puerta núm. 22.'

Gorden 1974 systematically studied the cultural conflicts that ensue when American students stay with Colombian host families. As a sociologist, his main emphasis was not linguistic, but he found copious cases in which misuse of linguistic rituals led to misunderstanding, mutual estrangement, and reinforcement of negative stereotypes. Some of them are given here:

(1) The American student grits his teeth and endures a primitive cold shower before retiring. Wondering at his spartanism, the *señora* asks if he prefers cold showers at night. The American misunderstands and says yes. Actually, she was using an indirect approach, which Colombians value for its politeness, to imply that *warm* showers were available in the morning,

when one normally bathes (in Colombia), but that the water heater could be turned on specially for him if he wished (p. 41).

(2) The *criada* pours concentrated Colombian coffee into the cup before adding warm milk, and expects the drinker to say 'when'. The American says *Bastante* but she keeps on pouring. It turns out that *bastante* is elliptical for 'quiero bastante', not 'es bastante'; the correct signal is *¡Ya!* (p. 41).

(3) Americans acknowledge some favors with a simple *thanks*—if at all (silence or a nod is more tactful sometimes in the United States); Colombians accept *gracias* for a simple favor like lending a match, but expect more verbal profusion for larger favors. Several Colombian families were therefore upset when an expensive excursion they had set up for their lodgers was acknowledged by a mere *gracias*. Those few lodgers who waxed on and on in appreciation—excessively, by U.S. standards—were admired as *bien educados* (p. 107).

(4) Americans thought they were polite in greetings and farewells, but felt that Colombians gave very confused signals as to coming or going. The Colombians complained that Americans were clumsy with the proprieties. Apparently, the Americans did not know that Colombians (a) expect frequent greetings, (b) expect personal touches to be added to greetings (*¿Qué tal está la familia?*) and to farewells (*Saludos en tu casa*), (c) acknowledge each other in passing with *adiós* (vs. *hi* among Americans), and (d) use *buenos días* and *buenas noches* for both greetings and farewells (vs. Eng. *good morning* and *good evening* for greetings, *good day* and *good night* for leave-taking) (pp. 107-109).

It is very easy for the student to get the idea that he still does not know the language when, despite his language studies, he constantly seems to be saying the wrong thing. His hosts may share this impression with him, and the escalating misunderstandings will give the student a sense of personal rejection and failure. Unless he is strongly motivated, he may call it quits at this point, if he has not done so already.

16.4 Aptitude and attitude in language learning and use. The road to communicative competence is fraught with a constant correcting of errors and a never ending list of new vocabulary and new usages, and many students give up long before any major pragmatic hurdles are reached. Even those who continue onward may regress and, to the frustration of their teachers, 'forget' usages after demonstrating apparent mastery of them in drills or on tests. The teacher can present the facts of the language and practice them intensively, but knowledge alone does not ensure native-like performance in the target language.

Part of this problem is that foreign languages were formerly taught as content courses instead of skill courses; many students still approach Spanish and French as they do history or political science. As a corrective, modern texts emphasize the 'four skills', 'communication', 'function', and other aspects of the conversion of knowledge-about to proficiency-in. There is a greater awareness that knowledge of, say, gender and mood must evolve into unthinking, automatic use of these in active communication. Consequently, students should be given as much contact as possible with the language in a variety of situations; some educators have, in fact, promoted total immersion in the target language, reasoning that foreign language learners (adults) need the same continuous stimulation available to first language learners (children), in all contexts and for all their needs.

But although total immersion has enjoyed some success—after all, everyone agrees that more contact helps—its underlying analogy between adults and children is not entirely valid. Children learn a language effortlessly, rapidly, even joyously, and through it they build their personalities and cognitive systems. Adults, on the other hand, tend to be more plodding and analytical, and they are already set in their ways culturally and linguistically. Moreover, children can learn a second or third language with the same ease and maintain them as distinct systems (COORDINATE bilingualism), whereas adults seem to construct their second language on top of the first (SUBORDINATE bilingualism), which yields source-to-target interference. It is well known that when a family spends an extended period abroad, the children can pick up the new language just by playing with peers, while their parents achieve more limited success and retain features of their first language (allophones, intonation, rhythm, lexical usage, favored syntactic patterns and pragmatic strategies) that betray them as foreigners.

Two theories have attempted to explain this difference between children and adults. The first, which can be called the 'Ability' or 'Aptitude' Theory, is based on rationalist traditions, and postulates that children are born with a special inductive and deductive capacity for figuring out rules (grammar) from raw data (speech). Adults retain only an attenuated degree of this aptitude. Studies suggest that the cutoff point is around age 12, so that the first decade or so of life is the 'critical age' for language learning. Afterward, speakers make additions to their lexicons and stylistic repertoires, but these are mere accretions on an already congealed system; they can no longer start from scratch as children can. According to Chomsky (1959 and subsequent writings), who has been one of the foremost exponents of the Ability Theory, this developmental pattern is genetically preprogrammed into human development.

The opposing theory (or cluster of theories, perhaps) proposes that the difference between children and adults has less to do with innate ability than with sociocultural conditioning of attitudes; this will be called the 'Motivation Theory'. Many of its supporters draw their tenets and terms from behaviorism, which hypothesizes that children do not 'figure out rules' but form habits in imitation of their parents' behavior; the parents moreover direct this habit formation by teaching, reinforcement, and control of input. The older the child becomes, the stronger his habits become and the harder they are to modify, though this is not altogether impossible. The critical age is explained in terms of maturation and socialization; increasingly, the child's self-image becomes fixed, he values his peer relationships, he is inured to one kind of behavior, and his approach to new information is entrenched. In short, the post-puberty language learner will have less motivation to adopt completely new behavior, although in principle new behavior can be acquired under conditions that favor different habits.

As with the larger Nature versus Nurture debate, the truth here may lie between the extremes, for each side can marshal cogent evidence from developmental studies. On the side of the Ability Theory are facts such as the following, which resist explanation unless some innate basis for language acquisition during childhood is posited.

(1) Parents do not overtly teach, drill, or explain linguistic structure; most, in fact, would have no idea how to describe phonological rules, tense systems, or the morphology and meanings of copulas. Nevertheless, their children somehow determine complex rules and patterns with amazing efficiency and rapidity.

(2) Parents do not specifically reinforce mastery of each unit, rule, construction, etc.; if anything, they unwittingly reinforce children's errors by remarking on their cuteness and by adopting them in their own speech with their children. Without direct reinforcement (or in spite of it) children still learn, and the only reinforcement they seem to require for language is the opportunity to use it.

(3) Although children are imitative to some extent, from the start they take building blocks of their parents' language and recombine them spontaneously to create sentences that they have never heard before. Evidently, they do not memorize sentences, but learn rules for producing them. They learn morphological rules as well, as shown by their ignoring adult models and producing forms that do not exist. Resnick (1981:116-117) illustrates this point as follows:

> Oímos a un niño de dos o tres años decir, por ejemplo, *yo cabo. Si el niño aprendiera principalmente por imitación, entonces diría yo quepo, como lo dicen los adultos que lo rodean. Sin embargo, el niño dice *cabo por la abrumadora evidencia de otras formas verbales . . . El niño formula su hipótesis en base a los datos que oye y a la necesidad humana de buscar orden y estructura en el aparente caos de la producción verbal de sus interlocutores . . . Y no importa cuántas veces la gente le corrija su palabra juvenil, el niño no la suelta hasta que se convence de que su hipótesis está al menos parcialmente errónea y de que tiene que formular una o más reglas aparte para producir la forma anómala quepo.

(4) Regardless of the language, the surrounding culture, and the conditions of upbringing, children follow uniform paths through rather

clear-cut stages in learning language. Comparative studies are showing that the uniformity in phonological, grammatical, and lexico-semantic development is quite striking. In phonology, intonation comes early, /t/ comes before /r/, /n/ before /l/, /s/ before /θ/; lest this be attributed to ease of articulation, it should be recalled that /s/, for instance, is articulatorily more complex than /θ/ (v. 2.1.4.2). In syntax, all children tend to establish basic phrase structures before proceeding to most transformed patterns, with no linguist to point out PSRs and transformations to them (see, for example, the study of the acquisition of Spanish syntax by González 1978).

(5) The reason for adults' difficulties with language acquisition is not simply entrenched habits that interfere with new ones; it turns out that even with no prior linguistic experience, older learners undertake language learning differently from children. Fromkin et al. (1981) report on the case of Genie, an adolescent rescued from a home where she had been kept from hearing or using language; she soon began learning some English, but haltingly and with problems that young children do not have. The 'critical age' does seem biologically determined.

Before the teacher gloomily asks '¿Por qué me esfuerzo entonces?', we turn to those who ascribe the difference to motivation, for they also have a point. Even if adults do not attain perfect foreign language competence or native proficiency, they can make considerable headway with a favorable attitude and a flexible outlook. In this regard, Lambert 1963 and others have distinguished three kinds of motivation in foreign language study and explored their consequences. With INSTRUMENTAL motivation, one studies the language as a means to some end, e.g. to get ahead or for access to information; he may have no intention of joining another group or directly communicating with it. With MANIPULATIVE motivation, one studies the language for the specific function of getting people to satisfy his personal or business needs; he requires some active skill, expressive and receptive, but need not assimilate to his interlocutors. With INTEGRATIVE motivation, one identifies with the foreign culture and seeks to join it through its language; he wants to sound like and act like the target group, and to be accepted by it. Some examples of the three types:

(1) Instrumental: the student who studies Spanish to sing Spanish folksongs or to read Mexican anthropological journals.
(2) Manipulative: the business graduate who plans to use his Spanish in the Caracas branch of a U.S. company, or the nurse who will practice in the Los Angeles *barrio*, or the tourist who wants to know enough to 'get around' in Mexico.
(3) Integrative: the student who studies Spanish because he likes Spain or Mexico and wants to live there among its people.

The three yield progressively greater proficiency in the language. With an instrumental motivation, one need not learn the full system of the target language (basic pronunciation alone might suffice for the singer), or achieve all skills in it (the reader of Mexican journals will not have to express himself in Spanish). With a manipulative motivation, one will need more active ability but can dispense with a full range of argots and styles, and he does not require a flawless command of pronunciation, grammar, and the lexicon. Since he is an outsider and may not wish to pass for a native anyway, his messages can be of a rather simple, formulaic type; as long as these are fairly clear and intelligible, despite an accent or a decidedly unidiomatic flavor, his needs are met. With neither of these two motivations must lifelong habits or attitudes be greatly altered.

Integrative motivation leads to more success, but it requires constant and drastic adaptation. One seeks to become at one with the target group, and tries to adopt its pronunciation, grammatical strategies, mannerisms, idioms, pragmatic conventions, belief systems, and cultural outlook. Eventually, he may assimilate fully, or become a bicultural bilingual at home in both societies. But this motivation poses a special danger. Many have noticed that well-motivated students may progress steadily up to a point and then flag, stagnate on a plateau, or even regress. For Lambert 1972, this condition results from the integrative students' discovery that they are caught midway between leaving the monolingual comfort and security of their native society and attaining the foreign norms; they have cast loose from one niche but are not yet secure in the next one, and they may even harbor doubts about the desirability of proceeding further. Exacerbating their position is the fact that they have learned just enough to get into trouble by seeming more communicatively competent than they are. Native speakers make allowances for the foreign tourist or businessman but have higher expectations of someone with a better command of the language and with ambitions to live among them; one who uses the allophones, intonations, and past subjunctive conditionals of a native will have to act like a native too (Gorden 1974:169). Moreover, since successful integration requires a readjustment of personality and self-image, students may hold back from what is turning out to be a sociopsychological transformation. Lambert and his followers call this syndrome *anomie*, and predict two outcomes: students fall back on the security of their native identity, or they emerge determined to take the final steps to join the foreign culture, at least to the extent possible for them.

As with other classifications of humans, this one oversimplifies. In reality, a student's motivation can change, and he can make apparent progress with yet other goals: to get good grades, to pass a requirement, for entertainment, for purely academic study, for verbal pats on the head by an admired teacher. Yet the theory makes the points that (1) some individuals do achieve some proficiency in a foreign language, even after puberty; (2) even if not flawless to the last allophone, their speech may become as native-like as one might reasonably hope for; and (3) success in mastery (and resistance to further mastery) can depend on extralinguistic factors such as personality, attitude, and goals. The more positive these factors are, the greater the overall command achieved; the more negative, the sooner that foreign language acquisition grinds to a halt. Indeed, many students are quite unmotivated from the start; they enter the classroom with hostility toward the whole undertaking, and they may resist at every step of the way a teacher's tampering with behavior with which they are comfortable and which they see no reason to change.

The foregoing is an important point that is seldom taken into account in the classroom. In asking students to modify their pronunciation (e.g. /d/ → [ð], /r/ → [ɾ], /a/ does not → [ə]), to revise their scheme of word order, to keep track of beginning/middle/end or of experienced/unexperienced, to show subjects by verb endings alone, to relexify the entire world, to change their verbal and nonverbal gestures, and to empathize with an alien people, the teacher is challenging them to remake themselves into new persons. This has been lucidly argued by Stevick 1976, who maintains that each linguistic unit and pattern will interfere because it is a meaningful act to students. Even pronunciation has meaning in this sense, for if the student attains any more than the grossest phonemic accuracy, he risks sounding foreign to himself and to his peers. Even good mimickers merely reproduce the foreign pronunciation in (Stevick's phrase) the spoken equivalent of quotation marks; they soon drop it in real communication. Stevick also points out that some phonetic advice only worsens this problem, since when students are told that Spanish /ř/ is an imitation of a motor or that French /ʀ/ is a dry gargle, they may disdain trills as unreal speech sounds. Failure to adopt and use a foreign element is meaningful in itself: a rejection of complete assimilation and a way of keeping foreignness at arm's length.

We began this chapter with a discussion of what else native speakers bring to the task of communicating besides knowledge of phonology, grammar, and lexicon. However much this communicative competence embraces, it is clear that an infant born to a Hispanic family will acquire it for Spanish in a different way from a teenaged or adult English speaker who labors over it in a classroom. To the extent that the difference is determined by innate developmental programming, there is nothing the teacher can do but reassert the need for beginning foreign language study in grade schools instead of high schools and universities; but to the extent that it depends on psychological and sociocultural factors, the teacher can try to facilitate an adjustment process that can be painful even for the well motivated. Stevick and others have espoused certain methods and techniques designed to ease students' discomfort and dread and to obviate the tension between teachers and students with different expectations of what is to happen; but there are no magic formulas for eliminating these hurdles entirely. Second language study does require the acquisition of a new phonology, grammar, and lexicon, and these can differ from their source language counterparts in many ways; the teacher who is aware of these systemic differences can anticipate specific errors and give students a precise account of the problem. Yet knowledge alone of these components does not ensure native-like use of them, for second language acquisition involves the appreciation of—and optimally, the gradual assimilation to—new ways of thinking, new norms for behaving, and new strategies for interacting with others. Unlike the contracting of *de* and *el* or the accents on demonstratives, these can reach down into the very soul of the language learner.

Notes for Chapter 16

1. As one teaching assistant from Buenos Aires put it when she used the LaMadrid text, 'I've never heard those *refranes* and feel awkward pretending they're natural for me.'

2. For an excellent and very thorough coverage of some of these categories in Spanish (mainly Venezuelan), see Gómez de Ivashevsky 1969. For example, she illustrates about 200 vocatives: *Ven(ga) acá paisano/joven/m'hijito/llave/tripón/polla/licenciado/compadre/cráneo* . . .

Exercises for Chapter 16

1. Part of communicative competence is the ability to use gestures, body contact, and speaking distance correctly. What differences between English and Spanish speakers are you aware of in this regard? Are any of the differences sex-linked?

2. In testing some grammatical points, it is common to use single sentences with spaces left blank, and to instruct students to fill in the correct tense (mood, article, preposition, copula, etc.). Though this procedure is convenient and time-honored, many teachers feel uncomfortable with it. Why? What is, and what is not, being tested? Is there a practical alternative, in your opinion?

3. Many texts and readers include Hispanic political cartoons and comic strips. What advantages do these have? What problems can they give to students?

4. Second language learners are often petrified by the prospect of using a telephone in the foreign country. Why should telephone calls seem difficult?

5. English *okay* is used in a variety of situations and some Spanish speakers have adopted it too. Aside from the borrowed *oquey*, how might a Spanish speaker convey each of the following? (Add other examples that occur to you.)

   (1) '*Okay*, now turn to page 32.'
   (2) 'I think I'll leave now, *okay?*'
   (3) 'Let's meet for dinner tomorrow, *okay?*'

6. Contrast Y's answers in the following situations to how an English-speaker might respond:

(1) X: ¿Me hace Ud. el favor de pasarme ese horario?
    Y: Tome Ud.
(2) X: ¿Me hace Ud. el favor de abrir esa maleta?
    Y: Ya está.

7. Three situations discussed in Handelsman et al. (1981:122-123) are the following:

(1) X tells Y any of the following:
    'Quisiera que Ud. escriba el informe ahora.'
    '¿Una entrevista? Pues, reunámonos mañana.'
    'Nos vemos esta noche a los ocho. ¿Conviene?'
(2) X meets Y for some item of business. They do not *ir al grano* right away, but instead digress to discuss a current festival or to inquire about each other's family.
(3) X proposes to Y: 'Vamos a tomar un cafecito.'

Now, consider how Y might construe the time references in (1), the chit-chat in (2), and the proposal in (3) (hint: who pays?), depending on whether Y is Hispanic or 'Anglo.' Can you think of other cases in which English and Spanish speakers might misunderstand one another because of the cultural conventions underlying speech?

8. Study the following list of words and phrases; then, (1) suggest English equivalents, where possible, and (2) pinpoint the communicative function each item carries out in speech acts or discourse.

al contrario	¡chócala!	gracias	pues
anda	de todos modos	hola	se me ocurre . . .
a ver	dime/dígame	lo siento	total
bueno, bien	eh, este	mira/mire	¿vale?
claro	en cambio	no hay de qué/	¿verdad?
¿cómo?	en fin	de nada	¿y qué?
¿cómo no?	excelente, fantás-	nomás	ya lo creo
	tico, etc.	puede que sí	

9. Repeat the above instructions for the following interjections:

ajá	caramba/caray	huy	qué barbaridad/ho-
ay	dale	Jesús	rror/lástima, etc.
bah	Dios mío	ojo	qué va
basta	epa	palabra	uf
			vaya

10. The following is a small sample of Spanish proverbs. Contrast them with equivalent English proverbs you may know for similarity of metaphor and of meaning. Even if English has no ready equivalent familiar to you, would the cultural values behind the Spanish proverb be representative of English speakers' values too? Can you add any other Spanish proverbs to this list?

(1) Donde una puerta se cierra, otra se abre.
(2) Por todas partes se va a Roma.

(3) Agua pasada no muele molinos.

(4) A quien madruga, Dios le ayuda.

(5) Aunque la mona se vista de seda, mona se queda.

(6) Antes que decidas nada, consúltalo con la almohada.

(7) No hay mal que dure cien años, ni cuerpo que lo resista.

(8) A caballo regalado no se le mira el diente.

(9) A mal tiempo, buena cara.

(10) Cría cuervos y te sacarán los ojos.

(11) De la mano a la boca se pierde la sopa.

(12) Cada cabeza es un mundo.

(13) Haz bien y no mires a quién.

(14) No digas nunca 'de esta agua no beberé.'

(15) Quien siembra vientos recoge tempestades.

(16) No se ganó Zamora en una hora.

(17) Con pan y vino se anda el camino.

(18) Padre mercader, hijo caballero, nieto limosnero.

(19) Dijo la sartén a la caldera, 'quítate de allá, que me tiznas.'

(20) La vida no es senda de rosas.

11. Construct a questionnaire on the use of second person pronouns in Spanish. (You might bear in mind not only *tú* and *usted*, but dialect variants, v. 9.2.) The basic format might be the following; try to include as many variables as possible.

¿Qué pronombre suele usar en las siguientes situaciones?

(1) hablando con su esposo o novio (esposa o novia)?

(2) hablando con una prima menor/mayor?

(3) quejándose de algo en un almacén?

(4) diciéndole a un perro que se vaya?

(5) insultando a un chofer que acaba de abollarle el carro?

(6) conversando con otra persona de su edad que acaba de conocer?

(7) en una rencilla con su papá?

(etc.)

After eliciting responses from a native speaker, compare your results with those of your classmates.

12. Reread *Don Quijote* and determine (1) the pronoun forms Don Quijote and Sancho Panza normally use with one another, (2) those with which they address other characters, and (3) where their usual T/V relationship is temporarily inverted (this does happen). Try to explain your observations in terms of Brown and Gilman's theory.

13. Contrast the connotations of each of the following Spanish/English pairs, and speculate on how they might derive from cultural differences.

(1) perra/bitch

(2) profesor/professor

(3) engañar/cheat

(4) compadre/godfather

(5) piropos/compliments

(6) animal domesticado/pet

(7) siesta/nap	(10) tertulia/bull session
(8) arroyo/creek	(11) azotea/flat roof
(9) mono/cute	(12) anciano, viejos/elderly, seniors

14. A woman named Catherine Thompson might be called any of the following in English: Catherine, Cathy, Mrs. Thompson, Ms. Thompson, Miss Thompson, Aunt Cathy, President Thompson, Doctor Thompson, Reverend Thompson, Miss Cathy (in some areas), Thompson.

What are the vocative possibilities in Spanish, and how do they differ from those in English?

15. In conjunction with the American Council on the Teaching of Foreign Languages and the U.S. Defense Language Institute, the Educational Testing Service (1982) has developed criteria for evaluating oral proficiency in language apart from, say, reading ability or purely academic tests on verb endings and the like. At what are called the novice, intermediate, and advanced levels, grammatical variables (e.g. correct use of preterite/imperfect) and functional variables (e.g. ability to describe, narrate, converse) weigh about equally; but for the so-called superior levels, grammatical and lexical accuracy are taken for granted and the testee is expected to do things such as the following:

(1) conjecture and argue on abstract issues

(2) negotiate, persuade

(3) tailor language to the situation (e.g. introduce a distinguished guest)

(4) use appropriate references to native-like experiences

Why—apart from general fluency, grammatical accuracy, and lexical richness—would these tasks require a special level of competence in a language?

16. Refer to the discussion of 'styles' of language. How much of both kinds of style are students typically exposed to in the foreign language programs with which you are familiar? How might stylistic limitations reflect on the nonnative as a person? What, if anything, could be done to facilitate stylistic diversification?

17. In what ways does attitude toward a foreign language and its speakers affect mastery of it? In your opinion, what stereotypes or preconceived ideas get in the way of foreign language acquisition, and what can a teacher do to ease the problem? Given a variety of student motivations in one classroom, what should the teacher aim to do?

18. Collect examples of argot (v. 16.1.3) of an area that interests you, whether professionally or as a hobby. Assume that this is for introducing students to the vocabulary needed for a reading on, and discussion of, that area, and try to include all specialized terms that might be needed in your English-Spanish (and/or Spanish-English) glossary. Indicate which words in your glossary would be for active mastery by students, and which ones would be for passive recognition purposes. One basis for your decision might be the difference between words that educated native speakers outside the area might know and use, as opposed to words that only serious specialists would employ.

Appendix 1:
English/Spanish glossary
of linguistic terminology

The following glossary is offered in order to facilitate class discussion of the material in Spanish, if desired, and to introduce readers to the terminology they may encounter in writings by Spanish-speaking linguists. Although it is not exhaustive, it covers the major linguistic terms used in this book. It should be noted that Spanish-speaking linguists are still in the process of working out suitable terms for generative grammar, and while the author has verified all the Spanish terms offered in writings by native speakers, some linguists might prefer a different equivalent in some cases.

Gender of nouns should be assumed to be masculine if ending in *-n, -o, -r, -s, -e, -l* and feminine if ending in *-a, -d,* or *-ción/sión,* unless otherwise indicated by (M) or (F). Adjectives used as nouns—*(los) adverbiales* for 'adverbials'—are usually masculine except for phonetic labels, which tend to be feminine as nouns in Spanish linguistics: *la nasal, las fricativas, una vocal alta, estas vibrantes, la consonante,* etc.

As in other fields with a more or less 'international' vocabulary, many linguistic terms are cognates. For economy in this glossary, the equals sign (=) will indicate orthographically identical equivalents and the congruence sign (≃) will stand for almost identical equivalents with predictable orthographic differences. For example, the entry 'nasal:=' abbreviates 'nasal:nasal', and the entry 'derivative, -ation:≃' abbreviates 'derivative, derivation: derivativo, derivación'.

Spanish terms for verb categories are omitted from this list since they were presented in Chapter 6 (see Figure 6.1).

absolute: absoluto
absorption (of yod): absorción (de yod)
accent: acento, acentuar(se) (ú); accented: acentuado, tónico; accent
    mark: acento, tilde (F)

acquire (a language): adquirir (ie), aprender; acquisition: adquisición, aprendizaje

add: agregar(se)

address: tratamiento; addressee: interlocutor

adjective: adjetivo; adjectival phrase: frase adjetival (F)

adverb: adverbio; adverbial:=; adverbial phrase: frase adverbial (F), complemento circunstancial

affix: afijo

affricate: africado

agree: concordar (ue); -ment: concordancia

allomorph: alomorfo

allophone: alófono

alternation: alternancia

alveolar, alveopalatal:=; alveolar ridge: alvéolos

antecedent: antecedente

antonym: antónimo

apex: ápice, punta de la lengua

apocope: apócope (F); apocopate: apocopar(se)

apply (a rule): aplicar(se)

appositive:≃

argot: lenguaje profesional, jerga

article: artículo

articulate: articular; -ation, -atory: ≃; manner/place of articulation: modo/punto de articulación

aspect: aspecto; beginning, middle, end: iniciativo, imperfectivo, terminativo

aspirate: aspirar(se); -ation: ≃

assibilate: asibilar(se)

assimilate: asimilarse; -ation: ≃

auxiliary: (verbo) auxiliar

back (vowel): (vocal) posterior, velar

become: volverse, convertirse (ie); X becomes Y in the environment of Z: X se convierte en Y en el contorno de Z

bilabial, labial: =

bilingual: bilingüe; bilingualism: bilingüismo

boundary: lindero, frontera, linde (F)

branching (structure): (estructura) ramificada

case: caso (nominativo, dativo, acusativo, preposicional)

category: categoría; -ization: ≃

causative: ≃

central: =

circumlocution: circunlocución

clause: cláusula (relativa, nominal, adverbial)

clitic: clítico, enclítico, proclítico

cluster: agrupación
coda: =
cognate: cognado, (palabra) cognada
collocation: locución
colloquial: coloquial
command: mandato; mandar
comparison: comparación; (of adjectives) gradación; comparative: ≃
competence: competencia
complement: complemento; -ary: -ario; complementizer: conjunción
    complementaria, complementante
complex: complejo, compuesto (*oración compuesta* is sometimes applied
    to both compound and complex)
compound: compuesto, (palabra) compuesta; -ing: composición
conjugate: conjugar; -ation: ≃
conjunction: conjunción; coordinating/subordinating...: ... coor-
    dinante/subordinante
connotation: ≃
consonant: consonante (F); -al: consonántico
constituent: constituyente, sintagma (M)
construct: construir; -tion: ≃
contract: contraer(se); -tion: contracción
contrast: contraste, oposición; contrastar; -ive analysis: análisis
    contrastivo
copula: cópula, (verbo) copulativo
count (noun): (nombre) contable

declarative: aseverativo
deep (structure): (estructura) profunda, latente
definite: definido, determinado
deictic: deíctico
delete, drop: suprimir(se), elidir(se); deletion: supresión, elisión
demonstrative: demostrativo
dental: =
derive: derivar(se); -ative, -ation: ≃
determiner: determinante
devoice: ensordecer(se); -ing: ensordecimiento
dialect: dialecto; -al: =
digraph: digrama (M)
diminutive: ≃
diphthong: diptongo; -al: diptongal; -ize: diptongar(se); falling/rising
    diphthong: diptongo creciente/decreciente
direct object: see object
discourse: discurso, decurso

ellipsis: elipsis (F)
embed: incrustar, incorporar

emphasis: énfasis; -atic: enfático
ending (inflectional): desinencia
environment: contorno, entorno; contexto
epenthesis: epéntesis (F)
epicene: epiceno
Equi-NP: equivalencia de FN
event: suceso
etymology: etimología
express: expresar; -ion: ≃, (special phrase, collocation) locución
extraposition: ≃

feature (syntactic or phonological): rasgo
feminine: feminino
flap, tap: vibrante simple (F)
focus: enfoque
form: forma; formar; -ative, -ation: ≃
fricative: fricativo
friction: fricación; (of /j/ in particular) rehilamiento
front (vowel): (vocal) anterior, palatal
function: función; funcionar
functor: gramema (M), palabra gramatical

gender: género
generate: generar: -ative, -ation: ≃
Germanic: germánico
gerund: gerundio
glide: semivocal (F); gliding movement: deslizamiento
glottal: glotal; . . . stop: golpe de glotis
govern: regir (i)
grammar: gramática; -arian; gramático
grammatical: gramatical; grammaticalize: ≃

head (of phrase): núcleo
hearer: oyente
height (of vowels): altura
hiatus: hiato
high (vowel): (vocal) alta, cerrada
homonym: homónimo

idiolect: idiolecto
idiom: modismo
impersonal: =; unipersonal (verb such as *haber* or *llover* that is 3sg.)
inchoative: incoativo
indefinite: indefinido, indeterminado
indirect object: see object
Indo-European: indoeuropeo
infinitive: infinitivo

inflection: inflexión, flexión; -al: flexivo
insert: insertar (se); -ion: inserción
intensifier: intensificador
interference: ≃
interrogative: ≃
intonation: entonación; -al: -al
irregular: =

jargon: jerigonza
join, link: unir(se)

language: lengua, idioma (M); (speech, way of talking) lenguaje
larynx: laringe (F)
lateral: =
lax: laxo, lenis, relajado
length: duración; -en: alargar(se)
level: nivel; llano
lexicon: léxico, lexicón; -cal: =
liaison: enlace
linguist: lingüista; -ic: ≃; -ics: lingüística
link, linking (between words in pronunciation): enlazar; enlace; linking
    (verb): (verbo) copulativo
liquid: líquido
loanword: préstamo, extranjerismo (anglicismo, galicismo, etc.); loan
    translation: calco
loud: fuerte
low (vowel): (vocal) baja, abierta

main, matrix: matriz (F), (cláusula) principal
masculine: masculino
mass (noun): (nombre) de masa
mean: significar; -ing: significado, sentido
mid (vowel): (vocal) media
minimal pair: ejemplo de oposición
modal: =
modify: modificar; -ier: modificador
mood: modo
morpheme: morfema (M); morphology: morfología; -ical: morfológico;
    morphophonemic: mor(fo)fonológico; morphophoneme: mor(fo)
    fonema (M)
move (a constituent): trasladar(se), desplazar(se); movement: traslado,
    desplazamiento

nasal: =
negate: negar(se) (ie); -ative, -ation: ≃
neuter: neutro (*lo, esto,* etc.), asexuado (*el libro,* etc.)
neutralize, -ation: neutralizar(se), -ización

node (in a phrase marker): nódulo (de una estructura ramificada), nudo
nominalize (a NP): sustantivar(se) (una FN); -ization: sustantivación
nonfinite: infinito, (forma) infinita
noun (N): sustantivo (Sust), nombre; noun phrase, NP: frase nominal (F),
  FN; noun clause: cláusula nominal
nucleus: núcleo
number: número

object: complemento, objeto; direct..., indirect...: complemento
  directo, indirecto; object of a preposition: término de preposición
obstruent: obstruyente
onset: cabeza (de una sílaba)
optional: facultativo, optativo
oral: =

palate: paladar; palatal: =
paradigm: paradigma (M)
part of speech: parte (F) de la oración
participle: participio
particle: partícula
passive: pasivo, (voz, oración) pasiva
pattern: pauta, patrón
periphrastic: perifrástico
person (1, 2, 3): (primera, segunda, tercera) persona
phone: fono; phonetic: fonético; phonetics: fonética
phoneme: fonema (M); phonemic: fonemático
phonology: fonología; phonological: fonológico
phonotactics: distribución fonemática
phrase: frase (F), sintagma (M); phrase structure rule: regla de estructura
  de frase, regla ahormacional; set phrase: frase hecha; phrasal collocation: locución; phrase marker: estructura ramificada, diagrama
  arbóreo, marcador de frase
pitch: tono
place, put: colocar, poner; place in front: anteponer(se);...after:
  posponer(se);...next to: yuxtaponer(se);...in between: inter-
  poner(se); placement: colocación
plural: =
polyseme: palabra polisémica; polysemy: polisemia
possession, -ive: ≃
pragmatics: pragmática
predicate: predicado;...element: atributo predicativo
predict: predecir: -able: predecible
prefix: prefijo
preposition: preposición; prepositional phrase, PP: frase preposicional,
  FP

progressive: ≃
pronoun; pronombre; pronominal: =; -ize: pronominalizar(se)
proverb: refrán; pro-verb: proverbo, sustituto verbal
pseudoreflexive: seudorreflejo

quantifier: cuantificativo
question: interrogación

raising (of vowels): cerrazón (F)
reciprocal: recíproco
reduce: reducir(se); -ction: ≃
reflexive: reflejo, reflexivo; ... verb: verbo pronominal (meaning-
    changing and inherent *se*), verbo reflexivo
related: relacionado; (etymologically) ... : emparentado; relation: ≃
relative: ≃
relator: nexo
replace: reemplazar a, sustituir a; -ment: reemplazo, sustituto
restrictive: ≃
retroflex: retroflexo; -ion: ≃
rheme: rema (M), predicado lógico
rhyme: rima
rhythm: ritmo
Romance: románico
rounded: redondeado, labial(izado); rounding: redondez (F)
r-sound (for flaps and trills only): vibrante (F)
rule: regla

schwa: schwa, vocal reducida
scope (of negation): abarque, alcance (de la negación)
semantic: semántico; -s: semántica, semiología
sentence, S: oración, O; -tial: oracional
sequence: secuencia
sibilant: sibilante
singular: =
slang: argot, caló, habla vulgar
sonorant: sonante
sound: sonar (ue), sonido
speaker: hablante
speech: habla
speech act: acto de elocución
spelling: deletreo (de una palabra), grafía (de un sonido), ortografía (en
    general); ... change: cambio ortográfico
spirantization: espirantización
standard: estándar, normal
stem: raíz (F), lexema (M); ... change: cambio radical
stop: oclusivo, plosivo

strengthen: reforzar(se) (ue); -ing: refuerzo
stress: acento (de intensidad); stressed: tónico, acentuado; stress-timed: acentualmente acompasado
string (of words): cadena (de palabras)
strong (verb): (verbo) fuerte
structure: estructura; -al: ≃
style: estilo
subject: sujeto
subordinate: subordinar; -ing: subordinante
substitute: sustituir a, sustituto; -able: sustituible
suffix: sufijo
suppletion: supletivismo
suprasegmental: =, prosodia, prosodema (M)
surface (structure): (estructura) superficial, patente
syllable: sílaba; -ic: silábico; syllable-timed: silábicamente acompasado; syllabification: delimitación silábica
syncope: síncopa
syncretism: sincretismo
syneresis: sinéresis (F)
synonym: sinónimo; -y: sinonimia
syntax: sintaxis (F); -actic: sintáctico
system: sistema (M); -atic: ≃

tense (vowel): tenso, fortis; (of verb) tiempo
terminal (of intonation): cadencia; falling/rising . . . : . . . descendente/ascendente
theme: tema (M); . . . vowel: vocal temática
theory: teoría; -etical: teórico
tip (of tongue): ápice
transform: transformar(se); -ation: ≃; transformational grammar: gramática transformativa, transformacional
transitive, intransitive: ≃
tree (for representing structure): diagrama arbóreo
trill: vibrante múltiple (F)

underlying: subyacente
ungrammatical: agramatical
unstressed: átono, inacentuado
utterance: enunciado

vary: variar (í); -iable, -iant, -ation: ≃
velar: =; velum: velo (del paladar)
verb: verbo; -al: =
verb phrase, VP: frase verbal (F), FV
vocabulary: vocabulario
vocal cords: cuerdas vocales

vocative: vocativo
voice: voz (F), sonoridad; sonorizar(se); voiced: sonoro
vowel: vocal (F)

weaken: debilitar(se)
word: palabra, voz; word order: orden de palabras

zeugma: = (M)

Appendix 2: Phonological index

For easier access, most phonological terms and symbols have been extracted from the General Index and are presented separately here. This special index consists of seven parts:

(a) and (b): Spanish and English phonemes, along with the allophones generally recognized for each (although phonemic analysis is sometimes controversial). The phonemes and allophones are described, and references are given to those sections that discuss their articulation and/or phonological behavior. Phonemic symbols are listed alphabetically, with nonroman symbols placed at the end. Alternative symbols used by some linguists are indicated in parentheses following the symbols used in this book.

(c): diacritics (marks such as accents that are added to phonetic symbols)

(d): boundaries

(e): descriptive terms, with references to sections that explain them

(f) and (g): rules and processes of Spanish and English, with references to sections that describe them.

(a) Spanish phonemes and their major allophones. (See Figures 2.1 and 2.6 in Chapter 2.)

1. /a/ low central or low front unrounded vowel: 1.1.4, 2.2.1
2. /b/ voiced bilabial stop: 3.1.6
   [β] (ƀ) voiced bilabial fricative: 3.1.6, 3.1.7
3. /č/ (tʃ, ŝ̌) voiceless alveopalatal affricate, sibilant: 1.1.3
   [š] (ʃ) voiceless alveopalatal fricative, sibilant: 1.1.3
4. /d/ voiced dental stop, [d̪]: 2.1.2, 3.1.6
   [ð] (đ) voiced dental fricative: 1.2, 3.1.6, 3.1.7
5. /e/ mid front unrounded vowel: 2.2.1
6. /f/ voiceless labiodental fricative: 3.1.8
   [ɸ] (ᵽ, φ) voiceless bilabial fricative (in some dialects): 3.1.8
7. /g/ voiced velar stop: 3.1.6
   [ɣ] (ǥ) voiced velar fricative: 3.1.6, 3.1.7
8. /i/ high front unrounded vowel: 2.2.1
   [j] (i̯, y) corresponding palatal glide: 2.2.3, 3.1.1.0
9. /j/ (y) voiced palatal glide, 'yod': 2.1.4.1, 2.2.3
   [ɟ] (ɏ) voiced palatal fricative: 3.1.1
   [ɟɟ] (ŷ) voiced palatal affricate: 3.1.1
   [ž] (ʒ) voiced alveopalatal fricative (in some dialects): 3.1.1
10. /k/ voiceless velar stop
11. /l/ voiced alveolar lateral, 'clear' [l̜]: 3.2.5
    [l̪] voiced dental lateral: 3.1.3

12. /m/ voiced bilabial nasal: 3.1.2
13. /n/ voiced alveolar nasal: 3.1.2
    [ɱ] voiced labiodental nasal: 3.1.2
    [n̪] voiced dental nasal: 3.1.2
    [ñ] voiced alveopalatal nasal: 3.1.2
    [ŋ] voiced velar nasal: 3.1.2, 3.1.8
14. /o/ mid back rounded vowel: 2.2.1
15. /p/ voiceless bilabial stop: 3.2.1
16. /r/ voiced alveolar flap, [ɾ]: 2.1.3.3
    [ɹ̆] assibilated alveolar flap: 3.1.8
17. /r̄/ (rr) voiced alveolar trill: 2.1.3.3
    [r̃] assibilated alveolar trill: 3.1.8
    [R] uvular trill (in some dialects): 3.1.8
    [x] voiceless velar fricative (in some dialects): 3.1.8
18. /s/ voiceless alveolar fricative, sibilant (grooved): 2.1.4.2, 3.1.4
    [ś] apicoalveolar fricative, sibilant (in some dialects): 2.1.4.2
    [z] voiced alveolar fricative, sibilant: 3.1.4
    [h] voiceless glottal fricative, aspirate (in some dialects): 2.1.2
19. /t/ voiceless dental stop, [t̪]: 2.1.2
20. /u/ high back rounded vowel: 2.2.1
    [w] (u̯) corresponding labiovelar glide: 2.2.3, 3.1.1
21. /w/ rounded voiced labiovelar glide: 2.2.3
    [w̵] (ɣʷ, gʷ) rounded velar fricative: 3.1.3
22. /x/ voiceless velar fricative, the 'jota': 2.1.3.2
    [h] voiceless glottal fricative, aspirate (in some dialects): 2.1.3.2
23. /ʎ/ (ĺ, ļ) voiced palatal lateral (in some dialects): 2.1.4.1
24. /θ/ voiceless dental fricative (in some dialects): 2.1.4.2
25. /ɲ/ (ñ, n̦) voiced palatal nasal, the 'eñe': 2.1.3.1, 3.1.2

   (b) English phonemes and their major allophones. (See Figures 2.1 and 2.6 in Chapter 2.)
   1. /ɑ/ (a) low back (or central) unrounded vowel: 2.2.1
   2. /b/ voiced bilabial stop
   3. /č/ (tʃ, tš) voiceless alveopalatal affricate: 1.1.3
      [čʰ] aspirated: 3.2.1
      [ʔč] preglottalized: 3.2.2
   4. /d/ voiced alveolar stop: 2.1.2
      [ɾ] (D) voiced alveolar flap: 2.1.3.3, 3.2.3
   5. /e/ mid front unrounded tense vowel, usually diphthongal [ej] (ey, ei): 2.2.1, 3.2.6
   6. /f/ voiceless labiodental fricative
   7. /g/ voiced velar stop
   8. /h/ voiceless glottal fricative, aspirate: 1.1.3
   9. /i/ high front unrounded tense vowel, often diphthongal [ij] (iy): 2.2.1, 3.2.6

10. /j/ (y) voiced palatal glide, 'yod': 1.1.1, 1.1.3, 3.1.1
11. /ǰ/ (dʒ) voiced alveopalatal affricate, sibilant: 3.1.1
12. /k/ voiceless velar stop: 3.2.1
    [kʰ] aspirated: 3.2.1
    [ʔk] preglottalized: 3.2.2
13. /l/ voiced alveolar lateral, generally dark [ɫ]: 3.2.5
14. /m/ voiced bilabial nasal
15. /n/ voiced alveolar nasal
16. /o/ mid back rounded tense vowel, usually diphthongal [ow] (ou):
    2.2.1, 3.2.6
17. /p/ voiceless bilabial stop: 3.2.1
    [pʰ] aspirated: 3.2.1
    [ʔp] preglottalized: 3.2.2
18. /r/ voiced retroflex approximant, [ɹ]: 2.1.3.3
    [ɹʷ] rounded: 1.2, 2.1.3.3
19. /s/ voiceless alveolar fricative, sibilant: 2.1.4.2
20. /š/ (ʃ) voiceless alveopalatal fricative, sibilant: 1.1.3
21. /t/ voiceless alveolar stop: 2.1.2, 3.2.1
    [tʰ] aspirated: 3.2.1
    [ʔt], [ʔ] preglottalized or replaced by glottal stop: 3.2.2
    [ɾ] voiced alveolar flap: 2.1.3.3, 3.2.3
22. /u/ high back or central rounded tense vowel, usually diphthongal
    [ʉw]: 2.2.1, 3.2.6
23. /v/ voiced labiodental fricative: 2.1.3
24. /w/ voiced labiovelar glide, rounded: 3.1.1
25. /z/ voiced alveolar fricative, sibilant
26. /ž/ (ʒ) voiced alveopalatal fricative, sibilant: 3.1.1
27. /ð/ voiced dental fricative: 1.2
28. /θ/ voiceless dental fricative: 2.1.4.2
29. /ŋ/ voiced velar nasal: 3.1.8
30. /æ/ low front unrounded vowel: 2.2.1
31. /ɛ/ mid front unrounded lax vowel
32. /ɪ/ (ɪ) high front unrounded lax vowel
33. /ʊ/ (ɷ) high back rounded lax vowel
34. /ʌ/ mid back unrounded lax vowel: 2.2
35. /ɔ/ mid (or sometimes low) back rounded lax vowel
36. /ə/ mid central reduced vowel, 'schwa': 1.1.4, 2.2, 3.2.7, 3.2.8
37. /ər/ mid central retroflex vowel, [ɚ] (ɝ): 2.2., 3.2.8
38. /aj/ /ɔj/ /aw/ (aɪ ɔɪ aʊ) rising diphthongs: 1.1.4, 2.2.2

(c) Diacritics.

CV́ ('CV CV́) primary stressed syllable
CV̀ (ˌCV CV̀) secondary stressed syllable
CV̆, CV unstressed syllable

V: lengthened vowel
Ṽ nasalized vowel
C̥ V̥ devoiced consonant or vowel
C̩ syllabic consonant

(d) Boundaries. (See also 3.0.)
+ morpheme boundary
# word boundary
|| phrase boundary, pause
. syllable boundary (also $)

(e) Descriptive terms.
See 1.1.1 for: consonant, glide, liquid, nasal, obstruent, vowel
See 1.1.2 for: sonorant, stress, voiced/voiceless
See 1.1.3 for: affricate, alveolar, alveopalatal, bilabial, coronal, dental, fricative, glottal, labial, labiovelar, labiodental, oral, palatal, sibilant, stop, uvular, velar
See 1.1.4 for: assimilate, back/central/front, diphthong, high/mid/low, lax/tense, rounded/unrounded
See 2.1.3.3 for: retroflex approximant, flap, trill
See 2.2.2 for: diphthongs (falling/rising), hiatus, syneresis
See 2.3 for: ambisyllabic, cluster, geminate, syllable

(f) Rules and processes of Spanish phonology.
See 2.2.4 for: linking
See 2.3 for: E-Epenthesis (also 3.0), weakening of syllable-final consonants
See 3.0 for: Vowel Nasalization
See 3.1 ff for: Fricativization of /č/, D-Deletion (Fricative Deletion), F-Bilabialization, Glide Strengthening, Lateral Assimilation, Liquid Leveling (*igualación*), N-Velarization, Nasal Assimilation, R-Assibilation, S-Aspiration, S-Voicing, Spirantization (of voiced stops), Vowel Gliding, Vowel Weakening

(g) Rules and processes of English phonology.
See 2.2.4 for: Glottal Stop Insertion
See 3.0 for: G-Dropping, Vowel Nasalization
See 3.2 ff for: Aspiration of Voiceless Stops, Diphthongization (of tense vowels), Flapping, L-Velarization, Palatalization (before yod), Preglottalization, Schwa Deletion, Vowel Reduction
See 4.1, 4.1.3 for: Vowel Lengthening

References

Agard, Frederick B. 1984. A course in Romance linguistics. Vol. 1: A synchronic view. Washington, D.C.: Georgetown University Press.

Aid, Frances. 1973. Semantic structures in Spanish: A proposal for instructional materials. Washington: Georgetown University Press.

Alonso, Amado. 1967. Estudios lingüísticos: temas hispanoamericanos. Madrid: Editorial Gredos.

—, 1974. Estilística y gramática del artículo en español, in Estudios lingüísticos: temas españoles. Madrid: Editorial Gredos.

Alonso, Damaso. 1950. Vocales andaluzas. Nueva revista de filología hispana 4:209-230.

Alvar, Manuel, A. Llorente, G. Salvador, eds. 1964. Atlas lingüístico y etnográfico de Andalucía (ALEA). Granada: Universidad de Granada.

Amastae, Jon and Lucía Elías-Olivares. 1982. Spanish in the United States: Sociolinguistic aspects. Cambridge, U.K.: Cambridge University Press.

Atlas lingüístico de la península ibérica. 1962. Madrid: Consejo Superior de Investigaciones Científicas.

Babcock, Sandra. 1970. The syntax of Spanish reflexive verbs. The Hague: Mouton.

Bell, Anthony. 1980. Mood in Spanish: A discussion of some recent proposals. Hispania 63:377-389.

Bello, Andrés (and Rufino Cuervo). 1958 (originally 1847). Gramática de la lengua castellana (edited by Alcalá-Zamora y Torres). Buenos Aires: Editorial Sopena Argentina.

Bergen, John. 1978a. One rule for the Spanish subjunctive. Hispania 61:218-234.

—. 1978b. A simplified approach for teaching the gender of Spanish nouns. Hispania 61:865-76.

—. 1980. The semantics of gender contrasts in Spanish. Hispania 63:48-57.

Bolinger, Dwight. 1954. English prosodic stress and Spanish sentence order. Hispania 37:152-156.

—. 1972. Adjective position again. Hispania 55:91-94.

—. 1974. One subjunctive or two? Hispania 57:462-471.

—. 1976. Again—one subjunctive or two? Hispania 59:41-49.

Bordelois, Ivonne. 1978. Animacy or subjecthood: Clitic movement and Romance causatives, in Suñer 1978:18-40.

Bowen, J. Donald and Robert Stockwell. 1955. The phonemic interpretation of semivowels in Spanish. Language 31:236-40.

Boyd-Bowman, Peter. 1960. El habla de Guanajuato. México: Imprenta Universitaria de la Universidad Nacional Autónoma.

Briscoe, Laurel and Enrique LaMadrid. 1978. Lectura y lengua: curso intermedio. Boston: Houghton Mifflin.

Brown, Roger and A. Gilman, 1960. The pronouns of power and solidarity, in T. A. Sebeok, ed., Style in language. Cambridge, Mass.: MIT Press. 253-76. Reprinted in P. P. Giglioli, ed., Language and social context. 1972. Middlesex, U.K.: Penguin.

Bull, William. 1965. Spanish for teachers: Applied linguistics. New York: Ronald Press.

—. 1972. The visual grammar of Spanish. Regents of the University of California and Houghton Mifflin.

Campbell, Joe, Mark Goldin, Mary Wang, eds. 1974. Linguistic studies in Romance languages. Washington, D.C.: Georgetown University Press.

Canfield, D. Lincoln. 1981. Spanish pronunciation in the Americas. Chicago: University of Chicago Press.

Cárdenas, Daniel. 1967. El español de Jalisco. Madrid: Consejo Superior de Investigaciones Científicas, Revista de filología española, anejo LXXXV.

Carnicer, Ramón. 1977. Tradición y evolución en el lenguaje actual. Madrid: Editorial Prensa Española.

Carratalá, Ernesto. 1980. Morfosintaxis del castellano actual. Barcelona: Editorial Labor.

Casagrande, Jean and Bohdan Saciuk, eds. 1972. Generative studies in Romance languages. Rowley, Mass.: Newbury House.

Champion, James. 1979. Derivatives of irregular verbs. Hispania 62: 317-320.

Chomsky, Noam. 1957. Syntactic structures. The Hague: Mouton.

—. 1959. Review of Verbal behavior by B. F. Skinner. Language 35:26-58.

—. 1965. Aspects of the theory of syntax. Cambridge, Mass.: MIT Press.

—. 1981. On binding, in Binding and filtering, ed. by F. W. Heny. Cambridge, Mass.: MIT Press.

—. 1982. Some concepts and consequences of the theory of government and binding. Cambridge, Mass.: MIT Press.

Contreras, Heles. 1974. Indeterminate subject sentences in Spanish.

Bloomington, Ind.: Indiana University Linguistics Club.

—. 1979. Clause reduction, the saturation constraint, and clitic promotion in Spanish. Linguistic Analysis 5:161-182.

Cook, Walter, S. J. 1969. Introduction to tagmemic analysis. Washington, D.C.: Georgetown University Press.

Cressey, William, 1969. Teaching the position of Spanish adjectives: A transformational approach. Hispania 52:878-881.

Dalbor, John. 1980a. Observations on present-day *seseo* and *ceceo* in southern Spain. Hispania 63:5-19.

—. 1980b. Spanish pronunciation: Theory and practice (2nd ed.). New York: Holt, Rinehart and Winston.

DaSilva, Zenia Sacks. 1982. On with Spanish. New York: Harper and Row.

— and Gabriel Lovett. 1965. A concept approach to Spanish. New York: Harper and Row.

Davis, J. Carey. 1969. The IO of possession in Spanish. University of Southern Florida Language Quarterly 7:2-6.

Dinnsen, Daniel. 1972. Additional constraints on clitic order in Spanish, in Casagrande and Saciuk 1972.

DiPietro, Robert. 1971. Language structures in contrast. Rowley, Mass.: Newbury House.

Dowdle, Harold. 1967. Observations on the uses of *a* and *de* in Spanish. Hispania 50:329-334.

Drake, Dana, Manuel Ascarza, Oralia Preble. 1982. The use and non-use of a preposition or other word between a noun and the following infinitive. Hispania 65:79-85.

Duden Español: Diccionario por la imagen. 1963. (2nd ed.) Mannheim, Fed. Rep. of Germany: Bibliographisches Institut.

Educational Testing Service. 1982. ETS oral proficiency testing manual. Princeton, N.J.: Educational Testing Service.

Fasold, Ralph and Roger Shuy, eds. 1977. Studies in language variation. Washington, D.C.: Georgetown University Press.

Fidelholz, James. 1975. Word frequency and vowel reduction in English. Chicago Linguistics Society 11:200-213.

Fillmore, Charles. 1968. The case for case. In Bach and Harms, eds., Universals in linguistic theory. New York: Holt, Rinehart and Winston.

Fish, Gorden. 1961. Adjectives fore and aft: Position and function in Spanish. Hispania 44:700-708.

—. 1967. *A* with a Spanish direct object. Hispania 50:80-85.

Fontanella de Weinberg, María Beatriz. 1974. Un aspecto sociolingüístico del español bonaerense. Bahía Blanca, Arg.: Cuadernos de lingüística.

Flórez, Luis. 1951. La pronunciación del español en Bogotá. Bogotá: Instituto Caro y Cuervo.

Fromkin, Victoria et al. 1981 (originally 1974). The development of language in Genie: A case of language acquisition beyond the 'critical period,' in Language: Introductory readings, ed. by Virginia Clark, Paul Eschholz and Alfred Rosa. New York: St. Martin's Press.

— and Robert Rodman. 1983. An introduction to language (3rd ed.). New York: Holt, Rinehart and Winston.

García-Pelayo y Gross. 1983. Pequeño Larousse Ilustrado. Vitoria, Spain: Larousse.

García, Erica and Ricardo Otheguy. 1977. Dialect differences in *leísmo*: A semantic approach, in Fasold and Shuy 1977.

Gili Gaya, Samuel. 1973. Vox curso superior de sintaxis española. Barcelona: Bibliograf.

Goldin, Mark. 1972. Indirect objects in Spanish and English, in Casagrande and Saciuk 1972:376-383.

—. 1974. A psychological perspective of the Spanish subjunctive. Hispania 57:295-301.

Gómez de Ivashevsky, Aura. 1969. Lenguaje coloquial venezolano. Caracas: Instituto de filología Andrés Bello, Facultad de humanidades y educación, Universidad Central de Venezuela.

González, Gustavo. 1978. The acquisition of Spanish grammar by native Spanish-speaking children. Rosslyn, Va.: National Clearinghouse for Bilingual Education.

Gorden, Raymond. 1974. Living in Latin America: A case-study in cross-cultural communication. Skokie, Ill.: National Textbook Co. and the American Council on the Teaching of Foreign Languages.

Graham, Carol. 1978. Jazz chants. New York: Oxford University Press.

Greenberg, Joseph. 1963. Some universals of grammar with particular reference to the order of meaningful elements, in Greenberg, ed., 1963:73-113.

—, ed. 1963. Universals of language. Cambridge, Mass.: MIT Press.

Guitart, Jorge. 1978. Aspects of Spanish aspect: A new look at the preterite/imperfect distinction, in Suñer 1978.

Hadlich, Roger. 1971. A transformational grammar of Spanish. Englewood Cliffs, N.J.: Prentice-Hall.

Hagerty, Timothy and J. Donald Bowen. 1973. A contrastive analysis of a lexical split, in Nash 1973:1-71.

Haiman, John. 1983. Iconic and economic motivation. Language 59:781-819.

Hammond, Robert. 1980. Las realizaciones fonéticas del fonema /s/ en el español cubano rápido de Miami, in Scavnicky 1980:8-15.

Handelsman, Michale, William Heflin, Rafael Hernández. 1981. La cultura hispana: dentro y fuera de los Estados Unidos. New York: Random House.

Harris, James. 1969. Spanish phonology. Cambridge, Mass.: MIT Press.

—. 1983. Syllable structure and stress in Spanish. Cambridge, Mass.: MIT Press.

Holton, James. 1960. Placement of object pronouns. Hispania 43:584-5.

Hooper (-Bybee), Joan. 1976. An introduction to natural generative phonology. New York: Academic Press.

Hurst, Dorothy. 1951. Spanish case: Influence of subject and connotation of force. Hispania 34:74-78.

Jacobs, Roderick and Peter Rosenbaum. 1968. English transformational grammar. Waltham, Mass.: Xerox College Publishing.

Jelinski, Jack. 1977. A new look at teaching the Spanish subjunctive. Hispania 60:320-326.

Jorge Morel, Elercia. 1974. Estudio lingüístico de Santo Domingo. Santo Domingo, Dom. Rep.: Editora Taller.

Kany, Charles. 1951 (originally 1945). American-Spanish syntax. Chicago: University of Chicago Press.

Kendris, Christopher. 1963. 201 Spanish verbs fully conjugated in all tenses. Woodbury, N.Y.: Barron's Educational Series.

Keniston, Hayward. 1937. Spanish syntax list: A statistical study of grammatical usage. New York: Holt.

King, Larry and Margarita Suñer. 1980. The meaning of the progressive in Spanish and Portuguese. Bilingual Review 7:222-238.

Kirshner, Robert. 1951. Let's do away with idioms. Hispania 34: 87.

Klein, Philip. 1984. Apparent correspondences in Spanish to English infinitival *to*. Hispania 67:416-419.

Kliffer, Mike. 1979. *Levanto la mano/me lavo las manos/me levanto la mano*. The Canadian Modern Language Review 35:217-226.

Kurath, Hans. 1949. Word geography of the eastern United States. Ann Arbor: University of Michigan Press.

— and Raven McDavid, Jr. 1961. The pronunciation of English in the Atlantic states. Ann Arbor: University of Michigan Press.

Kvavik, Karen. 1980. Las unidades melódicas en el español mexicano, in Scavnicky 1980, 48-57.

Ladefoged, Peter. 1982. A course in phonetics (2nd ed.). New York: Harcourt, Brace, Jovanovich.

Lakoff, George. 1971. Presupposition and relative well-formedness, in Danny Steinberg and Leon Jakobovits, eds., Semantics: An interdisciplinary reader, 329-340. Cambridge University Press.

LaMadrid, Enrique, William Bull, Laurel Briscoe. 1974a. Communicating in Spanish. Boston: Houghton Mifflin.

—. 1974b. Communicating in Spanish: Instructor's guide. Boston: Houghton Mifflin.

Lambert, W. E., et al. 1963. Attitudinal and cognitive aspects of intensive study of a second language. Journal of Abnormal and Social Psychology 66:358-368.

—. 1972. A study of the roles of attitudes and motivation in second-language learning, in Fishman, Joshua, ed., Readings in the sociology of language, 473-491. The Hague: Mouton.

— and G. Richard Tucker. 1976. *Tu, vous, usted*: A social psychological study of address patterns. Rowley, Mass.: Newbury House.

Lantolf, James P. 1978. The variable constraints on mood in Puerto-Rican American Spanish, in Suñer 1978.

Lindstrom, Naomi. 1980. Making the bilingual dictionary safer for students. Hispania 63:718-722.

Lipski, John. 1978. Subjunctive as fact? Hispania 61:931-34.

Lombardi, Ronald and Amalia Boero de Peters. 1981. Modern spoken Spanish: An interdisciplinary perspective. Washington, D.C.: University Press of America.

Lope Blanch, Juan. 1963. En torno a las vocales caedizas del español mexicano. Nueva Revista de Filología Hispana.

Lozano, Anthony. 1972. Subjunctives, transformations, and features in Spanish. Hispania 55:76-90.

—. 1975. In defense of two subjunctives. Hispania 58:277-283.

Marrone, Nila. 1974. Investigación sobre variaciones léxicas en el mundo hispano. The Bilingual Review/la Revista Bilingüe I:152-168.

Meyer, Paula. 1972. Some observations on constituent order in Spanish, in Casagrande and Saciuk, eds., 1972. 184-195.

Michalson, Dorothy and Charlotte Aires. 1981. Spanish grammar: un buen repaso. Englewood Cliffs, N.J.: Prentice Hall.

Miles, Cecil and Romelia Arciniegas. 1983. *Tener a*—a Spanish myth. Hispania 66:84-87.

Moody, Raymond. 1971. More on teaching Spanish adjective position. Hispania 54:315-21.

Moreno de Alba, José. 1978. Valores de las formas verbales en el español de México. México: Universidad Autónoma de México.

Mujica, Bárbara. 1982. Entrevista. New York: Holt, Rinehart, Winston.

Nash, Rose. 1973. Readings in Spanish-English contrastive linguistics. San Juan, P.R.: Inter-American University Press.

Navarro-Tomás, Tomás. 1948. El español en Puerto Rico: contribución a la geografía lingüística hispanoamericana. Río Piedras, P.R.: Universidad de Puerto Rico.

—. 1967. Manual de pronunciación española (6ª edición). New York: Hafner.

—. 1975. Capítulos de geografía lingüística de la península ibérica. Bogotá: Instituto Caro y Cuervo.

Navas Ruiz, Ricardo. 1963. *Ser y estar*: estudio sobre el sistema atributivo del español. Salamanca: Talleres gráficos Cervantes, Acta Salmanticensia.

Obaid, Antonio. 1973. The vagaries of the Spanish *S*. Hispania 56:60-67.

Oroz, Rodolfo. 1966. La lengua castellana en Chile. Santiago de Chile: Facultad de filosofía y educación, Universidad de Chile.

Osgood, Charles E. 1963. Linguistic universals and psycholinguistics, in Greenberg, ed., 1963. 299-322.

Otheguy, Ricardo. 1978. A semantic analysis of the difference between el/ la and lo, in Suñer, ed. 241-257.

Ozete, Oscar. 1981. Current usage of relative pronouns in Spanish. Hispania 64:85-91.

—. 1983. On the so-called Spanish gerund/participle. Hispania 66: 75-83.

Perissinotto, Giorgio. 1975. Fonología del español hablado en la ciudad de México: ensayo de un método sociolingüístico, traducido por Raúl Ávila. México: Colegio de México.

Perlmutter, David. 1971. Deep and surface structure constraints in syntax. New York: Holt, Rinehart, Winston.

Pike, Kenneth. 1954, 1955, 1960. Language in relation to a unified theory of the structure of human behavior. Glendale, Calif.: Summer Institute of Linguistics.

Pilleux, Mauricio and Hernán Urrutia. 1982. Gramática transformacional del español. Madrid: Ediciones Alcalá.

Poplack, Shana. 1980. Deletion and disambiguation in Puerto-Rican Spanish. Language 56:371-85.

Prado, Marcial. 1982. El género español y la teoría de la marcadez. Hispania 65:258-66.

Quilis, Antonio and Joseph A. Fernández. 1975. Curso de fonética y fonología españolas para estudiantes anglo-americanos (8ª edición). Madrid: Instituto Cervantes, Consejo Superior de Investigaciones Científicas.

Quirk, Randolph, Sidney Greenbaum, Geoffrey Leach, Jan Svartvik. 1972. A grammar of contemporary English. London: Longman.

Ramsey, Marathon. 1956 (revised by Robert Spaulding; originally 1894). A textbook of modern Spanish. New York: Holt, Rinehart, Winston.

Real Academia Española. 1924. Gramática de la lengua española. Madrid: Perlado, Páez y Cía.

—. 1956. Diccionario de la lengua española (19ª edición). Madrid: Espasa-Calpe.

—. 1979. Esbozo de una nueva gramática de la lengua española. Madrid: Espasa-Calpe.

Resnick, Melvyn C. 1975. Phonological variants and dialect identification in Latin American Spanish. The Hague: Mouton.

—. 1981. Introducción a la historia de la lengua española. Washington, D.C.: Georgetown University Press.

Rivero, María-Luisa. 1971. Una restricción de la estructura superficial sobre la negación en español, in Heles Contreras, ed., Los fundamentos de la gramática transformacional. México: Siglo Veintiuno.

Roldán, Mercedes. 1971a. The double object constructions of Spanish. Language Sciences: 1971, no. 15:8-14.

—. 1971b. Spanish constructions with se. Language Sciences: 1971, no. 18:15-29.

—. 1973. Reflexivization in Spanish, in Nash, ed. 1973. 197-219.

—. 1974. Constraints on clitic insertion in Spanish, in Campbell et al., eds., 1974. 124-138.

Sallese, Nicholas and Oscar Fernández de la Vega. 1968. Repaso: gramática moderna. New York: Van Nostrand.

Sánchez, Rosaura. 1978. Our linguistic and social context, in Amastae and Elías-Olivares, eds., 1982. 9-46.

Saporta, Sol. 1956. A note on Spanish semivowels. Language 32:287-90.

—. 1959. Morpheme alternants in Spanish, in Henry Kahane and Angelina Pietrangeli, eds., 1959, Structural studies on Spanish themes. Universidad de Salamanca: Filosofía y letras, tomo XII, núm. 3: 15-162.

Saussure, Ferdinand de. 1959 (originally 1915). Course in general linguistics. (Compiled by Charles Bally and Albert Sechehaye, trans. by Wade Baskin.) New York: McGraw-Hill.

Scavnicky, Gary, ed. 1980. Dialectología hispanoamericana: estudios actuales. Washington, D.C.: Georgetown University Press.

Silva-Corvalán, Carmen. 1982. Subject expression and placement in Mexican-American Spanish, in Amastae and Elías-Olivares, eds., 1982:93-120.

—. 1983. Tense and aspect in oral Spanish narrative. Language 59:760-780.

Spann, Susan. 1984. To translate the English gerund into Spanish, don't use the infinitive. Hispania 67:232-239.

Steel, Brian. 1975. Checklists of basic 'americanismos' and 'castellanismos.' Hispania 58:910-20.

Stevick, Earl. 1976. Memory, meaning, and method. Rowley, Mass.: Newbury House.

Stiehm, Bruce. 1978. Teaching Spanish word order. Hispania 61:410-34.

Stockwell, Robert P. and J. Donald Bowen. 1965. The sounds of English and Spanish. Chicago: University of Chicago Press.

— and John Martin. 1965. The grammatical structures of English and Spanish. Chicago: University of Chicago Press.

Studerus, Lenard. 1979. A model of temporal reference for Spanish verbs. Hispania 62:332-336.

Suñer, Margarita. 1974. Where does the impersonal se come from? in Campbell et al., eds., 1974. 146-57.

—, ed. 1978. Contemporary studies in Romance linguistics. Washington, D.C.: Georgetown University Press.

—. 1981. *Por* vs. *de*: Agential prepositions? Hispania 64:278-83.

—. 1982. Syntax and semantics of Spanish presentational sentence-types. Washington, D.C.: Georgetown University Press.

Szabo, Robert. 1974. Deep and surface order of the Spanish clitics, in Campbell et al., eds., 1974. 139-45.

Terker, Andrew. 1985. On Spanish adjective position. Hispania 68:502-509.

Terrell, Tracy and Joan Hooper. 1974. A semantically based analysis of mood in Spanish. Hispania 57:484-94.

Terrell, Tracy and Maruxa Salgués de Cargill. 1979. Lingüística aplicada a la enseñanza del español a angloparlantes. New York: John Wiley and Sons.

Tesnière, Lucien. 1959. Éléments de syntaxe structurelle. Paris: Klinksieck.

Torreblanca, Maximiliano. 1978. El fonema /s/ en la lengua española. Hispania 61:498-503.

—. 1980. Factores condicionadores de la distribución de los alófonos consonánticos españoles. Hispania 63:730-36.

Uber, Diana Ringer. 1985. The dual function of *usted*: Forms of address in Bogotá, Colombia. Hispania 68:388-92.

Van Els, Theo, with Theo Bongaerts, Guus Extra, Charles van Os, Anne-Mieke Janssen-van Dieten. 1984. Applied linguistics and the learning and teaching of foreign languages. Trans. by R. R. van Oirsouw. Baltimore: Edward Arnold.

Wells, J. C. 1982. Accents of English. Cambridge, U.K.: Cambridge University Press.

Whitley, M. Stanley. 1986a. *How*—the missing interrogative in Spanish. Hispania 69:82-96.

—. 1986b. Cláusula e infinitivo tras verbos y preposiciones. Hispania 69:669-676.

Whorf, Benjamin Lee. 1956. Language, thought, and reality. Cambridge, Mass.: MIT Press.

Wonder, John. 1981. The determiner + adjective phrase in Spanish. Hispania 64:348-359.

Zamora-Vicente, Alonso. 1967. Dialectología española. Madrid: Editorial Gredos.

Zierer, Ernesto. 1974. The qualifying adjective in Spanish. The Hague: Mouton.

Zlotchew, Clark. 1977. The Spanish subjunctive: Non-experience or emotion. Hispania 60: 938-9.

General index

The following index includes topics, terms, and abbreviations featured in this book. See also the Phonological Index (Appendix 2).

relative (pronouns, clauses), relativization: 13.3 ff
relator: 10.1 ff
reverse construction: 8.1.4
rhythm: 4.1.3
RP = recalled point

S = sentence
SAAD = simple active affirmative sentence type
semantic field: 15.4.1
semantics: see meaning
sentence: structure 11.1.1; permutations of subject verb object order 11.2-11.3.1; sentence adverbials 10.2.3, 11.1.2.4; see also compound, complex, negative, question, passive
ser/estar: 15.4.2
seseo: 2.1.4.2
Sg = singular; 1, 2, 3 sg = first, second, third person singular
speech acts: 16.3
spirantization: 3.1.6
stem changes: in verbs 6.1.2 ff; in nouns and adjectives 15.1.3
stress: 1.1.2, 4.1 ff
style: 16.1.2
Subj = subject
subject: vs. direct object 8.1-8.1.1; vs. topic or theme 11.3.2; subject (pronoun) deletion 11.1.1, 11.2
subjunctive: vs. indicative 7.3 ff; vs. infinitive 13.1.2 ff
SVO (SOV, VOS) = subject verb object ordering
syllable: 2.3; syllable timing 4.1.3
syneresis: 2.2.3, 3.1.10

tagmemics: 5.2
tenses: nomenclature 6.0; meaning 7.1 ff; tense mergers in the subjunctive 7.3.1
TG = (generative) transformational grammar
theme/rheme, topic/comment: 11.3.1

topicalization: see theme/rheme
transformation: 5.2, 11.0; see also specific transformational rules (agreement, clitic promotion, extraposition, imperative, negation, nominalization, preposing/postposing, question, reduction, relativization, subject pronoun deletion, topicalization)
transformational grammar: 5.2
tú/usted: development of 9.2.1; social meaning of 16.1.1

V = verb; vowel
V-cop = copula, copulative verb
V-ger = verb in gerund form
V-inf = verb in infinitive form
V-intr = intransitive verb
V-tns = verb with tense ending
V-tr = transitive verb
variable rule: vs. categorical rule 3.0; specific variable rules 3.1-3.2
verb: morphology, forms 6.0-6.3; verb + verb 6.4, 7.2, 13.1.3.5-13.1.3.7; reflexive 9.3 ff; verb + preposition 10.4.2; two-word verb 11.1.2.4; meaning of tenses and moods 7
verb phrase, VP: 5.2, 11.1.2.2
vos, voseo: 9.2
vowels: general description 1.1.4; phonemes 2.2 ff; processes 3.1.9-3.1.10, 3.2.6-3.2.8; see also diphthong, reduction, syllable
vocabulary: see lexicon
VP = verb phrase
VP-ger = gerund phrase, VP in gerund form
VP-inf = infinitival phrase, VP in infinitive form

word order: 5.2; specified by phrase structure rules 11.1-11.1.4; altered by transformations 11.2-11.3; see also question, passive, reduction

GEORGETOWN UNIVERSITY PRESS
Romance Languages and Linguistics Series

ROMANCE COLLOQUIA

1975 COLLOQUIUM ON HISPANIC LINGUISTICS
Frances M. Aid, Melvyn C. Resnick, Bohdan Saciuk, editors

SPANISH AND PORTUGUESE IN SOCIAL CONTEXT
John J. Bergen and Garland D. Bills, editors

LINGUISTIC SYMPOSIUM ON ROMANCE LANGUAGES: 9
William W. Cressey and Donna Jo Napoli, editors

COLLOQUIUM ON SPANISH AND LUSO-BRAZILIAN LINGUISTICS
James P. Lantolf, Francine Wattman Frank, Jorge M. Guitart, editors

CURRENT STUDIES IN ROMANCE LINGUISTICS
Marta Luján and Fritz G. Hensey, editors

1974 COLLOQUIUM ON SPANISH AND PORTUGUESE LINGUISTICS
William G. Milan, John J. Staczek, Juan C. Zamora, editors

LINGUISTIC APPROACHES TO THE ROMANCE LEXICON
Frank H. Nuessel, Jr., editor

DIALECTOLOGIA HISPANOAMERICANA: ESTUDIOS ACTUALES
Gary E.A. Scavnicky, editor

CONTEMPORARY STUDIES IN ROMANCE LINGUISTICS
Margarita Suñer, editor